Published, February, 1941
First printing, 5,000 copies
Second printing, 1,000 copies, August, 1952

Printed in the United States of America

THE
FORTIETH YEARBOOK

OF THE

NATIONAL SOCIETY FOR THE STUDY OF EDUCATION

ART IN AMERICAN LIFE AND EDUCATION

Prepared by the Society's Committee

Thomas Munro (Chairman), Alon Bement, George Sheldon Dutch
Raymond P. Ensign, Royal Bailey Farnum, Ray Faulkner
Melvin E. Haggerty, Robert Stose Hilpert, Ernest Horn
C. Valentine Kirby, Felix Payant, Leon L. Winslow
and Edwin Ziegfeld

Assisted by

Milton S. Fox and William L. Longyear
and Some Fifty Associated Contributors

Edited by

GUY MONTROSE WHIPPLE

This Yearbook Will Be Discussed at the Atlantic City Meeting of the
National Society, Saturday, February 22, 1941, 8:00 p.m. and
Monday, February 24, 1941, 9:00 a.m.

Distributed by

THE UNIVERSITY OF CHICAGO PRESS
CHICAGO 37, ILLINOIS
1941

TO

MELVIN E. HAGGERTY

This Yearbook on "Art in American Life and Education"
is dedicated
by the Board of Directors of which he was Chairman for several years
and
by his Associates on the Yearbook Committee
of which he was Chairman at the time of his death, in October, 1937
and to which, because of his conviction that Art was truly a "way of life"
he had devoted himself with zeal and assiduity

iv

OFFICERS OF THE SOCIETY
FOR 1940–1941

Board of Directors
(Term of office expires March 1 of the year indicated)

WILLIAM C. BAGLEY (1942)
Columbia University, New York, New York

LEO J. BRUECKNER, *Chairman* (1941)
University of Minnesota, Minneapolis, Minnesota

FRANK N. FREEMAN (1943)
University of California, Berkeley, California

BESS GOODYKOONTZ (1944)*
Office of Education, Washington, D. C.

GRAYSON N. KEFAUVER (1942)
Stanford University, Palo Alto, California

GEORGE D. STODDARD (1944)†
State University of Iowa, Iowa City, Iowa

RALPH W. TYLER (1943)
University of Chicago, Chicago, Illinois

GUY MONTROSE WHIPPLE (*Ex-officio*)
Clifton, Massachusetts

Secretary-Treasurer
GUY MONTROSE WHIPPLE (1941)
Clifton, Massachusetts

---

* Reëlected for three years beginning March 1, 1941.
† Elected for three years beginning March 1, 1941.

THE SOCIETY'S COMMITTEE ON ART IN AMERICAN LIFE AND EDUCATION

ALON BEMENT, Formerly Director of the Maryland Institute, Baltimore, Maryland, and the National Alliance of Art and Industry, New York, New York.

GEORGE SHELDON DUTCH, Professor of Art, George Peabody College for Teachers, Nashville, Tennessee.

RAYMOND P. ENSIGN, Secretary, The Eastern Arts Association, New York, New York.

ROYAL BAILEY FARNUM, Executive Vice-President, Rhode Island School of Design, Providence, Rhode Island.

RAY FAULKNER, Head, Department of Fine and Industrial Arts, Teachers College, Columbia University, New York, New York.

* MELVIN E. HAGGERTY, Dean, College of Education, University of Minnesota, Minneapolis, Minnesota.

ROBERT STOSE HILPERT, Associate Professor of Art Education, University of California at Los Angeles, Westwood Village, California.

ERNEST HORN, Professor of Education and Director of the University Elementary School, State University of Iowa, Iowa City, Iowa.

C. VALENTINE KIRBY, Chief, Art Education, Pennsylvania Department of Public Instruction, Harrisburg, Pennsylvania.

THOMAS MUNRO (*Chairman*), Curator of Education, The Cleveland Museum of Art, and Chairman, Division of Art, Western Reserve University, Cleveland, Ohio.

FELIX PAYANT, Editor of *Design*, Columbus, Ohio.

LEON L. WINSLOW, Director of Art Education, Department of Education, Baltimore, Maryland.

EDWIN ZIEGFELD, Assistant Professor of Fine Arts, Teachers College, Columbia University, New York, New York.

COMMITTEE ASSOCIATES

MILTON S. FOX, Instructor, Department of Education, The Cleveland Museum of Art, and Instructor, The Cleveland School of Art, Cleveland, Ohio.

WILLIAM L. LONGYEAR, Supervisor, Department of Advertising Design, School of Fine and Applied Arts, Pratt Institute, Brooklyn, New York.

---

* Originally Chairman of the Committee. Deceased.

ASSOCIATED CONTRIBUTORS

FLORENCE TILTON AHLFELD, Art Supervisor of Rural Schools, Sussex County, Delaware.

IRIS BARRY, Curator, Museum of Modern Art Film Library, Inc., New York, New York.

WALTER CURT BEHRENDT, Technical Director, Buffalo City Planning Association, Buffalo, New York.

BELLE BOAS, Chairman, Art Department, Horace Mann School for Girls, and Assistant Professor of Fine Arts, Teachers College, Columbia University, New York, New York.

E. RAYMOND BOSSANGE, Dean, School of Architecture and Allied Arts, New York University, New York, New York.

JAMES C. BOUDREAU, Director, School of Fine and Applied Arts, Pratt Institute, Brooklyn, New York.

MORSE A. CARTWRIGHT, Director, American Association for Adult Education, New York, New York.

MARTHA CHENEY, New York, New York.

SHELDON CHENEY, New York, New York.

GEORGE J. COX, Head of the Art Department, University of California at Los Angeles, Los Angeles, California.

DOROTHY F. CRUIKSHANK, Worcester Art Museum, Worcester, Massachusetts.

VICTOR E. D'AMICO, Head of the Fine Arts Department, Fieldston School, New York, New York.

JANE DRIVER, Director of Art Education, Wilmington, Delaware.

LOUISE M. DUNN, Associate Curator of Education, The Cleveland Museum of Art, Cleveland, Ohio.

OTTO F. EGE, Head of the Teacher Training Department, Cleveland School of Art, and Assistant Professor of Art, School of Education, Western Reserve University, Cleveland, Ohio.

HUGER ELLIOTT, Director of Educational Work, The Metropolitan Museum of Art, New York, New York.

MARGARET FAIRBANKS, Instructor, The Cleveland Museum of Art, and Instructor, Art Department, Flora Stone Mather College, Western Reserve University, Cleveland, Ohio.

ALMA C. FIELD, Supervisor of Art, Providence Public Schools, Providence, Rhode Island.

THOMAS M. FOLDS, Art Director, The Phillips Exeter Academy, Exeter, New Hampshire.

HENRY SAYLES FRANCIS, Curator of Paintings and Prints, The Cleveland Museum of Art, Cleveland, Ohio.

MARGARET F. S. GLACE, Head, Teacher Education Department, The Maryland Institute, Baltimore, Maryland.

HAROLD GREGG, Supervisor of Art, Sonoma County, California.

WALTER E. HAGER, Secretary, Teachers College, Columbia University, New York, New York.

TALBOT F. HAMLIN, Avery Librarian, Columbia University, New York, New York.

ANN V. HORTON, in charge of Museum Instruction, Cleveland Public Schools, Cleveland, Ohio.

ALFRED HOWELL, Director of Art in the Cleveland Public Schools, Cleveland, Ohio.

HELEN McIVER HOWELL, Instructor in Art, Hollywood High School, Los Angeles, California.

ELLA BOND JOHNSTON, Director of The Art Association, Richmond, Indiana.

ELIAS KATZ, Director, *Art Films*, New York, New York.

WALTER H. KLAR, Supervisor of Fine and Industrial Arts, Public Schools, Springfield, Massachusetts.

BARCLAY S. LEATHEM, Professor of Drama and Theater, Western Reserve University, Cleveland, Ohio.

SHERMAN E. LEE, Instructor, The Cleveland Museum of Art, and Instructor, Western Reserve University, Cleveland, Ohio.

FLORENCE N. LEVY, Director, Art Education Council, New York, New York.

LESTER D. LONGMAN, Head of the Department of Art and Professor of the History of Art, State University of Iowa, Iowa City, Iowa.

JOHN MARTIN, Dance Critic, The New York *Times*, New York, New York.

FRANK JEWETT MATHER, JR., Director of the Museum and Curator of Renaissance and Modern Art, Princeton University, Princeton, New Jersey.

NORMAN C. MEIER, Associate Professor of Psychology, State University of Iowa, Iowa City, Iowa.

ULRICH MIDDELDORF, Associate Professor of Art, and Acting Chairman of the Department of Art, University of Chicago, Chicago, Illinois.

EDITH L. MITCHELL, State Director of Art, Department of Public Instruction, Dover, Delaware.

L. MOHOLY-NAGY, Director, School of Design, Chicago, Illinois.

ALFRED H. MORTON, Vice-President in charge of Television, National Broadcasting Company, New York, New York.

RICHARD J. NEUTRA, Consultant, United States Housing Authority, Washington, D. C.

EDNA PATZIG, Associate Professor of Art, State University of Iowa, Iowa City, Iowa.

ALFRED G. PELIKAN, Director of Art, Milwaukee Public Schools, and Director, Milwaukee Art Institute, Milwaukee, Wisconsin.

ARTHUR POPE, Professor of Fine Arts, Harvard University, Cambridge, Massachusetts.

MARION QUIN, Lincoln School of Teachers College, Columbia University, New York, New York.

RUTH RAYMOND, Chairman of the Department of Art Education, University of Minnesota, Minneapolis, Minnesota.

GORDON L. REYNOLDS, President, Massachusetts School of Art, Boston, Massachusetts.

GRACE W. RIPLEY, Rhode Island School of Design, Providence, Rhode Island.

GILBERT ROHDE, Industrial Designer, New York, New York.

VINCENT A. ROY, Supervisor of Art Education, Pratt Institute, Brooklyn, New York.

GRACE SOBOTKA, George Peabody College for Teachers, Nashville, Tennessee.

ELMER A. STEPHAN, Director of Art Education, Pittsburgh, Pennsylvania.

SALLIE B. TANNAHILL, Associate Professor of Fine Arts, Teachers College, Columbia University, New York, New York.

CLIFFORD M. ULP, Director, School of Applied Art, Rochester Athenaeum and Mechanics Institute, Rochester, New York.

DANA P. VAUGHAN, Dean, Rhode Island School of Design, Providence, Rhode Island.

WILLIAM G. WHITFORD, Professor of Art Education, University of Chicago, Chicago, Illinois.

EDITOR'S PREFACE

At the Cleveland meeting of the Board of Directors, February, 1929, there was a brief, informal discussion of the desirability of initiating a yearbook on some phase of the general problem of " Education in the Fine Arts." Three months later, at the Chicago meeting, Director Horn, reporting at the request of the Board, stressed the importance and also the difficulty of securing as chairman of any yearbook committee in this field a person of nation-wide repute in the fine arts who at the same time would be fully conversant with the educational issues involved. He also suggested that there might well be a series of yearbooks on different branches of the fine arts — music, drawing, and the like — as they affect the school, but the Board was so impressed with the difficulty of committee personnel and also with the difficulty it apprehended from the rise of controversial issues that it then voted to lay the proposal on the table.

When the Board met at Atlantic City, in December, 1932, however, the proposal for a yearbook on some branch of the fine arts was revived, and at that time the late Dean Uhl was asked to report on the possibility of preparing a volume on " Music in the Public Schools." Dean Uhl's subsequent report led eventually to the appearance in 1936 of the *Thirty-Fifth Yearbook*, Part II, entitled " Music Education." (Parenthetically, it may be observed that " Musical Appreciation " had been suggested as a desirable topic as long ago as 1924, when the Board of Directors held its very first meeting for planning the Society's future yearbook program.)

It was not, accordingly, a totally new proposal when, at the meeting of the Board in February, 1935, the late Dean Melvin E. Haggerty, of the University of Minnesota, then Chairman of our Board of Directors, who had previously distributed in manuscript form his " Art a Way of Life," urged a yearbook on art because he was convinced that the point of view of the schools on art was definitely wrong, that the teachers of art were poorly prepared, and that there would be need, within a few years, for a general overhauling and new orientation in the field of art education if the place of art as a social agency affecting the lives of all was to be properly recognized. Coincident with Dean Haggerty's proposal was the arrival of a suggestion from J. C. Morrison, of Albany,

xi

that the Board consider the desirability of a yearbook on " The Fine and Practical Arts in the Elementary Schools."

About a year later (July, 1936) Dean Haggerty submitted at the Chicago meeting of the Board a specific proposal for a yearbook on Art Education, and the Board appropriated the sum of $500 to meet the expenses of a conference of Messrs. Bement, Farnum, Kirby, Payant, and Winslow with Dean Haggerty to lay out general plans, recommend contributors, and suggest the personnel of a directing committee. By the summer of 1937 there had been secured from the Carnegie Foundation for the Advancement of Teaching a grant of $5000, with the understanding that the Society should be prepared to invest $1500 — approximately the amount invested in yearbooks financed regularly by the Society. In view of the fact that there has been expended in the preparation of the manuscript of this yearbook virtually all of these two appropriations, it is obvious that the production of the Yearbook that follows would have been quite impossible without the Carnegie grant and that the members of the Society and others who read and use this contribution owe a very real debt of gratitude to Mr. Carnegie and those who administer his benefactions.

It is not the place here to record all the details in the development of committee personnel or of plans for the content of the Yearbook. Mention ought to be made, however, of the appointment of Dr. Thomas Munro, of the Cleveland Museum of Art, to the post of Chairman of the Yearbook Committee, made vacant by the unfortunate death of Dean Haggerty, October 7, 1937. The task to which Dr. Munro fell heir has been complicated and arduous. Great credit goes both to him and to other members of the Yearbook Committee for their unremitting effort, and no apology needs be made for the occasional overlapping of contents in a book written by so many hands upon so many aspects of so broad a field.

The editor, who makes no pretense to be other than a layman in the visual arts, now finds himself really excited about art and entirely convinced that a wide gulf stretches between art as " a way of life " and art as at present taught in the schools. To bridge this gulf and to glimpse what lies on the further brink ought to be a matter of concern to every curriculum-maker and every school administrator, and any treatment of the problem that makes that possible ought to be welcome. That is what this *Fortieth Yearbook* strives to do.

Guy M. Whipple

TABLE OF CONTENTS

INTRODUCTION

THOMAS MUNRO

SECTION I.— ART IN AMERICAN LIFE

FELIX PAYANT

WALTER CURT BEHRENDT

TALBOT F. HAMLIN

RICHARD J. NEUTRA

EDWIN ZIEGFELD

MARGARET FAIRBANKS

FELIX PAYANT

ALON BEMENT, SHELDON CHENEY, and MARTHA CHENEY

SECTION II.— THE NATURE OF ART AND RELATED TYPES
OF EXPERIENCE

INTRODUCTION

INTRODUCTION

THOMAS MUNRO
Chairman of the Committee
Curator of Education, The Cleveland Museum of Art
Chairman, Division of Art, Western Reserve University
Cleveland, Ohio

I. THE PLAN AND BACKGROUND OF THIS YEARBOOK

Of the thirty-nine yearbooks that this Society has already issued, none has dealt directly and systematically with the visual arts. Keenly interested in these arts himself, and aware of their growing importance in American life and education, the late Melvin E. Haggerty, Dean of the College of Education at the University of Minnesota, proposed in 1936 that some future yearbook be devoted to them. With the approval of the Society's Board of Directors, Dean Haggerty called together a preliminary conference of six art educators on September 10, 1936, in New York City. He then presented his project for the yearbook and his conception of art in a broad sense as an inseparable aspect of a rich and satisfying human life.

Dean Haggerty had already expressed this philosophy in a substantial and eloquent essay entitled *Art a Way of Life*.[1] It was issued as part of the Owatonna Art Education Project, of which he was the director and guiding spirit — an experiment begun in the public schools of Owatonna, Minnesota, in 1933. " Can the pattern of life here outlined," he asked, " a pattern that makes art interest, art need, and art activity integral with the business of institutional organization and effectiveness, be carried over and made the basis of an art curriculum? " The Owatonna project was to test the conviction that it could be. " The essence of that conviction is that education in art is a common need of all young people. They need the understanding, the appreciation, and the modicum of skill that will set them on the route to an ever-improving taste as regards the common, as well as the occasional, experiences of life."

Since Dean Haggerty's philosophy was to give the impetus and the basic plan of this *Yearbook*, his concise expression of it in the essay

---

[1] See references at the end of this Introduction for a fuller citation.

quoted might well serve as a preface to the present volume. He vigorously opposed the artificial separation of art from life, as an esoteric cult for the specially trained or gifted. " Its evil effects upon schools have been pronounced," he said, " making art seem alien to basic education, a fad tolerable in times of plenty but negligible when economic pressures increase, a field that can be ignored by all teachers except specialists, its program of activities having little relation to the ordinary affairs of life." He went on to show how many activities of the home and of ordinary life, in regard to the house and its furnishing, clothing, industry, commerce, and the printed page, involved esthetic sensibility and enjoyment as well as creative expression for everyone. He touched upon theoretical problems regarding the nature of art and related forms of experience, advocating a broadly functional point of view. Appreciation and creation were both active processes, he urged, involving intellect as well as emotion; and neither should be neglected in the educational development of ability.

As to what the schools should do in the name of art, he condemned " the gross neglect that art has everywhere suffered in education."

For persons above the level of mere existence, the arts of life are probably more pervasively important than anything the schools now teach except the mere rudiments of learning. At least they must share importance with a knowledge of science and the duties of citizenship. Measured by any standards of human value, by their contribution to human happiness, by the promotion of sound character and personality, by their enhancement of pleasurable and useful social relations, even by the economical use of time, money, and material resources, the standards of taste in an individual or a community are of the most profound import. Society has suffered merciless penalties for this neglect in our educational program. The results are all too obvious — cities unbelievably ugly, homes devoid of comfort and the benevolence of beauty, dwarfed and distorted personalities, marred and disfigured landscapes, crude manners, and a world of things uglier than they need to be.

He added these significant words on the preparation of art teachers:

This conception of art as a way of living offers very important implicacations as to the character and education of a teacher. He must, of course, be competent to some degree in the techniques of art activity, but vastly more important is it that he shall understand life, the interests and impulses of living individuals. . . . It thus appears that the basic equipment of a teacher who would lead his students into such realms of art as are here set forth is an intuitive and scholarly understanding of the minds of men. Without this sensitive understanding of how people work and think and enjoy the things they see and lay their hands upon, technical equipment is like a machine devoid of power. It may perform the tricks of the trade; it may create a museum, or a discourse upon the history of art, but it cannot make art a vital thing in human life. . . . It is this conception that must be clarified and dramatized in concrete ways if art is to take its place in the schools as a major and vital instrument of cultural education.

It was Dean Haggerty's hope that this *Yearbook* would aid in clarifying that conception through more specific examples, and thus in giving art its due place in the schools and in American life. His plan was destined to be carried through by other hands. Realizing that the book falls considerably short of the mark it would have reached if he had lived to complete it, the Committee has at least endeavored to carry on the project along the lines he proposed.

The Carnegie Corporation of New York, which had aided the Owatonna project, also contributed financially to the present *Yearbook*. The Committee was thus enabled to hold a number of conferences and to develop in detail the brief outline Dean Haggerty had prepared.

In a memorandum issued early in 1937, he described the " audience to be addressed " by the *Yearbook* as consisting primarily of those persons who are responsible for art education in public schools. They included, he said, the following groups: " (a) superintendents and principals responsible for the administration of schools; (b) teachers in elementary grades and all teachers in high schools; (c) supervisors of instruction and those responsible for the preparation of curriculums; (d) teachers of art and supervisors of art; (e) the interested public." A diversity of views was to be encouraged.

The book was to fall into four main parts, following the same order of topics as in *Art a Way of Life*. Section I was to " set forth the relationship between art broadly conceived and the institutions and activities of current American life." Section II would contain " discussions of theoretical problems, from the psychological, philosophical, sociological, economic, and educational points of view." Section III would cover the " agencies effective in art education," including schools and others. Section IV would discuss the education of teachers of art.

Terming this memorandum the " First Plan," the Committee developed it at subsequent meetings into fuller and fuller outlines, the fifth of which was adopted as the final one in 1939. This plan was a detailed topical syllabus of fifteen mimeographed pages. Names of persons believed most competent to write upon each topic were proposed and discussed, with the aim of finding authors who were not only competent but also representative of different points of view and different parts of the country. Members of the Committee were grouped into sub-committees, each under its own leader, and each to be especially responsible for one section of the book. Messrs. Bement and Payant were in charge of Section I, Mr. Faulkner of Section II, Messrs. Farnum and Winslow of Section III, and Mr. Dutch of Section IV. These sub-committees met separately and together, corresponded with prospective authors, collected and discussed manuscripts, and themselves wrote on topics that had not been adequately treated by outside writers. The manuscripts, as usual, were slow in forthcoming. In the spring of 1940, all those in the possession of sub-committees were turned over to the chairman, who has endeavored in the time available before going to press to fill in numerous gaps by last-minute assignments. This explains the unexpectedly large number of articles from the chairman's own home town.

It is an open question whether this is the best way to write a book. Doubtless many members of the Committee felt that each one, if left to himself, could have written a better book on the same subject — certainly a book that was more consistent and even in quality. But doubtless none would have done so; and if he had, the book would have represented only his own point of view. The actual book, as discerning readers will see, is uneven in quality and varied in mode of treatment; it is original, specific, and substantial here, vague and platitudinous there; dogmatic and personal here, objective and experimental there. Many topics that the Committee regarded as highly important have been omitted or scantily treated; it was impossible to hold every author of a chapter to the detailed covering of points assigned. Sometimes he would agree to do so; then shift to topics that seemed to him more important. This outcome had its advantages and disadvantages. Sometimes the Committee or the chairman returned a manuscript with suggestions for revision or addition; they cut and rearranged, but did not presume to alter the papers fundamentally. In short, the method followed has some of the values and defects of democracy itself and of all conference procedure in education. It has not produced a smoothly organized treatise of uniformly high quality, but has turned up a good many unexpected ideas, facts, and suggestions that may be useful in ways not foreseen.

No attempt was made to secure the Committee's agreement on all points. Many divergent views are expressed. It is not to be assumed that the Committee as a whole endorsed any particular ones, or that a member who includes various individual statements in his chapter necessarily agrees with them. Nevertheless, the extent of disagreement should not be overestimated. On the whole, divergence has been on details rather than on fundamentals.

It is open to question whether either the personnel of the Committee (mostly selected by Dean Haggerty) or the list of authors (mostly selected after long discussion by the Committee) was the most suitable. In both cases several individuals invited were too busy with other matters to coöperate; the work was a labor of love that appealed only to persons convinced of the great potential importance of a book of this sort. The Committee expresses its cordial thanks to the many capable writers who did take the time to contribute.

It is open to question, also, whether the attempted scope of the *Yearbook* was too great. Many authors felt with some reason that it was impossible for them to cover adequately the topics assigned, in the short space allowed. Some protested that the range of topics listed would require a whole library of books for proper treatment. Certainly it was impossible to ensure that every topic be treated from every point of view, and thus allow full representation to every shade of opinion. Nevertheless, the Committee held to its course, retaining and considerably augmenting the list of topics proposed by Dean Haggerty. It believed that there was a certain value in merely bringing together, in systematic order, so many topics, issues, and points of view that had never been assembled before. The outline alone might help to organize future thinking, and stimulate more thorough treatment of the topics listed. Furthermore, the *Yearbook* is not intended for advanced specialists, but as a general introduction for administrators, many of whom are laymen in the field of art. It was believed that even a very brief statement on each topic, followed by a list of references, would serve to start the reader off on a line of investigation he could follow up for himself if interested. However, writers differ considerably as to their powers of being brief without dissolving into vague generalities.

In spite of Dean Haggerty's desire to have the subject discussed from a practical, everyday-life point of view, most of the contributions included are by teachers. These naturally tend to emphasize the point of view of the schoolroom, the museum, or the library, rather than that of the studio, the workshop, the salesroom, or the street. This has not come about through the Committee's desire, but automatically and almost inevitably, because of the type of person likely to be interested in writing for an educational yearbook. Many persons of other types were asked to submit contributions, and some did. But writing is an art and a medium in itself; and some whose ideas and experiences might have been illuminating were unwilling or unable to express them in clear and original words. It is to be hoped that their view is indirectly expressed in the words of others. Moreover, many of the contributors to this *Yearbook* are practising artists in their own right as well as teachers, authors, and consumers of art.

In comparing this volume with previous yearbooks of the Society, the reader may find it relatively unscientific and unobjective, lacking in experimental data, full of unsupported generalizations. To a large extent, these criticisms are justified. But they are true, not of this *Yearbook* alone, but also of most current thinking and writing on art and art education. The field as a whole is backward from the standpoint of scientific method, by comparison with other fields that the yearbooks have discussed — necessarily so because of the considerable difficulty of dealing with esthetic problems scientifically. Where data are not already available, and researches not in progress, the writers have been unable to supply them at short notice. Some experimental researches are utilized in the text; some have been avoided as unsound. No doubt much valuable information is omitted merely because it did not come to the attention of the Committee. Again, the Committee hopes that the *Yearbook* represents some progress in the gradual development of realistic, informed, and open-minded thinking on the subject of art education.

These and other shortcomings the chairman wishes to acknowledge in advance, not from any desire to forestall criticism or apologize for faults, but to make clear that the Committee is fully aware of them. The Committee hopes that criticism will be vigorous, and that the *Yearbook*, though useful for a time to students and administrators, will be soon superseded.

II. Art in American Life

There is much doubt and confusion as to the meaning of the word *art,* and as to the types of phenomena it covers. This concerns the nature of ' art ' as a vocation or avocation, ' art ' as a type of human product — works of art — and ' art ' as a subject, an activity, or an area for study in the educational curriculum. In a very broad sense, the word is sometimes applied to all skill in the adaptation of nature to human uses, thus including all applied science; in a very narrow sense, it is sometimes restricted to the so-called fine arts of painting, drawing, architecture, and sculpture, with or without the inclusion of poetry, music, dancing, and dramatic art. College catalogs, in listing courses and departments, usually restrict the scope of ' art ' or ' fine art ' to the first four of the arts just mentioned, with the possible inclusion of certain ' decorative arts,' such as textile design. They are sometimes distinguished as ' visual arts,' appealing primarily to the sense of vision. If included as ' fine arts,' architecture and decoration are usually studied mainly with respect to their esthetic, religious, symbolic, and expressive aspects, rather than with respect to their utilitarian functions.

Teachers of art in schools and colleges have usually emphasized drawing, painting, sculpture, and the less utilitarian aspects of architecture and applied design. Students' technical experience in art has often been limited to drawing, painting, and clay modelling. Accordingly, this is what the school administrator is likely to think of when someone mentions art education. It is largely responsible for his tendency to disparage art as a useless frill. On the college level, there has been heavy emphasis on the archæological approach to art, on exact historical scholarship, and on the ' fine art ' of certain past cultures, especially the Egyptian, Babylonian, Grecian, Roman, Near and Far Eastern, Medieval European, and Renaissance. There has been, at least until very recently, a tendency to neglect and look down upon the more practical, everyday arts of all peoples, upon the controversial modern trends, upon machine products, and upon the claims of primitive art to be taken seriously from an esthetic standpoint.

Very recently, however, there has been a strong tendency, especially in the United States, to regard this conception of art and art education as snobbish, effete, and pedantic. Philosophers, especially John Dewey,[1] have argued that there is no such thing as ' fine art ' in the sense of art that is purely esthetic, entirely devoid of functional utility; that the so-called ' applied,' ' useful,' and ' practical' arts, the handcrafts, industrial and commercial arts, are at least as estimable from the standpoint of esthetic and other human values. They have praised the esthetic quality of many buildings other than temples and palaces, including modern utilitarian structures; of both primitive and modern utensils, furniture and accessories of daily living; of machines and machine products when severely and intelligently functional. Edu-

---

[1] See first and second references at the end of this Introduction.

cators have urged that studies of art on all levels should be extended
far beyond their former, narrow scope, to include more kinds of art,
more periods of art, especially the present, and more of the practical
functions of art. Dean Haggerty wrote:

> The outward activities and inward experiences that are called art are
> the efforts of human beings to make life more interesting and more pleas-
> ing. Art objects which are the product of these activities and experiences
> are meaningful to the degree that they increase human enjoyment. . . .
> Art is the making of things, all sorts of things, in the fittest possible way.

Thus in recent discussion, the common implication of the term *art*
has been considerably expanded, though not so far as the all-inclusive
definition first mentioned. In other words, *art* still implies especially
the visual arts, and especially those products and activities having
some claim to beauty; to power of pleasing the observer through sensory qualities and forms. But it is commonly taken to include at least
certain finer examples of industrial, commercial, and other practical
arts, whether made by hand or by machinery.

Section I of the *Yearbook* is an attempt to advance and illustrate
this broader view of art, with the especial hope that administrators and
educators will come to adopt it and thereby realize more fully the
great importance of art in that inclusive sense, as an element in life
and in education. The Committee believes that laymen generally are
unaware of how many different types of activity in the visual arts
exist today, how they ramify into every part of the social fabric, and
how influential they are from economic, sociological, and psychological,
as well as purely esthetic, standpoints. It has sought to correct this
misapprehension by some explicit reference, however brief, to the principal areas of modern life that should be included within the idea of
art. It has sought to stress on the whole the consumer's view, although
that cannot be wholly divorced from the artist's. At least, it has
avoided details of technique, and stressed the ways in which the finished
products function in American society. There is no special significance
in the order of discussing the various arts, and it does not imply order
of importance.

In the Committee's outline, it was proposed that each art should be
discussed with reference to the following points.[1]

---

[1] This intention has been only partially achieved, but the points are worth
quoting to indicate the aspects of art that the Committee believed to be most significant educationally.

1. Problems the field presents.
2. Materials with which the field is concerned.
3. What the artist in this area attempts to do.
4. Importance of this field in current American life.
5. The economic status of the artist in this area.
6. Art patrons; the extent to which art is privately or publicly supported; recent activities of American government in various arts; Federal Art Projects, P.W.A., and others; support by corporations, foundations, and individuals.
7. Art and mass production; the extent to which art is mechanized, produced by machines rather than by hand; the extent to which art is produced by large scale, mass production; the dissemination of art by reproduction and publication.
8. Foreign influences on American style versus American claims to originality; inherited traditions; successive waves of foreign influence; Colonial, ' Modernistic,' International Style, and other influences.
9. Opposing, or divergent tendencies, forces, factions, movements, issues, ' isms '; those concerned with artistic issues (*e.g.*, naturalism versus distortion); those concerned with political and economic issues (*e.g.*, individualistic versus collectivistic; radical versus conservative).
10. Relation between producer and consumer; the consumer as artist; his influence on community taste.
11. Relation between the arts.
12. Brief historical retrospect of each art in America.

As it has turned out, most of the chapters in Section I are predominantly factual — attempts to inform the reader on what the workers in a certain realm of art are doing, and how these tasks fit into the social setting. They also contain an evaluative element; each writer tends to praise certain trends with which he is in sympathy. Between the lines, one can discern some recurrent questions of policy as to American art itself, over and above the educational issues, which will be considered later. They are, for example,

1. How important and socially valuable are the arts traditionally recognized as ' fine ' (especially painting and sculpture) by comparison with those sometimes distinguished as practical, useful, industrial, and commercial?
2. Within a particular art, such as architecture or even painting, where it is possible to stress either utilitarian or decorative aims, which should be stressed? What is the relative value of the more purely esthetic? To what extent should art aim to be purely functional and to produce visual design only as incidental to function? To what extent is it worth while to produce art for the sake of visual beauty, apart from other

functions? Is art always most beautiful when it is most purely functional?

3. In the representative arts, such as painting and sculpture, on the one hand, to what extent should art be realistic, true to natural appearance, perspective and anatomy; or, on the other hand, alter natural appearances for the sake of design, fantasy, significant emphasis, and so forth?

4. To what extent should art try to be distinctively American, nationalistic, or even regional and local, as opposed to being cosmopolitan or building directly on older European traditions?

5. To what extent and how can the machine and industrial civilization produce good art? To what extent is it desirable to replace hand by machine techniques in art? To what extent should art become closely allied with scientific technology? Coöperative, involving division of labor, rather than individualistic?

6. To what extent should art be government-supported? Supported by foundations and other semi-public institutions? Supported by private business enterprise? By individual patrons?

7. What attitude should artists take in relation to social and political issues of the day, such as war, fascism, communism, the class struggle, social injustices?

III. The Nature of Art and Related Types of Experience

Section II of the syllabus was at first entitled, simply, "Theoretical Considerations." It was to contain discussion of art and art education from the psychological, sociological, economic, and educational points of view, so as to "provide an outline of such principles and theoretical issues as appear essential" for a proper understanding of the educational program to be discussed later. Some twenty chapters under this heading were proposed at the May, 1937 conference, including

1. The psychology of creative experience.
2. The incidence of art interest and need, of art ability.
3. The psychological basis of visual art.
4. Standards of value.
5. Principles of art; nature and elements of form, color, design.
6. Psychology of appreciation; intellectual and emotional elements; participation and appreciation.
7. Measurement of art abilities, achievement, judgment, appreciation.
8. The character and activities of the creative artist.
9. The social uses of art.
10. Genetic approach to art; relation to development of the individual.

This list and the space allotted to Section II were cut down considerably because of the Committee's wish to emphasize concrete details and practical issues rather than abstract theory. Nothing like a systematic treatise on esthetics or the psychology of art was attempted. A few central problems of theory were, however, treated at some length. These problems are concerned with both fact and value; with the nature of art and of the activities related to it, and with modes of evaluating them as good or bad, beautiful or ugly. They are 'theoretical' because of their comparatively abstract and general quality, and because they deal with controversial points on which little verified knowledge exists as yet.

No study of art and art education can be thorough or intelligent if it avoids fundamental questions completely. In education, it is impossible to avoid making assumptions and hypotheses on these fundamental points, whether one realizes it or not; and the assumptions made have a far-reaching effect on curriculum-building, choice of content, and teaching methods.

For example, it implies an evaluative assumption to urge that a certain type of art be shown to students, as worth studying and 'appreciating.' Similarly, it implies evaluation to urge that certain techniques in art are worth learning, and that certain qualities are desirable in a finished work of art. Assumptions on such points are commonly so vague and dogmatic, accepted with so little evidence as 'art principles,' that it is well to devote a little space to explicit discussion of this problem of value in art.

Uncritical assumptions about the psychology of activities connected with art are constantly being made. Teachers speak of having their students 'create' and 'appreciate,' with little definite understanding of the nature of these processes. What does it mean to be 'creative'? What happens when we 'appreciate' art? Can one learn to appreciate without actually using an art medium? How can real appreciation be taught, or powers of appreciation be developed, as distinct from mere book information or superficial verbal and emotional responses? What types of art ability exist, and how do people differ in these regards? Can they be measured or recognized in early life? How many people have potential art ability? How are creative and appreciative ability developed and affected by schooling and other environmental factors? To what extent are these abilities correlated with intelligence?

There is considerable disagreement among writers on esthetics and art theory. This applies not only to the nature of art and related psychological phenomena and to the standards of value for appraising art, but even to the methods of investigating these problems. Some writers believe them to be fundamentally beyond the reach of scientific methods like measurement, controlled observation, and experiment. Others believe that these methods can be applied — and indeed, have been applied — to the psychology of art with great success. Still others believe that they are applicable only in a superficial way, at least for the present; that much recent work of this sort has been unsound and unenlightening; and that scientific progress in esthetics can and should proceed for a time without much effort at exact measurement. Similar controversy exists in regard to the fruitfulness of psychoanalytic hypotheses and procedures in interpreting art and esthetic experience. (These are less used in American than in European writings on esthetic theory.)

These issues are not settled with any finality in Section II, but they are at least stated in some detail, so as to bring out their relation to the educational process. We are concerned in this *Yearbook*, not with art in itself or art education in itself, but with both in relation to life. Unless the word *life* is to be empty and meaningless, it must be translated into fairly specific psychological, sociological, and other terms denoting particular life activities, individual and collective.

A well-considered policy in regard to art education should involve some reasoned philosophy on the social and economic functions of the visual arts. What is the place of art in a democracy such as ours? The dictatorial states, communist and fascist, are fairly clear and consistent in this matter. They consider art as a means of securing unanimity of thought, feeling, and action in support of the ruling group and against its adversaries. In such regimented states, methods of teaching art are consistently worked out in relation to this end. So is the amount of government subsidy to be given the arts, and the choice of artists and types of art to be favored. In democratic states, including our own, the function of art is often ignored in framing social policy. Art is often put aside as a luxury, an idle enjoyment and recreation apart from the serious business of life. But in recent years, the United States has also seen a trend toward systematic government support of art, partly as relief to artists, and partly as a means of beautifying public buildings. Future conditions may force us to think out more thoroughly our social policy toward art, including the problem of propagandist art expressing social conflict, and the wider use of art as a leisure avocation. When we do, our conclusions will have far-reaching effects on the nature of art education.

Moreover, when we undertake to teach the details of art history, and the practice of various arts, we find ourselves more and more compelled to consider social and economic aspects. Art history is coming to be written, not as an isolated strain in the story of mankind, but as intimately bound up with religious movements, social orders and upheavals, scientific and intellectual progress, industrial and financial developments. When we teach an art such as city-planning, we find it necessary to urge the student not to regard it merely as a problem of designing beautiful façades, parks, and avenues; but to conceive the visible form of a city in relation to transportation, factories, business centers, economic levels of population, and all the manifold factors that make up the city as a social mechanism within the larger mechanism of the nation.

To the educator, such questions appear as problems of how to organize the teaching of a certain subject, and of how to integrate that subject with others. But integration can never be genuine or thorough if it is merely a matter of classroom procedure or of combination in a syllabus. It must be based on a genuine understanding by the teacher and administrator of the deep connections in actual life between the activities with which school subjects and school activities deal.

IV. Art Education: Its Aims, Procedures, and Agencies

Having begun in Section I with a broad conception of ' art ' as including many different arts and media, the *Yearbook* should now go on to discuss how all of them are, and should be, taught. It should not limit itself to the work of teachers explicitly called ' art teachers,' or of ' art departments ' in schools and colleges, or of ' art academies '; for these are often limited to art in a much narrower sense: to drawing, painting, sculpture, and a few restricted types of handcraft. That fact does not imply that the attitude toward art of such schools and teachers is necessarily narrow or effete. It has come about through ambiguous terminology, in the process of distinguishing subjects and departments in the curriculum. Much that has been included in Section I under the heading of ' art ' is taught under other names; as, architecture, stage design, dancing, costume, and so on. Much of it does not come within the administrative province of art teachers or art departments, and they are not to be held responsible for good or bad features in its teaching. We should distinguish clearly in our thinking between art in a broad sense and the work carried on by art departments explicitly so designated in our educational system. The latter covers but a small area of the former.

Unfortunately, to cover the educational aspects of all the arts mentioned in Section I, even briefly, would have expanded the *Yearbook* to impossible proportions. So it has come about perforce that ' art education ' is taken on the whole in a fairly restricted sense in Section III. More than the Committee would have wished, it is limited to the work of art schools and art departments. Although these have been expanding their scope considerably in recent years, they do not — and perhaps should not (for administrative reasons) — attempt to deal with instruction in all the arts mentioned in Section I. No doubt further rapprochement between teachers of all these arts should develop in future years; but whether it should be brought about by merging of present departments or by entrusting a greater area to art teachers is a debatable question of policy. Enough is said to indicate the Committee's belief that all the arts included in Section I should somehow find a secure place in our educational program — not that all children should study all the arts intensively; but that all arts should be made available to those specially fitted for them; and that a basic acquaintance with most or all of them should develop in the process of general education.

Moreover, much of what is said about art education in the narrow sense, or even about instruction in drawing or picture appreciation alone, will apply by implication to the other arts also. The same general issues apply to all of them; and a definite educational policy on one carries over into many related fields.

What, then, are the chief current issues in regard to art education, in a broad or narrow sense?

In the first place, all the issues mentioned above in regard to art, itself, as an adult occupation and a type of product, carry over into art education. According to the way we answer the questions, " What are the best kinds of art? " and " How can art best serve American society? " certain implications will follow as to the best ways of teaching art. As a matter of fact, methods of art education have on the whole followed successive trends and styles in art itself: once setting the student to emulate Classic, Florentine, or Dutch masters; now gradually opening the doors to Impressionist and Post-impressionist aims and techniques. As leading architects and industrial designers come to stress functionalism, simplicity, and new materials, the teachers of these arts follow suit; not all at once, but after the new trend has become respectable.

The issues raised in Section II with regard to the psychological, sociological, and evaluative aspects of art are also educational issues, or have an immediate educational bearing. What we believe as to the nature of art abilities and the mental processes involved in creation and appreciation will influence our ways of trying to develop these abilities in students. If we believe that art ability is restricted to the talented few, we shall be inclined to restrict art instruction to these gifted students; but if we believe it to be more universal, we may favor making such opportunities available for all. If we believe that art is an effeminate luxury of the idle rich, we shall not be inclined to spend much money on it in the public schools. What we believe as to the social functions of art will influence our ways of relating art to the rest of the curriculum, will make us present it as detached and trivial, or as an integral, vital factor in society. If we adhere to strict academic standards of value in art, we shall probably insist that students be drilled in accordance with them, made if possible to like such art, and to produce it. If on the other hand, we like to see an artist express his personal outlook in unusual ways, even if these are not always beautiful by accepted standards, we shall be more tolerant of children's experiments in self-expression. If we believe that painting and sculpture are the only arts worthy of the name, we shall restrict the scope of art courses accordingly; we may react to the opposite extreme of looking down on the ' fine arts ' as trivial, and restricting educational recognition to the ' practical arts ' alone.

Any policy can be carried to an unwise or absurd extreme. The one which Dean Haggerty expressed with moderation, and which this Committee endorsed, is no exception; that is, the policy of according more recognition to the useful, everyday manifestations of art, and of avoiding the narrow, genteel snobbishness of the ' fine art ' tradition in the past. No doubt the latter has been heavily overemphasized in many college art departments and museums. But it should not be inferred that the value of art is to be appraised entirely in terms of everyday utility or of the greatest enjoyment of the greatest number of people. Painting and sculpture should not be too hastily brushed aside as unimportant, in the new enthusiasm for practical arts. There may still be a place for the production and enjoyment of visual, as well as musical, forms that have no utility other than to provide objects for esthetic contemplation. There may still be a place for the types of art that stress pure decoration, fantasy, amusing entertainment, and the expression of abstract ideals remote from immediate needs. In our eagerness to make art function in the lives of common men, and in our insistence that art ability is not confined to the aristocratic few, we need not rush to an indiscriminate leveling of values. There may still be certain kinds of art that are too difficult for untrained or insensitive minds to enjoy, yet quite as valuable socially as the popular forms of art. There may be talented individuals, and a few geniuses, who deserve special treatment. They may come from any social or economic class.

Just how to balance these sets of values is a perennial issue in art and art education. At present, there is perhaps greater danger of a too narrowly practical attitude toward the claims of art on the part of school educators than of the opposite extreme. It would be unfortunate if this *Yearbook* should be understood as approving it, and as justifying art only on the basis of tangible returns in cash, comfort, or that vague catchword ' social adjustment.' It would be unfortunate if potential leaders in art were lost to sight through exaggerated emphasis on mass education.

Not all the issues in art education arise from issues in the outside world of art production and consumption. Some are more indigenous to the educational realm itself. Education in youth is not now regarded merely as preparation for later life, but as a period of life that has its own intrinsic values. Deciding on the right sort of art education is not, therefore, merely a matter of deciding what sort of mature artists or art appreciators we wish to produce. Even if we knew that none of our students were to become artists, and that none would have access to art, there would still be reason — so much the more reason — for letting them practice and enjoy the arts in school. Art is coming to be recognized, in other words, as a necessary part of general education for all persons, on all age-levels — necessary to the full exercise and development of personality, especially in its sensory, emotional, and imaginative aspects, and in muscular coördination.

But how shall art as an element in general education for all be related to art as vocational training for the few? What relative emphasis shall be placed on the two modes of approach? To what extent shall a broad, cultural view of art be required of all? To what extent shall intensive technical skill be sacrificed to it? To what extent shall free, individual experimentation be encouraged in all? To what extent shall the money available for art education be spent on students for whom it is to be a vocation? And to what extent shall these students be taught specific, salable techniques and styles? To what extent and how early shall they be given the practical viewpoint of factories and commercial studios? Shall students be encouraged to be original and experimental, to express their own interests and outlooks, or to please the public? Or can both be done at once? Some kinds of originality are salable, of course. And it is not without value in character development to learn how to do a technical job in a professional way. In overemphasizing personality, students' preferences, emotional adjustment, and so on, as aims of art, there is danger of sentimental vagueness, of losing the real educational values of self-discipline, habits of work, respect for sound craftsmanship, and definite knowledge. Yet few educators to-day, in democratic countries, propose returning to the set rules and repressive disciplines of the old academic education.

In so far as art is regarded as a phase of general education, rather than as training in a marketable skill, certain definite problems are raised. How can the stages in art education be adapted to those in personality development and general education, so as to become a phase in normal growth? How can they be made continuous from age-level to age-level, from lower to higher grades, avoiding the gaps and dislocations that now exist? How can studies in the appreciation, history, and criticism of art best be coördinated with those in technique and creative production? How should the emphasis be placed as between the two groups? Should there be much or little study of past art? How can museum or other studies of past art be made to contribute to creative originality, instead of making students imitative or merely scholarly? How can studies of art best aid in conveying the cultural heritage of past civilization and also give the student an ability to understand and cope with present civilization? What manual skills and technical knowledge are of value in general education for the student who will not become a professional artist? Should every child acquire some facility in using his hands to control a visual art medium, as he learns to use words for expression and communication? Which media should he work with; how many; and at what ages?

Each art and each medium raises its own additional problems. For example, in drawing, should students draw directly from observation of nature, and from past works of art, or only from memory and imagination? If from all, in what proportions? Is copying other works of art necessarily bad? If not, how and to what extent can it be done beneficially? To what extent should historical and other factual knowledge of the subject matter of art be required of students; and to what extent should students be allowed to ' use their imaginations ' in representing a subject?

How can art activity be used to develop mental and emotional health and stability in the student? What does psychoanalysis imply as to the possible psychotherapeutic uses of art, and how reliable are these implications?

From the administrative standpoint, with which many of our authors and readers are concerned as directors and supervisors, other problems may appear as most important. What teaching personnel and what physical equipment are necessary for art work on various levels, and in various types of school? What portion of the total budget does art deserve? How important is supervision, and what should the supervisor do? Should art be taught mostly by regular classroom teachers or by special teachers? If the latter, how should art be related to other subjects? At what school level should art and other subjects be departmentalized? How should elementary-school art differ from junior- and senior-high-school art, and these from college, graduate, and professional-school art? How can continuous progress in art from one school level to the next be facilitated? How can students' achievements on each level be evaluated and recorded? What standards of achievement can fairly be demanded on each level, for promotion to the next higher? How can attention to individual needs, especially of gifted students, be reconciled with the needs of ordinary students? How can large-scale education in art be standardized in desirable ways (*e.g.*, equipment and schedule) without becoming inflexible? How large should art classes be, and what maximal teaching load is desirable?

Still heatedly argued back and forth is the question of ' integration ' versus ' isolation ' — shall art be taught as a separate subject and department, or be merged with others, as in the project method, core curriculum, and similar procedures? If the former, how can it be kept from excessive specialization, aloofness, and artificiality? If the latter, how can it avoid being overwhelmed by other approaches and made a mere handmaid to other departments, as in the making of posters for English and Social Studies? Shall it be taught with emphasis on distinctively artistic aspects, such as color, design, and perspective, or with emphasis on ' social significance ' — on art as a means of social reform, realistic description, and propaganda?

To all these questions more than one answer is possible, and no answer has so far been proved right. On most of them, art teachers tend to divide into two main camps: first the so-called ' progressive ' wing, favoring comparative freedom for the student, a psychological and sociological approach, and integration rather than the subject curriculum; second, the more conservative wing, sometimes called ' academic,' favoring more discipline, required knowledge and technique, and more intensive, directed, systematic study of a limited realm of art. The former camp inclines to be more sympathetic to modern Post-impressionist art and to liberal politics; the latter to conservative politics, Realism, and traditional standards in art. But such views do not always go together, and most art teachers object to being definitely labelled. They are conscious of the unwise extremes to which both attitudes have been carried: the one to absurd freakishness and pampering of children's whims; the other to stodgy, repressive conventionality. Most art teachers regard themselves as being at a happy medium between the two extremes, and as combining in their approach both sets of values. Nevertheless, vigorous disputes still arise over details of method and content.

Another administrative problem that is coming to the fore is that of providing opportunities for students to see good art, past and present, originals and reproductions. To try to teach art without showing good examples reduces art instruction to students' groping experiments or to rules and teachers' demonstrations. It is like trying to teach musical composition to students who never hear good music; yet all too often that sort of teaching is attempted. Some extremists of the ' free expression ' school defend it as encouraging originality, and the extreme academic type of teacher still prefers to teach by demonstration and criticism only. But on the whole the demand is growing vigorously for opportunities to make good art familiar to students. If there is a museum nearby, this raises the question of fitting visits into the schedule, or of securing loan exhibits for the school. What should the school have in the way of exhibition space, lantern-slide projectors, and so forth? How can systematic observation of art be best fitted into the program? If far from a museum, the school can still borrow traveling exhibits. But what should it own in the way of permanent art material, such as lantern slides, photographs, color-print reproductions, casts, films, and (if possible) original works of art and craftsmanship? How can these be circulated from class to class or school to school? Government art projects have recently supplied thousands of original works of art to urban and rural schools. Yet these do not satisfy teaching needs, and sooner or later the school budget must face the task of supplying necessary materials for art as it does for chemistry. These will include, of course, artists' materials also — the traditional types, such as paints and clay, and the more complex apparatus of twentieth-century art, especially in the industrial fields and in theater arts.

V. The Preparation of the Art Teacher

One's attitude toward the preparation of art teachers tends, if consistently thought out, to be largely determined by one's attitude on the problems mentioned above. If one believes that a certain kind of art is best, and that students should be trained to produce and like it, then one will believe that teachers in turn should be trained so as to make them capable of achieving these results. Methods of educating art teachers, accordingly, tend to proceed from beliefs or assumptions regarding the best kinds of art, the most valuable kinds of skill in producing or appreciating art, and the principal values to be derived from a study of art. In defining ultimate objectives, the emphasis may be laid on the student's own benefit through vocational skill, culture, and development of personality, or both; or on the student's potential contributions to society. The latter may be interpreted in terms of a liberal ideal of free creative enterprise, or in terms of economic production, or in terms of solidarity, obedience, readiness to fight and die for the state, as in dictatorial regimes today. In any case, the rightness of any teacher-training program is decided largely on instrumental grounds — in terms of what kind of instruction we wish the prospective teacher to be able to give.

Naturally, various lines of thought part company on this question, as on the prior esthetic and educational issues themselves. There are teachers of prospective teachers who believe their charges should be fitted primarily to convey certain techniques of art as effectively as possible, including the requisite manual skills and technological information, and also a certain set of artistic ideals and standards. There are those who believe their task is to develop highly trained research scholars in art history, who can in turn make their own students into highly trained scholars. There are those who believe the art teacher's primary task is to develop in students a broad culture, independent habits of imagination and expression, emotional adjustment, and similar personality traits. They will believe, accordingly, that the art teacher's own training should be organized primarily to make him capable of developing these traits in students.

Of course, it is not necessary to choose one or another of these policies exclusively. Most American teacher-training institutions would probably recognize all (except some of the dictatorial ones) as desirable, and would claim to be working more or less for all of them, directly or indirectly. But real and considerable differences of emphasis arise in practice. They are manifested most obviously in the relative amounts of work in various fields required of prospective art teachers. The reader should examine the comparative data in Section IV, on the course requirements of various institutions, with this in mind.

Time was when no very complicated requirements were imposed upon a prospective teacher of art. The guild system was often fairly strict in recognizing a man as a master craftsman, whose qualifications would fit him to rule the lives of apprentices and to convey to them the ideals and skills of his craft. Under the freer individual methods of instruction that followed, anyone who could persuade others that he knew his craft could set up as a teacher or employ apprentices. Later on, vocational schools, some of them managed by craft unions, have again raised standards and organized systematic courses of instruction; but they have been almost entirely concerned with technique. Hence the principal requirement for teaching in them was technical. If a man was a good craftsman himself, it was assumed that he could teach his craft without bothering to study methods of teaching.

Meanwhile colleges and universities in this country were teaching art from another aspect; mainly from that of history and literature, especially of the Classical, Medieval, and Renaissance periods. They were interested very little, if at all, in producing artists, but rather in conveying knowledge about the history of art. Positions were opened for men and women to teach art history and appreciation in the increasing number of colleges throughout the country. Graduate instruction was arranged — primarily for prospective teachers of art history — and degrees were established requiring advanced knowledge and ability in historical research. But ability to practice art was not (and still is not) considered a necessary qualification for college art professors. Nor is there much disposition to require courses in education of a prospective college art teacher. Ordinarily he is exempt from state certification requirements. But he does, in a liberal college, have to study many other academic subjects besides art, and hence presumably he does acquire a fairly broad cultural background.

The tremendous rise of 'education' as a profession and a subject of study in this country has altered the situation considerably, especially with respect to the preparation of teachers for public and private schools of the elementary and secondary levels. Along with this has gone the increasing belief that studies in art are of value in the general education of all children, even for those who will not become artists; also that art instruction should aim at a variety of goals in addition to technical skill. It should help produce personality traits, integrate the curriculum, and so on. For these reasons it is urged that a prospective art teacher should devote a considerable amount of time to studying educational courses, such as the philosophy and psychology of education, teaching methods, and so forth, in addition to practice teaching. State teachers' certificates have enforced this tendency by demanding a certain amount of prescribed work in education. Professional art schools, universities, and teachers colleges have all been drawn into service to supply art teachers. They have been required to provide (at least by coöperation with some other institution) for the pedagogical, as well as the technical, training of their charges.

. The course of study for the prospective teacher of school art is continually being widened to include more and different studies, each of which can be reasonably defended as desirable. Teachers of the practice of art, however, usually oppose giving up much time from the technical work that they believe necessary. Not a few leaders in the subject of education are coming to agree with them, and to point out that required courses in education are often of little value as actually taught, and that, in any case, too many are required. At the same time, it is said that too little work in art history and theory is required in many teacher-training institutions.

It is difficult to generalize, because of the diverse conditions prevailing in different institutions and localities, but it seems fairly evident that various types of institution for preparing art teachers have developed on very different lines, and that much dislocation has resulted in the field as a whole. Teachers of art in the colleges are being prepared with heavy or exclusive emphasis on the historical approach to art, with fairly good cultural background, but with little or no technique in the practice of art, and little or no study of educational methods. Teachers of art in the schools below college level are being prepared with some technique and some educational methods, but often with little art history or theory, and little general cultural background, as evidenced by the small number of courses required in literature, history, and science. Teachers of professional art or craft instruction tend in their preparation to specialize on technique and to sacrifice all the other alternatives to some extent, except as they are forced to a broader preparation by certification requirements.

One result of these divergent lines of training has been to differentiate excessively between various types and levels in art instruction. College art has been decidedly different from, and unrelated to, the type of art done in secondary schools. Secondary-school art is often very different from elementary art, because of greater departmentalization and concentration on technique. Art work in vocational high schools again is very different from art work in general, academic high schools. This dislocation appears as lack of continuity in progression from grade to grade, lack of definite requirements for each grade, and lack of coöperative understanding between art teachers at various points in the educational process.

Progress is being made in improving the training of art teachers, mainly through the gradual recognition by each institution and school level of what it has been neglecting. College art faculties are coming to include practicing artists as well as historians in their faculties, and to recognize practical art experience as desirable, if not strictly necessary, for the college art teacher. Prospective teachers of school art are being required to study more art history and theory, which they have lacked. But the exact distribution of time and the organization of curricula still present many issues, which are discussed in detail in Section IV.

Ideally, it would seem that all courses for the training of art teachers should be made longer, with more possibility of including all the desirable types of subject matter. But it is hard for any one institution alone to raise the requirements. Moreover, the profession of teaching art must compete with practical opportunities afforded by the industrial and commercial arts, in which financial rewards are sometimes high and educational requirements low. No doubt further progress can be made through having administrators place a premium on adequate preparation in appointing teachers, and through concerted action by teacher-training institutions and teachers' associations. It should always be remembered that the problem is not solved by putting down on paper a fine array of required courses, topics of study, and so on. Everything will depend on how well these are taught and learned; and this in turn will depend on the quality of the persons engaged in them. It is to be hoped that the profession of art teaching, as well as the practice of art, will attract more broadly qualified persons to enter it, by its financial as well as its intangible rewards. This will necessitate better conditions of work, an easier teaching load, more secure tenure of position, and salary and retirement provisions commensurate with ever-rising standards of proficiency.

REFERENCES

(1) DEWEY, JOHN. *Experience and Nature*. (Open Court: Chicago, 1925) 443 pp.
(2) DEWEY, JOHN. *Art as Experience*. (Minton, Balch: New York, 1934) 355 pp.
(3) HAGGERTY, M. E. *Art a Way of Life*. (University of Minnesota Press: Minneapolis, 1935) 43 pp

SECTION I

ART IN AMERICAN LIFE

CHAPTER I

THE SOCIAL BACKGROUND OF AMERICAN ART

FELIX PAYANT
Editor of *Design*
Columbus, Ohio

Art, broadly conceived, is an inseparable aspect of rich and satisfying human life. Since education is, above all, the instrument for extending culture, any consideration of the validity of educational procedure must of necessity involve the art factor. In studying the place of art in education, it is well to begin with an analysis of the major activities encompassed by our complex social scene.

Primitive man carved and painted the walls of his cave. Today man surrounds himself with those things that he considers beautiful in order to avoid being stultified by everyday routine. There has been a constant urge for man to make things about him meaningful, to intensify the realities of his existence. Human values may vary among peoples, epochs, and regions. Available materials change and needs fluctuate. Yet the compelling force of giving life significance remains.

The materials of life are the materials of art. Art begins where nature leaves off. This relationship holds true throughout life, though it is less discernible in complex modern society. Man soon learned that where there is life, there may be drama; where there is sound, there may be music; where there is movement, there may be dance; where there is color, there may be painting; where there is mass, there may be sculpture, architecture, and cities. Ultimately there is a symphony of life relationships, with the various themes appearing either singly or in contrapuntal relationships.

Because man has striven to give meaning to materials in the world wherein he lives and has felt the joy of creating, he has elevated himself above the beast. Art is the precursor of science and a dominant factor of culture, today as in the past.

Art permeates the very warp and woof of our contemporary social fabric, so that man's conduct is constantly influenced by it. The planning of a great city so that life therein may reach its fullest significance

29

for all those persons and activities within it is an art of vast social import. The successful solution of this problem demands creative imagination supported by science and industry. Public architecture affords an insight into the ideals of society. The building of homes, with all the vividness of the domestic scene, is the very nucleus of society. Modern industry, in providing a wealth of commodities, demands art at every turn, not only in production, but also in distribution, where controlled appearance is a dominant factor.

Personal attire at its best depends upon the harmonizing of materials, physical needs, structure, and refinement. The printed page, closely interwoven with our lives today, is an attractive means of disseminating ideas in our complex world. In the theater, motion picture, radio, and television, the life-giving force is the esthetic quality.

One of the dominant factors with which modern civilized man has had to cope is the machine. It connotes mechanization, quantity production, division of labor, and crowded urban life. Man's rhythms and social forms have been decidedly disturbed by these phenomena and the complexion of life has had to be adjusted to them. Incoherencies of our age have had to be eliminated for the sake of harmony. The materials of art have changed. Through art, man is replacing confusion with organization, and incongruity with meaning. Each age has its own esthetic. Ours may be closely allied with the machine, the skyscraper, and the motor car. Thus our ideals of beauty are expressed in terms of the materials, standards, and rhythms of our age.

Civilization in its present conception, as in the past, is an art. The unfolding of the better life is a realization of art in its fullest sense. Man is finding that the machine is not his foe but perhaps a powerful force for good. It is a tool capable of producing articles of merit in quantity and at a cost within the means of everyone. Well-fashioned articles, reproductions of major expressions of our time, suitably printed volumes of the best thought of our age, and increased leisure are among the benefits derived from mass production.

By some strange misconception the fine arts — painting and sculpture — have been isolated as *art*. Perhaps because of the ease with which these may be handled and the comparative simplicity of the materials involved, this fallacy has taken root. But not only painting and sculpture, but also all those significant materials of life from the simplest act to the creation of a vast city with its innumerable agencies, necessarily contribute to rich community enterprise. The attributing of art to painting and sculpture alone is a concept reminiscent of the late nineteenth century, when the professional picture-maker and esthete became detached from society. It was the age of the 'ivory tower,' where the artist avoided the realities of life. Today the artist's place is close to the most vital activity and thought of society.

What is the artist's problem? What does the artist do to the materials of life to make them meaningful? How does he intensify the various elements in his environment to make life interesting?

When man found that life became drama through *emphasis;* sound became music through *harmony;* motion became dance through *rhythm;* color became painting through *composition;* mass became architecture through *order,* he learned the basic principles of creative experience or art. These fundamentals of art hold true today. Throughout new materials, expanded needs, and a more complex social environment these principles have remained intact. They are not veiled in mystery. They affect every man's art job. Too frequently has society considered art as something akin to magic. The real artist has never waved a magic wand. Although he was associated with a realm somewhat detached from the realities of the world, an indestructible tie checked his complete escape.

Today the fulfillment of the desire for art is the privilege and responsibility of all. The creative pattern of attack is not foreign to that in other pursuits. Craftsmanship is not 'fancy work.' Design is not mere embellishment or art 'applied.' It is a quality of construction.

In attacking a problem the artist analyzes the needs to be satisfied, the limitations implied, the materials to be used, suitable construction, and those qualities that might be referred to as 'refinements' — refinements of line, form, ornament. For example, in building a house the architect must be aware of the nature of the site, the amount to be spent, the materials to be used, and countless other matters. His is not unlike the approach to a scientific problem. The attack must be made step by step to insure the best result. Imagination is important; equally important is all available factual information. To make use of the knowledge attained by others is as important in art as in any other field. The solution of a problem, based on such an analysis, is expressed in the artist's statement. The manner in which the artist makes his statement is referred to as his technique. Too frequently technique is considered as the art itself rather than as a device or a method peculiar to an individual, a racial, religious, or social group.

Techniques must follow, rather than dictate, the manner of solving an art problem. They evolve from materials and structure.

There is an art quality in the things with which the consumer surrounds himself. There are urgent creative elements involved even in his selection of the 'readymade.' It is his job to assemble chairs, carpets, lamps, desks, and pictures into a unified functional room, and to fit himself with suitable wardrobe of suits, shirts, shoes, coats, and accessories. The consumer's problem is not so much the making of things as the organization into meaningful relationships. In so doing he is, to some extent, experiencing art. In selecting a proper chair or a suit of clothes he exercises a form of creative power. He identifies himself with those things to which his sensibilities respond. The consumer by his approval of material objects is to that extent an artist.

Because our nation has been a melting pot of institutions, standards, manners, and customs of many nations, our arts obviously are the result of this blending. In the early periods England dominated. As time moved on, other European nations and influences made their impressions. America exemplifies this potpourri. From the very first, however, the Colonists were faced with limitations in their new environment. When they sought to satisfy their needs by making those things to which they had become accustomed at home, they encountered new situations. They were forced to meet new limitations of locale, materials, equipment for working, not to mention differences in the kind of utensils necessary. This gave rise to a difference in the design of buildings, furnishings, clothing, and transportation. Their art from necessity was a part of their new life. It was a material expression of their attitude toward the new American culture.

Rarely in history has a people been composed of a greater variety of nationalities and accompanying influences than has the United States. This has meant a rich kaleidoscopic inheritance of art that from the very beginning was filled with the vigor, adventure, and freedom of expression peculiar to this heterogeneous population. Out of this, American art has derived its form, refinement, honesty, and simplicity of character spurred by the religious Puritanism that dominated the New England Colonists. These were factors that colored the folk arts of early America. Much of this restraint exists in the folk arts that have survived. Such art expressions as the Cape Cod cottage, the Windsor chair, the carved wooden ships' figure heads, the portraits by the itinerant painters (called 'limners'), the carved ivory and scrimshaw made by the whalers along the New England coast still exist as indisputable evidence of the desire for esthetic expression. They objectify with no little intensity the ideals of the time.

The rich art of the Pennsylvania Germans, with their architecture so well suited to the locale, fractur painting in the form of birth certificates and other family documents, ceramics of high order, hand-woven fabrics, the cast-iron stoves, Stiegel glass — all give ample evidence of an exuberance and a healthy joy of living.

New Orleans, with a strong intermingling of French and Spanish colonization, contributed a type of architecture with wrought- and cast-iron balconies. The Southwest, with a different set of geographical conditions and the early Spanish influence — colored by the Indians — has given us Mission architecture, furniture, the santos, silver, and leather accessories.

With these as typical of the influence of racial inheritance on the growth of our folk art it would be well to turn to the various socialistic and sectarian groups to consider their contributions. The Shakers, with their religious view, have left us excellent examples of housing, furniture design, and inspirationals (a type of painting not well known but extremely revealing of their moral code). The Zoarites in Ohio were architects, ceramists, cabinetmakers, and landscape architects; and are worthy of study as a social group in which art was coexistent with society. Canvassing the American scene would add further testimony to the already powerful evidence that through multiplicity of racial, religious, and social influences, largely from Europe, America at an early date established an art that was attuned to its own temperament and indigenous to its soil. The story of the arts here has been a vivid one, integral with man's deepest aspiration. Every region has made its peculiar statement regarding beauty embodied in the materials of that area and couched in the idiom of its particular entity. If we are convinced that art is coexistent with life, we cannot but feel the vitality and creative force of the early Americans.

While these arts were essentially the arts of the people, and available examples are usually anonymous, a few names have come down to us, among which are those of Edward Hicks, whose painting of Biblical scenes has been the inspiration of persons attuned to art ever since, and Schimmel of Pennsylvania, whose wood sculpture is unsurpassed as an expression in three-dimensional form.

It was natural for those arts pertinent to the physical necessities of life to be developed first. But as the rigors of early pioneer days passed and fortunes were made, the artist, as we have learned to think of him, made his appearance. His presence implies a certain amount of leisure and means with which to pay him for this work. Frequently in Colonial times the artist was not able to live on what he earned from his art, and he had to turn to other things for his support, as did Paul Revere, the silversmith. As fortunes grew, American architecture, home furnishing, and painting emerged as unsophisticated, unschooled craftsmanship up to 1700.

Talented young American architects and artists turned to England to further their education. English artists visited the Colonies. This fostered the adoption of English ideals here. In the middle of the nineteenth century those persons and institutions that supported art were engulfed by the Industrial Revolution. After the Civil War art was influenced by the chaotic conditions in America. It was a difficult time for the artist.

The period immediately following the Civil War introduced Whistler, Eakins, Ryder, and others among the painters; and Richardson, the architect. The late Victorian Age is sometimes spoken of as the ' Gilded Age ' of American art. The romantic and the bizarre were the vogue in architecture, in painting, in home furnishing, and on the printed page.

From that time on, America has been the scene of a succession of divergent tendencies, forces, contradictory factions, and innumerable issues. Each generation found art characterized by emphasis upon different methods: Impressionism with its theory of split color; *l'art nouveau* and its flowing curves; and in more recent years Cubism, Futurism, Surrealism — all of these emanating from Europe.

The introduction of electricity has done much to develop stage *décor*. Photography has had its influence on painting and has considerably affected the art of portrait-painting. The motion picture is one of four most influential arts, as gauged by the number of persons who patronize it.

Depression years and the collapse of huge personal fortunes revolutionized the position of the artist. Generous patronage of previous years disappeared. Government patronage of the arts marks the beginning of a significant epoch. Federal art centers dot the country. Numerous projects reintroduce murals as a component part of architecture. The Historical American Building Project through its study of architecture has provided a new source of material. The Index of American Design has done much to study and record significant arts indigenous to America. These are but a few of the powerful agencies for general education in the arts.

Among the immediate problems on the new horizon are demands for better community and city planning, functional architecture, and better machine-made art. To facilitate the solution of such problems there exist several foundations that give generous financial aid to research and study of art in its relation to the major aspects of life. The valuable results are made available for the public through educational institutions and other agencies.

Vast art expressions, like city planning, public architecture, and the home arts are all of widespread social import. The artist's place in industry, where the material necessities of life are produced in mass, the distribution of materials from one region to another, and the transportation of people by various means call for a careful study. Among those activities universally considered as of great cultural significance are painting, the graphic arts, sculpture, photography, motion pictures, theater arts, handcrafts, and personal attire.

These various problems are arresting, especially from the consumer's point of view. It is of vital importance that the consumer obtain that satisfaction and enrichment of living which the arts provide. It is assumed that every citizen is interested to some extent in the problems and materials with which art is concerned, in what the artist attempts to do, and the bearing that this has on current American life.

The economic status of the artist in any culture is important to consider. As has been noted, the American artist has had to look for his support to a variety of sources, for example, to persons of wealth, more recently to the government; in the future perhaps industry may be the chief patron of the arts. A striking phenomenon of the age is the extent to which the machine and the processes of mechanization have overhauled our way of living. Quantity production has made it possible for persons of little means to enjoy many more privileges than they have ever had before. Here lies a new type of art of which education must be cognizant.

Yet the handcrafts are still a force. While they are no longer of any import as a competitor of the machine-made, there is much to be said for them as a recreation, as a means of personal expression, as avocation, and in education.

The relation between producer and consumer and the responsibility of the consumer as an artist naturally become important items in an age dominated by the machine. What the consumer demands must ultimately be imposed upon those concerned with production. It is difficult to isolate the various institutions and activities of life. Art is eminently a quality of all those factors that make up our contemporary society. A historical retrospect of the arts in America will reinforce the significant conclusion that, from the disembarking of the first settler to the present time, man's social and economic activities have been inseparable from art.

CHAPTER II

CITY PLANNING

WALTER CURT BEHRENDT
Technical Director, Buffalo City Planning Association
Buffalo, New York

From a recent report by the National Resources Committee, entitled *Our Cities: Their Rôle in the National Economy*, it is to be gathered that the American city, at present, is heading for a serious crisis: an alarming intimation, indeed, but no news to those who, for any time, have worked and lived in a city. They know, from their own experience, that the unrestricted growth of cities threatens a serious crisis in urban life.

I. DIAGNOSIS OF THE CITY

Any diagnosis reveals that the city's structure is ailing. Unsound it is from a technical point of view. If the streets have been called the arteries of the city, then its organism suffers from some sort of arterio-sclerosis. The inner structure of our cities, which is the result of the rapid growth during the last century, has not yet been adapted to the new means of motor traffic that, with increasing velocity, flows through their arteries.

Nor has the pattern of layout ever been adjusted to the manifold changes that took place in the use of land. Unscrupulously, and without any thought, tall office buildings and skyscrapers have been erected on streets and blocks that were laid out and designed to accommodate single family houses of modest height. A great proportion of our urban population is badly housed, and particularly those who form the broad basis of the industrial structure.

Unsound, too, is the economic situation of the cities. They are burdened with ever-increasing expenses for administrative services, for new highways and street-widenings, for slum clearance and better housing, and, at the same time, they are faced with diminishing returns from tax revenues. Blighted areas, still figured in the cities' assessment rolls as having high values, do not yield the expected revenues. And slum districts involve expenditures to the city for their maintenance and for their fire, police, and sanitary protection that are heavily pressing on the city's budget. The larger the city, the more complicated and difficult becomes urban life, and the smaller the opportunity for the average urbanite to enjoy the contact with nature, with the good earth, and with the stimulating and refreshing effects of its green grass and growing trees — an enjoyment rare and badly needed in this unbalanced, one-sided urban environment.

These are just a few selected facts, well known to everybody and mentioned only to illustrate the urban situation in which we find ourselves. This situation is threatening, indeed, asking for immediate action and concerted effort toward reconstructing and redeveloping our cities. For, as the report of the National Resources Committee rightly points out, considering the important part the city plays at present in the national economy: " If the city fails, America fails."

II. The Task of Planning

In this situation the public looks at the planner who, as the professional expert, is expected to hold the key to the solution of the present problems. The trend of public opinion is clearly evidenced by the fact that, in recent years, perhaps no other word has been so often on the front page and in the headlines of our papers as the word *planning*. There has been a continuous discussion of all sorts of planning: social and economic planning, city planning and regional planning, state planning and even national planning. Why all this talk about planning?

Planning, shortly defined, is a way to order. And there is a familiar tendency to talk most about the things one needs most. All this talk about planning emanates from our present lack of order. The new and widespread movement towards planning indicates our longing for order. And so, this growing interest in city planning and regional planning, proved by the rapidly increasing number of planning agencies all over the country, is to be interpreted as a succinct reaction against the haphazard growth and the uncontrolled expansion of our cities, against the disastrous deterioration of the countryside. And it is from our sufferings that we realize the immediate need for reconstruction, for reconstruction of life in all fields of human activities.

III. New Cities or City Rehabilitation?

Many ideas and concepts have been fashioned by city planners aiming at the regeneration of our distressed cities. There is one school of thought that believes the present situation of our cities to be so hopeless as to necessitate their wholesale demolition and the establishment of new ones on virgin soil. These radical ideas, however, offer no practical solution. Too large investments are represented by the old cities to permit us simply to abandon them. As it is improbable that we can start city life and city building all over again, the question arises: What can be done in the way of planning to reshape the structure of our old cities in order to create a more desirable community pattern and a better-balanced urban environment?

It is more acute to discuss this question with the present generation, since the great period of population increase, which came with the beginning of the nineteenth century and stamped the structure of the modern city, is apparently drawing to a close. As pointed out in another recent report of the National Resources Committee on *The Problem of a Changing Population*, " the slowing down of population growth in the nation as a whole will also involve a general slowing down in the increase of city population." The phenomenal expansion of our cities, characteristic of the nineteenth century, can hardly be expected to continue. However, a marked decrease in the rate of growth in many cities, as pointed out in the report, " while necessitating certain economic adjustments, will provide an excellent opportunity for the improvement of municipal administration."

Indeed, the fact of the slowing down of urban growth, instead of depressing local pride, should be taken as a challenge. All our activities should be revised and our planning concepts reconsidered in the light of this new fact. In the past our cities were rejoicing in mere quantitative growth; the time has come when they have to concern themselves with their qualitative growth.

IV. The Masterplan

The modern city-planner aims at an integrated development of the urban structure by means of a general plan, or masterplan. Such a masterplan is not to be imagined as an effective design showing on a map an imposing number of broad avenues, tree-bordered boulevards, and monumental plazas. The modern planner has entirely abandoned this academic idea of the City Beautiful; his concept is more comprehensive. The modern planner thinks, not in terms of lines, but in terms of areas. His plan, as a matter of fact, is not a plan of street and building lines, but an area plan, a layout for the wise use of urban land.

In developing a masterplan the modern planner conceives the city as a living organism: an organism that, in its structure, has to be developed according to the various functions it has to fulfill, so that it can serve these functions with the highest degree of efficiency.

To increase efficiency, modern technique in its constructions follows the pattern of nature as it is manifested in its organisms of the higher order. Thus modern technique seeks efficiency through functional division of labor. The various functions that the organism of a machine or a building, or any other structure, has to fulfill are plainly separated and assigned to special organs adjusted in their form to the function they have to serve.

The same principles are followed in developing a comprehensive plan for a city. We must admit that the city is a complicated organism. Surveying its various functions, we have to realize that the city has to serve, first, for *work*. Included in the manifold ramifications of work are the various activities of trade, commerce, and industry. The city must also provide for communication, for housing, and finally, for recreation.

These various functions, however, are closely interrelated. As a living organism, the city practices these vital functions in permanent mutual interaction. Thus, industry, for its effective function, is dependent upon efficient systems of transportation and communication, which, in turn, are dependent upon a system of railways and a good harbor development equipped with all the necessary factors, such as docks, wharfs, and railroads. Similarly, labor, which forms the broad basis of the entire industrial structure, can only fulfill its important function if it is supplied with decent and wholesome housing at rentals that are within the reach of its wage scale. Finally, the urban dweller must be provided with a system of parks and recreation grounds dotted about the city to provide the necessary facilities for rest and play.

Thus, in preparing his comprehensive plan, the modern city-planner provides in advance various areas of the urban land for the purposes for which they are best suited according to their local or physical features. Trade and commerce will be concentrated in the downtown district. Industry, however, will be assigned areas throughout the city in order to avoid traffic congestion and overcrowding in the residential sections of the workers. Further decentralization will be provided by mapping off large areas of cheap land along the fringes of the city near transportation lines and main freight yards, as well as waterways, canals, rivers and harbors, because water traffic is still considered the cheapest for all sorts of bulk freight. Residential sections, particularly for workmen's dwellings, must be provided near industrial sites in order to shorten the daily travel between home and working place. These housing developments, if possible, will be located close to the factories, enabling employees to walk to their places of work. To secure quiet and to protect the residential areas against smoke and noise of the factories, the planner will try to separate these residential sections from the industrial districts by large green zones of parks and playgrounds.

Recreational areas, distributed throughout the city, should be developed into a continuous park system, spreading all over the urban territory, including any areas of natural vegetation, any brooks or lakes that offer picnic places and bathing beaches. Penetrating the whole city, this system of public greens should extend as far as possible, even into the core of the city, thoroughly loosening the density of building in the central districts where it is most needed.

By so allocating the various functions of the city to special areas, the planner prepares the proper and economic utilization of the urban land. The art of city-planning, then, consists in distributing these special areas so as to integrate their various functions and to develop the city's structure into a real organism.

V. Zoning, an Integral Part of Planning

With the development of such a land-use plan much of present zoning practice will become superfluous. Zoning was introduced in this country as a policy of prevention. With the rapid growth of the cities it was soon discovered that the unrestricted use of urban land was detrimental to property owners. A district invaded by factories and work shops, large or small, was no longer desirable for residential purpose. People began to move out and houses were left vacant, to the loss of the owners and the community.

To avoid these damages and to protect property owners, zoning was established with its regulations restricting the use of land. As a policy of prevention, however, zoning came too late to offer any effective control. Zoning ordinances were established at a time when most of the urban area was already built upon. Thus, zoning was restrictive rather than constructive in its effects on future building. Zoning regulations, however, should be imposed on land at the time it is first planned and subdivided. That is to say, zoning should be an integral part of the masterplan. Thus the newer forms of legislation assign the making of the zoning plan, not to a separate zoning commission, but to the planning commission, where it logically belongs.

Let it be emphasized that the comprehensive plan is not a fixed blueprint or a design to be immediately followed by building. It is just a framework, elastic and flexible, to be filled in with local developments and subdivisions as soon as a real need for them arises. Taking the city as a living organism, the modern city-planner realizes that life is always in evolution, and that every economic and technical change brings about a change in human conduct, manners, and habits. Thus, his plan must be dynamic rather than static, subject to adjustment to meet changes in the social and economic structure.

In short, the comprehensive plan is to be understood as a long-range program for the physical improvement of the city. It is a guide for the local authorities in directing and controlling the city's growth. And, as each problem of city development is closely related to all the others, it is only on the basis of a plan that decisions can be made securing the proper succession in these improvements. It is only by having a *plan* that we can avoid that wasteful practice of hit or miss, where we do one thing this year only to discover, next year, that the improvements we have just created with great expenditure are a stumbling block in the way for another improvement now imperative.

VI. A MUNICIPAL LAND POLICY

City-planning, however, is not only a technical problem, but also, and to no small degree, an administrative one. The best plan doesn't help very much if the municipal authorities have no power to get it officially adopted and carried through. To secure progress in planning, every city should do what the City of New York has recently done by amendment of her charter; namely, establish a strong City Planning Board, a body as independent of political control as possible, but entrusted with the power to set up a comprehensive plan and embodied with the necessary authority to carry through this plan, in accordance with the capital budget.

Furthermore, to make city-planning really effective, there is needed a municipal land policy enabling the city to acquire land not only for immediate and actual use, but also to assemble and to hold a certain reserve of real estate from which, in case of future needs, the necessary sites can be provided for all sorts of public uses — for school buildings, firehouses, public libraries, recreation centers, low-rent housing, and so forth.

Such a municipal land policy is an entirely foreign concept for this country, and it is probably bound to meet considerable opposition —

the same opposition that in this country turns against any idea of public control. However, in European countries, where the cities have a much older history, and people, living closer together, have for a long time conceived the need for public control, such a municipal land policy has long been adopted. Many European cities, following an old tradition inherited from the Middle Ages, always had large real estate holdings, administered by special departments under expert and responsible officials. Many towns in Germany and the Scandinavian countries own from one-third to a half of their entire municipal areas. The towns, anticipating their future needs, not only purchased large areas of land but also endeavored to distribute their estates as equally as possible throughout their administrative territory, so that they could make felt their influence as proprietors upon the land market in as many directions as possible.

This ' land storage ' policy proved a very successful means for controlling the development of the city; with its possession of land the city was enabled to determine in which direction it should expand and also frequently to check the abuses of professional land speculation. In times of increasing demands, the community could lower the price of land by bringing communal land upon the market.

In this country the concept of a public land policy has not yet found a foothold. Early efforts to build up a public domain and to make it a source of revenue have failed. It has been frequently pointed out, for instance, by such an eminent scholar as Professor Frederick Jackson Turner in his *The Frontier in American History* that " the policy of the United States in dealing with its lands is in sharp contrast with the European system of scientific administration."

Perhaps it was the frontier spirit, with its feeling of abundance of free land, characteristic of any age of colonization, that created this obsession against the idea of public land. American cities have never made any efforts to build up a land reserve, to make it a source of revenue, and to withhold it from subdivision in order that urban settlement might be more compact.

However, as with many other traditional habits, this attitude may change under the force of circumstances. It is worth while mentioning that, among the recommendations made by the National Resources Board in its report already quoted, is a strong advocacy of such a municipal land policy and a more liberal interpretation of the fundamental laws of the states regarding the acquisition of land by municipalities. With the urban situation as it is today, an excellent oppor-

tunity is offered to start such a policy on account of the many
tax-delinquent lots within the city area and the large amount of land
that has thus reverted to the cities.

VII. THE STREET PLAN

After having established a land-use map, the next step in the planning process is the development of a major street plan. This task, if it is
conscientiously done with the aim of rehabilitating our cities, means the
reshaping of the street pattern as it is inherited from the past in such
a way as to adapt it to the needs of the present motor age.

Most of the American cities have been developed on the basis of the
checkerboard system, which makes a city into a mere accretion of rectangular blocks of identical size, separated by streets of standard
widths. This type of plan, created for, and adapted to, the conditions
of the horse-and-buggy era, failed to discriminate between traffic
streets and residential streets. The old street pattern, with its numerous
delays, affected the efficiency of the private cars as well as that of the bus
and all other sorts of surface transit. What is needed today is a street
pattern designed to segregate through from local traffic. First, a network of main arteries has to be developed, consisting of radiating and
cross-town thoroughfares. The theoretical distance between through
roads, according to traffic experts, would be, at best, half a mile.
Through roads, then, would define the boundaries of a block containing
an area of about 160 acres. This super-block, with an area of one-
half mile by one-half mile, forms a new planning unit, just large enough
to be equipped with a public school and to be developed as a neighborhood community equipped with playgrounds, shopping facilities, meeting halls, branch libraries, and the like. Within these new neighborhood communities all but local traffic will be excluded, the streets
being designed to serve only as local access to the houses, built either as
grouped houses or as apartments.

VIII. THE NEIGHBORHOOD UNIT: THE CYCLE IN REAL ESTATE

In our cities the outskirts of the inner districts are spotted with
blighted areas. This defect, of course, is of our own making. By over-
zoning the business districts far beyond any justifiable demand, those
areas adjacent to the present business districts, now used for residential
purposes, are expected to be turned into more intensified utilization.
The land owners, under this illusive expectation, begin to let down in
upkeep and maintenance of their property, and the blighted area comes

into existence. We are complaining, today, about the damages these blighted areas do to the city's budget; but we are not realistic enough to adopt a method that would help to eliminate them. The best cure for blighted areas would be to prevent them from coming into being by accepting a scheme that is blightproof. The 'neighborhood unit' is such a scheme. Of course, to accept it means a definite change in the attitude of real estate, a change amounting almost to a complete reorganization of this important branch of private enterprise. It means a shift from a speculative tendency, working for quick profits, to a policy of long-term investments looking for a secure income from property.

Our rehabilitation plan also involves a reform of our methods of taxation — a reform long overdue. At present, assessments are based on anticipated (and mostly illusive) values. They should, however, represent the real value based on the earning power of the property and its rent-yield capitalized. And when the value of the building declines by obsolescence, no landlord should be granted the right of deriving the same revenue from his property. To prevent him from doing so, when in the process of obsolescence the property changes from use in a higher classification to use for lower income groups, drastic precaution should be taken by sanitary codes and building regulations to prevent overcrowding and substandard housing conditions.

With such provisions approved and recommended by enlightened real-estate men, we may be able to reëstablish a normal cycle in real estate wherein houses, when their normal life time expires after forty or fifty years, can be replaced by new ones, built on the same land, if it is still suited and still wanted for residential purposes, and on land available again at a reasonable price. New houses could be built in large-scale construction, and developed as neighborhood units, carried through by private companies, organized as limited dividend corporations, or similar organizations looking for long-term investments on a sound basis.

The redevelopment of our cities on the basis of this pattern calls for certain other, and even more drastic, administrative amendments. One of the main obstacles to be overcome before we can accomplish this new pattern is the present difficulty in ' land assembling ' — the task of bringing the various parcels needed for such a large-scale development under one ownership. The Germans have a law enabling local authorities to enact the pooling of privately owned lots in order to achieve an improved layout in the interest of public welfare. In this country the National Real Estate Board has drafted a Neighborhood Improvement Bill, which proves that these new planning ideas are felt to be favorable to real estate's own interest, but the bill is still rather vague and too complicated in its detail. The English have done a better job; they have worked out a more definite scheme, which was included in their Housing Act of 1935. With this act, the local authorities were invested with important powers for replanning and redeveloping large central areas, wherever overcrowding was manifested. They are carrying through these redevelopment schemes (which are designed to provide adequate housing accommodations for those who, for occupational or other reasons, still require to be centrally housed) partly by purchase of the land in the area, partly by entering into arrangements with owners for development in accordance with the plan. Where compulsory powers are exercised, compensation at market value will generally be paid.

IX. A REHABILITATION PROGRAM

To sum up, as we can't afford to abandon our cities and start anew, we must try to reconstruct them by developing new patterns of planning. The concept of neighborhood planning offers new possibilities for the redevelopment of the inner districts, too long neglected under the spell of the suburban trend. This suburban trend is disastrous for the city budget, since it destroys the basis of its revenues, and, as it takes place in the form of an uncontrolled and excessive decentralization, its result is the present overexpansion of our cities. We know it, but, although we complain about it, we still encourage this overexpansion by permitting new subdivisions in the outer areas long before they are really needed. We even go so far as to pay an indirect subsidy to these premature subdivisions by providing all sorts of public utilities and investing large sums of money in highways, streets, sewers, and so forth. Interest on the investment accumulates during many years and adds to the price of land, which makes the cost of building prohibitive.

By all means, we should try to arrest this wasteful overextension of our cities, caused by premature and speculative subdivisions. New sections of the urban area should only be opened if there is a definite need for further subdivision. New subdivisions should be made to comply with the comprehensive plan. Surrounding lands should be kept open as long as possible to keep them in use for gardening purposes, or even for farming, so that they would form some sort of green belt, so necessary as a breathing space for every city.

Assume we will be able to arrest the present centrifugal trend by reconstructing the inner districts of our cities on the basis of the neighborhood principle. Cities will then become attractive not only as places of work but also as places in which to live. Then it is very likely that we shall regain certain parts of the population now living in the suburbs. Among those people who are wasting every day a few hours of their leisure time by driving their cars back and forth through congested thoroughfares during the rush hours, there are certainly many who would pefer to have their homes within walking distance of their places of work, if only they could find decent places in such a vicinity.

X. The Parking Problem

By following this pattern for the rehabilitation of the inner districts of the city, we may also be able to relieve, at least to a certain degree, the serious traffic problem our cities have to face. This problem is not only confined to the acute congestion of the main thoroughfares, but also includes the growing need for parking space in the main business districts. It is doubtful whether we can any longer endure having the limited space of our thoroughfares and main traffic streets further narrowed by parking cars. The paved street is much too expensive to have its space used for standing cars. With cars parking at the curb, a four-lane traffic street is reduced to two lanes. Moreover, to widen a street just to provide parking space is too expensive. The City of Pittsburgh, for example, some years ago widened Grant Street in the downtown area from 36 to 50 feet, thus providing two additional traffic lanes. The cost of this improvement was $1,860,340. If the additional lanes are used for parking, only 144 parking spaces can be provided, making the cost of this public parking area per car space $13,302.

A recent survey made for Midtown Manhattan revealed that, in the area bounded by Fourteenth Street, Second Avenue, Seventy-second Street, and Eleventh Avenue, during an average working day no fewer than 80,000 motor vehicles come to park at the curb. To realize what this figure means, note that, in a procession headed west, the first car in this cavalcade would approach the city limits of Detroit as the last car left Columbus Circle.

New York City has recently made regulations forbidding curb parking entirely in a number of main cross streets. In other cities, similar attempts have been made to prohibit curb parking or to restrict parking time by police regulation or other devices, such as parking meters.

However, if we prevent street parking, we have to provide for off-street parking facilities. We shall probably be urged, within the near future, to consider new regulations to be included in our building codes such that building permits for structures attracting by their purpose a great number of people (as department stores, movie theaters, music halls) will be granted only on condition that there be provided a proportioned space for parking on the building site. This convenience for the customer is often enough to secure business that pays for the space, particularly if a cheap location is acquired.

XI. Society's Responsibility in City Planning

Having discussed some of the planning problems arising from the acute need of redeveloping our cities, the question remains: Is society courageous enough to endorse the necessary amendments and new administrative arrangements that, by restricting certain individual liberties, would create better human values and higher standards of living for the community as a whole? The planner cannot solve these problems alone. He cannot solve them at all unless society is willing to accept the premises on which the new planning patterns are based.

References

(1) Bauer, Catherine. *Modern Housing.* (Houghton Mifflin Co.: Boston, 1934)
(2) Carpenter, Niles. *The Sociology of City Life.* (Longmans, Green & Co.: New York, 1931)
(3) Mumford, Lewis. *The Culture of Cities.* (Harcourt, Brace & Co.: New York, 1938)
(4) Thorndike, E. L. *Your City.* (Harcourt, Brace & Co.: New York, 1939)
(5) Turner, Frederick Jackson. *The Frontier in American History.* (Henry Holt & Co.: New York, 1920)
(6) United States National Resources Committee. *Our Cities — Their Rôle in the National Economy.* (U. S. Government Printing Office: Washington, D. C., 1937)
(7) Wright, Frank Lloyd. *The Disappearing City.* (William Farquhar Payson: New York, 1932)

CHAPTER III

PUBLIC ARCHITECTURE

TALBOT F. HAMLIN
Avery Librarian, Columbia University
New York, New York

If public architecture is defined as all the architecture built by and for public bodies — that is, by governmental agencies — then the field of public architecture in the United States is not only large, but also increasing yearly. The growing complexity of the economic and social relationships of twentieth-century life has necessitated more and more governmental regulation. Unemployment has created inexorable demands, both for remedial building, such as the brilliantly conceived migratory labor camps now being built by the Farm Security Administration, and for an increased public building program as a means of stimulating employment. New concepts of the responsibility of the government to its citizens have arisen, and these have been represented in architecture by the vast amount of building in national parks, and by the construction of municipal swimming pools, playground buildings, and other recreational structures.

Even modern transportation has tended to widen the field of public architecture. The automobile has created a need for roads. Roads demand bridges, culverts, tunnels, and gasoline stations, and all of these may become necessary and beautiful works of public architecture. Similarly, the rapidly developing use of waterways, the necessities of irrigation, and the study of possible water power have demanded vast structures of enormous cost, which only the government is able economically to carry out for the common good of the citizens.

I. THE GROWTH OF PUBLIC ARCHITECTURE

In the early New England Colonial village but one public structure was necessary — the church — which served also as legislative chamber and courthouse. The later Colonial world of the eighteenth century needed more; the courthouse was built beside the church on the village common, and in the provincial capitals important and impressive

49

statehouses, like Independence Hall, arose. Later, as commerce developed, the customhouse became a necessity. Market buildings, like the Second Street Market in Philadelphia, were constructed; the cities began to exhibit the greater complexity of the nineteenth century. And after the Revolution, as Washington came slowly into being, the Capitol was but one of the necessary governmental structures; buildings for the Treasury, for the State Department, for the Army and Navy, for the Patent Office, all were needed. The complexity of a modern government was by 1840 already represented by a large number of different kinds of buildings in Washington, and the need for government building was recognized by setting up the post of government architect and the appointment of Robert Mills as the first incumbent.

The process thus easily recognizable in this growth of public buildings has continued ever since; recently, with increasing rapidity, as mass production and the growth of corporations have more and more forced their problems upon the government. Education became a government function towards the middle of the nineteenth century. Recreation came in on the heels of conservatism with the creation of the public park. Flood prevention, inland navigation, and soil conservation all combined to bring problems of industrial building design within the functions of government; the superb structures of the Tennessee Valley Authority are an example. And, finally, city growth and degeneration, the development of slums, and the failure of the current real-estate and land-value systems to build houses for low income groups forced the government into the housing field. Yet even if we except all domestic architecture, the field of public building today is enormous.

II. PUBLIC ARCHITECTURE EXPRESSES THE IDEALS OF SOCIETY

The architecture of public structures must be, to a certain degree, objective. Public buildings express the ideals of no single individual; they are necessarily communal, paid for by the taxes of thousands. Ideally, as the buildings the people themselves have built for their own delectation and their own use, they should serve to express the dreams, the hopes, the form sense, of an entire city or an entire nation. They should be buildings in which the ordinary citizen can feel pride, buildings that he can love and make emotionally his own. Thus esoteric architecture of any kind is fundamentally out of place in public architecture; public structures should speak a simple language, intelligible to the ordinary man in the street.

This is, alas, sometimes interpreted by building committees as meaning that public architecture must be dictated by the tastes of the stupidest part of the public. It is not a matter of taste, this question of public architecture; it is a matter of structure, of intent, of creative power. To make public buildings popularly intelligible does not mean to make them vulgar. The public taste is always better than the purveyors to it believe. The public is starved for visual beauty, and the very best that an architect can give of imagination, freshness, logic, and composition is not too great. All that the demand for popular intelligibility means is that the architect, in designing a public building, does not intrude his own personal prejudices, does not give the public ' styles ' that demand intellectual discrimination for appreciation, but *buildings* — useful, simple, dignified, built of as lovely materials as the money available will allow. And the public will love such buildings; rest assured of that. What the public dislikes is cheap ostentation, waste, cantankerous and obstreperous and obstinate design, in which the architect seems more anxious to ' put over ' and display his own ideas than to solve the problem in the best and simplest way. It is not a question of modern versus historic styles. The good building, however modern, will win its way to popular approval as surely as good music does.

III. GOVERNMENT ARCHITECTS VERSUS PRIVATE

Public buildings are designed in two different and contrasting ways. According to one usage, which seems at the moment to be increasing, they are designed by architectural departments that are integral parts of government agencies. Thus the architect of the Public Works Department of the United States Government (formerly the Supervising Architect of the Treasury Department) designs great numbers of the smaller post offices of the entire country, and a host of other work of all kinds in Washington and elsewhere. Similarly, many of our large city schools are designed by the architectural departments of boards of education, with more or less assistance from state education departments. The other system is for individual architects or architectural firms to do the work as part of their regular practice. There are advantages and disadvantages in both systems.

The first system — that of governmental architectural offices — allows the accumulation of much specialized knowledge. It favors the adoption of adequate standards. It works to produce an apparent economy in design costs, allows the most direct supervision of the designing and drafting processes by those who, as governmental officers, are directly responsible for the finished result. To the draftsman, it offers regular and continuous employment, usually under Civil Service protection. All these features make the system attractive to governmental agencies. At times the question of political patronage also enters in.

The other system — that of employing architects in private practice — offers independence of mind, vividness of creative imagination, the inducement to good work given by the opportunity for self-expression, and, above all, freedom from official conventions and out-worn standards. It allows local architects to take advantage of their deep knowledge of local sites, local contractors, local building materials, and even local tastes, for they have a knowledge of these important elements that no centralized bureau in a distant capital city can ever attain. Moreover, the private practitioner is usually more abreast of the times, keener in his approach to design problems, than is the member of the usual official bureau.

IV. STANDARDIZATION OF ARCHITECTURAL PLANS

Behind this controversy between the supporters of official bureaus and private architects lies another, deeper question — the question of the standardization of architectural design. A certain amount of standardization leads to economy, without a doubt. But standardization often leads also to mental laziness; it tends to make people ready to accept the usual as the best. All advances in architecture, whether in design or in construction, entail the abandonment of past standards in some degree. Standards — particularly standards approved and adopted by governmental bodies — have a way of persisting in use long after their usefulness has ceased. Many hospitals and schools of recent construction are not so good as they might be just because of an unthinking adherence to out-of-date official standards. The architect in private practice has been in general much freer from this hampering slavery to standards than have official designing agencies.

An interesting by-product of the employment of private architects has been the growing importance of the competitive system as a means of selecting them. Free and open competitions for this purpose have many advantages. If well conducted, competitions eliminate the dangers of political selection — a boon to legislators, administrators, and the general public. They assure the choice of an architect whose own work proves his grasp of the problem. They set many minds working independently on the task, and accordingly often give rise to new conceptions. Furthermore, public exhibition of the drawings (which should be required in all public architectural competitions) serves as a definite educational influence to both architects and laymen.

V. Recent Increase in Public Architecture

There has been tremendous activity in public architecture in the United States during the last few years. Unemployment relief programs have fostered it. It has varied from such monumental structures as the last buildings of the Washington " Triangle " through the whole range of post offices, town halls, and educational buildings, to park shelters. As a whole, it is difficult to evaluate. Much of it is routine building of the most banal type; especially disappointing are large numbers of the small standardized pseudo-Colonial post offices. It is encouraging to learn that the present policy of the government is to give more and more of this work to private designers, chosen by competition, and to work for greater variety in the rest. The Washington work, however rich in material, is chiefly distinguished by its size. Attempting a harmony with the work of the century-old Classic revival period, it has generally succeeded only in absolute failure to realize the real lesson of that work — simplicity, directness, reticence — and instead there has been produced a carnival of arrogant exhibitionism, with little regard for such practical necessities as parking space, light, and air. Fortunately, some of the larger post offices, designed by architects in outside practice, have been less superficial in design, and less bound by precedent.

VI. State and Municipal Architecture

State and municipal architecture has exhibited the same extreme variations as has federal work, and for the same reasons. Fixed ideas of some acceptable official style seem to control the thinking of legislators and official administrators. Generally speaking, they fear any architectural originality. This makes progress in design difficult. It is so much the more commendable, therefore, when the exception occurs. The State of Nebraska made a daring step forward in accepting the late B. G. Goodhue's design for its capitol, and carrying it out slowly and sympathetically. Following its lead, three other states have built capitols in which the past precedent of classic orders and a central dome was abandoned: Louisiana, in using the design by Weiss, Dreyfous, and Seiferth; North Dakota, the design by Holabird and Root; and

Oregon, that by Trowbridge and Livingstone and Francis Keally. Of these, the North Dakota Capitol is by far the most important as an interesting attempt to use contemporary ' sky-scraper ' forms in public building design, and to express frankly the two portions — legislative and administrative — of which the modern state house consists.

VII. PUBLIC WORKS

The two most creative classes of modern American public-building design have been the educational buildings and the vague class called " public works." Bridges erected by many public bodies have been striking and well designed. The San Francisco bridges across the Golden Gate and the Bay are excellent examples; even more beautiful have been the later bridges around New York, especially the arched Henry Hudson bridge across the Harlem River, and the exquisitely pure and refined Whitestone-Bronx bridge, perhaps the most beautiful suspension bridge yet erected.

Most interesting, too, has been much of the dam and powerhouse work necessitated by our great water-supply, navigation, and conservation projects. The enormity of the scale in itself makes this work impressive, as in the case of Boulder Dam. When to this size is added the quality of brilliant creative design, as in most of the work of the Tennessee Valley Authority, the result is magnificent. Norris, Guntersville, Chickamauga, all have dams and powerhouses that are among the noblest, as they are among the most useful, of all the works of recent American architecture.

VIII. DESIGN OF SCHOOL BUILDINGS

School-building design is obviously in a state of transition. Progressive school ideals necessitate an entirely different sort of structure from the old conventional knowledge-factory. Movable classroom furniture, more working space for pupils, new ideas of the benefits of open-air study, increased demands for recreation have all played havoc with the older accepted standards. Even the design of conventional schools has been profoundly affected by these revolutionary concepts, especially in the kindergarten and lower-grade fields. The net result has been considerable confusion. The new ideals require more square feet per student; this necessity, with its resultant extra costs, conflicts with the need to build as many schools as possible and with the drive for municipal and state economy. In general, the smaller cities have solved the problem more effectively than the great metropolitan centers, which frequently cling, out of pure inertia, to outworn building types; and the West has been generally more daring and more successful than the East.

It is in school design, too, that the problem of styles is particularly hampering. Eastern cities and states have been loath to abandon what they call ' Colonial.' They fear what they term ' Modernistic.' They fail to realize that in the light of the actual demands of the problem — great glass areas, economical plans, safety, ease of maintenance, close relationship to outdoor recreation — style names have little meaning. The classroom units, the auditorium and gymnasium, the outdoor class spaces and playfields, if arranged in the best possible way, must inevitably generate basic forms of their own, which will have their own special kind of effect and beauty. Any compromise to make these effects agree with some foreordained concept of ' style ' is uneconomical. It not only makes for less good buildings, but it also definitely obscures the pure beauty that the schools might otherwise have. Fortunately many communities in the West and South have been bold enough to attack the problem in the direct, simple way; and such examples as the Fowler School in Fresno, California, by Franklin and Kump, and the High School at Idaho Springs, Colorado, by Frewen and Morris, reveal the new and exciting beauty that results. Interesting, also, is the experiment made in the Joan of Arc Junior High School of New York, designed by Eric Kebbon, to gain light, air, and play space in congested city surroundings by carrying the building eight stories into the air.

One important factor of contemporary school design is the growing realization that schools must be designed primarily for children. This affects the entire problem of scale. It calls into question the custom of constructing enormous elementary and high schools for thousands of pupils. Where possible, smaller units are more desirable, and even when great central schools are necessary, it is becoming the custom to subdivide them into groups of buildings rather than to force all the children into one vast and almost terrifying whole. A good example is the grouped buildings of the Thomas Jefferson High School in Los Angeles, by Morgan, Walls, and Clement.

Unfortunately, few contemporary college and university buildings exhibit even the amount of free and creative design that is to be found in the elementary and high schools. The problems of harmony with existing buildings, of pleasing the sentimental wishes of ' old grads ' or aged donors, have raised almost insuperable barriers to any logical approach. The competitions recently held for a new art department for Wheaton College in Massachusetts, and for a new plant for Goucher College in Baltimore, have been of the greatest significance in revealing the latent possibilities of a contemporary approach to college-building design. It is greatly to be hoped that the college architects and the college trustees, who usually control building, will ponder these competitive drawings, and eventually awake to the pressing demands for modernizing college buildings as college courses have been modernized. It is at least possible that four years in a theatrically designed, sentimentally conceived, 'collegiate Gothic' environment, overornamented and overluxurious, may not be the best possible educational environment.

IX. PUBLIC ARCHITECTURE REFLECTS CONTEMPORARY LIFE

The entire field of public buildings thus reveals the fact that public architecture, like public life in America, is in a state of unstable equilibrium, hesitating between the old and the new, the conventional and the daringly creative. Taste is slowly swinging over from its past slavery to precedent to a newer, freer position. More and more persons are becoming aware of the fundamental sterility of the old huge Classic or Gothic edifice and are demanding public buildings that are convenient, well-lighted, efficient, and beautiful with a new simplicity. In these respects public taste is far ahead of the taste of most public authorities and publicly financed official architectural offices. The hope of the future of American public architecture lies in the fact that, because of the slow, but irresistible, forces of democracy, sooner or later the public officials will awaken to the fact that the mid-twentieth-century world requires buildings that are themselves expressions of their own day.

REFERENCES

(1) BEHRENDT, W. C. *Modern Building*. (Harcourt, Brace: New York, 1937) 241 pp.

(2) CHENEY, S. *The New World Architecture*. (Longmans: New York, 1930) 404 pp.

(3) HAMLIN, T. F. *The Enjoyment of Architecture*. (Scribner: New York, 1921) 349 pp.

(4) HAMLIN, T. F. *Architecture through the Ages*. (Putnam: New York, 1940) 732 pp.

(5) PEVSNER, N. *Pioneers of the Modern Movement from William Morris to Walter Gropius*. (Stokes: New York, 1937) 240 pp.

(6) WRIGHT, F. L. *Modern Architecture*. (Princeton University Press: Princeton, N. J., 1931) 115 pp.

CHAPTER IV

THE DOMESTIC SETTING TODAY

RICHARD J. NEUTRA
Consultant, United States Housing Authority
Washington, D. C.

I. ARCHITECTURE REVITALIZED OPERATES WITHIN A STEADY TRADITION: THAT OF COMMON SENSE

Architecture of this day, even in its most untraditional appearances, is in no way a revolutionary departure. To fulfill with devotion the functional requirements of practical use and of psychological satisfaction has been an underlying ideal of good planners, builders, and consumers of building in nearly all recorded periods.

The average human being from the time of the cave to that of the colonizers of the Atlantic border and the West American pioneers has built his home as functionally as he could afford, and as his materials on hand, his knowledge, and his skill in handling them permitted him to do. But this simple moral example has been periodically disregarded in favor of arbitrary formal diversity, whenever the designer and consumer experienced a period of comparative freedom from economic worry.

II. THE NEW CONDITIONS OF INDUSTRIALIZATION

Modern industrialization, based on the manifold developments of technology in the last two hundred years, has gradually brought about a new set of social and economic circumstances with unprecedented modes of living. In the field of technology, it has more recently yielded a host of new building materials, vastly different from the primeval adobe dugout of the ground, the natural stone quarried in the nearby rocky hills, or the logs dragged from neighboring woods to the building premises. There are now plate glass, linoleum, sheet steel, rolled and extruded metal sections, hydraulic cement, diatom composition, plastics, pressed wood, asbestos board, expanded metal, spun glass, rockwool, and a multitude of other ingredients that, in varying combinations, make up the complicated material specification of each little structure. In marked contrast to this, even a colossal Greek temple in

ancient Sicily was built out of one single stuff: limestone, which served
as flooring, roofing, bearing wall, insulation, plastering material, and
all. There are now a thousand other elements that make up the building equipment of any modest home: intricate heating, lighting, plumbing, and housework-saving devices from electric dishwashers to automatic refuse disposal.

To clear obsolete slums, to rehouse huge masses of urban and rural
populations in civilized countries, and to do it, in spite of low cost, with
the desired integration of fire-resisting, sanitary structure, of adequate
installations and equipment, has for decades seemed to the writer a
task beyond the capacity of traditional individual production methods.
Industrialization of so many other processes ushers in the revision of
domestic building activity and tends to the introduction of shop fabrication on the basis of sharply studied typical details. Beauty and attractive diversity have not at all been impaired, for example, by the
thousand-year-old standardization of elemental dimensions and materials in Japanese house construction. The anti-individualistic approach there has, on the contrary, fostered subtlety of consumers'
judgment and esthetic discrimination. Such significant abilities wither
where broadly accepted rules are lacking, and stylistic fashions quickly
change, as in the residential streets of Hollywood, with their Moorish,
Norman, and Georgian bungalow courts.

III. Inconsistency of Historical Imitation

Considering all new circumstances and methods, both in consumption and production of a home to which we have alluded, it would seem
nothing short of a miracle if the current house could have an appearance very similar to that before the mentioned changes had come about.
But we know that this miracle has happened right before our eyes. We
see American white-collar workers and mechanics live in little buildings that supposedly portray the primitive home of a Mediterranean
fisherman, except that they are endowed with an overhead-door garage
for a new streamlined car, and that strange sounds emanate from a
radio through the roller screens of the opened steel sash.

IV. Basic Principles

For every truly contemporary house, whether built under the pressure of economy or with some indulgence to luxurious demands, certain
basic principles can be accepted.

1. Closer Relations with the Outdoors

We are less afraid of the hostile elements: we have not, like pioneers, to contend with the aggression of wild beasts. Against burglars we carry insurance, as there are no door locks or window guards to stand effectively their technologically equipped trickery of our day.

A habitation differs from a mere shelter and from a place of protection. It can help to expand contemporary home activity, and for this purpose must be endowed with flexibility of arrangement and elasticity in space dedication, including outdoor spaces.

The greatest present change in our relation with the outdoors lies in this: that we are incomparably better equipped than our ancestors to control room climate, as to moisture content, temperature, movement, purification, and restoration of the air volume, without, be it noted, losing the intimate psychological relation to the outside spaces. We owe this among other things to the exquisite and increasingly economical production of a variety of window glass answering specific biological-requirements. There is actinic, heat-reflecting, ultra-violet ray diffusing glass, besides a host of translucid glasses of special service properties, and glass masonry. The writer himself has devised and used an exact replica of daylight illumination on outside window hangings with influx through these windows into the evening interiors. In brief, *present technology can produce natural, pleasant outdoor conditions within the home.*

Similarly, garden spaces around the dwelling must be not only decorative but also true, comfortable living areas. The example of the traditional Japanese house shows that even a tiny back yard can bring much of the refreshment and charm of universal nature close to the dwellers. Intensive design goes before extensive design. Space economy here can also be a stimulus rather than an impediment. Comprehensive site planning replaces the narrow conception of a checkerboard subdivision. It yields cohesive communal green areas and foliage-screened patches of privacy.

2. The Combination of Comfort and Economy of Space

Modern comfort and economy of space are combinable. Even a luxurious motor car presents itself as " a plenty in a nutshell! " We cannot model our homes after the architectural pattern of the past, where comfort was produced by a busy crew of servants or slaves, who themselves needed space and again space. Second-class staterooms of elaborate ocean liners, sky sleepers, and the newest Pullman compartments, with all their built-in and handy gadgets, are likely to serve as examples, rather than the huge palaces of the Roman Emperor Diocletian or of the Sun-king in France, which devoured gigantic quantities of human service to produce for a few a proportionately moderate sum of comfortable livability.

What is true for the whole dwelling is true for each of its rooms. The small step-saving kitchen becomes, when carefully laid out, the ideal of the servantless housewife. The bedroom, used only for eight night hours, is transformed, with the installation of a day-and-night couch and a little built-in desk, into a small, permanently useful private study into which the individual can withdraw on occasions from the life of the family group. Here he may read a book, write a letter, or indulge in needed isolation. The living room proper will remain the largest quarters of the home, but here also fitted-in furniture and suitable shelving, collapsible tables, and a well-studied lay-out will lend even to a physically restricted room at least psychological spaciousness. The true value of a house plan can be gauged by square-foot-hours of usage per day, by space put to function, rather than by mere static area and floor footage. In a small house it can hardly be tolerated that rooms or appreciable portions of the floor area are used only for occasional brief periods. Spaces must be designed for multiple purposes and greater productivity.

A list of *storage requirements* made by a prospective home-owner and his wife is almost as informative as a psychological family portrait.

Listing, in general, men's movable belongings and items of consumption, one cannot but notice that they have, on the whole, increased in numbers, but decreased in specific bulk, in permanency, and in replacement value. The actual daily use of all personal articles seems to have an upward trend. Specialized compartments and devices easily reached and handled for neckties, cosmetics, and stationery; built-in revolving racks for women's hats or for fruits or magazines are characteristic.

A dresser in former centuries, in which clothes were stored over generations by nobility, burghers, and peasants, was kept locked and was opened on special occasions only. A number of treasured books, family silver, and china were preserved by wealthy families in other safe compartments. Sometimes these were exhibited through glass, every single article primarily representing a high value of mere static possession. The feeling of ' having,' of ' owning,' these things was obviously prominent; the use of them, the putting of them to function, however, was comparatively rare.

The household storage containers themselves reflected this attitude in various periods of design. Sculptured tall dressers with conspicuous and elaborate locking devices, carved linen chests, ornate china closets, and bookcases indicated the value of the treasure behind the doors. These pieces of furniture were frankly monuments to possession; indeed, wilful inaccessibility was often employed to emphasize ownership.

To our generation these artistic documents of permanent ownership are flavored with a wistful quaintness. Possession has become less enduring, more fluctuating; frequently it tends to be subordinated, even obliterated, by the emphasis upon use. There is a long way from treasured family linens to paper napkins, paper handkerchiefs, and underwear that are discarded after one use. There may be still in many of our generation an ingrained antipathy to such pronounced impermanence, but the tendency is unmistakable and seems unavoidable in a civilization of inexpensive commodities produced in quantity. The compensation offered for the abandonment of permanence is carefree and abundant use without subsequent toil to restore, to repair, to clean.

3. Provision for Cleanliness

Our ideas of household cleanliness are higher, more scientifically tinged, and wider reaching than in any preceding period, but we want to spend a minimum of time and energy on it. We detest ' dirty work ' and time-devouring chores, although some of us may be embarrassed when it comes to a wise use of the time gained by simplification of our housekeeping.

Concealed refuse and soiled-linen chutes that are easily cleaned, receptacles and compartments with smooth impervious surfaces, diversified and adcquate storage space within arm's reach, dumps for cigarette ash and used matches, ventilated shoe closets, electric installations for vacuum cleaning, air-filtering, ozonization were not found in palaces of the past. But they are the desire of the contemporary dweller and in brief time may become a matter of course in any housing scheme.

The modern home, as we have already stated, is not serviced by slaves and most frequently not even by servants. But this should not mean that the inhabitants themselves, and the housewife in particular, should slave to keep everything going and in convenient order. The novelty of the situation is intensified by the mentioned change in the conception of cleanliness. Many cleanable surfaces with a minimum of joints, surfaces hard to permeate by liquids and gases, the elimination of dust catchers, clear visibility of dirt wherever it may develop, good daylight influx into all nooks and corners to check them with the eye and by the various new and effective cleaning tools are fundamentals of present household cleanliness. They become increasingly significant for the mere psychological and esthetic satisfaction of the new inhabitant. Under these conditions coziness by uncontrollable dimness, inaccessibility of voids and hollows left in the cramped set-up of furniture, fixed draping of windows for ' dignified darkness,' high-pile upholstery goods and carpets become questionable, if not obnoxious. Intricate plastic ornamentation is being replaced by smooth, cleanable, durable surfaces of color appeal and attractive finish. Enamelling, glazing, plating, anodic oxidation, opaque glass, metals and metal foils gain importance as finishes, while technological industrialization invades this field of esthetic satisfaction.

V. FUNCTIONAL HOME DESIGN

In addition to desires for simplification, rhythmical repetition and geometrical regularity are part of our mental make-up. We conceive as esthetically attractive those features to which we have been accustomed in our infancy and early adolescence. This evidently explains why formal appearances must change slowly. However, we are all used to finding beauty in free nature; and, consciously or not, we feel that in nature, especially inorganic nature, all appearances signify definite functions of life. They strike us as beautiful just because they do so function. A fish is beautiful because its shape and even surface texture express its manner of life and locomotion within its liquid medium. A linden tree prefers certain soil, subsoil, wind exposure, and plant companies; it has characteristic looks and differs from other trees. In this complete functional adjustment lies clearly the beauty with which a carefully or even a casually observed plant fascinates us. Beauty and variety here are not an additional something, a decoration superimposed on a utilitarian machine. Form really follows function, as half a century ago the American architect and philosopher Louis Sullivan demanded also for buildings. Decoration has largely been a means to cover up the imperfection of man's products. In proportion to the fuller accomplishment of subtle perfection in essentials, decoration and ornamentation can recede. The thing itself becomes beautiful and begins to satisfy by its formal and functional integration.

The conclusion here is that in designing and finishing home or habitation we shall be less in a frenzy over hunting for nonessential decorative schemes. We must trust that a sincere, sparing design to meet well-digested practical and psychological requirements will not tire the inhabitants. It will best leave space and unbiased freedom for their own happy individual expression, and for the daily consumption of creative art, outside of frozen patterns.

REFERENCES

(1) GEDDES, NORMAN BEL. *Horizons*. (Little: 1932) 293 pp.
(2) GROPIUS, W. *The New Architecture and the Bauhaus*. (Museum of Modern Art: New York, 1937) 80 pp.
(3) HITCHCOCK, H. R., and JOHNSON, P. *The International Style: Architecture since 1922*. (Norton: New York, 1932) 240 pp.
(4) MUMFORD, L. *Sticks and Stones*. (Norton: New York, 1934) 238 pp.
(5) TALLMADGE, T. E. *The Story of Architecture in America*. (Norton: New York, 1936) 332 pp.

CHAPTER V

LANDSCAPE DESIGN

Edwin Ziegfeld
Assistant Professor of Art
Teachers College, Columbia University
New York, New York

Landscape design, broadly speaking, is the fitting of outdoor areas for human use. These areas range from small back yards in congested cities to national parks of hundreds of square miles; from service-station grounds to complete highway systems. Although at one time the profession centered chiefly in the design of private gardens, the present trend, accentuated by the depression, has been towards community and regional planning, city and highway beautification. The field is referred to by several names: *landscape architecture* stresses its relation to architecture; *landscape gardening*, its affinity with plants and plant care; while *landscape design* has the advantage of being broader than either of the first two.

By its character and functions landscape design relates to many other fields of human activity, among which the following are important: *architecture*, because landscapes generally contain buildings, and in urban areas are often dominated by them; *painting*, because the visual effects are pictorial; *engineering*, because the construction of roads, lakes, bridges, and the like depends on the engineering sciences; *sociology*, because the planning of parks and communities is essentially a sociological problem; and *economics*, because of the cost factors involved in all landscape projects.

The characteristic of landscape design that differentiates it most clearly from the other arts is its concern with living materials, plants, which give the art a dynamic quality. The seasonal changes — the new greens of spring, the June blossoms, the fall color, the winter nakedness, and the gradual development and maturation of trees, shrubs, and vines — constantly alter the effects, and the planned control of these ever-varying materials constitutes a unique art problem.

I. LANDSCAPE DESIGN IN THE UNITED STATES

Landscape design as a profession, in this country, is scarcely over a century old. The first American practitioner was André Parmentier, who came to this country from Belgium about 1824 and practiced in Brooklyn. A. J. Downing, the second well-known leader, exerted a great influence through his writings, as well as his work. Our greatest landscape designer was Frederick Law Olmsted, who really established landscape design as a profession in this country. In 1856, he, along with Calvert Vaux, was placed in charge of the improvements of Central Park in New York City. This development exerted a tremendous influence, as did the many other commissions executed by him during his fruitful career. During the last half century the number of professional landscape designers has greatly increased, and many colleges and universities now offer excellent professional courses.

If the profession is relatively new to this country, gardens are not. The early Colonists brought with them the traditions of seventeenth-century European gardening, but they found little opportunity to follow them, for the task of merely existing in a wilderness required most of their energies. However, during the eighteenth century, with the possibility of more graceful living, gardens were designed to enhance the Georgian architecture of the period. These gardens, following the English tradition, were generally geometrical in pattern with clipped hedges and formal features. Although few of them remain, such examples as the gardens planned by Washington at Mt. Vernon and the restored garden of the Governor's Palace at Williamsburg are proof that a real garden tradition was built up during the Colonial period.

The era of industrial expansion and the westward movement offered fewer opportunities for garden design to flourish. People were too much occupied pushing back physical and technological frontiers to think of saving the natural beauty they were destroying or of creating other beauty in its place. With the disintegration of the Colonial culture came new ideas with respect to building and gardening. The Romantic movement, influencing all forms of art toward naturalism, found expression in gardening in the creation of ' natural ' landscapes, as opposed to the formalism and geometrical quality of the Georgian gardens. Here nature was used as a model, and a shibboleth of the Romantic gardeners was that " nature abhors a straight line." Central Park in New York City as designed by Olmsted and Vaux is a consummate example of Romantic planning. With minor exceptions the roads and paths are all winding, the open areas are treated as meadows with natural wood edges, and the sought-after effect is one of untouched, if concentrated, naturalness. Landscape work in this tradition is familiar to everyone; the curving shrub border found in most suburban yards is a logical descendent.

During the nineteenth century, eclecticism, in reality a part of the Romantic movement, became dominant in architecture. Buildings for over a century ceased to be American, and were Greek, Gothic, Romanesque, English, or any other of the many styles that were appropriated in our eagerness to acquire culture and distinction. Landscape design, always following architecture closely, became eclectic, and gardens were thought of in terms of the English, the French, or the Spanish styles, or whatever was the vogue of the moment. This tendency existed side by side with, and at times fused with, the Romantic naturalness described above. The practice of the eclectic architect or landscape designer was not to turn to European examples for ideas he could use in the American scene, but to come as close as he could to transplanting the European scene to these shores. Founded on a false premise, this concept of eclecticism was in general a disastrous one for American gardens, even though it produced some attractive, and at times distinguished, results.

Landscape design as it is now practiced exhibits two divergent tendencies, *formalism* and *informalism:* the first characterized as definitely man-made with straight lines, geometrical shapes, clipped and formalized plant materials; the second, nature-inspired with natural, curving, and meandering shapes and free-growing plants. While these are often presented as conflicting practices, it seems better to consider them as two extremes of treatment, with need for both, depending upon the situation under consideration. Thus, areas that are to be used intensively, as small city parks or areas close to houses, seem better suited to a formal treatment with paved areas and direct broad walks, whereas larger and less intensively used areas, often because of their very size, are better treated informally or naturally. As a matter of fact, most landscape developments exhibit characteristics of both formality and informality. While the best effects are not secured by their indiscriminate mixing, a judicious combination of the two can be satisfactory and attractive.

II. DOMESTIC LANDSCAPE DESIGN

Although most persons in the United States live in detached houses surrounded by land suitable for garden developments, very little attention has been given to the latter, and as a result the typical yard is neither useful nor attractive. Several factors have produced this situation. First, unlike the English, we have no well-established tradition of small-garden design to act as a guide, nor has there been any social impetus to develop such a tradition. Second, the professional landscape designers have not succeeded in offering their services at a price that the typical citizen can afford. Third, many of our houses, set high from the ground with the kitchen and garage commanding the most desirable garden space at the rear of the property, suggest few possibilities for developing usable gardens. Thus, lacking tradition and expert advice, the home-owner has had little help. One source of possible encouragement and education is the attention that several widely read magazines on homes and gardens have recently given to this problem.

A study of current practices in the design of home gardens shows the following trends:

1. *Landscape planning is based on the interests and activities of people.* During the height of eclecticism gardens were designed in imitation of historic foreign models and often failed to meet human needs. An even more serious threat to functional gardens because it is always present is the tendency to design gardens for plants rather than for people. However, the present salutary tendency is to design gardens that meet human needs squarely. In general, such functional gardens have a design that is easy to maintain, areas (such as outdoor living rooms) carefully planned for outdoor activities, and paths or means of circulation that are easy and direct. To obtain pleasant and useful garden areas, the side of the house away from the street is receiving most attention.

2. *The design is suited to the geographic and climatic conditions.* Every property constitutes a special problem, and any natural features — good trees, attractive views, outcroppings of rock — are important factors in the design. Flat or steep sites, different exposures, and prevailing winds, and the plants suited to the locality will likewise influence the development. Regional differences are beginning to produce distinctive garden types, the most characteristic of which is the California garden with its patios and subtropical plants.

3. *The garden areas are closely related to the house.* Gardens are more and more being regarded as extensions of the house, as outdoor living areas, and this demands a close relation between the two. Of first importance is the character of the house: a formal house generally suggests a formal garden, whereas a sprawling, romantic house calls for an informal development. Use of the same material in house and garden walls or other features fosters a close relation, as does the extension of the house with garden walls, hedges, or enclosing plants. The use of open or covered terraces at or near the first-floor

level of the house is probably the most direct way of achieving this desirable relationship.

4. *The available land is used efficiently.* In most urban and suburban properties space is at a premium, and working within this limitation the home-owner wants his development to give the impression of spaciousness as much as possible. The key to the matter is house placement. A house placed near the street and one property line leaves the back yard open for garden development, whereas placing the house far from the street often leaves a large but unusable front yard and a cramped back yard. It is customary in small properties to have one area dominant and as large as possible rather than several small ones of equal size.

5. *The garden is designed to be esthetically pleasing for a large part of the year.* A certain amount of attractiveness in a garden is almost unavoidable because no one to date has discovered a way to keep plants from being attractive. This natural beauty of plants, however, is greatly enhanced by attention to careful grouping, adequate backgrounds, and judicious use of heights and textures. The good garden is attractive to look into as well as to move about in. It should be designed to provide new and unexpected relations as one moves about. The effectiveness of the garden is under control only when one can regulate the views both on and off the property, which indicates the importance of screens or enclosures. Well-placed evergreens, shrubs with colored barks, and some garden features will do much toward making the gardens attractive during the monotonous winter months.

In summary, the trends are in the direction of common-sense, functional gardens, integrally related to the lives of the people who will use them and to the localities in which they are built. These trends are equally apparent in present-day architecture.

As was mentioned above, the typical home-owner is not financially able to enjoy the services of a professional landscape designer, a situation unfortunate for both parties. The home-owner must get along without special advice, and the landscape designer's clientele is sharply limited to a small fraction of the population. No satisfactory solution of this difficulty has been found, although several have been tried. Some magazines publish articles on garden design, and one periodical commissioned well-known designers to produce 'typical' garden plans, which were then sold in much the same way that dress patterns are. This practice had a very short life. In many instances nurserymen offer quasi-professional advice to all customers purchasing fairly large quantities of trees or shrubs. The quality of such service is on the average low, but it is probably better than no service at all. There seems no reason to believe that the small home-owner will be able to afford professional advice unless the profession of landscape design effects a radical change in practice. And until this situation is changed, only a few landscape designers will be able to make a living from designing private gardens.

III. PUBLIC LANDSCAPE DESIGN

Landscape design of public areas is considerably more complex than the design of residential developments, and it is interwoven with economics, sociology, traffic control, and politics. Public areas are generally much larger in scale, must accommodate large groups of people, and must serve a wide variety of interests and needs. However, the same general principles hold true as have been set forth in connection with landscape designing for private residences.

1. Public Buildings

The problems here concern the settings of civic buildings and the approaches to them. These are often given a monumental character in keeping with their communal, state, or national importance. Their large scale and the provision that must be made for the accommodation of many people generally demand a relatively simple design. The landscape treatment of many of the buildings in Washington, D. C., such as the Lincoln Memorial, and the new capitol of Louisiana at Baton Rouge are outstanding as typical of the better trends.

2. Parks, Playgrounds, and Parkways

The need for breathing and play spaces in a city is being realized as never before. The present tendency is to relate all parks in one community into a network or system, as is being done in Chicago and Minneapolis. There the large city parks are connected with parkways and boulevards that form rings of green around the different sections of the cities. Similar to this is the work being done on highways in many states. The edges of cuts and fills are carefully and gently graded, shoulders and ditches are turfed, in open stretches trees are planted, and at frequent intervals picnic areas are provided.

The designs of parks are varied, depending on their location, their function, and their size. Small city parks must provide for many people, and therefore are generally intensively developed with many walks and benches. They are often given an architectural character in keeping with the buildings that crowd in from every side. Large city or suburban parks often attempt to bring the country to the city by the use of features like meadows and lakes, but these may be supplemented by such special attractions as zoölogical gardens, rose gardens, or conservatories. Extensive recreation areas are invariably provided. Large country parks, as those developed by the state or national governments, are usually concerned with conserving some outstanding natural feature or features. The problem then becomes one of making these available to large numbers of people. In this field, the national government has done an enormous amount of work during the last decade.

One of the most stimulating trends in the field of public landscape design, and one that bids fair to transform the appearance of our cities, is the planting of trees in business districts. The tradition of tree-planting in residential areas is rather well established, but the commercial areas of our cities are characterized by a baldness that throws into prominence the all too mediocre design of the architecture. Trees in business districts in most communities were rejected during our rapid period of development and their rejection was rationalized by the statement that trees would not grow under such city conditions. We chose to forget that some European cities made great use of trees in business districts and that this was largely responsible for their attractiveness. But there are some trees that will grow even under the most trying of city conditions, and the effects they have on the appearance of a street are almost miraculous.

3. Housing Developments

In housing developments, the tendency, as discussed by Mr. Behrendt in Chapter II, is to construct neighborhood units, each a self-contained community, as a means of stabilizing urban residential areas and of providing more of the amenities of life for the residents.

Present indications are that public landscape design will continue to grow in importance as it has during the last decade. More significant work is being done in this field than in the field of residential design, and large numbers of landscape designers are now being employed on projects that will give many people opportunity to observe well-designed landscapes.

REFERENCES

(1) AMERICAN SOCIETY OF LANDSCAPE ARCHITECTS. *Colonial Gardens: The Landscape Architecture of George Washington's Time.* (Washington, D. C., 1932)
(2) BAILEY, L. H. *Manual of Gardening.* (Macmillan: New York, 1925)

(3) BOTTOMLEY, M. E. *The Art of Home Landscape.* (A. T. De La Mare Co., Inc.: New York, 1935)

(4) CARHART, A. H. *How to Plan the Home Landscape.* (Doubleday, Doran and Co., Inc.: Garden City, N. Y., 1935)

(5) ELWOOD, P. H., JR. *American Landscape Architecture.* (The Architectural Book Publishing Co.: New York, 1924)

(6) FINDLEY, H. *Garden Making and Keeping.* (Doubleday, Page and Co.: New York, 1926)

(7) HUBBARD, H. V., and KIMBALL, T. *An Introduction to the Study of Landscape Design.* (Macmillan: New York, 1927)

(8) PRESIDENT'S CONFERENCE OF HOME BUILDING AND HOME OWNERSHIP. Volume I, *City Planning, Subdivisions, Utilities, Landscape Planning.* (Washington, D. C., 1931)

(9) SHEPHERD, J. C., and JELLICOE, G. A. *Gardens and Design.* (C. Scribner's Sons: New York, 1927)

CHAPTER VI

FLOWER ARRANGEMENT

MARGARET FAIRBANKS
Instructor, The Cleveland Museum of Art
and Instructor, Art Department
Flora Stone Mather College, Western Reserve University
Cleveland, Ohio

The art of arranging flowers in the West is as old as any other art, but until the last fifteen years or so, flower forms have been used by amateur and professional alike as parts of larger decorative schemes. They have had their indispensable place in the ceremony of living, at weddings, banquets, and funerals, and here they have been consciously arranged in forms that followed the tastes of the people and the time.

Egyptian lotuses in formal pyramids crowned the offerings to the dead; tightly packed Byzantine garlands festooned the walls and tables at their banquets. The artist of the Renaissance, whom we generally think of as a painter or a sculptor, was a member of his patron's permanent household staff and was expected to design anything that the life of the household demanded: goblets, vases, the decoration of rooms for parties, and of gardens with their pavilions for outdoor festivals and pageants. The presence of flowers was expected and the manner of their disposal important. The way in which they are painted by Botticelli, Piero di Cosimo, and others shows such intimate understanding both of the flowers themselves and of the decorative handling of them that it is clear these artists were familiar with flower arrangement in real life. The garlands of Squarcione, Crivelli, and Mantegna were surely painted by men who had made real swags of flowers and fruit. Mantegna, we know, cultivated and took delight in his own garden. Louis XIV had his household artist, Charles LeBrun, who designed the settings of this sovereign's life down to the last door lock, and there is particular reference to the vases and flower creations that LeBrun created both for the palace rooms and for the garden bosques. At this time, as can be seen in tapestries and pictures of the period, carefully arranged flowers in vases were placed at points of vantage outdoors. During these important periods the forms followed the spirit

73

of other decorative forms — delicate and perfectly balanced in the Renaissance; in large, bold, heavy swirls in the seventeenth century (witness the Dutch seventeenth-century flower pictures, notably those of Huysum). In the last fifteen years flower arrangement has emerged from the fabric of everyday living into the world of conscious art.

The situation in the East, especially in Japan, has been entirely different. There the art has had its masters, schools, traditions, and students for centuries. Flower-arranging contests with the beguiling achievements of great masters are described in very early literature. Books of pictures, illustrating principles of design, vases, and other equipment, and describing techniques to be followed in preserving the blooms, trimming and bending the branches, have been published for several centuries. The art goes back in the written records of the *ikenobo* masters to the sixth century. (The forty-third master in the direct line of descent from the founder of this school was in 1935 the Head Priest of the Rokkaku Temple in Kyoto.) Then, as now, the art was closely associated with Buddhist tradition, has always received imperial patronage, and has been the fruit of an old and secure culture, long familiar with leisure and its opportunities for reflection.

The symbolism of Japanese floral arrangement is not obscure, but rather unobtrusive and subtle, and concerned with man's effort to understand and relate himself to nature. The arrangement, usually of a few blossoms or branches, is designed for a niche (unless it is made to stand before the image of the Buddha) and to be seen from one position only. The artist strives, as he does in the landscape art of Japan, to present nature, majestically, abundantly, or very simply. Sometimes he uses dead, sparse, or broken branches at the back of the arrangement, which is always understood to be the north, as the spectator is the south, or the sun. The season of the year and the time of day can be suggested, too, by the sensitive artist, and recognized by the keen observer. The arrangement is never flat, but, like the Japanese garden, is carefully constructed to suggest deep space, with foreground, middle ground, and distance. Large flowers and deep colors are therefore placed low and in the foreground, and tall branches with lighter foliage at the back of the arrangement. Sometimes a poem hangs on the wall behind the flowers, and near it is placed some object that further develops the experience of nature that the artist has tried to recapture.

Through the centuries many schools and styles have developed: *shokwa* arrangements for both tall and flat containers, generally of bronze, which preserve the oldest traditions; *moribana,* or ' piled up ' flowers in flat vases, which is most adaptable to American use; and *nageire*, or ' thrown in ' schemes. These all have their formal, semi-formal, and informal aspects. The mind of the flower master is not in the least hidebound or rule-ridden, but most flexible and inventive. " Beware, the beaten path may lead astray. Flowers bloom everywhere," said one of them. Americans are finding many suggestive ideas here without following any one style too closely.

Emerging today as a living art in our own country, this form deserves special attention and offers an unusually fruitful field for art education. The study of the organization of flowers and vase into a composition that illustrates principles of design, often today studied abstractly or with color and line on paper alone, gives the student sympathetic, because living and familiar, material to work with. Most significant of all, the tangible nature of the mediums (containers of all shapes and materials, and the plants themselves — evergreens, flowering shrubs, or the more familiar flowers of the average garden) makes it possible to demonstrate the importance for the artist of understanding the medium with which he is working. Although these materials are not at the moment as easy to put one's hands on as are crayons, water color, and paper, once there is a demand for their use, they will be forthcoming as they have been for many decades in Japan, where the art has been taught as a part of the normal education of young people.

The flower artist in America has at hand a constantly growing range of materials: vases of all kinds of materials and interesting shapes; plants, familiar and exotic, from all over the world. With these he works to present forms that will be a joy in themselves and will enliven and enhance the places for which they are designed. And the places where we now see that flowers can be used are increasing every day. Many public meeting places use them. They are finding a constant place in department-store window decoration, often combined with interesting lighting. Many commercial photographs are taken with flower arrangements as an integral part, along with clothes, automobiles, or other products. Art exhibitions and museum galleries (as has long been the case in Japan) are beginning to see their value.

The greatest danger that we face in exploring this field of artistic expression, which offers so much for discriminating choice and judgment, is that we will use the medium as we do any other, and not take the time to understand its own intrinsic possibilities. This is understandable when we review the early history of the art in the West. It is a danger that has never been faced in the East, where man has long

made an art of understanding and observing nature apart from her relation to man.

That the art of flowers is becoming an increasingly absorbing interest to a large number of people in our American communities is very
obvious to anyone who follows the activities of our garden clubs, with
their private flower-arrangement exhibitions, as well as their community shows and the great metropolitan exhibitions held in so many of
our large cities. In these the flower-arrangement entries are among the
most important and generally attractive parts of any horticultural
show. The exhibitions of the commercial growers and the horticultural
exhibitions are usually visited by ardent flower-arrangement enthusiasts, pencil and paper in hand, to make note of new and unusual material for their art.

The professional rôle of the artist of flower arrangement has an increasingly important place in our communities. Window decorators
in our important department stores, hospital nurses, professional arrangers of parties, people employed to maintain the vivid and living
charm of many of our national monuments, such as Williamsburg and
Mt. Vernon, are all making a serious study of the art, because it presents material important to their special problems. Still the person
who makes most constant demands on the art and the person who is
most consciously awake to the need of direction in this field is the
amateur and the home-maker. There are also fields in which the art
has not yet been explored, notably in the field of therapy. Nervous
patients would find in this gracious field a most rewarding and nourish-
ing activity.

The most important patron today is the public enterprise. The
Rockefeller Foundation at Williamsburg employs a flower-arranger;
the Coca Cola Company uses illustrations of flower arrangements in
its advertising and sells a booklet with arrangements in full color. In
the West several newspapers run a weekly column conducted by a professional artist, who uses a large illustration with a brief comment
calling attention to the quality of the vase and its relation to the flowers, the holder necessary to keep the branches in their proper position,
and the line or mass that the branches achieve. As a rule, the private
patron will call upon the artist only on unusually important occasions,
feeling that the arrangement is so transitory a creation that she had
best be her own artist. This is a very healthy situation, of course,
especially as the woman who is at all awake to the lovely forms that
can be made with flowers is eager to learn about the art, and attends

classes and lectures or uses the books that are appearing on the subject. In England the specialist in this art has found many private patrons. Constance Spry arranges flowers throughout the year in town houses and on country estates. She is commissioned to take charge of all the flowers used at important weddings and parties. Her activities are so extensive that she maintains large greenhouses, runs a school of flower arrangement, and is connected with a shop and school in New York City. It is very probable that we in this country will develop a much larger field for the artist with a private patron.

The style of this art in America naturally shows the influence of many European traditions, especially the Baroque, Georgian, and Victorian styles, which easily find their place in the majority of American houses. Constance Spry, who has had some influence here, has a predilection for very full and massive Georgian arrangements. The Japanese influence has been strong, especially on the West coast where people have consciously followed Oriental traditions. This influence has been most beneficial, partly because it so consistently emphasizes the importance of understanding flowers as a medium of expression. In the West, because the art has been treated as a part of decorative art in general, flowers have been handled as though they were paint or clay, and their intrinsic beauty has often been eclipsed. The Japanese have always emphasized the importance of studying the medium and letting it dictate the nature of the form.

Many other stylistic fields have been exploited in the career of this art. The Garden Club of America, most demanding on its members, presented the problem of creating arrangements in a Byzantine, a Greek, and a South Sea Island manner. The research in these fields, while it led to an understanding of these art forms, did not create any important tendencies. The Garden Club's competition for containers resulted in the creation of most interesting containers (notably wooden goblet shapes turned on a lathe) that might well be exploited by manufacturers who think that the ordinary glass vase is the last word in flower containers. In some sections of the country, at least, metal and pottery containers have practically replaced glass, and many truly artistic pottery products have been sold at very low cost, as, for instance, importations from Czecho-Slovakia. American artists have made their own contribution.

A distinctly American style has developed within the last two or three years that has close affiliations with modern European trends in architecture and painting. The style is as clear-cut, abstract, and mechanical as it is possible to achieve with flowers and foliage, and it has surprising possibilities if the material used is chosen with care. Calla lilies, the bird of paradise, many cacti, tropical plants, anthurium, caladium, flax, sanseveria, and a host of others can look as streamlined as an airplane and as machine-made as a metal disc. The containers used are clear-cut and shining; rectangular, square, or sphereshaped; of gleaming metal, black glass, or shining glazed pottery. In the prize-winning arrangement at the New York Flower Show in 1940 the leaves were clipped into rectangular shapes, and mushrooms wired onto bare branches were used with them. Naturally such formal arrangements are suitable primarily only for very modern interiors. This very abstract tendency does not crowd out much regional variety, the character of which is determined by the prevailing flora. Florida and Hawaii have tropical foliage and large, brilliantly colored flowers, which, when combined with striking shells and coral, often give a surrealistic effect. In Southern California tropical plants and fruit are placed in Samoan wooden bowls, and in New Mexico Indian baskets and pottery are used with flat primitive colors: orange, yellow, and beige, and simple shapes like those of the daisy, marigold, and zinnia. At Williamsburg, where the atmosphere of Colonial America has been reproduced with authentic dignity and charm, the flowers found in early American gardens are grown especially for the bouquets. The forms follow those found in paintings and textiles of the period. It is this style of arrangement, full and heavy, mixed in color, that is found in the average American house.

The amateur interested to find ideas and ways of handling flowers has ample opportunity to do so. Not only have many excellent books appeared in the last few years, but most magazines and newspapers print pages, often in color, of flowers, the prize-winning entries in flower shows, and the work of professional artists. Commercial advertisers often combine very fine flower arrangements with their products, and women's fashion magazines are full of lovely ladies peering into expensive vases of ravishing flowers, startlingly and often beautifully arranged.

The burning issue is no longer, as it once was, whether to give thought to arranging flowers at all or to dump them into the first container that came to hand, but whether to work for natural or formal and distorted effects. Even this issue is not a very important one, for the place and occasion will determine whether a natural or a formal style is suitable, and the medium lends itself to either.

The art is in the liveliest of health, engaging the interest and study of a constantly growing group of men and women. It has opened people's eyes to the infinite possibilities of color, of shape, of line and mass that this very rich medium presents. When it comes to the expression of ideas or moods, the ground can become more treacherous, but there are possibilities here, as the Japanese discovered long ago. One of the most important things that has come out of the consciousness of flowers as material for artistic expression is an increasing and intelligent interest in one's own garden; in planning it, too, with thought for its color and form, and in searching out beautiful foliage and unusual (not necessarily more expensive) plants.

REFERENCES

(1) ARMS, JOHN TAYLOR, AND ARMS, DOROTHY NOYES. *Design in Flower Arrangement.* (Macmillan: New York, 1937)
(2) FERGUSON, DONITA, AND SHELDON, ROY. *Fun with Flowers.* (Houghton Mifflin Co.: Boston, 1939)
(3) KOEHN, ALFRED. *The Art of Japanese Flower Arrangement.* (Houghton Mifflin Co.: Boston, 1934)
(4) KOEHN, ALFRED. *The Way of Japanese Flower Arrangement.* (Kyo Bun Kwan: Tokyo, 1935)
(5) OSHIKAWA, JOSUI, AND GORHAM, HAZEL H. *Manual of Japanese Flower Arrangement.* (Nippon Bunka Renmai: Tokyo, 1936)
(6) PREININGER, MARGARET. *Japanese Flower Arrangement for the Modern Home.* (Little, Brown, and Co.: Boston, 1936)
(7) SPRY, CONSTANCE. *Flowers in House and Garden.* (G. P. Putnam's Sons: New York, 1938)

CHAPTER VII

THE HANDCRAFTS

Felix Payant
Editor of *Design*
Columbus, Ohio

I. Introductory

In the days of the earliest settlers in America, practically every home was of necessity a busy workshop where everything needed for the family was made. The pioneer's art was a provincial one, for he made what he needed under the stress of his environment, and with the materials, tools, and skills that were available, so that his buildings, furniture, and utensils speak that dialect. But the vigor of these early arts provided a life force that gave meaning to the work of the pioneer, though it lacked sophisticated qualities.

The frontier moved gradually westward. This meant new racial influences, new geographical conditions, and new materials, which gave rise to many and varied handcrafts. These were a valuable and important contribution to us. Until the establishment of the machine age the handcrafts were numerous and they reached a high quality, with excellent examples of honest use of materials. They were developed in terms of those materials, with a simple directness of attack. A few persons became more skilled than others, so that we hear of itinerant artists, among them weavers, who moved from one household to another. The hand-woven coverlets in many cases show the name and trace the movements and techniques of the weaver. Often these coverlets incorporated interesting local events, such as the building of railroads.

Today the handcrafts as an art expression are reasserting themselves, not only in the lives of the young and the economically underprivileged, but also as highly desirable emotional expressions for all. The handcrafts force us to realize that art was a way of life before it was exhibited in museums.

From the earliest days the American colonists made their useful things interesting. They expressed in their handcrafts their zealous attitude towards life, their sincere convictions, and their desire to carve

81

for themselves a life based on their ideals. It is not strange, then, to find their utensils, their furniture, their ships, their simplest household utensils so made as to convey how they felt towards their new country. It was a vigorous statement and at the same time a simple one, humble and refined. Our early art inheritance is far from a crude one. Not until later did it assume the affectations and sentimentality of the Victorian Age, when surface decorations were popular.

II. Types of American Design, as Shown by the Index of American Design

Never before has any agency attempted such a work as the *Index of American Design*. It is a pictorial record of handcrafts in America, conducted as part of the Federal Art Project of the Works Progress Administration. The making of record drawings of handcrafts indigenous to American culture and the collection of data on these native arts form the groundwork for a nation-wide pictorial survey of design in the American decorative arts. Through the handcrafts we may understand the philosophies and ideals of our early American culture. We may likewise learn much to help us in solving some of our present-day problems relating to activity during leisure time and the proper use of materials.

The *Index of American Design* includes art objects that were made from the period of the earliest settlement up to 1890. First begun in New York, the work has progressed in various sections of the country from New England to California, with workers concentrating on the characteristic American art of their respective localities.

1. Furniture

One of the largest portfolios of the *Index of American Design* is devoted to furniture. Here may be seen reproductions of the early carved chests of Massachusetts and Connecticut; the block-front furniture of Newport; the finely proportioned mahogany and cherry of the cabinetmakers of New York, Philadelphia, and Charleston, which carry the main body of American design from seventeenth-century severity into the revived Classicism of the early Republican period.

The admiration of prosperous residents of the coastal cities for English fashions is reflected in the interpretations of Chippendale, Hepplewhite, and Sheraton styles, but distinctive American types also are shown in their adaptation to the living conditions of a new country and the frequent necessity for using native woods.

Victorian pieces are charming, despite their admixture of several styles. The less significant, but familiar phases of the furniture group include Shaker pieces (which anticipated modern design in their functional simplicity), the gaily painted chests and cupboards of the Pennsylvania Germans, and the picturesque adaptations of Spanish styles in the Southwest.

2. Ceramics and Glass

In the field of ceramics emphasis has been placed upon the decorative pottery of the eighteenth and nineteenth centuries.

American glass, as developed in New York, New Jersey, and Pennsylvania, ranges from the clear engraved glasses of " Baron " Stiegel in Pennsylvania to the brown and green flasks stamped with busts of such popular idols as Jenny Lind and Lafayette. The wares of Wistar and other South Jersey factories, the Amelong glass of Maryland, and the pressed Sandwich glass were popular in the Eastern and Middle Western States during the later period. Glassmaking was the best known of the early industries in New Jersey. Caspar Wistar made glass in Salem County as early as 1789, and later a German family named Stenger started a factory in Glassboro. Rare glass was made at Redfield near Syracuse, New York.

Ohio produced four general groups of ceramics: earthenware, comprising glazed and unglazed redware and glazed yellowware; salt glazed stoneware; Upper Muskingum Valley pottery lamps; and miniature examples of pottery. Glass of fine quality was also produced in Ohio, at Zanesville, Ravenna, and Mantua.

3. Metal

We are impressed with the native skill of American craftsmen in their handling of various metals for definitely practical use, and with the beauty of design and surface that they achieved in their household utensils, lighting fixtures, fire irons, stoves, and similar products. Silverware is essentially aristocratic in tradition. The elaborate architectural ironwork in Louisiana is strongly flavored with French tradition.

4. Textiles

The textile group includes the patterns of crewel work done in New England in the seventeenth century, the geometrical variations of coverlets woven on hand looms by the women of the pioneer era, and the

not-so-practical but quaint, expressions worked in samplers and em-
broidered pictures. Quilts, representing many types of design popular
throughout the country between 1750 and 1850, range from early designs, such as " King David's Crown," through such political and historical motifs, as " Tippecanoe and Tyler Too " and " Whig Rose,"
to such good old standbys as " The Pine Tree " and " Star of Bethle-
hem."

Costumes and accessories, devoted mainly to the fashions worn by
women, range all the way from the hooded severity of a Shaker Cape
to late eighteenth-century elegance. They include the elaborate bro-
cades and wide hooped skirts of late Colonial times; the straight, slender
dresses worn everywhere immediately after the French Revolution.
The short full skirts, the furbelows that ushered in the early days of
the reign of Queen Victoria, the bustles, bows, and trains of the early
seventies — all these find their colorful reproductions in the story of
milady and her fashions, and reveal significant phases of American life.

5. Wood Carving and Stone Carving

Only recently has there been an appreciation of the importance of
wood carving and stone carving in its relation to American sculpture.
Hardly an aspect of American civilization could be named that is not
reflected in these carvings. Maine sculpture forms a category by itself;
the wooden figureheads, billetheads, mast sheaths, and stern pieces so
frequently mentioned in American literature all are recorded in the
Index, along with the cigar-store Indians that had their greatest vogue
between 1850 and 1880. In Michigan an almost complete census of
cigar-store Indians has been compiled, including almost every type in
use during the eighteenth century. Incidentally, the Indian, although
most popular, was not the only figure used by cigar stores. Sir Walter
Raleighs, Lord Dundrearys, Punches, Bandmasters, Turks, and naturally enough, more than a few Uncle Sams were as typical in their day
as the striped barber pole in our day. These figures were made at
first by carvers in American shipyards, but later the art was continued
by Swiss and Germans, among them Julius Melchers, father of Gari
Melchers, who later was to reach fame as a painter. Along with the
cigar-store Indian must be placed the weather vane — a simple, bold
silhouette that ranks among the oldest craftwork of the United States.

Of primary interest have been the religious carvings, represented
by wooden saints (*santos*) and crude pictures on wood or buffalo hide.
Bultos, or wooden statues of the saints, were very crude and stylized.

Most of them were church property, but each family had a special patron saint. There are many theories to account for the presence of *santos* in New Mexico. Probably the padres taught the Indian converts how to carve and paint the little statues when they found that Mexico could not supply their needs. Undoubtedly the best craftsmen became professional *santeros,* for bultos from various parts of the state can be recognized as the work of one man.

6. Toys

Toys and puppets likewise have received attention from artists who are studying the types, history, and evolution of the playthings fashioned from whatever materials were at hand, to delight the hearts of children. Music boxes with carved figures, a Noah's Ark of the late eighteenth century, and an elaborate toy theater with automatic dancers reflect the imagination and ingenuity of the toymakers of a bygone day.

Michigan possesses an unusual number of early-day puppets and marionettes, many of them belonging to David Lano and used in his family for three generations. They give a good idea of the type of folk carving that this family brought to a high art.

There are also in many regions examples of superior artistry shown in miniature furniture, ceramics, and glass made by able parents for their children.

III. Sectarian Groups

A decided influence on handcrafts has been exerted by the many religious groups who established colonies throughout America. The Shaker sect was organized in this country by Ann Lee, an immigrant from England in 1774. Early in the nineteenth century no fewer than eighteen colonies had been founded, and today there still exist Shaker colonies at Hancock, Massachusetts; Canterbury, New Hampshire; New Lebanon and Watervliet, New York; and Sabbath Day Lake, Maine. Believing labor to be synonymous with worship, their doctrine was " Put your hands to work and your hearts to God." Their ingenuity and originality of style entitle them to a distinguished place in the history of American art; their furniture, with its emphasis on essential forms, its fine proportion, and its exclusion of superfluous ornament, was decidedly of artistic merit.

So, too, have the Pennsylvania-German handcrafts made a permanent impression on the nation's culture. Their ceramics, cabinets, textiles, toys, and ' Fractur ' drawings (made for births, baptisms, weddings, and deaths) all reflect the piety and prudence, love of color, and reserved desire for beauty of this sturdy section of America's people. Of all the Pennsylvania German objects, there is nothing more beautiful than the painted dower chest. The desire for cleanliness, however, is responsible for the scrubbing out and painting out of much of this early decoration, so that fine chests are rare and treasured possessions. Some pieplates and dishes of fine design date back to prerevolutionary days. The carving of butter molds and the making of toys were among their arts. Tiles made by Stiegel of Manheim in Lancaster County bear Biblical designs in purple line and white ground.

In the Southwest there was a rich folk art that flourished in the Rio Grande and Taos valleys from the sixteenth century through the nineteenth. In New Mexico wood sculptures and plaques of saints adorned the churches, while in Southern California there was rich material in the missions.

The communistic community at Zoar, Ohio, was settled by Separatists from Wurtemburg. The " community of goods," established as an expedient economic measure, was secondary to their primary objective of religious freedom. During its existence from 1817 to 1898, the colony produced household and personal articles of substantial merit. The Zoarites made clothing and bedding from textiles woven from flax, rye straw, and wool grown in Zoar; pottery, tin, and iron from local raw materials; and furniture from native fruit and other trees. The Amish made a contribution in carved wooden toys and austere furniture designs.

IV. THE ATLANTIC STATES

Maine was rich in many folk arts. Among them are embroidery and wood carving, such as weather vanes and ship figureheads. Massachusetts, besides being the center of the Shaker group, had a wealth of carved wooden ship figureheads, toys, portrait busts, and scrimshaw (etched bone).

In Rhode Island there were many ship figureheads and cigar-store figures, but wood carving also took the form of trade insignia, toys, weather vanes, butter molds, wooden pitchers, and kitchen utensils. Furniture-making was unlimited in this little state.

Connecticut was rich in ceramics, seventeenth-century furniture, wood carving, painted chests, carved chests, textiles, bandbox designs, crewel embroidery, and stencilled subjects, such as chairs and decorated walls. Research has established that bandbox paper was an important and lucrative business in the early years of the nineteenth century.

Maryland produced much furniture as early as 1746, and her early cabinetmakers include such names as John Shaw of Annapolis, and Robert Renwick. Virginia offers a wealth of handcrafts, including many ship figureheads and carved wooden figures of Jenny Lind and Daniel Webster. Vermont, of course, had much to offer in pottery, glassware, pewter, silver, and textiles.

V. The Midwest

Illinois was a state heterogeneous in its peoples and materials, both of which were marked by a welter of influences: the French, the Scandinavian, the German, and other nations. Illinois was for many not a mecca but a stopover. The state, however, was spotted with vestigial communities founded in the main on religious bases, and in these communities may be found the Swedish crafts of Bishop Hill, the Moravian relics of West Salem, the abandoned materials of Mormon and Icarian Nauvoo, and the spare means of Amish Arthur. The majority of other communities, including the French settlements and the Mississippi River towns, changed with the times, and later settlers brought with them the more elegant things from older parts of the country.

In Bishop Hill, the now forgotten village of Bishop Janson, the adaptation of Swedish forms in and by the extinct community was of considerable interest. Nauvoo is the city built by the Mormons; then abandoned at the time of their exodus to Salt Lake City and Independence. The Icarian colony, which moved into Nauvoo under Fournier, is interesting for tremendous community kettles, numbered chairs, provincial French sabots, and, finally, for the primitive wine-making implements of the succeeding German influx. Similarly, the early French communities and the existing Amish settlements contributed their share to this earlier culture.

Early Iowa handcrafts included wooden ladles, fruit jugs, tables, baker's cabinet and table, desks, tools, trunks, footstools, whisk-broom cases, and sewing cabinets; also forks, flails, hatboxes, single ox yokes, candle molds, weathervanes, mortars and pestles, lard-oil lanterns, shoe scrapers, woven blankets, drawn-work towels, dresses, bonnets, scarfs, capes, and boots, a Particle Host, a Holy Water font, and carved altar pieces of extremely interesting design. The Amana colonies, which emigrated to Iowa from Ebenezer, New York, in the early 1800's, were a part of pioneer Iowa. These people left many articles of interest, including a shoe scraper that has been in use since it was placed on the door step of the Amana Bakery in 1860.

Likewise one might study each state of the Union and find indications of art expression in the lives of the early settlers. Kentucky has its excellent hand-woven coverlets made as early as the late eighteenth century. Kansas for fifty years produced much wood sculpture in the form of merry-go-round horses and circus-wagon decoration. Oregon was settled late, but its settlers expressed their desire for beauty in their implements, kitchen utensils, furniture, and quilts.

VI. HANDCRAFTS TODAY

The handcrafts should help to solve many current problems concerned with developing good taste, the proper use of leisure, and the vitalizing of American life and traditions in our classroom work. Such objects as are preserved in the *Index of American Design* are a most valuable source of reference material for our artists and designers in industry today.

Just how does the person engaged in the handcrafts for a livelihood fit into our machine-controlled society? Obviously, the handcrafts have some importance as a direct economic factor. Quantity production, being what it is, makes it impossible to produce objects of value in quantity. Yet in many — usually remote — sections, such as exist in New Hampshire, Maine, Kentucky, North Carolina, and South Carolina, there is a definite move towards developing the handcrafts as a source of income. In occasional isolated places there are potters, cabinetmakers, weavers, and metalworkers who can make a livelihood by selling their products, though in general this source of revenue is somewhat uncertain and depends on tourists for support.

There are those, however, who believe that handcrafts in the home may be a means of materially reducing the cost of living. In his book, *Flight from the City*, Ralph Borsodi says:

> Nothing had developed to stop the factory in its successful competition with handicraft industry, so far as costs of production were concerned. Our economists, therefore, took it for granted that the superiority of the factory in competition with the home would continue indefinitely into the future. What they overlooked, however, was that while production costs decrease year after year, distribution costs increase. The tendency of distribution and transportation to absorb more

and more of the economies made possible by factory production was ignored. Transportation, warehousing, advertising, salesmanship, wholesaling, retailing — all these aspects of distribution cost more than the whole cost of fabricating the good themselves. Less than one-third of what the consumer pays when actually buying goods at retail is paid for the raw materials and costs of manufacturing finished commodities; over two-thirds is paid for distribution.[1]

It is undoubtedly true that some artists in such fields as metalwork, pottery, and textiles whose names are recognized and well known in America are unable to make an adequate income through the pursuit of their art, even when well located geographically. Private patronage of such arts is small. Museums and other institutions from time to time buy pieces for their collections. The large foundations occasionally subsidize artists in these fields for short periods.

The government, through the W.P.A. and its various projects, has done much to promote handcrafts in several states, where excellent work has been produced on the Federal Art Project. In some states there are handcraft projects in which craftsmen are producing under competent directors work of high esthetic value. Among these may be mentioned the handcraft project in Milwaukee and the one in St. Paul.

Allen Eaton, who wrote *Handicrafts of the Southern Highlands,* says:

> Living conditions today favor a continuation of the practice of handicrafts in the Southern Highlands. . . . many things have been made especially for sale because there 'fireside industries' often afford the only opportunity for meager earnings. It is this economic pressure which forms the natural basis for the continuation of handicrafts both in the homes and in the schools of the Highlands.[2]

Throughout America the recreation groups under a great number of auspices, both public and private, are facing the problem of how participation in the crafts can be provided on a recreational basis and still advance constructively towards an understanding of the arts. Here is a difficult situation, yet it has implications that are of national import. If the countless participants in handcrafts can experience the joy of creation with esthetic qualities in three-dimensional material, a definite improvement of public taste will result.

The social advantage in remote districts cannot be overlooked, for

---

[1] Borsodi (1), p. 16.
[2] Eaton (4), p. 34.

in such places there are few if any occasions that afford an opportunity for people to gather in groups. It has been found that groups meeting regularly to promote their work in handcrafts derived many advantages. In one case forty widely separated homes were affected. They met in a coöperatively built community house to discuss materials, instruction, marketing, and all questions conducive to their common good.

Since the World War occupational therapy has proved the great value of handcraft as a rehabilitating influence. Institutions for the blind and otherwise handicapped persons have found this type of esthetic experience invaluable for emotional stability, mental alertness, and real physical betterment. The economic factor has also been of significance in some of these cases. Of recent years, too, the handcrafts have grown rapidly as an avocation for all types of adult.

VII. The Past and the Future

Throughout the past hundred years, with the influence of machine production various recurrent and often conflicting attitudes have affected the American craftsman. Ruskin and William Morris were among the first to advocate a general movement against the machine-made product. America was soon to have its share of craft guilds and publications encouraging them. China-painting and pyrography are but two of the activities that were very popular; but from the esthetic point of view the emphasis was misplaced in these movements.

Today, our outlook is broader and we are keenly aware of our social needs. How can the craftsman influence the quality of mass production in America as he does in Sweden? How may the esthetic factor function properly in a technological world? Can the handcrafts that spoke the vigorous dialect of the pioneer speak the language of our age? In the answers to these questions lies the possibility of enriched living for America, in which the arts are co-existent with life.

References

(1) Borsodi, Ralph. *Flight from the City.* (Harper and Brothers: New York, 1933) 190 pp.

(2) Bruce, M. *The Book of Craftsmen.* (Dodd Mead and Co.: New York, 1936) 282 pp.

(3) Dewey, John. *Art as Experience.* (Minton, Balch, and Co.: New York, 1934) 349 pp.

(4) Eaton, Allen H. *Handicrafts of the Southern Highlands.* (Russell Sage Foundation: New York, 1937) 346 pp.

(5) GARDNER, H. *Understanding the Arts.* (Harcourt, Brace and Co.: New York, 1932) 336 pp.

(6) KEPPEL, F. P., and DUFFUS, R. L. *Art in American Life.* (McGraw-Hill Book Co.: New York, 1933) 208 pp.

(7) MUMFORD, LEWIS. *Technics and Civilization.* (Harcourt, Brace and Co.: New York, 1934) 435 pp.

(8) TOMLINSON, R. R. *Crafts for Children.* (The Studio, Ltd.: London, 1935) 120 pp.

CHAPTER VIII

ART IN INDUSTRY

ALON BEMENT
and
SHELDON CHENEY AND MARTHA CHENEY
New York, New York

I

THE DEVELOPMENT OF INDUSTRIAL DESIGN IN AMERICA

ALON BEMENT

When the effects of the depression are accounted, when stock is taken and a final evaluation is made, it will be found that a considerable number of human endeavors have been put forward by it. Among other things on the credit side of the ledger there is found written a renewal of interest in the arts: not so much in the arts of the *Salon* — of painting or sculpture or of high fashion, though favorable attention has been drawn to them — but rather in the art that has to do with daily living in association with common objects of utility.

The cause of this revival is traceable in part to the difficulty commerce and industry had in selling goods after the market disaster of October, 1929. For a considerable time confidence was so impaired that the exchange of money for commodities was reduced to an unheard-of low. The predicament of a merchant with a normal supply of goods on his shelves or of an industrialist with a reserve stock in his warehouse was an unpleasant one. In the endeavor to move these stocks every known selling inducement was tried and tried again. And, in the end, after the old expedients of drastic price reduction and extra advertising campaigns had proved futile, it became apparent that good appearance was a more important selling factor than it had previously been thought to be. In combination with reasonable price and sound utility, appearance became a controlling factor. This thought, once firmly fixed in the mind of the industrialist, added him to the ranks of the art-conscious. A new and vigorous proponent of good design

93

came into being — one capable of translating his interest into innumerable forms and colors suitable for distribution to the homes of the country.

Thus redesigned stoves, iceboxes, pans, knives, forks, spoons, motor cars, streamlined trains, and airplanes have already done something more than attract our attention by their increased utility; they have aroused an interest in how things look, and this interest has been intensified by the appearance in the open market of new materials, such as rayon, celanese, and nylon in the synthetic textile field; bakelite, plaskon, and durez among the plastics; and chromium, stainless steel, and monel metal in new treatments of copper and steel. This interest is growing and already is widespread enough to affect our whole environment and give hope that before long it may produce a betterment of that blight of the average small town, its business section, and presage a return to the good taste that is our heritage and that prevailed before the Industrial Revolution.

For two centuries, from 1620 to approximately 1840, art in the United States had a normal and natural development. In this period, the word *art* had no other meaning than the right way of making things — ' things ' being anything that was needed by man, either physical or spiritual. The maker of things was an artist. His product was accepted as a part of daily life. It was contrived according to the need for it, made not for the connoisseur but for the customer, not for the museum, but for use. During this epoch, the artist's only peculiarity lay in his exact knowledge of the way in which his work should be done. This knowledge was known, quite simply, as his ' art.' Artist and consumer were culturally of one mind, for they lived against the same background; they shared the same views and tastes. The artist was potentially the consumer, the consumer was potentially the artist. No one, least of all the maker himself, thought of the maker as more intelligent or more sensitive than any other man; he was regarded only as expert in his particular craft.

This rational attitude toward art was the cause of the immediate improvement in both the utility and the appearance of objects imported by the Colonists and their immediate descendants, from the Old World. It began with improvement of household utensils and implements of the field, and led in the end to such products as the famous Conestoga wagons, which carried the pioneers across prairie and mountain to the Pacific, and the graceful clipper ships, which bore American goods to all corners of the earth. Art, through such creations as these conveyances of land and sea, led us to a true expression of our national ideals of design. Unfortunately, this normal development halted midway in the nineteenth century, with the Industrial Revolution. The power-driven machine replaced the craftsman artist; the inferior appearance of quantity production overshadowed the artistic value of the single hand-made object. Quantity production meant low prices, and the people enthusiastically responded to their appeal. But quantity production at that time also meant a sacrifice of beauty in the product. Taste declined, and the American home was soon crowded with objects cheap in price, cheap in appearance, and too often cheap in inherent value as well.

A change in attitude toward the artist also resulted. The course of art was more and more directed by an élite of taste. Museums and private collectors, art dealers and schools, artists themselves, and finally the general public, in the end, believed that art was the prerogative of wealth and privilege, that its pursuit and enjoyment belonged to leisure.

The problem now is to bring about a balance between these two extremes of attitude, and to revive in the average man a consciousness of his responsibilities and his privileges as a creative artist. Toward the achievement of this end, two courses seem to be necessary; to create a state of mind in the general public that will demand beautiful things for homes and communities; and, since the power-driven machine has been perfected to an almost human ability, to induce the manufacturer — the controller of the machine — to meet this need. Intelligent self-interest on the part of industry, with the assistance of a numerous young and rapidly developing corps of artist-designers, seems to promise an increased industrial production of beauty.

The artist-designer is not a new figure in the American scene. With the appearance of the machine he became a permanent fixture in industry, and replaced craftsmen's instincts for design that were operative before the Industrial Revolution. But in spite of service beginning in the mid-nineteenth century, artist-designers achieved only a very modest place for themselves until the end of the first quarter of the present century. The designer was regarded as *paid help* and was treated as such — he punched the time clock with other employees. The usual procedure was to call him to the front office after the officials, including the sales and production manager, had decided what the next production would be; present him with a folio of plates — acquired from traditional sources; and instruct him to make " something like " one of them or possibly a combination of two. Except in the rarest case he was not consulted at all as to the type of design to be used.

The Art Alliance of America, the first association to interest itself in improving the appearance of American manufactured products, was organized in 1914. In 1917 the difficulty of obtaining European designs because of the submarine blockade for the first time focussed full attention upon the abilities of American designers and gave them an opportunity to prove their worth. The Alliance took advantage of the situation and organized an exhibition of textiles. This is believed to be the first exhibition of American machine-made products declared to be art and held in an art environment. Later the Metropolitan Museum of Art staged an exhibition of the same character in rooms adjacent to those occupied by the great masters in the fine arts.

Soon thereafter (1923) free-lance designers, without affiliation with any given firm, appeared and achieved minor success in services to the industries. By 1927 ultra-modern foreign designers, attracted by tales of the generous fees paid by American industrialists, began to trickle in from Western Europe. They were in the main capable, but were not sufficiently familiar with the taste of the American consumer to warrant sustained acceptance of their creations. Under the circumstances, therefore, it was only a matter of time before some serious doubts developed in the industries that had underwritten their talent, with the result that a number of powerful firms declared themselves against designers and redesigning. Fortunately, by this time the revival of interest in appearances had developed sufficient momentum to overcome the temporary setback, and by the beginning of 1929 the American designers had partially reassured industry by bringing out a number of convincingly good designs.

Then, without warning, the major catastrophe of the depression involved the financial world and from it emerged the present-day practical procedure in design. The pinch of poverty again proved its efficiency in energizing creation. In the ensuing fight for existence the superficial aspects of design began to disappear, and by 1931 a group of able designers had developed who were willing to consider with the manufacturer practical methods of producing and distributing articles suited to the taste of the buying public. As an indication of the importance designing had acquired during the depression period, it is interesting to observe that several free-lance designers earned $75,000 each in 1934 and one over $100,000. It is obvious that these men were no longer to be considered ' paid help ' and punchers of time clocks. They had establishments of their own, impressive suites on the upper floors of the best business buildings, and staffs of well-paid helpers. Their counsel fees were on a par with those of the most famous and skillful engineers. To raise the question here as to whether they were worth the enormous fees paid is futile. The depression had convinced the industrialist of the importance of appearance as an aid in selling, and these designers were first in the field. Artistic design was something the manufacturer had to have.

The criticism of one American writer that the major part of designers' work has been superficial — " face-lifting," as he puts it — should not be taken too seriously, though there are numerous instances, such as the imposition of gilded stripes on a heavy traction unit and the decorating of a transcontinental bus with grotesque and meaningless wave lines, that seem to bear him out. These represent only minor weaknesses, incidents in the development of a new profession. In observing them it must be remembered that there have been numberless instances of contributions to utility as well as to appearance in many American products in the last few years.

The statement that a large number of the more highly publicized designers have achieved prosperity through their shrewd business acumen rather than through their ability to design probably deserves more thought. There are among the less well-known men in the offices of design establishments and in the field outside, individuals who produce better designs than some who are now known as leaders; but here again it must be remembered that the young men devote all their time to designing and are not under the strain of directing an office, controlling a staff, and paying the overhead. In the natural course of events, the young man of today will move up tomorrow, and, as the profession becomes established, it will develop a more equitable code of ethics favoring the beginner. There will be a larger group at the top who will probably have to be satisfied with smaller fees and the secondary group will receive more in proportion. Every industry will have its own designers. More will be spent in the improvement of appearances, but it will be spread over a larger field, so that the service to industry will cost less, and the public will be better served.

Among the men who are devoting their time to the redesigning of American industrial products appear such names as: John Vassos, Walter D. Teague, Harold Van Doren, Norman Bel Geddes, Lucien Bernhard, and Raymond Loewy.

Sporadic attempts have been made to organize associations of which the many members of the profession could become active supporters, and through whose unity of purpose they could advance the cause in which they are interested; but to date the only one in operation is composed of men from the Middle West — the American Designers Institute. It holds its annual meeting in Chicago. In an address before the Institute this year Mr. Vassos made the following criticisms and suggestions:

> It appears to me that the efforts of the industrial designers have of late been directed too much toward the simplification of surfaces rather than to the building up of basic structural form. In the minds of the consumer as well as the designer, the habit of 'lining,' 'grooving,' and 'streamlining' is becoming too strong to be easily overcome. These habits can lead very easily away from the production of functional design. . . . The disheartening part of it is that many electrical appliances, things for the kitchen, the bathroom, the cellar, in pleasing and simple design, have been accepted by the public, but practically no interest has yet been evidenced in a corresponding redesigning of furniture; by that I mean furniture in simplified functional form, not merely repetitions of traditional pieces "modernized" by chromium handles, rounded corners, built-to-the-floor forms, and other superfluous affectations supposedly denoting modernity.

> Industrial designers have contributed much to the most popular room in the house, the kitchen. Their efforts in functionalizing gas and electric stoves by the introduction of lighted tops, time and heat control clocks, clear vision ovens, have been important. The same holds true of ice boxes. Not only is their form pleasing, but such things as space for vegetables, cold and semi-cold chambers, lighted interiors, drinking water receptacles, have been introduced. The lowly kitchen sink has been made a thing of beauty, and with the automatic electric washer as part of the sink, dish washing is no longer a dreaded or a tiring task. In the smaller appliances, such as electric mixers and toasters, not only have they been beautified, but their practicability has been greatly increased. We also see the skillful hand of the designer improving and beautifying even such a traditional item as cutlery by better form, better balance, and by the introduction of plastic handles which add a higher sanitary quality as well. The significant part of all of this styling in the kitchen is the fact that when assembled, the result is a coherent and harmonious whole.

Walter D. Teague, industrial designer, takes an optimistic view of the accomplishments of his profession. In an address delivered before the members of the School of Architecture at New York University in November 1926, he said:

There are but two categories of art: if a thing — anything — is made well enough, it is fine art, and beautiful; if it is made badly, crudely, clumsily, it is vile art, and ugly. So that while Mr. Cézanne and Mr. Brancusi are artists, so are Mr. Smith, who makes refrigerators, and Mr. Jones, who makes milling machines; not such distinguished artists, perhaps, but artists none the less. And the vast mass of fireside and curbstone art produced by the Smiths and Joneses of our factories, art that surrounds us every minute of our waking and sleeping hours, is of far greater importance to the general run of people than the minute fraction of the artistic total which we shut up in museums and picture galleries and visit, alas, so rarely. The real need of this world is that people, all people, should live among beautiful chairs and tables, in charming houses set in gracious streets of fair cities.

We are even beginning to question every man's inalienable right to make his own property as hideous as he pleases in his neighbor's eyes. We are beginning to ask ourselves if the ugliness so rife in our towns is not a reflection on our intelligence and a just cause for shame and remorse.

Out of this critical spirit may come a new world redesigned for human living. By eliminating waste, confusion, and blunders, we shall eliminate ugliness. By creating, instead, economy and efficiency, we shall substitute beauty.

II
ART AND THE MACHINE[1]
SHELDON AND MARTHA CHENEY

I. PRINCIPLES OF THE NEW INDUSTRIAL DESIGN

The principles are broad and general. The resulting style marks are few and simple. Honesty, simplicity, and functional expressiveness are the primary values involved and are basic alike to the streamline train, the cigarette lighter, the saucepan, or the grand piano as these emerge from the industrial designer's studio.

1. Materials are used honestly, each in accordance with its own intrinsic properties, its adaptation to machine processes, and its appear-

----

[1] Quoted from *Art and the Machine*, pp. 14f., 182f., 208f., by Sheldon and Martha Cheney (1936) by permission of the publishers: Whittlesey House (McGraw-Hill Book Co.), New York.

ance values. Sheet metal is not artificially grained to imitate wood, and wood is not machine-turned in simulation of hand-carved forms or finished with laid-on surface patterning of any kind.

2. Simplicity is observed in the number and kinds of materials employed, and in the form given to the object, in keeping with the requirements of mass production.

3. Functional expressiveness is the artist's foundation. It is insistence upon engineering integrity as the starting point. The bed is not to be disguised as a bookcase; the telephone is not to be hidden in the petticoat of a perfumed Paris doll or in a handicraft cabinet. The anatomy of the bed or telephone — or clock, or camera, or cook spoon, or motor truck, or grand piano — is accepted as the basic design fact, and the artist's undertaking is to bring out this fact in a characteristic and expressive appearance, an appearance that is as beautiful in its own machine-age way as are the dynamo and the ball bearing in their way or the clean, bright, efficient surgical instrument.

Because the approach is fundamental, and because the designer is artist-technologist, more than visual values emerge as a result of industrial-design procedure. The efficiency of the commodity is often increased, greater economy in its production is realized, and not infrequently a revolutionary new product appears to replace the old. This is now so well understood that representative industrial designers find demand for a large part of their services in the field of preliminary study: study in the field of rational engineering and in what is known as 'consumer engineering.' The specific contract to design is based upon such study and recommendations that follow it.

And we come to know the style marks as compounded of the engineering functional rightness of the product and the artist's confirmation of that rightness; of tangible, and intangible elements; elements that are rational and esthetic. " Efficiency, economy, and right appearance " — these the typical industrial-design practitioner will state as his objectives in any design undertaking, regardless of the nature of the product. Whenever he sufficiently realizes them, wherever he achieves that unanalyzable plus quality of art in merchandise, we recognize with a thrill the same characteristic machine-age style being produced by a new generation of architects, interior designers, mass-housing designers, and planners of model communities, by a range of new creative technological workers busy throughout the fields which are determining the larger contemporary visual environment.

The machine, which has become the dominant fact of life, we begin to see also as the bringer of a complex of arts significant to the age. Today, for the first time since the Middle Ages, we are at a new major beginning, with new dimensions, new proportions, new possibilities, new freedom everywhere asserting themselves. We have the superb fact of twentieth-century engineering, and a generation of artists competent to take the dominant fact of their own age as the basis of a new expression throughout the useful arts. The airplane, the skyscraper, the new domestic architecture, organic community design: these are the most conspicuous marks of machine-age achievement on the average man's horizons. The artist-designer has won from them today's outstanding esthetic realities in the streamline, the sheer wall, the new horizontality in houses, the unit and multiple, each announcing in its own way an advance beyond the limitations of what was formerly accepted as ' natural law.'

The airplane, with its symbol the streamline, is the most conspicuous object of the new age. But automobiles in steady flow along a pleasure parkway, projectile-formed busses, trolleys, trains, even ambulances, become examples of a new mobile architecture, units in a rhythmic repeat pattern. They, too, are streamlined. The same freedom in space which is symbolized by the streamline in fast-traveling machines is written into the steel-construction skyscraper, where floor hangs airily above floor a thousand feet above the earth, or higher, with only slim steel uprights evident as support between floor and floor. The skyscraper may, we already suspect, endure merely as a monument of a transition time and of its confused economic and social values. But we are learning to build into today's homes the same knowledge of machine-age materials and methods. We have long lines and sheer walls, broad areas of glass and slim bands of metal, extending and multiplying the resources of light and air and sunshine. But planning is organic and human as well as scientifically efficient. The house is no longer huddled close to its neighbors, but with the free spaces around it is an orderly unit in a larger design organism, the community.

Streamlined machines for rapid travel, skyscrapers, homes, neighborhood and community units have, then, a common esthetic which they now share with the smallest furnishing, object, or appliance of daily use, because the same design principles have produced them. In the large they are all examples of industrial design. They represent the artist's ingenuity and vision added to what the machine can produce efficiently and economically. Altogether, they form the new synthesis of use and beauty to which all humanly useful things may be made to contribute, as rapidly as industrial-design ideals come to be understood and industrial-design standards are demanded in individual products.

What is spurious passes automatically. The eye, sensitized to the new values, comes to demand the subtle repetition of forms and proportions, the design character and style brought over from the larger realm into the more intimate environment. The objects on the dressing table, the typewriter, the clock, the cigarette lighter, the humidifier, and the thermostat begin to appear appropriate examples of industrial design when they have the same machine-age expressiveness blent of the utilitarian and the esthetic. Individually judged, they must fulfill the expectation that they will bring into the smaller circle of everyday living, each in its own way and to its own degree, an added element of machine-age freedom by widening control·over the minutiæ of the daily routine. When the industrial designer's willed intention sufficiently succeeds in bringing out of whatever object he works upon, the peculiar beauty which first thrilled the public in machines and machine products of an elemental order, the inspiring streamline beauty of the airplane, the sheer, soaring, mass-and-line simplification that is a silo or a skyscraper (which is beauty because first it is usefulness in an intense age-of-the-machine sense), we know beyond a doubt that in it we have an example of the new useful art emergent; and that it shares a machine-age esthetic with Modernist design products now becoming increasingly apparent on all our horizons.

II. Furniture and Interior Design

The interior architect is the industrial designer working as a specialist. This is Modernism's successor to the old-time ' interior decorator,' the man or woman who would have arrived with his repertory of style fittings and his function of selecting and grouping objects appropriate to enhance the interior effect. That person might have been commissioned to travel over the world to discover *objets d'art* for a particular *décor;* but nobody would have expected him to design anything. The new worker, on the contrary, has an ideal that is architectonic rather than decorative. His central effort is identical with that of the exterior designer, and is directed toward unity.

Donald Deskey, Kem Weber, Gilbert Rohde, Eleanor LeMaire, Russel Wright, William Muschenheim, Wolfgang Hoffman, Marianna von Allesch, and Robert Heller are among originators of a volume of work which has gone far toward establishing a prevailing consciousness of modern interior design appropriate to take its place in the new industrially designed complex. They are creating a new ' geometry of forms ' that is beginning to dominate American interior schemes, be it for home, office, little luxury shop, or large recreation center.

This is the industrial-design group which the public has come to know best. It is exerting the broadest and most permeative influence, because there is a universal appeal in the immediate everyday environment and whatever has to do with changing its appearance. Through individual and group exhibitions, through creations illustrated and discussed in leading periodicals, and shown (though not always discriminatingly) on the stage and in the moving pictures, a very wide educational service has been done. The design work of the group has passed into mass production, too, on a scale which will soon permit the homemaker in the most remote part of the country to plan her own interiors representative of modern design. Provided only that she has a reasonable budget and fundamentally sound personal taste, she can obtain well-designed pieces or sets representing any reasonable degree of simplicity or luxury. It is becoming possible to find them offered in the catalogs of leading mail-order houses.

Some of the workers have arrived initially at interior design in the large through special industrial designing in some minor quarter of the field. Almost every one designs such articles as metal and glass tables, clocks, toasters, and sweepers, and originates new accessories and appliances. Between those whose approach is from the side of the architect and the others who came in first as industrial designers there is essentially no distinction so long as the product is organic and creative. Both types of worker are furthering, each to a degree conditioned by individual ability, the production of that new geometry of interior forms already mentioned.

In the field of interior architecture and modern furniture design, indeed, there is no possible hard-and-fast rule regarding admittance of machine-multiplied materials or objects and nonadmittance of those which are handmade or custom designed. In the nature of the varying problem of furnishing, and the limitations of machine manufacture and construction, there is continual alternation between the custom-made thing and the organization of predominantly mass-produced elements. The first test of Modernism is in the approach by way of a conceived unity of impression, and a sound reliance at all points upon the typically simple, clean, honestly expressive effect. The parts may be made to order or be purchasable in the nearest shops; but if conception, plan, and assembly are unified and organic, the result cannot at this stage be denied the title of Modern. As a matter of fact, today's mass-produced chair or bed or curtain is likely to have appeared yesterday as a specially made object in a custom ensemble by Deskey or Rohde or Russel Wright.

Deskey designed a candy-vending machine in 1927, and later an oil burner and a motor truck. In 1930 his metal-tubing chairs were being turned out by a factory near Grand Rapids. The quality that gave them general acceptance before common use of metal had been made in stock interiors led to continuous demand for wider production of his furniture by separate pieces and in ensemble groupings. A conservative manufacturer in the early days exhibited a modern room of Deskey's design where revolutionary use was made of cork, asbestos, glass, and metal, in a scheme the total effect of which was extremely simple. Upon astonished comment that he had taken a sudden turn toward " the new Modern style," the manufacturer showed surprise. " That's not Modern style," he replied, " that's good contemporary American." The incident illustrates Deskey's peculiar ability to present advanced ideas in a completely acceptable form. There is a growing conviction about " good contemporary American " as embodied in the work of the group as a whole. William Lescaze sometimes remarks with a degree of certainty even greater: " We are the classicists of tomorrow, and none of us doubts it."

Kem Weber, practicing in California, is a member of a small group specializing in the design of Modern furniture, a group in which Gilbert Rohde and Russel Wright are most representative in New York. Their contribution is in general less exciting than that of a Dreyfuss or a Loewy, for tables and chairs have not the thrilling connotations of locomotives and skyscrapers and X-ray machines. The manufacture of furniture, moreover, has long been an art-using mass-production process, and there has not been the sudden revolution in design evident elsewhere. But there is a Modern movement nevertheless in the field, and artists of the stature of Rohde and Wright and Weber are not to be overlooked in an account of contemporary industrial design. Their best work is as truly advanced and functional in spirit as the ensembles we are considering, and often finds place in them.

Rohde has been a pioneer in reconsidering the engineering aspects of furniture, and has contributed new types of bentwood chairs and unit bookcases and cabinets. In regard to furnishing, he points out that efficient use of room space is first to be considered, that a sense of unification through grouping is second, and that the individual piece is to be considered only after those factors. Thus he designs in lines, stressing standardized units which can be used elastically, yet harmoniously. He considers first the purpose the room is to serve, and then undertakes to supply a related and consistently beautiful grouping for that purpose.

Rohde is insistent upon the point that typical Modern furniture is merely a return to original expression and logical production in terms of our own time, and therefore in line with the best creative design of the past. He believes that in this decade artists are making the progress that would have been made through a whole century if the machine had not been senselessly utilized to imitate handicraft prototypes. In developing a special type of design suited to new materials and the machine processes, designers are obeying a law valid in the Stone Age and among the Greeks and under the Louis's: that craftsmen produce what is natural to the tool. Modern is not a breaking from tradition, nor is it a fad. It is this age's true answer to controlling conditions.

Russel Wright believes also in the value of traditional influences. He calls industrial design an American social art. " American design," he says, " should spring from native sources. Deflections such as *compromise classic* or *classic-modern* only tend to disturb the true course of modern design in this country. They have a decadent sophistication that is unpalatable to the average consumer." He sees the essence of true functionalism in American colonial furniture. We are to express something of the same character, but in terms of our own times. The mark of the machine tool has supplanted that of the handicraft tool and the manual processes, but the unchanging values of honest construction and good proportions remain.

Wright is equally well known for his furniture lines and for his metalwares. As in the cases of Geddes and Dreyfuss, his early experience of the arts was in connection with the theater. From brilliant and promiseful work in theater-design laboratories and theater production, he merged gradually, by way of manufacturing stage properties in a studio laboratory of his own, into making custom furniture and decorative metal accessories. Because of the success and reputation of designs for which he was his own manufacturer, in national markets, he began to be called on to design for industry. His " American Modern " furniture is extensively marketed throughout the country. He has originated scores of service accessories, particularly of spun aluminum. He believes that much of the characteristic decorative effect of modern rooms arises from the gleam of simple informal service pieces, such as chafing dishes, trays, decanters, and cocktail shakers — where a decade ago it would have been a matter of vases and shells and statuettes.

Robert Heller, of New York, was for a time particularly concerned with interior architecture. In that period he designed outstanding apartments for several people prominent in New York theater circles; and he is responsible for the broadcasting rooms of two radio stations — typical modern problems — and for salesrooms. His later design work ranges through a wide field of electrical accessories, toasters and percolators, electric fans and air-conditioning equipment, and includes pianos and bicycles.

It is primarily the architectural conception of the whole that distinguishes the products of the men and women who are working today as interior designers. The essential principles of their design work are identical with those of the architect. Unity and structural integrity are basic. The use of new industrial materials, or the new use of old, familiar materials, enters as an important determining factor in every undertaking. In interior architecture there is, of course, a special significance in qualities of surface capitalized in terms of texture and color. The final, the most distinctively machine-age element, is electric light, used as the harmonizing and unifying element, now a marvelous flexible instrument in the hands of the designer. These are the emphasized Modern means: distinctive totality of impression, truth to structure and materials, creative manipulation of texture and color, functional and esthetic lighting.

In 1900 no housewife could have been led to believe that the kitchen of 1936 would be the gleaming, clinically clean, light, and attractive place it is in today's progressive homes. The small windows, the smoky walls, the varnished wooden icebox, the musty pantry shelves, the long distances from stove to work table to sink, the involved and dust-catching pipes and boiler and chandeliers: what hint did they hold of the compact, bright, efficient machine kitchen of today? Here, of course, because the room design actually began with a group of mechanisms, the sense of industrial design first came into home architecture. Here still some of the most typical interior ensembles, and the most attractive, are to be found. To say that the kitchen in Contempora House or the Mandel house is a delight to the eye, is to express appreciation of a quality that grows characteristically out of machine-age inventiveness and the new feeling for abstract design.

The bathroom, too, is functionally honest, immaculately clean, joyously bright. It has claimed the attention of leading architectural and industrial designers. It is here that the inventor-artists have made their first large gains in marketing prefabricated units, comprising the whole room or a single major plumbing unit and its adjacent wall. It might be noted that in thus perfecting and standardizing the bathroom and the kitchen — not to say establishing their esthetic — the Moderns have glorified first those parts of the home that used to be considered mere utility adjuncts not of any importance in the artistic architect's work. The basement, and particularly the furnace room (soon to be generally known as the weather room), is next in line for revolutionary development. Already many waste spaces, formerly untidy, damp, and forbidding, have been salvaged for recreational use by reason of improved heating and air-conditioning mechanisms. Even heat pipes and air ducts have been used by a few designers as a new sort of abstract composition in the basement recreation room, yielding a pleasure akin to the esthetic.

The same spirit that is inspiring the modern appearance of home furnace rooms and baths is also active as a transforming influence in the executive offices of great corporations: redesigning the visible mechanical elements, expressing functional purpose, reorganizing and emphasizing for visual unity and harmony. In their way some of the well-known directors' rooms and presidential suites are as bright and fresh and livable as modern home interiors. The oil paintings of past presidents, impressively gilt-framed, the oak paneling, and the marbled columns have disappeared along with the narrow windows, velvet curtains, and mahogany book cases. Today all is clean, light, colorful — but still rich.

The richness here, of course, is occasionally aided by introduction of individual pieces from the handicraft studios. A hanging, a rug, a vase may be used to set off or enhance the composition; or a weaver of patterned textiles may contribute an arresting spot of color. The extreme Functionalists deprecate such revivals of the arts and crafts. But having established that the unity comes out of truth to mechanism and to use, that the sheerness and cleanliness and horizontality are capable of dramatization with their own sort of distinction, the designer often is ready to admit that there are desirable values that are not yet to be found in the range of machine-made materials and commodities.

REFERENCES

(1) CARRINGTON, N. *Design and a Changing Civilization.* (Lane: London, 1935) 140 pp.

(2) CHENEY, SHELDON, AND CHENEY, MARTHA. *Art and the Machine.* (Whittlesey House, McGraw-Hill Book Co.: New York, 1936) 307 pp.

(3) FRANKL, P. T. *Machine-Made Leisure.* (Harper and Brothers: New York, 1932) 192 pp.

(4) GEDDES, N. B. *Horizons.* (Little, Brown, and Co.: Boston, 1932) 293 pp.

(5) GLOAG, J. *Design in Modern Life.* (Allen and Unwin: London, 1934) 138 pp.

(6) HOLME, C. G. *Industrial Design and the Future.* (The Studio, Ltd.: London, 1934) 160 pp.

(7) KAHN, E. J. *Design in Art and Industry.* (Charles Scribner's Sons: New York, 1935) 204 pp.

(8) KIESLER, F. J. *Contemporary Art Applied to the Store and Its Display.* (L. Scall: New York, 1938)

(9) MOHOLY-NAGY, L. *The New Vision.* (Harcourt, Brace and Co.: New York, 1932) 191 pp.

(10) MUMFORD, L. *Technics and Civilization.* (Harcourt, Brace and Co.: New York, 1934) 495 pp.

(11) MUSEUM OF MODERN ART. *Machine Art.* (Museum of Modern Art: New York, 1934) 109 pp.

(12) PEVSNER, N. *An Enquiry into Industrial Art in England.* (The Macmillan Co.: New York, 1937) 234 pp.

(13) READ, H. E. *Art and Industry.* (Harcourt, Brace and Co.: New York, 1935) 143 pp.

(14) TEAGUE, W. D. *Design This Day.* (Harcourt, Brace and Co.: New York, 1940) 291 pp.

CHAPTER IX

CLOTHING AND PERSONAL ADORNMENT

Grace W. Ripley
Rhode Island School of Design
Providence, R. I.
and
Milton S. Fox
Instructor, The Cleveland Museum of Art
Instructor, The Cleveland School of Art
Cleveland, Ohio

I

ART IN DRESS

Grace W. Ripley

When style in dress reaches perfection, the costume is perfectly suited to the physique and to the personality of the wearer. The reason for the perennial admiration of Greek dress lies in the presentation of beautiful figures that are enhanced by very simple treatment of drapery. Every part has style, and, therefore, we have the very essence of style in the whole.

Since we recovered from the artificial Gay Nineties, the women of America have developed true style in sports attire. This development is truly American. Helen Wills on the tennis court is spoken of as being costumed as were the Greeks. We merely mean that the relation between her perfectly coördinated body and her dress is as functionally perfect as were the costumes of the Greek athletes. If we examine the case, we will find that the sports attire today is more functionally perfect than were the costumes of the Greeks.

We have only to search through history to see that the basic idea of dress as drapery to enhance the lines of the figure never disappears. This is the opposite of the tailored concept, which was really born in Persia, where the sleeve, the fitted coat with flaring skirt, and the well-fitted collar originated.

The emancipation of women at the beginning of the twentieth century changed the concept of woman's dress. In 1900 one could hardly breathe for the dust raised by women's long skirts. The body was imprisoned, symbolizing the restrictions imposed on women.

The body itself is our first concern, and it is the body free and beautiful in play that we should study. America's contribution to active-sports attire has evolved slowly, becoming more nearly perfect in cut, in fabric, and in color. The dress functions in harmony with the lithe body. In teaching costume design in the school, simple, functional dress should be studied first; that is, the active-sports dress.

The problem of dress, however, is not that of clothing only the body beautiful; it is also the problem of clothing every type of person in such a way as to provide both protection and expression of personality. In all art endeavor we start with ideal concepts and proceed to the difficult problems resulting from imperfect and difficult conditions. Most style shows deal only with the ideal conditions, but a recent exhibition showed models weighing from 115 pounds to 300 pounds. All heights from 5 feet to 6 feet were represented; also all faults of posture. It was shown what might be done in each case.

The problem today is very different from the problem of forty or even twenty years ago, for the little dressmaker has almost disappeared. It may prove to be more expensive to make a dress in the home than to buy one. Who in the home can produce a trim tailored suit for $10.95 or a neat apron for 35¢? At the opening of the twentieth century, class distinction indicated by dress largely disappeared. The spread of democratic ideas, inventions like the automobile, and mass production in dress have brought both men and women into close similarity. There are more women wage-earners, more clothes can be had, and, owing to quantity production, at relatively less money. The people of modest means wear copies of the custom-made garments of the well-to-do. Through radio, motion pictures, magazines, and now even television, ideas and ideals in dress have become universal, tending to level all classes and unify humanity.

The style, fit, and finish of even the cheapest grades of clothing have come to be a technical triumph. Costly and elaborate machinery and processes enable garments to be turned out that are superior in style to the dresses of dressmakers of the pre-mass-production era and the cost is about one-half. This unquestionably makes it possible for most people to have twice as many clothes as was formerly possible.

American manufacturers set a standard of excellence in the making of apparel of both men and women for all the world to follow. America removed the reproach that was attached to the ready-made. In the

United States above all countries, a man or a woman of almost any size or proportions can walk into a shop and obtain garments of good style, fabric, and fit.

It is important that Americans learn to be intelligent consumers, and also that they are taught the esthetic and the economic values of garments.

First, the body must be studied and understood, as in an art school. Second, the textile must be studied and understood. Neither is easy to understand. We all know and appreciate the great difficulties lying before the student; but we must remember that the great artists in costume have arrived at their understanding, not only through study of anatomy, but also by training their senses to observe, appreciate, and evaluate.

The study of textiles is no longer the simple matter that it was in our grandmother's day. Then everyone knew pure wool, or rather, "virgin" wool. They knew their cottons and their linens, and they knew that their silks were one hundred percent natural silk. Now no one but a trained person can evaluate the tremendous number of synthetic fibers on the market. Man-made products are vying with nature-made; for example, man has actually made a fiber four times finer than that which the silk worm makes.

Costume illustrating is not usually original costume design. Costume designing is best done in the actual material in relation to the living model.

The highly paid designers in America today are those making the original costumes in material that are the models to be used in mass production. These men are artists as well as craftsmen. We have been told of a young woman whose salary is $10,000 more than that of the President of the United States. She designs dresses that sell for about $10.98. She earns her salary because she serves so many women. Salaries of dress designers up to $10,000 a year are plentiful in this remarkable age, but the costume illustrator seldom, if ever, reaches the $10,000 class.

Men design women's dresses, but aside from Elizabeth Hawes, women do not design men's clothes. Women design necktie fabrics; women and men design gloves. Men design shoes; only three women shoe-designers are famous today. The informal sports shoe and the bathing shoe are often designed by women.

Dress accessories and jewelry are designed by both men and women. The American boy with creative capacity should be encouraged to read about the men who have succeeded in the realm of costume. It is only in the last hundred years that men have abandoned colorful styles in dress. Now there is a tendency away from the somber.

The *New Yorker* has recently published an account of the work of Raymond G. Twyefort, a New York custom tailor, who is teaching his distinguished clientele to dress in color. His theories in color are sound and are being accepted by men sufficiently strong to dare to be individual. Such an article would be good reading for boys being taught to attack the problem of color and design in costume.

Many of our greatest American designers have received their earlier training in the theater, and have emerged with versatile imaginations. Theater arts give invaluable training in color, line, and form design. Here again men and women work together.

The father of modern theatrical costume design is Leon Bakst, the great designer for the Russian Ballet. He was the first designer to make lively interpretations of Persian, Greek, Turkish, Egyptian, Medieval, and fantastic costumes, purely imaginative. Fortunately, his wonderful costume designs have been reproduced and are available for study. All museum libraries and major city libraries have portfolios of Leon Bakst. The simple and direct technique employed by him should be studied.[1]

The costumes of two American designers, Norman Bel Geddes and Robert Edmond Jones, are simply rendered and imaginative. It is difficult to get examples of their work except in large libraries. The work of these two American artists should be studied by talented young artists. Doing research in costume for period plays is invaluable experience. Authentic material can always be found in the *National Geographic Magazine*. Back copies of this magazine can be bought for a small sum and so a library of peasant and folk costume can be built up at small expense.

Bulletins issued by the Metropolitan Museum of Art (New York City), the Museum of Fine Arts (Boston), the Museum of the Chicago Art Institute, the Museum of the Rhode Island School of Design, and the Natural History Museum of New York supply valuable reference material. Postal cards showing costume and design of great periods can also be had from all great museums. Usually great portraits show authentic reproductions of costume. To prepare for a career in cos-

---

[1] It is possible to obtain examples both good and bad of cinema costumes, designed by American and European designers of note — from Photo Play Studios — published by Educational and Recreational Guides, Inc., 138 Washington Street, Newark, New Jersey.

tume design it is important to build up a background of knowledge and at the same time to develop creative capacity. At all times the teacher of costume should remember that the searching out of original ideas, lines, and color combinations is especially important. Nature herself is one of the greatest teachers.

In costuming a play the best result will be obtained if period research is a separate exercise, and creating designs a separate exercise. Color comes first in making a stage layout. Great designers often use colored papers and cloth and juggle them about on a neutral background seeking for fine combinations and arrangements. Norman Bel Geddes always has a rag bag of color samples and it is through experimentation that he finds the combinations he wants. Children with adequate material will not infrequently excel adults in color and design.

The young girl who designs for herself only may not be aware of it, but she is missing an opportunity of studying personalities and their preferences, and of acquiring the greatly desired technique necessary to a broad understanding of the designer's real problem, which always concerns the satisfactory relation between the consumer, the material, the design, and the maker. Thus in school, pupils can be induced to design for each other, and so gain a more professional point of view. The pupil who designs for many different types is gaining a real and many-sided education. Theory and practice can go hand in hand in the teaching of costume-designing. The French, who are the greatest technicians in the field of costume, always design with fabrics draped on a carefully chosen mannequin. The choice of fabric is the first problem to be considered.

Through the generosity of the great American textile houses it becomes possible to get samples of many appropriate materials. Advanced designs and colors can thus be obtained. One usually starts in costume designing with cotton material. A few dress lengths should be available, so that the pupils may acquire the important knowledge of how a given material will drape, fold, and hang.

The rewards awaiting the individual who, as a professional, will use science and education in meeting the wants of men and women in the field of clothing are large, and the opportunities are many. It takes courage, understanding of human beings, the ability to live in and value the present, and to work for the future. America is about to grow up; her industries will undergo many changes, and will be refined, and more esthetic, more differentiated. There is much room at the top for designers and stylists.

II

CLOTHING AND PERSONAL ADORNMENT AS EXPRESSIONS OF AMERICAN LIFE

Milton S. Fox

One of the surest indexes to the character of a period or a people is its dress and appearance. The other arts, such as painting, literature, and music, are apt to be more formal and self-conscious, more often regulated in such a way as to rule out the direct expression of much of social importance. They have, so to speak, an eye on posterity. But dress, as a form of expression, may be likened to conversation: it is more immediately revealing because it is more direct and spontaneous. From the one, as from the other, we can have direct insight into the aspirations, the morals, the economic status, the beliefs and superstitions, the psychology of the subject.

The American tradition in general, with its strong formative influences of the Puritans, the Quakers, and others, has tended to discourage ostentation in dress, particularly and persistently in man's clothing. To this must be added the fact that our men's costume has largely been derived from an England of generally conservative taste. The measure of our growing independence from English behavior is seen in the creation of new types of garment more characteristic of native customs and activities. Furthermore, it would seem natural that people living in a democracy would exhibit fewer differences in appearance than are found in an aristocratic society.

The result is a certain uniformity in our ordinary street wear that is in contradistinction to the diversity of racial stocks that form our population. These various groups have entirely given up their native costumes (except in celebration of national functions) and have striven to lose at least the outward mark of their alien identities by adopting innocuous standard fashions. This standardized appearance — in men, still largely patterned on the ideal of the English gentleman; in women, according to the mandates of Parisian designers — is but one aspect of our national dress. For there is probably no country in the world as variously dressed for different occasions as our own is. In sports wear, for men and women both, we lead the world in variety and originality of conception. Some of our most brilliant and functional apparel is found in this field; and nearly every wardrobe, except those of the lowest income groups, will contain a number of these items. Each is designed for a rather specialized use, and broadly speaking, they are among the most notable achievements of our designers.

In passing, it might be remarked that most of these outfits are so comfortable, while at the same time so flattering to the appearance, that people get into them as soon as the restrictions of convention will permit. It seems unavoidable that sports wear will sooner or later cause a radically new attitude towards men's clothes. The enhancement of color will be the most obvious of these changes, but the long-suffering male will one day not be forced to wear undergarments, shirt (his thighs well swathed in feet of shirt tail), belt, tight collar, tie, coat, and trousers on sweltering days. Because of their popularity, slack suits, tee shirts, shorts, and the like must strike any but Victorians as closer to the ideal of summer wear, not only in the country or at play, but also in business and street wear. Certainly some such development may be expected when the most stubborn stronghold of propriety gives way before new tastes. I refer to the acceptance of color in evening clothes for men — midnight blue and deep wine red — a flower on the lapel of the dinner jacket (which may now be also double-breasted), a colored bow tie; and for summer evening wear, the admissibility of white jackets with black trousers. Another stronghold that would seem to be the last to fall has been attacked — academic robes may be had in white or blue.

The youthfulness and casualness of our nation are attested in such developments. We are gradually breaking away from subservience to hallowed tradition and European prescription. The restrictions of our own immediate past are rapidly being discarded. It was not long ago that any tampering with nature was considered indecent. The wrath of the Lord was to be visited on women who shaved their legs or used depilatories, or who removed moles. It was the mark of a frivolous woman to emphasize or call attention to her natural physical endowments, even if this were only through the use of a little innocent make-up. But this prudish and unhealthy attitude is happily dead; the other extreme of unrestrained transformation, altogether ignoring natural appearance, is common. Women make use of foundation garments in order to discipline their contours, the uplift brassiere is frankly advertised and purchased (even built into bathing suits!). The cosmetic industry is one of tremendous proportions (one can even buy make-up for children and patronize beauty parlors catering to juveniles). Beauty parlors will bestow a perfect artificial sun-tan in short order, will alter and transform the face, the style and color of the hair.[1] Fingernails and toenails may be treated with many different types of polish. Reducing has been carried to the point where the alteration of the actual contours of the body is an art in itself — for example, one may now reduce only at selected points through classes in limbering, diet, massage, and other more mechanical treatment. Orthodontia is an important form of beauty aid, and plastic surgery has become a commonplace. Through ' posture study ' the whole bearing of the figure can be controlled.

The modern woman, in most of these activities, is merely repeating what her sisters have done at other times in highly sophisticated civilizations, whether they were Egyptian, Chinese, Renaissance, or any other. At such times a degree of emancipation stimulates the exploitation of their natural gifts and makes manifest the changing ideals of femininity. This is especially true of our own time, when women are exceptionally free (symbolized, perhaps, in their usurpation of trousers). They reflect the times not only in their ubiquity in sports, business, politics, and the professions, but, typically, also in the almost callous disregard of nature's mandates. What was once regarded as irrevocably fixed by nature is now transmuted, toyed with, in high disdain of the categories. Similarly, women have never so imposed their will on their natural appearance. Fashions in facial make-up will give us, at one time, ravishingly buxom apple-cheeked maidens, at another time boyish faces and flat-chested, narrow-hipped ladies, and now faces chiseled according to the sculptural severity of primitive African statues. Eyebrows are placed according to design, the lips and eyes strongly emphasized, and the appearance of the whole shape of the head altered to taste, through make-up and extreme care for coiffure.

A good deal of this can undoubtedly be accounted for by the highly organized and publicized businesses involved; nevertheless the fact remains that they would have no success if they did not satisfy a demand. Occasionally the beauty business will overreach itself; most women will not go beyond a certain point in impracticability. The late attempt to popularize the upswept type of coiffure was a failure because it was too costly to maintain, too fragile, and because it was not suited to the everyday activities of any but idlers — not to business, shopping, sports, or social interests. The tendency to the ' long bob ' has been the bane of the hairdressers' business; it is well suited to the life of the

---

[1] A new trick is ' color personalysis,' which " establishes your color affinities! "

active woman of today, but it has forced hairdressers to try all sorts of
dodges to sustain business.

It is worth noting in this connection that although men's hairdress
seems to change slowly, it nevertheless varies according to the times.
Beards are now the prerogative of the remaining Civil War veterans,
some professional men, particularly the physician, and a few former
Bohemian expatriates left over from the '20's. Mustaches, once a luxu-
riant mark of rugged power, are now a mere whiff of ornament, or they
have disappeared altogether. We have left behind the flowing mane,
the slick center part, the short-cropped tonsure of the early post-war
years, and the pompadour. The Jazz Age produced the patent leather
manner of the sheik, as popularized by Valentino. Today a rather un-
presumptuous side part, with the hair worn moderately long, is almost
universal. But contemporary men are not immune to the more delicate
graces, as may be gathered from a somewhat clandestine patronage of
beauty parlors, and the appearance of *parfums pour l'homme.*

Taken all in all, it may be gathered that one important form of
popular artistic expression today deals with the materials of the actual
human body, and more frequently than not the models for these creations are the current motion-picture stars.[1] The ideals of human beauty
are constantly changing, and the human face and figure are literally
not what they were at other times, as may be seen in a study of paintings and sculpture of the past. The ideals of femininity and of mascu-

---

[1] In a chapter as short as this, many important phases of the subject cannot
be touched upon. One of these is the relation between personal adornment and
sex. The monotony that American industry and business impose on the lives of
millions of urban dwellers tends to enforce rather extravagant forms of release
for emotions and feelings that demand some sort of satisfaction, even if only
symbolical. The great freedom of women, plus the revolt against the inhibitions
of the nineteenth century, and the standardization of contemporary life, all contribute to this situation. The cinema and advertising capitalize on it. 'Glamor'
and 'allure' have become almost necessary commodities, as is well seen in our
habits of dress, even for ordinary wear; one of the major deliberate objectives
of our dress is to create sexually stimulating and desirable objects. The extreme
emphasis on the mouth, for example, and the elaborate treatment of the eyes may
be cited. The breasts are strongly emphasized; the hip region is emphasized by
the use of high-heeled shoes, which throw this part of the body out, and exaggerate its movements. Women have found this posture so to their taste that even
in sport shoes (called " wedgies ") this effect may be had. Backless evening gowns,
strapless gowns, brassiere bathing suits, sun suits, silk stockings, and many others
show a great mastery of the art of suggestive concealment and controlled revelation. Merchants of make-up and dress offer to make the ugly duckling as 'kiss-
able' as the debutante.

linity have changed, and nowhere are these better expressed than in clothes and appearance; nowhere are society and the relation of the individual to society more clearly brought out. (Note, for example, the prominence of military costumes in totalitarian states.)

No article of apparel escapes these changes, from underwear to top hats. Even military costume is altered to suit new needs and new strategies. The diversity of occupational garb is itself an involved study in American costume. Gas-station attendants, delivery men, clerks, factory workers, motorcyclists, and many others have costumes suited to their needs, and made from fabrics devised for these purposes. Regional occupations produce their distinctively suitable coverings, as do peculiarities of season, climate, and to some extent, local legend. The unique dress of college youths staggers the imagination. The influence of the more specialized types of dress mentioned here on garments for ordinary use is seen most clearly in children's clothing. Boys, uninhibited by the proprieties, will wear a 'streamlined' aviator's helmet to cover ears and cheeks in a howling wind, instead of a silly fedora hat perched on the crown of the head. The snow-suit — patterned on the ski costume — keeps the wind away from one's bones. There are many such sensible usages that will sooner or later be adapted to everyday costume.

New materials will contribute to this evolution. Already plastics have become important in the accessories field and in footwear. Zippers allow new freedom of design. Latex and other rubber derivatives allow further adventures in corseting the figure and in the hang of garments (a rather startling use is the latex and satin bathing suit). Cellophane is used in raincoats. From time to time we hear of experiments with paper clothing. Of more immediate interest is the further development of fabrics, as for example, lighter and more porous materials for summer wear and for occasional use.

The diversification of our dress demands all of these explorations. New occupations often demand specially created wear, and this in turn, newly created materials, or new uses for old. In short, the high degree of specialization in American life is shown in the specialization of working clothing. Equally, the specialization of clothing for everyday and leisure wear indicates that perhaps we are beginning to understand the art of enjoying free moments: we have seen the creation of lounging pajamas and hostess gowns, gayer and more comfortable off-time garments for men. One may suspect, however, that in this not altogether perfect democracy, some usages are devised for the express purpose of satisfying an urge for distinction from the mass. In this category would certainly fall some of the fabulous costumes worn by secret societies — one answer to the universal, even though suppressed, desire for bright plumage. We may note this too in the giddy costumes so often assigned to ushers, elevator girls, waitresses, and so on.

Diversification and the pursuit of novelty encourages eclecticism. Upswept hair is frequently patterned on Baroque exuberance; patterns for fabrics are borrowed from the Balinese, peasant materials, the Aztecs. Cowls lately were modeled on Mughal Indian dress; the various decades of the nineteenth century have supplied themes for variation, as have other times and places. Despite this variety and diversity, and despite the local influences, there is a general uniformity in our dress from one end of the country to the other. Mass distribution and nation-wide advertising campaigns have been instrumental.[1] Ease of travel and communication, and a similarity of behavior and activities have tended to break down regional differences. The New Yorker and the Peorian wear the new creations of Hart, Schaffner, and Marx; the Floridan and the Oregonian, the new creations of our alert couture. There are few real differences in the dress and make-up of the city dweller and the farm lass; and these are restricted to our most cosmopolitan centers, because our ideas of hygiene, of functionalism, of suitability are fairly universal in the land, and our national psychology is growing more homogeneous.

III

MASS PRODUCTION AND MERCHANDISING IN WEARING APPAREL

MILTON S. FOX

As befits a highly industrialized democracy, one of the most notable facts about American clothing and accessories, for men, women, and children, is mass production and mass sales. From these flow many consequences, embracing design, profits, relations with contributing industries, taste, and labor conditions. Generally speaking, the designers

---

[1] See the next portion of this chapter.

and makers of Paris, and the originators of fashions for men in London have been specialists for the luxury trade; competent designers gave scant attention to the needs of the great mass of the people. The *salons* of Paris exposed to the world, with great éclat, the newest whimsies of their ' class ' designers, and the rest of the world humbly and gratefully accepted the new sartorial gospel for the season. Buyers rushed back with originals; a limited number of copies or duplicates were made in expensive fabrics for carefully controlled distribution at selected centers.

Presently these in turn would be adapted for production on a mass scale; and women in every town in the land could have something resembling the elegant pictures they saw in the magazines not long before. Certain changes may have been necessary due to the exigencies of quantity machine production. For large-scale merchandising each design must be adaptable to a full range of sizes, from 12 to 20 and up, to longs and stouts, and to an equally wide range of purses. Obviously, then, changes will be made in the basic pattern so that a minimum of skilled work is necessary, and a minimum of cutting operations. Sometimes a slight change in the design of some part — a neckline, a seam — will result in less waste per bolt of cloth, or less costly finishing procedures. These changes will forthwith be made in order to reach even the lowest income groups.

The production of clothes in great quantities for distribution in hundreds of stores tends to standardize design. But even though stylists will insist that certain fashions are suited only to certain types, the pressures of clever advertising and publicity, plus the effects of the motion pictures, lead to what is almost a neurotic emotional necessity. These agencies contrive to make women — and men, to a certain extent — feel that the proffered object is essential to their happiness. It is on this basis of a wide general demand, thoroughly exploited, that our clothing industry is founded and our popular taste nourished. Nevertheless, the level of clothing design for both men and women has been raised substantially with the result that, through our mass production and marketing facilities, we are probably the best dressed nation in the world.

It may be true that our dress is somewhat lacking in character (as this is achieved through slow evolution) ; that we tend mainly to ' smartness '; but it is also true that good designs are easily available at modest sums for those who know how to choose them. A great variety of accessories of all sorts, for both sexes, allows adequately for personal variation. It is also true that most people can afford more clothes than formerly, as machine production brings prices down.

The mass nature of our apparel industries (as distinguished from those abroad) demands quick turnover for the manufacturer; this in turn leads to the necessity for rapid changes and diversified garments for special uses. With this must go tremendous publicity to make the populace 'style conscious,' to break down habit and routine selection. It means that there will be pressure on our designers to produce variations on an item that is selling well, and when signs of surfeit appear, to produce a radically new creation. Thus, after many variations on the short skirt idea have been run, the designers 'stun' the market with long skirts; at one moment the waist will be low, at another, high; men's hats will have narrow brims until the market is fairly well supplied, and then a wide-brim hat will make its appearance; double-breasted coats will be the 'latest thing' this season, and single-breasted the next.

But in spite of the best intentions of the industry to regulate and control the demand, often a popular whim will assert itself, sometimes at great cost to some branch of the industry. For example, most men will not be persuaded to wear caps. At one time these were very popular; cap-manufacturers have made several 'high-powered' attempts to revive their popularity, but always unsuccessfully. Hat-manufacturers have been distressed by the preference of men to go bare-headed (although there was a notable revival of soft straws during the past summer). The manufacturers of garters, starched collars, and heavy sweaters have all suffered from idiosyncrasies regarding their product. Women too often — according to manufacturers — go stockingless and gloveless; too often they supplant hats with bandannas or some variety of cheap turban. Exactly what causes shifts in mass taste is often hard to determine. The motion pictures are of enormous importance in influencing our clothing tastes and habits. Sometimes altogether unlooked-for consequences arise from the most harmless incidents; and when they affect the country at large, they may be almost disastrous. For example, Margaret Farrand Thorp (16, p. 117) says,

> The story is told so often that it must be true that the fashion of going without undershirts began when Clark Gable undressed in the tourist camp in "It Happened One Night." The sale of masculine underwear declined so sharply immediately afterwards that knitwear manufacturers sent delegations to the producers asking them to take out the scene.

Mrs. Thorp points out:

No fashion magazine, however skilfully edited, can compete with the movies when it comes to making it seem imperative to own a particular hat or frock or necklace (p. 108) . . . The movies have little else to compete with as the dictators of fashion. (p. 110)

Recognizing this fact, there is a tendency for manufacturers and motion-picture producers to get together, so that the newer fashions may be presented in a subtle way, and a demand built up. Indeed, the Modern Merchandising Bureau, Inc., to quote Mrs. Thorp once again,

works in coöperation with the designers in all the big studios, who have no objection at all to creating for the screen with one eye upon the average American woman. (p. 109)

Following the release of a new picture, the average woman, if she should decide that a gown like that worn by one of the leading characters would do nicely for herself, will find her desire anticipated.

The apparel industries, as a matter of fact, are beginning to work in much closer coöperation with all the related industries. They now plan and consult with the makers of fabrics and the creators of new materials, with furriers and leaders in the leather industry, with the makers of accessories. Color experts and stylists are called in to advise and contribute to the general harmony in the new ensembles. No longer will the textile industries suffer such severe setbacks as that they suffered some years ago when women decided to give up superabundant clothes in favor of fashions using much less material. Since the fall of France, there is every likelihood that some sort of central clearing house for new ideas, to set the trends, will be created in this country. The designers and manufacturers, if they coöperate intelligently and make use of the vast productive facilities and talent available, may well, during this period of France's distress, take from her the fashion leadership of the world — or, at the very least, usurp a great part of her American market.

A consequence of the last war, for example, was a great boost to the American textile industries. Speaking of those who willy-nilly put European fabrics ahead of American, Pola Stout says,[1]

These people who do not know, who have not looked at American fabrics for years, and who take for granted whatever is said against them, have

---

[1] " Aura of Paris dims our style strides," by Kathleen McLaughlin, *New York Times,* August 11, 1940.

a tremendous surprise in store. It will stagger them to see how honest, how beautiful, how long-wearing and sturdy these fabrics are, how softly they drape and how easily they tailor.

Why should America, which has done such a marvelous job in cotton, for one fabric, not take the credit that is due? Nowhere on earth can you find such designing, such styling, such wearable, smart cotton clothes, cut to fit and planned to serve consumers well. Why not look at our shoes — the best designed shoes in the world, the most serviceable? Our silk stockings — where can you find such products as these, at a price for every person, whether they have much money or little?

Similarly, the complaints about our dyestuffs grow less justifiable; great improvements have been made in American dyes. The World War enforced invention, and offered opportunities (largely through patent confiscation) to learn the secrets of European formulas. Today our dyes are generally fadeproof, sunproof, and washproof. An enormous variety of beautiful hues, tints, and shades is available, some of extreme delicacy, some bold and harsh. These dyes have been adapted especially to different kinds of materials, for the chemistry of dyes in relation to stuffs is now an important field of investigation.

We have, of course, a class, or custom-made, couture, but this is not the distinctive characteristic (even though there are now many who claim that our designers are the equal of the Parisian). The machine-made, mass-produced garment — competently styled, durable, not too expensive, and easily available — is our great contribution. Naturally, in this category there is almost no handwork, although in some instances, notably for moderately priced lingerie, machines have been invented that imitate handwork. However, the cheapness and accessibility of good designs tend to discourage hand production, especially in articles of commonplace wear. Students of society may find this regrettable, but on the other hand most persons may have a larger and more varied wardrobe. Men's clothing has long since become so standardized as to make hand production in the home virtually non-existent. Mass production has made great changes in children's clothing, which until quite recently was in large part home-produced. With this development has also come the introduction of many innovations that will keep the factories running — novelties of all sorts based on current heroes and activities (even candies follow the headlines).

Within the apparel industries themselves is to be found the most thoroughgoing organization of American labor. The garment unions are extremely strong and influential, a protective situation that has its

rise in the fact that now the importance of the individual worker is at
a minimum in the making of clothes.[1] His services can easily be replaced; he does only one small task, but one of the total number of
tasks involved in the making of a coat, for instance. What was once an
important form of self-expression for a great many people is now largely
a matter of tending machines. Self-expression is left for the designers
and stylists; and for the public, is limited to selecting and organizing
an ensemble.

REFERENCES

(1) BYERS, MARGARETTA, and KAMHOLZ, CONSUELO. *Designing Women.* (Simon
& Schuster: New York, 1938)

(2) *Decorative Art of Leon Bakst.* (Fine Arts Society: London)

(3) DOOLEY, WILLIAM H. *The Economics of Clothing and Textiles.* (D. C.
Heath and Co.: Boston, 1934)

(4) ELLIS, HAVELOCK. *The Evolution of Modesty.* (Vol. I. in his *Studies in the
Psychology of Sex.*) (Random House: New York, 1936)

(5) ELLIS, HAVELOCK. *Man and Woman.* (Houghton Mifflin Co.: Boston, 1929)

(6) FISCHEL, OSKAR, and VON BOEHN, MAX. *Modes and Manners of the Nineteenth Century.* (E. P. Dutton and Co.: New York, 1927)

(7) GOLDSTEIN, HARRIET, and GOLDSTEIN, VETTA. *Art in Everyday Life.* (The
Macmillan Co.: New York, 1932)

(8) HAWES, ELIZABETH. *Fashion Is Spinach.* (Random House: New York,
1938)

(9) HOTCHKISS, G. B. *An Outline of Advertising.* (The Macmillan Co.: New
York, 1940)

(10) HURLOCK, ELIZABETH BERGNER. *The Psychology of Dress.* (Ronald Press:
New York, 1929)

(11) LEVEN, MAURICE, and OTHERS. *America's Capacity to Consume.* (Brook-
ings Institution: Washington, D. C., 1936)

(12) NATIONAL ASSOCIATION OF BETTER BUSINESS BUREAUS, INC. *Facts about
Jewelry, Facts about Furs, Facts about Cosmetics.*

(13) NOURSE, EDWIN G., and OTHERS. *America's Capacity to Produce.* (Brook-
ings Institution: Washington, D. C., 1936)

(14) NYSTROM, PAUL. *The Economics of Fashion.* (Ronald Press: New York,
1928)

(15) *Official American Textile Directory.* (McGraw-Hill Book Co.: New York,
1937)

(16) THORP, MARGARET FARRAND. *America at the Movies.* (Yale University
Press: New Haven, 1939)

(17) TRACEY, M. E. *Our Country, Our People, and Theirs.* (The Macmillan
Co.: New York, 1938)

(18) TUGWELL, REXFORD GUY; MUNRO, THOMAS; and STRYKER, ROY E. *American
Economic Life.* (Harcourt, Brace and Co.: New York, third edition, 1930)

---

[1] For a good discussion of these matters, see *American Economic Life* (18).

CHAPTER X

ART IN COMMERCE

WILLIAM LONGYEAR
Head, Department of Advertising Design
Pratt Institute
Brooklyn, New York

Art in commerce, as presented herein, will be limited to the visual aspects of advertising and its related merchandise. The allied subject of industrial design is treated more completely elsewhere. While copy (the written word) and art (the design and the illustration) are inseparable, this discussion focusses on design and illustration rather than on copy.

I. THE ART OF ADVERTISING AS A PROFESSION

Advertising as a profession, a business, and an industry has kept pace with the great economic development in America. The advertisement is a composite of art and copy, which share the responsibility of carrying the sales message.

That art in the form of illustration or decoration is an important factor in advertising has never been disputed. It is stimulating, educational, and amusing. Without art, commerce and industry, the sponsors of advertising, would lose much of their romance. That these facts are recognized is testified by the caliber of the talent engaged and the high prices paid for advertising art. Today commercial drawing and painting are factors in the success of countless industries, and the artist is accordingly recognized and featured as part of the campaign. The advertiser realizes that a high caliber of talent is an asset in the promotion of his sales message. Hence, advertising constantly demands new talent with fresh points of view; change is typical of the profession; and there is little tolerance for the designer whose work becomes stereotyped. This makes for opportunity and ready recognition.

The avenues of art in advertising are diversified. Few designers are capable of filling the requirements of the field as a whole. The average man specializes in one type of art work and is cataloged accordingly. This practice is regrettable, as it narrows the individual's

vocation accordingly. Advertising and its component part, art, are
influenced by economic trends. In a depression when there is curtailed
buying, advertising budgets suffer. A limited budget means limited
funds for art. Cheaper drawings, photographs, and other mechanical
means of evolving the pictorial sales message are resorted to.

II. The Function of Art in Advertising

' Art work,' the term professionally used in advertising, applies to
all kinds of hand-lettering, layout, decoration, and illustration. It
has been said that one picture is as effective as a thousand words, and
advertisers are well aware of this fact. Cartoons for political, war, and
other purposes prove this contention. Posters are characterized by
their dominant use of pictures to impart an idea forcefully and quickly.

The function of art in advertising is to obtain attention, to explain,
and to induce. Design also has the more esthetic function, that of arrangement, decoration, elaboration. Art work may carry the sales message alone or supplement the copy. Dull, indeed, would be our newspapers, magazines, and books without decoration and illustration.
Typography, too, begins with design. As each letter is a created design,
it is evident that art work is indispensable in publishing. *Life* and
Fortune magazines have been a great influence in stimulating America's
interest in art. Such magazines are the acknowledged force behind
the phenomenal sale of expensive art books.

In an age preceding extensive advertising the church was the great
patron of the arts. Today industry and commerce are the incentives
for much of the best art being produced. Only industry can bear the
cost of originals, their reproduction, and their widespread distribution.

Much advertising art is worthy of use for home decoration. Because
of this modern benefactor, the poor as well as the rich may enjoy fine
reproductions that once were a luxury, but today are commonplace.
Art in advertising has also had considerable influence in raising the
standards of taste in America. Witness the fashion designs and the
examples of interior decoration in our magazines. These furnish, especially to those in the rural districts, standards of art created by
leading designers. Taste as conveyed by advertising in recent years
has improved. The standards of taste among the multitudes must have
been accordingly affected. This same art work inspires many youngsters to take a lively interest in advertising art and to choose it as a
profession.

III. The Important Advertising Mediums

It is generally conceded that from the standpoint of volume, the *newspaper* is the most important medium of advertising. Most people buy and read a newspaper. All newspapers make use of art in layout, illustration, and decoration. The large metropolitan dailies average twenty pages of advertising.

Drawing for newspapers is a specialized branch of art. Illustrations apply to merchandise, household goods, figures, and clothing. Because of inferior paper and the rapidity of reproduction, the artist must have a knowledge of special mediums and techniques for newspaper work. Each large newspaper has its own art department, supplemented by free-lance artists. Because of the extent and endless demands for drawings, the newspaper field is one of the most important to the artist. Color and improved methods of reproduction are rapidly widening the opportunities of artists engaged in the newspaper field.

Direct mail refers to all advertising employing the mails for distribution. This is one of the most important fields of advertising from the standpoint of volume, influence, and art absorption. Many products and businesses depend almost entirely on direct mail as their advertising medium. This is exemplified by the so-called 'mail-order houses,' which purchase thousands of illustrations annually. These drawings are executed by staff and free-lance artists. Manufacturers of medical supplies and hospital equipment are extensive users of direct-mail merchandising and consume a large volume of art work. As their advertisements are directed to professional men, the standard of taste is high.

Materials used in direct-mail advertising range from simple leaflets to deluxe booklets. This field consumes a great volume of advertising designs, much of which is considered high grade. The manufacturer of fine automobiles needs dignified, forceful, and stimulating paintings as a setting for his product. His direct-mail pieces must carry fine lettering and typography.

The *magazine* is a great advertising medium. There are hundreds of different magazines appealing to all social classes. These range from the so-called 'comics,' of which there are over seventy different titles, to the deluxe magazines, such as *Fortune* and *Esquire*. Fifty years ago reproductions were limited to lithographs, as represented by A. B. Frost, and wood engravings, as represented by Timothy Cole. Later came the perfection of the line engraving, the half-tone, and modern photomechanical methods of reproduction. As reproductive methods improved, better talent was absorbed into the commercial fields. Today outstanding names in art may be found in magazine illustration.

The *poster,* because of its prominence and popularity, is the symbol of advertising to many. Typified by simple forceful design, the poster is the most dramatic medium of visual advertising. Posters are divided into two groups, indoor and outdoor. Each is a vast and important field. Indoor posters are typified by car cards, store posters, and travel posters. The billboard presents outdoor posters, although a variety of smalled signs are used on express trucks, busses, and in various other places. Poster designing has a strong appeal to the beginner in commercial design. Many designers are employed in this important branch of the graphic arts.

Displays range from poster cutouts in the store window to elaborate lighted and animated structures in a world's fair. They present either a sales message or actual merchandise. The greatest volume of displays is found in lithographs for general use in stores. Other types of displays are hand- and machine-fabricated in limited production. The display manufacturer is in a highly competitive field and generally submits designs on speculation. This practice is frequently shared by the freelance designer against his will and at the expense of his income. Three-dimensional displays are rapidly gaining in popularity and volume. This field offers interesting opportunity to the designer.

Because of its cost, the *electrically lighted display* is used only in centers of population, main streets, or at crossroads of traffic. Illuminated displays are created by direct or indirect use of bulbs or tubular neon lights. The neon display has several advantages over the massed bulb display. It is much more effective in daylight, when it is frequently used in shaded locations, such as store windows and interiors. Illuminated displays have great attention-compelling power, especially when isolated against the night sky, since the surrounding darkness eliminates diverting influences. While electric display is an important branch of advertising, the field for designers is now limited.

The primary purpose of the *package* is to hold and protect its contents, but hardly less important to the merchandiser is the advertising value of the *package label.* This permits the product to catch the eye, to appeal, to speak. The package should typify the product, whether it be a beauty preparation or a household appliance. Package design ranges from the exclusive use of typography to elaborate designs in fancy materials. Illustration is frequently used to show the product or the result of its use. Every canned food label on the store shelf requires the services of a designer. Each bottle or jar of cosmetics with its label represents a problem in design. Packaging in general has enjoyed a remarkable expansion and interest owing to new materials, a higher standard of living, and improved merchandising standards. The American housewife buys the product that presents an attractive, sanitary, and practical appearance. Package design, until recent years, offered limited opportunity to the designer, but today hundreds are employed in creating packages for new products or redesigning old standbys. Several of the more important professional art schools offer courses in package design. Most of these courses deal with the superficial, surface treatment of the container, whereas the first consideration should be materials. Much packaging depends entirely on effects created by a clever use of cellophane, plastics, foils, and novel accessories.

The following brief on the *motion picture* in advertising is presented by T. H. Westermann, of New York City:

In spite of their many specialized uses, motion pictures can be analyzed on the same general standard as other advertising media. Media in general belong to two divisions — 'mass media' and 'class media.' This same division can be made in the case of motion pictures.

Pictures designed for distribution through regular theaters fall into the 'mass media' classification. Although large numbers of people can be reached by theatrical distribution, there are very definite restrictions as to the type of picture which can be used. The following are the most common types:

Trailers. These consist of short episodes, from one to three minutes in length, and are spliced right on to the end of a news reel or feature. They are usually devoted to direct product selling.

Shorts. These are usually ten minutes or less in length, and must be entertaining, or the theater owners will not accept them. Obviously, high entertainment value is essential in any picture to be shown in theaters. Therefore, the advertiser must be satisfied with a minimum of promotional material for his own product or business.

All the other types of motion pictures are shown through *non-theatrical* channels. These channels include clubs of all kinds, schools, colleges, and other specialized groups, and an advertiser's own customers, jobbers, dealers, and sales force. Although most pictures are designed to do more than one job, and therefore overlap the objectives listed below, these are the main general classifications into which non-theatrical motion pictures will fall:

(1) *Institutional* films, designed to present an individual company, or an entire industry, as a progressive, forward-looking organization which forms an important part of the economic structure as a whole.

(2) *Labor relations* films, designed to present a company's story to the rank and file of employees as effectively as possible.

(3) *Product-selling* films, designed for showing either to the ultimate consumer, or to individual customers. This type of film usually includes considerable institutional material, in order to establish the company name as well as sell the products.

(4) *Sales information* films are usually released at the same time as a new product, and are designed to present essential sales points to retailers and jobbers.

(5) *Sales-training* pictures are concerned rather with a specific selling technique than with an individual product. These usually take the form of some dramatic episode, and illustrate the correct and incorrect ways of selling types of merchandise.

(6) *Demonstration* films, which are used as factual material to demonstrate the operation of large pieces of machinery to engineers or purchasing departments. Naturally, each of these divisions has many subdivisions into films for specialized uses, but they constitute the chief general groups.

That commercial art is a factor in motion-picture production and advertising is a recognized fact. It occurs, for example, in settings, costumes, lettering of titles, posters, and direct mail. The field employs hundreds of designers and features this talent as an inducement to the public. The moving picture has great influence on public taste. Some pictures illustrate good interior decoration, architecture, and style in clothes.

Aërial displays, typified by sky writing or towed banners, are classed as visual advertising. Creative design is a minor factor in aërial display. The execution of aërial advertising requires the services of an aviator rather than those of an artist.

IV. The Relation of the Designer to the Field of Advertising Design

Unusual art ability in the child generally manifests itself in the elementary school. Talent should be encouraged in a normal way rather than by forced methods. The talented child, whether he be in the elementary or the high school, should be taught that a well-rounded education is indispensable to a successful career in art. High-school graduation is most important. There is a growing percentage of college-trained students enrolled in the better art schools. A successful career in advertising design calls for a normal, healthy, well-educated student. The profession requires good judgment, good taste, and talent.

As the advertising-design profession is highly competitive, a specialized training is also necessary. The better art schools are constantly improving their courses to meet the high standards of the field. In selecting an art school, both student and parent should carefully examine catalogs and visit schools, if possible. The number and the professional standing of the faculty are valuable guides. The better schools require a three-year course for graduation. The first year is devoted to general fundamental training, followed by two years of specialized work in which practice and theory are combined. The following are typical of the special subjects studied: drawing, design, color, illustration, layout, lettering, typography, processes of reproduction, packaging, display, business procedure. The objective of the course in advertising design should be at least a minimal professional level of achievement upon graduation.

The advertising profession is universal, but it centers in the larger cities. It offers many and varied opportunities to qualified young men and women. The young designer must decide between free-lance work and a salaried position. Each offers certain advantages. The ' job ' will be found with an advertising agency, an art service, or a concern having an inside art department. Department stores and publishers are in this category. The job offers an average beginning salary of twenty dollars a week; betterment in position and salary is generally steady. Ultimately the job pays a capable designer from fifty to two hundred dollars a week. The free-lance artist is one who maintains his own studio and works on particular orders. He must develop a clientele. The most fortunate designers have one or more clients on a yearly retaining-fee basis. Such a plan precludes the ' feast or famine ' characteristic of free-lance practice. Free-lance artists do not enjoy a regular salary, but they have opportunity to make larger incomes, all other factors being equal.

Opportunities for women in the advertising field have grown. A well-trained woman is valuable as a package and merchandise designer. These specialties call for her natural point of view. Women make good letterers and illustrators of books, especially for children, but agency jobs favor men.

The advertising-design profession offers unlimited opportunity to the talented, well-educated student. Imagination, skill, perseverance, and dependability are invaluable. As advertising is decidedly an up-to-the-minute profession, it demands a modern point of view. As a profession, it rewards well those who have the ability to produce drawings that move people to action.

REFERENCES

(1) BINDER, JOSEPH. *Color in Advertising.* (Studio Publications: London, 1934) 29 pp. and 29 plates.

(2) CHARLTON, DEMETRIUS E. A. *The Art of Packaging.* (Studio Press: New York, 1938) 127 pp.

(3) CHORD, J. T. *The Window Display Manual.* (Display Publishing Co.: Cincinnati, Ohio, 1931) 240 pp.

(4) KIESLER, FREDERICK. *Contemporary Art Applied to the Store and its Display.* (Brentano's: New York, 1930) 156 pp.

(5) WEISS, E. B., KENDALL, F. C., and LARRABEE, C. B. *The Handbook of Advertising.* (McGraw-Hill Book Co.: New York, 1938) 530 pp.

CHAPTER XI

ART IN PRINTING AND PUBLISHING

WILLIAM LONGYEAR
Head, Department of Advertising Design
Pratt Institute
Brooklyn, New York

Printing and publishing include particularly the book and magazine field. Their function in commercial art has been discussed in the previous chapter. The creative, artistic aspects, rather than the material side of publishing, will be presented here. These include typography, decoration, and illustration. All type and illustration involve design. As such, they demand the imagination and skill of great designers. Type, illustration, and decoration are inseparable in producing visually interesting books and magazines.

I. TYPOGRAPHY

Gutenberg is generally given credit for having produced, at about 1450, the first practical movable type. Previously books were laboriously lettered by hand or rubbed one page at a time from engraved blocks. Each of these wood blocks carried a minimum of copy and illustration because of the laborious cutting necessary. These slow hand processes placed a high price on books, which were possessed only by the rich or by the church. Gutenberg's type process of combining separate letters into words, to be printed on a hand press, made possible the printing of three hundred pages a day. Books became common property. Paper, ink, and printing processes were developed to keep pace with the demand for more books.

In 1803 Foudrinier Brothers developed the paper-making machine. In 1814 Koenig's power press printed one thousand sheets per hour. In 1885 Mergenthaler produced the linotype machine, which enabled a man at a keyboard to set type six times faster than it could be done by hand. Today modern photomechanical processes have stepped up production to fabulous figures and improved quality into the bargain.

Type as we know it is based on what are called ' Roman ' letters. These in turn were developed from the Greek and the Phoenician alphabets. Although hundreds of type styles have been created, all those that survive have much in common with the early Roman forms. The trend is toward sans-serif styles (letters without serifs) in a variety of proportions. Type's primary purpose is to be read. It is judged on the basis of legibility. Legibility depends on simple forms carefully spaced.

II. Illustration

The reproduction of illustrations has kept pace with the development of typography. Methods of reproducing illustration were perfected through the wood engraving, the line cut, the half-tone, the lithograph, and finally through the photomechanical processes. Perfected reproduction has been an incentive to the illustrator. Until the present century mass production of excellent illustrations was impossible.

Mediums for illustration include pen and ink, pencil, prints from wood or linoleum, painting in oil or tempera. The choice of a medium depends on the project to be carried out, the artist's individual preference, the method and cost of reproduction. Styles in mediums change. The past few years have witnessed an increase in the use of the lighter mediums, water color and crayons.

Book illustration is frequently styled to take on the character of the typography and to harmonize with it. Illustrations are given a definite decorative quality and the originals are frequently engraved by hand.

Illustration for books or magazines begins with the covers, the purpose of which is to attract the attention of the prospective purchaser. Inside illustrations for stories are expected to entice the reader. A good illustration never gives the story away. Illustration is widely employed in textbooks, where its primary purpose is to explain and clarify. Cartoons provoke thought. Comics tell a complete story. There are many styles and purposes of illustrations, as is evident by the constant flow of books and periodicals.

III. Design in Publishing

Design in publishing is generally thought of as an arrangement of lines, spots, spaces, tones, and colors. In book publishing, design begins with the binding and includes the type, the layout, and other decoration. Decorative illustration is especially well suited to books, as it harmonizes with type. Decoration is less likely to be dated and remains in style longer than realistic illustration. Decoration may be composed of a few simple lines carefully spaced or may be an elaborate pattern. It is found in spots, borders, headings, or full-page designs. Maps and statistical diagrams may be decorative as well as factual.

IV. The Relationship of the Artist to the Field of Publishing

The requirements of talent and training for a successful art career in the publishing field are similar to those described in the chapter on advertising design. A thorough training in a reputable art school, the student's tendencies, and the advice of the faculty are the bases for guidance into the publishing field rather than into other fields of art endeavor.

Some students have a decided leaning toward decoration. They should be encouraged, as this type of art work is in constant demand. Design, being fundamental, is less susceptible to violent change in style than realistic illustration. A good sense of design enables the artist to solve a variety of design problems. The publishing field utilizes a great deal of design. It is one of the most active, dependable, and lucrative for the artist.

V. Processes of Reproduction in the Graphic Arts

There are three basic principles of graphic-arts reproduction. These are sometimes referred to as the subway, or intaglio, process; the surface car, or planography, process; and the elevated, or relief, process. All variations of printing are based on one of these three principles.

The *intaglio* process is typified by the etching, where scratches are made on a metal plate, ink is rubbed into the scratches, and the plane surface of the plate is wiped clean. The plate is then applied to a piece of dampened paper under pressure. The paper pulls the ink from the scratches in the plate and retains it as a picture called an ' etching.' The intaglio process includes rotogravure, which is used especially for long runs in newspaper supplements and magazines. This process gives excellent results at high speed, which makes it economical. Under the heading of intaglio may be included photogravure, copper and steel engraving, aquatints, and mezzotints.

The *planographic* process is typified by lithography, where a drawing is made with grease pencil on a stone or metal plate. The non-image areas are made and kept ink-repellent. Paper is applied under pressure, the ink is removed, and a fine reproduction of the original results.   No raising or lowering of the stone's or plate's surface is necessary in this process.   The lithography may be printed directly on the paper or offset by printing on a rubber blanket, which in turn is printed on the paper.   The collotype and equatone process is also under the heading of planography.

The elevated, or *relief*, process is typified by the line cut or half-tone. A drawing is made and then photographed on a sensitized metal plate. The whites and light tones are etched away with acid, leaving printing surfaces in relief.   These plateaus are inked, applied to paper under pressure, and the reproduction results.   Linoleum and wood blocks are other examples of this proscess.

Nearly all modern reproduction is *photomechanical;* that is to say, the picture to be reproduced is applied to the sensitized plate by photography and mechanically processed.   This gives scientific control and fine results not possible by the older hand methods.   Furthermore, the modern mechanical processes make possible the handling of great quantities of material in a limited time, as is witnessed by our daily and weekly publications.   A few generations ago, when all reproduction had to be done by hand, drawings were engraved on wood or metal with hand tools.   In the hands of a master craftsman noteworthy artistic effects were produced; witness the fine wood engravings of Timothy Cole.

Great progress has been made in the development of *printing presses*.   From simple hand presses making possible but a few hundred prints a day, we progress to the great multicolor presses that print four colors at high speed in one operation.

The amazing progress in the processes of reproduction and printing has had a definite influence on the graphic arts.   Once reproduction was laborious, the results crude.   Today the artist is relieved of all the drudgery of reproducing his work and the results are nearly perfect. This serves as an incentive to the artist, to the publisher, and to the layman who is the consumer of reproduced art.

To substantiate this contention one has only to examine the several de luxe publications of great works of art recently printed.   Although high in price, these books are best sellers, largely because of their beautiful reproductions.   Popular magazines frequently present fine reproductions of art.   All this is having a great influence on the taste and discrimination of the average American.

REFERENCES

(1) *Advertising-Publishing Production Yearbook.* Ettenberg, E. M., editor. (Colton Press: New York. Issued annually. 1939 edition) 424 pp.

(2) FRIEND, LEON, and HEFTER, JOSEPH. *Graphic Design.* (McGraw-Hill Book Co.: New York, 1935) 407 pp.

(3) HAVINDEN, ASHLEY. *Line Drawing for Reproduction.* (Studio Publications: London and New York, 1933) 96 pp.

(4) LEECH, GEORGE W. *Magazine Illustration.* (Pitman: London, 1939) 56 pp.

(5) LUND, HUMPHRIES and Co. *The Penrose Annual.* (12 Bedford Sq., London. Issued annually. Vol. 41 in 1939)

(6) POORTENAAR, J. P. *The Art of the Book and its Illustration.* (J. B. Lippincott Co.: Philadelphia, 1935) 182 pp.

(7) WHITING, J. D. *Practical Illustration.* (Harper and Brothers: New York, 1920)

CHAPTER XII

THE AMERICAN THEATER, PAST AND PRESENT

Barclay S. Leathem
Professor of Drama and Theater
Western Reserve University
Cleveland, Ohio

When tribal leaders first expressed in words and movement the feelings of the group, theater was born. Stage arts interpret emotionally man's relations to himself, his environment, his gods. Essentials of this interpretation are actors, audience, place, and playwright. Plays may be read and enjoyed, but the masterpieces of drama have had their greatest appeal when performed. A play is something to be seen and heard publicly. " Of all the arts, drama is closest to the people." [1] It appeals to mimetic instincts rooted deeply in the experience of the race. One of the earliest expressions of drama was probably the attempt of a primeval hunter to show others how he had made the kill. The child's love of play-acting is perennial. Few ever outgrow the urge to imagine themselves other characters in other circumstances. " Let's pretend " is the basis of the drama's hold upon man's curiosity and imagination. In the theater we seek vicarious satisfactions. We like stories well told. Adventure, conflict, spiritual catharsis are concomitants of the best tales the dramatist can unfold. People go to the theater because they want to be entertained. In the best sense great drama entertains (in the root sense of ' holding ' — *tenēre* to hold) ; whether tragedy or farce, it holds the audience in the spell of its emotional excitement.

I. Historical Background

Theatrical history in the United States really begins with the arrival of Lewis Hallam's company in 1752. Before that date there were some performances by amateurs and professionals, but the theater did not have the early support of the colonies. As Professor Arthur Quinn

---

[1] Milton Marx. *The Enjoyment of Drama.* (F. S. Crofts & Co.; New York, 1940.)

points out, to Puritan and Quaker the symbol was repugnant. They " associated it with monarchical forms in politics as well as religion and they had no use for it." Common objections were that the theater was too expensive and that it had been a part of Restoration loose living. Despite these handicaps, the Hallams won favor. Interesting among their activities was the production on April 24, 1767, of " The Prince of Parthia," the first play written by an American to be presented professionally upon the American stage. When, however, the Continental Congress, October 20, 1774, passed a resolution condemning " every species of extravagance and dissipation," the first period in the history of our theater ended.

During the Revolutionary War theater traditions were kept alive by the desire of British officers for entertainment. Satires were written dealing with Tory and Whig politics. With peace came a revival of the theater closely linked with an awakened national consciousness that stimulated native playwriting. Royall Tyler's comedy " The Contrast " was played at the John Street Theatre in New York during April, 1787. Other figures prominent in late eighteenth-century theater development were William Dunlap, playwright and first historian of the theater, and David Douglass, America's first theater-builder. The most important theater at the close of the century was the Park in New York City. Designed by a French engineer, it followed European models and had pit, gallery, and three tiers of boxes.

The first half of the nineteenth century saw the spread of theaters to cities throughout the country. The first show-boat made its picturesque appearance about 1830. A few years later, in 1841, the magic name P. T. Barnum flashed into prominence with the opening in New York of Barnum's Museum. Both there, and in the Boston Museum that opened the same year, ' moral lectures ' cloaked the appearance of some of the greatest actors of the day. Among the stars, or visiting ' lecturers,' who adorned the theater of 1800 to 1850 were Edmund Kean, William Charles Macready, Junius Brutus Booth, Charles Kemble, Charles Kean, and the native-born James H. Hackett, John Howard Payne, Charlotte Cushman, and Edward Davenport. In playwriting, foreign influences predominated. John Howard Payne, by adapting works of Kotzebue, and by translating from the French, led the writers who tried to model the American stage according to the London examples at Drury Lane and Covent Garden. Some ' Yankee plays ' were given, however, and the way was prepared for the presentation in 1845 of " Fashion " by Anna Cora Mowatt. This play is one of the great successes of the American theater. It satirizes uncritical imitation of foreign customs.

By 1850 theaters were still unsanitary and rowdy. Between 1820 and 1845 twenty-five burned down, a large percentage for that period. Scenery, costuming, and lighting were approximations of foreign practice.

The last half of the century brought Dion Boucicault, whose traveling company led to abandonment of the system then prevalent: the visiting star supported by local stock companies. It saw the technical innovations of Steele MacKaye, who in 1885 installed the first electric lighting system in a theater. It witnessed the rise of Augustin Daly, playwright and theatrical manager, who assembled the greatest collection of actors ever to play together as a permanent company. The period 1850–1900 is also noteworthy for the following: formation of the first theatrical syndicate in 1896; the minstrel show; the famous melodrama " The Black Crook " in which the leg show was a faint forerunner of the ' strip tease ' of modern burlesque; fireman drama; the first managerial success of David Belasco; rise of a tradition of distinguished acting, as illustrated by the performances of Edwin Booth, Joseph Jefferson III, Fanny Davenport, and numerous others; and finally the gradual emancipation of the American playwright from European influences.

The turn of the century found the syndicate laying foundations for its strangle hold on theaters, and on producing units of all kinds. Before the advent of motion pictures, stock companies flourished in every sizable town. The peanut gallery, admission one dime, attracted the audience lost later to the nickelodeon. The Little Theater movement arrived from Europe soon after 1910. Although often self-consciously ' arty,' this movement was so well established by 1923 that, beginning in that year, a tournament was held annually in New York City for nine years. The best of these theaters, notably the Provincetown Players, gave opportunity to playwrights and designers to open fresh vistas in stage arts. It was at Provincetown that Eugene O'Neill's one-act plays were first given. Here, too, Robert Edmond Jones introduced the principles of designing he had observed in Europe. Lee Simonson applied the theories of Adolphe Appia and the Meiningen Players in his early work with the Washington Square Players, later the Theater Guild.

But David Belasco and the realism of the box set were dominant influences until well into the nineteen twenties. Plays mirrored current life. Summarizing the season 1924–1925, Burns Mantle writes: " The season, as a season, will probably figure in theatrical history as that sensational period when questionable plays flourished amazingly and the life of the drama was threatened. The bold play and the profane play, the play concerned frankly with the lives of harlots and their social kin, suddenly became the issue of the year." The popularity of this kind of entertainment was short-lived. By 1929–1930, the best plays included such varying types as " The Green Pastures," " The Criminal Code," " June Moon," " Death Takes a Holiday," and " Rebound."

The Group Theater and Clifford Odets led the way for plays of social significance. The most marked recent tendency is toward the theater of satire, illustrated by " Pins and Needles " and " Meet the People." These musical revues ridicule in song and skit the foibles of the day. Though now defunct, the Federal Theater Project did much to restore drama to the people, and to encourage new forms. " The Living Newspaper " is a conspicuous example. Since 1905, playwriting has been stimulated by university courses in that subject, first introduced at Radcliffe College by the late George Pierce Baker. American Folk Drama continues to have the inspirational leadership of Frederick H. Koch at the University of North Carolina. The historian of the future, analyzing the period 1925–1950, will probably turn to the educational theater and to the influence of the Rockefeller Foundation as the developments, now barely under way, whose ultimate effects upon the American theater are most significant.

II. THEORIES OF CONTEMPORARY STAGE DESIGN

To understand present trends in the American theater, it is necessary to examine briefly the theories influencing not only Jones and Simonson, but also Joseph Urban, Norman Bel Geddes, Aline Bernstein, Donald Oenslager, Cleon Throckmorton, Jo Mielziner, and other outstanding designers in the American Theater.

The two words *Realism* and *Expressionism* are used loosely to sum up the broad tendencies in contemporary stage arts.

In general, Realism is representational; truth-to-life is the test. An audience sees in the play, and in the design of costumes, sets, and lighting, an adaptation of actuality. In the same sense Expressionism is presentational; here the artist is concerned with truth to his medium, the stage. An audience sees in play, and in design, not a representation of life's normal processes, but either frank distortions thereof, or portrayal of those characters and experiences that belong to life in the theater rather than to life outside of it. For example, a clown or an animal act has existence only in terms of circus or stage; neither is a representation of something we see in life outside the theater. The defender of Realism says: " Let us make the audience forget they are in the theater; let us have our stages resemble life so accurately that the audience will accept the illusion of reality." The expressionist, or presentationalist, answers: " Let us rather strive to have the audience remember they are in a theater; let us have them see what can be seen only in a theater."

There are many types of Realism. They range from the cluttered details of " The Doll's House " setting first used by the Moscow Art Theatre to the stylized Realism of Aline Bernstein's designs for " Camille." Frequently overlooked by critics of Realism is the fact that its most distinguished exponents — the directors of the Meininger Theater in Germany — were striving to relate the plastic form of the three-dimensional actor to a similar three-dimensionalism in the scenery. Until approximately 1875 theater scenery consisted almost entirely of painted perspective sets in imitation of the work of seventeenth-century Italian Baroque architects and painters. The Meininger's emphasis upon archaeological accuracy in plastic built-up sets, and the theories of Adolphe Appia and Gordon Craig are largely responsible for the best current practice in American stage *décor*. Theodore Komisarjevsky, discussing settings and costumes in Europe, states,

> In the last sixty years the change from the perspective painted decorative scenery has been extraordinary. Having passed through the waves of various *isms* — Naturalism, Symbolism, Stylism, and Expressionism — the advance-guard theatrical workers in Europe came to Constructive and Synthetic-Realistic methods of production and completely destroyed the decorative principles of the painters of illusionistic perspective scenery.

The strongest influence upon American designers is the Swiss artist Adolphe Appia. In his designs he simplified, or stylized, the forms of nature. He pointed out that light is mobile. He solved the esthetic problem of reconciling the movement in space of a three-dimensional actor against static three-dimensional backgrounds by moving light to harmonize with movements of the actor. Today, even in a so-called realistic play, audiences accept non-realistic changes in intensity and direction of light as part of the illusion of the theater.

It is a mistake to assume that Expressionism or any other ism is dominant in America today. Designers interpret and intensify the values inherent in the playwright's script. American stage *décor* is as varied as the plays themselves. In the New York season of 1939–1940, the majority of successful plays were comments upon modern life, conceived in terms of Realism. They were so designed and mounted. What can be said to the credit of our designers is that at all times they have matched the imagination of authors and directors.

III. Economic Status of the Theater

In 1925–1926, 80 theaters were used in New York. Within ten years the number had dropped to 46. The seasons 1926–1927 and 1927–1928 each had 302 theatrical productions. By 1938–39 new entertainments, dramatic and musical, were approximately eighty. Only one of every five shows produced is a financial success. The scenic artist, therefore, faces a shrinking market in the professional theater. Moreover, he will find that admission to the United Scenic Artists of America, the union he must join if he is to earn commissions, is almost impossible. He must pass a stiff examination and pay an initiation fee of $500. The union defends its policy on the ground that the field otherwise would be filled with incompetently trained artists. Although a few may earn as much as $20,000 in a season, the average for even successful designers is $5,000 to $8,000. Many are lucky to receive from $250, the union minimum, to $1,000 for a single show. If the play for which the designer was employed happens to be among the 80 percent of failures, he will probably not receive the final instalment of his fee. These economic conditions apply to other aspects of the New York stage. Newcomers have no difficulty joining Equity, the union for actors, but there are scores of applicants for every available rôle. Without financial backing, a director or producer has virtually no chance to break in. As a result, many of the best young men are now turning to the community and university theaters, where opportunities for development appear unlimited.

IV. Importance of the Theater Arts in Current American Life

Despite the recent decrease in plays and playhouses in New York, the American theater is more lively and provocative than at any time in its history. The level of artistic production in New York is not excelled by that of any other metropolis in the world. The closest rival, Moscow, cannot match it in the variety and distinction of its writing, acting, designing, directing, or technical proficiency. International exhibits of settings and costumes find American designers predominant.

The most significant evidence of America's leadership, and of the rising importance of stage arts in American life, is to be found in two developments: the growth of community theaters, and the spread of dramatic arts throughout the entire educational system.

The moving and talking picture helped bring to a close the stock company era. It influenced the collapse of the road show sent on tour from New York. It did not, however, destroy the people's desire to see plays enacted on a stage by living actors.

There are now more than five hundred community theaters in America and the number is increasing. In addition, there are performances by church groups, Y.M.C.A.'s, settlement houses, lodges, granges, and numerous similar organizations. In these latter groups, standards often are low, but each year sees an improvement as the effect of education in dramatics becomes evident. The standard in leading community theaters, however, is distinctly above the average of the New York theater if we consider all the plays produced in a given season. This opinion is not wishful thinking; it is one supported by the dramatic reviews of such discerning professional critics as William McDermott of the Cleveland *Plain Dealer* and John Rosenfield of the Dallas *Morning News.*

Community theaters no longer exist as small bands of enthusiasts with more ambition than skill. The Kansas City Resident Theater under the direction of Zolley Lerner plays to 15,000 people — more than turn out to see the best-known stars of the Broadway stage when they come to Kansas City. At Kalamazoo, Michigan, the community theater plays regularly to ten percent of the potential theater audience. The Jameses at the Seattle Repertory Playhouse reach a more representative audience than does any travelling professional troupe.

A community theater is part of the civic consciousness of a city in a way that stock companies never approached. Active on Boards of Directors are the same persons who support local symphony orchestras, art museums, libraries, hospitals, and universities. Typical of this sort of organization is the Cleveland Play House. The staff operates two theaters playing every week from September to June. They employ twenty or more trained directors, actors, and technicians. Their budget is $90,000 per year and the theater operates without endowment, subsidy, or deficit. No single theater entity on Broadway can point to a comparable record of sustained achievement in satisfying a public. The Pasadena Playhouse is another excellent example of a theater meeting regional needs in drama.

It is too soon to evaluate the full effect community theaters will have upon stage arts in America. One salutary benefit will be the gradual decentralization of the theater. When men and women can be assured adequate salaries by well-established local theaters in cities having populations of 100,000 or more, it will no longer be necessary for everyone to look only to New York or to Hollywood. Unquestionably the lure of the pay check will continue to draw to those centers talent of all kinds. It is just as likely that many will choose to remain where they are, for the same reasons that actuate members of other professions.

Another benefit to the American theater of indigenous communal drama is the encouragement of local art. The playwright, the designer, and the actor all need more opportunity for development than is now available. Audiences everywhere still prefer the tested play, the Broadway success. But gradually community theaters are finding support for trial performances of new manuscripts. For the subject matter of drama, a writer need not confine himself to his immediate locale. It is more important that a playwright in Arizona have a theater there to work in than that his play deal with the western scene, although inevitably writers are influenced by environment, and decentralization of the theater will enrich thereby the literature of regional interpretations of American life.

Important as is the rise of the community theater, it is the educational theater that has made the most astounding progress. From the kindergarten through the university graduate schools, stage arts are practiced and taught. Plays are given in 10,000 high schools. In hundreds of them, play-production is an established curricular subject. There are 800 colleges and universities that give dramatic performances regularly. One or more courses are offered in at least 250 institutions. There are 28 universities that give a Master of Arts degree in drama and theater. At the University of Iowa a student can earn the doctorate for creative excellence in playwriting. Beginning next year, Western Reserve University will be the first American university to accept as a candidate for the doctorate degree a man who will specialize in the producing and directing of plays.

The newest and best theaters in America are being built for universities. At Indiana University, Professor Lee Norvelle, head of the Drama Department, has guided the architects toward new functional forms in architectural design for the theater. The cost of the new Indiana drama plant will be approximately at $1,100,000. Good theaters of varying types are to be found at Stanford University, University of Wisconsin, University of Iowa, Cornell University, Yale University, Carnegie Institute of Technology, Amherst College, University of Georgia, Western Reserve University, University of North Carolina, and the University of Washington.

University faculties no longer look upon dramatics as an extra-curricular activity to be tolerated, but not encouraged. They accept the fact that stage arts form the basis of a sound liberal education. A student majoring in drama and theater prepares effectively for life outside the theater. In short, drama in its own right compares favorably with other established academic disciplines. It is no accident that many directors in New York and elsewhere are lawyers. The same analytical processes applicable to law are necessary to the theater. Universities stress production of period plays. Every student who takes part in a Greek, a Roman, or an Elizabethan play must familiarize himself with the artistic and historical backgrounds that influence style in settings, acting, and direction. He studies the folkways and customs that form the cultural heritage of the race.

For most students in American universities the theater will, of course, be an avocation. The future lawyer, doctor, or business man will not only have the direct benefits of training in voice, movement, posture, interpretation of character, teamwork, management, scene design and construction; he will also carry over to later life a vital interest in creative artistic processes. The effect of this is already being noticed in the improved quality of community theater productions. At Kalamazoo the president of the local bank played Caesar. In the same cast was a prominent physician whose delineation of Cassius was good by any standards, professional or amateur. The universities are breaking down the notion that only long-haired dilettantes turn to the theater for recreation.

Another fact overlooked by spokesmen of the Broadway Theater is the effect of universities and community theaters in building a new audience, one whose judgments are critical and informed. It will not accept the meretricious work of a number three company out of New York. It fills theaters for the best plays as acted and produced by the best representatives of the professional stage; it absents itself from anything less competent.

Not all students will follow the theater as an avocation; some will use it as a profession. Here, too, the university emphasis upon stage arts is justified by recent trends. The largest source of positions lies in the public and private schools. Every year the demand is increasing for teachers who can direct plays and teach courses in all aspects of play-production. Another field is provided by similar demands in the college and the university. Radio takes many. So do the picture companies in Hollywood, whose talent scouts state that the college-trained actor is their most promising recruit. Even industry offers new openings. The General Electric Company has advertised its products for the past few years by sending small acting companies on tour. Several performers for this project were taken fresh from universities. The professional theater is another source of employment. Though limited, it still attracts a few annually. The number will certainly increase as more directors and producers with college backgrounds take places held formerly by men who came to prominence by way of the now defunct stock companies.

All this promises much for the future of our theater. As Charles Coburn points out, the actor of the future will have advantages of education that were generally denied to those who entered the professional theater as youthful apprentices. Nor will the gain be limited to one field. Playwriting, technical methods, scene- and costume-design will all profit by university experimentation. The effect of education in the drama itself cannot be judged so soon. It is a comparatively new subject in our institutions of learning. There is every reason to anticipate an influence in stage arts comparable to the leadership universities now provide in science, social studies, business administration, law, and other areas of knowledge.

V. Theater Art Patrons

Until last year, the United States Government was for a time the greatest patron of stage arts in America. The Federal Theater Project proved that audiences still exist for entertainment by actors in the flesh. It demonstrated the dynamic force of the theater in a democracy. Under the imaginative direction of Hallie Flanagan the foundation was laid for any future venture by the government as a patron of drama. A grant from the Rockefeller Foundation is financing Theater Research, through which the full story of the Federal Theater Project will be made available.

The Rockefeller Foundation is also supporting the National Theater Conference. This organization of leaders in universities and community theaters has its roots in every section of the country. It coördinates regional activity in drama. It is a ' holding company ' for the vast interests of the American theater as represented by thousands of closely integrated social and educational groups. The scope of the National Theater Conference's activity is described in detail elsewhere in this *Yearbook*. The Rockefeller Foundation also has strengthened regional centers of university training for leadership in theater arts at Yale, Cornell, North Carolina, Western Reserve, Iowa, and Stanford.

Some support for drama has been given by the following: General Education Board, Carnegie Corporation, Guggenheim Memorial Foundation, Munson-Williams-Proctor Institute, Kosciusko Foundation, and the Julius Rosenwald Fund.

The land-grant colleges have benefited by federal aid through the P.W.A. and W.P.A. The University of Iowa and the University of Washington are among the many beneficiaries of this kind of assistance. State and local governments have given aid. The Municipal Outdoor Theater, in St. Louis, and Cain Park Theater, in Cleveland Heights, illustrate what can be done when local civic leaders take an interest in drama.

Federal, state, and local aid may very likely increase when people everywhere realize the importance of drama in plans for national defense. The theater is close to the pulse beat of an aroused citizenry. It can mold opinion, stimulate morale. To a loosely knit social organism it can restore clarity of purpose. To soldier in camp, to worker in field, factory, or office, it can bring salutary enlightenment of democracy's objectives. The theater is a weapon that cannot be ignored.

REFERENCES

(1) ANDERSON, JOHN. *The American Theatre*. (The Dial Press: New York, 1938)

(2) *Billboard Index of the New York Legitimate Stage*. (Billboard Publishing Co.: Cincinnati. Issued annually.)

(3) Bricker, Herschel L., Editor. *Our Theatre Today. A Composite Handbook on the Art, Craft, and Management of the Contemporary Theatre*. (Samuel French: New York, 1936)

(4) BROWN, JOHN MASON. *The Modern Theatre in Revolt*. (W. W. Norton and Co., Inc.: New York, 1929)

(5) CHENEY, SHELDON. *Stage Decoration*. (John Day Co.: New York, 1928)

(6) CHENEY, SHELDON. *The Theatre. Three Thousand Years of Drama, Acting, and Stagecraft*. (Longmans, Green, and Co.: New York, 1929)

(7) EUSTIS, MORTON. *B'way, Inc.! The Theatre as a Business*. (Dodd Mead and Co.: New York, 1934)

(8) HUGHES, GLENN. *The Story of the Theatre. A Short History of Theatrical*

Art from Its Beginnings to the Present Day. (Samuel French: New York, 1928)

(9) Koch, Frederick H., Editor. *American Folk Plays.* (D. Appleton-Century Co.: New York, 1939)

(10) KOMISARJEVSKY, THEODORE, and SIMONSON, LEE. *Settings and Costumes of the Modern Stage.* (The Studio Publications, Inc.: New York, 1933)

(11) MACGOWAN, KENNETH, and JONES, ROBERT EDMOND. *Continental Stagecraft.* (Harcourt, Brace and Co.: New York, 1922)

(12) MANTLE, BURNS. *The Best Plays* of 1919–1920, 1920–1921, etc. (Dodd Mead and Co.: New York, 1919–1940. Issued annually.)

(13) MARX, MILTON. *The Enjoyment of Drama.* (F. S. Crofts and Co.: New York, 1940)

(14) MODERWELL, HIRAM KELLY. *The Theatre of Today.* (Dodd Mead and Co.: New York, 1923)

(15) OENSLAGER, DONALD. *Scenery Then and Now.* (W. W. Norton and Co., Inc.: New York, 1936)

(16) QUINN, ARTHUR HOBSEN. *A History of the American Drama. From the Civil War to the Present Day.* 2 vols. (Harper and Brothers: New York, 1927)

(17) Sobel, Bernard, Editor. *The Theatre Handbook and Digest of Plays.* (Crown Publishers: New York, 1940)

(18) TRAUBE, SHEPARD. *So You Want to Go into the Theatre?* (Little, Brown, and Co.: Boston, 1936)

CHAPTER XIII

PUPPETS, MARIONETTES, AND SHADOW PLAYS

Louise M. Dunn
Associate Curator of Education
The Cleveland Museum of Art
Cleveland, Ohio

Any form of art that has survived at least three thousand years, has been enjoyed by young and old, rich and poor, and has flourished in every country of the world is worthy of our consideration.

In 1862, in Paris, there appeared the first great modern work on marionettes, Charles Magnin's "*Histoire des marionettes en Europe depuis l'antiquité jusqu'à nos jours,*" the work to which all subsequent writers on puppetry are largely indebted. This scholarly work for the first time brought together the widely scattered knowledge of the puppet and gave an impulse to further research in this form of theater art.

With the turn of the twentieth century and the quest for newer forms of art the puppet was rediscovered. The possible stylization of its forms and movements and its almost uncanny ability to suggest touched the imagination. Bernard Shaw found that it had " an intensity to which few actors can pretend, an intensity like those images in immovable hieratic attitudes on the stained glass of Chartres Cathedral." Gordon Craig, who did much to bring about this renaissance, believed that " the puppet is the actor in his most primitive form," that in its " obedience " and " silence " lay its spell. Max Von Boehn, the German authority, says that the true puppet is " not an individual but a type."

Let us ignore its primitive beginnings and the extraordinary automata and movable images of the Egyptians, and come to the acrobatic mimes of the Greek puppet-makers, possibly as clever as any ever devised. Xenophon describes these small, cord-controlled figures that mathematicians and engineers created. Puppet shows were common in all of the larger Greek cities. Their triumph came when the Athenians gave over a part of their great theater of Dionysus to the puppet showman, Potheinos. We find puppets in Rome and her colonies in many forms. Their importance in the dramatic ceremonies of the early church is well known. Figures of great scale enacted through at least five centuries the rôles of the Holy Family, of saints and martyrs, of angels and demons. In the service of the church they crossed the Alps. Germany, Austria, France, and Spain welcomed them. During the Reformation in England they were protected when all other forms of the theater were placed under the ban.

With the coming of the early Renaissance, puppets left the churches for more adventurous freedom in a changing world. Puppet showmen originated the *Commedia dell'Arte*. Italy has been the homeland of the puppets of the western world, ever since they migrated there from Greece. They belong to its cities and towns and still perform the stirring hero tales in its open squares. Of the puppets that emigrated at an early time to the East, some found Russia to their liking; others went on to Persia, India, China, and Japan. In each of these lands they took on new forms and new rôles. They exchanged naturalistic for decorative forms and allied themselves with music, poetry, and the dance, giving up most of their clever mechanical perfection.

In China, India, Bali, and Java they fell under the spell of the mystic shadow world, and took on the shapes of new gods and goddesses, new heroes and heroines, playing all the rôles in the great religious dramas. In China they shared the more intimate life of the court and of the common people. They were invited into the seclusion of their gardens, where nightly they presented episodes in cycles of folk tales. Japan adopted them in a very different spirit, one more nearly like that of the Greek engineers and mathematicians. The creation of Japanese puppets is an art in itself. Each puppet must be an esthetic experience to its slightest detail. Japanese puppets are created to be seen, enjoyed, and marveled at for their perfection.

It may be of interest to see how the puppet, through its " silence " and " obedience," has adapted itself to our own country. The early chapters of this include the wandering Italian puppet showmen and their families who followed their countrymen over the seas to New York, Chicago, Cleveland, New Orleans, and San Francisco. Here thirty years and more ago in the over-crowded Italian districts they set up their sturdy stages, and with their puppets in full armor, were ready to do battle, nightly, for most appreciative audiences. Ariosto's *Orlando Furioso* is the source of the stirring adventures that required months for their acting. Occasionally those with ' a taste for it ' ventured in and sat enthralled for long uncomfortable hours catching something of the satisfaction and enjoyment of the work-a-day audiences. These

American visitors invited their theater-minded friends and the cult grew.

Meanwhile Americans visiting Europe discovered the city-owned marionette theater of 'Papa' Schmidt in Munich and the delightful puppet booths in the Luxembourg Gardens and the Bois de Bologne in Paris. Brander Matthews as a young boy returned with a complete set of these French puppets, which he continued to cherish and finally gave as his last gift to The Museum of Theater Arts at Columbia University. Collections of puppets began to appear in American museums: in the Brooklyn Institute Museum, the American Museum of Natural History of New York, the Field Museum of Chicago, and the Cleveland Museum of Art.

In New York the young artists, Tony Sarg and Raymond Bufano, near the Italian tradition, began to create modern marionettes, scenery, and lighting, and adapted plays suitable for puppet production. They visited other American cities. Success followed. Hundreds of Americans for the first time saw fine marionette plays. Following the popular demand, Sarg and Bufano opened a school of puppetry in connection with their studio in New York.

In Detroit, William Duncan and Edward Mabley organized the well-known Tatterman Puppeteers, while Paul McPharlin began his experiments and the gathering together of material that finally led in 1930 to his publication of the magazine *Puppetry*. Mrs. Maurice Broune experimented with various types of puppets and presented her plays in Chicago's Little Theater. Raymond O'Neil included puppetry in the activities of Cleveland's first little theater — The Cleveland Play House. In California, Percy Dilley carved and constructed puppets of such outstanding excellence that he finally became a member of the Drama Department of the University of California. By such steps American puppeteers have developed their art and formed a fellowship.

Artists and craftsmen as teachers in schools soon saw in puppetry an almost ideal means of interesting young people and of correlating art activities with music, history, and literature.

Books and magazine articles on the history and educational possibilities of puppets began to appear in Europe and America. Popular demand made this material available in public libraries. Normal schools, colleges, and a few courageous universities, including the Catholic University of America, began to offer credit courses in puppetry. Teachers in smaller communities read books on puppetry and articles in educational magazines. Travelling puppeteers again are seen, this time in automobiles with trailers. Today thousands of American school children make puppets and present plays in their schools. The puppet has invaded the home. Basements and attics have become marionette workshops. There is now a national conference that meets annually and an official yearbook published by Paul McPharlin in Birmingham, Michigan.

Such growing popularity could not long escape the eagle eyes of alert commercial advertisers. Why not call upon clever young puppeteers to enter a profitable new field? We have all seen some form of this latest adventure. At the Chicago World's Fair puppets demonstrated the history of food-preservation for the Kelvinator Company. Now super-marionettes show us the ways in which Mrs. Cinderella sets about modernizing the castle with the aid of General Electric products — all to a modern script and music especially written to catch and please the thousands of visitors to the New York World's Fair.

With its immortal genius for taking advantage of the present, it is not surprising to find the puppet appearing on the radio and screen. Through the ability of Edgar Bergen, Charlie McCarthy has become one of the most entertaining and popular characters of our time.

One may well ask why this amazing renaissance of the puppet has come about in America. The reasons seem obvious as we list some of them. The American genius is active, restless, visual; it likes to make, to experiment, and to participate. We are social; boys and girls, old and young, parents and children enjoy life together. We are democratic with but few class prejudices. For these reasons the puppet in all its forms — guignol, shadow figure, and marionette — seems to have taken us to its heart and found its place among us as it did in the days of its sway in ancient Greece.

There are other reasons. The possibilities of stage effects through modern electric lighting, movable spots, and dimmers are in contrast with the limitations of centuries of candles and lamps. There are new materials to appeal to any craft interest among us. Balsa wood from South America (easy to carve), rubber, cellophane, rayon, new composition boards of lightness and strength, papers, tools, and gadgets, wire, paint, paste, and string make the modern ten-cent store a treasure house for the puppet-maker.

Of the future of puppetry in America, who can predict? Thus far our puppets have been like ourselves — young, vigorous, joyful, healthy, talking, singing, dancing, popular in the fullest sense of that word. It is true that they have grown up, and accomplished difficult rôles. In our hands they have kept something of their age-old ability to touch the heart.

However, there are still other worlds to explore, deeper and more universal emotions to stir, and new forms of beauty to express. We have rarely called upon the puppet to use keen wit and humor, irony and caustic satire in the cause of right and justice as the times seemed to demand. Since the untimely death of Joel Cutler nothing outstanding seems to have been undertaken. Our puppets as yet have found little time for a better understanding of the use of form, color, and light as means of art expression through relations and abstractions, movement and design. When the puppet finally reaches its maturity among us, we may all say with Gordon Craig, but in a newer sense, " Gentlemen, the marionette."

REFERENCES

(1) ANDERSON, M. *Heroes of the Puppet Stage.* (Harcourt, Brace and Co.: New York, 1923) 420 pp.

(2) BEAUMONT, C. W. *Puppets and the Puppet Stage.* (The Studio Ltd.: London, 1938) 144 pp.

(3) CRAIG, E. G. *The Mask.* (Florence, Italy, 1929) 60 pp.

(4) INVERARITY, R. B. *A Manual of Puppetry.* (The Metropolitan Press: Portland, Oregon, 1938) 220 pp.

(5) JOSEPH, H. H. *A Book of Marionettes.* (W. B. Huebsch: New York, 1920) 241 pp.

(6) KENNARD, J. S. *Masks and Maricnettes.* (The Macmillan Co.: New York, 1935) 125 pp.

(7) MAGNIN, C. *Histoire des marionettes en Europe depuis l'antiquité jusqu'à nos jours.* (Michel Lévy: Paris, 1852) 346 pp.

(8) MAINDRON, E. *Marionettes et Guignols, les poupées agissantes et parlantes à travers les ages.* (Felix Juven: Paris, 1900) 381 pp.

(9) McPHARLIN, P. *Puppetry Imprints.* Yearbooks of Marionettes. 1930–1940. (Birmingham, Michigan: 155 Wimbleton Drive)

(10) MILLS, W., and DUNN, L. M. *Marionettes, Masks and Shadows.* (Doubleday, Doran and Co. Inc.: New York, 1927) 270 pp.

(11) SERRURIER, L. *De Wajang Poerwâ.* (E. J. Brill: Leiden, Holland, 1896) 352 pp.

(12) SIBBALD, R. S. *Marionettes in the North of France.* (Humphrey Milford. Oxford University Press: London, 1936) 134 pp. (Also University of Pennsylvania Press: Philadelphia)

(13) VON BOEHN, M. *Dolls and Puppets.* Transl. by Josephine Nicoll. (Harrap: London, 1932) 522 pp.

CHAPTER XIV

THE MOTION PICTURE

Iris Barry
Curator, The Museum of Modern Art Film Library, Inc.
New York, New York

Edwin Ziegfeld
Assistant Professor of Fine Arts
Columbia University
New York, New York
and
Milton S. Fox
Instructor, The Cleveland Museum of Art
Instructor, The Cleveland School of Art
Cleveland, Ohio

I

THE DEVELOPMENT OF MOTION PICTURES IN AMERICA [1]

Iris Barry

The motion picture is unique in three important ways: first, it is the one medium of expression in which America has influenced the rest of the world; second, it has had a marked influence on contemporary life; and third, it is such a young art that we can study it at first hand from its beginnings (the primitives among movies are only forty years old).

Though many experiments and inventions had gone before, the motion picture as we know it did not come into being until, upon Eastman's inventing film to take the place of photographic plates, Edison perfected the kinetoscope. This peep show machine made its first appearance at Broadway and 34th Street in New York in April, 1894. At first it was regarded only as a semi-scientific curiosity, even after other inventors had taken the animated pictures out of the peep show and projected them upon a screen. For a time the public was satisfied merely to see things move. Scenic views, actual street scenes, or simple

---

[1] Quoted with minor alterations by permission from *Art in America*, edited by Holger Cahill and Alfred H. Barr, Jr. (Reynal & Hitchcock: New York, 1934)

actions — a woman dancing, an engine puffing towards the audience, a boy playing a prank — provided the subject matter for these early movies. Little improvised comic or dramatic incidents were screened before the close of the nineteenth century, but very few attempts at sustained story-telling or drama were made until about 1903. In that year an Edison cameraman, Edwin S. Porter, combined several popular ingredients into a distinct plot in " The Great Train Robbery," which was a whole reel long. Italy, France, and England contributed many of the crude one-reel historical dramas, condensed plays, and novels that followed, while America became identified with the livelier, more graphic, and more purely cinematic cowboy dramas and slapstick comedies. Gradually films grew longer. The most famous of the early multi-reel movies was undoubtedly the French " Queen Elizabeth," with Sarah Bernhardt, made in 1911.

In 1913 Italy sent over the super-spectacle " Quo Vadis," complete with crowds, lions, and the Colosseum, in eight reels. D. W. Griffith, an ambitious young director who had then been with the American Biograph Company for five years, determined to outdo " Quo Vadis." The result was " The Birth of a Nation," the film with which the history of the motion picture as a great popular art is usually judged to have begun. Griffith had already realized that the camera need not confine itself to action like that of the stage, with the players always seen at full-length at a constant distance from the spectator. He had already brought the camera closer to both actors and inanimate objects, and now found how to alternate more distant scenes of action with closer and more intimate scenes of emotion, making the film at once more fluid and expressive and less literal. He made dramatic use of the ' dissolve,' the ' close-up,' and other technical tricks, and employed the old ' ride to the rescue ' motive of the early Western films, along with ' cutbacks,' to achieve a contrapuntal method of pictorial narration. " The Birth of a Nation," because of its magnitude as well as its subject and its treatment, and Griffith's colossal " Intolerance," made two years later, had a lasting effect on the developing motion picture. It is noteworthy that " Intolerance," perhaps the most momentous of all movies, was, like most of the interesting early American pictures, based on a story written specially for the screen and not on an adaptation of a novel or play.

From 1914 to 1918 the work of Griffith and others in America carried the motion picture out of the nickelodeon stage with its exaggerated gestures, rapid action, and psychological crudity. It was during these years that Charlie Chaplin progressed from the rough-and-tumble farces of his beginnings to that brilliant succession of tragicomedies that were tender and sardonic as well as funny, filled with a profound knowledge of human nature, and assembled with an instinctive feeling for the medium. Both Griffith and Chaplin brought more complex situations and characters to the screen and taught it to find a purely visual expression unlike that of the drama or fiction. Chaplin developed a sure feeling for the exact length of time each single shot should last; he, particularly, is a master of editing and of timing. Other men in this country made contributions, but many of them unhappily relied on famous stage actors or on plots drawn unchanged from plays and novels; they too eagerly exploited sensationalism and personalities, and they were more concerned with creating an impression of opulence than curious about the potentialities of the medium.

From the time filmgoers acclaimed the Biograph Girl with the golden curls, long before she was known as Mary Pickford, through to the time of Rudolph Valentino and Greta Garbo, the star system has done much to injure motion pictures. The great popular favorites themselves have all been exceptionally expressive players, but their popularity was abused when motion-picture companies stressed who rather than what was in a motion picture.

The years following the Armistice brought technical innovations and an added sophistication from Germany. German films, from the expressionist " Cabinet of Dr. Caligari " (1919) to Dupont's " Variety " and Murnau's " The Last Laugh " (1925), left a marked impression. The use of camera angles and of the traveling camera, the designing of scenery for pictorial rather than for theatrical effect, both came from the German studios. It was the example of the Germans that influenced Hollywood to use artificial lighting as a rule rather than as an exception, and to construct artificial ' outdoor ' scenes within the studio in place of natural settings. With their slower movement, their exploration of somber moods and psychological bypaths, the beautiful German films themselves were seldom to the public taste. But they were closely studied by American directors, and the innovations they presented were incorporated into the general technique of production, again widening the film's range of expression. During this period, many German directors, actors, and cameramen were brought over to Hollywood.

The American movie on its own account had by no means stood still, despite the frankly commercial attitude of its makers. Cruze's " The

Covered Wagon " (1923) was a far cry from the one-reel Westerns but was equally pure cinema. Erich von Stroheim's " Blind Husbands " (1919) — a remarkable piece — and his " Foolish Wives " (1922) were followed in 1923 by a movie that Chaplin directed but did not act in, " A Woman of Paris." All three of these assumed a considerable degree of visual and intellectual alertness on the part of their audiences, and all of them contrived in a way, which at the time seemed startling, to suggest rather than to illustrate the finer shades of moods and of situations. Vivid and subtle as we found the American-made movies of the German director, Ernst Lubitsch — such, for instance, as " The Marriage Circle " and " Forbidden Paradise " — their sparkle and eloquence had been foreshadowed in von Stroheim's and Chaplin's pictures.

In the years that followed, movies as different as Fairbanks' " The Black Pirate," in color, documentary pictures like " Chang," " Moana," and " Tabu," the farces of Harold Lloyd and Buster Keaton, and the incomparable Chaplin's " The Pilgrim " and " The Gold Rush," besides Ford's " The Iron Horse," von Stroheim's " Greed," Stiller's " Hotel Imperial," and Vidor's " The Big Parade," showed many indications of an intelligent struggle to explore the screen's possibilities.

In 1927 after the appearance of " The Jazz Singer " every motion-picture studio set about making ' talkies.' The movies had achieved a remarkable degree of eloquence through pictures alone. There was a temporary setback with the coming of audible dialog. Canned plays threatened to sweep away most of the advances made by the silent films. It is well to remember, however, that except in unusual productions like Chaplin's " The Woman of Paris " and Murnau's " The Last Laugh," one-third of the footage of the average silent film consisted of printed subtitles. Silent films, too, were invariably accompanied by both music and sound effects from the theater orchestra.

By 1929 talkies like Victor Fleming's outdoor " The Virginian " and von Sternberg's German-made " The Blue Angel " succeeded in shaking off the restrictions at first imposed by the mechanics of sound-recording. A French movie, René Clair's " *Sous les Toits de Paris*," indicated to what an extent intelligently used sound could become an asset. The screen quickly regained its range and wealth of pictorial expression, dialog became briefer, less continuous, and more natural. In the brilliantly edited " Mickey Mouse " and " Silly Symphonies," the animated cartoons equipped with sound have shown a new vitality and inventiveness beyond that displayed by other branches of the art.

The influence of many remarkable films made in Soviet Russia has not been very marked. The Russian directors, of whom Pudovkin and Eisenstein are best known, avowedly derive in part from D. W. Griffith. With a metronomic, machine-gun fire of rapid and realistic shots (usually close-ups) in place of the customary sustained scenes, they have achieved an almost physical intensity of expression. The present tendency to choose players physically well-suited to interpret each part rather than established favorites may well be due to them. But their influence in this country was more noticeable in an increase of productions with a sociological flavor, such as " I Am a Fugitive from the Chain Gang " and " Wild Boys of the Road."

The many types of films — documentary, spectacular, historical, Western, comedy-drama, slapstick, animated cartoon — were established in the early days of the cinema. Not a single type has yet been fully developed, though recent years have seen considerable advance both in photography, *décor*, and acting, and three or four notable extensions in the technical use of the medium. From the first, progress has been retarded by the necessity for producing companies to entertain their immense public, their consequent neglect to explore the innate possibilities of the film itself and their insistence on proven ingredients and glamorous personalities. Almost all purely experimental movies have been the work of amateurs — painters like Charles Sheeler, Fernand Leger, Viking Eggeling, Salvador Dali (on whose scenario the striking surrealist *" L'Age d'Or "* was based), Jean Cocteau, with his surrealist *" Le Sang d'un Poète,"* or Melville Webber and Dr. Watson whose " Fall of the House of Usher " and " Lot in Sodom " were among the most interesting non-commercial films made in this country.[1] Very seldom, as with " The Cabinet of Dr. Caligari " and Chaplin's " A Woman of Paris," and then only under special conditions, have experimental films been made within the industry itself.

Another grave detriment has been the passing of almost all motion-picture theaters into the hands of the producing companies, so that mass-produced films are automatically poured out through chain-store theaters. The result is necessarily mediocre, as though all book publishers and booksellers strove to issue nothing but best-sellers. Good films are produced and are sometimes overwhelmingly successful, whether nationally advertised (as is usual with superfilms good or bad), or whether brought back time and again by popular demand.

---

[1] The documentary film has recently sponsored some of the most interesting and original work done in America, but this special branch of cinematography lies outside the scope of this brief survey. — *I. B.*

Others are shown only in a fugitive way to small, and often the wrong, audiences or cannot find an outlet at all.

Much could be done to remedy this state of affairs by organization on the part of discontented filmgoers. It has been proved that active local demand can dictate what shall be shown in neighborhood houses. Much could also be done by discriminating film fans with letters written to producing companies and to cinemas. These would not be disregarded. Unfortunately, it is usually the undiscriminating and not the critical filmgoers who write letters. Nevertheless, it is undoubtedly in the hands of the few creative directors and of the general public that the future of this great twentieth-century art still lies. They will determine whether it shall remain, as now, largely a diversion in which mere photography and secondhand theater play all too large a part or shall develop fully its unique methods of expression.

II

RECENT TRENDS IN AMERICAN MOTION PICTURES

Edwin Ziegfeld

Visually, the most significant of recent developments has been the increased use of *color film*. Color is by no means new (the first color film was released in 1916), but until the introduction of the Technicolor process it remained distinctly a novelty. It is interesting to note that the introduction of color in the pictures was in many ways reminiscent of the introduction of talking pictures, indeed, of the introduction of the pictures themselves, in that people were satisfied at first merely to see objects in color (demonstrated by the many short subjects of circuses and flower gardens and similarly colorful subjects and events that first appeared) and that only portions of feature pictures were produced in color. When the motion-picture public had been prepared and indicated approval, full-length pictures in color were produced and distributed. Attempts have been made to use the emotional aspects of color, as in " *La Cucaracha*," for whose color Robert Edmond Jones was responsible. We can look forward to its more significant use as an expressive medium as it becomes further incorporated into motion-picture production.

Another innovation has been the development of *full-length animated cartoons*, the first being Walt Disney's "Snow White." Only a few such pictures have been produced, but the phenomenal success of "Snow White" has assured the continuance of this new type of feature picture, offering as it does a medium remarkably suited to the portrayal of comic and imaginative themes.

Perhaps the most significant recent development in the motion pictures has been the change and increase in popularity of *documentary* films. They are by no means new. News reels are, of course, of a documentary nature, and they have occupied an accepted place in motion-picture programs for many years. In character they are comparable to superficial reporting, such as one might get in newspaper headlines. There have also been travelogs that have enjoyed unfailing popularity for many years, but for the most part they have dealt with foreign lands and peoples and with scenes and events that had little or no relation to our own lives. They were planned primarily as diversion, but with a strong educational flavor. The change that has taken place in documentary motion-picture production is that there is now a distinct tendency to be concerned with immediate and often controversial issues.

Pare Lorenz' films, "The River" and "The Plow That Broke the Plains," produced in connection with the Farm Security Administration, were the first in this country to attract wide attention. They both deal with questions of importance that are facing the country today, presenting in a factual, if somewhat dramatized, form the issues that have arisen in connection with rapacious deforestation and unwise plowing under of the Western grasslands.

This documentary development began in England before it did in this country. For many years the British Post Office produced films that were visual documents of various areas and activities in Great Britain, such as "The Fishing Banks of Skye" and "Airmail." Paul Rotha, in writing of the production of documentary films in England, observes: "It has raised the movie from its status of providing popular amusement to a status of dignity and public service" (12). In this country "The March of Time" has introduced, in its own words, "a new type of pictorial journalism."

Another noteworthy development has been the founding of *film libraries* to preserve and make available to the public the great films that have been produced. The two most famous are at the Museum of Modern Art in New York City and the British Film Institute in London. The Museum of Modern Art, as part of its regular program, has frequent showings of many of the famous films that have been carefully selected and preserved, indicating that the motion picture, the youngest of the arts, has become conscious and proud of its own development.

III

THE MOTION PICTURE AS ART AND AS PATRON OF THE ARTS

MILTON S. FOX

The motion picture provides the means of selecting and juxtaposing fragments of the visible world in such a way as to sublimate details, as to make the part greater and more expressive than the whole. The forcefulness of the medium derives largely from the fact that the whole repertory of natural shapes, animate and inanimate, great or small, elemental or tentative, is the substance with which the creator deals. From these he strips their incidental and casual character, their fortuitous surroundings, their transient significance.

No other medium can achieve this in quite so definitive and immediate a manner. Powerful as the visual image is in any case, much more powerful is the image-in-time. In the best of motion-picture usage, it most closely parallels our mental activities, in sleeping or in waking hours, and in the in-between states of floating reverie. The cinema artist can revive the past and dress a cherished moment for us with all the tinsel loveliness of errant memories — and at the next instant crush it with the bare truth. He can speed up time, or slow it down. He is free from all the restraints of the earth-bound body. With the arbitrariness of a whim he disdains gravity, opacity, distance, condition, distinctions between real and imagined things, between physical objects and mental events. The microscopic can momentarily fill the whole of the conscious mind, can become the sole existing reality. Or, suddenly, infinite vistas may be presented, great magnitudes and vast armies; the catastrophes of nature can be documented. There is no event too heroic or massive, no action too commonplace, no shading of mood or thought too slight to be bodied forth in this art. The incredibility of the fairy tale and the myth, which has fascinated man almost since the beginning, has been reinstated and verified by the camera and sound track: flowers sing, they grow old, wither, and change into something else before our very eyes; we may be in more than one place at one time; inanimate things have sentience; we hear the voices of the dead. There is absolutely no limitation, in short, to the movies' treatment of time, place, bulk, or any of the other material exigencies of actual being — of what we might call 'the logic of everyday reality.'

The heart of this art form is the selection of images of crucial significance, no matter what they may be, and the conditioning of these images by preceding and subsequent images to make a series; and, again, the same process as regards these image-series. Image follows image, conditioning, qualifying, sometimes coalescing with one another. Cinema style is analogous to poetic expression, as distinguished from prosaic: it distils and enforces; it speaks through metaphor, simile, figures of speech; it evokes; it endows the commonplace and humble with greatness and power and surprise.

The artist of the pictures has at his disposal a multitude of camera effects, effects of lighting, processing, and trick-work. He can make use of illusions, printed words, or drawings and animations. In parallel or in counterpoint to the visual image he may use all varieties of sound, natural, musical, industrial, or speech, or silence. He has as movement, action in the photographed objects — horses running, men fighting; movement in the camera, which approaches, turns from side to side, swoops, falters; and finally, the movement that comes from cutting — the phrasing: a staccato succession of short shots, or alternations of short and long, or a continued flow of the same sort of material. Through the 'fade,' the 'dissolve,' the 'wipe,' the 'iris-in' and 'iris-out,' alteration of focus, and other devices, he bridges from idea to idea, further qualifying and conditioning mind and image. All of these may be varied endlessly through all sorts of rhythmic effects. The treatment of sound adds further complexities; and color, properly used, has tremendous esthetic possibilities in connection with the representational, the abstract, and the fantasy film. The great masters who will be able to mold these vast materials according to their intuitions are yet to come. We are still the primitives in the ways of this art.

It will be noted that I have not mentioned actors. This omission is deliberate, since the essence of the art is the cutting and assembling of vital and pertinent images, no matter who or what the identity of objects from which the images are made. In a picture dealing with human activities, it is obvious that satisfactory actors will contribute more than unsatisfactory ones; but to say that a picture is competently acted does not yet say that it is a good example of motion-picture art.

These notes only hint at the formal and esthetic problems of the motion pictures. The mass-produced pictures of Hollywood plants are often of genuinely impressive quality, but still more often the exigencies of the market and of profit stultify the creative imagination. The result is that the run of Hollywood pictures bears the same relation to great motion-picture art as popular magazine literature does to great, or even good, writing. Hollywood's pictures — and magazine ' literature ' — evidently meet important popular needs; but those interested in the art of the motion picture are determined that its future shall not be neglected because of unrelieved subservience to these needs.

The motion-picture industry increasingly becomes a patron of the other arts. Artists are needed to design sets, to make sketches on location, to make compositional sketches for proposed shots. Architects are needed for structures of all sorts; sculptors; art historians; lighting and photographic experts; interior decorators; costume designers, fashion designers; make-up experts; experts at hairdressing — all these and their allied crafts are needed. For sound in general are needed (not to mention the technical side) composers, arrangers, historians, instrumentalists of all kinds, experts at sound effects. Scenario and script are the work of writers, sometimes especially trained in the field, often individuals who have made a name in *belles-lettres;* some beautiful dialog comes our way occasionally on the screens of America. That branch of the industry that gives itself over to the creation of animated cartoon pictures (perhaps the most daring and brilliant side of the industry today) utilizes the services of hundreds of artists in all kinds of tasks, from the most routine to the extremely creative.

References

(1) BARDECHE, M., and BRASILLACH, R. *The History of Motion Pictures.* (W. W. Norton and Co.: New York, 1938) 412 pp.

(2) COMMISSION ON EDUCATION AND CULTURAL FILMS. *The Film in National Life.* (George Allen and Unwin: London, 1932)

(3) DALE, EDGAR. *How to Appreciate Motion Pictures.* (The Macmillan Co.: New York, 1933)

(4) DALE, EDGAR. *The Content of Motion Pictures.* (The Macmillan Co.: New York, 1935)

(5) HAMPTON, B. B. *A History of the Movies.* (Civici: New York, 1931) 456 pp.

(6) NAUMBERG, NANCY. *We Make the Movies.* (W. W. Norton and Co.: New York, 1937)

(7) NICOLL, ALLARDYCE. *Film and Theater.* (Thomas Y. Crowell Co.: New York, 1936)

(8) NILSEN, VLADIMIR S. *The Cinema as a Graphic Art.* (George Newnes, Ltd.: London, 1937)

(9) RAND, H. M., and LEWIS, R. *Film and School.* (D. Appleton-Century Co.: New York, 1937) 182 pp.

(10) ROTHA, PAUL. *Celluloid: the Film Today.* (Longmans, Green, and Co.: New York, 1933)

(11) ROTHA, PAUL. *Documentary Film.* (American Photographic Publishing Co.: Boston, 1939) 272 pp.

(12) ROTHA, PAUL. *Movie Parade.* (The Studio Publications, Inc.: New York, 1936)

(13) SELDES, GILBERT V. *The Movies Come from America.* (Charles Scribner's Sons: New York, 1937) 120 pp.

(14) THORP, M. F. *America at the Movies.* (Yale University Press: New Haven, 1939)

CHAPTER XV

TELEVISION

Alfred H. Morton
Vice-President in Charge of Television
National Broadcasting Company
New York, New York

Before our eyes a new miracle in mass communication is taking shape. Television, long heralded and much publicized, has made its debut in America, thus marking the beginning of the second phase of an invention in which many millions of dollars and more than a decade's intense labor by hundreds of scientists and practical engineers have been invested.

Years have gone into the development of television; the measure of its use in actual day-to-day telecasting is in months. Despite its extreme infancy, however, telecasting has already given some amazing demonstrations of its significance. Some of these have attracted nationwide press comment. The opening of the New York World's Fair was hardly more notable, and probably future historians will consider it less so, than the telecast of President Franklin Delano Roosevelt, Sir Lewis Beale, and others who delivered addresses in the Court of Peace on the Sunday afternoon of April 30, 1939.

Later, but still within the year, the National Broadcasting Company, which instituted the country's first regular high-definition service in television, presented a succession of significant programs over its New York City station. Among these were telecasts of certain major sports events, the visit of King George VI and Queen Elizabeth to the New York World's Fair, many dramas presented in our studios, and several parades, including the entry of the United States Army's famous ' Iron Horses ' into New York City. Of particular interest to the educator were several television book reviews, art presentations, a lesson in photoelectricity by Dr. C. C. Clark, of New York University, and a demonstration of ' brain waves.' Dr. Georg Roemmert presented his microvivarium, revealing the bacterial life in a drop of water by means of a projection microscope, to the amazed members of our television audience.

Enough has been said to indicate something of the scope of the infant industry. Something of television's potentialities has been envisioned by David Sarnoff, president of the Radio Corporation of America. " The ultimate contribution of television," he said, " will be its service towards unification of the life of the nation and, at the same time, the greater development of the life of the individual." Again, it is " a new art so important in its implications that it is bound to affect all society. It is an art which shines like a torch of hope in a troubled world. It is a creative force which we must learn to utilize for the benefit of all mankind."

It may be well to define television. Television is concerned with the transmission and reproduction, by electrical communication methods, of transient images in motion. It finds its subjects in the television studio and in the field, and in the vast resources of entertainment and educational material stored in motion-picture film. On occasion it may, and does, resort to still photographs, maps, and documents, to illustrate certain types of program.

Few persons in the United States have witnessed television at work either in the field or in the studio. Its cameras, in both instances, are nearly as mobile as motion-picture cameras, and although the mobile equipment at present operated by NBC must be transported in two large motor vans, newer apparatus recently delivered is so compact that a complete basic unit for wire-line relay may be carried in an ordinary motor car.

Electronic television, as developed by the Radio Corporation of America, has as its basis two large vacuum tubes. Both are inventions of Vladimir K. Zworykin. Dr. Zworykin's pick-up device is called the 'Iconoscope.' His reproduction tube bears the name of 'Kinescope.' These tubes are, of course, without a single moving mechanical part, as is the entire electronic system of television.

It is not the place here to discuss in detail the structure of this marvelously ingenious system. Those who are interested may refer to more extended discussions, both popular and technical. The iconoscope, which has been called a ' light microphone,' has the function of registering an optional image, of translating it into electrical terms, and of dissecting the resultant electrical image into its elements in a definite, predetermined manner. To carry out this operation the iconoscope has a photosensitve plate, corresponding to the film in an ordinary camera, which registers the image and converts it to electrical values. These are released by an electron beam in the tube, which explores each part of the plate in turn.

Owing to this operation, the television image issues from the iconoscope as a series of electrical impulses of varying strength, corresponding to the light intensities comprised in the optical image. Magnified a millionfold, these impulses are eventually radiated from the television antenna array to home receivers.

In the receiver the kinescope is the instrument that converts the electrical impulses into a visible image. The kinescope is a funnel-shaped tube on the large end of which the image is traced in a translucent and fluorescent screen. Within the neck of the tube is an electron gun that focuses a beam of electrons on this screen. At the point of contact it creates a spot of light that varies in intensity with the strength of the beam. The beam itself is drawn over the screen by electromagnetic means. The incoming impulses modulate the beam, thus varying the intensity of the light spot from instant to instant as it proceeds over the screen. Since the entire image is scanned thirty times a second, the illusion of a composite, moving image is created.

The television image, as transmitted at the present time, under technical standards adopted by the radio industry, is in 441 horizontal scanning-lines. The usual reproduction tube creates an image in black and white. The size of the image depends on the diameter of the tube, of which the largest now available in commercial receivers gives an image approximately eight inches by ten inches in size.

Apparatus based on this system has been installed at Radio City for the telecasting of live talent productions and motion pictures. In the field, as I have mentioned, mobile equipment is mounted in motor vans for the coverage of public events of news value, sports contests, and other happenings or scenes of general public interest. This mobile unit has relayed programs over a directed radio beam from points as far distant as twenty-seven miles from the NBC transmitter in the Empire State Building tower. The service area of our transmitter, in turn, extends more than fifty miles in all directions from the building. In this area, I believe, reside more than 20,000,000 persons.

Our own station will shortly be joined in telecasting, in the eastern part of the United States, by that of the General Electric Company near Schenectady, and the Columbia Broadcasting System's station in New York City. On the Pacific Coast, the Los Angeles station operated by the Don Lee Broadcasting System is already on the air regularly with high definition television.

The problems of television programming have, naturally, been explored more deeply by our organization since we took the air regularly last year. Prior to 1939, however, NBC had transmitted experimentally for a period of nearly three years, with the object of acquiring a knowledge of the rudiments of television showmanship. This, I must point out, is a highly important element. For regardless of the merits of any given program material, it is sure to lack appeal unless it is presented with a certain zest and skill that implies a knowledge of the methods of catching and holding the interest of large audiences.

The demands on the performer are, therefore, very heavy. I use the word *performer* here in its broadest sense, to include speakers, educators, and every kind of non-professional who appears before the Iconoscope cameras. The material to be presented must be thoroughly mastered, so that there shall be no halting in the delivery; yet the presentation must be characterized by a certain spontaneity.

The use of several cameras simultaneously makes it possible to present to the viewer that interesting variety of ' angles ' and ' shots ' that Hollywood technique has made familiar in motion pictures. Television has adopted this technique; it has been found most helpful to alternate close-ups, where small detail is to be emphasized, and longer views that depict the overall scene. Citing an example of peculiar interest to educators, we focused on Dr. C. C. Clark and his apparatus for intercepting and recording ' brain waves,' then switched to a close-up of the needle tracing the record on a paper tape. In the telecast of Dr. Roemmert, again, we were able to give the viewer an image of the entire equipment, of the principal placing his drop of water on a slide and then under the microscope. By a quick switch to another camera we immediately shifted to a view showing the creatures living and moving in the water. Both these programs were fine examples of the educational job that can be done by television.

The responsibility for the presentation rests on the director. It is he who rehearses his characters and cameramen before the program goes on the air. He also sits in the control room during the actual telecast and performs a function analogous to that of the film editor in Hollywood. The apparatus is so arranged that the images registered by the several cameras in the studio are visible to him in this control room, so that he may choose which one will telecast from moment to moment. This method of production, which suggests at once the techniques of the stage, the motion picture, and radio, also suggests the future possibilities of a distinctive art form.

Program material at the disposal of the director should be of the widest range. It must certainly encompass the entire scope of present-day sound broadcasting and include, additionally, much that is now found unsuitable to radio. There may, however, be a considerable difference in the balance of the program schedule. Today's radio emphasizes those programs that may be enjoyed without the aid of vision. Thus music has been heavily emphasized. Television, naturally, will turn to those subjects where visibility adds materially to the enjoyment, or the usefulness, of a program. The visual arts, therefore, should at last find encouragement in a radio art.

Already, I may point out, we have presented a brief series of art programs in an endeavor to develop methods of popularizing painting and sculpture. We hope to do for the visual arts something that sound broadcasting has done for music. It is common knowledge, I believe, that sound broadcasting has made musical classics appreciated on a wider scale than ever before in our history. The task will be difficult, perhaps, but with the coöperation of persons interested in a broader dissemination of knowledge of the arts I feel certain that much can be done in this direction.

The drama is an obvious and rich source of program material and one we are already exploiting with considerable success. Politics and government, too, should take on new meaning for the average man and woman through the medium of television. News events are of highest importance. For it is here that television's unique quality of instantaneous visual transmission of scenes takes on its most spectacular guise. The suspense that inheres in a happening the outcome of which still remains unknown — this in itself would guarantee television's success.

But far less spectacular material will also find new opportunities in television. Dr. Roemmert's program, for instance, opened up a new and fascinating world to lookers-in. And I am sure that a majority of our audience found a recent cooking lesson, a demonstration of the making of an apple strudel, an exciting event. Within these limits, most of those who have the gift of teaching the masses of our citizens will find ample scope for their activities.

Before such things can come to pass on a broad scale, however, television has some perplexing problems of its own to solve. First among these is the creation of a network, first regional and then national, to carry television to American homes. I am happy to report prospects are very bright for the creation of a limited network within a comparatively short time. The introduction of an ingenious automatic radio relay, now ready for practical tests, should give considerable impetus to the spread of television.

Our great problem, however, is economic. We believe that if television is to be forever free of the danger of regimentation, such as characterizes sound broadcasting at present in some nations of Europe, then it must be developed within the framework of the American system of radio broadcasting. Television must earn its own keep. Fortunately, television has qualities that, I firmly believe, will enlist the support of American business and industry. Our experiments with advertising programs confirm this belief. So that eventually, when television offers a daily schedule of many hours of varied programs, the entire structure should be supported by the comparatively small percentage of sponsored presentations. This system has made American sound broadcasting successful and free; it can do as much for television, so that through it, as Mr. Sarnoff has written, "America will rise to new heights as a nation of free people and high ideals."

REFERENCES

(1) BRAGDON, E. L. *Television Amateur's Handbook*. (Thomas Y. Crowell Co.: New York, 1939)
(2) KIRBY, P. *Victory of Television*. (Harper and Brothers: New York, 1939)
(3) MOSELEY, S. A., and McKAY, H. *Television*. (Oxford University Press: New York, 1939)

CHAPTER XVI

DANCING [1]

JOHN MARTIN
Dance Critic
The New York *Times*
New York, New York

In her autobiography, which was still in manuscript when she met her tragic death in 1927, Isadora Duncan recorded her " vision of America dancing," and the dance she saw was one of such heroic sweep and nobility as to match the prophecy of Whitman that she paraphrased. It was " the living leap of the child springing towards the heights, towards its future accomplishment, towards a new great vision of life that would express America."

It was many years earlier that Walt Whitman wrote:

> I hear America singing, the varied carols I hear. . . .
> Each singing what belongs to him or her and to none else.

But his prophecy, for all its priority, is still for the future, while hers is in the process of being fulfilled. America is dancing, and just such a " new great vision of life " infuses its dance. It is fairly safe to assume that Isadora would not recognize it as the dance of which she spoke, for its forms have departed radically from her forms; but it is nonetheless deeply and fundamentally the fruit of her prophecy, her ideal, her work. As her great insurgency in the closing years of the century dated an epoch in the arts, so at the end of her life her foresight led her to announce the arrival of a new period.

It is possible now to look back and see that in that space of two years of which Isadora's death marks almost the middle point, many of the individual forces that have put their mark upon the new movement began to emerge. For example, in the spring of 1926 Martha Graham made her New York début as an independent artist; the same

---

[1] Excerpts quoted with minor changes from *America Dancing*, by permission of the author and of the publishers (Dodge Publishing Co.: New York, 1936). Pp. 3f., 36f., 289f.

year the dance was introduced into a university for the first time in history as a major subject leading to a degree, at the University of Wisconsin under the direction of Margaret H'Doubler; Tamiris made her début in 1927, and the same year for the first time in history three New York newspapers established independent departments of dance criticism; the following spring, Doris Humphrey and Charles Weidman left the ranks of Denishawn and appeared with their own concert company. On such bases and others like them has been built the contemporary dance movement that has become labeled as ' modern.' The decade that has passed since then has served to bring into focus these and other influences and events, which in their own time seemed unrelated and without significance, and to give shape and direction to the period.

To be sure, there is still a widespread incomprehension of what is taking place in the dance. Only yesterday it was the last word in frivolity, and no one of serious mind gave it more than passing attention; now it has become the most active and the most serious of American arts. The dance is very obviously confined no longer to the categories of amusement and recreation, but has achieved notable proportions in the fields of art and education as well.

There have been no subsidies such as have been lavished upon symphony orchestras, opera companies, and art museums over the country; there has not even been any assistance from the ordinary commercial agencies, which have stood aloof, according to their ancient practice, from all but the showier attractions from abroad. The dancers themselves and a few enthusiastic laymen have simply rolled up their sleeves and gone to work. They have faced financial losses, gratuitous insults, and what is probably harder to bear than either, a generous measure of indifference in high places, but the result of their efforts is a mass of conclusive evidence all testifying to the existence of a large and vital interest in the various branches of the dance from one end of the country to the other.

There is, to begin with, the professional field in New York, which has become the dance capital of the world. Whereas in 1926 it would have been difficult to force the total number of dance events in a single season up to as many as fifty, there were in the season of 1935–1936 upwards of three hundred. These figures do not include any subsidiary dance performances, such as those which are introduced into the operas, the Broadway revues, or the moving picture presentations, but consist entirely of independent recitals, ballet performances, lectures, and the like, given during the regular season between the first of October and the first of June.

Though these subsidiary fields do not concern the present survey directly, they are worth notice even at the cost of a digression, for they have their own tale to tell. With the reorganization of the Metropolitan Opera Company at the beginning of the 1935 season, the ballet began to come into its own there after a generation of virtual banishment. The old régime, always inclined to be suspicious of the dance, had its predisposition in this direction strongly reënforced when in 1916 and 1917, against the advice of its then new director, it sponsored the Diaghileff ballet for two seasons and lost half a million dollars in the venture. Since then the dance program at the opera house has been negligible until, with the reorganization, it was put into the hands of the American Ballet. In all the years between the Diaghileff *tournées* and the reorganization, the opera presented a total of six ballets, which is one less than the number offered in the first season of the new régime.

In the matter of resident ballet companies, the one at Radio City certainly cannot be ignored, for it holds the world's record for consecutive performances. When it is considered that this company has been continuously active since it opened under the direction of Leon Staats at the Roxy Theater in 1927, and that its schedule averages thirty performances a week, its grand total is seen to mount to staggering figures. By the end of the season of 1935–1936 it had passed the fourteen-thousand mark. In order to equal this record, even with the feature of consecutiveness disregarded, an ordinary opera ballet would have to have given two performances a week all the year round since 1801, which, as it happens, is the very year when the son of Catherine the Great summoned Didelot from Paris to remake the Imperial Russian Ballet.

In the field of revue and musical comedy, dancing has always played a considerable part, so that the difference here to be noted is not so much a quantitative as a qualitative one. The old days of drilling chorus girls, precision units, acrobatic adagio teams, and hotcha specialists have given way completely to an era of better taste, more imagination, and greater skill. What is more remarkable in the theater field is the extent to which the dance has become an integral part of so-called ' legitimate ' productions. Dancers have collaborated, both as performers and directors, in any number of independent productions, and the Group Theater, followed by several younger organizations, has consistently included dance instruction as a regular part of the rehearsal schedule, no matter what the play. In this, to be sure, it is only following the long-established custom of the best Continental theaters.

In this connection, Hallie Flanagan, director of the Federal Theater Project of the WPA, declared:

> It is impossible to think of the modern theater, without thinking of the dance. The theater director, learning from such unconscious sources as " Mickey Mouse," " Aeschylus," " Mei Lan-Fang," and " The Daring Young Man on the Flying Trapeze," gradually realizes that he must have a movement score as well as a script. Particularly on a stage such as that of a Federal Theater Project, where there can be no lavish expenditure for scenery and costumes, where the actors must move us without benefit of Bergdorf-Goodman, it is necessary for the director to learn the hard lessons of the dancer — how to emphasize and distort line, how to assault by color, how to design in space.

Thanks to Mrs. Flanagan's high evaluation of the dance, the Federal Theater Project authorized in January, 1936, the creation of a Federal Dance Theater, with Don Oscar Becque as its director, Glück-Sandor, Doris Humphrey, Felicia Sorel, Tamiris, and Charles Weidman as supervisors, and provision for a company of 185 dancers.

But all these things by no means tell the whole story. The stability of the dance as an independent enterprise must depend on something stronger than any number of New York performances. From the financial standpoint many of these are actually given at a loss, in spite of capacity audiences, for their entire initial investment must be covered by a single performance, or perhaps two. From the standpoint of healthy national significance, such a comparatively small audience as these performances can reach might very well constitute, as they have sometimes been accused of doing, nothing more vital than a select group of connoisseurs, a clique. From both points of view, the test of the issue rests with the country at large, for here is where the dancer must turn for a livelihood, and here also he must arrive at a *rapprochement* with popular taste. That test is now being made with notable results.

Until fairly recently, ' the road ' offered little reward for American dance attractions, for they had, and still have, by and large, no money to spend on publicity build-ups. By the slow and laborious bootstrap method, however, the situation has been changed, and the improvement is now gaining of its own momentum.

The season of 1935–1936 found no fewer than twenty-two dance attractions on tour, sixteen of which were of native origin. When it is realized that this number compares very favorably with the number of theatrical productions that toured during the same season, it becomes evident that something is stirring. Nor were these tours merely little fly-by-night affairs. Ted Shawn, for example, played nearly 140 dates with his company of men dancers, and Carola Goya and Angna Enters both covered the country pretty thoroughly in all four directions. The previous season, Doris Humphrey and Charles Weidman and their company leaped rather perilously about between Canada and Texas on the first tour to be attempted by a company of American dancers of the modern school, and later both Tamiris and her group and Martha Graham ventured forth on extended travels with a success that surprised even themselves.

It is perhaps less spectacular that the De Basil *Ballet Russe* has for several seasons played a fabulous number of engagements on the road, for European attractions have always had a definite advantage in this respect through the coöperation of the commercial managements. The reason for this coöperation is to be found no doubt in part in the fact that these managements are generally directed by men of European origin and background, who naturally lean to the kind of dancing on which they have been brought up, and in part in the fact that there is a ready-made box-office appeal in what the local manager of the De Basil troupe has described as " a kind of three-ring circus of the arts." Nevertheless, this company's success on tour is not without significance in measuring the American appetite for dancing of all sorts.

The manifestations of interest outside New York are significant and many. Local centers have arisen in almost every section not only to sponsor touring attractions, but to produce their own dance movements as well. The activity on the Pacific Coast, for example, is second only to that of the New York area. Chicago, Cleveland, Detroit, Philadelphia, Baltimore, Boston, have all developed their own fields to greater or lesser degree, and no doubt the same thing has taken place in other localities. Without the trumpetings of high-powered press agents, such achievements are likely to make little noise outside their immediate environs.

Perhaps the most widespread type of independent center is the community in which there is an even fairly progressive college. The interest of the colleges, especially the women's colleges, is little short of amazing, and the twofold contribution that this interest is making to the subject can scarcely be overestimated. From the cultural standpoint, it is preparing an audience qualitatively, and from the commer-

cial standpoint it is creating an audience numerically. The result thus
far is that some of the best dance audiences, both in size and intelligence, are to be found in towns that are scarcely on the map at all as
far as population goes. The climax of this achievement to date is the
annual festival held at Bennington, Vermont, in connection with the
summer dance school of Bennington College. Here in the summer of
1934 was held the first American dance festival, and the quiet little
New England town began to hear itself referred to as " the Salzburg of
America " and " a choreographic Bayreuth."

Both in the colleges and the lower schools, especially those which
are known as ' progressive,' the teaching of dancing has become a matter of great interest, and there is scarcely a national or a regional convention of the American Physical Education Association or the Progressive Education Association that does not pay considerable attention
to this newest educational medium. In at least six colleges it is possible to major in the dance and to obtain either a B.S. or an A.B. degree.
What this movement will necessarily do toward the building of a
nation-wide audience capable of a highly intelligent response to dancing
is self-evident, though its full fruits will not be seen, perhaps, for another generation.

Other forces are also at work in the same ultimate direction. There
are, for example, the workers' groups, such as the New Dance League
and the Rebel Arts, with branches in many cities, which not only sponsor periodical professional performances, but, what is more important,
develop recreational groups for laymen who wish to learn to dance
for their own pleasure. Certain individual trade unions carry on the
same idea. The International Ladies Garment Workers Union, for
one, has in the neighborhood of two hundred students in its New York
classes.

In the department of lay dancing, there has been a notable revival
of interest in the folk-dance throughout the country, and festivals
held in the parks of Manhattan and Brooklyn have drawn crowds of
more than twenty thousand. A large and thriving business is conducted from coast to coast in the teaching of ballroom dances, and
another sizable industry is devoted to their practice. The public
dance hall may not be a particularly elevating place of assembly, the
profession of ' taxi-dancer ' may not be one to which the ambitious
would aspire, but the prevalence of both of them is indicative of the
hold of the dance on large sections of the general public.

It is not yet possible to report much progress in the films, for in spite of the magnificent opportunities offered by such a medium, nothing of any consequence has been accomplished. Most of the banalities that have passed from the revue have found themselves magnified a thousandfold in the sumptuous revels of the screen musicals. To be sure, Fred Astaire, Bill Robinson, and Escudero have spread their excellences over a much wider sphere than they could have otherwise done, but in the solider realm everything remains for the future.

Public libraries in various parts of the country have begun to make collections of dance books, no doubt inspired by the success of the still small, but growing, collection instituted by Dorothy Lawton in the Music Branch of the New York Public Library, of which she is librarian. Under Miss Lawton's general supervision, a remarkable bibliographical project has been started by the W.P.A., which, when completed, will rank as one of the greatest sources of dance reference to be found anywhere.

Courses in dance ' appreciation ' have begun to be established in various schools and museums in a number of cities, where the layman is enabled to make an intelligent contact with the dance. The model for these courses is the annual lecture-demonstration series that the New School for Social Research started in New York as long ago as 1931.

Certain churches have introduced, or rather reintroduced, the subject of dancing in religious ritual; the dance has been applied to therapy, and, indeed, there is practically no field in which some trace of it is not to be found.

The causes for this great increase of interest have been the source of much questioning. Is it that as a nation we are becoming more esthetically minded? Examination of the other art fields would scarcely uphold such a theory. Though there is, no doubt, a rise to be noted in the level of nearly all the other arts, none of them can report anything so spectacular in the way of growth, nor has the general rise in level in any of them been characterized by a heightened estheticism, but quite the reverse. . .

As a matter of fact, it had its beginnings as long ago as the turn of the century, when Isadora brought a new concept of dancing to the world, and except for a certain lapse during the abnormal war years, it has been progressing steadily ever since. When the character of this new concept is given its due consideration, the whole question resolves itself. It is not that we have lifted our heads higher into the clouds esthetically, but rather that the dance has come down to earth.

It has taken its stand against pedantry and become popular. It has refused to be a class art any longer and has made up its mind to be a mass art. All its manifestations in America from the very beginning have been characterized by this tendency, but only now has it gained sufficient momentum to make itself clearly understood.

Back in the romantic beginnings of the last century, the dance became imbued with an etherealism that clung to it assiduously up to our own day. The *spirituelle* Taglioni and her sisterhood left a legacy of such supernatural creatures as *sylphides* and *willis;* numerous enchanted princesses were transformed into swans and released by Love; endless successions of *papillons* and *libellules* fluttered through the air with insect daintiness; flowers waltzed, and roses shed their petals in sentimental tragedy.

Indeed, the nineteenth-century dance world concerned itself almost exclusively with coquetry, acrobatics, and horticultural and zoölogical impersonations. There was never a touch of genuine human emotion, of the life of the contemporary world, or of anything tainted with the actualities of experience. Even down to our own day the finest dancers spent their genius on " The Sleeping Beauty," " The Fairy Doll," " California Poppy," and the like. A random glance at current programs reveals how differently our leading contemporary dancers are occupied. Here we find such items as " Strike," " Heretic," " Cycle of Unrest," " Traditions," " Atavisms," " Stock Exchange," " Lynch Town," " Strange American Funeral," " Work and Play," " Harvest 1935," " American Provincials," " Dominion." Though they are not all in this iron vein, the accent has shifted completely away from the safely remote and romantic realm of flora and fauna to the immediate world of men and women. " Willis " and " libellules " are left to do their airy pirouetting for the aloof spirits who inhabit their heaven of well-bred dreams, and only one heaven below them are to be found the ' esthetic ' and ' serpentine,' and the general ' fancy ' dancers, waving their pretty scarfs for disembodied lovers of Beauty.

It is frequent cause for comment that the audience seen at dance performances of the contemporary type is made up predominantly of young people, and in this is to be found the key to the new popularity of the art and a sound prophecy of its future. If the graybeards are satisfied with the old conventional ideas of dancing, the youngsters demand something with more vitality. They have no interest in comparing bits of decorative design with other bits of decorative design for the sake of testing their discipleship; they demand that their personal experience of living be touched. A new order is in the making, and the arts must be made to serve it. No doubt there are also many oldsters, not too set in their ways to change their minds when they are subjected to a new experience, who have embraced the new dance with enthusiasm, but the movement is clearly one of youth. Young people are not usually conspicuous for their patronage of the serious aspects of the arts, and it is therefore distinctly worth noting that this outstanding art movement of our day is a young people's movement. Perhaps it is characteristic of such a movement that it should have turned its back on the lavender and old lace of yesterday, that it should have doffed its high hat, white tie and tails, unwound its chiffon veils, pulled its head in from the stratosphere, and planted its feet solidly on the earth.

The characteristic contribution of the American Negro slave to the arts was the now obsolete minstrel show. Designed originally to entertain the white families on the plantations, it was often considered so successful in specific instances that a white owner would send a whole show intact to neighboring plantations, by way of boasting. After the Civil War, it became a professionalized entertainment, and by the turn of the century had worn itself out, but not before it had made familiar the distinctive qualities of Negro rhythm in both music and dance. Indeed, the Negro musical style that we know as ' blues ' has had an influence outside the bounds of its own field, and the Negro form of the ubiquitous clog dance ranks as the finest development of this almost universal folk manifestation outside Spain. In the ' blues ' there is to be seen the germ of a creative art, as opposed to an art merely of amusement, a slave art. There is also a potentially great art to be developed out of the ingredients of the Negro dance. But as yet these manifestations have not got beyond the folk stage; they are still waiting for the creative artist to use them consciously for their expressional values. When he arises, it will be against heavy odds, for in spite of the formalities of emancipation, Negro art is still expected to be humorous or erotic.

Thus, however great the art of the Indian, which we have virtually never seen, and the art of the American Negro, which has not yet been created, we have no claim to them whatever beyond that of the plantation owner to his minstrels' performances. They are the arts of the subject peoples of America, who go by the separate names of Negroes and Indians. But whether we claim them or not, they are the only American art with any value on the international market. The arts of the white races represented here are all of European origin, and their art is therefore nothing but inferior quality, colonial-grade European art. American dancing consists of jazz and Indian war dances; the dance of Isadora Duncan was Greek; of Ruth St. Denis, Oriental; of Martha Graham and Doris Humphrey, Central-European or some-times frankly German. . .

Obviously, by reason of its materials, it is the dance that has led the way; no other art could possibly have done so. Isadora Duncan and the Turkey Trot, the sublime and ridiculous manifestations of a single impulse, enunciated in their several spheres a common gospel of emancipation. It was a lonely gospel to begin with, but it had the virtue of being demonstrable; and now, with less than a half century of life behind it, it is entering upon its period of universal application. The entrance is as yet a tentative one, but it has got its foot across the threshold, and there is no retreat. The dance must still assume the leadership — must ever do so, indeed — but about it are gathering strong and eager lieutenants, so that at last there is a practical hope for the building of a genuinely kinesthetic generation.

There is, for example, the work that is being done in the field of general education. It is not generally known to what an extent modern education has awakened to the value of the dance, not merely as a kind of finishing-school touch, but as a fundamental instrumentality of the learning process. The tendency to break down the dividing line between psychology and physiology, which has been gaining ground ever since Professor Pavlov's experiments with the conditioned reflex, has resulted naturally in a consideration of the impracticality of trying to educate an isolated section of the individual called ' the mind ' without reference to another isolated section called ' the body.' Latin and mathematics and the like become at once less dominating forces and even less practical mediums of education than those subjects which set up more interplay between the two heretofore separated depart-ments of human behavior. Simultaneously, physical culture, the old business of acquiring large muscles and learning a few elementary prin-ciples of hygiene, has been compelled to retire before physical educa-tion, which concerns itself with the integration of the individual rather than the enlargement of his biceps. In such a program the dance must take an important place in its own right, for the creation of expressional movement, with its synthesis of physical and emotional action, is peculiarly its province.

REFERENCES

(1) BEAUMONT, C. W. *A Short History of Ballet.* (Beaumont: London, 1936) 40 pp.

(2) CHUJOY, A. *Ballet.* (Robert Speller Publishing Corp.: New York, 1936) 108 pp.

(3) CHUJOY, A. *The Symphonic Ballet.* (Kamin: 1939) 47 pp.

(4) HUGHES, R. M. *Dance as an Art-Form.* (A. S. Barnes and Co.: New York, 1933) 198 pp.

(5) KIRSTEIN, L. *Dance.* (G. P. Putnam's Sons: New York, 1935) 369 pp.

(6) LIFAR, S. *Ballet, Traditional to Modern.* (G. P. Putnam's Sons: New York, 1939) 302 pp.

(7) MARTIN, J. *America Dancing.* (Dodge Publishing Co.: New York, 1936) 320 pp.

(8) MARTIN, J. *Introduction to the Dance.* (W. W. Norton and Co., Inc.: New York, 1939) 363 pp.

(9) MARTIN, J. *The Modern Dance.* (A. S. Barnes and Co.: New York, 1933). 123 pp.

(10) SACHS, C. *World History of the Dance.* (W. W. Norton and Co., Inc.: New York, 1937) 469 pp.

(11) SELDEN, E. S. *The Dancer's Quest.* (University of California Press: Berkeley, Calif., 1935) 216 pp.

(12) SHAWN, T. *The American Ballet.* (Henry Holt and Co.: New York, 1926) 136 pp.

(13) STEWART, V. *Modern Dance.* (E. Weyhe: New York, 1935) 155 pp.

CHAPTER XVII

PHOTOGRAPHY

RAYMOND P. ENSIGN
Secretary, The Eastern Arts Association
New York, New York
and
MILTON S. FOX
Instructor, The Cleveland Museum of Art
Instructor, The Cleveland School of Art
Cleveland, Ohio

I

THE ART OF PHOTOGRAPHY

RAYMOND P. ENSIGN

Its devotees maintain, and the rest of us should gratefully agree, that photography is an art. Certainly it is an important field in this day and age. The output ranges from a snapshot of baby in the bath to large photomurals for wall decorations; from a picture reproduced in today's newspaper and then forgotten, to documentary photographs designed for unlimited periods of time.

In what follows we shall consider the development and artistic significance of photography other than in motion pictures.

It is barely a hundred years since Niepce and Daguerre gave the first real start to photographic recording. It is a far cry, however, from those days, when a sitter held a pose for five full minutes in direct sunlight for a single photographic impression, to the present day of high-speed work that records fifty stages in the impact of club against golf ball within the space of 1/1000 of a second.

Though photography was hardly out of its infancy at the time of the Civil War, Matthew Brady made a collection of war pictures at that time that stands as the first such recording of large-scale activities of any kind. Great honor is due him for that accomplishment. The physical handicaps to be overcome were enormous. He had to handle and transport a cumbersome stock of glass plates and negatives, and all his equipment was comparatively crude. How different the case of the news photographer of today with his compact camera, varied lenses, and lightweight, flexible film!

Many of us can remember the photographic studios at the time when the nineteenth century was nearing its end. The painted backdrops of the old stone fence or tasseled drapery, the grip of the viselike headrest (which incidentally did not rest but developed a real 'pain in the neck'), the inadequate lighting and slow lenses made 'watching the birdie' an experience not soon to be forgotten.

About that time George Eastman and others introduced the 'Kodak,' popularized the taking of amateur pictures, and laid the foundations for the present vast use of photography with all its ramifications. The amateur of today has at his command, without excessive financial outlay, a choice of cameras, lenses, films, and accessories to suit his every whim, need, and purpose. He may start with a dollar camera and penny film. If he runs true to form, he will soon be a proud producer of motion and full-color pictures.

Photography since its early days has been held closely akin to painting. Essentially a medium for realistic recording, it was soon recognized to have infinite possibilities for personal interpretation in terms of composition, lighting, choice of subject, subordination of the unessential, as well as projection of character and mood. It has been affected by, and has in turn doubtless affected, the changing trends in the painter's art. In the romantic and realistic period of art that marked the latter part of the nineteenth century, photographers, too, were content with accurate portrayal, flavored with sentimentalism. At the turn of the century, it was perhaps the influence of Impressionism that led to the 'soft focus' era in photography. This simplification and striving for effects naturally called for the same general approach that marked the painter's development of his concept. By this time, too, improved cameras, lenses, emulsions, and printing papers and perfected methods of manipulation made for elasticity in the use of photography as a medium.

Somewhat paralleling the various isms that have arisen in the world of 'modern' art has been the photographer's seizure upon unusual viewpoints, arresting composition (play of line and dark-and-light), sometimes stark realism and an awareness of the interest in social problems. If the painter be free to develop his concept by accent or disregard of the normal physical articulations of the human figure, for instance, the man behind the camera also departs, within his limitations,

and according to his creative fancy, from the traditions and tenets of
more earth-bound souls.

It is in the field of professional and commercial photography that
the outstanding achievements of recent years have taken place. We
have our portrait photographers who catch the underlying character,
perhaps the fleeting mood, and spurn the retouching skill that years
ago reduced all surface textures to smoothed-out masks that effectually covered the subtle variations of the sitters. Renown has come to
many whose talents have led to concentration upon the portrayal of
'children. There are those who specialize in work with animals and,
if portraiture may cover inanimate objects, there is that group which
has the architectural subject as the focus point of its ability.

Supplementing the telegraph, radio, and newspaper column in bringing last-minute happenings to the ken of a waiting world, the news
photographer seems always on the spot and almost as soon presents his
visual record to the preponderantly eye-minded public. In association
with travel pictures, this work has been an important contributing factor in our knowledge and understanding of other peoples throughout
the world.

The marts of trade, through advertising, present an ever-widening
field for photography and call for technical excellence, a broad range
of interest, and real understanding of consumer reactions. There are
varied departments. Some photographers find themselves more than
busy in a single, specialized field, as for example, fashions or food products. As those working into advertising photography soon find out,
technical expertness is important, but it is only one factor in success.
One must be a master of composition (picture arrangement), understand the manipulation of lighting, and be ready to conceive and seize
effective angles of approach. He must have a wide knowledge of the
subject matter. A fashion photographer must know styles and have a
flair for interpreting their characteristics adequately. When foods are
photographed, the camera man must know the correct setting and associated paraphernalia. In all these special fields, the photographer must
be adept at posing and setting up. He must use psychology in handling
models and understand the psychology of the audience to which the
published picture is designed to appeal. The manufacturer or merchandiser who is paying for the picture (and not inconsiderably) may be
interested in art, but first of all he is interested in attracting profitable
orders. In passing, it may be noted that the successful advertising photographer must be a business man himself; he must be able to get busi-

ness, hold it, and produce a reasonable financial return for himself. The overhead in a modern, fully equipped photographic studio is enormous.

Space does not here permit discussion of the many other special fields of modern photography, such as its use in medicine, astronomy, aerial mapping, detection of crime, and many other activities. Photomicrography is fascinating to amateurs and professionals alike. One of the outstanding accomplishments of recent years is the development of super-high-speed photography. When the minute fragments of glass are ' stopped ' mid-air in the smashing of an electric light bulb by hammer blow, we must believe that the exposure was 1/100,000 of a second, though the ordinary human mind finds such a figure vague and incomprehensible.

Youth naturally inquires into the desirability of photography as a vocation and how to go about finding a place in the field. To the question, " Are more photographers needed? " it must be truthfully said that there is no particular need for more photographers, but there is always need for better photography. The young man or woman looking forward to professional participation in this field should have a very good background of training and general culture. An inquiring mind is essential. It must be understood that in any art, there is no such thing as graduating. One must be forever alert to new developments and eager to apply them creatively. In addition to the usual school studies, courses in optics, color, and psychology should be helpful. The attainment of excellence in the technique of photographic processes must, of course, be taken for granted. This may be sought in schools of photography and small studios. Some training in art is highly desirable. The photographer with artistic instinct or with some art training is, of course, most likely to produce artistic results.

II
PHOTOGRAPHY AS A POPULAR ART

Milton S. Fox

There are many students of society who deplore that modern civilization has discouraged handicraft and ' divorced art from life.' They hold that at some other time nearly everybody was an artist, or at least performed an artisan's task of some sort, thus partaking of the spiritual values of the period and a more completely integrated life. The man of the Middle Ages — so runs the argument — or of colonial America built what he needed, adapted it nicely to its function, and hence it was beautiful as an expression of life as well as beautiful in itself, esthetically. Our time, on the other hand, has specialized so highly that our culture is compartmentalized; the average man performs a routine task that allows little reflection, and the arts are of another realm.

That this view is not the whole story is suggested in other articles in this section. What is too often overlooked is the fact that artistic expression may lie in other practices than the traditional ones. For the agencies of creative expression evolve and develop as the substance of the expression itself does, and, as certain practices disappear, others take their place. Modern America has not only brought the traditional arts closer to everyday life through popularizing painting and sculpture and through excellent design of commonplace materials; it has also fostered other means of expression that must be called authentic. Photography is one of these means.

It will not do to argue, as some do, that photography is hopelessly mechanical, that it is less personal than, say, etching or drawing; for, using exactly the same mechanical devices, two photographers may secure two pictures of the same scene that will be as unlike as the versions of two different painters. As a matter of fact, a good photographer is apt to be less simply ' photographic ' than an academic painter. It seems pointless to argue whether photography is as much an art as painting or carving; suffice it to say that it is a complicated form of expression to anybody who has gone beyond the snapshot stage. It involves the selection of a suitable, meaningful theme or subject, and the determination of its most completely expressive aspect. This is arrived at by the relative position of the subject to the camera, to its frame, and to the other material in the scene; the proper angle must be found so that the finished image will be a veritable ideograph; the lighting must be selected for descriptive and emotional flavor. The photographer must think of exposure, filters, film stock, of developing and printing. In short, he must visualize the realization of his original intuition in terms of the complex medium with which he is working. He ' sees ' in terms of the finished work, as a water-colorist ' sees ' in terms of his water colors. This fitting of means and processes to a previsioned outcome can be an artistic act of first magnitude. Its emphasis is on the concept at the heart of the finished work.

Photography has made a form of artistic expression possible to the great masses of our people, and the eagerness and universality associated with it attests the fact that a great need is being met. From a popular standpoint the major discouragement to the practice of the more conventional arts has been that, under academic guidance, disproportionate emphasis is laid on process. (The director of a well-known art school in the Middle West some years ago praised the drawings of the Slade School in London because " there were so many strokes in the shadow areas that they could not be counted.") Photography is a great democratic form of expression because it puts into the hands of the average man (cameras can be bought for less than fifty cents) an instrument through which he can record what he finds beautiful or significant. Obviously, the more time he spends with it, the more proficient he will be in the control of this instrument; yet he is not called upon to go through months and years of arduous drill before he can produce something acceptable, as he would have to do in the graphic arts.

The growing popularity of color photography adds another resource to the medium. It is as yet too expensive for wide use, and limitations arise from the fact that there is no satisfactory, popular way of making prints, instead of, as at present, projecting the pictures on a screen. Undoubtedly new developments will remedy the situation, allowing the photographer to handle his color negatives in his own darkroom, as he does the black-and-white. Some purists resent the intrusion of color in photography, but overwhelmingly it is anticipated as a new adventure.

Rayograms (sometimes called photograms) — the process of exposing sensitized paper to light and interfering with the light by means of objects laid on, or held above, the paper, which is then developed — adds another possibility in this field. *Montage* — the clipping and pasting of sections of photographs to make an original composition — is still another variation.

No other form of expression has been able to attract to single meetings attendances, running well into four figures, to hear discussions of balance, composition, lighting, and the significance of color and of subject matter. Magazines and books by the dozen carry on the debate over esthetic principles and practical devices, often with a good deal of competency. Thousands of youngsters all over the country will learnedly argue over the effectiveness of prints, discussing selectivity, placement, lighting, subject. It would be well for educators not to overlook the potentialities of this interest.

REFERENCES

(1) ADAMS, ANSEL. *Making a Photograph.* (Studio Publications: New York, 1939, rev. ed.)

(2) ANDERSON, PAUL L. *The Technique of Pictorial Photography.* J. B. Lippincott Co.: Philadelphia, 1939)

(3) CLERC, L. P. *Photography — Theory and Practice.* (Pitman Publishing Corp.: New York, 1937, 2nd ed.)

(4) DESCHIN, J. *Finding New Subjects for Your Camera.* (McGraw-Hill Book Co.: New York, 1939)

(5) HENNEY, KEITH. *Color Photography for the Amateur.* (McGraw-Hill Book Co.: New York, 1938)

(6) *How to Make Good Pictures.* (Eastman Kodak Co.: Rochester, 1938)

(7) MEES, C. E. KENNETH. *Photography.* (The Macmillan Co.: New York, 1937)

(8) MELTMAR, WRAY. *Photographic Make-up.* (Pitman Publishing Corp.: New York, 1938)

(9) MOHOLY, LUCIA. *A Hundred Years of Photography.* (Penguin Books, Inc.: New York, 1939)

(10) MORGAN, W. D., and LESTER, H. M., and Others. *Leica Manual.* (Morgan and Lester: New York, 1937, 3rd ed.)

(11) *Photography of Colored Objects.* (Eastman Kodak Co.: Rochester, 1938)

(12) *Photography 1839-1937.* (Museum of Modern Art: New York, 1937)

(13) NEBLETTE, C. B. *Photography: Its Principles and Practice.* (D. Van Nostrand Co.: New York, 1938, 3rd ed.)

(14) SCACHERI, MARIO, and SCACHERI, MABEL. *The Fun of Photography.* (Harcourt, Brace and Co.: New York, 1938)

(15) STENGER, ERICH. *The History of Photography.* (Mack Printing Co.: Easton, Pa., 1939)

(16) TAFT, ROBERT. *Photography and the American Scene.* (The Macmillan Co.: New York, 1938)

CHAPTER XVIII

THE GRAPHIC ARTS

ALON BEMENT
New York, New York
and
HENRY SAYLES FRANCIS
Curator of Paintings and Prints
The Cleveland Museum of Art
Cleveland, Ohio

I

INTRODUCTION

ALON BEMENT

From the early days of the fifteenth century when crude prints of a religious character were distributed to churchgoers, the graphic arts have exercised a greater influence upon the taste of the average person than have the arts of painting and sculpture. The reason for this is not hard to discover. The graphic arts hold this enviable place by virtue of processes of duplication.

The purist of the past held that the term ' graphic arts ' applied to those blocks cut, or those plates graved or etched, by the original artist, who also inked the plates and ' pulled ' his own proofs. Today the term is accepted to cover all printed pictures, regardless of the medium of reproduction.

It is obvious that the spread of education would be greatly handicapped without the means of precisely duplicable prints. To cite but a few instances, consider how inadequate would be the facilities of transmitting definite knowledge of geography, anatomy, or floriculture without printed pictures precisely duplicated.

Duplication does not lessen the educational or esthetic value of a print, but it does reduce the monetary value to collectors in the inverse ratio to the number printed. By this process excellent educational and art values are made available to persons of moderate means at extremely reasonable prices.

195

Handwork, as represented by these processes, was augmented toward the end of the nineteenth century by mechanical reproduction that was made possible by the appearance of the power press and the use of photography in photoengraving. As is inevitable when mechanical methods are first employed, there was some loss of esthetic value in the early photoengraved, half-tone prints, but this was offset by the advantage of the number of reproductions that could be made. The most important aspect of the development was that the new processes made it possible to reproduce photomechanically and in great numbers half-tone likenesses of the handwork of the masters of art.

By 1915 photography began to replace drawings for illustrations. In the meantime, color photography was being developed and, as technological growth continued, four-color half-tone engraving and printing and offset printing in color became possible. Today admirable reproductions of the great masters by both these mediums can be obtained at very reasonable prices. Recent publications in the field of color printing warrant and receive the closest attention of the artistic fraternity and will, beyond any question, serve to increase appreciation in all levels of society.

Since printed pictures cost so much less than even the oil paintings of good copyists, subjects may be changed much more frequently in homes. And, nowadays, printed pictures are made available through lending services and picture clubs. These services rotate to subscribers framed prints at intervals, much on the same basis as books are distributed by lending libraries and book clubs — and at correspondingly low fees. All these services develop appreciators, widen the opportunities for sales to creative artists, and facilitate education.

II
THE GRAPHIC ARTS IN AMERICA

HENRY SAYLES FRANCIS

I. THEIR HISTORICAL BACKGROUND AND DEVELOPMENT

In the fifteenth century the artist, looking round for some convenient method of making many original designs for popular consumption, hit upon the idea of designing a key plate, a block, or a stone, inking it and then pulling, or printing, as many impressions on paper as the metal or wood materials would permit. Yet, by comparison with the mechanical processes of today, the reproduction of prints is limited; editions of from one to two hundred, or in the case of lithography, editions of several hundreds of impressions are as much as can be attempted by the print-maker. With such a relatively small number, it is possible for the artist to print each plate, or at least to supervise its production. Each impression gains thereby a certain personal attention, and, in the printing of proofs, often a luster and individual richness that is unobtainable by more mechanical means. And, since the block or plate from which these impressions are taken is designed, etched, lithographed, or cut by the artist himself, prints are in great measure original works of art, in considerably greater measure than the commercial pictures of the present day, which are made by machine processes of reproduction, achieved through rotogravure, photomechanical processes, and other means.

The earliest efforts in print-making were in the woodcut field and were made as illustrations for the first printed books, both in Germany and Italy; such illustrations were calculated to assume the rôle taken by miniatures in illuminated manuscripts. The woodcut, being a relief process, with the design cut free of its background and high above its foundation, is exactly like moveable type, and designs so cut on the blocks can be bound and printed with type.

Simultaneously there arose another variety of graphic art called ' engraving.' In this case, lines incised in copper plates were inked, and paper, under pressure, pulled the ink from these incised lines. It was the armorers and metalworkers who first used this so-called ' intaglio ' method to see how their designs were progressing on breastplates, shields, or on whatever object they were working, and powdered charcoal was what they dusted into these engraved lines. The artists soon imitated this idea, substituting ink for charcoal, thus making the impressions more permanent, and making a plate specifically for the purpose, which, in the case of the goldsmith, was to retain a particular design he considered worthy, or that he wished to distribute to his apprentices and pupils or to other goldsmiths; and which, in the case of the painter or sculptor, was to record his own drawings and preliminary ideas for himself and for his students.

From about 1450 onward, these ideas rapidly took individual forms in one method of technique or another; and the proofs drawn from these various plates and blocks were used as art works of an inexpensive nature, were sold at fairs, religious or secular, as souvenirs, and were cherished as such; or they were cherished, by those who could not afford the larger forms of the representative arts, as works by currently great artists and designers. In this manner, the graphic arts rapidly became a popular form of art serviceable to artists and public alike.

Since the fifteenth century, the history of the graphic arts has been varied; the numerous processes have been put to many uses; and a wealth of material remains. From the sixteenth to the nineteenth centuries, the graphic processes acted as a handmaiden to painting, in many instances playing the lowly rôle of the copyist, as the camera does to-day. In the case of such engravings, a high degree of perfection was obtained in the technique in order to approximate as closely as possible to the original work; and by the same token, a uniform dullness of result was achieved. This vogue for engraved reproductions in large measure obscured the important original material produced by the graphic artists during the period. In the late eighteenth century, for instance, taste in prints of such collectors as Sir Joshua Reynolds included, on the one hand, the superlative etchings of Rembrandt, and on the other hand, large, uninteresting engravings by Raphael Morghen after Renaissance paintings such as Leonardo's "Last Supper." In other words, there was little discrimination for original work, and the primary attitude was an embracing curiosity for all pictorial art, with no keeness of perception as to its shades of esthetic value; the interest was an intellectual and literary one rather than an artistic appraisal. To be sure, there were a few discerning and critical collectors, but the prevalent taste was in the opposite direction.

In the nineteenth century the rôle of the artist changed. Princely patronage, until then the mainstay and supporter of the arts (which were treated as a craft, and as a useful if pleasurable commodity), largely disappeared, and a bourgeois public, fickle and wayward, became the patron instead. From this circumstance rose the condition of "Art for Art's sake" and art became a separate vehicle of expression of the artist's personality, and not art that represented subject matter for the sake of the contents or for sundry other purposes, such as decoration. The artist was therefore forced to create a public of his own, to stimulate a vogue for his work so that persons would vie with one another, in a sense, to buy his production. Prior to that date, artists had flourished, and others had fared less well; but in the nineteenth century, the odds against the artists became great. Rembrandt, in his time, had been universally acclaimed solely upon his own merits, by specialists and ordinary citizens alike; but Meryon, around 1840–1850, the architectural etcher of Paris, and easily the best etcher of his time, languished in obscurity and died because he could not obtain state commissions, which were available to the 'right' persons, and because he did not produce work that was the vogue at the moment. Today, the situation is much the same as it was in the past century, except that, once again, as in Rembrandt's time and in the late Medieval Germany of Dürer, there is an embracing curiosity for all types of prints. Discrimination remains of a personal nature, and does not depend so largely upon transient popularity.

In reviewing the historical development of the graphic arts in America, it should be remembered that all cultural and intellectual pursuits in Colonial times stemmed directly from Europe. For nearly two hundred years, except as provincial variations changed them slightly, the European contact underlay the basis of such manifestations. Thus, such examples are the eighteenth-century mezzotints by Peter Pelham, who, according to Hind (8, p. 270), deserves mention " for the honor of having introduced mezzotint (engraving with a tone process) into America. He migrated and settled in Boston in 1726 and his portrait of the Rev. Cotton Mather (of 1727) is probably the first mezzotint produced on American soil."

European influences prevailed in the numerous engraved portraits of Washington and many other influential figures in public life, and in such famous engravings as Paul Revere's " Boston Massacre." Revere — silversmith, dentist, engraver, and patriot — created an engraving of artistic merit more by accident than intention in this instance, for his intention was merely to depict the scene as a commemorative broadside. He was typical of his profession at the end of the eighteenth century, devoted not to art so much as to the practical ways of existence. Most of these early engravings and many of those produced throughout the nineteenth century have little claim to artistic merit and are interesting solely as historical documents.

From 1835 on, the firm of Currier and Ives developed the technique of lithography and in this medium published numerous current themes for popular consumption. They reproduced many rural scenes after landscapes by the Hudson River School and other painters — lithographs that had much real merit. The commercial success of these charming efforts was so great that the firm was led to disregard the discriminating eye of the persons initially responsible — whoever they may have been — and to produce cheap and worthless souvenirs. The whole venture ultimately disappeared and with it nineteenth-century interest in the lithograph. Only today has it been revived, and quite differently.

Three distinct manifestations of the later period, roughly from 1850 to about 1890, are worthy of note. One was the technique of wood engraving, in which illustrations of current events were made by artists for *Harpers Magazine* and other papers. Through the invention of the process-block, wood engraving came to be the chief style for reproduction in newspapers and magazines, and the artists who drew for these periodicals were often of considerable stature. Capable men, like Winslow Homer, designed many of these interesting pictures. (A similar project is being prompted today by the illustrated newspaper *PM*.) Second was the group of etchings done by Peter and Thomas Moran and other members of their family, and those of the etchers Charles Platt and Stephen Parrish. These etchings were the result of the influence of the currently popular Barbizon School, introduced to this country from France by William Morris Hunt. They possessed a pleasant style and sprang from the naturalist's observation of the outdoors in terms of the French idea. Third, and of considerably more importance, were the etchings produced by James A. McNeill Whistler. Though an expatriate who lived most of his life in London and Paris, he did not forget his American origin and exhibited an independence of view and an individuality of technique that was definitely outside the European trend. His etchings, drypoints, and lithographs easily rank with the best in the past, and his " Thames Set " and " Venetian Set " are outstanding graphic productions.

Frank Duveneck, of Cincinnati, working with Whistler in his early days in Venice, followed in Whistler's wake, as also did Otto Bacher, of Cleveland. The later phases of Whistler's style were inherited and enlarged upon by Joseph Pennell, Whistler's chief follower. Indeed, it is hardly too much to say that it was Whistler and his followers, and this American impetus in general, that formed the link to most of the graphic work in Europe and America today, especially as the English School, through Whistler's brother-in-law, Sir Francis Seymour Haden, derived much of its spontaneity from this connection. In the 1890's one other outstanding contributor to the American graphic arts was Mary Cassatt. Her debt to her French master, Degas, is notable; yet, her aquatints in color, of women and children, were done largely in this country and are among the most felicitous and beautifully achieved efforts of their kind.

Of the recent past, as a draughtsman, George Wesley Bellows is of
the stature of Whistler, but his field was lithography alone. In a few
years his brilliant output of some three hundred items not only made a
permanent record of that period of America in vivid portrayal, but also
gave immeasurable promise for the future, which was cut off by his
untimely death. His influence also has been one of the most potent on
contemporary graphic arts.

II. Contemporary Expression

To do justice to all those men and women making prints concurrently in the United States would require considerable space and explanation; yet an attempted summary should be made and one is best
attained through a classification within mediums rather than in style
and content. Many techniques are used, combinations and complicated variations of the best known in etching, woodcutting, and lithography.

1. Etching

The traditional style of etching, savoring remotely of Whistler and
Pennell but vigorous and individual in technical approach, is the work
of Frank W. Benson, whose nature studies, if limited in content, are
nevertheless extremely well accomplished. In the same style, and much
closer to the source, are the immensely capable architectural plates of
John Taylor Arms and Ernest Roth. Whereas Whistler fully, and
Pennell partially, caught the esthetic feel, apart from representation,
of the places and buildings they portrayed, Arms and Roth are more
preoccupied with the architectural exactness of their subjects, or the
astounding versatility of their own techniques. Childe Hassam, on
the other hand, partaking of Impressionism, reaches a more subtle
degree in interpreting his subjects, if less actual; and Donald Shaw
MacLaughlin has a real line in landscape, expressive and vigorous in
his Rocky Mountain subjects.

Of a more local content, Harry Wickey and Edward Hopper, the
latter using a rather hard, untamed, brittle line, give a homely crudeness and strength to their portrayal of city sights: corner drugstores
seen at night from oblique angles above, hot nights in boardinghouse
rooms with curtains blowing out windows, or congregations of people
milling to and fro in streets. Martin Lewis, in the drypoint technique
with crosshatching, has achieved a style of his own in night scenes,
using for contrast patches of sharp light and deep darks. Reginald
Marsh uses a simple, straightforward line in etching, is mostly pre-

occupied with his subject, and is addicted to beaches and locomotives. Peggy Bacon, a chronicler of the foibles of mankind, draws her victims inimitably and caricatures them unmercifully. George "Pop" Hart used the etched tone process of aquatint, combined with etching, to create his Mexican cockfights and lounging figures, in a unique style; and John Sloan, a contemporary of Bellows, commented faithfully and with humor, but impartially, upon our native scene. For the abstract approach, the most successful creator is John Marin, confined in his subjects to landscape.

2. Woodcutting

In woodcutting, a style of heavy blacks with sheer starkness and arresting force is to be found in the early blocks of Rockwell Kent. His figures and the details surrounding them are simple in monumental structure and suggestive of sculpture. For the older and extremely careful style of the nineteenth-century woodcut, with subtle gradations of planes and softness of design, Thomas Nason is easily the leader, with Asa Cheffetz and J. J. Lankes his peers, the latter especially in cutting the designs of Charles Burchfield. In four- or five-block chiaroscuro woodcuts — prints done in several colors — Rudolph Ruzicka has established a well-merited reputation. In both etching and woodcutting, founded as they are in styles on a rich background, the notable force of originality is very evident in the present output.

3. Lithography

Particularly is originality true of the contemporary process of lithography, a medium facile and strong in appearance, which is in keeping with the spirit of the time. Stow Wengenroth, who does vigorous snow scenes and seascapes, Thomas Benton, whose gnarled and writhing figures are individual expressions of the rural scene, and Louis Lozowick — to mention but three outstanding lithographers at random — hold a place of real popularity in a wide collectors' public, and a reputation also through their commercial affiliations.

4. The Cartoon

The realm of the cartoon deserves specific mention as one feature in contemporary prints, possessing the full vigor of social importance. There is a group of character draughtsmen too numerous to enumerate, excepting in two particular instances. Boardman Robinson is the first of these men who sees the sterner realities of a wayward life, as well as the humorous ones. His humanitarian interest places him, apart from the striking force of his drawings, as a champion of the right causes. William Gropper, who, in addition to many newspaper ventures, also does lithographs, strikes viciously at the injustices of the social structure, and he takes the place currently of the French lithographer, Daumier, in nineteenth-century Paris.

These few are but a handful of a long list of capable graphic artists who could be discussed.

III. Economic Features

The position of the graphic artist today is potentially one of moderate security. His output of ideas can be greatly multiplied and he does not rely, as the painter and sculptor do, upon the single example of an idea; his work can be utilized in a number of ways. He does not limit his editions to a very few impressions, as did the nineteenth-century printmaker, whose theory was to make a rarity of his productions, both to enhance the price and to stimulate rivalry among collectors. Today the artist can return to the methods of the earlier times, where, by a reasonable price and large editions, he creates a wide and varied public, and disseminates his wares. Only recently, for example, a sale was held in Macy's Department Store, in New York, over a period of months, where the etchings and lithographs of the leading draughtsmen of the day were sold over the counter as low as two dollars a print, much to the chagrin of the art dealers, whose business is to promote a specialized interest. This widespread distribution was certainly valuable to the artists, whose work went into the homes of a public much larger than would have conceivably been reached through the activities of the specialized salesroom, and the curiosity of the public was aroused to a new interest.

Several forces have combined to bring about the new attitude. One notable milestone in public taste was the exhibition of American and European contemporary art called the "Armory Show," held in 1913. This exhibition, very large in scope, included all the current and non-academic work in painting, sculpture, and graphic arts both in this country and, notably, from Paris. The undertaking was supervised by Arthur B. Davies, a well-recognized printmaker himself. There is little doubt that this caused a revolution in the popular mind, and increased contact with Europe after the World War further awakened public interest in artistic values. The vogue for the up-to-date and the ' chic ' has taken the form of familiarization with art pictures, which has

been furthered by such magazines as *Life* and *Fortune*. Those who
stood to gain by this interest have encouraged the collecting of the
graphic arts, and partially because of them ' Print-A-Month ' Societies
and ' Print Clubs,' like those of Albany, Cleveland, and Rochester, have
sprung up throughout the country; even the Brooklyn and Chicago
Societies of Etchers received considerable impetus from this public
interest. In the wake of this enthusiasm, publishing houses issued reproductions of prints, as well as fine color reproductions of contemporary painters' works. Museum policies have been oriented to this
trend: witness the Museum of Modern Art, in New York, with its
varied and stimulating exhibitions; The Art Institute of Chicago, with
its annual exhibitions of prints as well as paintings; the purchase policy
of the Metropolitan Museum, in New York, through the Hearn Fund
for contemporary art; the biennial exhibitions of the Whitney Museum
of American Art; the annual exhibition of the Carnegie Institute at
Pittsburgh; and such regional exhibitions as the " Annual Exhibition of
the Cleveland Artists and Craftsmen " in Cleveland. All such activities not only call public notice to the existence of current American art, but also create a conscious desire on the part of the public to participate in the whole scheme.

Furthermore, at the time of the depression, Federal projects were
set up to assist artists, and these not only put the government's stamp
of approval upon the art, but also provided the wherewithal for many
artists who might otherwise have disappeared from the field.

There is little question that this government approval added its
portion to the stimulus that was given particularly to the graphic arts,
yet it remains to be seen what the economic future of the graphic artist
will be, whether in society as it is constructed today there is a place for
a vigorous artistic existence that is self-supporting. It seems hard to
believe that the total economic stability of the individual artist can be
based solely upon the sale of created objects. The printmaker has the
advantage because, prints being small and inexpensive, more can be
sold. Yet, on the other hand, the graphic artist has to sell more prints
to obtain the same sum that a painting or a piece of sculpture would
bring. Probably in most instances the artist will have to include some
commercial application of his work; in the case of the printmaker this
could take the form of doing cartoons for magazines or periodicals, of
illustrating books, of making greeting cards, or of doing advertisements.
Only thus can the artist of today make his remuneration commensurate
with the demand of the present economic system. More and more,

artificially stimulated interest, such as is stirred up by government patronage or private subsidy, is unsound and, under changing social conditions, impossible. The most logical scheme is for the graphic artist to merge his efforts with commercial organizations that operate large-scale reproduction of prints. The artist must take a less personal rôle in creating his plates and in making hand-proofed editions and must be content to design and supervise his output, so that large editions may be produced and marketed, on the order of a postcard or newspaper, for relatively little cost.

Since the tendency of the graphic artists has been to dwell increasingly upon the local scene and the aspects of current life, such a scheme would seem logical. It does not necessarily preclude the efforts of the artist who is not preoccupied with indigenous topics. For abstract design will appeal to a public whose taste embraces a large territory of thought.

REFERENCES

(1) ARMS, JOHN TAYLOR. *Handbook of Print-Making and Printmakers.* (The Macmillan Co.: New York, 1934) 255 pp.

(2) BLISS, DOUGLAS PERCY. *A History of Wood Engraving.* (J. M. Dent and Sons, Ltd.: London, 1928) 263 pp.

(3) BROWN, BOLTON. *Lithography.* (FitzRoy Carrington: New York, 1923) 27 pp.

(4) CAHILL, HOLGER, and BARR, ALFRED. *Art in America in Modern Times.* (Reynald and Hitchcock, Inc.: New York, 1934) 100 pp.

(5) CUMMING, DAVID. *Handbook of Lithography.* (A. and C. Black, Ltd.: London, 1932)

(6) DREPPERD, CARL W. *Early American Prints.* (D. Appleton-Century Co., Inc.: New York, 1930) 232 pp.

(7) FURST, HERBERT. *The Modern Woodcut.* (John Lane, The Bodley Head, Ltd.: London, 1924) 271 pp.

(8) HIND, ARTHUR M. *History of Engraving and Etching.* (Houghton Mifflin Co.: Boston, 1923) 487 pp.

(9) HOLMAN, LOUIS A. *The Graphic Processes: Intaglio, Relief, and Planographic.* (Goodspeeds: Boston, 1929)

(10) LAVER, JAMES. *A History of British and American Etching.* (Ernest Benn, Ltd.: London, 1929) 195 pp.

(11) LUMSDEN, E. S. *The Art of Etching.* (Seeley, Service and Co., Ltd.: London, 1925) 376 pp.

(12) PENNELL, JOSEPH, and ROBINS, ELIZABETH. *Lithography and Lithographers.* (The Macmillan Co.: New York, 1915) 319 pp.

(13) WEITENKAMPF, FRANK. *American Graphic Art.* (The Macmillan Co.: New York, 1924) 328 pp.

(14) WEITENKAMPF, FRANK. *How to Appreciate Prints.* (Charles Scribner's Sons: New York, 1922) 330 pp.

CHAPTER XIX

SCULPTURE

FELIX PAYANT
Editor of *Design*
Columbus, Ohio
and
GEORGE J. COX
Head of Art Department
University of California at Los Angeles
Los Angeles, California

I

SCULPTORS AND THEIR WORK

FELIX PAYANT

I. THE SCULPTOR'S PROBLEM

Sculpture is primarily an art of three-dimensional form. Its message is spoken in terms of materials such as wood, clay, stone, and metal. Because of this fact it is concerned primarily with expression through mass, bulk, quantity, and such natural laws as govern them. Weight, gravity, stresses, and strains cannot be overlooked, regardless of the idea to be expressed. These are not only the limitations of the art but they are also the very means through which the sculptural idea is conceived and becomes vital and human. Hence sculpture, by the very nature of its means and materials, is allied to architecture, which also relies on such material and basic natural laws. Sculpture is, however, unlike architecture in that it usually presents the subject matter of life and expresses it by devices that, to some degree, are recognizable and identified with life. Sculpture depends upon nature for its content; but that does not limit it to imitation of nature. It seeks through experience and study to find those basic relations, easily understood motives, and generally accepted truths that are suitable to its method of expression. " Not life, but the mathematics to which life has been

reconciled," is the problem of the sculptor.[1]   Mere imitations of the
spatial aspects of nature without the dignity of the internal structure
and architectural qualities of the materials make for sham.   " In no
case, however, is artistic ability manifest in willfully ignoring the requirements of the materials worked in." [2]

Sculpture implies a statement made in terms of mass about some
significant phase of life. It is an art that objectifies life, its ideas, and
expressions. Sculpture takes recognizable life forms and places them
in space. It should be the sculptor's aim to express his ideas forcefully
and truthfully rather than to reproduce the appearance of nature.
While the sculptor depends on nature and must study her himself, his
responsibility is to select such meaningful elements as he deems important. It is these ideas that he must objectify in his three-dimensional material.

Sculpture, like painting, is representational. However, the latter is
basically a two-dimensional art, while sculpture exists in space. It
depends largely upon the relation of forms and the play of light and
shade to convey its meaning. In this respect it is much like architecture and has flourished throughout the ages in close mutual alliance
with it. " At first there is no difference between architecture and
sculpture. The memorials that were consecrated to the dead or to the
gods — cubes, or cylinders, or pyramids, or wood, or stone — share the
rhythms of vases and implements. As simple in their organism, as
little the product of observation or of conscious thought, they have like
these the immediate objective beauty of harmonic masses set in space
and revealed by light." [3] Certainly we have a right to expect that in
America sculpture, like architecture, will frankly and fearlessly express the materials of which it is made, whether it be wood, clay, stone,
concrete, metal, glass, or any of the new materials such as the plastics.

II. What the Sculptor Attempts to Do

The sculptor may attempt in the use of his material to reproduce
convincingly such things as a human figure. The result in this case may
be an identical translation of the figure used as a model as, " The
Plunger," by R. Tait Mackenzie.[4] The artist may have set out to present an event, historical or otherwise, using a group of figures in such

---

[1] Hudnut (7), p. 8.
[2] Hildebrand (5), p. 13.
[3] Hudnut (7), p. 3.
[4] Dodd (4), p. 61.

a way as to illustrate that event. For example, the " Shaw Memorial " in Boston, by Augustus Saint Gaudens.[1] The figures need in no sense be reproductions of any particular models.

Abstract sculpture, such as the Cubist type, emphasizes design of line, plane, and mass. Even representative sculpture usually seeks to achieve some amount of such design.

The sculptor may aim to express some emotional quality. To produce this result he has the choice of many different means. He may produce this effect by the idea involved or through his manner of expression; or again by the use of both. An excellent example of this is the " Stations of the Cross " by Alfeo Faggi.[2] The artist may wish to emphasize the medium or material with which he works and to a large extent may allow the material to determine the manner in which he works. At present the sculptors of America, as well as the public, are especially interested in the artist's use of the medium. In sculpture, as in the various arts, the artist must work *en rapport* with his medium. Obviously, if he is modelling a figure in clay, which is later to be cast in bronze, there will be possible a greater sensitivity of line and surface quality than if he is carving from a piece of granite. And it is easy to see how a miniature carved in ivory will have a delicacy and a line tracery very different from a figure carved from a piece of oak.

III. Sculpture in Contemporary American Life

In the recent past sculpture has functioned as a supplementary aspect of architecture. It found its place in mouldings, various types of ornamentation, and surface embellishments. While that is not as true today, modern sculpture finds a somewhat different outlet in relation to architecture. Today it is not necessary for sculpture to become a component part of a building and take its place as an actual part within or without the structure. Much recent architecture includes little or no sculpture. That the sculptor has lost something by this estrangement cannot be denied.

An excellent recent example of the use of sculpture is Rockefeller Center, New York, where the important focal points are accented by the work of such sculptors as Paul Manship and Lee Lawrie. There is every reason why sculpture should enhance the beauty of architecture, as the latter gives force and stability to sculpture by lending an im-

[1] Dodd (4), p. 14.
[2] Rindge (9), pl. XXXIII.

posing background. This relationship may be seen in the fact that both are arts of form, bulk, and mass; their very mass implies permanence; they are not easily moved; they belong to their environment; in short, because they are made of the materials of the earth, they are a part of it and serve their best when they are closely related to it.

The small sculpture, or figurine, is seemingly more popular now than it has ever been, perhaps because of a change in our mode of living. Many persons, including Carl Walters, Waylande Gregory, Archipenko, and Vally Weiselthier, have done much to have the ceramic product accepted in the realm of sculpture in America. No little influence has been exerted on our sculpture by the advent of new and synthetic materials. The plastics offer a challenge. The constant investigation and adventure with old materials put to new uses has produced results of considerable merit, among which might be included glass and terra cotta. The return to wood as a medium in sculpture is another characteristic of recent years.

The sentimental, allegorical figures that once graced the squares of American cities are now seldom produced. Something of the revival of the ideal reappeared in World War memorials, but they never deluged America as at the close of the Civil War.

IV. FOLK SCULPTURE

From the very earliest days in America, as soon as the acute necessities of food, shelter, and clothing were satisfied, the Colonists showed a strong aptitude for work in three-dimensional materials. They were especially aware of the sculptural possibilities of wood. There were several important outlets for this expression, notably in connection with shipbuilding. As early as 1623 shipbuilding began in Plymouth, creating a demand for suitable figureheads, headrails, and stern boards. Most of these were beautifully carved and sometimes painted. From among these early makers of ships' figureheads came our first real American sculpture.

Besides the ship figureheads the art of carving manifested itself in gravestones, weather vanes, inn signs, and wild-fowl decoys. The carving of ivory reached a high degree of perfection in such articles as jagging tools carved for their wives and sweethearts by the whalers in the long trips spent away from home.

Because it was so intimately involved with the lives of the people and was carried on by unschooled persons, this early type of three-dimensional expression may well be called ' folk sculpture.' It was naïve and in the dialect of the pioneer. While the craftsmen had little or no opportunity to study, they did understand basic principles of form and suitable use of material. Because the work of the folk sculptors was so intimately related to the lives of the common people, they exemplify a sincerity, an integrity that is not always evident in the sculpture of later periods.

Most of the early carvers learned their trade in England, but the new materials and the new conditions in America gave a distinct quality to the work done here. Most of the figureheads used on the ships represented the shipowner, his wife, or persons prominent in public life. The whaling museum in New Bedford, Massachusetts, and the Peabody Museum in Salem, Massachusetts, house a great number of carved, wooden figureheads that give us an insight into a significant art-expression that was discontinued with the passing of the wooden ships.[1] Folk sculpture continued to exert its influence on America well on into the nineteenth century. There are certain names that began to stand out and identify themselves with the art, even though these men were essentially the artists of the common people. Among these were William Rush of Philadelphia, 1756–1833, and Samuel McIntire of Salem, 1757–1811. An itinerant folk sculptor by the name of Schimmel of Pennsylvania was a prolific worker. His work covered a great range of subjects, such as eagles, roosters, dogs, hunters, and sometimes more pretentious groups.[2]

Since sculpture may be considered both as relief and ' in the round,' no discussion of it would be complete without mention being made of the cast-iron stove plates made by the Pennsylvania Germans.

These rectangular cast-iron plates, generally about two feet square, formed parts of the first house warming stoves used in this country. The front and two sides of each stove were decorated, the top and the bottom plain. Though there were few allegorical subjects, the upper panels were almost all illustrated Biblical scenes; and generally the verse from which the scene was taken was inscribed in the lower panel. The sincerity of their work makes it appealing as well as amusing, and in spite of the naïveté of conception and crudeness of drawing, the plates have dramatic spirit and sound design. These early pictorial plates are the freshest and

---

[1] An interesting revival of the hand-carved figurehead, hand-wrought fastenings, the Great Cabin, and other aspects of early shipbuilding is exhibited in the *Swift of Ipswich,* a topsail schooner based upon the old Baltimore clippers, and in other sailing craft recently designed and built by Robinson and Chapelle at Ipswich, Massachusetts. — *Editor.*

[2] *American Folk Sculpture* (2), p. 41.

the most vigorous floral design which was used almost entirely between 1756 and 1760. The last record of the making of a five-plate stove is dated 1768.[1]

II

SCULPTURE TODAY

George J. Cox

The carving of wood, the shaping of clay to be fired with colored glaze, and the modelling in wax or clay for later reproduction in metals are usually held to fall within the sculptor's realm, but today, as immemorially, the ponderable bulk and immense duration of stone makes it an instinctive choice when men desire to give eternal shape to noble concepts.

Apart from recent mechanical alleviations of his toil, the tools and materials of the real sculptor remain unchanged since carving came of age in Egypt, and certain lessons learned centuries ago are valid yet. On the other hand, cultural, social, and economic pressures have modified the scope and purpose of the art. It seems to be not so much the greatness of an age but the end its sculpture serves that has everything to do with its real virtue. We can take over the techniques and forms of earlier epochs, but their motivations are no longer ours. The cult symbols of Prehistoric Man and the fetishes of the Negro were functional items in their lives; the monumental works of Egypt — extolling the might of the Pharaohs and emphasizing the importance of the hereafter — had a definite use and purpose. The democratic Greeks put sculpture to a wider use and its enjoyment was extended to the common man. In the age called ' Romanesque ' the practice of sculpture was imperative. It was a veritable language for illiterate common folks. In their churches they perused old Bible tales translated into stone.

Today's situation is complicated by contemporary eclecticism, experimentation, and revolt. Much of our modern sculpture is excellent, but little of it is functional in the manner understood in the great epochs. Some of it is a very personal expression, and much of it is remote in thought and expression from the civilization in which its authors live —

---

[1] *American Folk Sculpture* (2), p. 86.

all of which are phenomena that no great age of sculpture ever witnessed. We can of course draw certain physical comparisons. The plastic values of sculpture, dealing simply with the competent arrangement of line, contour, plane, and mass, can be evaluated with some confidence whenever the critic applies himself with the industry and intelligence equal to that used in judging literature or music. But when we attempt to relate emotive and psychological values, there seems no common ground upon which the modern and the ancient plastics meet.

The one common principle is a respect for the medium. The primitive worker intuitively recognized the limitations of his stone or wood and thus, perhaps unconsciously, obtained maximal results. The modern sculptor will draw his own line, but his business is not naturalism, or even realism, much less is it animation after the manner of waxworks.

Another imperative even less easy to achieve is the recovery of sculpture's natural environment. The magnificent effigies of Egypt, the gaunt austerities of Gothic masons, even the baroque extravagance of Versailles, were alike set out for men to see. Supplied with air and space, they dominated a vista, enriched a façade, or gave point to formal gardens. They were approached slowly and grew upon a spectator who could then adjust eyes and mood to changing perspectives. We are only now recovering from the defective taste of the nineteenth century that stuck beaver-hatted worthies on the crowded steps of stock exchanges and state capitols. Even yet well-meaning architects continue to give unnecessary jobs, so that we often approach our sculpture preoccupied with traffic hazards and parking speculations. Not all sculptors are as fortunate as Carl Milles, whose works are mostly set in landscaped parks where their baroquely modern spirit, not untouched by humor, gives and receives the compliments that art and nature merit. Sculpture still demands breathing space and leisure for its appreciation.

There is another handicap that modern sculpture has to surmount. Fashions of the day being what they are, the sculptor much prefers his models nude, and authentically inspired, the creator is likely to assert his right to simplify, accent, or disregard the normal physical articulations of the human figure. This invites the criticism of those adults who instinctively apply to sculpture the simple rules they would employ in choosing mates.

In their location, and more particularly in their style, our great buildings offer little opportunity for sculptural embellishment. Even new museums and art galleries have foregone its decorative touches. Theaters and amusement centers now depend upon arresting forms made possible by new methods of construction and new materials, and upon flood and neon lights, to attract the patron who perforce must snatch at pleasure. Even our churches have surrendered to the stripped austerity of functional architecture. To all these generalizations, there are of course exceptions. It is clear that under conditions such as these, if architectural sculpture is to live, then the sculptor's work must show a strong and stern delight in forms. So, too, our architects should abate the excess of functional zeal and study sculpture as a contributing art.

Lighting is an important factor, and though light, as an end in itself, is being increasingly used with imagination and effect, the controlled lighting of sculpture has been neglected. Flood lights, above or below, side lights, lights behind to silhouette clean shapes, spot lights, and even radiant or interior lights securing new effects and stimulating changes, call for the experimental mind. With light and color and creative imagination sculpture may take on another lease of life — a different life, which ministers to opportunities and moods patently, if not profoundly, different from those of our forefathers.

Moreover, the new materials and new processes demand new concepts. A growing abstract art, with scope for beauty and surprise, engages the creative artist. Here they will not be limited by any representational norms, or any necessity to conform to nature, though the organic structure and exquisite logic of nature will be the source of inspiration. Here, too, the magnificent materials and faultless processes that science has placed at the disposal of industry will also function. Plastics, still in their infancy, metallic alloys, glass, and synthetics will supply colors and textures of great variety and beauty. Their lightness, tensile strength, and comparative cheapness will facilitate reduplication and ensure wider markets. Though even intimate sculpture can never be broadcast to anything like the same extent as pictures are by way of color prints, sculpture should find its way more and more into the home.

The foregoing deals with professional aims, but there is a personal end of high value. To amateurs, the sculptor's art provides an admirable activity for leisure hours. Mentally soothing and physically stimulating, the progressive development of a concept in the round can offer a complete escape from daily cares.

The human form will still remain the sculptor's first resort. For less profound and less exacting themes, the wider range and more utilitarian function of abstract design and decorative work increasingly command attention. Thus between the amusing figurine, the balanced thought and feeling of the abstract, and the emotional depth of the heroic statue, the sculptor's art can still supply extremes of taste. Given sincere encouragement, a vital art would reassert its use in life again.

REFERENCES

(1) AGARD, WALTER RAYMOND. *The New Architectural Sculpture.* (Oxford University Press: New York, 1935) 124 pp.

(2) *American Folk Sculpture.* (The Newark Museum: Newark, New Jersey, 1931)

(3) CAHILL, HOLGER, and BARR, H. H. *Art in American Life.* (Halcyon House Publications: New York, 1939) Chap. 2 — Chap. 5.

(4) DODD, LORING HOLMES. *The Golden Age of American Sculpture.* (Mount Vernon Press: Boston, 1936) 108 pp.

(5) HILDEBRAND, ADOLF. *The Problem of Form.* (G. E. Stechert and Co.: New York, 1932) 141 pp.

(6) HOFFMAN, MALVINA. *Sculpture Inside and Out.* (W. W. Norton and Co., Inc.: New York, 1939) 330 pp.

(7) HUDNUT, JOSEPH. *Modern Sculpture.* (W. W. Norton and Co., Inc.: New York, 1929) 90 pp.

(8) PUTNAM, BRENDA. *The Sculpture Way.* (Frederick A. Stokes Co.: New York, 1939)

(9) RINDGE, A. M. *Sculpture.* (Payson and Clarke, Ltd.: New York, 1929) 221 pp.

(10) TAFT, LORADO. *The History of American Sculpture.* (Oxford University Press: New York, 1903) 604 pp.

(11) WILENSKI, R. H. *The Meaning of Modern Sculpture.* (Frederick A. Stokes Co.: New York, 1932) 171 pp.

CHAPTER XX

PAINTING

Milton S. Fox
Instructor, The Cleveland Museum of Art
Instructor, The Cleveland School of Art
and
Sherman E. Lee
Instructor, The Cleveland Museum of Art
Cleveland, Ohio

I

CONTEMPORARY AMERICAN PAINTING

Milton S. Fox

I. Nationalistic and Conservative Tendencies; Story-Telling

Throughout its history American painting has alternated between homespun practices and admiration for European artistic enterprise. Today, overwhelmingly, American art wants to be 'American,' to slough off obvious reminders of indebtedness to recent European art. For nationalism, which already has transformed (one is tempted to say 'distorted') the mentality of Europe, is having its way with our art.

Nationalistic tendencies, generally speaking, produce an art that is anecdotal in nature, and sometimes downright hortatory or propagandist. Its function is to celebrate the particularities of place and group. In this respect, America is behaving as the rest of the world is behaving. We, too, are caught up in the world-wide tendency; and the predominant strains in our painting are those that thrive on nationalism. These strains have always been pretty close to the surface. Ours may be epitomized roughly as a common-sense esthetic, which asks that painting deal with what is present and tangible; and so long as the subject, or story element, is not obscured by it, we do not object to technical refinements or invention. This has always placed considerable restraints upon our more enterprising artists, as may be gathered from this statement by Henry Billings (2),[1] one of our leading painters:

> The European audience [pre–1933] allows much greater professional freedom in the plastic arts, and Picasso's range has been possible because of the willingness of Europeans to extend the metier of painting to include not only the use of a variety of media, but also to allow the painter to move about in related fields: book illustrations, ballet *décor*, tapestry, murals, and sculpture. With us, once a painter's performance has come up to standard of excellence and once he has indicated his direction and receives his personal identification tag, he must be ready to show his tag on all occasions or run the risk of jeopardizing his professional standing.

The pressure on American artists of what might be called a ' cultural conservatism ' has always been great. We have never been very sympathetic to modern art, for example. To quote Suzanne LaFollette (15)

> . . . notoriety [of the Armory Show in 1913, America's first important contact with the ' new ' art] by no means implied an easy victory for the radical element. The modernist galleries that were opened in the enthusiasm aroused by the success of the show were obliged eventually to close their doors; the established dealers were slow to take up modern works, and the modernists were obliged to get along as best they could until the public should begin to catch up. (p. 315)

This native wariness has many roots, among which are the lack of a tradition that has witnessed changes and that would thus guarantee a degree of catholicity, and the native American distrust of Europe's beguilements. As a nation, anything foreign is apt to strike us as ' highfalutin.' And so it was that, when a large number of American artists did finally begin to produce modern art of one sort and another, it was a little too late. For the social and artistic trends of the Western world had begun to change. The art of the '20's began to ' mean ' something, to tell stories, to excite associations. The one-time Fauve was now painting a woman, not merely a rhythm of lines and color; the Surrealists were conjuring up pictures of demons walking abroad.

Presently there set in a period of reëstimation of the European tradition. One interesting consequence of this was the discovery, for our own time, of other media than oil and water color. Fresco has become an important medium for the first time since the Renaissance; tempera likewise has been rehabilitated; even the mosaic business is looking up.

---

[1] For details see first group of references at the end of this chapter. — *Editor*.

In sculpture there is a good deal more direct cutting in stone. Undoubtedly there is another reason for American interest in the exploitation
of the resurrected media: if experimentation in esthetic was blocked,
some measure of satisfaction could be had through experimenting in
materials.

At the same time, artists began to look less at primitive African
statues and to spend more time with the familiar names of the Renais-
sance and the outstanding names of European art in general. Soon
Americans discovered for themselves three amenable old masters:
Winslow Homer, Thomas Eakins, Albert P. Ryder. An 'American
School' suddenly appeared.

This return to 'tradition' reënforced our native storytelling, conservative tendencies. Sophistication suddenly became 'effete'; 'foreign' art was to be abandoned; 'obscurities,' removed. Popular and
social art became almost an historical necessity. Then came the re-
crudescence of mural (public) painting. Here came to a focus nationalism, the rediscovery of fresco, the revolt from modernist studio practices, and the artist's desire to feel that he was a needed and welcome
member of society. Anecdote, or message, or sentiment became supreme. At this point came government sponsorship of art (to be discussed more fully later on) giving a tremendous impetus to these already strong tendencies.

Now arose a great hue and cry about an 'American art.' Sounder
criticism, to quote Munro (18), expressed itself as follows:

> I propose, nevertheless, to invite trouble by laying down a very unpopular
> thesis; namely, that there is no such thing as an American school of art
> with any marked traits in common. I should like to follow it up at once,
> however, with the statement that the so-called French, German, and
> other national 'schools' of painting are also largely figments of imagina-
> tive patriotism. Also, I will add that there is nothing disgraceful in the
> lack of a national school, for it indicates at least that some individualism
> and zest for experiment still exist within our shores. (p. 202)

Soon there followed that *reductio ad absurdum* of nationalism, regionalism, which says that each section of the country must produce a
local, distinct, and unique art. This dogma still has currency, even
though it would be impossible, from looking at pictures alone, to determine the origins of the artist or even the section of the country depicted,
and further whether it was done by an artist native to the locality
or by a casual visitor. To quote Devree (9):

Let it be also said that the consideration of the regional aspect of the exhibition [of American art at the New York World's Fair, 1939] gives the lie to regionalism except in some cases of local-color subject matter. (p. 266)

Even stronger is Margaret Breuning's assertion (4, p. 100): " We all know that there are no real local ' schools,' or any great divergences in regional art."

II. Eclecticism

Indeed, one of the leading traits of American painting is *eclecticism*, as it is of twentieth-century civilization in general. The borrowing runs not merely to European material or to the far past; it includes as well a distinctive borrowing by trained and sophisticated artists from our own ' primitives ' or ' naïves ' (as sometimes by Arnold Blanch, Doris Lee, Philip Evergood, Ernest Fiene). In work so influenced there is a rough-and-ready innocence of vision which resembles that found in unschooled ' popular ' painters: awkward and frozen poses; proportions strange and sometimes fearsome; abrupt transitions from light to dark; a free handling of perspective; lack of the conventional visual unity given by a fixed point of focus; drawing that is guileless and lacking soft grace; attention to unexpected details. In short, we are reminded of the fourteenth- and early fifteenth-century primitives, the works of colonial journeyman limners, and the so-called ' popular ' painters generally. When it has somewhat less of the deliberately ' untutored ' look about it, it results in blocklike houses, simple doll-like and wooden figures, pipelike trees, bright flat color (and too often, alas, an indifference to the beauties of pigment as such; the paint is more like a stain), and a tendency to the panoramic view, as in many works by Grant Wood, Dale Nichols, Paul Sample, Alexandre Hogue, and others.

The net result is a type of painting that carries with it the illusion of forthright statement, direct and ' close to the soil ' (since it is so unlike academic painting on the one hand, or what was called ' Modern ' art on the other). It has a crispness that is paralleled in much of our writing. This flat treatment of paint, taken with the tight enamel-like surface introduced by the Surrealists, and the wide use of fresco and tempera represent the newer developments on the technical side; they challenge the predominance of the showy, more graphic brushing that derives from Greco, Rembrandt, or Manet; and the gossamer technique of the Impressionists has been left to doddering academicians. In short, technique today is not the *raison d'être* as it was of much painting only a few years ago. Then the subject — anything would do — often was a mere peg on which to hang dazzling virtuosity; or more accurately, the subject was the cleverness of the artist in handling his materials. But today a restrained, often lackluster, technique is frequently used, for it is the subject matter to which attention is to be drawn, especially in painting that is illustrational rather than evocative.

III. Frank Social Commentary

These matters are as nothing, however, in comparison with what seems to me to be far and away the most important thing about American painting today. This is the freedom and the willingness to deal with every phase of American life, every aspect of the American scene; and to call a spade a spade. Never before in the history of painting has there been anything like it. In this, and in this alone, this country does not follow or parallel Europe. As far as one may judge from exhibitions in this country, from a wide survey of European and American magazines, and from reproductions of art from other sources, no European art has had the courage to deal so frankly with the problem of society. American art presents the drouth-stricken farm, the emaciated Joads of the country, the floods, the strikes, slums, politicians: catastrophes man-made and catastrophes natural. These are presented in many tones, sometimes disinterestedly, sometimes satirically, sometimes with bitter condemnation; our art may be compounded of hate, or indulgence, or supplication, or fun; but as a body it confronts the issues of the day squarely.

The magnificence of this phenomenon lies in its deep social significance: it indicates that the American artistic conscience is still free — and impelled — not only to choose between this technique and that, or between landscape and still life, but also to say out what weighs so heavily on the nation's mind. There is no cheap trimming of the issues. American art in this phase of its output says, these things exist here; this is what they look like, and some of them are terrible; even, says some American art, these things must change, for they are nightmarish beyond all Surrealism. There is little poetizing about it. In contrast to this, recent European art gives no direct clue as to how life is really lived. When real occurrences are painted, the subjects are selected from the ' glorious ' moments of party history, or they exalt war, or heroism, or the Leaders, or the most prolific families. It is a positivism, but shallow and transparent; least of all is it an optimism.

As Elizabeth McCausland wrote (17, p. 5) : " If the white oxen of Italy hunger, we do not know it.   But on Western plains cattle die for lack of food and water; and on city and farm human beings die also of lack of food."

This strong reportorial or journalistic strain is commented on by Whiting (23) : " No sluggard was it who saw in American art a good complement to stark news photographs " (p. 50).   It is at once a sign of artistic immaturity, and a valuable quality.   It would not be an exaggeration to say that, for the first time in history, art really presents a fairly complete picture of the society that produced it.   This is the mark of American painting today.   In the past, it has always been more or less understood that art would undertake certain tasks, and keep away from others.   We had to guess at many of the processes of everyday life or piece them out from other sources, for the art of painting concerned itself little with such matters in the past.   But the historian of the future will know exactly, from American painting of the last decade, what went on in the minds of Americans, and how it was with the land.   There has never been an art so detailed in this respect, so accurate, and so frank.   (The only thing that comes near it is the Dutch painting of the seventeenth century, but this is pale by comparison in both intensity and range.)   Examples are to be noted in the work of George Grosz, Joe Jones, William Gropper, the Soyers, and many, many others.

IV. BOLDNESS, BIGNESS, AND ACTION

But it would be ill-proportioned to dwell too long on the painting of social and natural and economic devastation; there is yet greatness and beauty in our country.   Our plains and rivers and mountains, our deserts and our skies, our endless and pregnant fields, our good-natured and sentimental people — these things exist too.   To quote Miss McCausland (17, p. 3) again:

> Yet life, even in crisis, is rich with conscious beauty; and the pictures displayed show joy as well as suffering. . . . Social strife is a frequent theme; but so is the positive aspect of our industrial civilization, mass production, technology's triumphs, illustrated in the pure formalism of flour mills. . . . Vanguard artists record the abundance of life, as well as its starvation: the brilliant sun that lies warmly on western wheatfields.   Loving eyes observe the historic beauty of America's land, prized and pictured through three centuries of American life.   This land is our land, the artists say with passion; its beauty shall be reclaimed and made whole.   This world, threatened by war and aggression, yet so wide,

so beautiful, so potential, is our world; it shall be saved for peace and human happiness.

This aspect of painting may be noted in the work of such artists as John S. Demartelly, Georges Schreiber, John Steuart Curry, Waldo Peirce, Millard Sheets, Grant Wood, and Clarence Carter. Let us note, then, the quality of boldness — boldness in manner and boldness in conception — and with this, bigness of scale. It is as though American painting today is fulfilling the sentiment of an unnamed critic, quoted by Burroughs (6: p. 148), who said in 1853: "The future spirit of our art must be inherently vast like our western plains, majestic like our forests, generous like our rivers." Far horizons, great sweeps of land-scape, and the high point of view are now common.

The second main characteristic of our painting today (after its greatness in dealing with life in America) is *action*. One of the most striking things about any good exhibition of our recent art is the feeling of activity, of things being done, of people doing things — take, for ex-ample, the work of Jon Corbino, Paul Cadmus, Eugene Higgins, Hen-drick M. Mayer, Fletcher Martin. Note this activity in two aspects: first, people and objects in movement (for example, the extraordinary importance of animated and spacious skies in our painting); and sec-ond, flowing, agitated composition. It would be shortsighted not to recognize in this phenomenon one of our most obvious traits as a people; Americans are always moving, always going somewhere. Reflected in painting, we find in murals a compounding of anecdote and action that disregards the unities of time and place and recounts in a single panel the whole development of a community or of an industry. European art seems to lack this unrestrained, superactive, fidgety movement. The reader may interpret this lack in European art however he chooses; perhaps a fatalistic submission may be read into it.

V. Melancholy and Humor

But I must call attention to a strong and growing note of *melancholy* in our recent art. Many painters are producing grand and beautiful canvases in this vein. Some are compounded of melancholy, haunting nostalgia, and sheer romanticism; others are brooding and somber blends of social ills and melancholy: war, the homeless, the orphans, the wanderers. Still others find a sadness and eternal melancholy in the heart of nature. One wonders whether this is the complement in our art of the extraverted noise of the professional 'regionalist.' Artists exhibiting this mood are Mitchell Siporin, Charles Shannon, Edward Millman, Karl Fortress, Yasuo Kuniyoshi, Hobson Pittman, Henry Mattson.

A third prominent trait in our recent art is *humor*. It is not the vicious satire of some European art, nor is it sly and witty, marked by *double entendre*. It is what we call ' kidding ' in the slang of the day. Seen in this light, some of the current painting of social realities becomes a little less grim. Has not Charlie Chaplin taught Americans that humor and adversity are not necessarily strangers? How much of this manner of expression may be attributed to the influence of magazines like the *New Yorker?* (Consider Doris Lee, Morris Kantor, Louis Guglielmi, Franklin Watkins, Reginald Marsh, for example.) In any case, humor frequently appears in *genre painting*, now again important, and also in what is called the ' conversation piece.' There are stirrings of a revival of this idiom — paintings, like those by Peppino Mangravite, that portray definite personalities, the family, friends, in intimate surroundings.

VI. The Influence of Photography, Motion Pictures, and Advertising

The fact that many of our painters have served as illustrators at one time or another, taken together with the ubiquity of the illustrated magazines and the even greater ubiquity of the snapshot, has undoubtedly been of great importance in forming the image-making propensities of the American artist. *Photography* has had a great influence, as it has had on art in general since the second half of the last century. But in recent years it has added a new order of visual images to the pictorial repertory. This, combined with Surrealism (I refer particularly to the element of surprise and novelty due to unaccustomed juxtapositions) and new esteem for the integrity of the object (for example, in the work of the French Pierre Roy, the English Edward Wadsworth, and the American Charles Sheeler), has led to paintings in which detail is mirrored to life; sharp edges are restored, and a taste for pattern-making is joined with extreme, but selective, fidelity (as in the work of Alexandre Hogue, Aaron Bohrod, Edward Hopper, Henry Billings, Charles Sheeler). The mark of the photograph is seen in the poses of figures. Not always are they the familiar artistic conventions; we now have the slouch, the sudden twist of the head, the moment of shift of balance from one foot to another, novel foreshortenings.

The *motion picture* [1] has been important here, too. It changes locale rapidly; it is composed of many little subsidiary plot developments; it changes scale — mid-shot, long shot, big close-up; at its best it searches out the telling detail. American painting has taken over many of these traits. And recently another interesting influence affecting painting as well as drawing has appeared in the form of the animated cartoon.

Advertising, both as advertising photography and advertising art, has unquestionably definitely affected American figure painting and portraiture, for our standards of ' looks ' are set by these agencies. Many painters affect the same ' chic ' that we find in fashion drawings: the postures, the facial types, the slender, well-groomed appearance; e.g., the work of John Carroll, Frederic Taubes, and Abram Poole.

VII. Portraits; Figures; Textures

Let us note that portraiture is a relatively moribund art today. Academicians continue to supply the required pastiches for the social élite, employing all the proved salon artifices, with some of Hollywood's best glamor inventions added thereto. Our best portraiture comes from painters not considered specialists in the field: Franklin Watkins, Grant Wood, George Biddle, Peter Hurd, and others. As against the older aristocratic and pretentious portrait painting we now have an informal " take me as I am " attitude — *en pantoufle,* as the French say. Similarly, figure painting still seems to be left to more academic souls. Few changes have appeared in pictures of the nude; the studio appurtenances are somewhat different, and there is a shift in technique from that founded in a general way on Manet to a fuzzy, softly glowing, light-impregnated one based on Renoir. Examples are supplied by the work of Eugene Speicher, Gladys Davis, Bernard Karfiol, and Alexander Brook. On the whole, American painting is still very reserved about one of the traditional accomplishments of the artist, the celebration of the charms of the female nude for no other reason than sheer sensuous pleasure.

An interesting reaction in the direction of sensuous pleasure is appearing, however, in the form of elaborate studies of textures — variations on the theme of tactile qualities. I have already remarked on the new respect for the integrity of objects; now we have further explorations, not of the ' look ' of things, but of their ' feel.' Recent work of

---

[1] For an extended treatment, see the chapter on the motion picture. — *Editor.*

Thomas Benton and George Grosz may be cited. Will this new tendency start a reaction from the school of crass canvas-staining?

VIII. FANTASY AND ABSTRACTION

It remains now to mention a few aspects of our painting today other than those generally realistic and anecdotal, already mentioned. For, despite the American-art-even-if-it-kills-us school of criticism, not a few painters are working at certain of the late European tendencies. These artists seem to feel (and rightly so, I think) that the mere fact of European priority in their development does not make the psychological bases of Surrealism, or Expressionism, or Abstract art any the less universal. Surrealism, at bottom, is common to all men: in the dream, in fairy tale, in accidents, in the fantastic. Expressionist behavior — subjectivism heavily colored emotionally — is equally common. Abstract art has been extremely influential in the design of objects of everyday use. (What may be called the ' instrumental value of modern art' is of great importance in any consideration of the art of the Western world). American Abstract art is extensive and varied. Some of it is purely geometrical, calling for resource in the adjustment of shape to shape, line to line, and for extreme attention to the use of materials; some less severe, recalls the shapes of life. There are variations that compromise between geometrical figures and natural appearance, some giving more emphasis to the geometrical side, some to the other (as in the work of Ralston Crawford, Georgia O'Keefe, Charles Sheeler). Among the Abstract painters are Stuart Davis, George L. K. Morris, Raymond Jonson, Louis Schanker, Arthur Dove, Karl Knaths.

The American painters in the Surrealist vein, as a rule, use this manner in connection with expression on the state of man. The contemporary world, it need hardly be pointed out, offers ample proof that the fantastic, the incredible, the diabolical, are actual and present. Freud, modern science, and the dictators have made this plain. Most of our Surrealists use the idiom in a watered-down version, and many other painters, not Surrealists, have been influenced. In the Surrealist vein may be named Peter Blume, Anton Refregier, James Guy, John McGrady, Castellon, Julien Levi, Walter Quirt, and others, while a strong Expressionist flavor is to be found in the work of Marsden Hartley, Mervin Jules, Matthew Barnes, William Gropper, Charles Burchfield, and Nahum Tschacbasov.

In this brief account of American painting today, many important names, and several tendencies, have not been mentioned. I have not discussed the mass of conservative, academic art, which plods along, oblivious of great change, pretty much as it did twenty-five or even fifty years ago. Suffice it to say that many writers, lately becoming dismayed that painting has come to grips with everyday experience, are beginning to call for a return to hothouse exaltation; one even begins to read wistful remarks about "that old Ivory Tower." There are some other disquieting hints that American painting may become less outspoken about America, and yield to studio mentality, but the balance appears to be all in favor of a greater and finer body of art. We have many wonderful painters; we have the freedom, the vigor, and the dignity; and as, in one European country after another, painting is reduced to a mere adjunct of politics and a mockery of the creative imagination, America has become the artistic hope of the world.

IX. Some Functions of the Art of Painting Today

In the last two decades or so, painting has become more important in American life than ever before. While formerly reserved for the celebration of the wealthy (in portraiture, for example) and for the creation of objects for gentle relaxation, painting today serves a broad social function.

It is no longer regarded as mainly an agency through which the artist may express emotions that in their origins were of interest only to himself. Partly this is due to the great importance of *mural painting*, which by its very nature demands a more social outlook on the part of the artist; partly it is due to the general trend of recent art already discussed. The hundreds of murals and thousands of paintings that have been produced under the patronage of the Federal government have made the artist more conscious of his place in society. It has brought art directly into the lives of millions of people for probably the first time, on such terms of intimacy, in their lives.

Painting under Federal sponsorship serves more than an esthetic function; most of it deals with history, local or national, or with matters of information and instruction. Painting today serves to some extent *to foster a sentiment for the nation* and to illustrate the close kinship of the peoples who inhabit the land, the community of their problems, their common aspirations. It serves, if you will, a patriotic function, but in the best sense of this term. It spreads its message of dignity, travail, and aspiration on the walls of public buildings of all sorts, entering into the daily lives of the people. But our painting is not by any means a smugly complacent " little Sir Echo." One of its great qualities is the fact that good painting has been combined with *social criticism.* In America today this is an outstanding function of painting, and, as a mass, in respect to its daring, its understanding, and its completeness, it surpasses anything yet produced in art.

Sometimes painting has become frankly *propagandist;* and while it may be pointed out that art at all times has to some extent advanced the values of the sponsors, it is a new development in recent art for painting deliberately to expound one cause or another. This kind of art is also frank in declaring that the function of art is first of all to persuade, to effect the goals advanced, and only secondarily to be of interest because of artistic or formal qualities. Indeed, the latter, it is held, may distract from the force of the message. But propaganda need not always be blatant. There are other forms of persuasion. The Federal government and various other agencies have been organizing exhibitions of American art that are to tour the Latin-American countries in the interest of good will. The basic belief here seems to be that if one likes a work of art, some feeling of sympathy between the creator and the appreciator will have been fostered. All of us know that to a certain extent this is true; and this use of art is not being neglected in our present attempts to build friendships.

More so than in the recent past, painting now serves *an instrumental function in relation to industry and commerce,* affecting the appearance of the workaday environment. The designs of all kinds of artifacts have been influenced by the stylistic innovations of modern art. Fashion designers, designers for the stage and the screen draw heavily on painting of all sorts for ideas. The so-called ' fine arts ' serve in relation to everyday use as ' pure ' science does to ' applied.' Printing, advertising, posters, packages, book illustrations have been influenced. The appearance of the interior of the home has undoubtedly been modified by the brighter color and relative simplicity of the painting of the modernists' schools.

Pictures themselves are more common in American homes than ever before, and serve there *a directly decorative function.* For various reasons (to be mentioned later) they are more accessible to the general public and less expensive than formerly. Most homes, except those in the lower income groups, include paintings of some sort as adjuncts to their decorative schemes. In this connection one must mention the extensive use of decorative painting (often carrying subtle ' educational ' implications) in commercial exhibits and on buildings of the numerous

World's Fairs. Modern motion-picture emporia generally have availed themselves of decorative murals to add ' tone.' Thus, while museums have been reluctant about bringing art to the public, other agencies have made great strides in this direction.

Generally speaking, people have been inclined to regard painting as primarily — if not only — *a source of esthetic pleasure*. This function of course continues. Thousands of paintings are turned out annually in all parts of the country that aim consciously only to provide pleasure in color, line, technique, and the associations aroused by the subject. There is more of this sort of painting now than at any time in our history. The general public is in much closer daily contact with art in the ways already mentioned and this is supplemented by the efforts of museums, schools, and other educational agencies that now make art appreciation an important part of their activities.

Museums are perforce becoming more lively, owing in part to the challenge of other aggressive uses of painting. We have a tendency to more liberal purchasing policies. More important, there has been a strong attempt to increase attendance through lively *museum exhibitions* based on the ' theme ' idea, thus giving the pictures displayed some ' point '; for example, " The Nude in Painting," " The Streets of New York," " The World of Today," and the like. This use of art is related to the one just described: painting for esthetic enjoyment. But it must also be mentioned that the educational departments of American museums plan their exhibitions for other reasons. Some of these are *the study of costume, manners, and the cultural trends of various periods* as interpreted in art. Painting is more closely related than ever before in our *educational* schemes with other studies. Teachers of economics, geography, the crafts, literature, and the like, all make use of painting as it bears on their particular fields. In addition, it is felt that the analysis of paintings and discussion of their fine points lead to the *general improvement of taste*, as in suggested color schemes, ensembles, textural qualities, and so on, that may be applied to home decoration or personal adornment.

It is now recognized that the reproduction of pictures in magazines has *a definite sales value*. Many of the popular magazines and most of the ' class ' magazines carry color plates after paintings (which in some cases are even commissioned especially for this purpose). Surely this considerable expense has been found justified in increased prestige and sales.

With the greatly renewed and extended common interest in painting, and its present-day ubiquity, it is to be expected that painting will become a more important form of *leisure-time activity*. The increased size of evening classes, the increase in number of correspondence courses, and the greater number of exhibitions of painting by non-professionals in the field of art (doctors, business men, and the like), taken with the large and enthusiastic attendance of Federal Art Projects classes, give some indication of the extent of active participation.

It is important to mention at this point the *therapeutic value* of painting, and of the enjoyment of pictures. Any ' art appreciation ' has a certain sedative effect, since it turns attention away from the hard facts of life. But painting, in both appreciation and creation, allows a certain objectification of feelings that might not find satisfactory release otherwise; it allows the sublimation, we are told, of desires and urges difficult to gratify. This function of painting has become important these days with psychiatrists and psychoanalysts. However, the value of painting as a means of emotional release, as an aid in easing conflicts within the self, can easily be seen in the work of children, where painting performs a great service if the child is not too restricted in his creative activities.

Let us note in passing that one of the great historic functions of art, that of *service to religion*, is practically dead today (if one except the esthetically regrettable ' art ' of church supply houses). There are some signs, however, that we may see a revival of this type of artistic endeavor.

X. The Economic Status of the American Artist

While, as a specialized group, artists in America still live precariously, they no longer take it for granted that picturesque squalor is their sole proper reward any more than it is the doctor's or the insurance salesman's. Even though there are many more persons professing art than at any previous time, and even though, for most of them, life is a severe struggle for bare subsistence, nevertheless, their economic status is better than at any other time in our history.

There are many causes for this change, some of which are devious. For example, the public turned to our own less extremist art because it was weary of attempts to ' understand ' the various *avant-garde* movements. Sophisticates and connoisseurs, on the edges of satiation, welcomed a new turn; Americans became bored with the constant insistence on European artistic superiority and the belittlement of American talent. All these tendencies were nourished by the rise of nationalistic sentiment.

But unquestionably the greatest single consideration in these notes on the economics of American art production is Federal sponsorship — the State as patron. In our time private patronage had become completely inadequate, and the artist found himself pursuing a hazardous financial existence, rivalling the lowest income groups in any other occupation.[1] Once the church, then the courts and princes, later the petty aristocrats, were the patrons of art. But by the middle of the last century the artist was on his own; for his livelihood he could only hope that the whim of some wealthy individual would lead to a purchase. To a large extent this situation still obtains.

The Federal patronage of art, however, has brought great changes. It has given employment and commissions to thousands of painters, sculptors, craftsmen, and allied workers through its various agencies: the Public Works of Art Project, December, 1933 to June, 1934; the Section of Painting and Sculpture (now the Section of Fine Arts) of the Treasury Department, established in 1934; and the projects under the Works Progress Administration, inaugurated in August, 1935. Millions of dollars have been spent in a greater and more extensive program than has ever been fostered by a modern nation. The assignments for mural paintings, easel pictures, sculpture, the graphic arts, and so on, have been distributed to artists all over the country without regard, on the whole, for reputation, race, sex, or artistic tendencies. Sometimes the artists have earned their commissions on a competitive basis, at other times on the basis of their record in earlier competitions; most often the artist is engaged in part-time employment and paid an established per-hour rate.

As the times have seemed to stimulate expression and interest in the arts, many small galleries have appeared, given to the sales of moderately priced objects. They have made it somewhat easier for the artist to show his works by demanding less extravagant returns and have stimulated public interest by more adroit methods of selling and exhibiting. The dealers have thus built up regular followings that look for new exhibitions with all the zeal of confirmed first-nighters. The dealers will contract with artists for a quantity of works, or arrive at agreements to handle certain artists exclusively, or invite artists for an occasional show, or rent their facilities to the unattached artist.

---

[1] I am referring specifically to 'progressive' artists, as some use that term. Slick society portrait painters, pasticheurs, animal portraitists, receive fabulous amounts for their services. Nor am I referring to industrial or commercial artists, whose work is often very lucrative.

Numerous other plans have been devised to sustain purchases —
for example, the print-a-month and other plans for selling graphic art.
These may not bring in large amounts for the artist, but over a period
of time they provide a welcome addition to the net income. Let us note
also that several museums now make a concerted effort to sell the works
they display, particularly the local product. One of the pioneers in
this respect, and still outdistancing all others is the Cleveland Museum
of Art, which in twenty-two years has sold $200,000 worth of the work
of Cleveland exhibitors.

The business world, too, has discovered that it can exploit ' fine
art ' to its own profit, and this naturally benefits the artist as well.
Commercial art and industrial design need hardly be mentioned in this
connection. Similarly, publications like *Life, PM, Esquire,* and others
commission original works; again, the International Business Machines
Company made collections of paintings for display at the World's Fairs.
Recently there was an interesting tie-up between an enterprising gallery in New York and a motion-picture company that led not only to
commissions for several artists handled by the dealer but also to excellent publicity for the company.

The field of commercial and advertising art has more and more
been using the talents of the nonspecialist in the field. One frequently
finds artists like Georgia O'Keeffe and Millard Sheets commissioned
to produce pieces for advertising use. The motion pictures have availed
themselves of the talents of artists in the publicity and production departments; and the studios of Disney and other makers of animated
cartoons give employment to hundreds of artists. The publication of
illustrated books has led to many commissions for artists.

New tendencies in architecture and interior decoration have led
to a greater demand for art objects in the home and in the place of
business. The murals and other large-scale decorative painting of the
World's Fairs have familiarized the American public with uses of art
for other than pure exaltation; as a result, many an artist is called upon
to decorate a recreation room or to provide panels for a dining room.

As the demand for art grows, there grows a demand for training;
and now professional artists find themselves invited to join the faculties of universities, sometimes in the enviable position of ' artist-in-
residence.'

All this would seem to make for economic ease for the American
artist. Actually, not many artists are troubled by income-tax problems.
If they exist on earnings from the sales of their art alone, most artists,

it is safe to say, earn considerably less than $2,000 a year. It must be remembered that the artist produces an article that is not exactly essential to the maintenance of daily life; he cannot peddle it, and he cannot take an office or storeroom. He must continue to invest his meager funds in canvas, pigments, brushes, stone, clay, tools of various sorts, printing facilities (for graphic artists), frames, mats, and the like, while his stock-on-hand increases.

His training is decidedly circumscribed and unadaptable to unforeseen needs. In most cases he learns how to paint, draw, or carve, and he learns very little else — nothing through which, in an emergency, he can turn an honest penny. The investment for his training is large, involving tuition fees and a continuous outlay for materials that are consumed on first use. In return, he gets a degree or a certificate, but the history of art shows that a truly competent artist can get along without these.

To sum up, then, few artists maintain themselves through their art alone.[1] They teach (art, art history, or whatever they can). They lecture occasionally, illustrate books, and do commercial art when they can; or they try to snare an occasional portrait commission (which they frequently regard as potboiling). Sometimes they frankly engage in some remunerative occupation outside the field of art entirely, painting and sculpturing whenever they find the time.

In recent years we have seen attempts by artists to organize for the sake of their social and economic welfare. There have long been artists' organizations of an honorary sort, and many artists' clubs. But increasingly the tendency has been to organize for the purpose of eliminating flagrant abuses of the profession, and of regulating relations with the public. Among the notable developments of this kind are the United American Artists (a national organization affiliated with the C.I.O.), the Sculptors' Guild and the Mural Artists' Guild (affiliated with the A.F. of L.), and the American Artists' Congress. The latter (now disrupted by internecine quarrels over charges of Communist domination) at first seemed destined to assure that artists would get their just deserts. Some of these groups, and several others, were active in the late, unfruitful attempts to get through Congress legislation setting up a permanent Bureau of Fine Arts and some form of permanent Government sponsorship of art. As professional men, artists are still too individualistic to unite in common action for their common good.

---

[1] An excellent discussion of these matters may be found in von Wiegand (24).

What, then, can be done to improve the situation of the artist without resorting to the usual advice to go into commercial art or other activities? Perhaps one solution might be the encouragement of reproductions for the home, suited to more or less standardized frames, and cheap enough so that the general public could buy them often, alternating them on the walls of the home according to the mood. The publisher of the reproduction (like the publisher of books) would publicize the new works and see to their wide distribution amongst energetic merchants. He would either buy the original picture outright or pay royalties to the artist, in which case the artist might then sell his original. (A similar plan could be followed in sculpture.)

Many homes now have reproductions of paintings, but these, as a rule, are fairly costly, and the reproductions are most commonly after paintings by artists of some historic fame. To be of any real financial value to the living artist, a strong advertising campaign apparently must drive home the desirability of buying contemporary pictures, not for a permanent place on the wall, but as a form of artistic experience that should be renewed and varied from time to time, as one buys, uses, loans, and exchanges phonograph records.

The idea of renting, rather than of selling, pictures suggests itself, but the several attempts that have been made in this direction have seldom been conspicuous successes. The same may be said of the encouragement of installment buying, perhaps because the entrepreneurs have not been clever enough.

Are artists entitled to rental from museums and galleries when these show their works? The issue was violently debated only a short while ago. Many artists claimed that they were entitled to some compensation for their ' performance ' in the same way as composers get their fees from performances. The museums countered with the argument that they supplied the artist with the ideal place in which to show off his wares. More numerous well-run coöperative artists' galleries might be helpful. An interesting development is the attempt being made by some artists to retain a partial claim on their works, so that if their value is augmented in some considerable degree at any time after the sale has been made, they, or their heirs, will also benefit by the rise.

As for the public, let us note that all sorts of artistic work are available for decorative uses in the home; that enormous numbers of art works are on exhibition, making contact with the arts very easy; and that original art works can be had to fit almost any budget. The ownership of some kind of originals is no longer the exclusive prerogative of the rich. In general, the shift of patronage is one of the most notable things about the situation of the American artistic scene. With patronage on a broader and more popular basis than formerly, we obviously will have another kind of art, and new uses for art. Art will be increasingly brought directly and immediately into the everyday activities of more and more persons.

II

AMERICAN WATER–COLOR PAINTING [1]

SHERMAN E. LEE

I. ITS TECHNIQUE AND QUALITIES

Water-color painting possesses certain qualities that distinguish it from other methods of painting. Because of its cheapness and compactness it is used by great numbers of people, amateur and professional, child and adult. The apparent ease of application leads to the situation known as " dabbling in water colors." This ease combined with transparency and simplicity of effect makes the medium ideal for reproduction in such diverse fields as fashion drawing and magazine illustration. As a reporting instrument it is rivalled only by the camera, which is, however, less flexible. The passing moment, action, or scene may be caught by an adept water-colorist with a spontaneity and freshness that recreates the essentials of the scene for the spectator. This function leads to its importance as a sketching medium for notation of a significant and simplified view of a scene to be remembered or used in a later picture. In the hands of an expert the sketch can be more important than the finished picture; in the hands of a tyro the result is confusion. This results from the variety of effects at the command of the painter, which must be handled with near precision. Accidental effects are controlled by the competent professional.

Essentially, water color is a transparent stain of pigment and water applied to a light ground. The clearness of the color depends upon the brilliancy of the ground, just as the clearness of a red light depends

---

[1] For references applying especially to water colors, see the final page of this chapter.

upon the white source light behind the red glass. The paper can also function as a color, shape, or texture in itself, and for this reason it is often left blank in large areas. Water color can be applied in varying degrees of wetness, from the most fluid stain to a dry stain that leaves a scrubby texture and color of a low brilliance. The fluid technique generally results in blurred edges and soft, fuzzy textures that provide contrasts with sections painted in a less fluid manner. The brush may be used to apply broad washes with careful gradations, or it may define shapes with a linear ease that we associate with the Oriental water-colorists. The brush may apply color in the staccato strokes of Impressionism or in the careful washes of the Early English School. The tendency in water-color painting has been away from a tinted drawing towards a brushed sketch where the drawing is merely an indication of placement. After the color has been applied it may be varied as to hue and texture by blotting with a rag or by scraping with the brush handle, or the paper may be tilted to control the flow of paint already applied. Once a brush stroke has been applied, it may not be removed; consequently the organization of the picture must be clearly imagined before painting has begun. This requires a sureness of touch and a quickness of hand for the transference of the idea to paper, for there is no eraser or palette knife in the water-color method. This required technical skill leads to an emphasis upon the process of production that is probably stronger in water color than in any other medium. The movements that the hand makes as it guides the brush are important even after they are finished, for they are translated into the physical properties of the brush stroke on the paper. Some of the greatest pleasures of the water-color picture to the observer are the sensations: crispness, slowness, jerkiness, smoothness, lightness. These simpler perceptions may then be translated into the more complex moods of energy, calmness, or nervousness.

II. A Brief Account of Its Historical Development

1. Colonial Beginnings

The beginnings of American water-color painting are allied with the early efforts at colonization of the New World. Aside from American Indian work in the medium on dried skins, the first water colors done in America were by Governor John White of Raleigh's colony in Virginia. His productions were made at the end of the sixteenth century and were confined in subject matter to a recording of the aborigines and their culture. Confined and semiscientific in technique as these papers were, nevertheless two centuries later Audubon (1780–1851), in his description of the wildlife of America, took up where White's work left off. Audubon's work shows the advance in treatment of color, but retains the idea of a tinted or stained drawing, common to the Continental schools of topographical water color.

2. Derivative Elements

A summary of the history of American water-color painting must necessarily emphasize our derivative elements, for Continental influence has played a large part in the formation and development of the water-color medium in the United States. As colonies and cultural imitators of England, we could but be artistically responsible to her. Aside from Audubon, who was trained by the French academician, David, our early painters were so tied to the English tradition that many migrated there. The English tradition was carried on in landscape by the Hudson River School, which was also strongly touched by the French Romantic movement. Their work was generally done by means of glazes over a preliminary drawing. However, the work of Thomas Moran (1837–1926) shows the romantic grandeur and looser brushwork associated with the water colors of J. M. W. Turner.

3. The American ' Primitives '

In contradistinction to these derivative groups were the American ' primitive ' painters. The works of these artists are like other ' primitive ' groups only insofar as all works of this nature spring from similarly untutored, naïve, and original minds. Many of these men were transients, going from town to town along the roads and trails, selling their wares as any tradesman would. Another element in the primitive group was the dilettante, or amateur, usually a typical Victorian woman who painted for amusement, in the same spirit as one might embroider. Nevertheless, water colors of this group, on velvet, on paper, of flowers, funeral monuments, and landscapes, attain a somber and earnest dignity that sometimes places them above the more sophisticated, but derivative, work of the ' serious ' artists of the time. Chronologically, the primitives continue right down until the twentieth century, when growing contacts and increasing social stimuli make semisophisticates of all. It must be remembered that this was a popular art that circulated among the middle and lower classes of primarily rural areas; it was not a collector's art, though it has become so today.

4. Winslow Homer

The Civil War constituted a political, economic, and social break in our history. The war that helped produce a wealthy class that was more urbane than its predecessors, and hence was more interested in the fine arts, also helped produce our first significant water-colorist. Winslow Homer (1836–1910) received his early training as a staff artist, before and during the war, for the new magazine *Harper's*. It was here that he found the need of rapid and incisive notation of observed phenomena that is the essence of reporting in war or peace. When he turned to more peaceful subjects after the war, he carried this descriptive quality into his now-much-sought-after papers. He was probably strongly influenced by the English school in its broader, more cursive manner, which was well adapted to his visual descriptions of forest life, of the pounding Northern Sea, of the calm and brilliant Gulf Stream, of the profuse foliage of the Bahamas as against the spare, monochrome Maine coast. Homer's style is essentially the base of much American water-color work since his time. It reports accurately, and with no little quality of design, the way a scene looked to him at a particular place and at a particular time. As time went on, Homer's style grew more bold, more fluent, and we see an interest born in the qualities of a brush stroke for its own sake, aside from its descriptive qualities. This tendency was to find its development in later men under the influence of the French.

5. The American Water-Color Society

The acquisitive instincts of the *nouveau riche* and their desire for the patron's crown led to a demand for pictures, water colors among them. Partly to satisfy this demand in an orderly manner, and partly to imitate the English Water-Color Society, the American Water-Color Society was formed in 1868. Its motto, " To hold, as 'twere, the mirror up to nature," is illuminating. Thomas Wood, its first president, was typical of the Victorian *genre* painters, obviously derived from such English academicians as Mulready and Frith. A. T. Bricher (1837–1908) is typical of the landscape water-colorists of the academy, a more or less sentimental describer of American topography, strangely reminiscent of England.

For those who could not afford the original pictures, Currier and Ives supplied their now famous prints for which many of the sketches were made in water color, as well as the final hand coloring of the lithographs. Periodicals, too, particularly those that had fashionable pretensions, employed water color as a means of describing the proper style of dress for the Victorian lady.

6. Inness, Whistler, La Farge, and Sargent

With the growth of the United States as a world power and its extension into the world, and partly as a result of its estrangement from England during the Civil War and later, other views and other influences began to filter into our arts. George Inness (1825–1894) and his group were strongly molded by the French Romantic landscapists, with their interest in twilight, sunrise, and a golden glow of light. James MacNeill Whistler (1834–1903) was tremendously struck with Chinese and Japanese paintings and prints, and imitated them in their more precious, superficial aspects. Simple shapes of uniform hue and delicate coloration were the keynotes of this art. John La Farge (1835–1910) and Robert Blum (1857–1903) were influenced by Japanese art in subject matter if not too much in technique. John Sargent's (1856–1925) water colors are generally classed with the English School, though many of them are more broad in technique and closely allied to Homer. Sargent's use of brilliant sunlit color also shows the infiltration of the greatest innovation in Western painting since the Renaissance, namely Impressionism, largely a French movement.

7. Impressionism

With the influence of Impressionism in the 70's and 80's we come to the great body of American water-color painting and it will be most convenient to consider our water colors under the headings of successive waves of influence, noting the native flavor of the work and the changes in outlook. Study in Paris was the first means of influence. At the turn of the century the tempo quickened and the Armory Show of 1913, the Stieglitz Gallery among others, and the annual water-color show in Chicago provided the means for transmission of the new theories and methods. The dealers became extremely important in dictating the flux of the market; private collectors came more and more to be of an esthetic as well as a wealthy cast. On the whole, though the older traditions were bought by the majority, the intellectuals and the more daring of the collectors gravitated to the new works. In collecting, as in painting, the trend was to a cosmopolitan, an international, style. The American scene was to be a reaction against this urbane group, a revolt against growing estheticism, a revolt that in our time has become the main trend in American water color, a revolt that tends towards chauvinism and regionalism, and a self-conscious exploitation of obviously familiar scenes and events.

Impressionism, with its interest in effects of light, its use of the single brush stroke of color, and its desire to blend these strokes with the eye rather than the brush, was a tremendous influence for change in water-color technique. Glazes, grays, and the mixing of colors were discarded, and the colorful papers that we are accustomed to today were the result. The importance of the single brush stroke as a unit was influential in helping the development of a calligraphic technique that was partly derived from a more intelligent study of the great Oriental schools of water-color painting. These developments lie at the base of modern water-color painting, and there is hardly a painter alive today whose indebtedness to the movement is not apparent. Dodge MacKnight's (b. 1860) water colors of New England are probably the most important works of this Impressionist group. His sketchy renditions of light effects, particularly in winter scenes, developed into a technique unfortunately capable of easy imitation by a host of followers. The work of Childe Hassam (1859–1935) is also of importance in its use of divided color, if not in its spontaneity. George " Pop " Hart (1868–1933) in his tropical scenes used an extremely fluid wash of low brilliance. His illustrational style is noteworthy for the freeness of the pen drawing and the applied tints.

8. Postimpressionism

Postimpressionism was concerned with the possibilities of design inherent in color, shape, line, volume, or space. The picture was considered as a unit in itself to be arranged and manipulated with relation to the physical properties of paint and paper as well as to the objective appearance of nature. When the artist had achieved the thematic arrangement of the units used in the picture, it was complete, however sketchy or unfinished the completed work appeared to the casual eye. Thus many of Paul Cézanne's water colors have surprisingly few strokes of the brush, yet the existing arrangement is complete and satisfactory. His water colors, even more so than his oil sketches, tended to be rapid notations of arrangements in nature or imposed upon her. In these notations color, shape, and line worked together as a unit of construction. Color was not an added element to composition; it was one of the elements, often of first importance.. Cubism developed from Postimpressionism and may be summarized as a more analytical, abstract interest in construction by means of shape and volume rather than by color. In America, Charles Demuth (1883–1935) was most strongly influenced by Cézanne. But his interest in American folk art and a delicate crispness in his style served to save his work from obvious derivation. His illustrational style places more emphasis on the curve and the arabesque than his more familiar works, which emphasize the delicate aspects of angles and forms found in flowers, vegetables, and foliage. Demuth's delicate color is enhanced by the variety it achieves through his system of blotting and wiping the wet color after application to the delicate pencil drawing. Preston Dickinson belongs in this group because of his interest in architecture as a subject for water-color and a means of achieving a rigid organization of short lines, small shapes and volumes, and a rich jewel-like color that gains in richness by contrast with great expanses of untouched paper. Stuart Davis (b. 1894) and Charles Sheeler were both profoundly influenced by Cubism of a constructive, rather than an analytic, nature.

Maurice Prendergast's (1861–1924) use of flat color patterns is unique because of its nonstatic nature. Unlike the color decorations of Gauguin, a strong sense of movement is imparted to Prendergast's work by the wormlike movement of the colored brush strokes over the paper. The high saturation of the color makes for extremely decorative effects, and its luminosity is high because of his intelligent use of the paper as a means of illuminating the transparent washes of color. He has been classed as an Impressionist, but his organization of color and movement place him in the ranks of painters more conscious of design qualities. Not the least of Prendergast's qualities are his gayety of movement and richness of color, which give his water colors a sensuous quality. William Zorach (b. 1887) uses water color in a broader manner than Prendergast and with more interest in objective appearance. Zorach uses one stroke of the brush to describe a bush, where Prendergast would use from six to a dozen strokes. Zorach also is interested in contrasts of crisp areas with blurred areas, partly as a means of realization of space. Often combined with these qualities is a dramatic force approaching the aims of the Expressionists, whom we shall next consider.

9. Expressionism

Expressionism, derived largely from Belgium and Germany, attempts a statement of a psychological or an emotional state of mind with a technique appropriate and subordinated to that end. Broad technique, powerful color, and irregular shapes seem to be most typical of this group. George Grosz (b. 1893), a German emigré, brings this movement to us in the hands of a master. His satirical comments on modern society are expressed with a rawness of color and a use of a wet, blurred technique unknown to American water-colorists. His later works are less subjective in nature and show his interest in the study of textures, a study ignored since the work of Albrecht Dürer in the early sixteenth century. The American-born Max Weber has done water colors in the Expressionist idiom with the use of a dry brushwork that takes full advantage of the grain of the paper. The early water colors of Charles Burchfield (b. 1893) are Expressionistic in their subjective lyricism as well as in their childlike hobgoblin aspect. More than the others, Burchfield was conscious of decorative quality as an end in itself, but his work changed after the war to nostalgic picturizations of the American scene. Later, however, he has turned towards Expressionism again.

10. John Marin

With these developments of water color in mind, we can turn to the work of John Marin (b. 1872), generally accepted as the most significant of American water-colorists. Marin passed through an early Impressionist stage that helped to make his color extremely decorative. Though interested in the design of his papers, and the function of each unit in relation to the other, he has never lost his close contact with the subject matter he loves. The Maine woods, the sea, and tree forms are as much a part of Marin's work as his technical means. Added to this is a daring, a willingness to experiment, that has often impaired his work, but has inevitably led to greater results. He restored black to his palette and uses it for rich accents in the midst of his more brilliant colors. The various grays that flow from his brush are not only expressive of the forms they describe, but they are also sensuously pleasing in themselves. His interest in Cubism leads him to useful and striking contrasts between spare angular form and rich, luscious color.

11. The American-Scene Painters

The reaction against internationalism and ' foreign ' influence was not long in coming. The early twentieth century had seen its origins in the work of John Sloan, Robert Henri, George Bellows, and George Luks. But with the depression and the introspective, self-examining period of American culture there arose the American-scene painters.

Resting mainly on a straightforward representational technique, their work relies on Fords, Coca-Cola signs, and farms for subject matter. Thomas Benton (b. 1889), in his small water colors of the South and Middle West, achieves a pointed illustrational style that presents the more homely, awkward movements of American people. This quality has made him an excellent illustrator of Americana, notably in *An Artist in America*. Less famous American-scene water-colorists are Adolph Dehn (b. 1895) and Edward Hopper (b. 1882). The former varies from a soft, summery landscape style to a trenchant, satirical manner that places him in the forefront of the social commentators, along with William Gropper (b. 1897).

III. The Present Status of Water-Color Painting

The water color has become increasingly important in the field of commercial art. The magazine, in particular, has utilized the services of many facile water-colorists for illustration of fiction. The advertisers have taken advantage of possibilities in color reproduction, and for this work such decorative water-colorists as Millard Sheets (b. 1907) have been used. Fashion drawing continues with water-color sketches, but they are less representational, more stylized and sophisticated than ever before. The ultimate in sophistication and satirical humor is achieved by the numerous water colors done for the *New Yorker* magazine covers.

More and more, water color is becoming a people's art, an art that more people can afford to own. Reproduction, local shows, high-school art programs, and summer sketching classes have helped this trend. But even more than these, there is a water-color school that reaches an audience of millions with accomplished and revolutionary work. The development of the airbrush by industry has allowed a speed-up and mass production of water colors that was heretofore impossible. Out of this has come a new kind of water color. The Walt Disney Productions use water color on various ground materials for backgrounds, and on celluloid for figures, which produces a luminosity of light and color as a result of lighting from artificial sources. Hundreds of skilled water-colorists produce thousands of works designed for animated cartoons. The modern discoveries of cinema technique and the airbrush, with an ancient medium, combine to give water color a new and undeveloped dimension, movement through space in time.

REFERENCES

A. Applying to American Painting in General

(1) *American Art Today.* (National Art Society: New York's World Fair, 1939) 20 pp.

(2) BILLINGS, HENRY. "The Picasso exhibition." *Magazine of Art,* New York, January, 1940, pp. 27, 50.

(3) BOSWELL, PEYTON, JR. *Modern American Painting.* (Dodd, Mead & Co.: New York, 1939)

(4) BREUNING, MARGARET. "The Whitney's Enlarged Annual." *Magazine of Art,* New York, January, 1940, p. 100.

(5) BRUCE, EDWARD, and WATSON, FORBES. *Art in Federal Building.* (Art in Federal Buildings, Inc.: New York, 1934–36)

(6) BURROUGHS, ALAN. *Limners and Likenesses.* (Harvard University Press: Cambridge, Massachusetts, 1936) 148 pp.

(7) Cahill, Holger, and Barr, H. H., ed. *Art in America.* (Reynald and Hitchcock, Inc.: New York, 1935)

(8) CHENEY, (MRS.) M. C. *Modern Art in America.* (McGraw-Hill Book Co., New York, 1939)

(9) DEVREE, HOWARD: "Art and democracy." *Magazine of Art,* New York, June, 1939, p. 266.

(10) HAGAN, O. F. L. *The Birth of the American Tradition in Art.* (Charles Scribner's Sons: New York, 1939)

(11) HALL, W. S. *Eyes on America.* (Studio Publications: New York, 1939)

(12) ISHAM, SAMUEL. *The History of American Painting.* (The Macmillan Co.: New York, 1936)

(13) JEWELL, E. A. *Have We an American Art?* (Longmans, Green, and Co.: New York, 1939)

(14) KOOTZ, S. M. *Modern American Painters.* (Brewer and Warren, Inc.: New York, 1930)

(15) LaFOLLETTE, SUZANNE. *Art in America.* (Harper and Brothers: New York, 1929) p. 315.

(16) *Life in America.* (Metropolitan Museum of Art: New York, 1939)

(17) McCAUSLAND, ELIZABETH. Catalog of the exhibition *The World of Today.* (Berkshire Museum: Pittsfield, Massachusetts, July 26–Sept. 5, 1939) pp. 3, 5.

(18) MUNRO, THOMAS. "Present American painting: A report of progress." *Formes,* Paris, January, 1932, p. 202.

(19) *New Horizons in American Art.* (Museum of Modern Art: New York, 1936)

(20) OVERMYER, GRACE. *Government and the Arts.* (W. W. Norton & Co., Inc.: New York, 1939) 110 pp.

(21) *Trois Siecles d'Art aux Etats-Unis.* (Musée du Jeu de Paume; Paris, Mai–Juillet, 1938)

(22) Watson, Forbes, ed. *American Painting Today.* (American Federation of Arts: Washington, 1939)

(23) W[HITING], F. A., JR. "'Life' takes liberties." *Magazine of Art,* New York, January, 1940, p. 50.

(24) WIEGAND, CHARMION VON. "Can art sustain artists?" *The Nation,* New York, Aug. 24, 1940, p. 150.

B. Applying Especially to Water-Color Painting

(1) BENSON, E. M. *John Marin.* (The American Federation of Arts: Washington, D. C., 1935)

(2) BRUENING, MARGARET. *Maurice Prendergast.* (Whitney Museum of American Art: New York, 1931)

(3) DOWNES, WILLIAM. *Life and Works of Winslow Homer.* (Houghton Mifflin Co.: Boston, 1911)

(4) GALLATIN, ALBERT. *American Watercolourists.* (E. P. Dutton and Co.: New York, 1922)

(5) *John Marin.* (Museum of Modern Art: New York, 1936)

(6) MURRELL, WILLIAM. *Charles Demuth.* (Whitney Museum of American Art: New York, n.d.)

(7) ROURKE, CONSTANCE. *Charles Sheeler.* (Harcourt, Brace and Co.: New York, 1938)

(8) The Studio. *Famous Masters of Water-color Painting: J. S. Sargent.* (William Edwin Rudge: New York, 1930)

SECTION II

THE NATURE OF ART AND RELATED TYPES OF EXPERIENCE

CHAPTER XXI

THE PSYCHOLOGICAL APPROACH TO ART AND ART EDUCATION

THOMAS MUNRO
Curator of Education, The Cleveland Museum of Art
Chairman, Division of Art, Western Reserve University
Cleveland, Ohio
and Chairman of the Society's Yearbook Committee

I. AIMS OF ART EDUCATION FROM A PSYCHOLOGICAL STANDPOINT

Modern psychology has deeply affected education in all fields. It had led us to realize that, in all branches of education, we are trying to direct the development of human beings. These are the basic materials with which we work; and the more we understand them, the more effectively we can control them for their own benefit and that of society. Teachers, too, are human beings, each with a peculiar set of strong and weak qualities, desires, and emotions. They affect the educational process in ways not always foreseen or intended. The content of education itself consists of products and records of human thinking and striving. The ideas and skills, the books, machines, and works of art that we ask children to study are expressions of human nature, and all are to be understood more clearly in the light of psychology.

Art especially is a warmly personal subject, though not always so presented in schools and colleges. It is concerned directly and constantly with human individuals and groups, rather than with impersonal facts or logical abstractions. It deals with concrete experiences and their objects; with emotive sense images, aspirations, loves, and hates. The forms and activities of art can be fully understood only in the light of the motives that inspired them and the experiences they arouse. Psychology should and will illuminate these for us, although so far it has made only a slight beginning in the study of behavior and experience in the realm of art.

Success in art depends to an unusually high degree upon obscure personal factors in the student, the teacher, and the mature artist. It depends on configurations of desire, imagination, and feeling that we now understand very dimly. No amount of technical skill or informa-

249

tion alone will produce creative artists or discriminating appreciators. Routine methods, and even the most apparently logical courses of study, are often unavailing. Many teachers are eager to make their students ' creative,' and often fondly believe they have done so, only to see the capable student become a mediocrity, while some neglected ' ugly duckling ' of the class may go on to produce surprisingly original things. Educational idealists hold up the goal of producing a new, American culture, including new advances in art. But there is little evidence that we know how to educate for artistic creativeness.

The psychological approach to education regards teaching in all subjects, on all age levels, as an attempt to *develop abilities,* rather than to convey an inert mass of knowledge; as an attempt to foster inborn aptitudes, to harmonize and direct them into channels desirable from the social, as well as the individual standpoint. There are many sorts of mental ability, all involving a coöperation of basic functions, but differing to some extent as to what functions they emphasize. We recognize some abilities concerned especially with manual or with other forms of nerve and muscle coördination, some with powers of visual or other sense perception, some with various sorts of memory, some with understanding of abstract concepts. There are powers of creative imagination, powers of enjoyment, and powers of critical judgment. All are exercised in art and may be developed through it.

The teaching of any subject may be appraised in terms of how well it succeeds in developing valuable mental and bodily abilities. Too often we teach science without asking how we can best develop powers of scientific thinking, rather than mere understanding and memory of past scientific discoveries or mere ability to apply them in a mechanical way. Too often we teach art without asking how we can best develop the power to think and imagine artistically; to create and appreciate art. We teach it, in other words, as a set of mechanical skills or historical facts, apart from the mental ability to use these skills and facts constructively. We sometimes profess a desire to develop creative originality and powers of appreciation in students, and then proceed to teach as if the creation of art were merely a matter of manual technique and the following of set rules of composition, or as if appreciation were merely a matter of knowing historical facts about art.

Some theorists would reply that neither appreciation nor creative ability can be taught, and that all we can hope to do in art education is to train the hands and memories. Perhaps; but that is a psychological assumption for which there is no other evidence than the frequent failure of past educational methods. The fact remains that we know little about what constitutes the process of artistic creation or that of appreciation, or what factors enable some individuals to achieve greater ability in these processes than others do. Both are essentially problems of psychology. If we ignore them or rest content with dogmatic assumptions about them, our educational principles remain to that extent unscientific and unintelligent. The situation points to one outstanding need; and that is for more careful systematic study and experiment in the psychology of art — not in isolation, but in relation to general psychology.

That art is a powerful means of influencing children, and thus of educational control, is evident if we consider the hold of motion pictures, comic strips, and illustrated stories upon the imagination of youth. True, these are not always good art; but they do attract and stimulate to an extent that school art and other school studies often fail to achieve. Vivid, dramatic techniques of presentation, visual and otherwise, can vitalize all sorts of school work and make learning easy. Well-meaning efforts of educators and moralists, on the other hand, are often hampered by dullness and abstractness. These facts are bound up with the larger fact that art is a powerful means of social control in general. It operates effectively in the dictatorial state, and we should not forget the long history of religious art in the service of various creeds and cults or the present influence of advertising, political cartoons, and posters. Whether we consider the educational process in a narrow sense or consider the whole process of social control, the same fact is evident: that art is an instrument of incalculable power, too often left to selfish interests and neglected by the public-spirited. To use it better, we must understand better how it affects and can affect human nature; how it moves the springs of human action, belief, and emotion. This is fundamentally a problem for psychology, to be approached through a study, not of art alone, but of art in relation to the basic factors of personality as well.

A consistent analysis of educational aims from the standpoint of psychology leads again to the old Greek conception of a well-balanced, harmoniously developed *personality*. Each individual is born with a number of rudimentary functions, to which others are added during maturation. They develop into complex types of perception, imagination, reasoning, desire, preference, purpose, and evaluation, as well as into powers of manual and other bodily coördination. All these can be actively exercised, controlled, and refined through the activities of art — in some respects, more directly and effectively there than in any other branch of human culture. A consistent effort at balanced development of personality would include attention to these and to their manifestations in esthetic experience. In other words, the perceptive, imaginative, and affective components of personality should be fostered and developed through the educational process, along with the bodily and intellectual components. All are active and spontaneous in young children. But too often they become neglected, repressed, and atrophied in older students and adults, with the result that the adult personality is mutilated and disbalanced, with many of its potential functions arrested and immature.

This situation cannot be blamed entirely on formal education. In large part, it is a result of maladjustments inherent in our civilization. Life closes in upon the older child; repressive customs and competitive responsibilities force him to give up, one after another, the development of abilities he might ideally have pursued to fruition. But education could counteract these repressive forces much more than it does, through achieving a better balance in its own activities. From the psychological standpoint, an excessive share of the educational process — more and more as the child grows older — is devoted to intensive, and sometimes fatiguing, training of a few selected nerves and muscles, especially of those concerned with reading the printed page, understanding abstract ideas, and memorizing facts. The functions thus neglected by formal education do not become entirely inactive, however. They are stimulated outside of school, often by irresponsible agencies, in sensational and undisciplined ways, thus producing dissociation between the school and outside interests, and sometimes antagonism to the school as dull and prosaic. A considerable advance toward correcting this fault has been made in recent years, especially in the lower grades of school. Where made, it has always involved a greater emphasis on activities in the visual and other arts, including those of the theater.

In addition, art activities are being increasingly employed as a corrective for mental and nervous maladjustments in both children and adults. Their therapeutic value results in part from bringing into active play muscular, sensory, and other functions that may have been too little exercised in a sedentary life, thus restoring balance and helping to rest the overfatigued nerve centers. In part, it results from helping the individual to externalize his interests, and divert some attention from himself and his anxieties. Meanwhile, the growing popularity of art activities for leisure recreation on the part of normal people, especially professional and office workers, gives a clear indication of their value in helping to correct the tiring overspecialization of urban life.

It is not implied that the development of individual personality should be the sole aim of education. That would be to overwork a single psychological conception. We also aim, for example, at transferring to all children, so far as they are able to receive it, those elements in our *cultural heritage* that seem most important for intrinsic enjoyment and practical use. That choice can never be made with complete objectivity or finality, but must be made by each generation of educational leaders in the light of its best powers of judgment. It involves a compromise (different in different types of school) between the requirements of vocational training and those of a broad cultural background. The latter, as far-sighted vocational advisers realize, is not to be advocated merely for the sake of leisure enjoyment, but also for its direct contribution to powers of advancement in any skilled occupation. A wise selection from our social heritage should include careful attention to some of its artistic elements. Without this, no one can be said to have a broad cultural background, however skilled and learned he may be in a special field.

The task of transferring the cultural heritage of art, science, and other human achievements to the young raises many psychological problems. That heritage cannot be conveyed in mass, all at once, but requires selection and adaptation to the type of student involved. Individual differences of interest and ability require us to vary the selection and emphasis according to the student's mentality. Above all, the selection and emphasis must be adapted to the mental-age level of the student. Certain things can be understood, enjoyed, and used by older students and not by younger. Certain types of art can be appreciated and profitably studied by the twelve-year-old and not by the six-year-old. Certain technical activities, such as oil painting and enamelling, are too difficult for the very young. How shall these be graded, presented in order of sequence, so as to be adapted to the student's present stage of development? How can they be organized into a continuous program of advancement toward the more difficult and mature, without gaps or confusing dislocations? These questions can be answered, in regard to art or any other subject, only in the light of genetic psychology; after a study of the normal development of interests and abilities through maturation, and the principal types of deviation in such growth. We shall consider them more fully in a later section of this chapter.

As already stated, American education (not to speak of that in other countries) has been remiss in developing the artistic and esthetic, the perceptual, imaginative, and emotional strains in personality. This charge requires a little further amplification. Several causes have impelled many educational administrators in recent years to adopt a consciously 'hard-boiled' attitude, to disparage and disfavor expressions of imagination and feeling. Financial stringency has led to renewed attacks on 'frills' and fancies, including the arts. Some (by no means all) administrators and school boards are opposed to art that is not 'realistic' and practical. For the young child, they are intolerant toward fairy tales, myths, and fanciful pictures. They insist that children spend their time instead on 'factual' studies of modern industry, transportation, and the like. Even the 'progressive' wing of recent educators, consciously revolting from the classical, aristocratic education of yesterday, has tended toward a heavy emphasis on social and economic realism, often at the expense of imaginative art. The latter it sometimes condemns as 'escape from reality,' and many of its leaders would restrict the study of art to realistic portrayals of the contemporary social scene. Thus, whereas the old classical education at least paid some attention to the Bible and to Greek and Latin literature, with their rich content of myth, fantasy, and folklore, the modern education gives the child comparatively little of these cultural traditions, indispensable for appreciation of past art.

Even from the standpoint of realism, these attitudes are narrow and incomplete. They assume, and lead students to assume, a false psychology, which ignores the tremendous force of sensuous, willful, emotional, and often irrational factors in life; the proneness of all mankind to fantasy-building of one sort or another. They lose the great power of art to deal directly with such factors, and to refine and organize them into some degree of rational adjustment with the rest of life. Through ignoring the actual importance of art in present American society, they conceal from the student important vocational opportunities and resources, even in commerce and industry themselves.

Inadequate attention to art in American education is due in part to confusion between the broad and the narrow meanings of the term 'art'; in part, it has been due to a narrow conception of art in the minds of professional teachers of art. In a very broad sense, 'art' includes not only the visual arts, but also literature and music, so that educators sometimes feel that they are doing enough for art when they include some study of literature and music. Thus the development of visual ability is neglected. In a very narrow sense, ' art ' is often restricted to the ' fine arts ' of drawing, painting, sculpture, and decorative design. Overemphasis on these fine arts by art teachers tends to exclude the industrial and commercial arts, furniture, clothing, the handcrafts, city planning, and even architecture (aside from temples and cathedrals). As a result, the administrator gets an exaggerated impression of the impracticality and triviality of all visual art. He comes to think of art education merely in terms of flower painting, clay modelling, abstract decoration, and what seem to him crude efforts by children at pictorial self-expression. ' Art appreciation ' becomes identified in his mind with sentimental effusions about pictures, and ineffective attempts to make children like them. Those responsible for art in education have too often failed to put it forward so as to show its true power and substance, its true utility, practicality, and realism.

Psychologically, the goal of developing the esthetic and artistic strains in personality is not necessarily achieved by merely including one or more ' art courses ' in the curriculum. Such a perfunctory solution often serves merely to conceal the basic neglect. For art can be taught merely as trivial play — pleasant for little children, tedious to older ones — or as unimaginative technique or dry scholarship on higher levels.

The Yearbook has tried to help correct some of these misunderstandings by stressing in Section I the great variety of products and activities included in the concept of visual art and their vital importance in present American life. If we are to understand the psychological importance of art, we must first regard it broadly; not as a special accomplishment or luxury for the few or as a mere avocation for leisure amusement, but as covering a group of activities almost universal in scope and concerned with basic human interests.

The wide range of phenomena concerned becomes more evident as soon as we think, not only of the artist or producer of visual art, but also of the appreciator, the consumer, the enjoyer, and the user of art. For everybody falls in some way under this latter category. It includes, not only those addicted to art galleries and museums, but also every reader of illustrated books, magazines, and newspapers, whether the illustrations are drawings or photographs. It includes every patron of theaters and motion-picture shows; every wearer of clothes, jewelry, and other accessories of costume. It includes every inhabitant of a house and garden or an apartment; everyone who visits parks, playgrounds, and public buildings; and everyone who uses furniture and utensils in house, school, or office. It includes every rider in automobiles, trains, and airplanes; everyone who looks at advertising and buys packaged goods. In short, everyone is somehow a consumer of art, is affected by it, develops likes and dislikes towards it and standards of value in judging it. Most of these persons, of course, have no particular interest in ' fine ' art; in the refined and specialized products of painting and sculpture. Some persons, indeed, are distinctly scornful toward them; but this may signify only that they prefer another type of art, such as the plain, informal, and ' natural.'

The producers of art are perhaps fewer in number, but by no means so few as they are commonly supposed to be. In the first place, they include not only painters and sculptors, but also thousands of workers in many industries — not all the workers, to be sure, but those in any way concerned with affecting the visual appearance of products and services. And these are only the vocational, professional artists. Millions more practice some art or craft in an amateur way. Children from nursery school onward now construct pictures, clay models, and handcraft materials. Many unpaid and amateur artists are recognized as outstanding in their fields. Every amateur photographer, or hobbyist who ' makes things,' is to some degree an artist. Psychologically, it is not even essential that the art produced be technically skillful. Children's art is often quite lacking in this respect, by adult standards. The impulse to produce art of some kind, to express oneself in some art medium, is almost as universal as the use of art produced by others, if not equally so. Just as everyone uses words, and thus produces rudimentary literature, so everyone selects and rearranges, partly on a basis of their visual appearance, the objects presented to him for purchase, use, and further observation. To assemble the elements of a costume, of a home or an office interior, usually involves some rudiments of artistic arrangement, along with more purely utilitarian considerations. The ' consuming ' of art thus includes ' creative ' phases, in the form of active selection, reorganization, reëmphasis, and adaptation of given materials to a new situation, partly on a basis of their visual appearance. True, such rudimentary types of artistic production involve little, if any, special technical skill and perhaps no manipulation of a recognized art medium. It is well at times to make a clear distinction between artists in a broad sense and those in a narrow sense; between good and bad or mediocre art. But to see the psychological significance of the activity called 'art,' we should not set it apart too sharply from activities that differ only in the medium employed or in the degree of technical development.

II. The Educational Importance of Esthetic Standards

As there are many producers and consumers of art, so there are also many critics of art, and theorists on the subject of beauty and artistic value. Most of them, of course, have not studied the subject formally and do not realize the assumptions involved in expressing critical opinions about art. Many outside the field of art like to repeat the old saying, "I don't know much about art, but I know what I like." Sometimes these same individuals really believe that they know a good deal about art or at least about art values; about what makes a picture or a statue good or bad. Confidence in one's judgment of art values is often greatest in those who have little direct experience in that realm. As a rule, it does no harm; but it sometimes does very definite harm when the dogmatic critic is a school principal, a superintendent, or otherwise in educational authority. As such, he may ridicule and tyrannize over art teachers who wish to have their children study or experiment with new and unconventional types of art that he does not understand or like. Men who would hesitate to express opinions in other technical fields with which they are unfamiliar often become surprisingly self-assured in evaluating art. Since the field of art itself contains all shades of opinion, such an administrator can nearly always find persons in the neighborhood, claiming to be art authorities, who will support his repressive attitude. In recent years the hand of such administrative domineering has fallen heavily on attempts to modernize art education by allowing older students to experiment in unconventional forms, and by showing them examples of Postimpressionist art. "What's that supposed to be a picture of?" and "Are you trying to make these children into crazy modernists?"— with such remarks, the progressive teacher is gradually frightened into conformity.

It is not part of our present discussion to defend Modernism, or any particular styles in art. But it is relevant to urge upon administrators and other persons of influence in education the duty of studying the subject of art values open-mindedly before becoming actively partisan. This subject in its most theoretical form is called 'esthetics.' But without delving far into theory, the layman can at least read a little of both sides of the case in current works of art criticism dealing with modern tendencies.

Great disagreement exists among artists, art critics, and theorists as to what constitutes good art.[1] There is nothing new in this; such disagreement has always existed. It is well known that most of the artists whom we now recognize as great, and whose styles have become traditional classics, were met at first with violent attacks — often plausibly reasoned out — by conservative critics. Nor is visual art peculiar in this respect. Wide disagreement on values exists in regard to music and literature, and in regard to politics, economics, and morals. Some conflict and change of standards are signs of health and progress. But the clash of styles in painting and sculpture, and to some extent in architecture and furnishing, has been especially active in the last few decades. It has been vigorously publicized, and has attracted many of the lay public to take sides. Its causes are numerous and complex. One is that during the nineteenth century many strange, exotic, and primitive styles of art were introduced to the Western World by travel, anthropology, and archaeology. They commanded attention by their forcefulness, and by the passionate admiration of them on the part of some artists and critics. Their aims, qualities, and claims to esthetic value were often markedly at variance with those of late Greek, Roman, and Renaissance art, on which our traditional rules and standards had been based. Yet they were increasingly imitated and adapted, gained popularity, and helped produce new contemporary styles that violated classical canons of beauty. Machine industry, new materials and techniques, and social and national upheavals also contributed their devious influences, stimulating but bewildering in their variety, and hard to reconcile with older principles.

Though many of these events are now regarded as ancient history in European art circles, and by Americans who have kept in touch with them, the American public as a whole has taken several decades to realize their impact. Public education in America has shown a tendency to lag even farther behind general movements of taste and opinion, to approve for passing on to the young only that which has become unquestionably respectable.

One result of controversy and confusion in the world of art has been to produce a spirit of vagueness and uncertainty in art education. No longer quite confident of the old rules and 'art principles,' the art

[1] See Chapter XXVII, "Standards of Value in Art," for a further discussion.

teacher has nothing very definite to take their place. With so many
different artists, styles, and methods to choose from, he is sometimes
overwhelmed by the task of choosing among them. Moreover, as
we have previously noted, the whole subject of art education in this
country is relatively new and unorganized. Hampered by far-reaching dissension in its own field, it has had to feel its way and struggle
for a definite place in the American school and college curriculum.

In contrast with the representatives of other subjects, especially
the exact sciences, art teachers often seem to the administrator to be
tiresomely incapable of making up their own minds as to what they
want to teach and how, or even as to what materials and equipment they
need to teach it with. The administrator, however well-intentioned, often has no course but to put the whole matter aside and postpone the
development of art instruction until the art teachers can decide what
they want to do and can present some definite, convincing case for doing it.

A little more attention to fundamental esthetic issues on the part
of both art teachers and administrators might go far to improve this
situation. Not that such issues could or should be finally solved, and
complete agreement achieved, for that is not to be desired in a democratic society. But it would help, first, to bring a realization of what
the essential differences are, and, second, to show how much agreement
already exists on the aims to be sought in both art and art education.
It is easy to exaggerate the differences by stressing heated argument
over a few controversial moderns and primitives. Aside from these,
there is now almost universal agreement among artists, critics, and
scholars on the artistic merit of most of the past traditions and individual artists emphasized by current art histories. Discussion goes on
about the exact relative importance to be assigned to Giotto, Titian,
Tintoretto, and El Greco, for example; but no responsible critic today
denies that all these artists possess elements of greatness. The same
is true regarding Greek, Hindu, Romanesque, and Gothic sculpture and
architecture, Chinese and modern French landscape, Persian and Japanese decorative arts, and so on through a long list.

No esthetic theorist denies, in general, that a good work of art will
possess some unity and some variety; will achieve some harmony between material, form, and function; and so on. Dispute arises chiefly
when we come to the specific implications of these principles; for
instance, just what ' unity ' implies, and how much of it is desirable in
a particular case. No one who has studied the old masters can deny

that all of them to some extent alter or ' distort ' natural objects, including human anatomy, in the process of artistic representation; that, in fact, it is impossible to represent nature exactly as it is, since every artist must select and rearrange for himself. But dispute arises over just how much alteration, and what kind, is agreeable or disagreeable, justified or unjustified, in particular cases. No one questions that decorative design and utility, visual appearance and associated meanings, can all be valuable in art at certain times and places.

As to art education, no one denies that some technique and direction are valuable for a prospective artist and also some freedom to work out his own ideas. The dispute is over what compromise between the two should be worked out for students of various age levels and what kinds of technique and direction are most valuable in the light of all the educational goals to be considered. Intelligent solutions for these disputes can be achieved only by clear analysis and careful experiment over a long period of time. They must be constantly revised in the light of new conditions. It is not necessary, then, to decide all the moot points of esthetic theory before going ahead with the development of art education. Many of these points can be handled most advantageously by showing the student frankly that different schools of thought and practice exist in these matters and by helping him to work out intelligent opinions about them on a basis of study and experience, not of snap judgments.

III. Current 'Art Principles'; Their Uses and Dangers

Teachers of art sometimes oversimplify the problem of esthetic value by excessive reliance upon a few concepts known as ' art principles.' Besides ' unity and variety,' these include ' rhythm,' ' proportion,' ' balance,' ' dominance and subordination,' and a few others. Some of the textbooks used by art teachers lay these down as rules of good art, and as yardsticks by which to measure the value of art, including the work of children as well as adult artists. Accordingly, many art teachers use them in class as a sort of Decalogue of Esthetics, and as if they solved all evaluative problems.

The main trouble with these so-called ' art principles ' is not that they are definitely wrong or false, but that they are so vague and abstract as to mean very little in practice, or rather to mean whatever each individual writer or teacher wishes them to mean. The current definitions of them are so broad and general that almost any work of art can be shown to possess them to some extent, in one way or another. It is impossible to estimate that extent, or to compare two works of art as to their conformity to a certain ' principle,' without giving to the principle some special interpretation that makes it easily recognizable, perhaps measurable. For instance, ' good ' proportion may be defined in terms of some particular mathematical ratio between the sizes of parts. Then, however, the principle is likely to be so narrow as to be very debatable. Past works of art, commonly recognized as good, can always be found that do not conform to it. Creative artists, for the most part, pay much less attention to these rules than do teachers and their more docile students. In art education, their excessive use often indicates a desire to reduce all problems as quickly as possible to some simple, stereotyped formula. There are not a few teachers, unfortunately, who continue throughout a long career to base their teaching upon a few impressive catchwords learned in their period of training. Others, more eager to be modern, make the same mistake by scanning each new art teachers' magazine for some new, simple formula to apply in their class: for the latest ' method ' by this or that writer.

Many of these formulas, it is true, have a certain measure of truth and educational usefulness. They save the teacher and class from too much aimless groping. They call attention to some particular kind of art, or way of producing art, that is good in its own way, as far as it goes. The evil in their use arises when they are applied in an absolutistic spirit, rigidly and exclusively, as a substitute for studying different kinds of art, and for open-minded thinking about art; for analyzing the specific aims and qualities of each particular work of art in terms of what it is trying to do and of what it is expected to do under the particular conditions. The situations for which art is produced are so infinitely variable; the types of person who will make and use it are so variable; the ideals and styles of art in different times and cultures are so numerous and changing that no brief set of ' principles ' can possibly serve as an adequate yardstick of values. When such a set, narrowly defined, is imposed upon art students or seriously relied upon as a test of art ability, it becomes definitely repressive and harmful. Fortunately the common sense of most art teachers prevents them from doing so.

This does not mean that there are no standards of value in art, that any work of art is as good as any other, or that the task of evaluation is doomed to failure. Economic and political science cannot yet give us a simple yardstick for deciding what is a good law, a good form of government, or a good business practice. Democratic peoples are gradually evolving a general philosophy on the subject; but it is often hard to see its implications in a special case. Much experimentation and research are necessary, in the light of changing social conditions. The same is true of art values. There is much enlightenment in the old principles of esthetics, as explained and illustrated by wise philosophers. From studying them we can derive suggestive hypotheses, not empty catchwords or arbitrary rules. Then it remains to develop and revise them in the light of all the new needs and situations that art is trying to serve today. For this study we need not only psychological information about the human beings who make and use art, but also detailed information about the kinds of art being produced, and how they work in contemporary society.

IV. Scientific Approaches to Esthetic Value

For further study by advanced scholars, it is well to realize how the study of esthetics is being approached today in the light of both sociological and psychological considerations. Through studying social history and the differences among past and present cultures, we are coming to realize how art has been a phase of all cultural development. We learn in what ways the various types of art have expressed their social, political, and economic backgrounds; how art has interacted with these other phases in cultural history, being influenced by them and exerting a profound influence upon them in its turn. We come to see modern tendencies in art, not as whims, or aberrations of individual artists, but as intimately bound up with vast undercurrents in civilization. We become aware of the enormous variety of types of art that have been produced throughout the history of civilization, each with its own peculiar aims, functions, and standards of value. We see that each type has had certain reasons and certain justifications for its existence. As a result, we become less sure that our own personal tastes or familiar traditions represent immutable laws of good art for all the world. We look for common, broad principles in all of them. Finally, we ask in what ways it may be possible for education to help work out for our own time and culture those forms of art that are most suited to it and most conducive to social welfare.

The psychological approach to esthetics and the problem of value in art proceeds from the recognition that valuation itself is a psychological process. Individuals are born with certain capacities for desire, pain, discomfort, and enjoyment. Experience conditions and redirects our impulses, responses, and attitudes from primary objects of physical need to secondary, remote, cultural objects, producing what we describe as ' tastes ' and ' standards ' of value in art, ethics, and other realms. Innate endowment and cultural influences thus coöperate in determining what each individual's tastes and standards shall be. Sometimes works of art are liked and are judged good or beautiful mainly upon a basis of their immediate effects on our sense perception and feeling; at other times, upon a basis of their expected future uses or consequences. These and a few more broad generalities are fairly clear; but they leave much room for future investigation of details, especially as to how individuals come to differ in their tastes and standards. Most of the terms commonly used in describing value and valuation are extremely vague and hard to define, such as ' pleasant ' and ' unpleasant.' They undoubtedly refer to some actual types of experience and underlying physical processes, but we know little about them.

Psychological investigation in itself will perhaps never succeed in proving that certain kinds of art are really good or beautiful and others the opposite, or that certain standards of value are true or binding. For psychology is a descriptive science and does not in itself try to set up aims or standards of value. There will always need to be added a more normative approach, and this the traditional subject of esthetics has undertaken to provide. This approach can make use of data from other fields, such as history, sociology, and biography, to discover the specific effects and functions of various types of art in a civilized society. But psychology does throw much light on the problem of esthetic value and does aid us in forming judgments intelligently, if not with absolute certainty. It will contribute much in practice if it shows us the actual genesis in human motivation of those traditional rules and standards of art that have claimed to be absolute and universal. It will not limit itself to the study of liking and disliking, but will show as well how various types of art have the power to impel various types of attitude and action and to function in many other ways in human behavior and experience.

V. Methods and Difficulties in the Psychological Study of Esthetic Phenomena

What has been done in the psychological study of esthetic phenomena, and how can further progress be made? The first question can be answered quickly: very little has been accomplished by modern scientific psychology towards analyzing and describing, in any fundamental way, the processes involved in creating and experiencing art. Voluminous reports of the experiments and researches since the time of Fechner (who inaugurated experimental esthetics in the eighteen seventies) have produced verified, accepted results only when they dealt with relatively trivial and external aspects of these processes. The essential inner nature of artistic and esthetic experience is still obscure and open to speculative theory. Philosophical, literary, and introspective analyses often seem enlightening and plausible in certain respects, but turn out to be vague, abstract, and disputatious.

Esthetics, which undertakes to explain the general nature of art and beauty, has been recognized as a distinct subject only since the eighteenth century. But philosophers since the time of Socrates and Plato have theorized about art; hence the history of esthetics as philosophy of art can be traced back through many centuries. All sciences and fields of rational investigation can also be traced back to the parent stem of Greek philosophy. But the mathematical, physical, biological, and social sciences have broken away from it to some extent, and achieved increasing power to stand on their own feet through objective methods of observation, experiment, and measurement. Esthetics is apparently in process of doing so; but the transitional phase is long and difficult. It had perhaps to wait until general psychology had become at least partly scientific, changing over from its status as ' philosophy of mind ' to the experimental approach of Wundt, Helmholtz, and other comparatively recent students of mind. A half century or more of scientific psychology has succeeded in building up a considerable framework of verified knowledge about human nature. Within this framework, and with tested laboratory and statistical methods, it would seem that psychology could readily go on to study the phenomena of art, for much of what it has discovered, especially in regard to sense perception, learning, and the physical basis of emotion, seems obviously applicable to art.

One difficulty is that the phenomena of art are especially complex and subtle, involving configurations of thought and feeling as intricate, shifting, and finely differentiated as any in human experience. Another is that they are in large part inward, implicit, occurring in the depths of personality; often not manifested in overt behavior and expression, or manifested in delayed, indirect ways that partly conceal their nature. Often the work of art itself is our chief or only clue to what went on in the artist's mind, or the critic's words are the chief clue to how the work of art affected him. These are both difficult to interpret and not always to be taken at face value. A third reason is that the phenomena of art tend to arouse emotion and hence are hard to study objectively. The same can be said, of course, of attempts to study political, economic, and moral phenomena scientifically.

Opening any recent textbook of general or genetic psychology, one can see at once that by far the greater amount of space is devoted to relatively simple phenomena within each main division. There is much about the behavior of infants and animals; little about that of philosophers, scientists, and artists. The simpler manifestations of muscular control, of sensing, remembering, imagining, learning, and problem-solving are described and illustrated. How these function in the complex situations of art, religion, science, and political life is only briefly hinted. The case was exactly opposite in the old speculative ' philosophy of mind.' There the higher thought processes were emphasized, because they seemed most important. Modern psychology is more conclusive as far as it goes, but it will not have replaced pre-scientific psychology entirely until it likewise deals directly and fully with the more complex mental processes, including those which operate in art.

Will the general psychology of the future, then, include chapters on the psychology of art? Not directly, perhaps, for art may rather be considered a problem of applied psychology. In studying works of art, we immediately come into contact with specialized phenomena. Art itself, considered very broadly, is almost a universal human phenomenon, occurring in all cultures; but civilized art products vary greatly from one age and culture to another. The behavior, methods, and expressed attitudes of artists also differ widely in various cultural settings — for example, according to whether the artists work in the service of religion or of secular patrons, whether they use hand or machine methods, and whether the culture favors individual originality or strict conformity to convention. Thus it is a dubious step to set up such a concept as ' the artist,' and ask how he creates, as if all were of one basic type, or to assume that ' art creation ' or ' art appreciation ' is a single, constant process, similar under all conditions. Much of what is called ' the psychology of art ' is an account of certain behavior traits in a restricted, contemporary group of people, acting according to the customs in vogue at the time. It is comparable to ' the psychology of advertising,' of fencing, or of card-playing. Such studies are not properly a part of general psychology. There is little danger of confusion when they are labelled so as to indicate frankly their limited scope. But too often American psychologists observe a single group of children in one town or the behavior of a few college students and professors in one psychological laboratory; then imply that their findings are true of all children or of all humanity in every age.

Conversely, special cultural studies often do throw light on general psychology, however, by showing how given basic human traits operate in various special types of situation. It is rare, indeed, to encounter any mental phenomena that are not profoundly influenced by special cultural conditions, especially in the case of the higher mental processes of civilized adults. To progress into these realms, general psychology must examine many varieties of behavior under special cultural conditions, compare the behavior of people in different cultures past and present, and seek to find common, basic tendencies among them. Thus so specialized a field as the psychology of art, or even the psychology of modern concert-goers and museum visitors, may be a source of information for general psychology. Light might well be thrown upon the higher processes by making use of such sources.

With a still broader outlook, the psychologist may undertake to study not only fine art and the special modes of civilized behavior toward it, but also esthetic and artistic experience in general. For these are by no means limited to recognized art products and techniques. People experience many things as beautiful or ugly in addition to works of art. They observe, and respond emotionally to the perceptible forms of nature, of other persons, of cities, factories, machines, and other utilitarian objects. They react to the products of scientific as well as artistic thinking. What are these modes of response? In what ways are they similar to the experience of art, and in what ways different? Such phenomena are more universal than responses to art (in the narrow sense), and the study of them is more definitely a part of general psychology. Moreover, as we have noted, the professional artist is not the only one who arranges details into organized forms in such a way as to make them more satisfying to visual perception. Everyone does this to some extent. Everyone dreams, imagines visual forms, and builds phantasies expressing his desires, hopes, and fears. The life of phantasy in general, whether as idle reverie and escape from reality or as instrument to practical effort, is known to be closely bound up with the creation of art. It occurs there, but it also occurs apart from all relation to art, and its study is properly a part of general psychology. If the investigation of those types of phenomena needs a distinguishing label, or recognition as a branch of general psy-

chology, it is perhaps better described as ' esthetic psychology ' than
as ' psychology of art.'

The opinion has already been expressed that the attempts by experimental psychologists to study esthetic phenomena suffer characteristically from their limitation to the laboratory environment. This
criticism is peculiarly applicable to recent American psychologists.[1]
By contrast with such Europeans as Freud and Jung, they fail to realize
the importance of cultural history, biography, literature, and art as
sources of data for generalizing about human nature. They tend to
ignore all the opportunities for observing human nature in action outside the scope of their own laboratories and questionnaires. What
little can be observed within this limited scope is, in the case of art
at least, pathetically bare and fragmentary. It is hard to produce or
experiment with the phenomenon of genuine art appreciation under
laboratory conditions, and nearly impossible to do so with artistic creation. Of course, it is easy to get people to ' go through the motions,'
but the result is likely to be an empty imitation. The laboratory situation, by its very nature, inhibits spontaneous imagination and emotion. The extreme subdivision and simplification of problems that is
necessary for exact experiment and measurement substitutes artificial
arrangements of a few lines, dots, or colored papers for the rich complexities of art, and artificially simplified questions of yes-or-no preference for the intricate relativities of esthetic taste. Behavior in the
laboratory is not necessarily like that in the outside world; indeed, it
may be the direct opposite.

In reacting against the extremely unscientific speculation and intro-
spectionism of early psychology, recent psychologists in this country
have gone to an opposite extreme of exaggerated confidence in quantitative methods, with a tendency to distrust and exclude all observation
that cannot be made under exactly controlled conditions, or at least
expressed in quantitative terms. The result is sometimes to neglect
consideration of inner mental experience and of complex, variable behavior under actual life conditions; sometimes to produce specious
' researches ' that claim to have measured these realities and that are
convincing only to like-minded laboratory devotees. Recent attempts
at the psychology of art have suffered from both these tendencies.

Genuine progress requires, in the first place, a deeper understanding of scientific method on the part of psychologists, including the fact

[1] A more favorable view of American research in the psychology of art is
expressed in Chapter XXVI. — *T.M.*

that it is not necessarily quantitative, at least in its early and transitional stages. When the data are too complex and variable to be measured at once, much can be done through a gradual introduction of other phases of scientific method, as is common in anthropology and other social studies. Observations and hypotheses from all available sources, whether made under controlled conditions or not, can be assembled, compared, and tested out as far as possible through mutual checking of results among workers. When some of the phenomena are obviously inward experiences, inaccessible to behavioristic observation, more introspective methods must be used or none at all; but these methods also can be checked and controlled to an increasing extent through systematic coöperation.

In the second place, psychologists who wish to study art and other complex mental processes must become more widely educated in the humanistic subjects. They must learn more about actual works of art, about art's place in cultural history, about the biographies of artists, and about expressed responses to art in the form of critical writings. They must learn to interrelate these with the more exact findings of laboratory psychology, so that each can verify and augment the other. They must realize the potential value of researches that lie somewhere between exact science and the older introspective, speculative, and literary approaches in method and degree of conclusiveness — researches that strive gradually toward science and do not expect to reach it at one bound.

Attempts to theorize about esthetic psychology sometimes begin with works of art and people's responses to them. Here is a picture, and here is a person looking at it; the picture is a stimulus, and the person responds. How does he respond? What responses, inward and outward, does the picture arouse? The picture is a complex form, and no doubt the observer's total response is also complex, a highly differentiated *Gestalt*, or configuration. But how trace it further? Whether by questioning and introspection or in some other way, the psychologist usually hopes to analyze the response in terms of the basic functions of general psychology: of perception, emotion, volition, and so on, or whatever substitutes for these terms are in vogue. When instincts are in vogue, he hopes to trace the complex response back to original instincts; when conditioned reflexes are in vogue, he hopes to trace it back to these, and thus to explain it. This approach is on the whole analytic, from a complex to supposedly simple elements. It is a common approach among writers whose principal training has been in the arts and art criticism, rather than in scientific psychology.

Authors of textbooks and systems of general psychology usually proceed in an opposite, synthetic direction, beginning with the basic nerve centers, functions and mechanisms, the learning process, and so on, hoping to arrive toward the end of the book at some account of how these elements combine into complex types of behavior. Such culminating chapters are usually rather brief and perfunctory. If the author has committed himself to a rigorously scientific point of view, he has little to offer but reports of a few scattered researches on color preference and the like, which obviously do not cover the complexities of esthetic experience. As one approaches esthetic experience, the phenomena become not only more complex but more variable as well, so that no text of reasonable length could hope to describe even the main types of configuration. But if it could describe even one example of a complex esthetic response in terms of the primary functions with which it began, it would at least have shown how to bridge the gap between simple and complex, basic function and configuration in adult, civilized experience. This gap is never really bridged, although it is often concealed in the effort to present a systematic text.

Psychologists impressed by *Gestalt* principles tend to avoid the whole problem of linking up simple with complex, through insisting that the whole (the complex configuration) is different from the sum of its parts, or from the individual ' basic functions ' as conceived in any artificially simplified, isolated way. They attempt to present various typical configurations in behavior and to point out some of their recurring characteristics. *Gestalt* psychologists have so far done little with art or esthetic phenomena and have restricted themselves on the whole to fairly simple configurations. The *Gestalt* approach has not advanced very far toward describing or explaining any configuration because of its fear to analyze it into much simpler elements. It is even more opposed to attempts at synthesis of complex configurations out of supposedly simple elements. But how can any phenomenon be described or compared with another except in terms of some simpler constituents or factors, whose proportion and arrangement determine the nature of the complex phenomenon? Admittedly, all conceptions of psychological ' elements,' such as ' functions ' or ' instincts,' are abstractions. None ever operates alone or remains entirely constant, and none has ever been satisfactorily defined or described. But all psychological advance must somehow proceed in terms of showing the relations between relatively simple and constant factors and relatively complex, variable ones. New conceptions of the former will have to be invented if the old ones are too misleading. Usually the new are very much like the old. In spite of much denunciation, the old concepts of ' will,' ' instinct,' ' apperception,' and so on keep reappearing in slightly different terminology. The terms make little difference if the facts are correctly reported. Some American psychologists are overquick to brand others in the field as ' dated ' or ' old-fashioned ' if their terminology is that of yesterday. It prevents them, for one thing, from appreciating the valuable insights into complex mental processes achieved by earlier writers.

Whichever course is followed at the start, analytic or synthetic, it must be followed through to the other end if real understanding is to be achieved. Probably both must be followed to some extent. In the process, we shall learn how to describe both the basic factors and the complex resultants more accurately. Certainly, the concept of configuration is useful in esthetic psychology, and so is the implied warning that configurations in esthetic behavior are enormously variable, not to be hastily ' reduced ' to a few simple formulas.

In the old, purely speculative type of esthetic theory, one stumbling block has been overemphasis on verbal issues, with interminable debate over the proper definitions of ' art,' ' beauty,' and other abstract ideas. Such issues often distract the inquiries of psychologists as well. There is great need of an authoritative, accepted set of definitions for use in discussing the phenomena of art, but it is hard to get one because of the various controversial meanings attached by different writers to different terms.[1] It helps considerably if each writer, whatever terms he uses, defines them clearly and holds to these definitions consistently.

Another perennial stumbling block has been the tendency of esthetic theorists to adopt some one simple concept or formula and put it forward as all-explaining. Empathy, wish fulfillment, expression, communication — these and many others have held the spotlight for a few years or months, until the next appeared. There can be, of course, no one simple explanation for phenomena so widely variable as those of art.

Closely akin to this error is the tendency to adopt one extreme posi-

---

[1] An attempt, at least, to describe such terms has been made in the *Dictionary of Psychology*, edited by H. G. Warren (Houghton Mifflin Co.: Boston, 1934). — *Editor*.

tion or the opposite. For example, there has been endless argument in the field of art, as in every branch of psychology, as to whether special abilities are acquired or hereditary, produced by nature or by nurture. Is artistic genius inborn? If so, is education powerless to produce it, or even to know what means are best for its development? This view is common among artists and art critics, who like to believe that genius is altogether mysterious and unaccountable, beyond the reach of school-masters. Is genius due to environment, and can proper conditioning accomplish everything? In that case, a great responsibility seems to lie upon education. But as usual, when either set of extremists is backed against the wall, it has to admit that both heredity and environment are responsible; that both interact to produce genius and lesser abilities, as well as specific varieties of taste and creative impulse.

VI. DETERMINANTS OF ART ABILITY

The many extreme and one-sided theories advanced in recent years, if taken all together, would supply a useful set of hypotheses. There is probably some truth in all of them, and there is no need for selecting any one as all-sufficient. In other words, there are many different *determinants* of art ability, and of other esthetic phenomena. Some may be classified as mainly *hereditary*, and others as mainly *environmental*. Among the former, some pertain to *human nature in general*, and are relatively universal, such as the basic functions and the processes of maturation and learning described by general psychology. They are common to all normal individuals regardless of cultural environment. Then there is the possibility of inborn racial differences in equipment. This question is fraught with emotional dynamite among the theorists who maintain and oppose doctrines of racial superiority and inferiority. But that evaluative issue need not be raised at all. As the Negro differs from the white in pigmentation and shape of hair, does he also differ in nervous or glandular structure that might affect his behavior in realms of art? Little is known about this matter, mainly because of the difficulty in studying racial factors apart from environmental influences. There are hereditary determinants peculiar to certain *family strains*, as in the Kallikaks, the Adamses, and the Bach family of talented musicians. But again, what part of the final results is due to family heredity, and what to family environment?[1] Finally, there are apparently inborn differences in *individuals* within the same family;

---

[1] For a discussion of this aspect of psychology, the reader may consult the *Twenty-Seventh* and the *Thirty-Ninth* Yearbooks of this Society. — *Editor.*

for example, genius and mediocrity among siblings brought up under similar conditions.

Environmental determinants may be similarly distinguished. Some are *physical*, geographical and climatic. They include the differences between one locality and another. Some art historians have stressed this factor, as in attributing differences in pictorial and architectural style to the fact that one style arose in a sunny climate, another in a cold and cloudy. Certainly the presence or absence of materials, such as stone and wood, has had an influence on art forms. But to what extent does climate influence the personality of the artist?

Other environmental determinants are *social* or *cultural*. Here again they differ as to breadth of scope. In some respects all dwellers in the modern Western World are subject to the same cultural influences; to machinery, printing, and science, as contrasted with dwellers in medieval Europe or present-day Tibet. These are *major* cultural determinants. There are also *national* and *local* differences in culture, and these operate as determinants of artistic results. They involve language and special traditions. In what ways does the American environment in general predispose a child to different tendencies from those of France or Germany? That of New York City as compared with a small southern town? Marxist art critics stress the importance of *social* and *economic* class influences. What difference does it make whether a child grows up on a level of luxury, of modest comfort, or of bare subsistence? No doubt class distinctions in the Old World are on the whole more fixed and radical, more loaded with emotional attitudes, than are those of America. But in any locality, it often seems that an artist's aims, interests, and antagonisms are largely attributable to the fact that he thinks as a proletarian or as a property-owner. Some environmental influences are peculiar to a certain *type of school;* for example, to a free progressive school as contrasted with a strict military academy. Some are bound up with a certain set of *companions*, as a gang or snobbish clique. Some are centered in the *family;* in the peculiar drama of personalities provided by father, mother, brothers, and sisters. This last type of influence is heavily stressed by psychoanalysts and child psychologists. It is said to involve the Oedipus conflict, sibling rivalry, and parental overprotection or neglect.

Obviously, these various types of influence overlap and merge in ways not clearly distinguishable. They affect not only the artistic and esthetic sides of personality, but the whole personality and social culture as well. To study them adequately would take us far outside the usual scope of psychological investigations and into realms more commonly regarded as sociological, economic, and historical. Yet it is hard to see how general psychology can go very far toward understanding the civilized adult mind and its development without considering them. Here, as elsewhere, the old subject demarcations are breaking down, and discovery must proceed by coördinating many lines of inquiry. Esthetic psychology by itself cannot go far toward understanding the nature and genesis of behavior in the realm of art. For if any outstanding fact emerges, it is that such behavior is not an isolated phenomenon, but intimately bound up with the development of personality in general, and with the interplay of all cultural factors.

Merely to list the diversity of influences at work upon the civilized child must make for some modesty on the part of educators. For it is obvious how few are the factors subject to control in the schoolroom, how restricted are the opportunities for even the wisest teacher to control the child's development or to experiment with the factors that determine it. We often assume that the responsibility for satisfactory development rests largely with education in a narrow sense and that this responsibility will be met by devising proper methods of instruction. No one knows at present just how true or false this assumption may be, but certainly the cause is not helped by ignoring the complexity of the problem. We can at least go on to see how well the school can carry out its part in relation to the others; and perhaps that may help to modify the other influences. Certainly, educational psychology is beginning to influence the family environment and the attitude of parents toward their children. The school transmits many cultural influences to the child, including national and local traditions, which it can select and interpret as it thinks best.

VII. ESTHETIC DEVELOPMENT, INDIVIDUAL AND SOCIAL
1. Individual Esthetic Development

Art teachers are coming to realize the need for a psychological understanding of esthetic development, of how children's ability to create and appreciate art grows from one age level to the next. They are trying to reorganize the course of study in art so that it will fit in with this development, rather than be imposed in an artificial order conceived by and for adults.

In the past, the facts and skills of art have usually been presented to students in some artificial order. The cultural heritage of past art has been presented partly in historical, chronological sequence. In this case, it conforms partly, though not wholly, with children's growth. Moderately young children can be easily interested in primitive art and life and children a little older in that of Egypt and Greece, but the development of their interest and ability to understand is not an exact recapitulation of art history as a whole. Young children are also interested in certain phases of modern art that they can understand and enjoy. On the other hand, certain phases of primitive and ancient art are too difficult for them or are alien to their interests, as, for example, religious and sexual symbolism. To present the heritage of art mainly in chronological order does not fit in with normal individual development; it postpones the modern too long and fails to convey important aspects of early culture that only older students can grasp.

Another way of presenting art is in theoretical, synthetic order: to proceed from simple ' art elements ' and ' principles,' such as line and color, rhythm and balance, to complex works of art. But this procedure is too abstract and formal to fit in with the development of children. Power to grasp abstract elements and to be interested in them comes rather late in the child's mental growth, not at the start. Both these ways of organizing subject matter are more suited to older than to younger students. The old, academic way of teaching artistic techniques is similarly formal. It begins with supposed fundamentals of technique, such as drawing from a three-dimensional object in realistic detail, or copying a line drawing by some adult; in any case, with activities that young children do not ordinarily enjoy or do well and that fail to exercise their strong potential art interests at the time. (In much the same way, the conventional teaching of musical technique often begins with finger exercises on some difficult instrument.)

If we can work out some order of gradation in art studies that will be closely coördinated with children's natural growth, we may hope to gain the motivation of spontaneous interest as well as the many other values that come from properly adapting the content of instruction to stage of maturity. We need answers to the following questions: What can children on each age level be reasonably expected to do, learn, and enjoy in art, without undue pressure? What tasks in art are suitably difficult — not too hard or too easy — for the normal child of each age? What kinds of art are most likely to interest children of each stage and to help them progress to the next stage of development?

Some educators in the progressive and free-expression group have gone to the extreme of abandoning all definite gradation and direction, all planned, systematic courses of study, relying on student initiative to guide the sequence of steps. This has led to significant experiments, but in the higher grades it seems to result in much waste of time through aimless trial and error. Older students, even the more independent, usually desire to be helped in learning something fairly definite in the way of techniques, information, and understanding. They enjoy following a definite series of steps that seems to ' get somewhere.' Adapting a course of study to the basic processes of growth does not necessarily mean letting children take the lead in directing their own studies or letting them do at each moment what they wish to do. Teachers who possess a scientific understanding of personality development should be better able than the child himself to understand what the child needs and fundamentally desires or will desire, what problems lie ahead of him, and what he needs to learn in order to cope with them. They will not ignore the child's present conscious impulses, but will so interpret them as to help him to realize his best potentialities and to prepare himself for adult social living.

What is ' natural,' or ' normal,' development? It is a name for an abstract and somewhat idealized conception of the more universal and inwardly determined phases of individual growth, as distinguished from the more peculiar and apparently accidental traits that individuals develop under peculiar environmental conditions. It is, of course, recognized today that the two factors, nature and nurture, cannot be clearly distinguished. In talking of natural development, psychologists are not trying to imagine how individuals would grow if entirely uninfluenced by particular environments. Their conclusions must be drawn from observing how people develop under particular cultural conditions, usually those of modern urban civilization. In talking of normal development, they are not implying that there is any one right or ideal way of growing. The ' normal ' is not necessarily the best conceivable, and moralists, educators, or eugenicists may try to conceive of a still better, supernormal way for the future. But ' normal ' is not exactly the same as ' average.' Most of the children in a given region may be obviously stunted by faulty diet and living conditions. By studying how children grow under fairly adequate (not necessarily ideal) conditions, the scientist builds up a theoretical concept of normality. An account of normal development will be highly generalized, a sort of skeleton outline, stressing phases of growth common to all or to most individuals. However, it may mention some of the general ways in which individual differences develop through various combinations of inborn and environmental determinants. It may mention how deviate types of individual (some of them appraised as subnormal or super-normal) sometimes arise through departure from the normal process.

American psychologists have as a rule been cautious about general-izing on ' basic human tendencies ' or on ' types of personality.' Their accounts of development have been comparatively objective and veri-fiable, but somewhat superficial from the standpoint of those interested in the inner life of imagination, desire, and feeling. European psy-chologists have speculated more boldly from philosophic and literary starting points, often proposing theories of normal development and character types that, though dubious and unverifiable, deal more di-rectly with problems of major concern to art and esthetics. Thus the psychoanalysts, especially Freud (15), Jung (18, 19), and Ferenczi (10), have proposed theories of individual development and of the for-mation of personality types, neurotic and normal, that have direct bearing upon the development of esthetic tastes and creative or expres-sive impulses in children and adults. Especially noteworthy in this connection are Ferenczi's theory of the development of the sense of re-ality, and Freud's theory of successive transfers of the libido through various bodily zones and types of desired object. Psychoanalysis also offers a suggestive theory of fixations and regressions as neurotic devia-tions from normal personality development. Graphology, the study of handwriting as a clue to personality traits, is in better repute in Europe than here (46). It is significant for art in that handwriting is closely related to line drawing. Such theories and approaches should not be quickly dismissed as unverified, for a tremendous mass of clinical and other evidence is claimed for them. They should be tested further on this side of the water to determine what they may contribute to the psychology of art.

An account of normal development will include the order and ap-proximate age levels (allowing for the well-known principles of the distribution of traits) at which important physical and behavior traits appear, including the ability to learn various skills when opportunity and social stimulus present themselves. As cross sections of the process, there should be made composite, generalized descriptions of the normal person of each age level (again with due recognition of the usual range of sex, individual, and perhaps racial and cultural differences). An individual could then be classified tentatively as ' normal,' ' advanced,' or ' retarded,' either on the whole or in certain particulars. Tests of mental age and of intelligence quotient are based upon such a concept of normality, derived through comparing the ability of many children of different ages to perform a varied set of tasks. There is of course much danger of oversimplification in erecting such a concept of normal development and normal age-level abilities. We may be led to ignore important individual differences or differences between our own culture and others, so that what seems to us a basic, universal tendency may be only a limited culture pattern. But there are ways of guarding against this danger, especially through widening our field of vision with more case studies and more ethnological comparisons.

What art teachers could use to very great advantage would be a description of normal development and age-level traits with more explicit emphasis than heretofore on the interests and abilities and other traits most directly involved in activities dealing with art. In short, it would be highly desirable to have a measure of *esthetic age*, analogous to mental age, by which we could determine whether a child was normal, advanced, or retarded in those characteristics and abilities most active in the production and appreciation of art. We frequently make judgments of this sort without scientific accuracy, and it would seem that science could help us to refine them. For example, it is regarded as childish or infantile for a civilized adolescent or adult to prefer dolls, games, songs, and stories suited to early childhood or to be able to draw or model only crude schematic representations. There are, in other words, certain types of taste in art, and in toys and games involving art qualities, that are associated roughly with certain age levels. When an individual deviates markedly from them, down or up the scale, he is considered as retarded or precocious. Similarly, there are certain types of art product, in drawing and other media, that are regarded as natural and normal for children of a certain age, but as retarded or as precocious if made by a child much older or much younger. Furthermore, it is believed that neurotic, arrested, or distorted modes of development may manifest themselves in behavior towards art, as in markedly feminine tastes — love of dolls, dresses, and delicate textiles, quiet games, perfumes, and the like — on the part of an older boy. But such symptoms must always be analyzed in relation to the prevailing culture pattern, which may (as in the Orient) approve them for the masculine boy or man.

It is often hard to link psychological accounts of the general characteristics normal for a certain age level with behavior and ability in specific art situations. There is great need for closer coöperation between psychologists and art teachers on this problem. Psychologists could help by using the forms, materials, and activities of art more frequently as stimuli and test devices; even for problems of general psychology they might often be as suitable as any others. For example, power to perceive complex form in art is some indication of an individual's perceptual powers in general. Art teachers could assist by consciously thinking out their curriculum in terms of the psychological processes, skills, and motivations involved.

A psychological account of development, in so far as it is restricted to the more basic and universal human traits, will tend to minimize reference to specific art works, styles, and techniques, for the reason that such phenomena differ considerably from one cultural group or epoch to another. It need not, however, exclude all specific art or other cultural situations or the behavior traits thereby induced. In fact, it requires a few of them as illustrations of how basic traits manifest themselves in the normal person living in a social environment. A fully worked-out description of normal development should include some reference to how people develop habits of appreciation — tastes, standards of value, habits of perceiving, using, and enjoying objects of art and other esthetic phenomena; how persons of a certain age, a given sex, and so forth tend to some extent to resemble each other in some of these respects and to diverge in others. It should include some reference to how people develop ' creative impulses ' — tendencies to construct forms and express ideas in some way that can be broadly classified as artistic. (This includes practically everyone beyond infancy.) It should include typical similarities within the chief age, sex, and other groups, as well as accounts of the genesis of individual differences through various combinations of determinants.

The desired psychological account of development in the field of art will naturally draw many of its data and examples from art situations of our own time and place, but it will seek to bring out for emphasis the more universal types of product and behavior. For instance, city boys of today may like to play with and to draw toy airplanes and machine guns rather than toy chariots and battering-rams, but the tendency for boys to play with some kind of miniature weapon and vehicle is fairly universal. The wooden sword, the doll, the little clay animal, the schematized line drawing of a human figure, the beaded necklace — these occur in some form in all cultures and periods. In short, when we survey the behavior of present-day children in relation to art, some part of what we see is cultural and transitory — perhaps a momentary fad; another part is a manifestation of more deep and universal motivations. Genetic psychology should seek to discover and emphasize the latter, in so far as it aims at comparative universality in its account of human development. For this purpose, there is need of wide interests on the part of the psychologist, to take in data regarding the behavior of children and adolescents in other times and cultures.

As we have noted in regard to other problems of esthetic psychology, the main requirement is to bring psychology and art into closer contact. This can be approached from either aspect, but in either case the task requires some familiarity on the part of investigators with both fields. Unfortunately, the number of persons who receive training in both is very limited; the pressure toward specialization is still too great.

One can approach the question of esthetic development, first, from the standpoint of psychology. There are numerous partial summaries of genetic or developmental psychology in its broad outlines, notably that by Anderson (1). So far there is none, however, that adequately combines experimental research of the type favored in America with the psychoanalytic and other theoretical approaches. It still remains for each investigator to make his own synthesis of what he will accept from the many proposed accounts of the psychological development of children. When he has done so, he can use it as a set of hypotheses for interpreting children's behavior in relation to art and for conducting new experiments in that field.

The art teacher can use such an account in selecting art materials and activities for each age level that seem to meet the general needs of that level. He can derive many hints as to specific art activities from the general traits of muscular strength and coördination, intelligence, power to learn motor and linguistic skills, attention span, emotional control, personal relationships, and so forth that psychologists regard as normal for each level. He can be ready to recognize and to deal suitably with individual differences and with common deviations from the normal, such as maladjustment and accelerated or retarded development, prescribing in each case the proper artistic diet so far as educational conditions permit. He can understand the function of art in education more thoroughly by seeing it against the background of an inclusive educational process.

The other approach is through an open-minded, inductive study of children's behavior in relation to art, their tastes in art, and their own productions and performances with art media. A substantial beginning along this line has been made in the United States and in England. Much American work in this field, however, has suffered from serious limitations and false assumptions, as: (1) The tremendous amount of significant factual research conducted in Germany, Austria, and France between 1918 and 1933 has been largely ignored. Many thousands of children's drawings, some made by the same child over a period of years, have been collected and carefully analyzed; the results have been published in numerous books and articles mostly still untranslated and not easily available to American readers.[1]   (2) There has been a tendency in this country to assume without justification certain adult standards of value of correctness in children's art products and preferences, and to appraise them by these standards instead of observing them objectively.   (3) Excessive reliance has been placed on questionnaires of preference, which are easy to give but often superficial and inconclusive.   (4) The American work has been too much restricted to drawings and other pictures, instead of being widened to include the whole range of forms, among them craftwork, toys, and games, that function as art in the lives of children. (5) Finally, there has been a persistent tendency to generalize on the basis of inadequate data — the cases available for direct laboratory study in a certain year and locality — without consulting the wealth of data on children's art and esthetic behavior available in the history and literature of various peoples.

In spite of these five limitations, a body of information is slowly accumulating that permits us to classify children's art, especially drawings, according to types normal for various age groups.   The broad division into stages of drawing (the ' scribble,' ' schematic,' and ' true to appearance ' stages) is being refined in terms of intermediate, transitional types, of narrower age and sex groups, and of individual differences.   Children's preferences in art, many of them long recognized in an unscientific way, are being more precisely analyzed and correlated with other psychological factors.   Studies are being made of intelligence in relation to art ability, though as long as art ability itself is so dimly understood, so incapable of measurement, no definite correlation with intelligence tests can be expected.

2. Social Esthetic Development

Closely related to the problem of individual development in art is that of social or cultural development, as evidenced in the history of art and civilization.   There are obvious resemblances between children's behavior and primitive behavior, and between children's art and primitive art.   Children like to see and make pictures of primitive life, to

---

[1] Those of Eng (9) and Bühler (4), however, are already available in English.

hear stories about it, and to imitate primitive people (in this country, American Indians) in their play. Even without explicitly assuming a recapitulation theory, education often tends to act in accord with one, to feed children a heavy diet of primitive art and try to make them produce it. This procedure has its values as a corrective against academic methods, but it involves a misunderstanding of child psychology when carried too far. It is difficult to generalize about the relations between two kinds of development, each of which is only slightly understood at present. But the following brief comparison, showing some of the differences and some of the resemblances, may be hazarded.

' Primitive art ' is a rather vaguely defined concept that ordinarily includes art produced under tribal social conditions at any period from prehistoric to contemporary. Strictly speaking, it should not include that of early empires and city-states, like the Egyptian, Sumerian, or Mayan, after these peoples had advanced to urban civilization. Primitive art thus *differs* on the whole from modern children's art in many ways, especially in the following four. (1) Being made mostly by adults, it tends to express certain attitudes, interests, and motives that are typically adult, including those connected with adult sexuality. Modern civilized children and their arts are on the whole more naïve, ignorant, and repressed in this respect than are primitive children; hence, more unlike adults. Civilized children are made to differ more from adults than primitive children in many respects, in the effort to postpone sexual activity. Primitive children also tend to mature earlier in other respects through being less sheltered and having to care for younger children. (2) Primitive art expresses a primitive (tribal) social order, including certain characteristic institutions, beliefs, and attitudes in religious, political, economic, and family relations; for example, totemism, exogamy, fetishism, and magic. It also deals with the physical environment and equipment of such life, with the non-mechanical, with wild nature, or with primitive farming. Children's art in modern civilization tends to express and represent an urban, mechanized environment. (3) Modern children's art, through school influences, is affected by recent adult art, and by special educational methods, including those of art education. It tends to use the materials of contemporary adult art and to approximate the latter's techniques. It tends to adopt stylistic traits and formulas and to choose subjects that are not spontaneously childish. Modern education tends to accelerate children's intellectual and emotional maturation in certain respects (other than the directly sexual) ; to hurry children into many adult interests, attitudes, and techniques, including those of art. Art museums, stressing adult art, contribute to this effect. (4) Young children's schematic drawings are composites, assembled by combining more-or-less completely outlined parts. Paleolithic art often uses a continuous, flowing outline, showing grasp of the total contour of the figure as a whole, even in active movement. The young child's drawing is usually a rather loose assemblage of more-or-less separate memory images, which are added together without definite fusion into a single complex unit. Neolithic adult drawing regresses on the whole toward extreme schematicism. It resembles that of young children in some ways, but springs from a different motivation and mentality. It is associated with the origin of linguistic symbols, abbreviated pictographs.

On the other hand, the following *resemblances* are to be noted between primitive art and modern, young children's art. (1) Both are often comparatively simple and lacking in subtle differentiation of parts and qualities. However, some tribal art is complex in certain respects; for example, the design and symbolism of a Chilkat blanket. (2) In pictorial representation both tend to show such features as flatness; lack of three-dimensional modelling with shadows; lack of perspective; distortion of spatial, anatomical, and other relations and of natural shapes and sizes; the use of strong contrast of bright colors when possible; and strong rhythmic repetition of shapes and color areas.

What appears to the civilized art critic as ' distortion ' or ' conventionalization ' — in other words, lack of conformity to the usual appearance of things — probably springs from similar, though not identical, sources in primitive and modern children's art. It is not merely a failure, through lack of skill, to represent things accurately, but is also due to an emphasis on what seems important. Neither the primitive adult nor the young modern child sees any reason for representing the exact appearance of any single object. He is more concerned to set down his concept of the main, distinguishing features of each type of thing that interests him. A modern woman has a dress and long hair; a man has trousers, short hair, and sometimes smokes a pipe. A dog is horizontal, not erect, with short legs (at first an indefinite number, from two or three to a whole fringe) below its body. Both the primitive and the young child at first set down their concepts, in comparatively simplified, schematic form, of the few main types they have mentally and visually distinguished, such as man, house, tree, horse, and, today, automobile or airplane. Their representations include typical movements as well as shapes.

As adult art becomes more civilized its concepts are multiplied, refined, and subdivided. The development of an individual artist from childhood to maturity involves similar changes toward greater power to represent individuals and groups in a unified and realistic way. Some adult artists, to be sure, are deliberately unrealistic, and sometimes imitate primitive art for decorative or other reasons. The drawing ability of most adults is arrested at a childish stage. As a rule, not until comparatively late in either individual or cultural development is there much interest in representing subtle details in the appearance of a particular person or thing. Nor is there much interest in design, esthetic form or composition for its own sake, though such attributes often develop along with representation. Young children, looking at an adult modern picture, are not likely to be much interested in formal aspects or in small details of individual representation, but rather in general types of object and situation. These a child wants to learn about, not from impersonal curiosity, but as they may (or might conceivably) affect him personally. He likes to enter vividly into a story picture, through identification and projection, and to use it as an aid to active phantasy-building. This applies both to the pictures he makes and to those he notices by other artists. In all these respects there are parallels in primitive adult art and behavior toward it. But the term ' primitive ' covers so many varieties that no exact analogy is possible.

There has been much research on this problem in Europe, but much remains to be done. If we are on guard against oversimplified recapitulation theories, we can well afford to consider the many suggestive hypotheses regarding individual development that arise from a study of social development.

As to art education, there are important implications. It should take account of the peculiar functions that picture-making, picture-appreciation, and other art activities naturally play in the mental development of children. These functions include the forming of intellectual concepts based on visual and other sensory experience, as we have just seen. Psychoanalysts would counsel us also to pay close attention to the function of art in the child's phantasy life, both as means of escape from reality and as means of effectively dealing with reality. In any case, the art teacher is wise not to hurry the child artist or appreciator into adult attitudes toward art, but rather to let him derive from it what he needs at each step on the way.

VIII. The Evaluation of Children's Work in Art

In psychological studies of children's art, it is usually advisable to exclude so far as possible all evaluative questions and assumptions; for example, whether a child's taste is good or bad, his drawings beautiful or ugly. Failure to do so has vitiated many researches in the field in spite of an imposing array of statistics. However, the practical problem of evaluating children's art does remain to be faced, if for no other reason than that of administering grades, rewards, and special opportunities in school. And the theoretical problem of what standards should be used in judging children's art must sooner or later be faced clearly by art critics and teachers, if not by psychologists. We cannot go very far in talking about ' ability ' without making evaluative judgments. A narrow special skill or performance, like making exact freehand copies of a line drawing, can be measured objectively. But when we talk about ' art ability ' or ' powers of appreciation ' in general, we usually imply power to make or enjoy good art. Most applied sciences assume certain goals to be good; medicine, for example, assumes health as its goal. Science need not ignore evaluative problems entirely, but should try to distinguish them from descriptive ones and recognize its limitations in dealing with evaluative issues. It can throw much light on them even if it cannot settle them finally.

As to children's art, much depends upon whether or not we assume certain universal standards of value to be applicable alike to the art of adults and children. If we do, the task of appraisal becomes simple and dogmatic; we appraise a child's drawing on the basis of its approximation to what we consider good adult art. We appraise his taste from a standpoint of adult ' good taste ' as we conceive it. If we take a more relativistic view, in accord with modern trends in education, the task is harder. Then we need to consider what values art may have for children themselves. Of course, children do want to imitate adults in some things, but not in everything at once. There is danger in art, as elsewhere, of forcing and overaccelerating their maturation and thus of causing them to miss not only legitimate pleasures of childhood but also necessary steps in the development of abilities.

Psychological accounts of the normal development of children's art abilities — in drawing, for instance — may easily be made into a basis for evaluation. This is done by comparing a child's chronological age with the developmental stage of art that his product exemplifies. Thus it is now becoming possible to say that a given ten-year-old child can make drawings of a type that most children cannot make until twelve or fifteen years old. That may be taken as a sign of special ability as well as precocity; hence, as promising high art ability in later life, and, hence, as deserving present rewards and encouragements. There is no definite proof that such precocity is a reliable indication of adult ability, but the presumption is strong enough to act upon.

In such a case, the fact that the child's drawings are of an *older type* does not mean that they are necessarily *better*. It is not to be assumed that an adult type is the ideal of perfection for children. The young child's ways of producing art and his tastes in art are perhaps as right for him as the adolescent's are for the adolescent or the adult's for the adult. Furthermore, precocity of the sort just mentioned is not necessarily desirable or equivalent to total ability; it may even, at times, be an unhealthy symptom.

Again, *within each age-level type* there appear other variations that may be taken as criteria of value and ability. For want of a better word, we may call these for the present ' qualitative ' variations. Two children, six years of age, may both draw in a typical six-year-old way — highly simplified, flat, schematic, expressing general concepts rather than exact appearances. Yet the drawings of one will be inventive, full of imagined details and events, striking as designs, vivid in representing movement, interrelated as a group, while those of the other are bare and perfunctory, stiff, monotonous, awkward, unrelated. One seems animated, definite, effective in many ways; the other comparatively dead or vague and fumbling in every respect. Both stay within the limits of a single general type of form; yet the one realizes the possibilities of development within those limits more than does the other.

It is not easy to define such qualities as these in precise objective terms, or to prove that they do or do not exist in a particular case. Extreme examples, however, are obvious. It is not necessary to argue whether they constitute adequate standards of value; no brief list of abstract qualities will do so. The important thing to recognize is that, after children's art has been classified into a few main, developmental types of form, there still remains a possibility of wide individual variations within these types. Such variations are in a sense developmental also; they reveal different stages of development in certain abilities having to do with art. A six-year-old child can have most of the basic personality traits characteristic of his age and yet be more highly developed than another (by nature or nurture) in respect to certain component abilities, such as keen visual imagination, manual coördination, and power to translate mental concepts into objective forms through manipulating a medium.

Much the same can be said of adult art in various cultural stages. Some is primitive in type, some characteristic of advanced urban civilization, but within each type qualitative differences are found. Critics will distinguish good from bad primitive art; good from bad civilized art. Some primitive art is admired and kept in art museums; some adult art is rejected as mediocre. In other words, the difference between good and bad art is not the same as that between primitive and civilized art, or between childish and adult art. Flat, schematic drawings are not necessarily inferior to those with realistic perspective. Wide variations of development and personal style are possible within the former type, as in the case of much Egyptian painting by adult artists.

When art is taught for the definite purpose of vocational, technical skill, then it is reasonable to evaluate students' work on a basis of approximation to the adult skills and types of product desired; for example, those thought to be readily marketable. When art is taught as a part of general education, especially for younger children, exact evaluation is often less essential. When it is necessary, adult standards should be applied, if at all, with considerable modification. A premium should not be placed on conformity with adult taste or on perfection in the finished product. Habits of careful craftsmanship are desirable; but facile perfection and smoothness of finish in children's art is often less promising than vigorous, if clumsy, experimentation. Children should be encouraged to make and to enjoy the types of art appropriate to their level of general maturation and should be led gradually — not hurriedly — to those ahead. Within these youthful types of art form and behavior, the discerning teacher can look for those signs of alertness, sensitivity, inventiveness, and organizing power that distinguish excellence from mediocrity at every stage of development.

REFERENCES

(1) ANDERSON, J. E. " Child Development and the Growth Process." (In) *The Thirty-Eighth Yearbook, Part I,* of this Society, 1939, pp. 15–49.

(2) BAUDOUIN, P. *The Mind of the Child, a Psycho-Analytical Study.* (Dodd, Mead and Co.: New York, 1933) 282 pp.

(3) BRITSCH, G. *Theorie der Bildenden Kunst.* (Bruckmann: Munich, 1930) 152 pp.

(4) BÜHLER, K. *The Mental Development of the Child.* (Harcourt, Brace and Co.: New York, 1930) 170 pp.

(5) CHANDLER, A. R. *Beauty and Human Nature: Elements of Psychological Aesthetics.* (D. Appleton-Century Co., Inc.: New York, 1934) 381 pp.

(6) Child Study Association of America. (B. C. Gruenberg, editor). *Guidance of Childhood and Youth.* (The Macmillan Co.: New York, 1929) 324 pp.

(7) DELACROIX, H. *Psychologie de l'art.* (Alcan: Paris, 1927) 481 pp.

(8) DEWEY, J. *Art as Experience.* (Minton, Balch: New York, 1934) 355 pp.

(9) ENG, HELGA. *The Psychology of Children's Drawings.* (Harcourt, Brace and Co.: New York, 1931) 223 pp.

(10) FERENCZI, S. "Stages in the Development of the Sense of Reality." (In) *An Outline of Psychoanalysis,* ed. by J. S. Van Teslaar. (Modern Library: New York, 1924). 383 pp. (pp. 108–127)

(11) GOODENOUGH, F. L. *Developmental Psychology.* (D. Appleton-Century Co.: New York, 1934) 619 pp.

(12) GREENE, H. A., and JORGENSEN, A. N. *The Use and Interpretation of Elementary School Tests.* (Longmans, Green, and Co.: New York, 1935) 530 pp. (Ch. XIX on " Measurement in the Fine Arts ")

(13) HARTLAUB, G. F. *Der Genius im Kinde.* (Hirt: Breslau, 1930) 229 pp.

(14) HARTMANN, G. W. *Gestalt Psychology.* (Ronald Press: New York, 1935) 325 pp. (p. 271)

(15) HEALY, W., BRONNER, A. F., and BOWERS, A. M. *The Structure and Meaning of Psychoanalysis.* (Alfred A. Knopf: New York, 1931) 482 pp.

(16) JERSILD, A. T. "Education in Motor Activities." (In) *The Thirty-Eighth Yearbook, Part I,* of this Society, 1939, pp. 57–83.

(17) JERSILD, A. T. "Radio and Motion Pictures." (In) *The Thirty-Eighth Yearbook, Part I,* of this Society, 1939, pp. 160–173.

(18) JUNG, C. G. *The Integration of the Personality.* (Farrar and Rinehart, Inc.: New York, 1939) 313 pp.

(19) JUNG, C. G. *Psychology of the Unconscious.* (Dodd, Mead and Co.: New York, 1931) 565 pp.

(20) KINTER, M., and ACHILLES, P. S. *The Measurement of Artistic Abilities.* (Psychological Corporation: New York, 1933) 90 pp.

(21) LALO, C. *L'esthétique expérimentale contemporaine.* (Alcan: Paris, 1908) 208 pp.

(22) LARK-HOROVITZ, B. "On Art Appreciation of Children: I. Preference of Picture Subjects in General." *Jour. Educ. Res.,* XXI: 1937, pp. 118–137. "II. Portrait Preference Study." *Ibid.,* XXXI: 1938, pp. 572–598. "III. Textile Pattern Preference Study." *Ibid.,* XXXIII: 1939, pp. 7–35.

(23) LARK-HOROVITZ, B., BARNHART, E. N., and SILLS, E. M. *Graphic Work-Sample Diagnosis: An Analytic Method of Estimating Children's Drawing Ability.* (Cleveland Museum of Art: Cleveland, Ohio, 1939) 43 pp.

(24) LIQUET, G. H. *Le dessin enfantin.* (Alcan: Paris, 1927) 260 pp.

(25) MEIER, N. C. "The Graphic and Allied Arts." (In) *The Thirty-Eighth Yearbook, Part I,* of this Society, 1939, pp. 175–184.

(26) MEINHOF, W. *Die Bildgestaltung des Kindes.* (Teubner: Leipzig, 1930) 74 pp.

(27) MEISS, G. *Sinn und Wert der Kinderkunst.* (Goerlich: Breslau, 1931) 114 pp.

(28) MORGAN, C. D., and MURRAY, H. A. " A Method for Investigating Fantasies:

the Thematic Apperception Test." *Archives of Neurology and Psychiatry,* 34: 2, August, 1935, pp. 289–306.

(29) MULLER-FREIENFELS, R. *Psychologie der Kunst.* (Teubner: Berlin, 1923, 1933) 3 vols.

(30) MUNN, N. L. *Psychological Development.* (Houghton Mifflin Co.: Boston, 1938) 582 pp.

(31) MUNRO, T. "Adolescence and Art Education." (In) *Methods of Teaching the Fine Arts,* ed. by Rusk. (University of North Carolina Press: Chapel Hill, 1935).

(32) MUNRO, T. "Art Tests and Research in Art Education." *Bulletin of the Western Arts Association,* XVII: 6, December, 1933.

(33) MUNRO, T. "A Graded Program in Comparative Arts." (In) *Art Education Today: 1936.* (Teachers College: New York, 1936)

(34) MUNRO, T. "A Psychological Approach to College Art Instruction." *Parnassus,* November, 1933, and (In) *Methods of Teaching the Fine Arts,* ed. by Rusk. (University of North Carolina Press: Chapel Hill, 1935)

(35) MUNRO, T. *Scientific Method in Aesthetics.* (W. W. Norton and Co., Inc.: New York, 1928) 101 pp.

(36) Murchison, C. (ed.) *A Handbook of Child Psychology.* (Clark University Press: Worcester, Mass., 1933) 956 pp.

(37) MURPHY, G. *General Psychology.* (Harper and Brothers: New York, 1933) 657 pp. (pp. 236–252)

(38) MURPHY, G., and JENSEN, F. (supplement by LEVY, J.) *Approaches to Personality.* (Coward-McCann, Inc.: New York, 1932) 427 pp.

(39) MURSELL, J. L., and Others. "Growth." (In) *Readings in Educational Psychology,* ed. by C. E. Skinner. (Farrar and Rinehart, Inc.: New York, 1937) 630 pp. (pp. 77–91)

(40) OGDEN, R. M. *The Psychology of Art.* (Charles Scribner's Sons: New York, 1938) 291 pp.

(41) PFISTER, O. *Some Applications of Psycho-Analysis.* (George Allen and Unwin, Ltd.: London, 1923) 352 pp.

(42) PIAGET, J. *The Language and Thought of the Child.* (Harcourt, Brace and Co.: New York, 1932) 246 pp.

(43) READ, H. *Art and Society.* (The Macmillan Co.: New York, 1937) 282 pp.

(44) ROBINSON, E. S. and RICHARDSON-ROBINSON, F. *Readings in General Psychology.* (University of Chicago Press: Chicago, 1929) 812 pp.

(45) RUCKMICK, C. A. *The Psychology of Feeling and Emotion.* (McGraw-Hill Book Co.: New York, 1936) 529 pp.

(46) SAUDEK, R. *The Psychology of Handwriting.* (Doran: New York, 1926) 288 pp.

(47) SOURIAU, E. *L'avenir de l'esthétique.* (Alcan: Paris, 1929) 403 pp.

(48) STERZINGER, O. H. *Grundlinien der Kunstpsychologie.* (Leykam: Graz, 1938, 1939) 2 vols.

(49) *White House Conference on Child Health and Protection. Report of the Committee on Growth and Development: Part IV. Appraisement of the Child. I. Mental Status.* (The Century Co.: New York, 1932) 344 pp.

(50) WULFF, O. *Die Kunst des Kindes.* (Enke: Stuttgart, 1927) 407 pp.

CHAPTER XXII

CREATIVE ABILITY IN ART, AND ITS EDUCATIONAL FOSTERING

Thomas Munro

I. The Meaning of Creativeness: Mistaken Claims to It

The ideal of producing creative, original minds through public education, or at least of helping in their development, is characteristic of modern educational philosophy in America. It expresses our optimistic belief in social progress and in our own ability to accelerate and direct it. This optimism is perhaps uncritical in view of recent world events and our own economic troubles, but it has survived them with scarcely diminished enthusiasm. It is based on no very clear conception of what we mean by progress, especially in art, or of what sort of art we would like to see created. We realize that, so far, we have not filled many pages in the history of art, except perhaps with the motion picture and certain types of architecture. But we have a youthful confidence in the ability of our people to create worth-while things in this field, as in applied science and industry. As a democracy, we like to affirm, against the repressive systems of the day, our confidence that the masses can be trusted with freedom to think for themselves and to express themselves in art, and we have tremendous confidence in the power of education to remake the world and to produce the kind of people we desire. Among these will be individual leaders in art and other fields, supermen from all economic and racial groups, who will give personal concreteness to our progress and leaven the vast, impersonal standardization that characterizes so much of our social life.

Our own investigations of intelligence and learning ability should chasten this optimism a little, for they point inescapably to the limits set on individual development by heredity and inborn capacity. These would perhaps point rather to eugenics than to education as a means of producing mental superiority, but we are not yet ready for that mode of control. There are deterministic, old-world philosophies of history that would deny our ability to produce a really creative period by trying to do so. Such periods, they say, happen automatically at certain stages in a people's development, when all biological and cultural factors converge to produce them, as in ancient Athens and Renaissance Italy. There are others, more encouraging, who maintain that cultural creativeness follows historically from political power and economic prosperity. If so, we have some of the prerequisites. Most of all, we seem to have one powerful new tool in scientific psychology with all its possible educational applications. That tool has been scarcely forged as yet, but we are impatient to try out its possibilities.

Let us try to clarify the problem a little by analyzing what we mean by creative ability. The words ' creation ' and ' creative ' are now much used by art teachers, and often in a rather vague, sentimental way that arouses suspicion in the scientist. They convey a eulogistic implication, as if the child who ' creates art ' were doing something much finer than merely drawing a picture. And yet so much ordinary student work is labelled ' creative ' by the teachers in charge that skeptical outsiders wonder if all of it can possibly deserve the title. Of late, the words have fallen into some disrepute for this reason, but still they stand for some important ideas that are difficult to ignore in working out a philosophy of art education.

Webster's *New International Dictionary* defines *create* as follows: " 3. To cause or occasion; to form; — said of natural or physical causes and especially of social and evolutional forces; as, new environment *creates* new forms of life. 4. To produce as a work of thought or imagination, esp. as a work of art or of dramatic interpretation along new or unconventional lines; as, Irving *created* a new Hamlet." *Creation* is " 1. *b*. Act of making, producing, fashioning, or bringing into existence, in general. . . . *d*. The presentation of a new conception in an artistic embodiment." *Creative* is " 1. Having the power or quality of creating; given to creation. ' *Creative* talent.' *Irving*." The religious sense, in which things are said to have been created out of nothing by a divine power, is not relevant to any sort of human art.

Evidently, two main ideas are implied here, one broad and one narrow. These are often confused. In the broad sense, any sort of production, or making, is creation, and thus all student art can be so described, whatever its quality. In the narrow sense, the term implies novelty or originality, as contrasted with the imitation of earlier products. In addition, it suggests that the work is somehow important and valuable; it would not be applied to something that was new in a merely freakish, trivial way.

Art teachers who use the term often have still another idea in mind.

They mean that students' art is ' creative ' if it was spontaneously conceived and executed by the student, not done in accordance with the teacher's directions. Likewise, we sometimes contrast the creative adult artist with the mere artisan, however skilled, as one who conceives or thinks out the product, instead of following another's instructions in executing it.

If we wish a term for psychological purposes to include a wide range of phenomena — the making of art in general, whether important and original or not — it would perhaps be better to use a more neutral term, such as ' art production.' If we wish to narrow down the field, let us speak explicitly of ' original ' art production, and of ' spontaneous ' art production. Child art is often spontaneous (not directly influenced), but it is rarely original, in the sense of being new.

How much of students' art is to be called creative in the narrower senses will depend on the strictness of the standards we set for originality and spontaneity. This will also determine our answer to the question " How many people are creative, or can become creative, in art? " or in other words, " What range of creative ability exists in children? " There is no possibility of objective, quantitative answers to these questions, for they involve evaluation at the start. Anyone can produce some kind of art in a broad sense, even a person of very low intelligence and skill. But speaking strictly, the number of artists who are recognized by subsequent history as having made important, original contributions to art are few, indeed — a handful in any generation. Historians argue for centuries over which artists were the really creative innovators. Their answers involve not only controversial standards of value and importance, but also factual questions of priority and influence.

No young child or his products has ever been so recognized, and it would be remarkable if any should be. There are many child prodigies in *artistic performance*, especially in music and acting, but few in art production or composition. Children's drawings often seem to promise marked originality in later life. Those of young children often delight us by a comparative freshness of imagination and technique, as if the child has looked at the world for himself, selected what seemed interesting to him, and worked out his own way of putting it down on paper. Their designs are often refreshingly unlike those of older, academically trained artists, involving forceful rhythms and surprising distortions. None is perhaps *exactly* like any other picture, old or new. Child art in general is certainly a contribution to human culture. But it is hard to find definitely original characteristics in the art of individual children — that is, any radically new and important quality or type of form that would justify us in calling it an individual contribution to the world's artistic heritage.

We sometimes go from one extreme to the other in talking of children's art. The old attitude was to judge it by adult, academic standards, and thus to regard it as crude and lacking in all artistic merit. We have now discovered that it can please the adult observer in its own right, and that it deserves respect as an expression of a stage in development that is worth while in itself. It is not an unsuccessful attempt at adult art and hence cannot be fairly judged by adult standards. Moreover, there are reasons for encouraging young children to try out their own ideas in art and other activities. But to praise children's art in a wholesale, effusive way, in the same terms that we use to praise the work of mature genius, is to reveal a lack of standards for discriminating relative degrees of importance and originality.

There is much self-deception in the claims of progressive teachers for the utter spontaneity of their students' work. From Cizek on, the free expressionists in art education have ignored the constant, manifold influences that were playing upon the children in their charge. There are many ways of influencing students' art besides telling them explicitly " do it this way," or " copy this." No child who has lived for six or seven years in a world of cultural influences, including such popular art as magazine covers and cartoons, whose every thought is influenced by home and outside agencies, who goes to a school where certain kinds of art are praised and encouraged, can be called ' spontaneous ' in any strict sense of the word. The most that can be claimed is a relatively high degree of freedom from definite influence during the immediate process of production. But anyone who observes school art exhibits in one American town after another is likely to become first annoyed and then amused by the constant claims of originality and spontaneity on the part of proud teachers, in spite of the obviously stereotyped imitativeness of much of the work.

Furthermore, overemphasis by well-meaning teachers on the aim of individual originality may lead to undesired effects. The ninety-nine percent who can never be original creators may become discouraged and think of themselves as failures, missing the satisfaction and usefulness that should come with skilled craftsmanship and willing collaboration under the leadership of others. They may become self-conscious and conceited in the effort to express their own egos, turning out shoddy, 'half-baked' products that are never frankly criticized in the school, and they may thus become doomed to a rough awakening later on. Real originality has often emerged without being sought, and even from environments and teaching methods that discouraged it, through long, patient study of traditions, techniques, and current practices. Admitting that such originality is to be desired and fostered in all who are potentially capable of it, we are far from sure that the best way to achieve it is through explicit preaching and unlimited freedom in school.

Adult artists, too, often make excessive claims of complete originality. They feel it as an admission of inferiority to recognize that they have learned from their predecessors, and especially that they have learned from their contemporaries. To the trained observer, their indebtedness is usually quite apparent. But the basic error lies in the implication that any artist or any work of art can be completely original. All artists build upon the past, upon the traditions and recent tendencies in their field. There can be no justifiable stigma in admitting such debts; and the most any artist should presume to claim is that he has made some slight addition of his own, some relatively new adaptation of earlier achievements to a new situation, need, technique, or material.

The notion of an artist as a unique, isolated genius, creating something *de novo* through a mysterious flash of inspiration, is itself a survival from the romantic tradition we inherit. It has cultural connections with extreme individualism and *laisser faire* in social thought. It ignores the whole drift of modern practice toward collective action. There is less and less place for the purely individualistic artist, the genius in a garret, and more for the man who can coöperate with others in a vast undertaking like the making of a cathedral, an airplane, or a motion picture, without worrying too much about his incorruptible originality. Of course, credit for really new ideas has its place, too. Patent and copyright laws try to protect and reward them, but find it harder and harder to do so in this day of adaptations and collective art production.

Painters and sculptors, and other practitioners of the so-called 'fine arts,' are especially prone to regard themselves as 'creative,' and to look down on mere craftsmen and performers elsewhere. One even hears of painting and sculpture as 'creative arts,' as if everything done therein were creative, and as if the making of a chair or an advertising poster were necessarily mere craftsmanship or commercialism. It is one of the commonest delusions of painters and their admirers that anything done in oil paint and that is not a direct copy of some other picture is necessarily creative and original. To be sure, it is probably not exactly like any other picture, but the difference may be only in details of subject matter. Anyone can paint or photograph a costumed figure, a scene, or a group of still-life objects that has never been portrayed before. But originality from the standpoint of art history and criticism implies far more than that. It implies a valuable innovation in manner of treatment; in pictorial form, composition, expression, or technique; in what the artist himself contributes through selection and reorganization of his subject matter. The claim to creative originality is specious if the subject matter, though in some details unique, is in all important ways like that selected by earlier artists, and if the mode of representation is conventional. This is not to say, of course, that an imitative picture is without value. It may give pleasure to many and good experience to the student artist. The danger lies in obscuring the nature of real originality, so that we fail to strive for it intelligently or to recognize it when it appears.

By discounting the snobbery of the ' fine arts,' we shall be readier to appreciate the creative elements that often occur in less genteel arts — in the handcrafts, industrial and commercial arts, utilitarian architecture, motion pictures, and even in popular and journalistic illustration. Creative originality in art is not limited to any particular arts, mediums, or techniques, or to people who call themselves ' artists.' The maker of a picture frame may be more truly a creative artist than the maker of the picture it encloses. The discerning critic who advances new points of view toward art, and even the discriminating collector who assembles a unique, suggestively organized collection, may be more creative than the majority of dabblers in a fine-art medium.

II. Is There a Creative Type of Person?

Regardless of where it occurs, is there such a thing as a creative, original type of mind? If so, has it been possessed by the artists recognized as great innovators in the past? Is it a pecular type of mental ability or mode of thinking, absent in ordinary mortals? We are entering into speculative problems here, and our answers can be supported only by slight evidence. In general, the present tendency is definitely to deny the existence of any quite unique ability or method, even in the very great. The more we learn about them, the more they seem in certain respects like ordinary people, motivated by the same desires, some petty and some noble; faced by analogous difficulties and dealing intelligently with some, ineffectively with others. Essentially, creative originality and the abilities that produce it seem to be different in degree, rather than in kind, from the mental characteristics of the mediocre. Judgments of greatness in art are made on the basis of the value of the product, not on how it was produced. For all we can see, the world is, and always has been, full of capable workers in art and other fields, who possess tremendous skill, intelligence, and vivid imaginations, but whose products never achieve outstanding recognition. Other artists do gain recognition in spite of being very commonplace in most respects, like Cézanne, or psychopathic, like Van Gogh. Many show less than ordinary intelligence and *savoir-faire* in dealing with practical life problems and human contacts.

This surprising fact, and the conspicuousness of a few psychopathic artists, has led some theorists to maintain that genius and insanity are causally connected. There is no space here to discuss this theory in detail. But it may at least be noted that for every insane genius many others can be mentioned, like Bach and Titian, who showed no particular abnormalities. Probably the percentage of definite neurosis among artists, great or mediocre, is no larger than among other people. Indeed, Freud has pointed out that the artist has pecular opportunities for readjusting himself to reality through his art — through being able to objectify and use his phantasies in achieving success — and thus for correcting in part whatever neurotic tendencies he may have had in early life. Artists sometimes break down mentally or develop pathological traits in later life, but so do some scientists and business men. The artist often has the advantage that oddities of behavior are tolerated in him as a pardonable Bohemianism, thus producing less than ordinary conflict with society. At the same time countless artists, major and minor, lead the most conventional of lives, with no outward sign of abnormality or eccentricity. It may well be that the eccentric artist type is a product of special cultural trends or fashions, rather than of anything more basic psychologically. Extreme differentiation of the artistic or esthetic type from the practical is a sign of temporary cultural dislocation, of an artificial divorce between useful production and the pursuit of beautiful luxuries. It became a convention of the Romantic movement in Europe to think of the artist as an eccentric genius, living in a world apart, and not like other men. In the late nineteenth century the pose was fashionable, and many who were not seriously interested in art as well as some who were (Baudelaire, for example) cultivated its bizarre outward signs in costume and manner. At other periods, most artists have preferred to look and act like ordinary citizens.

On the other hand, there are reasons for believing that originality, especially in art, may involve some fairly distinct psychological traits. These are not necessarily differences in kind, but at least marked differences in degree and mode of development. For example, there is still debate among psychologists as to whether genius is the same as extremely high intelligence as measured by standardized tests. Terman has applied the term "studies of genius" to studies of children with unusually high I.Q. Others have insisted that genius, in the sense of creative originality, is something different from high I.Q.[1] Highly intelligent children, at least as measured by our present tests, often fail to develop anything that could be called creative originality in later life. They usually become capable, successful, and respected citizens, but that is not the same thing. There is not sufficient evidence to show whether persons recognized as creatively original always have high intelligence. One may concede perhaps that the very greatest always do, and yet maintain that persons of moderate intelligence sometimes do decidedly original things.

The experience of teachers would often corroborate the hypothesis that high intelligence alone is not enough, though it is one prerequisite for great achievement. Every teacher of long experience has been disappointed by the phenomenon of students who apparently have all the qualifications for notable creative work — intelligence, information, techncial skill, every home and educational advantage — yet who never go on to produce such work. Sometimes they even lose the desire to do so and settle down to lives of comfortable conformity, of mediocrity, as judged by their own youthful ideals and those of their teachers.

It may be that the reason lies partly in the realm of motivation; in what (to use the old-fashioned word) might be called the _will_ to create. As yet, this factor is not measured by our intelligence tests, although every educator admits the importance of interest and effort. A mild, diffused type of interest and effort in school days is not enough, however. Neither is an attachment to one's adult occupation so halfhearted as to be easily distracted by competing interests. Drastic concentration and sacrifice of other interests are often necessary to achieve the heights of creative eminence. The creators have been willing to make this sacrifice when necessary, or perhaps have been unable to

---

[1] For example, Witty (21)

adjust themselves to life conditions so as to achieve other goals in addition to the one supremely desired.

History and biography have made us familiar with the story of the genius who fails to achieve success in money and its comforts, in health, in love and family relations, and in the approval of his contemporaries — at least in his early years if not through life. Whether he made these sacrifices voluntarily or involuntarily is perhaps not essential. He is frequently unable to avoid them and at the same time pursue his chosen course along creative lines. Perhaps that course took too much of his limited health and emotional energy, or led him to a stand too violently counter to approved conventions; in any case, the sacrifice was made. True, there are happier stories of men like Titian and Rubens, who achieved greatness without giving up many of the ordinary values of life. Such men are shrewd, versatile, and fortunate enough to ride the crest of a wave, and their kind of originality happens to be socially approved. But bitter struggle and sacrifice are by no means uncommon in the story of greatness, in art, science, religion, social reform, or any other field. We do not know exactly what conscious or unconscious factors impel some to choose sacrifice, but we do see the common spectacle of others, including extremely intelligent people, who do not feel called upon to make that choice.

It is not for the psychologist to appraise the wisdom of either course, but to explain both if possible. Perhaps even the teacher has no right to condemn a student who prefers a happy, well-adjusted, useful social life to original creation. But let us not delude ourselves with the idea that no choice is ever necessary, and that originality is always easily reconcilable with social adjustment. The more potent the force of conservatism in any society, the more difficult the reconciliation.

How does the will to be original and to create in a particular field develop intensely in a given individual? To know that, we must trace his early history in detail, and as a rule its essential facts are inaccessible to the investigator. Psychoanalysis offers certain general hypotheses in terms of unconscious conflict and sublimation. It tells of how an early sense of guilt arising from the Oedipus situation carries over into later life; how the sensitive ego in adolescence and afterward needs to build up its self-esteem in some way; how this way may lead into neurotic symptoms, into overcompensation through egotism, conceit, cruelty, or pugnacity, or through sublimation into more or less approved channels, like those of art. This would perhaps help explain the discontent and restlessness, the egotism alternating with depression, the antagonism to conventional forms and people, that so often accompany genius. But even Freud admits ignorance of the fundamental reasons why some persons can adjust their conflicts only through crime or neurosis, while others achieve cultural sublimations. He hints that we may be driven back to inborn physiological differences for the final difference in power and mode of adjustment.

At least, the original genius would appear to be a person who has achieved a partial adjustment with his cultural environment, in that he has directed much of his libido into socially approved channels, such as art or religion. But he is not so completely adjusted as to seek conformity and immediate social approval at all costs; he retains a strong impulse to differ with his contemporaries, sometimes over trivial as well as important matters. He is often torn between the common desire for immediate social approval and a scornful resentment toward his contemporaries, which makes him disdain their opinions and dream of later approval by the judicious few, by posterity, or God; or he may try to find a lonely satisfaction in merely living up to his own standards. He usually maintains a rich phantasy life in dreams, waking reveries, or both, in contrast with the highly extraverted and adjusted person who lives more wholly in the external present. But he is not content to relapse into excessive, idle phantasy, for he has a grasp of reality to the extent of learning to manipulate a medium, to express his phantasies objectively, and to become a force among his fellows. He can discipline and redirect his imaginings into paths of systematic construction. Within this general type, there is much variation. Some geniuses have a strong grasp on practical reality; some relapse at times into escapist phantasies and neurotic symptoms or struggle blindly against hopeless odds. Some are comparatively tolerant of old traditions and present practices, even regarding themselves as conservatives and finding the old forms flexible enough to admit progress. They are less discontented and exhibit less sacrifice and struggle; but even they have the will to persistent, concentrated work, and the desire to improve on the past.

The will to be original is not enough in itself, for many have it keenly and fail nevertheless. Mere radicalism, as antagonism to the conventional and a desire to improve things, is not enough. There, perhaps, is where intelligence comes in, as a power to discern what possible lines of effort are most promising, and to adapt effective means to ends in following them. But even general intelligence will not necessarily suffice. It must be directed and implemented with specific skills and information, as in some technique of art. Physical equipment, as in sensory and muscular powers, must be adequate for the task set, but intelligence shows itself in choosing a task for which one has the potential means.

Besides a general disposition to produce and alter things, it is characteristic of the original mind to develop an intense, persistent attachment to some particular art or vocation, to some particular medium, material, or instrument for expression and construction. He becomes fascinated by the look and feel of oil paints, brushes and canvas, marble and chisel, machinery, the piano, the written word, the stage, or the speaker's rostrum. Whatever his choice, he can never be long content away from it and must be somehow occupied with it, even when not actually creating anything new. Such devotion varies in intensity, of course, but it is often most intense in the most original and powerful creators.

However strong, this devotion entails a corresponding sacrifice of other interests, of the values that attract ordinary people. It can become so extreme as to seem exaggerated and obsessive to the latter. Even family ties and responsibilities may be abandoned, father and mother forsaken, one's own economic interests as well as social duties ignored, and the world counted well lost for the sake of one's chosen work. This, of course, is the exceptional extreme, but in lesser degree it is common. The gradual concentration of one who has found his work involves a constant and often regretful cutting off of minor interests that had been delightful during the rambling explorations of youth, but that seem now to demand too much time and energy. This is not to say that the creative mind becomes narrow in every way. It may expand to a universal perspective, like that of Dante or Shakespeare, in its range of ideas. But it tends to focus its mental interests upon a systematic process of thinking out and objectifying these ideas in some chosen medium. Versatile exceptions, like Leonardo da Vinci, are rare indeed.

One reason for stressing this concentration or channelizing of interest is that it helps answer the question we have raised as to why so many highly intelligent and capable persons, promising as students, never become especially creative. In some of these cases the essential reason is an unwillingness to concentrate on a single goal to the necessary degree. Such persons are perhaps too adaptive; they can become interested in too many different things; they can shift too easily to a new one if the first choice demands too high a price. They have more varied, more widely distributed interests; no one job seems important enough to deserve the sacrifice of the many other values and obligations of life. Much can be said in defense of this attitude; it may lead to a more balanced, socially adjusted, and healthy existence. But again, it is for the psychologist to describe and explain rather than to moralize about values.

Why does such intense and persistent concentration occur in some individuals? It is certainly not wholly inborn; at least physiological predispositions would appear to be much more general, though they may give a broad initial bent in some direction, such as visual, rather than auditory, art. We must keep in mind the great number of possible determinants of personality. Once more, the theories of psychoanalysis would suggest that such a powerful, often abnormal, concentration of desire must be traceable in large part to unconscious mechanisms. The material or special activity chosen must somehow have become symbolic in the psychoanalytic sense, and a sublimation that is necessary to the individual for reasons he does not fully understand. His own rationalizations, of course, may be quite misleading, and here is where the questionnaires of descriptive psychology so often go astray.

The phenomenon also suggests an answer to the question whether art abilities tend to be versatile or specialized. Some researches have indicated that high ability in one field usually goes with high ability in others, and that the one-sided genius is a myth. Such a conclusion has been based mainly on studies of children and of ordinary capable, successful adults. It may be true of these, but not true of the exceptionally creative. It may even be true of the latter, in the sense that they have many of the potential capacities necessary for success in any field. But in another sense they could not succeed in any other field, if they are so constituted as not to want to; that is, if their volitional and emotional drives have concentrated in such a way that no deflection is now possible.

It is another common characteristic of genius, though not observable in all cases, to form an intense, persistent attachment for some particular type of form or product, for some type or style of art, some one ideal, aim, and standard of value; for example, if an artist, he may be a passionate partisan of the romantic ideal, and seek to embody it in everything he creates. To that extent, he tends to be intolerant or blind to the values of other and opposing types of art. Moral and political reformers often hold with bigoted ardor to a particular doctrine of the ideal state or the right mode of conduct. Their extremism, and the force and skill with which it is asserted, their consistent hammering away at one idea often enable them to make an impression on the world that more reasonable men, looking on all sides of the question, fail to make. This is especially the case in art, where success may depend not on truth or expediency so much as on the vividness and consistency with which a certain way of seeing things is expressed. It is less so in science and philosophy. There are so many ways of drawing a figure or painting a landscape, each pleasing and revealing in certain ways, and each perhaps as right as any other, that an artist equally interested in all may never follow any one very definitely. His products may become halfhearted, overloaded, or vague, eclectic, through his desire to combine too many values in one work of art. Great artists, on the other hand, are often narrowly intolerant toward other great artists, as were some of the giants of the Italian Renaissance. They are so intensely devoted to one way of doing things as to be irritated by any other.

Not that such an outstanding artist necessarily remains true to his first convictions or his first style of art. He may change radically in the course of his career, and either slowly or suddenly. Many original artists go through very different periods, in each of which they explore a certain approach with intense devotion. They may change to an opposite and previously hated style with little attempt at rational justification, being simply ' fed up ' with what they have been doing. But while in the grip of a particular attitude, they do follow it with intense conviction.

Again, such concentration and possible change of heart present to the psychologist interesting problems, as to their genesis and motivation. Let us note in passing but one educational question; namely, how far it is wise for the prospective artist to familiarize himself with many styles of art and to develop a catholic taste toward all of them. For the appreciator, there is every reason for so doing. And even for the artist, a wide acquaintance in art may provide valuable suggestions out of which he can select and reorganize for himself. So original an artist as Picasso (who, by the way, has gone through several radically different styles) is well versed in the history of art. He takes from it only what he needs at a particular time and usually produces therefrom a highly specialized, self-consistent form. But students often start their careers with some intense enthusiasm, then learn in college how narrow and ' immature ' it is, how much can be said on the other side, and how many other good ways of doing things exist. They gradually acquire a spirit of mellow tolerance and scholarly insight, but lose the creative impulse. Progressive education does try to keep alive this impulse, but there is little evidence so far that its methods will be effective. Its broad tolerance, its emphasis on a wide general education, the great latitude it gives students for experimentation may all operate to blur the student's vision and diffuse his enthusiasm. The stricter disciplinary methods of the past, which most great artists have undergone, may have the value of concentrating attention on a single line of approach, at least long enough for the student to grasp it clearly and to acquire habits of persistent work in following it. If he finds it too uncongenial, he may at least be goaded into a vehement counter-assertion, into an artistic revolt that is equally sharp and definite. Very liberal methods, in which the teacher carefully refrains from exerting any definite influence, often seem to turn out vaguely cultivated people who themselves have nothing very definite to say. This has been a weakness of complacent modern liberalism in general. It has helped open the door to fanatical extremists, who have captured mass emotion with their vivid and passionate advocacy of some particular course of action.

Before setting up ' creative originality ' as a goal of education, especially in art, it might be well for us to find out more about what it really is, what causes it, and how it behaves when it occurs. One may suspect that many teachers who praise it as a high-sounding slogan are thinking of something almost impossible: a sort of innovation that is always refined, decorous, and easy to get along with; that produces only beautiful works of art that please and inspire everyone and offend no one. They do not realize how shocking and unsettling extreme originality usually is. To be sure, they have read a little of the storms of abuse and ridicule that greeted Darwin in science, Beethoven and Wagner in music, Rodin in sculpture, Rembrandt, Courbet, Monet, and the Postimpressionists in painting; but these were far away and long ago. Of the men of today who shock and offend, like Freud and Havelock Ellis, Stravinsky, Picasso, and Frank Lloyd Wright, it is said that one cannot be sure whether they are really great or mere sensationalists who will be forgotten. But this is so of all geniuses in their own time. Teachers try to make students polite, respectable, and similar in tastes to themselves, not realizing that these qualities may be difficult to reconcile with high originality. There is more consistency in the Roman Catholic attitude, which condemns the tendency of modern education to glorify innovation and freedom of thought. If we do champion these traits in art and elsewhere, we should at least be prepared to accept the shocks and antagonisms they inevitably arouse.

Is it consistent to work for the ideal of originality in education and at the same time for that of harmonious personal and social adjustment? Only if we are prepared to qualify the latter and to admit that some harmony may have to be sacrificed in the interests of progress. The products of original minds must inevitably clash to some extent with accepted beliefs and practices. Even when the creative person has no desire for such conflict and is personally as mild and retiring as Darwin was, the intrinsic force of his ideas will produce explosive repercussions. Others will point out their negative implications if he does not, and will use them as weapons of attack.

Psychologically, we do not know how much inward neurotic conflict, if any, is necessary for artistic genius. Psychoanalytic theory would imply that a good deal is necessary. If so, when we try to promote normal, well-adjusted personality development in children, we may be unintentionally weakening the inner forces that make for creative genius. The answer may be, 'well and good; let us have the former instead.' Or, preferably, let us see whether a type of genius can be produced with the aid of proper education that can create in a more serene and reasonable way, with less inward conflict. Certainly, there is still no lack in the world of conditions that make for anxiety and conflict. If education can do anything to mitigate them, it need have no fear of doing too much. Liberal and progressive ideals of education have had too little time so far to work out really effective methods, especially in art, and in due time they may learn to avoid their present weaknesses.

Moreover, our chief concern in public education is not with the rare extremes of genius, but with more ordinary people. If we can succeed in developing a little more creative originality in the ordinary student, we need not fear the extremes of conflict that exceptional genius tends to involve. The latter is perhaps beyond our power to produce, and we have enough to do in encouraging a little more interest in art production on the part of great numbers of students. Incidental doubts and difficulties should not prevent us from going ahead to provide a few fairly obvious means to that end, such as a wider distribution in our schools of the basic equipment for art work in various media, of a chance to see good works of art, and of more time to spend on art under congenial conditions.

So far as our psychological understanding is concerned, there is a certain advantage in studying the extremes of genius, of superiority as well as of subnormality and pathological deviation. For all such examples help us to see in a magnified way, and sometimes in a detached, dissociated way, mental phenomena that occur to a less degree in the normal. It is useful to study genius, if only to see how its values can be cultivated apart from those traits that are considered undesirable. Certainly, there is need for more studies of genius in various fields carried out in the light of modern psychology. Freud's study of Leonardo da Vinci is a suggestive example, but it is limited to certain aspects of his personality and concerned with applying a special theory. Most of the data available are secondary and often unreliable, gathered from biographies and letters. Even the study of the artist's works is often misleading. But difficulties of this sort should not deter us from doing as much as can be done with so important a subject.

III. Creative Imagination

Common usage of the word *genius,* as expressed in dictionary definitions, emphasizes the factor of imagination in this type of personality. The most relevant in Webster's list of meanings is as follows: " 6. Extraordinary mental superiority; esp., unusual power of invention or origination of any kind." Genius is contrasted with mere talent as " original creative power, frequently working through the imagination, in contradistinction to a faculty for effective dealing with existent material; as the intuitive and spontaneous, in opposition to the merely disciplined and trained; as the inexplicable, unanalyzable, and as it were inspired, over against what works in the main by rule and line." This would seem to contradict the popular saying that " genius is only an infinite capacity for taking pains," although such a capacity might still be needed as a means to effective accomplishment.

Discounting the mystical suggestion in such words as *inexplicable* and *inspired,* we still have a valid psychological distinction. There is one kind of intelligent thinking that proceeds gradually, step by step, according to definite logical or technical rules, with each step fairly conscious and explicit. There is another kind that leaps through or over intermediate steps to a goal, to the hypothetical solution of a scientific problem or the image of a complete work of art. No doubt the intermediate steps are made somehow; but they are made with extreme speed and abbreviation and often in an unconscious or semiconscious way, as in dream or waking reverie. Past laborious struggles with detail are suddenly brought to fruition; blockings and obstacles suddenly overcome. Scientists have told of thus suddenly realizing the solution of a difficult problem; artists, of suddenly envisaging the total form they wish to produce. Such leaps of thought occur to some extent in all thinking, but in what we call ' genius ' they are more extreme and characteristic. The ' creative flash ' of original genius, which is recognized by common observation, is no less real because it is difficult to control in the psychological laboratory or to measure in standard tests.

There is a type of intelligent thinking that is effective in dealing with problems clearly stated in advance. This type is most easily tested in our standardized intelligence tests, so that those who excel in it receive high intelligence scores. But there is another kind of intelligent thinking, not so easily tested, that is likely to be impatient with artificially set problems; that prefers to set up its own problems and objectives; and that, impelled by strong inner motivations, dashes quickly to their solution. The quick, abbreviated thinking that is common in geniuses is by no means independent of discipline, technique, and ordinary step-by-step learning. But these come in advance, as necessary preparatory phases; later on, they enter as phases in detailed verification or technical construction.

Some psychologists distinguish between the ' creative ' and the ' reproductive ' imagination. *Imagination* in general is defined by Webster as the " 1. . . . formation of mental images of objects not present to the senses." It would include the recall of images of objects previously sensed; and this process, identical with one kind of memory is called ' reproductive imagination.' The other, called ' productive, constructive, or creative,' " starts with the notion of mental imaging of things suggested but not previously experienced, and thence expands, first to fantastic representation, or fancy, and later to the idea of mental creation and poetic idealization. . . ."

The fault in this distinction is that it tends to separate the two varieties too sharply. We rarely if ever imagine in a purely reproductive way. There is some ' creation ' (in the selection and reorganization of sense data) in all remembering and imaging and even in the process of sense perception itself. Every normal person learns to imagine objects and events he has not directly sensed, through mentally reorganizing details of his own past experience into combinations suggested by others. When we hear someone describe a journey to strange places, we are led to imagine places that are somewhat unlike any we have seen, although in doing so we recall and reorganize constituent details, such as colors, trees, and rocks that we have seen elsewhere before. All imagining is thus somewhat ' creative ' in a broad sense of that term. But it is true at the same time that some imagining tends to adhere, or tries to adhere, more exactly to the previous sense experience, as when we try to recall the exact words of an important conversation. Some imagining selects and reorganizes much more freely and extensively, as in dreams and wish-fulfillment phantasies or in reading a fairy story. Some individuals can perform the latter type of imagining more vividly and powerfully than others can. In contrast with the brief, fragmentary phantasy of a dull mind, the resultant forms may be unusually complex and systematic, as in imagining a whole novel or a picture of heaven. The imagery of other persons, not necessarily intellectually dull, is usually stereotyped,[1] whereas a more original mind organizes unusual forms out of the common data of experience. They may be on the whole realistic, in accord with scientific accounts of reality; or they may be 'fantastic' in the artistic sense, building up impossible, yet momentarily credible, worlds of spirits, monsters, and magic.

No one will know about these forms, of course, unless the imaginer also expresses them through a medium of communication, such as words or pictures. If these expressions have the power to interest and please other people, they will be called works of creative imagination in the strict and eulogistic sense. Thus we see again that the idea of creativeness can have a broad or a narrow sense, as applied to imagination. The latter implies an exceptional power to reorganize images into new types of form, as judged by other persons to whom they have been communicated.

Related to imagination is the little-understood process known as *empathy*, which Webster defines as " Imaginative projection of one's own consciousness into another being; esp., sympathetic understanding of other than human beings." Briefly, its place in artistic creation is as follows. In varying degrees, artists tend to project their own experiences into an unfinished work of art. For example, the sculptor imagines his block of stone as possessed of inner life and muscular tension. Van Gogh projected his own emotional agitation into his paintings of trees, clouds, rocks, and houses. In other words, he expressed his feelings in his pictures, and such art is sometimes called 'expressionistic.' Children often have a vivid power to 'make believe' that a doll, a drawing, or a clay model is living and doing things. But the artist goes further if he constructs a work of art so that observers are also stimulated to similar imaginings.

---

[1] It may be held, in the opinion of some psychologists, that, in certain types of mental activity at least, efficiency goes hand in hand with a reduction in the amount of concrete imagery. — *Editor.*

The theories of psychoanalysis have direct reference to the problem of the nature of creative imagination. Freud did not work out a very explicit, systematic application of these theories to the nature of art, nor have his successors done so. There is much to be done in this regard, for the general hypotheses are extremely suggestive and reinforced by vast amounts of clinical evidence. It is to be hoped that the assurance with which some present American psychologists dismiss the works of Freud as outmoded will not long prevent an open-minded testing of the psychoanalytic approach to esthetic psychology. Certainly, the more accepted American schools of psychology have produced nothing that begins to promise so much enlightenment along this line; in fact, they have almost ignored the whole problem of creative imagination and of phantasy-formation in general. Freud's theory of dream and phantasy production, if true in general, must be true of much creative imagination in art as well. His account of dream images as symbols unconsciously devised to mask and compromise internal conflicts in the individual, and of folklore and ritual as examples of such symbolism in social culture, offers promising hypotheses for the analysis of civilized art. But most efforts to work out this analysis have been oversimplified and farfetched, consisting of superficial references to erotic symbols and wish fulfillments. As Freud himself made clear, the processes of symbolization are much too variable, indirect, and subtle to be explained in any facile way. Art teachers interested in psychology should read Freud's introductory writings for themselves, and not be content with popular misrepresentations of them.

The educational applications of these writings are also far from clear. For if creative imagination arises in large part from neurotic conflict, and if rational education tends to remove such conflict by bringing its sources into consciousness, much of the motivation of artistic phantasy (or at least of certain kinds of it) may be lost. Again we have the problem of whether creative originality in art can always be achieved along with a normal, happily adjusted personality. If so, how?

IV. Component Functions and Abilities; Individual Differences

Whatever the answer, we may be very sure that it will have to be varied in relation to different types of individuals. It was stated above, and needs repeating, that there is no such thing as ' the artistic type,' in the sense of a distinctive kind of personality common to all practitioners of an art medium. Artists are as diverse as persons in any other great realm of human activity. There is no such thing as ' the creative process,' in the sense of a single, uniform mode of thinking and feeling by which all works of art are produced. Perhaps the nearest we can come to describing an artistic type is to recognize a sort of person who persistently seeks to produce objects and events, which, through their sensory form, will interest other persons. But the artistic type is not necessarily creative or original. The visual artist likes to make forms appealing to the eye; the musician, to make forms appealing to the ear; the writer to assemble words stimulating thought, feeling, or imagination. This is an obvious, external classification, and it includes numerous varieties of the creative process.

All these varieties are composite and diversified psychologically, in that they include the operation of many basic functions, such as perceiving, imagining, desiring, reasoning, experiencing emotions, and controlling the muscles of hands, voice, or limbs to manipulate some medium of expression. Now these same functions can be combined and used in any one of many different civilized activities; the same ones are used in art as in science, commerce, war, and sport. The most easily discernible difference is in the type of object produced, which, in the case of the artist, is primarily a stimulus to sense perception and imagination. None of the basic functions can ever be used in entire isolation. They can be coördinated into countless different configurations, some of which are momentary moods and attitudes; some, long-continued occupations, individual and collective.

Although they cannot be entirely isolated, the several functions do operate at different times with various degrees of emphasis or dominance. Sometimes we devote all our attention to seeing clearly, sometimes to hearing, sometimes to imagining, sometimes to reasoning, sometimes to directing the hand. The result in any case is a different main type of compound behavior, in which many component functions coöperate in a certain general configuration. Such general types recur in approximately similar form, and hence can be described by general psychology, although they admit of endless variation in detail.

Psychology is just beginning the task of describing these types of mental activity in relation to various types of external situation. When the task has progressed further, we may be able to use the descriptions in analyzing roughly the activities of art production. For example, it seems that every artist (like every other person) has some moments in which visual observation dominates his behavior and other moments in which each of the other functions dominates. In other words, while all, or nearly all, the basic functions operate to some extent throughout the creative process, it has various phases in which somewhat different configurations exist. These may occur in any order. With the visual artist, there are phases of attentive observing — toward nature indiscriminately, toward some particular object (such as a tree), or toward some work of art (such as a painting of a tree). There are phases when imaginative reconstruction dominates; as when the artist, far away from any tree and perhaps in a darkened room, tries to visualize his future painting of a tree. There is a phase of attentive effort to manipulate the medium; for example, to make oil paints look like the kind of scene he has in mind. There is a phase of reflective thinking, criticism, and evaluation, when he stands off and tries to decide what is the matter with his unfinished work, how it could be altered so as to improve upon it.

Such phases occur in any art or type of art to some extent. But different arts and styles of art lead to stronger emphasis on different ones. For example, if the art is representative and the style is realistic, the artist will tend to emphasize comparison between actual trees and his picture of one, so that the picture will resemble actual trees and tend to arouse an image of one in the mind of an observer. If the style is less realistic, he may devote more effort to imagining a strange, fantastic tree. If interested in decorative design, he will bend more effort toward organizing his imagery and the resultant picture in terms of repeated lines and colors, and of unified patterns. If making a statue of a god, he may have to compare his work with authoritative conceptions of the nature of that god, and with his own conception, rather than with any natural object. Some art has a strongly intellectual content, conveying philosophic or scientific ideas in some concrete embodiment, as through symbolism and allegory. If the art is on the whole utilitarian and practical, as in the making of a chair or a house, the artist will probably try to imagine how his product will work under specified conditions: how strong, comfortable, and salable it will be. He may have to do more reflective, planful thinking along functional lines, and less observation of nature. But he will still use his eyes at times in observing other chairs or houses, and his imagination in visualizing the intended one. He may still include decorative design as one factor to be considered. In short, the artistic process tends to vary to some extent among different schools and periods of art, according to the aims and standards adopted, and according to the medium and technique used, though in all of them a few basic psychological functions and a few types of composite attitude or configuration tend to recur.

Again, the process will vary to some extent according to the individual personality and habits of the artist. Such differences, too, may be approached from a standpoint of component function and composite attitude. Some artists in any medium are more imaginative than others, spend more time and effort in trying to visualize an intended work of art before it is produced. Some do a great deal of close observation of nature or of other works of art; others, comparatively little. Some plan their works with conscious system and many preliminary sketches, thinking the whole thing out logically; others proceed more through spontaneous impulse and emotion. These likewise are differences that are not peculiar to artists but characteristic of human beings concerned with various matters. They provide the data for psychologists to use in distinguishing main types of personality and character. The artistic process, then, will vary according to the general type of personality to which the artist belongs.

Questions of *artistic ability* may also be approached from this standpoint. Each of the various functions and constituent processes, mentioned above as entering the production of art, may be considered in terms of ability, of the amount of power the artist shows in that particular direction. ' Artistic ability ' is a broad, inclusive name for the net result of all of them in joint operation. For example, some artists have unusually high sensory ability. This may again be differentiated, to the effect that some have unusually high powers of color discrimination; others, of space perception. Some artists have more ability to organize vivid, complex visual designs than others do. Some have more ability to imagine the strange and fantastic, whereas others can deal only with the realistic and actually observable. Some have more ability to plan intelligently; some, to criticize their own work objectively. Many can think more intelligently in a nonverbal situation, as in manipulating a concrete material, than in the verbal situations that our present intelligence tests tend to emphasize. Some artists can think intellectually, in terms of philosophic and scientific concepts, but find it hard to embody these in concrete images; some can do both. Some have more manual dexterity than others in the physical manipulation of the medium. (A heavy-handed technician like the early Cézanne, if strong in vision, imagination, and planning, may outrank many facile wielders of the brush.) Some artists have more determined

will to create and be original than others do, more intense emotional
devotion to certain types of form and subject. This, too, must be classed
with the component abilities of creation — the ability to desire some
kind of achievement strongly enough to impel the necessary work and
sacrifice.

The total *character* of an artist and the net difference between one
and another can perhaps eventually be analyzed in terms of such traits
and abilities as these, with due attention to the relative strength and
dominance of each, and to the peculiar configuration they assume at
various stages of the artist's career. Discerning biographies of artists
have approached such analysis, usually in nonpsychological terms, but
with suggestive hints for scientific interpretation. Often our best clue
to them is in the nature of the artist's works themselves. One picture
has a strong element of color design, another of fantasy, another of
philosophic implication. One utensil or building has elaborate surface
pattern but little practical efficiency, another the opposite, and so on.
We tend to assume, then, that the artist was comparatively strong in the
modes of thought and execution necessary to the production of these
traits in the finished product, and strongly motivated toward them as
goals.

No doubt such an assumption is often warranted. But we must
remember again that what appears in a given work of art is not necessarily the sole, original creation of the artist whose name it bears. He
may have taken over and adapted certain elements from previous
sources and have given them a new particular embodiment without
having thought them out for himself or even thoroughly understood
them. It is one thing to recognize the elements of form and cultural
significance a work of art contains; another, to find out who really
originated them. Often a religious or ethical concept is advanced by a
thinker in that field, then translated by others into various art media.
A picture may contain profound suggestions of sublime tragedy or
poignant sentiment, even though the artist himself did not feel them
very keenly. This is not necessarily a mark of insincerity in a deroga-
tory sense. A playwright can express in words the emotional attitudes of hatred and jealousy and an actor can portray them without
either of them feeling these attitudes strongly himself. Similarly, a
painter can represent the facial expressions and gestures that tend to
stimulate an emotion in others, without feeling it himself. He can express and represent madness, and yet be quite sane.

For such reasons it is necessary, in tracing the mental processes and abilities that led up to a work of art, to look behind the finished product. We may discover letters and comments of the artist or opinions of contemporaries, each of which is to be taken with a grain of salt, though contributing its bit to the mass of evidence.

In another respect, too, works of art are inadequate clues to the psychology of artists. It is hard to infer from the finished product just what steps were involved in its conception and execution. To what extent was it systematically planned? Or was it done on the spur of the moment? The final product may seem extremely casual, impulsive, free, and irregular, as in typical romantic art; and yet every detail may have been meticulously calculated for those effects. Here it is useful to study, if we can, the preliminary notes and sketches, in chronological order. Living artists are easier to study in this respect and deserve more attention from psychologists. For the training of young artists, information on these settings and motives of art production would be of great value.

Psychological research has much to do in studying the specific components of art ability, through comparison of individual cases and through measurement when possible. Some of these component abilities are much more easily measured than others. For example, the simpler kinds of sensory discrimination have been accurately measured. The ability to perceive complex visual forms, such as those of art, has been less explored, but it is not incapable of measurement. The ability to imagine vividly has not been carefully studied, except for the special variety known as ' eidetic imagery.' The ability to imagine complex forms, or unusual, original forms, has not received much attention. The Rorschach and other ink-blot tests supply a promising approach to certain types of imaginative ability, including the difference between stereotyped and unusual tendencies, but so far little has been done to distinguish between creative and pathological varieties of unusual response. Many manual skills can be accurately measured, but those involved in artistic technique have not been systematically approached. The emotional and the conative or motivational elements in art ability seem least accessible to experimental study and measurement.

In general, it would seem desirable to do more in the way of preliminary analysis of the field, of distinguishing tentatively the many different types of ability involved in art, before launching forth on ambitious programs of detailed measurement that may turn out to miss essential factors. Such fundamental facts as the compound nature of art ability and the general way in which component abilities are present in varying degrees in various individuals have not yet been clearly recognized. (It must be remembered that even the functions and abilities that we here designate as ' component ' or ' basic,' because of their recurrence in various configurations, are themselves compound, joint operations of many sets of nerves and muscles. There are no purely elementary functions, but there are degrees of complexity.)

Let us return to the problem again from the point of view of education. It was mentioned that art education has an unusual opportunity to deal directly and constructively with a number of important factors in the development of personality. In terms of ability, this means that it can try to foster, harmonize, and direct into socially desirable channels the various special abilities involved in art production. The objectives and methods of art education on each age level should be examined and developed from this point of view: how so to select and to organize the specific materials and activities of art as to develop *all* the important component abilities to some extent. At present, the art course tends to exercise only a few of them directly, and even that is done without much psychological insight. College courses tend to overstress intellectual study and verbal memory; art academies, to overstress manual technique. All along the line, for both general education and professional training, more effort should be made to deal with those other mental and emotional factors the development of which is necessary for maximal creative and appreciative ability.

How can they best be dealt with? We do not know, but we can at least experiment consciously and systematically, through combining the approach of the psychologist with those of the scholar and the technician in art. Certainly, educational methods should be more carefully adapted to the requirements of different types of individual personality. To recognize these types is mainly a psychological problem. We cannot say in general how much intellectual training and information are conducive to creative originality. But what little we know at present about artists would indicate that some can profit by a great deal more intellectual training than others can; that there are intellectual, rational, planful types who can develop in this way without losing the spark of creativeness, whereas for others much intellectual study and rational analysis are uncongenial and even detrimental. We do not know how much discipline and definite guidance are good for the future artist; but, here again, certain types probably need more than others. Neither extreme free expressionism nor extreme academic discipline can be accepted for all cases; the two must be combined in varying degrees for various types of student.

It would be highly desirable in certain ways if we could recognize potential creative ability in art and other fields at an early stage of development. Democracy needs leaders, and mass education needs means of singling out gifted children for special opportunities. Leaders may arise from any racial, religious, or geographic group, and from any economic level. Special opportunities should be awarded without regard to these factors, though in ways to compensate for the disadvantages of unfavorable environment. At the same time, one may tremble at the thought of what would have happened to some geniuses of the past, had they been exposed too early to the spotlight of flattering attention or to the well-meaning solicitude of educational faddists.

We are still far from knowing the best way to treat superior children after we discover them: how much to segregate them; how much praise, freedom, and special training to give them. For the present, it is well to be cautious about premature devices for the selection and special nurture of children whom we believe to be superior in art. If better opportunities in art are provided for all children who desire them, the gifted may perhaps be counted on to make themselves known through better use of these common opportunities. At present, there is no brief, artificial test that can do more than hint at possible superiority. There is no set of measurable or easily recognizable characteristics in children's art that will guarantee later creative ability. Any that are singled out by present research must remain hypothetical until verified by adult achievement in later years. The judgment of art teachers is still mainly personal and subjective, with vaguely defined and conflicting standards. Of all available indices of potential creative ability, there is perhaps none more significant than *interest:* not mild or temporary interest, but the intense, persistent desire for art materials and activities that impels some students year after year to effort and sacrifice for the sake of working with them. If we can provide such students with a fair amount of opportunity and encouragement, we shall be reasonably sure of not failing in our first duty to the potential creators.

V. TECHNICAL TRAINING IN ART

The problem of technical training requires careful consideration in formulating a policy for art education. There is not only the general question of how much technical training should be required (as over against free expression), but also the question of what kinds to require.

Practically all educators agree that more intensive technical work is necessary for the higher ages than for the lower, where much free play is desirable. Older students need and demand technique, become dissatisfied with mere play, and want to know how to do a thing well (as judged by contemporary adult standards) if at all. They become more self-critical, impatient of awkward groping and mere self-expression; they delight in learning a technique for its own sake, as an interesting game. Almost any definite formula for drawing a figure or fastening two pieces of material together pleases them more than spontaneous experiment. To learn how to do or to make something difficult gives them an added sense of power and self-respect through control over environment. It helps them forget their anxieties and extravert their attention. Technical training exercises limbs and muscles and is thus of use in assisting a balanced development of the whole individual. For such reasons, some amount of technical training in art processes is valuable as a part of general education, even for students who will never use it professionally. It is coming to be recognized as a desirable part of all liberal education, even on the college level. For the prospective artist, and as part of a vocational course in high school, art academy, or professional institute, it is of course paramount in importance.

But what is technique? It is skill in executing the details necessary for expert production or performance. It is learned ability, as contrasted with innate; it involves ability to profit by accumulated cultural experience. The technique necessary to paint a picture is not restricted to the hand alone. The hand cannot be separated from the eye and brain. Broadly considered, the technique of creating a picture includes skilled use of all the abilities involved in the process. It includes skilled vision, skilled imagination, skilled planning, criticism, and concentration of energies. As we have seen, the fault of most academic training in art has been that it neglects most of the elements necessary for a full technique. It fails even to realize that there is such a thing as the technique of artistic perceiving and imagining. It leads students too directly and constantly to the final stages of execution and expression, with too little attention to the preliminary phases of creative thinking.

For some purposes, however, it is useful to distinguish between these broader mental techniques and the specific kind of skill concerned more directly with the manipulation of a medium. This skill does focus ordinarily on muscular control through the hands or other parts of the body (perhaps the whole body, as in dancing or acting). It focusses on the actual putting on of paint or cutting of marble, on playing the piano or writing one word after another, as distinct from working out the thoughts and aims that should guide any such process. Even here, the mental and manual are intimately bound together, at least for the creative artist. Perhaps this is the main distinction between the artist and the mere artisan, the uncreative worker, however skilled the latter may be in a mechanical way. In the former, direction of the hands and outer medium is controlled by an inner, self-developed aim and vision, whereas the factory machine operator can at times almost let his hands work by themselves, without conscious control; the hack worker does what he is told to do and does not have to think out ends and means.

Technique for the artist involves not only trained nerve and muscle coördination, but also knowledge of the medium, its properties and modes of operation. He must know how oils or water colors will spread and mix; how jade will break if not properly cut; what chemicals to apply before firing to produce a red or a blue glaze. Part of his technique consists in remembering accumulated knowledge, such as that of science; and part in having it organized for quick, adaptive use in overt action. Part of his technique consists in a developed habit of intelligent thinking, of adapting means to ends. He must be able to think out what he wants to do and apply the means for doing it. Such ability is especially evident in the industrial arts, where it must deal with the functional effectiveness of utensils, but it applies to the ' fine arts ' as well.

To enrich his background stock of potential means, it is good experience for the student to do much extensive manipulation of materials and instruments in his art, even without any specific aim at the time; merely to ' get the feel ' of them and learn what they will do or not do if treated in various ways. Ideas for works of art often arise from such direct experience of the medium and its properties.

As a creative artist, he will not be restricted to seeking the same ends that other artists have sought or that he learned in school. He will formulate other goals, and consequently, have to alter the methods he has learned. If his aim is relatively traditional, the old technical methods may be flexible enough to cover them. But the more original the artist, the more he has to devise new techniques as he goes along, or at least substantially revise and extend the old ones. If instruction is to stimulate creativeness, it should inculcate this attitude toward past and present techniques, as suggestions and starting points, not as final laws. Old materials have still unrealized possibilities. Through the acceleration of scientific technology, new materials and potential techniques are arising faster than the artists can effectively use them. Each year new machine processes, plastic materials, metals, dyes, colored lights, and so on are laid in endless profusion on the artist's lap. To the more adaptive artist, they suggest new types of art form. He goes ahead to learn their properties, and usually employs them at first in making types of form very much like the old ones; only later does the new medium stimulate more radical originations. This was the case, for example, with the motion picture, most of the early productions of which imitated stage plays and failed to utilize the peculiar advantages of the cinema for telling a story. Students who acquire one type of technique in any art too fixedly and unimaginatively are likely to be left far behind in today's competitive race. While applied science now provides new resources for the artist without his asking, there is no reason why artists should not be more active in asking science for desired assistance, as by envisaging new desirable art forms and letting science provide the means to actualize them.

Teachers sometimes speak of ' learning the fundamentals ' in an art, and doing one's experimenting or creative work later on. The ' fundamentals ' are certain technical skills, believed to be widely applicable. Academic art teachers have so regarded drawing from Greek and Roman casts, perspective, and life drawing, with emphasis on the correct representation of anatomy. These have been considered necessary preliminaries, not only for painting and sculpture, but even for architecture and the decorative arts. There is much to be said for this practice, and many highly original artists endorse it, but it has some debatable features.

Certainly, these studies and related skills are not fundamental in the sense that all modern styles of art directly involve them. Much modern art deliberately avoids or distorts naturalistic anatomy, perspective, and the classical type of light-and-shade modelling, and these are not involved in most Oriental, medieval, archaic, and primitive styles. The idea that they are fundamental is in part a heritage from the time when little was known of any style of art other than the Greco-Roman and Renaissance. Today, one could argue that a quite different set of skills and disciplines is necessary if one desires to paint in the Chinese or Persian way or to model in the Egyptian or Cubist way. The Greek and Renaissance styles are still fundamental to our culture to a much greater degree than these others are, but less exclusively so in these cosmopolitan times. Since we have learned to respect other great styles, we are less confident that the traditional European style is the right one or fundamental to art in any absolute sense. It is becoming more and more advantageous for the modern artist in any medium to acquaint himself with exotic and primitive styles of art, both visually and if possible through some experience with their techniques. They are providing our day with a wealth of rich materials for the artistic melting pot, to be transformed into new modern styles. Leaders in the Western arts have long been making use of them with profitable results. Yet our art schools, on the whole, have yet to begin giving serious instruction in them, even from the standpoint of visual appreciation. In this respect, college and museum instruction, stressing art history, is farther advanced. Vocational courses for prospective artists must soon follow their lead toward greater cosmopolitanism, at least to the extent of offering advanced students an opportunity to learn something of the esthetic principles and technical practices of exotic, archaic, and primitive arts.

Furthermore, it is a mistake to assume that students can acquire 'thorough grounding' in a traditional European technique and then easily change over to something very different later on. Intensive drill in any particular technique necessarily involves a tendency to acquire certain habits of thinking, imagining, and creating associated with that technique. Along with manual skill and knowledge of a medium, the student may acquire a belief that there are certain right ways of using that skill and medium. He may acquire traditional esthetic ideals, standards, and conventions of form along with the traditional technique, since the latter is never presented apart from them. If so, he can still free himself to some extent from them later on, perhaps through a rather violent reaction and exceptionally vigorous powers of original thinking. In music, a student who spends years in practicing Bach and Beethoven, Clementi and Czerny, is likely to acquire not only pianistic technique, but also a tendency to approach musical composition in the spirit of classical harmony and counterpoint. In visual art, a student who learns the technique of drawing through years of drawing in the style of Raphael will tend himself to see and imagine also in the style of Raphael. Only the more independent will avoid doing so. Often neither the teacher nor the student realizes that a particular style is being learned. He is so accustomed to seeing both art and nature from the standpoint of that style that it seems to him to be merely the ' true '

or ' correct ' way to represent nature, and hence as the necessary fundamental for any kind of art. The best cure for such narrowness is further
observation of the many past and present styles of art other than those
to which one has become accustomed.

At the same time, there are definite values in intensive, traditional
training, whatever style of art one desires to produce later on. We
have noted that there are values in following out clearly and consistently one particular approach to art at a time, to avoid the confusion
and vagueness of too much freedom and cosmopolitanism. (Which
approach is chosen first is perhaps not essential; but since the Greek
is closer to us than the Chinese or Gothic, it is doubtless the one to
emphasize.) One of these values is that of mental clarity and equilibrium — a matter of letting the student organize himself one stage
at a time and absorb the vast cultural heritage part by part, rather than
overwhelming him at the start by too many complex influences and
alternatives at once. Another value is that of acquiring systematic
habits of continuous work.

This brings us to the question of transfer of training. Drawing
skill acquired in making Raphaelesque pictures is not easily transferred
to the making of Postimpressionist pictures like those of Matisse,
based on the Persian style. But there is no doubt that some of that
skill can be transferred; that the development of the skill is not incon-
sistent with some flexibility and adaptiveness. One at least knows how
to handle a pencil or charcoal and approach the problem of dividing
up a picture-space into areas. It is for such reasons as these that very
radical artists often urge young students to begin with traditional training. " But," they sometimes add, " you don't need very much of it;
you can learn all that's necessary in a short time and then go on for
yourself." In other words, what is really fundamental for all drawing,
transferable to any style of drawing, and universal in applicability
is comparatively little and easily understood, though it may require
long practice for proficiency in execution. Much of the work that art
schools require as necessary grounding is really dispensable, since it
consists in learning some particular style of art that the student may
not want to use later on.

Where the exact truth lies in this issue is debatable. But it suggests
an approach to the problem of technical training; that of analyzing the
work to be required into different categories, from the standpoint of
ends and means. The elements of training that can be shown to be most
fundamental, in the sense that they promise to be most constantly and

urgently required in any sort of art work later on, should be distinguished as clearly as possible from the elements that will be needed only by those who decide to practice a particular type of art. The three R's of the elementary school are certainly fundamental to general education, whereas the calculus and Egyptian hieroglyphics are not. Skill in drawing with pencil on paper is more widely useful for more persons in later life than is skill in arranging mosaics. Again, with any particular medium, such as oil paints, there are certain fundamental properties and procedures that artists in almost any style will find useful. How to prepare the canvas, to mix pigment with oil and lay it on so the colors will not run or change in unintended ways, to protect the surface with varnish without affecting the colors — these are comparatively fundamental and often rather quickly explained. Where an art makes much use of applied science, as do ceramics, industrial design, and architecture, there is more to be learned about complex properties and procedures. On the other hand, how to apply oil paints in the Impressionist, broken-color style is not fundamental to the art of painting. It is useful chiefly to those who wish to paint Impressionist pictures.

A technical course should include some fundamentals for all students, mostly at the beginning; and also a choice of several optional skills from which a student may select what he expects to need. Unfortunately, it is hard to get artists or art teachers to agree upon what is fundamental and what is dispensable. Each tends to regard his own pet practices and tastes as fundamental to all good art. They may agree that pencil-drawing is more fundamental than mosaic or enamelling. But within a subject, such as ' life drawing,' ' perspective,' or ' composition,' what part of the work is really useful for any style of art, and what part is merely an expression of the teacher's own tastes? In figure drawing, such injunctions as ' bring out the main masses ' or ' get the true proportions ' are advanced as necessary laws, regardless of the fact that many leading artists, past and present, choose to draw the figure otherwise. Esthetic standards are still so controversial, and art teachers mix them so unconsciously and dogmatically with technique, that we are a long way from agreeing upon technical fundamentals.

The applied sciences are much clearer in this respect and could well be emulated by art instruction. In the medical school, for example, students learn about ' materia medica,' the properties of various drugs. But they are not told: " Always prescribe strychnine." They are told: " If the condition is thus, and you wish to produce a certain result, strychnine is a way to produce it." This is technique, intelligently thought out in terms of means and ends. Art educators also must learn to think out their technical materials and methods in terms of general and specific ends. Some ends are very general and unquestioned, such as manual dexterity and (let us add) the various types of mental ability that have been noted. Some are optional, but widely useful because of frequent demand later on. The ability to draw active figures with realistic anatomy and perspective, for example, belongs in this intermediate category. Some are transitory fads or individual whims, such as a preference for dark and subdued, or bright, contrasting color combinations; for the geometric lines of Cubism or the wavy lines of *art nouveau*. The student can profit by studying and practicing many of these optional methods. But he should be led to regard them as useful means to certain types of artistic effect, not as basic rules. Thus he may be helped to acquire a really flexible technique along with intelligent habits of planning his work and with adaptability in contriving effective means to new ends.

REFERENCES

(1) BENHAM, E. "The creative activity." *British Journal of Psychology,* 20: 1929, pp. 59–65.

(2) DEWEY, J., and Others. *Art and Education.* (Barnes Foundation Press: Merion, Pa., 1929) 349 pp.

(3) DOWNEY, J. *Creative Imagination.* (Harcourt, Brace and Co.: New York, 1929) 230 pp.

(4) EDMAN, I. *Arts and the Man.* (W. W. Norton and Co., Inc.: New York, 1939) 154 pp.

(5) FERENCZI, S. "Stages in the Development of the Sense of Reality." (In) *An Outline of Psycho-analysis,* ed. by J. S. Van Teslaar. (Modern Library: New York, 1924) 383 pp. (pp. 108–127).

(6) FREUD, S. *A General Introduction to Psychoanalysis.* (Liveright: New York, 1935) 412 pp.

(7) FREUD, S. *Leonardo da Vinci.* (Moffat, Yard: New York, 1916) 130 pp.

(8) GRIFFITH, C. R., and Others. "Creative Activity and Expression" (In) *Readings in Educational Psychology,* ed. by C. E. Skinner. (Farrar and Rinehart: New York, 1937) 630 pp. (pp. 270–289).

(9) HOLLINGWORTH, L. S. *Gifted Children, Their Nature and Nurture.* (The Macmillan Co.: New York, 1927) 374 pp.

(10) KRETSCHMER, E. *The Psychology of Men of Genius.* (Harcourt, Brace and Co.: New York, 1931) 256 pp.

(11) LANGFELD, H. S. "Conflict and Adjustment in Art." (In) *Problems of Personality,* ed. by C. M. Campbell and Others. (Harcourt, Brace and Co.: New York, 1925) 434 pp. (pp. 373–383).

(12) Löwenfeld, V. *The Nature of Creative Activity.* (Harcourt, Brace and Co.: New York, 1939) 272 pp.

(13) Montmasson, I. M. *Invention and the Unconscious.* (Harcourt, Brace and Co.: New York, 1932) 338 pp.

(14) Munro, T. " Creative imagination and nature " and " How the artist looks at nature." *American Magazine of Art,* June and July, 1932.

(15) Prescott, F. C. *The Poetic Mind.* (The Macmillan Co.: New York, 1926) 308 pp.

(16) Rank, O. *Art and Artist.* (Alfred Knopf: New York, 1932) 443 pp.

(17) Ribot, T. *Essay on the Creative Imagination.* (Open Court: Chicago, 1906) 370 pp.

(18) Rugg, H., and Shumaker, A. " The Psychology of the Creative Act." (In) *The Child-Centered School.* (World Book Co.: New York, 1928) 359 pp. (pp. 276–286)

(19) Spearman, C. *Creative Mind.* (Nisbet: London, 1930) 153 pp.

(20) Terman, L. M., and Oden, M. " Status of the California Gifted Group at the End of Sixteen Years " and " Correlates of Adult Achievement in the California Gifted Group." (In) *The Thirty-Ninth Yearbook, Part I,* of this Society, 1939, pp. 67–89.

(21) Witty, P. A. " Evidence Regarding the Nature of Intelligence from the Study of Superior Deviates." (In) *Addresses and Discussions Presenting the Thirty-Ninth Yearbook* of this Society, 1940, pp. 23–30.

CHAPTER XXIII

POWERS OF ART APPRECIATION AND EVALUATION

Thomas Munro

I. Educational Aspects of Art Appreciation

The appreciation of art is commonly contrasted with its creation. To use the language of economics, the artist, or creator, is the producer of art; the appreciator is its consumer, or user. 'Appreciation' implies also that he is a discriminating consumer, who knows and enjoys real values in this type of commodity or service.[1] Since there are many more consumers of art than artists, educators are coming to stress art appreciation, especially as a part of general education. It is not necessarily divorced from the technical practice of art, however. Indeed, some amount of the latter is widely regarded as contributing to appreciation; and the artist is supposed to be able to appreciate esthetic values, at least in his own field. But more attention is being given to the artistic needs of the layman, and to the value that art may have for his cultural background and leisure enjoyment.

The appreciation of art is also contrasted educationally with the history of art. College courses in art history try to stress objective facts: the sequence of major periods, styles, and outstanding examples of them; the lives, dates, and characteristics of leading artists, and the influences of one upon another. The scholarly approach to art tries to emulate science in excluding the writer's or teacher's personal preferences. No doubt there are evaluative assumptions even in selecting certain works and artists for emphasis and omitting others. But at least the scholar abstains from the sentimental rhapsodizing about beauty that often constitutes the bulk of popular lectures on 'art appre-

---

[1] To *appreciate*, says Webster, is " 5. To be critically and emotionally sensitive to the esthetic values of; as, to *appreciate* Shelley's lyrics or a Beethoven sonata; to admire critically the artistic or technical excellence of; as, to *appreciate* a violinist's fingering." *Appreciation* is " 1. . . . full recognition of worth; recognition through the senses, esp. with delicacy of perception . . . 5. Sensitive awareness or perception of worth or value, esp. esthetic value; as, his fine *appreciation* of painting." In education, it is defined as " 6. The study of esthetic values (as distinguished from historical values), as in music, art, or literature."

ciation.' Scholarly professors of art history, indeed, incline to the view that appreciation cannot be taught, any more than creative originality can be taught. The innately sensitive student of art will develop good taste as a personal characteristic, along with good manners and morals.

For children, however, and in popular lectures and introductory courses for adults, a less scholarly approach is considered legitimate. Here, too, the tendency has been away from mere emotional praise and toward pointing out why certain works of art are considered important. This is usually done through showing how they exemplify accepted standards of value or ' art principles,' such as rhythm, balance, and proportion. Progressive schools attempt to get children to express their own preferences in art and to discuss the reasons for them. All such courses in appreciation tend to include some amount of historical fact, even though not necessarily in chronological order. At least, an objective of such courses is to try to familiarize the student with a few main facts about artists and historic styles, so that he can recognize examples when he sees them. In short, the teaching of art appreciation is usually a rather superficial, unsystematic mixture of observation, history, and esthetic theory.

How can the results of such instruction be graded, and how can any differences in ' power of appreciation ' among individuals be recognized or measured? It is fairly easy, of course, to measure knowledge of historic facts and ability to recognize artists' works. One can grade as literary compositions the essays students write about art and why they like or dislike it. But these obviously do not deal directly and fully with appreciative ability.

If the teacher is sure he knows what works of art are best, what the student ought to like, and why, it is also fairly easy to grade on this basis. But most teachers and art critics are a good deal less dogmatic about such matters than they used to be. Not only are esthetic standards and the relative importance of artists in dispute, but it is also coming to be felt that there is no reason why children should always like the same kinds of art that adults do. Even for adults, some individuality in taste, some divergence from current authority, is recognized as valuable in a democratic society. Nevertheless, several alleged tests of art ability have been advanced and widely used that undertake to measure such ability on a basis of conformity to an established norm of taste. The psychologists who make these pseudo-scientific ' tests ' do not, as a rule, presume to decide what types of art are best; but they assume that somebody knows. Hence they proceed to ascertain the preferences of a number of established artists, teachers, and critics. Statistically treated, these will constitute a norm for judging other people as 'high' or 'low' in powers of appreciation, according as they agree or disagree with it. Another device is to alter or 'spoil' certain works of art, and ask the subject whether he likes the spoiled or the original version better. This assumes, of course, that the altered version is really worse, for all persons at all times. That is again a debatable assumption, particularly because it still involves the old absolutistic attitude toward art value, which conflicts with modern trends in both esthetics and education.

It is not at all necessary that we approach the question of appreciative ability on a basis of *what* people like in art, or even that we expect them to like the same things at all times. Certainly it is not necessary to assume they all should like the same thing, regardless of their differences in age and personality. *What* they like in art is perhaps less important on the whole than *why* they like it, *how* they come to form their judgments of value. The single issue of preference, of whether one likes picture A better than picture B, is far from being the whole of art appreciation. It is more important psychologically and educationally to find out what kind of total experience the individual is deriving from his contact with art, and what kind of subsequent experience and behavior it may lead him to. Psychologically, we should try to find out more about the nature and varieties of such esthetic experience, under different conditions and for different types of individuals. This will disclose various types of specific ability, cooperating to make up the composite ability we roughly designate as 'power of appreciation.' Educationally, we should then try to find out how these can best be developed, along with other factors in the growing personality.

II. Appreciative Ability in Relation to Creative Ability

To some extent, the abilities involved in appreciation are the same as those involved in art creation or in any other complex psychophysical activity. Visual ability in general enters into many activities, and so does imaginative ability. This is another way of saying that persons who are capable at one activity are usually capable at many others also. A superior artist is likely to have superior potential ability in appreciation, whether or not he has tried to train it directly. In fact, few persons ever try directly to develop powers of art appreciation; they do so incidentally, if at all, in the course of other work.

One might infer that appreciative ability is nothing more than a partial approach to creative ability. Some theorists have declared that appreciation should strive to be as nearly as possible a reproduction of the artist's experience in creating the work of art. But these conclusions are oversimplified and misleading. The processes and powers of appreciation overlap those of creation to a large extent, but are not identical, and there is no reason why one should necessarily be a mere imperfect repetition of the other.

If appreciation is, and should be, merely a partial approach to artistic experience, then the best training for appreciation is perhaps a course in artistic technique, followed by practical experience in art production. Artists sometimes scoff at the idea of anyone who is not an artist being able to understand art as well as they do. " How can he know what it's all about," they say, " until he's gone through the work of doing it? " There are educators who sympathize with this attitude, and urge " participation in art activities " as the only road to appreciation. It is fashionable to quote the Deweyan maxim of learning by doing, with the inference that one can never learn to understand any human activity or its products without physically engaging in it. Must one then try to dabble in all the occupations and techniques whose products interest one or else give up the hope of understanding them? The idea is absurd and is never consistently followed out. We do not need to repeat the bee's experience to enjoy its honey, or the glassblower's experience to enjoy the glass.

The appreciator's experience lacks some elements present in creation; but it may develop others even beyond the point achieved by the creator. In looking at a child's drawing, for example, the teacher, by reason of his broader experience of life and art, can sometimes understand and appreciate certain qualities in it more fully than the child did. When we look at primitive or ancient art, we no doubt miss certain meanings and functions that have passed away with the early artist, but we can also appreciate its importance in the light of cultural history.

Undoubtedly, to have practiced an art is a help to appreciation in certain ways. One has associations of the feel of the medium. One knows from experience the difficulty of achieving certain effects, and so can admire their successful achievement. Children, especially, like to be doing things with their hands and grow impatient if asked to concentrate long on looking or listening and thinking quietly about what they observe. Wide experimentation in productive techniques is valuable in the early stages of general education. To specialize intensively on appreciation and criticism is a task for mature minds. But it is none the less possible and worth while. No one can go far in technical production along many lines. He may choose to practice one or two, but he must study the others from outside if at all.

It is extremely doubtful whether technical producers are as a rule the best appreciators or judges in their own fields. As to their own products, they are more than likely to be biassed, as also to the products of competing artists. The judicious outsider can achieve more perspective for a fair evaluation. Artists of the past were sometimes impelled by motives and emotions that have little relevance to us; they portrayed the kings they admired, the enemies they hated, the gods they worshipped. Is it necessary for us to reproduce and share these feelings, or, can we appreciate the lasting importance of the work of such artists in some respects more clearly by the fact that we do not share their purposes and attitudes?

In certain respects, it is even a disadvantage in appreciation to be much involved in technical problems. One is likely to regard the products so much from a standpoint of how they were made as to neglect other important aspects.

Perceiving a complex art form clearly and fully in all its subtle details and relations of design and meaning is a task in itself requiring training and experience. The development of such ability is one of the essential phases in the training of appreciation. Such ability is usually neglected in the technical training of artists; it is pushed aside by the more practical question of how to get results through an external medium. Trained appreciation involves techniques of its own, which are not dependent on skill in manipulating a tangible material. They are none the less important for being perceptual and mental rather than manual.

As to the ideal of reproducing the artist's experience when we appreciate, it is easy to overestimate the quality of that experience. It was pointed out in the chapter on creative ability that a great deal of what the artist apparently ' creates ' — that is, puts down on canvas or otherwise embodies in a work of art — is really not his own creation. It is the creation of a long line of artists and thinkers before him; of the whole cultural tradition upon which his work is based. The element of real originality in all cases — even in the greatest artists of the past — is relatively slight by comparison. In the work of minor artists, practically everything can be traced to prior sources that the present ' creator ' has merely repeated with trivial alterations. It is not necessary for the artist to understand or appreciate fully the forms and ideas he thus repeats and adapts. If he is essentially an imitative mind, like most of the professional artists in any generation, the process will be rather superficial and mechanical. With some manual and technical skill, one can imitate or combine elements from a few great works of the past, and still understand or appreciate them little more than a camera would. To reproduce such a process of ' creation ' is a low ideal for the appreciator. Rather, he should seek to understand the full richness of the cultural heritage that enters consciously or unconsciously into each work of art, to distinguish also those elements of real originality that each artist has achieved, and to estimate them at their proper worth in the light of carefully thought-out standards. So regarded, appreciation can become to some extent creative in its own way; that is, it can involve an active, interpretive reorganization by each appreciator of the works of art he experiences, from the standpoint of his own mental background and ability.

From that stage, some appreciators will go on to a more fully creative response in the medium of verbal expression. The penetrating critic or teacher of art appreciation may be more genuinely creative than many artists if he makes an original contribution to social understanding. Such activity, however, passes beyond the limits of appreciation in a strict sense. Appreciation has values in its own right, even if it does not go so far. Indeed, extreme readiness to verbalize on one's reactions to art sometimes goes with shallowness and ostentation and is by no means a sign of profound inward experience.

III. The Process of Appreciation

' Appreciation ' is now used in a broad sense, as we have seen, which contrasts it with ' creation ' or ' production.' It refers to the whole process of responding esthetically to art, nature, or other objects. ' Esthetic experience ' is another term that vaguely covers about the same thing. Just what it means to respond in this way is a problem for investigation, but in common discourse certain general distinctions are recognized. Whereas the creative, or artistic, attitude emphasizes a disposition to change or reorganize outward things into a new form, to manipulate some objective medium of construction or expression, the esthetic attitude minimizes this and stresses sense perception more or less for its own sake; that is, for the immediate interest of the process and of the external object on which it is focussed. The artistic attitude is to a greater extent practical and purposeful, in that it involves an effort to adapt means to ends in achieving a future goal, the completed work of art. In esthetic appreciation, the practical element tends to diminish or disappear, in so far as the individual's whole attention is fixed on the present object and the phantasies it suggests, not divided between these and some external aim to be striven for.

Of course, there are countless different ways of responding to art; some combine the esthetic with the practical, as in the case of a collector who seeks to acquire a picture; some combine it with intellectual investigation, as in the case of an art historian or esthetician who studies a picture. Appreciation can be combined with practical use, as when one enjoys the appearance of a cup, a chair, or a house while using it. It may involve verbal expression, as in speaking or writing an ' appreciation ' of some work of art, an explicit statement of one's own feelings and opinions toward it. But even this outward manifestation does not always occur. Appreciation can be almost wholly a matter of quiet contemplation, of direct sense perception along with various inward mental and emotional processes aroused by perception. Psychologists now tend to overlook this distinctively esthetic type of response at this time when it is fashionable to lay heavy stress upon the active and purposeful aspects of behavior. The esthetic type is no less real and important, though harder for behavioristic psychologists to deal with and often ignored in consequence.

The sense of relaxation and recreation that often comes from enjoying art is intimately bound up with the temporary escape it can afford from the ordinary tension of solving problems and achieving ends. Competitive struggles and anxieties force people as a rule to neglect present enjoyments in order to pursue elusive future goals. Those experiences are esthetic when attention and interest are focussed more completely on a present source of enjoyment, on intrinsic rather than instrumental values. Such a source need not be art; it can be nature or any kind of human product or activity. But art affords especially effective stimuli to the esthetic attitude. One's attention does not need to be wholly on an object physically present; it can be on a phantasy suggested by the work of art, as in reading a story. The visible letters induce this phantasy, and the reader, if his attitude is esthetic, simply contemplates this phantasy with no thought of doing anything in particular about it. The esthetic attitude is in a sense compliant — not that one necessarily approves entirely of the work of art — but in the sense that one is willing to perceive and imagine more or less in accordance with its directions.

We must not say that esthetic experience is wholly passive, however.

One tends to be less active with the limbs and large muscles than when producing art or engaging in other practical activities, but one's sense organs and related nerve processes are active. To observe such an art as architecture requires a good deal of bodily movement, but in looking at a picture, there may be no outwardly noticeable movement except that of the eyes.

IV. FUNCTIONS INVOLVED IN APPRECIATION

Although the word *esthetic* means primarily a perceptual response, it cannot be restricted to perception without stretching that concept unduly. The esthetic response is set off by visual or auditory perception, which itself includes some recognition of meanings, some comparison with past experience to interpret the causal, spatiotemporal, and qualitative data presented. It may go on to include extensive phantasy-building in response to the outer stimuli, as in seeing a picture of a battle or reading about one. In reading literature, the element of direct sense perception is restricted to interpreting letters and punctuation marks, and the major part of the response consists in organizing the images and concepts they suggest into systematic forms, such as narratives, descriptions, and conversations.

Psychologists once used the term ' apperception ' to denote a process in which the organizing of sense data in relation to previous experience is especially extensive and systematic. This term is still useful in describing responses to art and to complex verbal forms, whether artistic or not. All perception contains some amount of this, but in describing esthetic experience it is especially important to notice the extent and order with which inner forms are built up more or less in compliance with the cues suggested by the outer form, the seen or heard work of art. Whereas the artist or the dreamer builds phantasies with comparative freedom (never complete, for he is impelled by inner forces), the person enjoying a story or a story-picture imagines more or less as he is directed. He may indeed launch forth upon independent reveries, but in that case he is no longer directly experiencing the work of art.

The apperception of art often involves some inference and reasoning, as in reading a detective story. In some types of art, such as religious symbolism, apperception involves understanding abstract ideas and theoretical relations. Even the understanding of a simple story-picture may require inference as to what is happening and why. Often the inference made is consciously false and illusory. In looking at a painted landscape, one tries to perceive the streaks of paint as trees, rocks, and clouds. Some types of art, those which depend more on the design and decorative qualities of lines and colors or of sounds, have correspondingly less tendency to direct the imagination or the reasoning of the beholder.

The esthetic response usually contains an affective element also, which may vary in intensity from mild feeling tone to strong excitement. All the emotions of ordinary life may be stimulated by art and directed upon the art-work itself or upon the images it suggests. All types of volitional or conative attitude can be aroused by art as a part of the total esthetic response; for example, welcoming or rejecting; desire or aversion; impulses to possess, escape, or destroy. Esthetic experience is not always enjoyable; it may involve displeasure at ugliness or evil as well as pleasure at their opposites. Whereas, in other attitudes, such emotions and volitions tend to issue in overt action, in the esthetic they may, or may not, do so. Most often they are recognized by the individual as having no direct reference to the art-work itself as a concrete object, but only to the images it suggests. Unlike the child or primitive, the civilized adult can usually inhibit with ease any impulse he may feel to caress or assault a portrait. He knows when there would be no possible, satisfactory outlet in present overt action. Hence the emotional and conative elements in his response may remain internal and rudimentary as far as action is concerned, though capable at the same time of great intensity and elaborate reference to systems of mental images and concepts. Of course, people often do respond to art with bodily action, immediate or delayed. Children and primitives commonly do so, and civilized adults do occasionally, as in dancing. Art can stimulate any kind of behavior. To respond with little or no immediate outward action is doubtless an artificial, culturally determined trait of civilized people. Even among these, some persons inhibit expressions of feeling more than others do.

Whether they issue in overt action and expression or not, the affective attitudes aroused by art include liking and disliking. These may be directed at something suggested by the work of art or at the work of art itself, in the latter case as a feeling that it is beautiful or ugly, good or bad. To call it ' beautiful ' is a projection of pleasant inward responses, affective and perceptual, upon the object. One attributes these responses to their supposed cause, as if they were intrinsic qualities of the object. Unless one is theoretically sophisticated, one does not realize that the pleasant or unpleasant nature of the response is conditioned, not only by the nature of the work of art, but also by one's own personality, one's previously acquired tastes or habits of liking and disliking. ' Preference ' occurs when two or more objects are presented for choice or comparison.

' Evaluation,' in the sense of an explicit judgment of value based on general standards, is a kind of appreciation that requires intellectual development in addition to likes and dislikes. It may even be performed in a purely intellectual, deductive manner when the individual feels no definite emotional attitude one way or the other. This is often the case with sophisticated connoisseurs who evaluate by rule and principle rather than by spontaneous feeling and impulse.

Esthetic appreciation thus involves a number of basic functions and attitudes that are much the same as those entering into the creation of art or into any other complex civilized activity. The difference between one such activity and another is a matter of configuration, of the relative emphasis or dominance of various component functions and their mode of coöperation in the whole process.

V. Varieties of Esthetic Response

So widespread an activity as art appreciation can be described only in a very broad and flexible way, since it varies greatly in different cases. Each esthetic response is a joint product of many variables interacting at the time, including (a) the nature of the work of art or other stimulus; (b) the nature of the respondent, stable and temporary; (c) the attendant circumstances.

The response tends to vary, as we have seen, in relation to the type of art that acts as stimulus; for example, music stimulates auditory perception primarily, while painting stimulates visual perception. Abstract textile design also emphasizes visual perception, but with comparatively little definite stimulus to imagination. Other forms, such as symbolic art and literature, offer explicit and detailed direction to imagination and reasoning. Again, some tend to suggest images and feelings of sadness and pity, as in portrayals of suffering; others, of joy or anger.

In addition, the nature of the response tends to vary in accordance with the type of individual who is responding at the time. Here we must have in mind not only the observer's general character, education, special training, and habits of preference, but also his mood and interest of the moment, eager and favorable or bored and indifferent. Further, the same person will respond to the same work of art in very different ways at different times, depending upon who else is present, whether the occasion is one of gravity or amusement, work or play, and so on. The emotion (if any) that he will feel *toward* the work of art may not be the same as the one the work of art expresses or the artist intended to arouse. For example, the artist may intend to arouse indignation in us through representing joy on the face of a villain; yet, as a result of our taste or present mood, we may be moved only to ridicule or boredom.

As an approach to understanding the nature of appreciation, we have been considering how the basic psychophysical functions coöperate in different configurations at different times. Appreciation and esthetic experience, we have seen, refer to a certain general type of configuration, as yet dimly understood, and hard to define because of its inwardness and variability. In following this approach, we must be careful not to conceive of the basic functions as remaining individually the same in all configurations or complex processes. That would be to take an antiquated, atomistic view of their nature. True, there is such a function as visual perception, that retains a few essential characteristics in all configurations, but in other respects visual perception or any other function is very different according to the total attitude and process within which it operates. It is not an independent, clearly delimited nerve-system or process in itself, but is always bound up with others. Perception not only coöperates with memory, affect, and reasoning, but always contains some element of these other functions as well. In some types of total behavior, perception is more strongly visual than in others; in some more strongly affective; in some more strongly conceptual and inferential.

Each function differs somewhat, according as it enters into the esthetic or some other type of attitude. We have seen that, in the esthetic response to art, volition and emotion do not tend, as ordinarily, to issue in immediate overt action, but to be felt as inward likes or dislikes, pleasant or unpleasant feeling tones that may or may not have even the slight outlet of facial or verbal expression. Perception likewise differs. In a practical, purposeful enterprise like hunting or commerce, it tends to be restricted and directed by the requirements of the end in view. Practical perception thus tends to be rather rigidly selective, ignoring features that are irrelevant to the present undertaking, and to stress the interpretation of sense data in terms of their probable causes in outer objects. The hunter interprets a mark in the snow as a deer's track. Esthetic perception, on the other hand, as in contemplating a natural scene or a painted landscape, tends to be less rigidly selective and directive, more freely wandering, attentive to a greater variety of presented objects and qualities. It often involves a sort of voluntary illusion, as in the tendency mentioned above for an observer of a painting to perceive the paint as grass or trees. Also, it often involves greater attention to sense qualities as qualities; as greens or blues, light or dark areas, straight or curved lines, patterns, and designs. The perception of visual design often involves a voluntary disregard of the representative or causal meaning of sensory data and a focussing of attention instead on their immediate sensory aspects. This shift can never be complete. There is no such thing as purely qualitative perception; it is always mixed with some association and inference. But there is a difference in degree of emphasis.

The artist must often be practical in attitude, rather than esthetic. He must think of how to control his medium and achieve desired results; for example, how to lay on strokes of paint so as to make them look like a tree. The esthetic observer is freer in this respect. He has no ulterior end to achieve; no task except to see, to understand, and, if possible, to enjoy. Hence he can let his attention wander more unrestrictedly over all the visible details of the scene or picture before him.

VI. Component Abilities in Appreciation

As in the case of creative abilities, we can consider those of appreciation from the standpoint of the component functions involved in the process. As we have seen, these are basically the same as those in art creation or in any other complex human activity; but they vary in certain respects according to the nature of the total attitude and process. There is no one right way to appreciate, to look at pictures, or to listen to music, any more than there is one right way to create art — though the market is full of books and teachers who insist that their way is the only right way. The ways and techniques of appreciation are as diverse as the types of art and of human personality. In other words, no author has a right to urge people to notice only ' pure form ' and to ignore subject matter in pictures or to think only of moral effects or sociological aspects. The world of art is there in all its richness, for each to use and enjoy in the ways that seem best to him.

Nevertheless, we can say that certain ways of responding to art involve highly developed skill and understanding, while others do not. Some ways are superficial and fragmentary, involving the experience of very few elements in the work of art. A young child, or even a dog, may look at a painting by Rembrandt, but cannot perceive it fully or appreciate its qualities. Many adults look at art in ways that are superficial and fragmentary by comparison with the experience of a trained observer. The child or untrained adult may enjoy art very intensely in certain respects and thus deserve the envy of the jaded connoisseur. There is no special training that can guarantee such conditions of enjoyment as the basic health, vigor, and happiness of the individual. Some persons are highly developed in their intellectual responsiveness to art; some in their perceptual responsiveness; some in their emotional sensitivity. It is possible to develop one's appreciative ability in one or more of several ways. Those who desire a diversified kind of experience, which utilizes the possible value of art in many ways, will desire to develop and use many different types of ability.

One group of abilities is concerned with visual perception. We already have a key to them in what has been said about the nature of esthetic seeing. Ordinary perception is likely to become strongly practical, through the pressure of gaining necessary ends. We learn to look at things mostly for their associated meanings (as in the case of letters, numbers, and other signs) with attention fixed on what they mean in relation to some practical interest. Intelligent laymen, confronted with a work of art, often approach it in the same spirit. They ask, what does it mean? What practical use has it? Now, these questions do apply to certain aspects of art. Some works of art do have utilitarian purposes, and some do undertake to convey meanings — religious, moral, patriotic, and otherwise. But there are other aspects of art that this approach tends to ignore. They are largely concerned with the values of direct sensory experience. Sometimes a work of art has little use or meaning save to present a design or texture of colors and shapes to the eye. Such forms have the power to arouse responses of interest and keen pleasure in the sensitive, trained observer. For him, they need not have any further use or meaning, but are worth while for their own sake, as musical melodies, harmonies, and rhythms are worth while. There is nothing especially mysterious about them, no hidden explanation. But to enjoy them, one must first be able to notice them; and it is just this ability that many educated laymen lack because long habits of practical perception have directed their attention elsewhere. This is especially true of busy people in our Western World, and much of our educational emphasis aggravates it. For this reason, it is important in teaching art appreciation at present to stress the technique of looking at things in terms of their directly visible qualities and arrangements, the technique of qualitative perception. One must develop the power to ignore, at times, the indirect uses and associations of things, in order to perceive more clearly their directly visible forms.

Representative art, pictorial and sculptural, presents a difficult task in this respect. For it usually combines some directly visible qualities of line, color, and design along with the portrayal of other objects, scenes, and persons. These may be interesting, too, and there is no reason to neglect them in the long run. But the usual tendency is to notice them only; that is, to perceive only the represented subject matter in a picture. Conscious effort and instruction are usually necessary to help students learn how to discern the design aspects in representative art. Their attention must be directed, in one concrete example after another, to subtle gradations of line, light, and color, to complex organizations of pattern. When realism of anatomy and perspective is partly sacrificed to design, as often happens in ancient as well as contemporary art, the untrained observer is puzzled and offended. He sees only the negative aspect, the 'distortion,' and not the design for which it was produced. The tremendous variety of effects in visible form and design that art contains is quite unsuspected by the ordinary layman. He ignores them under his very eyes in walking casually through a museum or down a city street. It may require long experience under capable guidance to open his eyes to the rich world of visible form. And it is unfortunately true that not all professional artists or teachers of art have themselves learned to use their eyes in this way. When one does learn to do so, through careful looking at art, one is constantly struck by the similar visible qualities in nature itself, and in all the life about one, a fascinating world of shape and color that an overly practical civilization has tended to obscure from us.

To develop powers of sense perception does not mean, however, that one must neglect or repress imagination and understanding. These are different functions, and may be developed in their own right. They are called forth in response to certain elements in art, over and above the directly sensible. In all visual art except abstract decoration (and even there to a less degree) there are stimuli to make the beholder build up a phantasy of things and events not present to the eye. It may be of a comparatively static scene, as in a landscape or the interior of a room, of a group of figures in action, or of a long narrative. Arts that present a changing series of images, like the cinema, the theater, and the dance, are especially capable of telling stories.

The ability to imagine as a work of art directs us to is in part dependent on our general cultural background, our stock of memory images, and our understanding of established symbols and meanings. Art suggests images at times by imitation, as in making paint look like grass; at times by arbitrary symbolism, as in words and signs like the cross or trident. By presenting sensory images in certain groups and sequences, the work of art influences us to call forth images and concepts from our own memories and to arrange them into forms we have never before experienced. These forms may involve not only sensory images, but also inferences and systems of reasoning. Thus we can follow an argument in a play or novel and apprehend its reasoning esthetically without necessarily agreeing with it. Insofar as ability to grasp the imaginative and rational content of art is dependent on one's general education, special training in art appreciation is inadequate to cope with it. This, incidentally, is one reason why art appreciation now suffers from the educational tendency to neglect classical, Biblical, and Oriental culture. Students often cannot recognize the events and personages depicted, because they have never heard of them before. But, conversely, art appreciation can be made an occasion for familiarizing them with cultural traditions.

In addition, there is a fairly definite technique of responding to the associative content of art. It is dependent on the general power to link up ideas in new relationships, which is akin to intelligence. But it is not the same as intelligence in practical affairs, and one may have it without being very original. It is, in part, a sensitivity to outward cues, a quickness in grasping what the work of art is trying to suggest, a facility in organizing ideas in accordance with these suggestions. This may be called ' esthetic imagination ' or ' apprehension,' in contrast with the more spontaneous and independent thinking required in creative work. Individuals differ markedly in their powers of ' catching on ' to what is intended. Some are slow and dull; others, bright. Some can grasp and follow very complex groups and sequences of ideas without losing track of subtle details or general outlines. High ability of this sort is required to follow a complex novel like *War and Peace*, with its many characters and vast march of events, or the symbolic and representative content of a great cathedral, as conveyed through the details of architecture, sculpture, and stained glass.

There are also differences of ability in regard to empathy, or the power to project oneself in imagination into some external object. Here the external object is the work of art, including the world of fancy it conjures up. Small children usually project themselves with ease into a world of make-believe; so much, at times, as to become more frightened or convinced of its reality than we intend them to. They forget themselves and become completely engrossed in the story or picture. More sophisticated adults often find it harder to forget their own self-conscious preoccupations and to enter vividly into the phantasy-world of art.

Knowledge about art can operate as a powerful aid in the apperception of particular works of art, through enabling us to recognize, classify, and analyze them conceptually. People who are ignorant of art history and theory sometimes feel that such knowledge would dampen their enthusiasm and destroy the fascination of art, through dissecting its mysteries. Yet it is doubtful whether anyone who has acquired it regrets the acquisition, and many feel that it multiplies the interest of art by endowing it with greater meaning. Certainly, there are persons, including capable artists, who know little about art from a scholarly standpoint and yet who can enjoy art with fine discrimination. Certainly, there are scholars of great erudition who cannot. Much depends on the extent to which such knowledge is linked with other abilities and modes of response. Factual information can be accumulated by itself, apart from perceptual and other direct experience of art, producing the dry pedant. A mass of verbal concepts can fill one's mind to the extent of obscuring the present object and diverting one's attention to problems of identification, date, and the like. These have a scientific value, but should not be confused with appreciation, as they often are by pedantic teachers.

However, information about art can be merged with other elements in a vigorous, diversified experience. It can be put into action as a means of understanding what one sees. All perceiving under civilized conditions is done with the aid of concepts, including verbal names for qualities, such as *red* and *blue*, *straight* and *curved*, *still* and *moving*. By their aid, we not only classify and understand what we see, in relation to our past experience and that of others, but we also are led to notice qualities and relations we otherwise would not perceive. Through scholarly education, one's conceptual apparatus can be developed to include names for types and styles of artistic form, their elements and modes of organization. It can include such historical concepts as Byzantine and Romanesque, Impressionist and Post-impressionist, Classic and Romantic; such esthetic concepts as tragic and comic, design and representation, function and symbolism. If these are not mere empty words in the mind, but linked in memory with vivid sensory and other experiences, they can be used in encountering each new work of art. They help one not only to notice characteristics that exemplify these types, but also to interpret their meaning and importance in relation to a wider cultural background.

VII. Taste and Evaluation

The affective phases of esthetic response are more shrouded in obscurity. We have little specific understanding of why works of art move us to volitional attitudes of approval or antagonism, mild or violent. Certain it is that the reasons given to oneself and others, the plausible esthetic and moral principles, are often not the real ones or the complete ones, and that these latter often lie deep in the history of individual personality. Taste in art is influenced by indirect association with one's personal joys, successes, conflicts, and frustrations that happened long ago and may now seem quite unrelated to art. We know also, mainly from study of neurotic symptoms, that the inability to accept and enjoy things that most healthy people like is often due to inward conflicts, repressions, and frustrations. To like very few things that others like, to be hypercritical and hard to please, is often a sign of inward maladjustment and unhappiness. The individual is full of mental sore spots, and these are constantly being irritated by ideas and images that come to him through art or otherwise. He fails to recognize the inner cause of his antipathies and rationalizes them with faultfinding. An occasional violent prejudice in the normal person may result from such inner causes, and their correction makes him able to enjoy what he formerly could not.

Of course, one can never prove to another person that he ought to like what he does not. He has a right to his own dislikes, and will probably cling to them proudly, even though he sees other people enjoying what displeases him. Moreover, there is no reason for saying that people ought to like everything or all kinds of art. There can be no discrimination of values without preferring some things to others, and intense devotion to what seems best may involve intense dislike of what seems evil, ugly, or dangerous. The apparent ability to like everything may indicate a lack of standards or of any strong enthusiasms. Nevertheless, it often seems fairly obvious to the outsider that an individual is cutting himself off from real potential values for no good reason and merely through groundless prejudice or lack of understanding. A great many adults are reasonable enough to suspect this about their own lack of interest in art or their antipathy toward certain kinds of art. Some study art appreciation for this very reason, in the hope of expanding their scope of interests and learning to enjoy some of the things others have found worth while.

In dealing with young students, the educator is on firmer ground in trying to develop their taste for art and especially for more of the types of art that have been generally recognized as great. From his own and others' past experience, he is justified in saying about art, as he does about certain kinds of food, exercise, or mental discipline, " Try this again, even if you don't like it now. You may learn to like it, and be glad you did."

Of course, urging people to like things or preaching about our own likes is not the most.effective way to get results. If the capacity to like is there, it may be sufficient to present the objects under favorable conditions, with a few hints as to their significance and what to notice in particular. Few things are more gratifying in education than to watch students develop, not only an understanding of great cultural achievements, but also a genuine interest in them and a desire for further experience of them. One has no right to hope that students will ever develop exactly the same tastes as one's own, but with due allowance for variation, one may hope that all will come to prize the central values upon which civilized people in all ages tend to agree.

Moreover, the wise teacher will not expect students to like all kinds of art at too early an age. The fact that some kinds are museum exhibits and interesting to mature scholars does not mean that they are, or should be, especially interesting to children. Like our foods, some kinds are especially needed by the individual at an early stage; others, at a later stage. Extreme precocity may be as unhealthy a sign in esthetic taste as in other matters; it may be a sign of maladjustment. It is absurd to suppose that active boys and girls should prefer Gothic Madonnas to athletics and dancing, or even to cartoons and motion-picture comedies. What they spontaneously like may turn out to have more genuine value for their growth in art and general education than what we mistakenly try to impose upon them. Certain kinds of adult art are too complex and involve types of motivation that are yet foreign to them. Certain aspects in adult art can interest young children, such as the obvious story element in pictures, and little by little, the more mature and difficult elements in a single great work of art, such as a cathedral, can be gradually imparted to a growing mind; but not all at once. Research in art education has much to do in discovering what kinds of art, and what approaches to art, can arouse vital interest in children of various ages and types of personality. It is not enough to find what they prefer spontaneously, before educational influence. We must find also what they can become interested in by proper presentation and use.

The power to evaluate art is in part an application of general intelligence and rationality. Valuation in a broad sense occurs on all levels of mental development. It develops out of innate organic tendencies to accept or reject various types of stimuli, with accompanying emotions of joy, disgust, anger, or the like. Conditioning transforms these into more subtle, mixed, and complex attitudes toward many types of civilized objects that do not directly affect us physically, but affect us mainly through their associated meanings. Even the educated adult responds at times with simple, direct impulses of welcoming, escape, or attack. These are evaluative in a broad sense, as expressions of approval or disapproval, but they are not value judgments. The educated adult or older child is also able to express his likes and dislikes in words and to give explicit reasons for them. He may even be able to describe and defend his affective habits in the form of generalized, intellectual standards, theories of what kinds of art are good or beautiful, and why. Thus, evaluation on the higher mental levels is usually a combination of affective response with conceptual thinking. As we have seen, it may become almost wholly intellectual, a matter of applying esthetic or moral principles deductively; in other words, one may be able to evaluate art in this way with great erudition and logic and yet have extremely meager esthetic experience or appreciative power in a broad sense.

Reasoning may coöperate with sensory and affective functions in evaluation. This occurs when the individual is able to suspend judgment — that is, to suspend the first impulse to a ‘ snap judgment ’ of like or dislike — and take time to perceive and understand the work of art as clearly and thoroughly as possible. No value judgment can be considered fair or rational that is not based on a moderately clear and thorough perception and understanding of the nature of the object. The ability to suspend judgment, to remain open-minded while exploring the facts of the case, is essentially intelligent, as opposed to crude impulse, prejudice, and dogmatism.

This is not to say that all appreciation or evaluation should be highly rational or thorough and painstaking. There is a place also for the quick, impulsive, and emotional type of response. Sometimes the situation is not important enough to justify detailed examination. Sometimes it is so obviously similar to others previously considered that one is justified in a routine appraisal. Life is too short to keep raising the same esthetic or moral issues time after time. The power of intelligent evaluation consists in knowing how to think out a problem carefully and experimentally when conditions seem to call for it, as in making up one's mind about the inclusion of some new, controversial type of art in an educational program. In minor cases, one simply expresses one's feelings at the moment, in a word or gesture of approval or disapproval. A smile or a frown cannot be criticized on logical grounds as true or false. But when the individual goes farther and undertakes to judge a work of art as ' harmful ' or ' lacking unity,' then he is venturing into more theoretical issues about the nature of the object and its probable consequences.

Even generalizations about one's own likes and dislikes are sometimes subject to question. Parents realize that a child does not always know what he really likes, that he sometimes expresses dislike of a thing without really understanding it, that he would like it better if he knew more about it or were in a better humor. Likewise, the psychologist may have grounds for thinking that adults do not always accurately express their own fundamental tastes when they make a hasty, careless judgment, based on superficial observation. Still more, when the individual ventures into statements about the power of a work of art to please or displease, to benefit or injure, other persons, the psychologist has the right to question the evaluation on factual grounds. Here, appreciation ceases to be a purely personal response and becomes a generalization about the effects of a certain type of art on human beings. The more one undertakes to verbalize and defend one's tastes in art, the more one enters the realm of esthetic theory. Development in this respect requires the use of scientific methods, clear definition of terms, and verification of evidence. Most art appreciation does not seek to go so far. It remains somewhere between primitive impulse and scientific generalization. Art criticism of a literary or journalistic type is intermediate between the two. It is not merely personal appreciation; it is also an attempt to express the feelings of the writer about some work of art in explicit verbal judgments, with examples and arguments to defend them in a more or less logical way. It varies from the comparatively personal and subjective to the comparatively scientific and scholarly. Ordinary art appreciation, by educated adults, often leads to an informal sort of criticism, usually brief and casual.

It can be pleasant and enlightening to exchange impressions of art with other people, in gallery, home, or classroom. There is no reason for disparaging such rudimentary criticism as inferior merely because it is undeveloped in accordance with scientific inquiry. It has its own values in education and immediate enjoyment, as an integral part of the process of appreciation. But we should realize how it involves abilities in reasoning and verbal expression, in which some persons are more capable than others. These abilities can be developed and equipped with requisite information through studies emphasizing the logical, psychological, historical, and sociological approaches to art.

VIII. Relativism in Evaluating Art

Much of the confusion and disagreement involved in judgments of esthetic value could be avoided by greater care in specifying the kind of evaluation one wishes to make, and by making limited, relative evaluations instead of sweeping and absolute ones. The common tendency, in appraising art, is to label it very simply and briefly as good or bad, beautiful or ugly, important or trivial, beneficial or harmful, pleasant or unpleasant. This evades the highly significant questions: " For whom? " " In what way? " and " Under what conditions? "

If one asks and clearly answers these questions in regard to the object of art under consideration, it usually turns out to be impossible to make a sweeping, brief evaluation, for the reason that the object is now seen to be good for some kinds of person, bad for others; good in some ways and under some conditions, bad in other ways and under other conditions. No one would think of evaluating other types of products so sweepingly — a drug or an instrument. Their goodness or badness is obviously relative to how and by whom they are used. Many works of art, especially in the handcrafts and industrial arts, are in part utilitarian devices, and their value thus depends in part on the value of the end they serve and how efficiently they serve it. Some works of so-called ' fine art,' also, have instrumental functions; paintings as historic records, as religious symbols, and as military or advertising propaganda, for example. To evaluate them fully, one must consider such instrumental functions.

The effect an object will have on the observer, as beautiful or ugly, pleasant or unpleasant, also depends on a variety of interacting factors: on the conditions under which the object is displayed, and on the nature of the observer — his or her age, sex, native capacities, training, habits, and present mood. In relation to these factors, a picture may appear to be good for adults and bad for children, beautiful in drawing and ugly in color, appropriate for a theater lobby and inappropriate for a church or hospital. It may seem attractive or amusing on first sight, yet likely to grow tiresome if permanently installed; or unattractive on first sight, yet with qualities likely to ' grow on one ' through longer experience. A chair may please the eye because of its pattern and texture, and yet be uncomfortable, weak, or hard to clean — in other words, unsatisfactory in a functional, instrumental way.

Some works of art are effective and pleasing in many important ways, for many sorts of people throughout long periods of time. They are likely to be rated, on the whole, as higher in social value than those of more trivial, limited, and evanescent appeal. To make so broad a generalization requires a great deal of evidence, however, and will involve many debatable issues. Each object will reveal certain actual or potential values — some instrumental and some directly esthetic — and certain limitations or weaknesses in relation to certain possible situations. It is difficult, and not especially important, to try to arrive at a total estimate of its worth. Long ago, debating societies gave up trying to decide whether fire was better than water. The important thing is to find out the specific properties, uses, dangers, and limitations of each.

An evaluation that is carefully limited, tentative, and supported with evidence is less likely to arouse disagreement than one that is sweeping and dogmatic. Two persons may seem to be in violent disagreement, one praising a work of art and the other condemning it, and yet be closer together than they seem to be. They are perhaps evaluating it from different points of view, for different sorts of quality or supposed effect, and the disagreement might be greatly reduced if each would explain and delimit his judgment.

IX. ORIGINALITY IN RELATION TO VALUE IN ART

One of the commonest sources of misunderstanding in evaluating art is the question of *historical importance*, of *priority and originality*, as against imitativeness. Laymen in art are sometimes perplexed and antagonized when their sincere enthusiasms are brushed aside by some supposed authority on art, on the ground that what they like is ' old stuff,' or ' just an imitation of so-and-so.' If the layman sticks to his guns, he may answer with some reason that he doesn't care how original the object is, that it gives him and many others like him a great deal of pleasure and perhaps other values as well. The authority on art is likely to be judging the work, not in terms of its present power to be of use or pleasure, but in terms of its position in the history of art. He thinks in terms of the chronological development of styles and tech-niques, of the milestones in artistic progress, the outstanding innova-tions of each age and the men who made them. He appraises artistic value in terms of original contribution to the world's artistic heritage. Consequently, he looks down upon the legions of imitators who follow in the train of every great innovator. Seeing an Impressionist land-scape in a shop window, he may recognize it at once as an imitation of Monet's style, with little or nothing added, and hence rank it low in value. In the same way, a trained music-lover would condemn a newly written symphony, however agreeable to the ear, if it contained nothing but slightly modified, unacknowledged quotations from Brahms and Debussy. Accordingly, connoisseurs will praise in ardent terms the work of some old master in any art who represented a great advance for his day or of some contemporary who has introduced a novel effect. The layman tries hard, perhaps, but can find little of interest or value in either.

Each, the connoisseur and the layman, has some right on his side. They are judging art from two different standpoints; the one in terms of its historical importance, the other in terms of its ability to please or serve the modern observer. The connoisseur has no right to argue that all persons should enjoy the original work more or appraise it higher. As a matter of fact, some imitations are so nearly perfect as to deceive the most respected experts. Their esthetic value cannot be far from that of the original, except as determined by the pleasure one may get from knowing (or believing) that one is looking at some-thing authentic and historically epoch-making. Art authorities often form the habit of considering art so exclusively in terms of authenticity and historic importance that they are, in fact, unable to admire any work that does not qualify in these respects. But there is no reason why all consumers of art should be required to feel the same way. If they frankly and explicitly evaluate a work of art in terms of its power to please or serve them directly, here and now, they need not be required to take the broad historical point of view, and their judgments are not necessarily mistaken or inferior. The five-millionth reproduction of a certain utensil or automobile may be quite as useful and beautiful as the first, and (assuming the reproduction to be exact) so may the five-millionth reproduction of a certain painting.

The problem is quite different, however, when one undertakes to appraise a work of art or an artist in regard to the amount of credit that it or he deserves for creative originality or contribution to the social heritage. For this reason we are apt to admire an inventor's first model and perhaps to keep it in a museum of science and industry as a concrete example of progress, without implying that it has great value as a machine today. It is quite possible for a critic to assign great historic importance to a work of art, recognizing intellectually its value as a step in progress, without getting much pleasure or profit from seeing or using it today. In practice, however, the two modes of evaluation are likely to be somewhat merged in the critic's mind; on the one hand, as he looks at the object, he enjoys realizing how great a contribution it was; on the other hand, in looking at an imitation of it, his enjoyment may be diminished by the thought that it is only an imitation.

If we desire to think out our evaluations clearly, we must try to distinguish between such different grounds for praise or blame. Very often, of course, the two modes of evaluation lead to the same verdict; the historically important object is found superior as a present object of use or observation, a source of esthetic enjoyment through its own form and meaning. In our age at least, the most capable artists do not often devote themselves to exact imitation or minor adaptation of others' works. The imitative work is apt to be also unskilled and unimaginative by comparison with the one it imitates. It deserves a lower rating for its own intrinsic qualities, without regard to its chronological priority. The connoisseur, in observing it, compares it with his memory image of the original work it imitates and rates it low accordingly. The layman has no such basis of comparison. He sees only what the present work contains, without knowing or caring that it is inferior to something else of the same kind.

While the layman's judgment has a certain validity in relation to his own present experience, it obviously has limited scope. He has not the right to extend his personal expression of like or dislike into a broad generalization about the object's general importance in the world of art or the artist's claim to social admiration and reward. Unfortunately, he often does just that. To justify such a broad evaluation, he needs some knowledge of past and present art and of the conditions under which and for which the present work was created, as a frame of reference for assigning the work its proper place in cultural history. He needs to know something about human nature and present society in general in order to say that the present work will, or will not, prove valuable for others besides himself.

It was mentioned in a previous chapter that modern civilization, especially in western Europe and America, sets a great premium on progress and originality in art as in other realms. In this we differ markedly from certain past cultures, such as those of Egypt, China, and medieval Europe. We profess a desire to encourage originality in mature artists and in students, even though in practice we do not always recognize or reward it. To admire an original product more than an imitation, even when they are practically identical, is one of our strongest social traits. This trait can be justified as conducive on the whole to further progress, although it is sometimes carried to an extreme of faddism, of ignoring the old, traditional values. On the whole, we are justified in praising originality in art; that is, in praising genuine, important innovation; not innovation for its own sake. We are justified in leading students to recognize and respect real contributions to social culture, past and present, to rank the original higher than the imitative work, and to prefer experiencing it when possible.

There is a great difference here between the frankly mechanical reproduction, such as a color print or phonograph record, and the ' hand made ' work of art that pretends to be original and is not. The student can enjoy the former as an honest, inexpensive substitute, in proportion to its exactness; it makes no claim to be creative in itself. The latter he can enjoy for what it is, though realizing that the present artist does not deserve full credit for it. It would be more honest, perhaps, if visual artists would somehow acknowledge indebtedness to their principal sources — say in a note at the bottom of a painting — as authors and musical composers often do in their texts and scores. Since this is not to be expected, teachers of art appreciation have so much the more obligation to help their students distinguish the original from the imitation. Under present cultural conditions such an ability is a necessary element in developed powers of art appreciation.

It should be reaffirmed that the principal thing to work for in teaching appreciation to children is not to make them like or dislike any particular kinds of art — even to prefer original art — or to make them use any particular standards of value. It is rather to help them experience art fully and vividly, under conditions favorable to use and enjoyment. For this, highly developed powers of intellectual evaluation are not entirely necessary. But those persons who undertake to criticize, teach, or direct the teaching of art professionally are under obligation to train such powers in themselves beyond the point strictly necessary for a layman's enjoyment. They should strive to clarify and support their judgments through especially careful perception and analysis of the factors involved in the interaction between works of art and human beings. These include both psychological and social factors in the individuals who create, use, and respond to art, and also factors in artistic form — the nature of the works of art concerned. The latter we shall consider in the next chapter.

REFERENCES

(1) BUERMEYER, L. *The Aesthetic Experience.* (Barnes Foundation Press: Merion, Pa., 1924) 183 pp.

(2) DEWEY, J., and Others. *Art and Education.* (Barnes Foundation Press: Merion, Pa., 1939) 349 pp.

(3) FINE ARTS STAFF, Teachers College, Columbia University. *Art Education Today: 1940.* (Teachers College: New York, 1940) 85 pp.

(4) GALE, A. V. *Children's Preferences for Colors, Color Combinations, and Color Arrangements.* (University of Chicago Press: Chicago, 1933) 60 pp.

(5) MUNRO, T. "The esthetic appreciation of nature." *American Magazine of Art,* April, 1932.

(6) MUNRO, T. "The case for art appreciation." *Journal of Adult Education,* 6: October, 1934, 392–394.

(7) MUNRO, T. *Great Pictures of Europe.* (Brentano's: New York, 1930) 289 pp.

(8) MUNRO, T. "Methods of teaching art appreciation." *Bulletin of the Western Arts Association,* 18: September, 1934.

(9) RICHARDS, I. A. *Principles of Literary Criticism.* (Harcourt, Brace and Co.: New York, 1926) 298 pp.

(10) SCHOEN, M. *Art and Beauty.* (The Macmillan Co.: New York, 1932) 230 pp.

(11) WHITFORD, W. G. *An Introduction to Art Education.* (D. Appleton-Century Co.: New York, 1937) 391 pp.

CHAPTER XXIV

THE ANALYSIS OF FORM IN ART

Thomas Munro

I. The Problem of Objective Description and Classification in Studies of Art

Through studying art from a psychological and sociological standpoint, we hope to learn more about its genesis, nature, and functions — what factors in the individual artist and in social conditions tend to produce various types of art, how various types of art affect various types of appreciator, what other uses they have in society, and how they can be further controlled for human welfare. To do this, it is necessary to observe and describe particular works of art in a fairly objective way and to distinguish various types of art in order to study in detail their interactions with other psychological and social factors.

The chief difficulty is to find ways of doing so without at the same time expressing debatable personal views about them. It is not objective to ' describe ' a work of art as beautiful or ugly, pleasant or unpleasant, well or badly drawn. On the other hand, it is not enough to describe art in terms of its size and physical structure, for these fail to bring out the differences in form, style, and expression that are important in determining its psychological and social functions.

No way of describing art or anything else can be purely objective, for all involve human responses of perception and thinking. But we can try to leave out the more emotional and evaluative terms for the time being and to emphasize those characteristics that are capable of dispassionate observation by other investigators. There are many descriptive concepts available for this purpose that have arisen through years of philosophical, historical, and critical discussion. Most of them are vague and ambiguous, however, and loaded with controversial associations. They are in great need of clear, consistent definition and systematic interrelation. This is a task of esthetic theory. Psychology can assist substantially, but its present concepts are not sufficient and must be augmented by others derived from a direct study of art.

The problem arises, for example, in planning a survey such as the present Yearbook. Its very title is ambiguous, for ' art ' in a broad

sense is often taken to include music and literature, but these are not
included in the scope of the Yearbook. College catalogs sometimes
refer to departments of ' fine arts,' but music and poetry can also be
considered as fine arts. ' Fine art ' is usually opposed to ' useful ' or
' industrial ' art, but literature, and even music, have industrial and
other useful functions. So does painting, as in making an advertising
poster. Architecture, usually classed as a fine art, has industrial and
other uses.

There is no single, satisfactory basis for naming and classifying
the arts. All involve overlappings and misleading suggestions. One
basis is in terms of material, or medium, as in speaking of the arts of
painting, wood carving, metalworking, ceramics, enamelling, and stained
glass. But to consider all the arts from this standpoint would be cumbersome. Architecture and sculpture use many different materials.
Moreover, it conceals the important fact that a picture is a picture,
whether made in oil, mosaic, or tapestry. For some purposes it is necessary to group together all kinds of pictorial representation, regardless of
material, all kinds of statuary in another group, and all kinds of buildings in still another. To speak in terms of material or medium tends
to restrict one to the standpoint of the artist, who thinks largely in
terms of handling a certain medium. To the public, this is often less
important than the final appearance or function of the object.

When we think in such terms as city planning, public and domestic
architecture, we are adopting a more or less sociological point of view
and distinguishing types of art on a basis of how they function in civic
and social life. ' Art in industry,' ' art in commerce,' ' art in clothing,'
' art in printing and publishing ' — these also refer to how the product is used, rather than to its materials or techniques. Yet sometimes
we wish to distinguish on a basis of technique, as in considering ' handcrafts ' apart from machine production, whatever their materials or
uses. ' Photography ' and ' motion pictures ' also refer primarily to a
technique of production and presentation. The ' theater arts ' include many kinds of art that are presented in a certain kind of building, such as acting, the ballet, costume, scene design, lighting, and
even motion pictures. They may be taken to include the literary, as
well as the visual, phases of drama.

Theorists sometimes speak of the ' visual arts ' in distinction from
music and literature, and perhaps this term would serve as well as
any other to mark off the general field that is covered by this Yearbook.
It takes the point of view of the appreciator and specifies the sense

primarily appealed to in appreciation. But literature is in a way visual when we read the printed page, and literature as well as music can suggest visual images.

Again, the arts have been classified into 'space arts' and 'time arts.' This cuts across several other classifications, and it is difficult to include any whole art in either category. Music and literature unfold in time, but can suggest images of space. Motion pictures and other theater arts are organized in both space and time. Furthermore, it takes time to perceive a picture or a cathedral, even though it is relatively static. Certain kinds of pictures, such as Chinese landscape scrolls, are to be seen in temporal order. In short, any single way of classifying the arts involves theoretical difficulties and may lead to mistaken generalizations. In a comprehensive survey of art, one is usually forced to adopt several different modes of classification, each to bring out certain distinctions and groupings that seem important from various points of view.

In education, it is well to have students consider art from all these points of view; otherwise their understanding will be very limited. For example, those who study one 'art' alone, in the sense of a single medium, such as oil painting or ivory carving, are likely to regard it too much in isolation and to ignore its relations with other arts. A great style or movement, such as the Romantic or the Gothic, spreads through most or all of the arts of its time, and indeed through all branches of civilization. It can be thoroughly understood only by a comparative study of the arts and other fields. Likewise, an artist working in any medium will miss valuable suggestions if he ignores what has happened or is happening outside it. If he is alive to broader trends in art, he may be able to deal with them in his own medium in a less narrow and stereotyped way.

As we look more carefully at the phenomena of art, we see how difficult it is to generalize about any one art as a whole; that is, about any art in the sense of a single medium or technique. For each of the principal arts has been used to produce a tremendous variety of forms. A certain general type of form can occur in many arts. It is often enlightening to put less emphasis on the particular art or medium and more on the principal types of artistic form.

It is questionable to divide the arts into 'representative arts' and 'decorative arts,' as is sometimes done, for the reason that many arts contain some decoration and some representation. Painting and sculpture involve both. Sometimes they tend to stress decorative design and sometimes realistic representation. In the same way, many arts contain a utilitarian, or functional, practical element. Architecture often combines it with elements of design and decoration. It may also include representation, as in the sculpture and glass of a cathedral. In other words, representation, decoration, and utility refer to types of form, or factors in form, that occur in many arts.

II. PRESENTED AND SUGGESTED FACTORS IN ESTHETIC FORM

What is *form* in art? In Webster's definition, form is " 8. Orderly arrangement or method of arrangement; as: order or method of presenting ideas; manner of coördinating the elements of an artistic production or course of reasoning." In brief, the form of a work of art is the way in which its details are organized.[1] Esthetic form occurs not alone in art but also in all types of object, natural or artificial. A flower and a machine have esthetic form; so does a city or a sunset. It is not the same as physical form (molecular and atomic structure), but consists rather in the structure a scene or other object *appears* to have as an object of esthetic apperception. The physical form of a painting consists in certain arrangements of the molecules in pigment; but this is less important in psychology than the way the painting functions as a stimulus to perception and understanding.

In terms of the psychology of perception, a work of art consists of certain stimuli to sensory experience and also to association and interpretation on the basis of memory and past experience. A work of visual art, like a painting, stimulates visual responses, such as those of shape, color, lightness, and darkness. It *presents* some visual images directly to the eyes. In addition, it has the power to *suggest* other images and concepts to a brain that has been conditioned through experience and education. Thus a painting can be analyzed into certain *presented factors* (the shapes and colors that are directly visible) and certain *suggested factors* (the other objects and events, such as trees, persons, battles, that it tends to call up in imagination; and also, in some cases, more abstract conceptions, such as moral ideals and religious doctrines).

No two persons will see exactly the same thing in a picture, for each is led by his nature and habits to select slightly different aspects for

---

[1] The word *form* is also used in a sense equivalent to 'shape' or 'solid shape,' as in speaking of the elements of visual art as 'line, form, and color.' This is a misleading sense, which makes it hard to compare the arts. The definition adopted here is applicable to all arts, as in speaking of 'musical form' or 'literary form.'

special notice. Further, no two will imagine or understand exactly the same things because of differences in mental constitution, habits, and education. But presented factors are comparatively easy to verify and agree upon. One can point out that certain lines are straight or curved; certain areas, light or dark, blue or yellow; and all persons of normal vision will agree substantially upon their presence.

As to suggested factors, there is often more disagreement on exactly what is meant or represented. Various modes of suggestion are employed by visual art. One is imitation, or *mimesis,* as in a picture of a tree. One is arbitrary *symbolism,* as in the use of a cross to suggest Christianity. In addition, certain visual qualities often derive suggestive power from *common association* in experience. Thus, reds and yellows may suggest warmth, blues and greens, coolness; horizontal lines, rest or stability; and diagonal, wavy or zigzag lines, disbalance, movement, or agitation.

Sometimes the associations suggested in one or more of these ways are so vague, conflicting, or fragmentary as to arouse different interpretations. A picture may look somewhat like a tree, but not exactly. A symbol like the swastika may have different meanings. Thus it is often impossible to say objectively just what the suggestive content of a work of art is. However, there is usually a nucleus of comparatively obvious meanings upon which most observers will agree. Within a particular cultural environment, common usage tends to attach fairly definite meanings to particular images and groups of images. Artists come to use certain images with a definite intention, and observers to understand them in the same way, by tradition and convention. Authoritative reference works, such as dictionaries, encyclopedias, and books on the iconography of art, confirm a number of these symbol-meaning relations. On a basis of social custom, then, it becomes possible to say with some objective authority that a certain picture has certain definite meanings, whether uneducated or disputatious persons understand it so or not.

In addition to these established meanings, the same work of art may have others that are less cogent, more subject to personal interpretation. These can hardly be classed as objective parts of the form. But the form of the work of art as a whole, from a standpoint of esthetic apperception, includes not only the directly presented images but also that portion of its suggestive content which is most definitely demonstrable on a basis of cultural usage.

The distinction becomes clearer if we compare a picture with a literary form, such as a poem. Here the directly presented factors may be auditory images (the sounds of spoken words) or visual images (printed words on a page). Whichever is used, the form of the poem evidently includes something more than these presented images. It includes also an arrangement of meanings, of other images and concepts that the words suggest. Words, written or spoken, are arbitrary symbols endowed with more or less definite suggestive powers through cultural usage. In the case of printing, the visible shape and color of the letters makes little essential difference to the form of the poem; it can even be conveyed through Braille type for the blind. Of course, the sound of the words is important, as in rhyme and rhythm. But that can be either presented (if spoken aloud) or suggested (if read silently).

In visual art, the presented factors tend to make up a conspicuous part of the total form and to be regarded as essential to it. Sometimes, as in abstract decoration, they make up almost the whole form, and there is little definite meaning. (There is always some, for all sense data call up some associations, individual and cultural.) At other times, as in narrative figure painting, the suggestive content bulks larger in the whole. In the case of useful art, such as a cup or a sword, part of the suggestive content consists of associations derived from use. To tell what the object means is, in part, to tell how it is used or is intended to be used.

III. The Components of Esthetic Form

We have not described the form of a work of art by merely dividing it into presented and suggested factors. It is necessary to observe what specific ingredients are presented, what ones suggested, and how they are organized. Psychology helps us considerably in describing them. For they are the same as in all conscious experience. The materials of art, from a standpoint of esthetic apperception, are not chemical pigments, bronze, and marble, but visible shapes and colors, joys and sorrows, desires, beliefs, and actions.

To classify the materials of art, we must look to psychology for a classification of the modes of human experience and behavior, and so far there has been no adequate classification. The traditional way is under such headings as sensation, emotion, conation, reasoning, and so on. This is open to objection as suggesting the old faculty psychology, but it has its uses at the present early stage in the psychology of art. However, any approach to general psychology is also, by implication, an approach to describing the materials of art. For art merely selects and rearranges details from life experience into concrete forms.

Inadequate as they are, the traditional psychological categories are useful in analyzing a work of art. 'Sensation' includes vision and other senses. In visual art, by definition, we are concerned only with forms the main presented ingredients of which are visual rather than auditory. There are certain concepts by which we compare and describe visual objects: especially shape and color. Under 'visual' come linear shape, or line, surface shape, and solid shape (sometimes called 'mass' or 'volume'). Under 'color' come hue; lightness and darkness (often called 'value' in art, 'brightness' in psychology, and 'brilliance' in physics); and saturation (often called 'chroma'). These are the principal visual attributes, but many others can be added. In talking of shape, it is often important to note the shape of voids, or empty spaces. In talking of colors, it is often important to notice their luminosity, as in colored electric lights. Effects of texture are produced by many small variations in color, shape, or both.

These visual attributes function as *components,* or elements, in esthetic form. They are concepts devised for describing objects visually and do not refer to independent realities. No such attribute ever occurs alone; line is always the linear shape of some colored area or solid.

Under the heading of each attribute or component, common usage recognizes a multitude of names for specific *traits* and *types* of quality. Under 'hue,' for example, come red, green, and blue; under 'lightness' or 'value,' the various shades and tints from very dark to very light. Under 'linear shape' come the various types, such as straight, curved, angular, wavy. Under 'solid shape' come the geometric types, such as cubical, spherical, pyramidal, and others more popularly designated, such as barrel-shaped or mushroom-shaped. Countless words are in use to describe the specific visual qualities of things. They occur in art as *component traits.* Any work of art may be analyzed as to its visual ingredients in terms of a peculiar set of such component traits.

It is important to realize that the psychological content of a work of visual art is not restricted to visual qualities. 'Visual' refers only to its mode of presentation to the observer, to its presented content. A work of visual art may *suggest* visual images that it does not directly present, as of solid shape and deep space in a painting. In addition, it can suggest a much wider range of sensory images. It can suggest tactile and kinesthetic images, sounds, and even tastes and odors, as in a picture of flowers, food, and wine. Its suggestive content can extend beyond the sensory to emotions, desires, and rational inference. In each case, if one asks what sorts of things are suggested, the answer will be in terms of general *components* of experience, such as emotion, and of specific *traits* or *types* under each, as joy, grief, and anger. Desire, aversion, indifference, and many more specific types of attitude may come under the general heading of volition. Art may suggest abstract concepts, religious beliefs, logical arguments, overt actions — in short, examples of any mode of experience or behavior.

Any work of art can be described as to its suggested as well as its presented ingredients, in terms of a peculiar set of specific types of emotion, conation, and so on. Some works of art are more *diversified* than others in terms of the different kinds of experience they present or suggest. Rembrandt's works are usually restricted in range of presented hues, but highly varied in light and dark. Dante's *Divine Comedy* suggests a wide range of human emotions and desires; a Shakespearean sonnet is more limited in range. A Cézanne still life is more specialized in suggestive content than Tintoretto's *Paradise* or Michelangelo's *Last Judgment*. A Persian rug is often more diversified in its presented shapes and colors than in its suggested meanings.

Strictly speaking, the ingredients of a work of art are not really ' in ' the object (for example, in the painting) as a physical thing, but in the interaction between it and human observers, the behavior of human beings toward it. People respond to a given type of art in a more or less similar way, because of similarities in their innate equipment and cultural conditioning, and tend to project these responses into the object that arouses them as if they were attributes of the object itself. Metaphysically, this raises difficult problems of distinguishing the real from the apparent, but they need not be raised in esthetics. To esthetics, the ' real ' in a metaphysical or physical sense is less important than the way things appear to human experience. And from a psychological standpoint, ' appearing ' is a fact in itself; a psychological phenomenon to be explained. One approach to this problem has been outlined in the chapter on appreciation. Here we take another point of view: the *description of esthetic forms* as they appear to human beings in a cultural environment, including not only the sensory but also the meaningful aspects of these forms.

IV. Organization in Space and Time

The description of esthetic forms, including works of art, may be compared with morphology as a branch of biological science. In both cases, it is necessary to describe *modes of organization* as well as ingredients. The ingredients of a biological form, such as a tree or animal, consist of molecules arranged in cells and tissues, roots and stems, bones and blood, nervous and muscular systems. The ingredients of an esthetic form are stimuli to sensory and other types of apperceptive response. We exclude from the analysis of form all question of whether the work of art is good, beautiful, or pleasant. What can be directly seen or heard in art or understood from it by interpreting socially established symbols is more capable of objective description in spite of occasional debatable aspects.

The organization of esthetic forms can be described in various ways. In other words, a work of art is usually organized in various ways at the same time. (Likewise, an animal organism can be described in terms of its nervous, muscular, circulatory, and other modes of organization.)

One way in which a work of art is organized is in certain dimensions of space and time. Various types of art can be contrasted as to their mode of *spatiotemporal* organization. For example, an oil painting is presented to the eyes as essentially a flat, two-dimensional area — the actual thickness of paint and canvas is usually not emphasized — yet as a suggestive form it can be three-dimensional; that is, represent a scene in deep space. It presents no moving images; its presentation is not developed in time, yet it can suggest movement and temporal sequence, as in the early Italian paintings that show successive stages in the ascent to Calvary. A carved relief, a statue, or a chair is directly presented to the observer as three-dimensional, even though the third dimension is read into it perceptually. It presents different aspects as one views it from different positions. A relief, as in the Ghiberti doors, can also suggest further three-dimensional development, in deep space. A marionette show, a stage, and a ballet are presented in three dimensions of space and in time, and more or less definitely determined in all four dimensions. There is usually little development in the vertical dimension, but there may be if action takes place on various levels of the stage, as through ramps, platforms, and balconies.

The relative complexity of a work of art depends in part on the degree to which it is definitely *developed* in these various dimensions. It may be highly complex in two-dimensional presentation and very simple or undeveloped in others, as in the case of a Persian rug design. Complexity, in one or in several dimensions, consists of differentiation and integration among parts. It differs from simple unity, as in a stone pyramid, and from disordered multiplicity, as in the wreckage of a bombed city.

Another way of interrelating the images presented and suggested by a work of art is *causal organization.* This occurs in literature, as in the plot of a narrative that shows the effect of one action or character on another. It also occurs in pictures that represent a dramatic situation, as in Leonardo's *Last Supper,* where the effects of Christ's words on the various disciples are shown. It is highly developed in drama and cinema. The observer must interpret and organize the successive images, not only in terms of before and after, but also in terms of cause and effect. Here again, the organization can be vague or definite, simple or complex.

As art forms become more complex, it often becomes necessary to deal with them in terms of components more complex than line and color. For example, motion-picture producers and critics discuss a film in terms of continuity, *montage*, photography, setting, and so on. Dramatists and novelists discuss plot, dialogue, and characterization. These are *developed components* in form, conceived as more or less complex combinations of several elementary components. In music, the elementary component, pitch, is developed into melody and harmony; that is, melody and harmony consist of the organized interrelation of tones, mainly on a basis of differences in pitch. In painting, we speak of drawing, modelling, tonality, color-harmony, perspective, and so on — all involving complex developments of visual shape and color. There is no brief, final list of the developed components in art. New conceptions of them appear in the course of development of a vital art, as means whereby artists plan and organize their works, and critics analyze them.

V. Modes of Composition in Art

Compositional organization is another way of interrelating the details in a work of art. There are four principal *modes of composition:* (*a*) utilitarian, (*b*) expository, (*c*) representative, and (*d*) decorative. Some of these were mentioned at the beginning of this chapter, with the remark that whole arts could not be distinguished on this basis. All the modes of composition are used in all the arts, though to a different extent at different periods. A single work of art may involve all four modes; many are organized in two or more modes at the same time.

Utilitarian composition consists in arranging details in such a way as to be instrumental (or at least apparently or intentionally instrumental) to some active use or end. ' Active ' refers here to overt bodily action and movement, or direct preparation for it, and in general to all the ordinary business of life as distinguished from esthetic and intellectual contemplation, dreams, and reveries. Utility is fitness for some use over and above being looked at, listened to, understood, or thought about. Utilitarian form is sometimes called ' functional.' But from a psychological standpoint, art has a function if it serves only as a stimulus to esthetic perception and enjoyment. Here we are thinking of additional functions in the world of practical behavior. In so far as a thing is organized in a utilitarian way, its form can be described in terms of fitness for some practical use; of means to an end. We can say this of the blade and handle of a sword; of the legs and seat of a chair; of the walls, roof, and openings of a house; and of each moving part in a machine. But that is not enough to describe the thing in full; for it usually involves decorative arrangements also, which may or may not coincide with the utilitarian.

Representative composition is arrangement of details in such a way as to suggest to the imagination a concrete object, a person, or a scene — or group of these — in space. Some representation goes further and suggests a series of events in time. It suggests a specific, concrete phantasy in the mind of a suitably trained and compliant observer. There are two main types of representation: mimetic and symbolic. In *mimetic*, or imitative, representation, the presented set of images (lines, colors, and so forth) resembles to some extent the set of images it calls up in imagination. In the *symbolic* type, especially in literature, the presented images are words or other conventional signs and usually do not resemble the images they suggest. In visual art, representation is usually mimetic. Some varieties are *static:* that is, motionless or presenting no determinate order of movements. These include most pictorial and sculptural representation; also the *tableau vivant* in pantomime and other less common types. Oriental flower and garden art sometimes involves representation, as of a small tray arrangement to suggest a landscape or a garden mound to suggest Fujiyama. Other varieties are *mobile;* that is, presenting images in a determined order. Mobile pictorial representation includes the cinema in its story-telling phases, whether in photographs or animated drawings; also the Chinese shadow play. Mobile sculptural representation includes marionettes and puppets. Dramatic visual representation includes certain phases (not the literary or musical) in acting, pantomime, and dancing. With auditory and literary representation we are not concerned.

Some composition is *expository*, in that it arranges details so as to set forth general relationships, as of causal or logical connection; ab-

stract meanings, pervasive qualities, common or underlying principles. This mode of composition is more highly developed today in
literary art than in visual art; but it has visual examples. Much religious art, such as the Dancing Siva in Hindu sculpture, undertakes
to convey theological, metaphysical, and moral ideas through visual
images. A great deal of medieval and Renaissance painting expresses
Christian belief through symbolism. Hieroglyphics and other types
of pictography are used, not only to suggest concrete descriptions and
narrations, but also to express abstract principles and arguments. A
coat of arms involves expository composition, in that it undertakes
to convey general facts about the owner's rank and privileges in feudal
society, and perhaps about his ideals and the accomplishments of his
family.

Decorative composition is a kind of esthetic form that is aimed at,
or apparently suitable for, stimulating direct perceptual experience in
the beholder, especially through the nature and arrangement of visual
qualities. It differs from utilitarian composition in that it does not
need to be suited for any use except to provide an object for perception.
A decorative object may also be utilitarian, but that is not what is
meant by calling it decorative. As contrasted with representative form,
the decorative does not need to look like anything else, or suggest anything else to the imagination. It may do so, as in a decorative picture,
but that is not essential. As contrasted with expository form, the decorative does not need to mean anything in particular, to convey any information, to express any attitudes or concepts, or to suggest any relationships over and above those directly observable in the sensory
details themselves. A decorative object may happen to do this, as in
a coat of arms; but again that is not essential to its nature as decoration.

When developed with some complexity, a decorative composition is
a *design*. It can be described in terms of *thematic relations:* the repetition and variation of certain component traits, such as blue areas and
curving lines, and perhaps their contrast with markedly different traits,
such as red areas and angular lines.[1] Design also involves the integration of such thematic relations by subordinating details to a comprehensive pattern. Design and thematic relations occur in music and
literature (especially in poetry) as well as in visual art, but the term
' decorative ' is not usually applied there. One of the most effective

---

[1] Thematic repetition is sometimes called ' rhythm,' but that word tends to
confuse it with rhythm in a more specific sense, as an auditory component.

ways of understanding design in general is to compare musical with complex visual design, as a fugue with a Persian rug.

A given set of component traits can be arranged according to any one of these modes of composition, or according to two or more at once. Some types of art are comparatively *specialized* from a compositional standpoint, in that they involve complex development in only one mode. These are sometimes called ' pure decoration,' ' purely utilitarian,' and so on. But it is impossible for a work of art to be completely restricted to one mode. Even if a tool, chair, or house is bare and unadorned, and intended only for utilitarian purposes, it is sure to involve some aspects of a decorative nature. In the chair, for example, the four legs will constitute a series of repeated cylindrical masses, which fit together as a thematic arrangement. However, the decorative development of the chair may proceed much farther than this, as through the addition of incised grooves and ridges, or the coloring of surfaces. These additions may, or may not, fit into the utilitarian scheme; i. e., may, or may not, be useful in themselves. They may, or may not, be integrated with the utilitarian scheme from a decorative standpoint, as through making the added lines repeat the contours of the legs, seat, and back. Furthermore, the chair may be developed along representative lines, as in a king's throne ornamented with carved animals in relief. Finally, these details may have expository significance if they fit together into a coat of arms. A Gothic cathedral is highly developed in all four modes of composition, through its functional basis, its decorative treatment of masses and surfaces, its sculptural and stained-glass representations, and its theological and moral symbolism. A Dancing Siva contains representation of a dancing figure, a design of masses, lines, and surfaces, and a complex religious and philosophic exposition. It also has utility for purposes of worship and spiritual advancement.

From the standpoint of form analysis, the modes of composition operate as *factors* in a particular work of art. In other words, a work of art can be described as to the various modes of composition involved in it, their relative emphasis and degree of development, and their interrelations in that particular object. For example, we speak of the ' design element ' or the ' decorative element ' in a painting, of the relation between decorative and functional elements in a building.

It becomes important, then, to notice, not only how each compositional factor is developed in itself, but also how, and how thoroughly, they are *integrated*. In a painting, we may ask how the design is related to the representative factor or ' subject matter.' Sometimes the design is conspicuous and clearly organized, while the represented objects are vague and distorted; at other times there is a highly realistic portrait or landscape with little or no definite design. However, there must always be some decorative element, if only from the simple lines and colors necessary for representation. Sometimes the design seems clearly integrated with the representation, so that neither can be easily distinguished from the other; the representative form provides a basic structure for the design itself. At other times, on the contrary, the decorative factor in a picture or a building is superficial and separate. Such distinctions are used as a basis for standards of value in art criticism, but the descriptive study of form is content to note them as facts.

One way of discovering whether compositional factors are integrated is to look at a number of individual details, and find out whether each is functioning as an element in more than one mode of composition. Does each decorative detail of a building also have a utilitarian function, and does each visible part of the utilitarian scheme contribute to the design? In a picture, a given spot of red may function as part of a represented flower, and also as part of a design of lines and colors.

Whatever compositional factors are present in a work of art, one of them usually acts as a basic *framework* for the whole form, while the others are *accessories*. For example, in the decorated chair, utility is the framework mode of composition, determining the basic structure. But it does not follow that the framework mode is necessarily the most important from a historical or evaluative standpoint. The utilitarian structure of the chair may be quite conventional, like a thousand others. Its decorative factor, though accessory, may be the only one elaborately developed, and the only one that is distinctive and original. The representation of a scene gives a basic framework to most pictures, but accessory effects of decorative color may give to a certain picture its most distinctive characteristic. Decorative composition may provide the general framework for an abstract design, whose representative factor is confined to occasional repetitions of a flower or animal motif.

The relation between modes of composition has important historical aspects, which can be only briefly touched upon in this chapter. They concern the *evolution of art forms,* and their relation to science. Important primitive and archaic forms are usually undifferentiated as to modes of composition, combining several. As historians have pointed out, there is no such thing as pure decoration, art for art's sake, or fine as opposed to useful art, in early society. Again there is little, if any, restriction and differentiation in Oriental or medieval culture. The tendency to differentiate sharply between beauty and use, the esthetic and the practical, the decorative and the functional or significant, is largely a sophisticated modern trend. A phase of dissociation of this sort followed the Industrial Revolution. It was manifested in many bleak utilitarian products, and on the other hand in an efflorescence of superficial, nonfunctional decoration. Recent years have seen a conscious effort to reintegrate the two, as in artistically designed industrial products.

However, there is always a certain pressure toward specialization for the sake of intensive, undistracted progress along one chosen path. The intensive, specialized development of utilitarian form has led to applied science or technology; that of expository form, to pure science. The cultural ancestors of modern machines and technical processes, and of modern scientific textbooks are the undifferentiated forms of early practical and religious art. Representation has a scientific development, in exact photographs, maps, models, and diagrams. But other types of representation remain within the accepted province of fine art. Decoration alone has shown no strong tendency to pass from an artistic to a scientific stage. Visual design reached a high intensive development in Islamic textiles (partly because of a taboo against visual representation) and in the products of certain other periods. Auditory design has been intensively developed in modern classical music.

After periods of specialization in one or another mode, there is usually a reaction toward diversity, as in the recent effort to combine design with representation in painting and sculpture, with utility in furniture and architecture, or the recent development of pictorial art for educational purposes, as in illustrations for children's textbooks, which, as in much ancient art, include not only representation and decoration, but also an expository element: the conveying of information and abstract ideas through concrete illustration. Advertising and propagandist art are similar in this respect.

VI. Types and Styles of Art

The description of a particular work of art is best accomplished by classifying it in terms of various *types*, just as in zoölogy a newly found animal might be described by classifying it as belonging to one type as to its bony structure, another as to its mode of locomotion, to another as to its mode of reproduction, and so on. Thus the whole is described as a specific combination of various characteristics. The Statue of Liberty in New York is the figure of a goddess from the standpoint of representation, and it is a lighthouse from that of its utilitarian structure. One should also indicate how the work under description *differs* from usual examples of each type. Its colossal size distinguishes the Statue of Liberty, for instance, from most statues.

In this chapter, we have already noted a number of artistic types. Some works of art are visual and some auditory in respect to principal mode of presentation. Some are diversified and some specialized in range of presented ingredients; some in range of suggested ingredients. Some are specialized in one mode of composition; some in another; some combine several. Some have complex presentative development in three dimensions of space; some in only two. Some are developed in time as well as in three dimensions of space. These are but a few examples of numerous types available for use as terms of description.

The traditional names for esthetic types, or categories, are often confusing because of their evaluative implications. For example, to call an object 'beautiful,' 'ugly,' 'sublime,' or 'pretty,' not only helps to describe it but also in part evaluates it, praises or condemns it. At the same time, there is an objective element in the difference between sublimity and prettiness that can be expressed in terms of observable characteristics without reference to value. Other esthetic types, such as 'romantic' and 'tragic' have a still larger element of objective meaning, and hence can be applied in describing art with less danger of confusion. The 'art principles,' which we have discussed in a previous chapter as supposed rules and standards of value, also refer to certain objective types of art and can be so considered apart from questions of value. Whether or not all art should be 'balanced' (and many will deny that it should), at least some works of art possess more balance than others. Some works of art contain more 'rhythm' than others do; some have more 'dominance and subordination' than others have. If defined as purely descriptive terms, these words are useful in comparative analysis. Any of them, however, may be very ambiguous; there is no reason for assuming that any one of the current meanings of a certain term is the correct one. Confusion can be avoided by explicitly selecting one definition and holding to it.

Sometimes objects can be compared in a way approximating quantitative estimate, though rarely with numerical exactness. For example, one can say that a certain Persian rug is more complex in its visual design than a certain Chinese bowl, or that a Rubens battle scene contains more suggested movement than a Chardin still life. These comparisons are obvious and will arouse little dispute, but quantitative estimates are often more difficult. At present, measurement can go but a little way in the description of esthetic form.

The description of *historic styles of art* presents an important and difficult task for esthetics. A style is a distinctive or characteristic mode of presentation, construction, execution, or expression in art. Historians attempt to define styles characteristic of certain nations, periods, schools, and persons, as the Greek, the Medieval, the Impressionist, or the Raphaelesque style. As a rule, the broader the scope thus taken in, the more difficult it is to define the style satisfactorily, for the reason that more varieties of form are encountered. Yet if one defines the style too narrowly, one must add that many exceptions to it exist in the historical field included. Even a single artist, such as Raphael, is likely to have painted in several different ways during his life; so distinctions are sometimes made as to the early, middle, and late styles of the artist. It is a perennial problem to define such terms as Gothic, Classic, and Romantic in brief yet adequate terms. A historic style is in some ways analogous to a biological species, as a complex type that persists through many successive individuals. (Even a personal style, like the Raphaelesque, can be followed by many artists.) It is to be described or defined, not in terms of any single characteristic, but in terms of a number that tend to be associated with one another. Thus, the Gothic style involves certain characteristics as to usual shape of doors and windows, height of vaults, thickness of walls, type of ornamentation, and so on. In whatever way one tries to characterize a style of art, one is likely to find examples that conform in some ways and deviate in others. Artistic styles are much more variable than biological species. They change more rapidly and merge imperceptibly into other styles.

Some of the difficulty arises from confusion in applying the names of styles both to abstract *types* and to particular, historic *periods* or *nations*. If one thinks of the Baroque period as equivalent to the seventeenth century in Europe, then the Baroque will include many different types of art. If one thinks of it as an abstract type involving large, sweeping curves, oblique and eccentric patterns, emotional excitement, and so on, then examples of the Baroque style will be found in other centuries and even in other civilizations, such as that of India. It is important for the study of cultural history to recognize such resemblances among the arts of remote peoples and places, but to do so we need clearer definitions of various styles as abstract, complex types.

Many terms used as names of abstract types are also used in the other sense. For example, ' Classic ' refers to the art of Greece and

Rome, and also to an abstract type involving comparative regularity, balance, symmetrical proportion, smoothness, gently flowing curves, rationality, and cool serenity of expression. 'Romantic' refers to European art in the late eighteenth and early nineteenth centuries, and also to an abstract type involving a tendency to irregularity, rough textures, sentiment, primitive impulse, and passion. Of course, the terms 'Classic' and 'Romantic' as abstractly defined will not characterize all the art of any one period or nationality, for every age exhibits divergence.

If such terms are to be used as names of abstract types, they should be clearly defined as such apart from special historical associations, but it is hard to exclude these associations. Even when the terms are abstractly defined, their application to particular cases is troublesome. Cases will appear that embody some, but not all, characteristics of the type as so defined. For example, Delacroix, Beethoven, and Keats are Romantic in some, but not in all, the traits just mentioned, and the individual works of any one of them vary considerably. However styles are defined, examples will be found that conform to none of them exactly — examples that are intermediate or transitional and that embody characteristics of more than one style. Such examples are found in biology also, but plants and animals are more 'true to type' than works of art.

VII. Comparative Analysis

In spite of the confusing ambiguity of esthetic terms, they contain enough definite meaning to provide a basis for descriptive study. They are gradually being refined through the aid of dictionary-makers and through theoretical analysis in the light of concrete examples. It would be a mistake to wait until they are defined to everyone's satisfaction before going on with research. In fact, endless argument over the definitions of 'beauty,' 'sublimity,' 'the classic,' and similar terms has too long delayed inductive inquiry.

In learning to analyze art, students usually go through several stages. The first stage, that of an untrained observer, is to notice only a few fragmentary aspects in a work of art. In painting and sculpture, they tend to notice an occasional conspicuous detail, a facial expression, a gesture, or an unusual garment, and to ignore the structure of the whole. Through practice and instruction, they can be led to notice many other types of detail and relation, including those of design, and to identify examples of the chief historic styles. At this second stage, the task of analyzing a single work of art in words is apt to seem endless. There are so many things to be said about it, so many details and relations to be noted in each case, that a single description could run into volumes.

The third stage is reached only by further comparative study in the light of historical knowledge. It is one of *abbreviation,* of singling out the few most important things to say of each particular case. This will of course vary considerably according to the interest or problem one has in mind. But in general, one acquires speed in observation and in finding the proper word to describe each characteristic observed. One learns to select the distinctive traits that demarcate each particular case from all others. For example, one may immediately recognize a painting as Impressionist, and probably a work by Monet. Having said that it is a typical Monet in most respects, one can take a great many details for granted as covered by this classification. The next step is to notice how it differs from many other Monets and from the usual Impressionist picture, as, for instance, through an exceptional emphasis upon definite perspective or upon linear design. A brief explanation may serve to bring out the principal ways in which this example is distinctive and original.

It does not follow that an appreciator should notice only these distinctive traits, but they are important for brief scientific reporting. Even in appreciation, as one encounters more and more works of art, most of them saying only what has been said many times before, one tends to look at each for its distinctive qualities, if any. The training needed here is in perception and understanding, involving sensory and intellectual elements in close coöperation. The emotional and evaluative elements in appreciation are not directly concerned. But the central ability to perceive and understand art will tend, if other conditions favor, to increase enjoyment and discrimination also. In science and education, it can lead to further investigation of the genesis and functions of art in society and thus to increased control of art as a means to human welfare.

REFERENCES

(1) BARNES, A. C. *The Art in Painting.* (Harcourt, Brace and Co.: New York, 1928) 560 pp.
(2) DEWEY, J., and Others. *Art and Education.* (Barnes Foundation Press: Merion, Pa., 1929) 349 pp.
(3) FRY, R. *Vision and Design.* (Brentano's: New York: n.d.) 302 pp.

(4) GARDNER, H. "The analytic approach to art." [In] *Art Education Today: 1940.* (The Fine Arts Staff, Teachers College, Columbia University) 85 pp. (pp. 26–38)

(5) GARDNER, H. *Understanding the Arts.* (Harcourt, Brace and Co.: New York, 1932) 336 pp.

(6) GREENE, T. M. *The Arts and the Art of Criticism.* (Princeton University Press: Princeton, 1940) 690 pp.

(7) PARKER, D. W. *The Analysis of Art.* (Yale University Press: New Haven, 1926) 190 pp.

(8) POPE, A. *An Introduction to the Language of Drawing and Painting.* (Harvard University Press: Cambridge, 1929)

(9) PRALL, D. W. *Aesthetic Analysis.* (Thomas Y. Crowell Co.: New York, 1936) 211 pp.

CHAPTER XXV

A SURVEY OF RECENT RESEARCH IN ART AND ART EDUCATION [1]

RAY FAULKNER
Head, Department of Fine and Industrial Arts
Teachers College, Columbia University
New York, New York

I. INTRODUCTORY

Serious attention to research and experimentation in art and art education is comparatively new in American circles, although there is already a relatively large body of literature available. Much of this research has been stimulated by the Carnegie Corporation, the Carnegie Foundation for the Advancement of Teaching, and the General Education Board. Supported in whole or in part by funds from these foundations, many projects have been directed by individuals connected with universities or art museums, so that the work has had the advantage of academic backgrounds and resources (26, 39, 87, 89). Another vital source of stimulation, just beginning to be felt, comes from educational organizations through committees that have proposed programs of research and experimentation for which they feel the need.

In addition to such projects clearly of a research nature are numerous programs that have added much to our understanding of art and art education. Thus, outstanding work in vitalizing art at the elementary- and secondary-school levels has been done at the Oaklane Country Day School near Philadelphia, the Lincoln and Horace Mann Schools of Teachers College, Columbia University; at the college level, at Bennington and Stephens colleges; and in the professional training of artists, at the Design Laboratory, Harvard's Graduate School of Design, and the New *Bauhaus* in Chicago. The Fine Arts departments of Harvard and Princeton universities have contributed much to our knowledge of the arts of the past through scholarly historical research.

---

[1] The presentation of the material in this chapter has been facilitated by helpful suggestions from Joseph C. Moore, Professor of Educational Psychology, George Peabody College for Teachers, Nashville, Tennessee. — *R. F.*

II. Typical Books and Articles Bearing upon Investigations in Several Aspects of Art

While it is impossible to present an adequate picture of research in art and art education in this brief space, its scope and variety can be indicated in the following bibliography by the mention of characteristic books and articles dealing with the topic, each one chosen from many similar studies of equally high merit and importance. Although there is considerable overlapping, the titles fall into such broad classifications as the History and Theory of Art, the Psychology of Art, and Education in the Arts. Certain of them offer suggestions for future work. Titles are presented according to these classifications.

1. The History and Theory of Art

The history and theory of art has proved a fertile field for investigations and researches ranging from careful studies of the work and influence of one man (6) to studies of the work of whole periods (1, 2).[1]

2. Studies of Color, Line, and Shape

Here the emphasis has been on scientific investigations of reactions to single and combined colors, different types of lines, and varied shapes. Although the work for the most part is above reproach scientifically, it seldom has as much immediate value for the art educator as studies of the nature and history of art or of appreciation and creative ability. It is invaluable, however, in adding to our fundamental store of knowledge concerning the arts. Chandler (12) presents convenient summaries of examples of this phase of research.

3. Talent and Aptitude

Long discussed by philosophers, the question of talent has also been attacked by psychologists, who have hoped through using the scientific method to throw new light on this aspect of man's ability. The work in this field, while inconclusive, is stimulating, and marks the beginning of an important quest.

4. The Development of Art Skills and Abilities

Though of great interest to the art educator, research in the skills and abilities analyzable in art work has received less attention than studies of shape and color, perhaps because of the serious difficulties

---

[1] See the references under A in the list at the end of this chapter.

this field presents to the research worker. However, progress is being made, and the items listed as typical references (under D) are significant contributions.

5. Perception, Appreciation, and Judgment

An understanding of the way in which art objects affect observers is of paramount importance to the art educator, and the search for a clear and valid explanation has stimulated considerable research and thought. As is the case with much art research, at present there is no completely satisfactory answer on this issue, but the groundwork for further study has been well established.

6. Art Interests and Preferences

Closely related to appreciations and judgments are interests and preferences, the sources of motivation in art activities. Because they provide the fundamental drives and bases for art activities, interests and preferences are of considerable import, not only to the teacher, but also to the artist, the advertiser, and the business man.

7. Feelings and Emotions

The rôle of the feelings and emotions in all art activities has long been the subject of discussion, and yet there is little pertinent experimental data. The small quantity of data is no indication of the importance of the topic, but rather of the difficulty of applying the scientific method to the study of feelings and emotions, particularly in relation to art.

8. Art Tests

The extent to which art abilities may be measured scientifically is still a controversial issue. Viewed objectively, few if any art tests have lived up to the expectations and promises of their makers; however, it would seem that the real trouble is with the extravagant claims advanced for them and with the failure to interpret the results wisely. Because our increased understanding of art and art activities is largely dependent on the perfection of measuring instruments, the field of art tests is one of promise, if not of conspicuous achievement. References 71 and 72 present summaries of past work.

9. Philosophy and Proposed Programs of Research

Although almost all the early research was done without benefit of a well-considered basic philosophy or a clear program of work, there has been an increasing tendency to consider such factors carefully. Also several writers have suggested directions for future work.

10. Bibliographies of Research in Art

Two highly useful bibliographies of research in art are available.

III. SUMMARY

That a conspicuous body of varied research in art exists should be evident from the references listed in this chapter, and more particularly from the many studies listed in the bibliographies (95, 96). However, the surface has hardly been scratched. If we are to predict and develop human behavior in the field of art, there is vital need for intensive investigation of many fields. Perhaps the most hopeful sign is the increasing interest of students in graduate work in the arts, a tendency that, if encouraged, can provide a more solid basis for art education than now exists.

It is important not only that more research be encouraged, but also that the research be of higher caliber. Effective art research demands two things: first, a genuine understanding of the field of art; and second, a familiarity and proficiency with the techniques of research. Neither is sufficient by itself, and the fact that few workers have combined both assets has limited the value of many projects. Research that ignores the basic nature of art is a useless, or sometimes harmful, pastime; research that is unsound scientifically can do little more than provide material for new arguments. There is little need for that; there is real need for honest, intelligent endeavor.

REFERENCES

A. The History and Theory of Art

(1) BERENSON, BERNHARD. *The Study and Criticism of Italian Art.* (Harcourt, Brace and Co.: New York, 1916. 3 v.)

(2) BOAS, FRANZ. *Primitive Art.* (Harvard University Press: Cambridge, 1927) 376 pp.

(3) CALLAHAN, J. L. *A Theory of Esthetic According to the Principles of St. Thomas Aquinas.* (Doctoral Dissertation. Catholic University of America: Washington, 1927) 132 pp.

(4) HAMBIDGE, JAY. *The Elements of Dynamic Symmetry.* (Brentano's: New York, 1926) 140 pp.

(5) HIRN, YRJO. *The Origin of Art.* (The Macmillan Co.: New York, 1900) 341 pp.

(6) HITCHCOCK, HENRY R. *Architecture of H. H. Richardson and His Times.* (Museum of Modern Art: New York, 1936) 311 pp.

(7) KEPPEL, F. P., and DUFFUS, R. L. *The Arts in American Life.* (McGraw-Hill Book Co.: New York, 1933) 227 pp.

(8) OGDEN, R. M. "Naïve geometry in the psychology of art." *Amer. Jour. Psychol.* 49:1937, 198–216.

(9) WARNER, LANGDON. *Japanese Sculpture of the Suiko Period.* (Yale University Press: New Haven, 1923) 80 pp.

B. Studies of Color, Line, and Shape

(10) BRIAN, C. R., and GOODENOUGH, F. L. "The relative potency of color and form perception at different ages." *Jour. Exper. Psychol.,* 12: 1929, 197–213.

(11) CALKIN, M. W. "An attempted experiment in psychological aesthetics." *Psychol. Review,* 7: 1900, 580–591.

(12) CHANDLER, A. R. *Beauty and Human Nature.* (D. Appleton-Century Co., Inc.: New York, 1934) 381 pp. Especially Chapters 3, 4, 5, 6.

(13) CHEVREUL, M. E. *The Laws of Contrast of Colour, and Their Application to the Arts.* English trans. by John Spanton. (Routledge, N. D.: London, 1857) 243 pp.

(14) DROUGHT, R. A. "A survey of studies in experimental esthetics." *Jour. of Ed. Research,* 20: 1929, 97–102.

(15) GORDON, KATE. "The aesthetics of simple color arrangements." *Psychol. Review,* 19: 1912, 352–363.

(16) LADD-FRANKLIN, C. *Colour and Colour Theories.* (Harcourt, Brace and Co.: New York, 1929) 287 pp.

(17) POFFENBERGER, A. T., and BARROWS, B. E. "The feeling values of lines." *Jour. Applied Psychol.,* 8: 1924, 187–205.

(18) THORNDIKE, E. L. "Individual differences in judgments of the beauty of simple forms." *Psych. Review,* 24: 1917, 147–153.

(19) WASHBURN, M. F., HAIGHT, D., and REGENEBURG, J. "The relation of the pleasantness of color combinations to that of colors seen singly." *Amer. Jour. Psychol.,* 32: 1921, 145–146.

(20) WEBER, C. O. "The aesthetics of rectangles and theories of affection." *Jour. Applied Psychol.,* 15: 1931, 310–318.

C. Talent and Aptitude

(21) DREPS, HILDEGARDE. "The Psychological Capacities and Abilities of College Art Students of High and Low Standing." *Psychol. Monogr.* 45: 1933, No. 200, 134–146.

(22) EURICH, A. C., and CARROLL, H. "Abstract intelligence and art appreciation." *Jour. of Educ. Psychol.,* 23: 1932, 214–220.

(23) GUILFORD, R. B., and GUILFORD, J. P. "A prognostic test for students of design." *Jour. of Applied Psychol.* 15: 1931, 335–345.

(24) LEWERENZ, A. S. "I.Q. and ability in art." *School and Society,* 27: 1928, 489–490.

(25) McCLOY, W. "Creative Imagination in Children and Adults." *Psychol. Monogr.,* 51: 1939, No. 5, 88–102.

(26) MEIER, N. C. "Factors in Artistic Aptitude: Final Summary of a Ten-

Year Study of a Special Ability." *Psychol. Monogr.*, 51: 1939, No. 5, 140–158.

(27) MILLER, JOSEPH. "Intelligence testing by drawings." *Jour. Educ. Psychol.*, 29: 1938, 390–394.

(28) PATRICK, C. "Creative thought in artists." *Jour. Psychol.*, 4: 1937, 35–37.

(29) SHOEMAKER, R. "Student pedigree-studies." *Eugen. News*, 22: 1937, 107–108.

(30) TIEBOUT, C. "The Psychophysical Functions Differentiating Artistically Superior from Artistically Inferior Children." *Psychol. Monogr.*, 45: 1933, No. 200, 108–133.

D. Art Skills and Abilities

(31) AYER, F. C. *The Psychology of Drawing.* (Warwick and York: Baltimore, 1916) 186 pp.

(32) BIRD, MILTON H. *A Study in Aesthetics.* (Harvard University Press: Cambridge, 1932) 117 pp.

(33) BUSWELL, G. T. "Learning to look at pictures." *Progressive Educ.*, 13: 1936, 422–426.

(34) CHILD, H. G. "Measurement of drawing ability of 2,177 children in an Indiana school system." *Jour. Educ. Psychol.*, 6: 1915, 391–408.

(35) CRAWFORD, C. C. "An experiment with three ways of teaching water-color painting." *Elem. School Jour.*, 36: 1935, 40–43.

(36) CROWLEY, EDNA. *An Experiment in Methods of Teaching Design.* (Master's Thesis. University of Chicago, 1931) 87 pp.

(37) ENG, HELGA K. *The Psychology of Children's Drawings from the First Stroke to the Coloured Drawing.* (Paul, Trench, Trubner: London, 1931) 223 pp.

(38) GOODENOUGH, F. L. "Studies in the psychology of children's drawings." *Psychol. Bull.*, 25: 1928, 272–283.

(39) LARK-HOROWITZ, B., BARNHART, E., and SILLS, E. *Graphic Work-Sample Diagnosis.* (Cleveland Museum of Art: Cleveland, 1939)

(40) MEIER, N. C. "Art Ability without Instruction or Environmental Background: Case Study of Loran Lockhart." *Psychol. Monogr.*, 48: 1936, No. 213, 155–163.

(41) MUNDEL, L. R. "The Effect of Lectures on Art Principles upon Art Production at the Fifth- and Sixth-Grade Level." *Psychol. Monogr.*, 51: 1939, No. 5, 127–319.

(42) RICE, CHARLOTTE. "Excellence of production in types of movements in drawing." *Child Development*, 1: 1930, 1–14.

E. Perception, Appreciation, and Judgment

(43) ALLEN, A. H. B. "A psychological theory of aesthetic value." *Brit. Jour. Psychol.*, 28: 1937, 43–58.

(44) BIRKHOFF, G. D. *Aesthetic Measure.* (Harvard University Press: Cambridge, 1933) 240 pp.

(45) BULLOUGH, E. "The perceptive problem in aesthetic appreciation of single colors." *Brit. Jour. Psychol.*, 2: 1908, 406–463.

(46) Buswell, G. T. *How People Look at Pictures.* (University of Chicago Press: Chicago, 1935) 195 pp.

(47) Clair, M. B. "Variation in the Perception of Aesthetic Qualities in Paintings." *Psychol. Monogr.,* 51: 1939, No. 5, 52–67.

(48) Hurlock, E. B., and Thomson, J. L. "Children's drawings: An experimental study of perception." *Child Development,* 5: 1934, 127–138.

(49) Kellett, K. R. "A Gestalt Study of the Function of Unity in Aesthetic Perception." *Psychol. Monogr.,* 51: 1939, No. 5, 23–51.

(50) Lund, F. H. and Anastasi, A. "An interpretation of aesthetic experience." *Amer. Jour. Psychol.,* 40: 1928, 434–448.

(51) Mitra, S. C., and Ghosh, R. "Studies in aesthetic perception." *Indian Jour. Psychol.,* 11: 1936, 115–122.

(52) Mueller, J. H. "Theories of Esthetic Appreciation." [In] *Studies in Appreciation of Art.* (University of Oregon Publications, Studies in College Teaching, 4, No. 6: Eugene, Oregon, 1934) pp. 7–30.

(53) Sisson, E. D. "Suggestion in art judgment." *Jour. Gen. Psychol.,* 18: 1938, 433–435.

(54) Thorndike, E. L. "Individual differences in judgments of the beauty of simple forms." *Psychol. Rev.,* 24: 1917, 147–153.

(55) Zane, N. B. "Appreciation of the Space Arts." [In] *Studies in Appreciation of Art.* (University of Oregon Publications, Studies in College Teaching, 4, No. 6: Eugene, Oregon, 1934) pp. 53–82.

F. Art Interests and Preferences

(56) Anastasi, A., and Foley, J. P. "Analysis of spontaneous drawings by children in different cultures." *Jour. Appl. Psychol.,* 20: 1936, 689–726.

(57) Ballard, P. B. "What London children like to draw." *Jour. Exper. Ped.,* 1: 1912, 186–197.

(58) Barnes, Earl. "A study of children's drawings." *Ped. Sem.,* 2: 1892, 455–463.

(59) Brighouse, G. "Variability in Preferences for Simple Forms." *Psychol. Monogr.,* 51: 1939, No. 5, 68–74.

(60) Gale, A. van N. *Children's Preferences for Colors, Color Combinations, and Color Arrangements.* (University of Chicago Press: Chicago, 1933) 60 pp.

(61) Lark-Horowitz, Betty. "On art appreciation of children: I. Preference of picture subjects in general." *Jour. of Ed. Research,* 21: 1937, 118–137.

(62) Lehman, H. C., and Witty, P. A. "Play interests as evidence of sex differences in aesthetic appreciation." *Amer. Jour. Psychol.,* 40: 1928, 449–457.

(63) Morrison, J. C. *Children's Preferences for Pictures Commonly Used in Art Appreciation Courses.* (University of Chicago Press: Chicago, 1935) 55 pp.

(64) Walton, W. E., Guilford, R. B., and Guilford, J. P. "Color preferences of 1,279 university students." *Amer. Jour. Psychol.,* 45: 1933, 322–328.

G. Feelings and Emotions

(65) Guilford, J. P. "The prediction of affective values." *Amer. Jour. Psych.,* 43: 1931, 469–478.

(66) Langfeld, H. S. "Rôle of feeling and emotion in esthetics." *Inter. Sym-*

posium on Feelings and Emotions, Wittenberg College, 1927. (Clark University Press: Worcester, 1928) 346–354.

(67) LUND, F. H. *Emotions: Their Psychological, Physiological, and Educative Influences.* (Ronald Press: New York, 1939) 305 pp.

(68) PRESCOTT, DANIEL. *Emotions and the Educative Process.* (American Council on Education: Washington, 1938) 323 pp.

(69) WASHBURN, M. F., and POWELSON, I. "The effect of verbal suggestion on judgments of the affective value of colors." *Amer. Jour. Psychol.,* 25: 1913, 267–269.

H. Art Tests

(70) DEWARS, H. "A comparison of tests of artistic appreciation." *British Jour. Educ. Psychol.,* 8: 1938, 29–49.

(71) FAULKNER, RAY. *An Experimental Investigation Designed to Develop Tests to Measure Art Understanding and Appreciation.* (Unpublished Thesis. University of Minnesota: Minneapolis, 1937) 246 pp. Summary in *Summaries of Ph.D. Theses: I.* (University of Minnesota: Minneapolis, 1939)

(72) KINTER, M. *The Measurement of Artistic Abilities: A Survey of Scientific Studies in the Field of Graphic Arts.* (Psychological Corp.: New York, 1933) 89 pp.

(73) KLINE, L. W., and CAREY, C. L. *A Measuring Scale in Freehand Drawing.* Part I. Representation: Part II, Design and Composition. (Johns Hopkins Univ., Studies in Educ. No. 5: Baltimore, 1922–1923) 119 pp.

(74) KNAUBER, A. J. *The Knauber Art Ability Test* and *The Knauber Art Vocabulary Test.* (Alma J. Knauber, 3331 Arrow Avenue, Cincinnati, Ohio, 1935)

(75) LEWERENZ, A. S. *Tests in Fundamental Abilities of Visual Art.* (Southern California School Book Depository: Los Angeles, 1927)

(76) McADORY, MARGARET. *The Construction and Validation of an Art Test.* Contributions to Education, No. 383. (Teachers College, Columbia University: New York, 1929) 40 pp.

(77) MEIER, N. C. *Meier-Seashore Art Judgment Test.* (University of Iowa: Iowa City, Iowa)

(78) MUNRO, THOMAS. "Some proposed tests and their fallacies." *Art News,* 33: 1934, 17.

(79) STEGGERDA, M., and MACOMBER, E. "A revision of the McAdory Art Test applied to American Indians, Dutch Whites, and college graduates." *Jour. of Comp. Psychol.,* 26: 1938, 349–354.

(80) VARNUM, W. H. *Selective Art Aptitude Test.* (International Textbook Company: Scranton, Pa., 1939)

(81) WINSLOW, L. L. *Integrated School Art Program.* (McGraw-Hill Book Co.: New York, 1939) 391 pp.

(82) FARNUM, R. B. *Art Education in the United States.* Biennial Bulletins — 1922, 1924, 1930. (Office of Education: Washington, D. C.)

(83) HISS, P., and FANSLER, R. M. *Research in Fine Arts in Colleges and Universities of the United States.* (Carnegie Corporation: New York, 1934) 223 pp.

(84) HILPERT, ROBERT. "A method of community study as a basis for curriculum construction." *Education,* 55: 1934, 211–214.

(85) Hilpert, Robert. *The Regents' Inquiry into Character and Cost of Public Education in the State of New York.* (Unpublished report. 1938).

(86) MacGowan, Clara. *Statement of Problems for the Committee on Research for Determining Teacher Qualifications in Art.* (Mimeographed report. 1939)

(87) Maclean, Malcolm, and Others. *Report on Problems and Progress of the General College, University of Minnesota.* (University of Minnesota: Minneapolis, 1939) 148 pp.

(88) Pierce, A. E., and Hilpert, Robert. *Instructions in Music and Art.* [In] National Survey of Secondary Education Monogr. No. 25. (U. S. Office of Education: Washington, 1932) 468 pp.

(89) Ziegfeld, Edwin. "Owatonna Art Education Project." *Curriculum Jour.,* 8: 1937, 143–149.

I. Basic Philosophy and Programs of Research

(90) Faulkner, Ray. "A research program in art appreciation." *Jour Educ. Research,* 33: 1939, 36–43.

(91) Hilpert, Robert. "Fine Arts." [In] *Suggested Studies in Secondary Education.* (Civic Education Service: Washington, D. C.) 43–46.

(92) Munro, Thomas. *Scientific Method in Aesthetics.* (W. W. Norton and Co., Inc.: New York, 1928) 101 pp.

(93) Mursell, J. L. "The application of psychology to the arts." *Teachers College Record,* 37: 1936, 290–299.

(94) Whitford, W. G. *An Introduction to Art Education.* (D. Appleton-Century Co., Inc.: New York, 1937) 391 pp.

J. Bibliographies of Research in Art

(95) Chandler, A. R., and Barnhart, E. N. *A Bibliography of Psychological and Experimental Esthetics, 1864–1937.* (University of California Press: Berkeley, Calif., 1938) 190 pp.

(96) Hammond, William. *Bibliography of Aesthetics and of Philosophy of Fine Arts.* (Longmans, Green, and Co.: New York, 1934. Rev. ed.) 205 pp.

CHAPTER XXVI

RECENT RESEARCH IN THE PSYCHOLOGY OF ART

NORMAN C. MEIER
Associate Professor of Psychology
State University of Iowa
Iowa City, Iowa

I. INTRODUCTORY

The interests of art-psychologists, insofar as they relate to art education, have included; first, the nature and variety of the child's efforts to express himself graphically and the ways in which this expression may best be cultivated and encouraged; second, the extent of variability in the performance; third, the detection of unusual products and their significance; fourth, the nature of talent and the interrelations of hereditary and environmental factors in its determination. On the side of appreciation, it has studied the conditions and factors that tend to explain the development of appreciation. In the course of this phase, psychology of art has thrown some light upon esthetic theory, chiefly upon the reasons why some pictures yield to the observer higher degrees of satisfaction than do others.

The psychology of art has hence attempted to provide suggestions and, in some cases, tentative answers to such problems as the following. First, does the young child, as in nursery school and the early grades, use crayon or other material for purposes other than play or self-expression? Second, what may account for the observed variability in the interests of different children and in the skill with which different children handle materials? Third, why does there seem to be in the later grades a gradual withdrawal of most children from art activities? Fourth, is there some ascertainable hereditary factor operative that makes it difficult, if not impossible to get, even with expert teaching, good results from all children? Fifth, what is involved in the creative process, and what, if anything, can education do to encourage its furtherance in more and more children? Sixth, what may seem to be the prospect for effecting a more adequate teaching of art appreciation for all children?

This chapter will review some of the more significant studies made by individuals in several fields with a variety of objectives. All the studies in the bibliography cannot be individually discussed, but those believed to be of particular interest are so indicated by asterisks. Not all these studies meet the requirements of rigid scientific procedure, since studies that enjoy ideal conditions, with an incontestable adequacy of subjects, permitting positive final conclusions, are rare in this field of psychology as in others. It is believed, nevertheless, that, in view of the limitations and paucity of resources, the results of any apparently well-planned study should be accepted provisionally for what they are worth until the findings have been revised or disproved by subsequent studies.[1]

Generally considered, the child in the preschool years uses graphic expression for a variety of ends, among which is chiefly that of play with materials, later taking the form of constructions that aid him in his concept development. In the early grades other objectives enter, in some cases spontaneously and in others fostered by the educational program. Here a variety of contrasted aims may be found, ranging from the requirement of the child to attempt to reproduce objects of nature very much as they appear before him to the complete liberty afforded in the so-called ' progressive ' philosophy that, in its more extreme applications, permits him to do anything he chooses on any kind of theme. The problem here is largely one of striking a balance between the procedure of finding what the child can do and the significance of his effort. Psychologically, the best results here follow from permitting the child to draw things with which he has had adequate sensory contact. This process usually confines itself to illustration of activities and experiences, either individual or participated in by the group. There seems to be a difference of opinion as to whether the child here draws what he really sees or what he knows, or a mixture of what he sees and experiences through various sensory avenues. The series of studies following will open up more clearly the nature of this problem.

II. Studies of the Process of Graphic Expression in the Child

The analysis of spontaneous drawings by children in different cultures by Anastasi and Foley (1),[2] based on 602 drawings by children

---

[1] A less favorable view of American research in the psychology of art is expressed in Chapter XXI. — T. M.

[2] Numbers in parentheses pertain to the list of references at the end of this chapter.

between the ages of 6 and 12 from 42 countries, disclosed principally that intercultural differences appear in the drawings, and that there was a general correspondence between the subject matter and details of the drawings and concrete cultural factors present where the drawing was produced. This, of course, is a verification of the widespread observation that children use the drawing medium to interpret and express their reactions to local stimulating conditions. A number of studies, however, disclose that the drawing process in children generally (assuming that an extensive international collection represents the better than average achievement) follows the pattern largely of concept delineation.

Kobayashi (62), studying the way children of ages 4 to 11 draw from models, found an inability to perceive and express an object as a divided whole, primarily through inadequate development of aids to spatial perception, with age, intelligence, and feeling-state also affecting the activity. It is maintained that the act depends upon the principles of stabilization, equilibration, and simplification of figures, which the child at this age range has not yet mastered. From their examination of the drawings made by 1648 Japanese children of both sexes from a direct impression of a moving train, Iinuma and Watanabe (52) reported that 71 were clearly influenced by models other than that immediately seen; 22 of the drawings were not trains; 12 were obscure as to the running direction; and 26 were front views of the train, while the remainder were abortive attempts. This study would seem to support the general belief that children in the early years draw, not what they see, but what they know. However, Huang (49), in a study of drawings of 351 Chinese children in the nursery school and early grades, concluded that the drawing behavior of Chinese children, while quite similar to that of Occidental children, was based on the phenomena of perceptual constancies, and indicated that the child draws what he sees naïvely, whereas the artist draws what he sees in a special sophisticated way, which presumes considerable knowledge and training.

This view draws apparent support from a strange source. Rouma (122) reports the free drawings of adult, illiterate Aymara and Ouechua Indians on the Bolivian plateau to be practically interchangeable with drawings of normal three- to six-year-old children, with the same hesitations, errors, and stages in drawing; but after three weeks' training they passed rapidly from one stage of performance to another, reaching one corresponding to the twelve-year-old child's standard. The adults exhibited marked superiority over children in animal drawing.

An earlier unpublished study by a psychologist in New Mexico disclosed that, in the drawing-of-a-man test, white children were superior to Indian children, but in a comparable drawing-of-a-horse test Navajo children were definitely superior to white children. A third study, made by Mott (102), supplies similar evidence that the child draws best that which is interrelated with significant behavior and experience in his immediate associations. Even such feeling-states as happy, cold, suffering, and the like are made materially more effective through overt movements, as in motor training through pantomime, dances, or gymnastics preliminary to the actual drawing. In the study by Schiebe (124), 478 children between the ages of 4 and 18 made 2,519 drawings of a tree to suggest states of feeling such as those mentioned. The experiment demonstrated that the specific tone of feelings and their cognate conditions or qualities of consciousness are determined and governed by empirical motor characteristics. This educational principle has been followed for many years in the art education department of a prominent university. Kröber's study (66) of the drawing of forms from memory supports one aspect of this view in that reproductions are not so much expressive of the *form* of the figure, as of the emotional (impressional) value of that form upon the drawer.

Block-building, usually considered as simply a play occupation of children, is believed now to have significance in indicating early vocational tendencies. This was indicated by the study of Czurles (23), who found from an intensive study of a single child during the first three years of life that there are definite recurrent organizational patterns in the handling of three-dimensional objects. This study is supported by day-by-day records and hundreds of photographic illustrations. Guanella (40), following diary records and laboratory observation, discloses that block-building activities proceed through four stages; namely, nonstructural, linear (about 97 weeks), areal (133 weeks), tridimensional (about 190 weeks), with the culmination of block-building arrived at between the ages of four and seven. Like Czurles, he indicates that there are probably some individual variations in these activities that have possible vocational reference.

Körperth-Tippel (Vienna), studying the reactions of children of 3 to 14 years, found that while rudiments of esthetic expression could be detected even among the youngest subjects, the attention of the typical child was up to the eighth year primarily upon the object of the picture. At the tenth year the esthetic attitude begins to dominate, and by the fourteenth the tendency to prefer the artistic picture begins to become fairly general.

In a prolonged and carefully conducted series of experiments with Iowa school children in the second through the sixth grades in two widely spread communities, Voss (144) arrived at the conclusion that, while considerable individual differences exist, children at these ages (7 to 11 years) were able to profit readily from guidance in the experiencing of esthetic principles and disclosed some degree of capacity without opportunity to experience art systematically. Since sampling procedures have disclosed a remarkable similarity in response where cultural conditions are approximately comparable, there is no reason to assume that these conclusions need be restricted to the two samplings of Iowa children.

In the matter of simple appreciation of pictures by school children, Kubo (68) had children complete imperfect pictures prepared by professional painters. The children added the objects or strokes they felt necessary for the completed work. This interesting experiment disclosed that, while in the first grade children like clear and distinct pictures, in the higher grades this tendency decreases and there is increasing preference for simplified, vague, and rough pictures, and there is an additional tendency toward attempting to build up a completed whole (in the younger ages the completions were enumerative and fragmentary). Pan (112), by a process of exposure through successive stages to repeated materials, found that the familiarization tended to guide preferences for pictures at the expense of other works seen later that had no common experiential element. In time, however, the familiarization tended to influence esthetic judgment less and less, until the effect ultimately disappeared. Another influence long known to affect esthetic judgment — suggestion — was reverified by Sisson (131), who exhibited plates from the Meier-Seashore Test to subjects along with, in some instances, suggestions and check marks, in other instances with check marks alone, and in a third group with no suggestions. The presence of the suggestions or check marks led to slight changes in previous indications of preference, but in the main the earlier judgments held. From a different approach and with a different objective, Cahalan (16) had subjects rate reproductions of artists' sketches and Meier-Seashore material. When, after a period of one year, she repeated the exercise, she found that the two sets of judgments corresponded very closely. In this case, there was no attempt at suggestion, but merely an effort to determine the consistency of judgment. In this study it was also disclosed that, if the subject had attained a more advanced understanding of the nature of esthetic principles and criteria of value in art, he was more likely to be consistent. Walton (148), in studying the empathic responses of children, found that, although well-marked individual differences were present up to the age of 12, a condition of maturity in esthetic response was not reached until that age, and that even then the maturity was less than that characteristic of adults.

With older subjects, such as are found in high school and colleges, some more ambitious and complex investigations of the appreciational processes have been accomplished. Hevner and Mueller (46) secured ratings on a nine-point scale from 180 subjects at different times on the same five mountain-landscape paintings. Each subject was then provided with material describing four of the five pictures. Four types of appreciative ideas were introduced: anecdotal and bibliographical data on the painter, literary interpretation of his work, the mood and meaning of the picture, and a formal analysis of each picture. Most preferences were for realism, and in the retests following the use of the ideas the largest gain came in response to the type of material most remote from the actual esthetic subject (also the less clear and comprehensible to the subject). The use of the appreciation aids tended to raise the rating of that picture on retest. Brighouse (12), using a carefully controlled technique of showing quick exposures of a work of art to subjects in the dark room, repeating the process sufficiently, and recording all responses as given, found that the ' non-art ' adult and the child are satisfied earlier than the artistically competent person, who continues to experience more and more aspects of the painting with prolonged exposures. Since this study eliminated the aspect of familiarity, confusion of constantly continued exposure, and inhibitions arising from too many experiences simultaneously, the conclusion must be drawn that the appreciational process is augmented by learning and by significant experience of other kinds. By a somewhat similar process, Clair (22), who used paintings having an almost inexhaustible number of esthetic qualities, attempted to record by means of a comprehensive check list the detection and enumeration of esthetic qualities observed in the picture by high-school art students. Her conclusion suggests that the teaching of art in the high school tends to feature two-dimensional comprehension of art products almost to the complete neglect of three-dimensional considerations, and that in the process the important aspect of unity is imperfectly conveyed, if arrived at at all, in the educative process.

The aspect of unity in a work of art was studied by Kellett (56). On the assumption that the casual photograph of a given setting would lack the many opportunities for unification available to the artist, she projected side by side, by a quick-exposure technique similar to that of Brighouse, a well-organized painting and a casual photograph of the scene from which the artist had constructed his painting. Since she found that the subjects did not consistently and uniformly prefer the organized painting to the photograph, it seemed logical to conclude that this condition is probably more general than is ordinarily assumed, and hence so much time is spent in piecemeal study of separate aspects of production that complete functional training is seriously handicapped. In fact, the binding, organizing, and unifying techniques are postponed in the training process so long that, if gotten to finally, they are usually inadequately treated. Hence Kellett concluded that art instruction in the secondary school has tended not to place adequate emphasis upon unity. At the college and professional level this short-coming is not probably much in evidence. The more complete organizational unity of every composition attempted is insisted upon, and in some instances also a complete working out to the last detail is required before any painting is permitted.

III. STUDIES OF THE CREATIVE PROCESS

Recent research has led to several broad generalizations regarding the creative process, but the process is still far from being adequately understood. There is less tendency today to regard creative imagination as anything other than a normal process carried to a more highly developed and specialized form than is ordinarily met with in common experience. Whether studied in children or in adults or in mature artists, it seems to devolve upon at least three conditions or factors: first, more adequate, accurate, and extensive perceptual experience than a normal situation involves; second, some greater degree of emotional reinforcement of the experience; and third, greater than usual intelligence applied to the handling or technique employed to express the experience or to translate it into an art product. Incidental data from experiments seem to support the growing conviction that most individuals have the ability to experience and utilize creative imagination to some degree, but that there are extreme variations and that these extreme variations are to be accounted for on the basis of a higher degree of the three aspects just reviewed, so that the introduction of an undemonstrable functioning of some metaphysical process is unnecessary.

In specific studies, such as the one by Markey (82) made on 54 children all under four years of age, individual differences are disclosed even at this tender age — differences attributable to such factors as more imaginative behavior, and association with older children. The imaginative play of children of lower socio-economic status was somewhat more prosaic than the play of children of higher status. Also, the imaginative behavior was found to be correlated somewhat higher with mental than with chronological age. It would seem that even at this very early stage differentiations in the three factors listed are beginning to show. Schildre (125), in a study of children's drawings, points out that, though children's drawings reflect primitive visual motor organization differing from that of adults, nevertheless the experience of *Gestalt units* is revealed in both cases. In both children and adults the emotional interest in the object depicted is the main factor and represents an expression of the desire for constructive adaptation to the world and the single objects therein.

In a recent work Löwenfeld (80) describes studies of art productions by blind and weak-sighted persons in comparison with those of normal children and primitive groups. From this vantage point, Löwenfeld observes that normal vision is by no means essential for artistic production; that it tends to handicap rather than facilitate expressive work. Indeed, complete dependence upon visual impressions tends to limit the work essentially to a reproductive character, whereas the individual (which Löwenfeld characterizes as the haptic type) who relies heavily upon kinesthetic and tactual experiences, fortified by a richly affective life, realizes a fuller expression. Pure haptic drawings are characterized by excessive emphasis upon a central theme with minor details omitted or glossed over and with considerable use of symbols that express feeling without much reliance upon visual anatomical facts. It would seem that this type of creative activity might in general secure a higher degree of unity, positively by its simplification and concentration upon gross forms and negatively by its avoidance of possibly irrelevant minor developments. Dwelshauvers (28) investigated creative imagination through the use of incomplete drawings that his subjects were asked to finish. Some of the drawings were meaningless; others were supposed to suggest meaning. He concluded from his study that persons with no imaginative invention are very rare, that subjects terminate their operations with a great variety of results, that drawing ability does not seem to be essentially tied up with creative imagination, but that there seems to be some correlation between drawing ability and inventive intuition.[1] His findings also included the indication that imaginative invention is more often reason than intuition. Patrick (114) adapted her procedure used in studying creative thought among poets to an investigation of fifty professional artists and fifty unpracticed sketchers. She reports that processes very similar to those found in the poets characterize the artists — a process that likewise is more rational than intuitive and that proceeds through four stages; namely, preparation, incubation, illumination, verification. The course of thought she also found is similar between artists and non-artists, but that artists arrive at their products apparently with less effort, yet spend about the same time in the thinking stage.

A wholly different approach involving several years' study and the construction of a novel apparatus by means of which compositions could be produced at will by manipulating colored light on gray-green colored figures and backgrounds was devised by the writer and utilized by him and W. McCloy (85, 86, 89). The apparatus offered the advantage of being suitable for subjects of all ages, regardless of training and skill in handling the media of art. By acquainting the subject with the apparatus and offering him for manipulation a wide study of ' properties,' he could manipulate the controls at will until he had achieved a composition to his own satisfaction. In this manner it was disclosed that creative imagination was present in some degree in practically all the subjects, that it was not correlated with age, and that some of the untrained subjects produced compositions that ranked with the best when evaluated by competent art judges. It is significant, to take examples, that some of the best compositions were made by a fifteen-year-old girl, a twenty-six-year-old holder of a doctorate in the psychology of art, and a nine-year-old boy. In a second approach to the study of creative imagination, abstractions were projected on a screen from colored slides and viewed by high-school art students, who indicated whether they were able to sense the expressive content of the picture. The results in this instance disclosed ability in some persons to approximate the artist's idea; in others, complete bafflement. Negative results were also obtained for the most part to compositions prepared by McCloy (87) by means of Dufay process film, and then exhibited to

---

[1] Inventive intuition, contrasted with creative imagination, refers to a more subtle process of developing an art product, implying that the stages are not to any real degree consciously realized.

subjects with the expectation that they could rank variations in the compositional themes and also identify the prevailing mood. A further approach (92) led the subject, when viewing an abstract composition that had been checked with the painter previously, through an involved process of progressive perception with opportunities to give a total reaction at each of five stages. In this study again high-school students with few exceptions were unable to grasp the universal concepts necessary for an adequate *rapprochement* to the artist's theme. At least two of these studies revealed clearly that complex imagination of the types studied — reconstructive, reproductive, and re-creative — is possessed only rarely and represents a maturity of social experience, cultural contacts, and vision that has been attained at the high-school stage by only a few individuals. This seems to be in accord with the findings of other investigators that superior artistic ability and creativity are not plentifully supplied in the general population; probably not more than one person in twenty is presumptive material for advanced development.

IV. THE DETERMINERS OF TALENT

Despite much controversy over the relative contribution of heredity and environment in this and other phases of human traits, the question is still unanswered, although recent research has greatly enlarged our understanding of the probable relationship of the two factors in determining artistic talent. It now seems a futile quest to assign the burden of influence to one *or* the other; rather one should regard the relation as an interlinkage of these two factors.

A number of studies need mention at this juncture for whatever light they may throw on the general problem. Sterzinger (135) holds artistic aptitude to consist of, first, certain general abilities, such as "sensory concentration," ability in recall, patience, and perseverance; and second, some specific function-complex expressed as ability to conceive and perceive form, to interpret, to approach relationships and harmony of color and line, and to imagine. The latter ability is characterized in the artist by precision in imagining and facility in enlarging, multiplying, and fusing images. Flemming (31), in an informal study utilizing teachers' ratings of high-school girls for personality traits, points to the following as often associated with artistic ability — idealism, originality, wide interests, cleverness, culture, and individuality. Manifestations of ability of the artistically gifted child, according to Cane (18), are the following: (1) quality of line, rhythm, and balance,

(2) dynamic imagination, (3) effectiveness of the design and organization, and (4) spirit and vitality of the whole composition. These gifted children she suggests " should be treated just as normal children, leading a healthy everyday life with regular work and play, only with more time set aside for the studies of their special gifts." Normal living is also suggested by Seeman (126) in his observation that the sequence in the growth of drawing activities is about the same for most children but that the time factor is different; the child with no genius progresses slowly, and the one with marked genius, rapidly. A rich artistic environment in early childhood stimulates the unfolding of the graphic abilities. In comparing the artistic ability of 100 American children between the ages of 18 months and 7 years with that of 100 Chinese children of the same ages, Seeman noted a similarity in the development of this ability, with whatever variation there may be (concerned chiefly with the degree of genius) conditioned somewhat by racial culture and immediate environmental conditions.

The Iowa Spelman-Carnegie project " Genetic Studies in Artistic Capacity " is, considering time continued, number of persons engaged, and subjects covered, the most comprehensive and sustained project to explore the nature of creative mind and the factors and conditions affecting the creative process. While little of the data from thirty published studies (volumes appearing in 1933, 1936, and 1939) can be reviewed here, several of the more significant findings should be mentioned. This project secured the collaborative effort of artists, art educators, and child- and art-psychologists, involved subjects ranging from nursery-school children to aged artists, and extended its inquiry into heredity as well as taking account of present activities. Most of the following items refer to my published summary (93).

The preponderance of evidence in the fifteen years' accumulation of data points strongly to the conception of artistic capacity as a complex of abilities and functions — six in number — *that are peculiarly interlinked*. Discarding the either-heredity-*or*-environment alternative as gratuitous, the investigations amass evidence to show that the six factors interlink and condition the development of one another in a way hitherto never suspected.

Three of the six factors — *manual skill*, or craftsman ability; *volitional perseverance;* and *esthetic intelligence* — are believed to refer primarily to heredity; the other three — *perceptual facility, creative imagination,* and *esthetic judgment* — refer more directly to learning. But the point of most interest and significance is that the latter three, while advanced most by learning, are in that very process conditioned by the craftsman attitude and manner of work. Since manual skill, a first essential to artistic production, appears now to be a concomitant of constitutional *stock* heredity (not direct specific inheritance), it is apparent that to have many craftsmen among one's ancestors is of far more significance than heretofore envisioned. Genetically, it means simply that such an individual is of the stock *from which the artist may develop* most readily and surely.

On this point five studies (54, 78, 98, 117, 130) contribute support. There is this difference, however, that mere finding of a preponderance of artists in a given family line presumptively tends to favor the heredity hypothesis, whereas the conclusions of the Spelman-Carnegie program point to constitutional *stock* inheritance as only the beginning of the full explanation. In the latter view it comes to this: without *some* craftsman heredity in the stock, little progress will be made by the art-student aspirant; with constitutional *stock* inheritance all other things will be added thereto, granting requisite energy, incentives, experience, and opportunities. The craftsman attitude is essentially deep regard for careful workmanship, painstaking interest in detail and completed effect, and a voluntary setting of high standards of accomplishment. It is, moreover, the determiner for *volitional perseveration* (self-election of a degree of persistent thoroughness requisite to a given end) and for *perceptual facility*. This factor refers to the manner of experiencing and organizing contact with one's world. The craftsman attitude features, compared to typical individuals, a more detailed, a more adequate, and a more retentive perception. This more rapidly accumulating, richer, and more varied [1] perceptual stock of material then, in turn, provides for the artistic personality a greater variety and number of suggestions for subsequent growth in use of themes, in selection of subject matter, and in manner of development — which is virtually most of what there is to *creative imagination*. It is thus observable that in the year-by-year development of the artist-personality it is the craftsman attitude that conditions that development at every turn. The two remaining factors are indicative of the *depth* of development of which the individual is capable. *Esthetic intelligence* — probably determined more by heredity — marks the facility and readiness with which the individual will profit from experience, particularly experience that is likely to advance the quality and effectiveness of his work from year to year. The final factor, *esthetic judgment*, regarded by ninety

---

[1] Differences are found to be present in six-year-olds.

percent of competent artists studied as a crucial factor in artistic capacity, is one that is never completely and finally mastered by anyone. But here, too, the perhaps most single dominant fact is that the craftsman manner, being basically a fine regard for *orderly arrangement*, makes the easy acquisition of a major degree of esthetic judgment inevitable and permits its sure functioning in time almost as second nature.

The education of the producer of art would thus follow, not disregard, the natural conditions that make it easy for some individuals, difficult for others, to attain eventual effectiveness in the field. While there lie in the body of research and investigations certain suggestions for a more effective education of the art consumer (appreciation), this field is still open to further more serious study.

V. Summary

It is my belief that psychological research can help to formulate and clarify the fundamental concepts of art. Careful research can go far in reducing internal dissension based upon personal opinion or lack of appreciation of the basic processes involved in art.

The art educator who is receptive to the enlarging conceptions of the graphic processes at all its stages finds that the mysticism still shrouding these natural processes is being dispelled and replaced by understanding of individual variations, and by scientific conceptions of special ability and of the creative processes.

A summary of tentative findings in the psychology of art can at best be inadequate in the light of all we would like to know, but some approximation would seem to be desirable.

Through research we find that in the nursery-school stage graphic activity commences as manipulative play, that it soon begins to play a part in concept development (along with speech), and that, even then, it is marked by definite individual differences. In the process the typical child may draw naïvely what he sees because of his imperfectly developed concept. With the artistically superior child progress is rapid; with others the pace varies. In all instances those concepts are featured that have some strong emotional interest to the individual child. With boys this may include aeroplanes and trains; with girls, figures and costume; with both, houses and various incidents of their individual experience.

In the early grades the process continues unless deflected. Faulty teaching procedures are often the cause of the deflection. Good judgment would indicate that best results would follow from effort on the part of the teacher, either to learn the dominant interests of her children and exploit those interests at the level of development concerned, or to provide common interests (class trips to fire-engine house, bakery, or farm) with encouragement of the child to perceive more adequately whatever his interest dictates and to express the object of his interest effectively and individually.

Appreciation may then follow — never precede — the child's own effort to organize graphically his emotionally reinforced experience. Principles (balance, rhythm, unity, and the like) may then be explained *as qualities inhering in successful organization;* and the more *ingeniously* a work of art is organized *with* attainment of such qualities, the more satisfying it becomes. *Unity* may profitably be set up as a desired goal from the start, not left until the twelfth grade or never gotten around to at all. The drawing of an orange may be a project of great interest if it is drawn *in a setting;* but merely as a task for imitative rendering it will be just another bore. In the one instance *ingenuity in arranging* challenges the drive of the pupil; in the other, mere manual skill.

Some production should be the experience of every child; it can be made the basis for the subsequent development of a sounder appreciation; certainly so if it affords a grasp of the fundamental conception that art rests upon principles attained ingeniously.

Progress in appreciation is best assured when tied up with the pupil's interests and environment, when a broad conception of art prevails, and when the applied phases are not neglected. Youth, particularly, is interested in motor-car design and aeroplanes (which exhibit unity, rhythm, transition) as well as in murals and regional Americana.

But it now becomes more than probable, in the light of continuous research, that only certain children may attain ultimate effectiveness *as artists.* Such a degree of effectiveness is now revealed as conditioned by an interaction of complex factors involving the type of stock from which the individual has descended, the way he utilizes his developmental opportunities, and the possession of certain personality traits and drives. Only close study of these significant findings will yield the clear understanding necessary to enable the earnest educator to plan educational facilities intelligently to take care of those whose potentialities should be identified and trained in order best to serve society.

References [1]

(1) Anastasi, A., and Foley, J. P., Jr. "An analysis of spontaneous drawings by children in different cultures." *Jour. Appl. Psychol.*, 20: 1936, 689–726.

(2) Anastasi, A., and Foley, J. P., Jr. "A study of animal drawings by Indian children of the north Pacific coast." *Jour. Soc. Psychol.*, 9: 1938, 363–374.

(3) Atwell, S. "Color vision in relation to artistic ability." *Psychol. Bull.*, 36: 1939, 647.

(4) Barnhart, E. N. "The criteria used in preferential judgments of geometrical forms." *Amer. Jour. Psychol.*, 53: 1940, 354–370.

(5) Barwell, J. S. "The nature of ugliness." *Brit. Jour. Med. Psychol.*, 17: 1937, 119–127.

(6) Bergemann-Könitzer, M. "Entwicklungsaufbau plastischer Gestaltung." (The structural development of plastic form). *Z. Jugendk.*, 5: 1935, 42–50.

(7) Beebe-Center, J. G., and Pratt, C. C. "A test of Birkhoff's esthetic measure." *Jour. Gen. Psychol.*, 17: 1937, 339–353.

(8) Birkhoff, G. D. "The present status of esthetic measure." *Sci. Mo.*, 46: 1938, 351–357.

(9) Bose, R. C. "On the construction of balanced incomplete block designs." *Ann. Eugen.* 9: 1939, 353–399.

(10) Bowers, D. F. "The rôle of subject matter in art." *Jour. Phil.*, 36: 1939, 617–630.

(11) Brighouse, G. "The effects of protracted observation of a painting." *Psychol. Bull.*, 36: 1939, 552.

*(12) Brighouse, G. "A Study of Aesthetic Apperception." *Psychol. Monogr.*, 51: 1939, 1–22.

(13) Brighouse, G. "Variability in Preferences for Simple Forms." *Psychol. Monogr.*, 51: 1939, 68–74.

(14) Burkhardt, H. "Ueber Verlagerung raümlicher Gestalten." (On the alteration of spatial forms.) *Neue psychol. Stud.*, 7: 1933, 158.

*(15) Buswell, G. T. *How People Look at Pictures: A Study of the Psychology and Perception of Art.* (University of Chicago Press: Chicago, 1935)

*(16) Cahalan, E. J. "The Consistency of Aesthetic Judgment." *Psychol. Monogr.*, 51: 1939, 75–87.

(17) Cameron, N. "Functional immaturity in the symbolization of scientifically trained adults." *Jour. Psychol.*, 6: 1938, 161–175.

*(18) Cane, F. "The gifted child in art." *Jour. Educ. Sociol.*, 10: 1936, 67–73.

*(19) Carroll, H. A. "A preliminary report on a study of the relationship between ability in art and certain personality traits." *School and Soc.*, 36: 1932, 285–288.

(20) Carroll, H. A. "A preliminary report on a study of the interrelationships of certain appreciations." *Jour. Educ. Psychol.*, 23: 1932, 505–510.

*(21) Carroll, H. A., and Eurich, A. C. "Abstract intelligence and art appreciation." *Jour. Educ. Psychol.*, 23: 1932, 214–220.

---

[1] References to which an asterisk is prefixed are especially recommended by the author of the chapter for further study of the topics discussed herein. — *Editor.*

*(22) CLAIR, M. B. " Variation in the Perception of Aesthetic Qualities in Paintings." *Psychol. Monogr.*, 51: 1939, 52–67.

*(23) CZURLES, S. A. " The Emergence of Art Abilities in the First Three Years of Life." (Master's Thesis, Syracuse University Library: Syracuse, 1938)

(24) DAVIS, F. C. " Aesthetic proportion." *Amer. Jour. Psychol.*, 45: 1933, 298–302.

(25) DAVIS, R. C. " An evaluation and test of Birkhoff's aesthetic measurement formula." *Jour. Gen. Psychol.*, 15: 1936, 231–240.

(26) DIDIER, J. " Comment travaille l'imagination créatrice." (How creative imagination works.) *Psychol. et Vie*, 4: 1930, 118–121.

*(27) DREPS, H. F. " The Psychophysical Capacities and Abilities of College Art Students of High and Low Standing." *Psychol. Monogr.*, 45: 1933, 134–146.

*(28) DWELSHAUVERS, G. " Recherches expérimentales sur l'imagination créatrice." (Experimental research on creative imagination.) *Jour. Psychol. norm. path.*, 32: 1935, 435–442.

(29) EIGLER, P. " The Kohs block-design test." *Child Development*, 1: 1930, 341–342.

(30) EURICH, A. C., and CARROLL, H. A. " Group differences in art judgment." *School and Soc.*, 34: 1931, 204–206.

(31) FLEMMING, E. G. " Personality and artistic talent." *Jour. Educ. Sociol.*, 8: 1934, 27–33.

(32) FOMENKO, K. E. (The perception of pictures of spatial and perspective relations in the preschool age.) [In] *Psikhologitchni doslidzennia. Naookovi zapiski.* (Derj. Ped. Institut: Kharkov, 1939) 101–199.

(33) GARRISON, K. C. " Psychology of special abilities." *Peabody Reflector*, 12: 1939, 11–13.

(34) GINSBURG, A. M. (" Proportions and equilibrium of mass in architecture.") *Psikhotekn. i psikhofiziol. truda,* 1931, 46–55.

*(35) GOODENOUGH, F. L. " Children's Drawings." [In] *A Handbook of Child Psychology.* (Clark University Press: Worcester, 1931) 480–514.

(36) GRAEWE, H. *Untersuchung der Entwicklung des Zeichnens.* (A study of the development of drawing.) (Schroedel: Halle, 1932)

(37) GRAEWE, H. " Das Tierzeichnen der Kinder." (Children's drawings of animals.) *Z. pädag. Psychol.*, 36: 1935, 251–256, 291–300.

(38) GRIDLEY, P. F. " Graphic Representation of a Man by Four-year-old Children in Nine Prescribed Drawing Situations." *Genet. Psychol. Monogr.*, 20: 1938, 183–350.

(39) GRIMES, J. W. " Values in a work of art." *Educ. Res. Bull., Ohio State University,* 19: 1940, 283–292.

(40) GUANELLA, F. M. " Block-building activities of young children." *Arch. Psychol.* (New York), 1934, 92.

*(41) GUILFORD, J. P., and GUILFORD, R. B. " A prognostic test for students in design." *Jour. Appl. Psychol.*, 15: 1931, 335–345.

(42) HARSH, C. M., BEEBE-CENTER, J. G., and BEEBE-CENTER, R. " Further evidence regarding preferential judgment of polygonal forms." *Jour. Psychol.*, 7: 1939, 343–350.

(43) HEATON, M. L. " The inheritance of artistic traits." *Eug. News*, 16: 1932, 211–213.

(44) HETZER, H. " Kind und Schaffen, Experimente über konstruktive Betäti-
gungen im Kleinkindalter." (Creative ability in children; experiments
on constructive occupations of preschool children.) *Quellen u. Stud. z.
Jugendk.,* 7: 1931, 108.

*(45) HEVNER, K. " Experimental studies of the affective value of colors and
lines." *Jour. Appl. Psychol.,* 19: 1935, 385–398.

*(46) HEVNER, K., and MUELLER, J. H. " The effectiveness of various types of
art appreciation aids." *Jour. Abnorm. Soc. Psychol.,* 34: 1939, 63–72.

*(47) HOLLINGWORTH, L. S. " Special Gifts and Special Deficiencies." [In] *A
Handbook of Child Psychology.* (Clark University Press: Worcester, 1931)
627–642.

(48) HOMMA, T. (The law of Prägnanz in the process of drawing figures.) *Jap.
Jour. Psychol.,* 12: 1937, 112–153.

(49) HUANG, I. " The Psychology of Children's Drawings." (Commercial Press:
Shanghai, 1938)

(50) HURLOCK, E. B., and THOMSON, J. L. " Children's drawings: an experimental study of perception." *Child Development,* 5: 1934, 127–138.

(51) HUTH, A. " Neigung und Eignung." (Inclination and talent.) *Z.
Jugendk.,* 4: 1934, 198–206.

*(52) IINUMA, R., and WATANABE, K. (Observations on moving objects drawn
by children. Orientation and motion of railway trains.) *Jap. Jour.
Psychol.,* 12: 1937, 393–408.

*(53) JACOBSON, W. " Basic Aesthetic Factors in Costume Design." *Psychol.
Monogr.,* 45: 1933, 147–184.

(54) KAHN, R. " Inheritance of ability in drawing." *Eug. News,* 16: 1931,
42.

(55) KATO, M. " Kantanna zukei ni okeru biteki wariai no jikken-bigaku-teki
kenkyü." (An experimental study on esthetic proportion in simple forms.)
Jap. Jour. Exp. Psychol., 5: 1938, 57–61.

*(56) KELLETT, K. R. " A Gestalt Study of the Function of Unity in Aesthetic
Perception." *Psychol. Monogr.,* 51: 1939, 23–51.

(57) KERR, M. " Children's drawings of houses." *Brit. Jour. Med. Psychol.,*
16: 1937, 206–218.

(58) KIENZLE, R. *Das bildhafte Gestalten als Ausdruck der Persönlichkeit.*
(Pictorial forms as expressions of the personality.) (Esslingen: Burg-
bücherei, 1932)

*(59) KINTER, M. *The Measurement of Artistic Abilities: A Survey of Scien-
tific Studies in the Field of Graphic Arts.* (Psychological Corporation: New
York, 1933)

(60) KLINE, L. W., and CAREY, G. L. " A Measuring Scale for Free-Hand Drawing. Part II. Design and Composition." *Hopkins Univ. Stud. Educ.,*
1933, No. 5.

(61) KNAUBER, A. J. *The Knauber Art Vocabulary Test.* (Published by the
author: Cincinnati, 1935)

(62) KOBAYASHI, S. (A study on a variation of facsimiles drawn by children.)
Jap. Jour. Psychol., 12: 1937, 375–392.

(63) KOESTER, H. L. " Ueber das Verhaltnis der intellectuellen Begabung zur
musikalischen, zeichnerischen, und technischen Begabung." (On the rela-

tions between intellectual aptitudes and talents for music, drawing, and technical skills.) *Zsch. f. päd. Psychol.*, 31: 1930, 399–403.

(64) Körperth-Tippel, A. (Child and picture.) (Deutscher Verlag für Jugend und Volk: Vienna; n.d.)

(65) Krause, W. "Experimentelle Untersuchungen über die Vererbung der zeichnerischen Begabung. I." (Experimental investigations of the inheritance of drawing ability. I.) *Zsch. f. Psychol.*, 126: 1932, 86–145.

(66) Kröber, W. "Über das Aufzeichnen von Formen aus dem Gedächtnis." (Concerning the drawing of forms from memory.) *Z. Angew. Psychol.*, 54: 1938, 273–327.

(67) Kruger, G. "Analyse der Denkvorgange beim Lesen von Werkzeichnungen." (Analysis of the thought processes involved in reading mechanical drawings.) *Psychotechn. Zsch.*, 1938, 24–33.

(68) Kubo, Y. (Children's appreciation of Japanese pictures.) *Trans. Inst. Child Stud.*, 17: 1937, 1–38.

(69) Kunde, L. A. "Aesthetic judgment of seventh-grade students of line in dress costume design." *Pittsb. Schs.*, 12: 1938, 141–154.

(70) Langford, R. C. "Ocular behavior and the principle of pictorial balance." *Psychol. Bull.*, 30: 1933, 679.

(71) Lark-Horovitz, B. "Interlinkage of sensory memories in relation to training in drawing." *Jour. Genet. Psychol.*, 49: 1936, 69–89.

*(72) Lark-Horovitz, B. "On art appreciation of children: I. Preference of picture subjects in general." *Jour. Educ. Res.*, 31: 1937, 118–137.

*(73) Lark-Horovitz, B. "On art appreciation of children: II. Portrait preference study." *Jour. Educ. Res.*, 31: 1938, 572–598.

*(74) Lark-Horovitz, B. "On art appreciation of children: III. Textile pattern preference study." *Jour. Educ. Res.*, 33: 1939, 7–35.

(75) Lark-Horovitz, B. "On art appreciation of children: IV. Comparative study of white and Negro children, 13 to 15 years old." *Jour. Educ. Res.*, 30: 1939, 258–285.

*(76) Lembke, W. "Über Zeichnungen von 'frechen' und 'schuchternen' Schulkindern." (The significance of drawings by "bold" and "shy" pupils.) *Zsch. f. päd. Psychol.*, 1930, 459–463.

(77) Levey, H. B. "A theory concerning free creation in the inventive arts." *Psychiatry*, 3: 1940, 229–293.

(78) Link, M. "Die Malerfamilie Tischbein." (The Tischbein family of painters.) *Arch. f. Rassen- u. Gesellschbiol.*, 27: 1933, 185–186.

(79) Loch, M. "Über Eidetik und Kinderzeichnung." (Concerning eidetic imagery and children's drawing.) *Arb. a. d. Psychol. Instit. d. München*, 2: 1931.

*(80) Löwenfeld, V. *The Nature of Creative Activity*. Translated by O. A. Oeser. (Harcourt, Brace and Co.: New York, 1939)

(81) Lucio, W. H., and Mead, C. D. "An investigation of children's preferences for modern pictures." *Elem. Sch. Jour.* 39: 1939, 678–689.

*(82) Markey, F. V. "Imaginative Behavior of Young Children." *Child Develpm. Monogr.*, 1935, No. 18.

(83) Martin, H. "Stile und Stilwandlungsgesetze der Kinderzeichnung, nachgewiesen an den Menschenzeichnungen der Volksschulkinder." (Styles and

laws of change in style in children's drawing as shown in drawings of a man by folkschool children.) *Vjsch. f. Jugendk.*, 2: 1932, 211–226.

(84) MARTIN, H. "Die Motivwahl und ihre Wandel in der freinen Zeichnung des Grundschulkindes." (Choice of motif and its change in spontaneous drawings of elementary pupils.) *Z. pädag. Psychol.*, 40: 1939, 231–241.

*(85) McCLOY, W. "Creative Imagination in Children and Adults." *Psychol. Monogr.*, 51: 1939, 88–102.

*(86) McCLOY, W. "Passive Creative Imagination." *Psychol. Monogr.*, 51: 1939, 103–107.

*(87) McCLOY, W., and MEIER, N. C. "Re-creative Imagination." *Psychol. Monogr.*, 51: 1939, 108–116.

*(88) MEIER, N. C. "Art Ability without Instruction or Environmental Background: Case Study of Loran Lockhart." *Psychol. Monogr.*, 48: 1936, 155–163.

(89) MEIER, N. C., and McCLOY, W. "An Instrument for the Study of Creative Artistic Intelligence." *Psychol. Monogr.*, 48: 1936, 164–172.

(90) MEIER, N. C. "What is special ability?" *Psychol. Bull.*, 36: 1939, 505.

(91) MEIER, N. C. "The perception of abstractions in graphic form." *Psychol. Bull.*, 34: 1937, 757.

*(92) MEIER, N. C. "Reconstructive Imagination." *Psychol. Monogr.*, 51: 1939, 117–126.

*(93) MEIER, N. C. "Factors in Artistic Aptitude: Final Summary of a Ten-Year Study of a Special Ability." *Psychol. Monogr.*, 51: 1939, 140–158.

*(94) MEIER, N. C. "Diagnosis in Art." *Thirty-fourth Yearbook* of this Society, 1935. Ch. XXII.

(95) MEIER, N. C. "The Graphic and Allied Arts." *Thirty-eighth Yearbook* of this Society, 1939. Ch. VIII.

(96) MEIER, N. C. "The Appreciational Arts." Ch. XIII, *1939 Yearbook, Nat. Educ. Assn. and Amer. Educ. Res. Assn.*

(97) MELLINGER, B. E. "Children's Interests in Pictures." *Teach. Coll. Contrib. Educ.*, 1932, No. 516.

(98) MERRY, R. C. "Art talent and racial background." *Jour. Educ. Res.*, 32: 1938, 17–22.

(99) MILLER, J. "Intelligence testing by drawings." *Jour. Educ. Psychol.*, 29: 1938, 390–394.

(100) MILLER, W. A. "What children see in pictures." *Elem. Sch. Jour.*, 39: 1938, 280–289.

(101) MORROW, R. S. "An analysis of the relations among tests of musical, artistic, and mechanical abilities." *Jour. Psychol.*, 5: 1938, 253–263.

*(102) MOTT, S. M. "The development of concepts. A study of children's drawings." *Child Develpm.*, 7: 1936, 144–148.

*(103) MOTT, S. M. "The growth of an abstract concept." *Child Develpm.*, 10: 1939, 21–25.

(104) MUELLER, J. "Studies in College Teaching." (*University of Oregon Publications*, 1934, 4, No. 6)

*(105) MUNDEL, L. R. "The Effect of Lectures on Art Principles upon Art Production at the Fifth- and Sixth-Grade Levels." *Psychol. Monogr.*, 51: 1939, 127–139.

(106) NATORP, F. "Ein Versuch zur Deutung von Kinderzeichnungen." (An investigation on the meaning of child drawings.) *Werdende Zeitalter,* 1930, 347–349.

(107) NEUBAUER, V. "Zur Entwicklung der dekorativen Zeichnung." (The development of decorative drawing.) *Zsch. f. angew. Psychol.,* 39: 1931, 273–325.

(108) OAKLEY, C. A. "Drawings of a man by adolescents." *Brit. Jour. Psychol.,* 31: 1940, 37–60.

(109) OAKLEY, C. A. "The interpretation of children's drawings." *Brit. Jour. Psychol.,* 21: 1931, 256–270.

(110) OVSEPJAN, G. T. (The evolution of observation in children.) *(Sci. Mem. pedag. Inst. Herzen)*, 18: 1939, 21–59.

(111) OYAMA, S., and KIDO, M. (An experimental study on plastic molding by children.) *Jap. Jour. Psychol.,* 14: 1939, 327–338.

*(112) PAN, S. (A study in esthetic judgment: the influence of familiarity.) *N. C. J. Psychol. nat. cent. Univ.,* 1934, 1, 10.

(113) PARLOG, C. *"Psihologia desemnului."* (Psychology of drawing.) Inst. de Psihol., Univ. Cluj: (Cluj, Rumania, 1932)

(114) PATRICK, C. "Creative thought in artists." *Jour. Psychol.,* 4: 1937, 35–73.

(115) PAUL, R. I. *Vieta Estetica.* (Esthetic life.) (Minerva: Cluj, 1937)

(116) PERKINS, F. T. "Symmetry in visual recall." *Amer. Jour. Psychol.,* 44: 1932, 473–490.

*(117) POPENOE, P. "The inheritance of artistic talents." *Jour. Hered.,* 20: 1929.

(118) RABELLO, S. Caractericas do desenho infantil. Contribução para o estudo psychologico da criança brasileira." (Characteristics of children's drawing. Contribution to the psychological study of the Brazilian child.) *Bol. Direct. tech. Educ., Pernambuco,* 2: 1932, 15–78.

(119) RATHE, K. *Die Ausdrucksfunktion extrem verkurzter Figuren.* (The expressive function of radically foreshortened figures.) (Warburg Institute: London, 1938)

(120) REINHARDT, H. "Studien zur Eignung zum Konstrukteurberuf." (Studies on aptitude for construction work.) *Indus. Psychotechn.,* 8: 1931, 263–265.

(121) ROBBINS, A. B. "The inheritance of designing capacity." *Eug. News,* 16: 1931, 192–193.

(122) ROUMA, G. "Dessins d'indiens quitchouas et aymaras. Le graphisme et l'expression graphique." (Drawings of the Quechua and Aymara Indians. Writing and graphic expression.) *Sem. univ. Pédag. Univ. libre Brux.,* 1: 1935, 133–147.

*(123) SAUNDERS, A. W. "The Stability of Artistic Aptitude at the Childhood Level." *Psychol. Monogr.,* 48: 1936, 126–153.

(124) SCHIEBE, G. "Erlebnismotorik und zeichnerischer (physiognomischer) Ausdruck bei Kindern und Jugendlichen. Zur Psychogenese der Ausdrucksgestaltung." (Empirical motor expression and graphic physiognomic expression in children and youth. On the psychogenesis of expressional representations.) *Z. Kinderforsch.,* 43: 1934, 40–76.

(125) SCHILDRE, P. "The child and the symbol." *Scientia,* Milano, 64: 1938, 21–26.

(126) SEEMAN, E. "Development of the pictorial aptitude in children." *Character and Personality,* 2: 1934, 209–221.

(127) Shabalin, S. N. (The objective-gnostic moments in the perception of form in preschool children.) *Sci. Mem. pedag. Inst. Herzen,* 18: 1939, 59–106.

(128) Shaffer, L. F. "Children's Interpretations of Cartoons." *Teach. Coll. Contrib. Educ.,* 1930, No. 429.

*(129) Shaw, R. F. *Finger Painting.* (Little, Brown and Co.: Boston, 1934)

(130) Shoemaker, R. "Student pedigree-studies. 51. Artistic ability in the Shoemaker family." *Eugen. News,* 22: 1937, 107–108.

(131) Sisson, E. D. "Suggestion in art judgment." *Jour. Gen. Psychol.,* 18: 1938, 433–435.

*(132) Spearman, C. "Is ability random or organized? *Jour. Educ. Psychol.,* 31: 1940, 305–310.

(133) Spielrein, S. "Kinderzeichnungen bei offenen und geschlossenen Augen: Untersuchungen über die unterschwelligen kinästhetischen Vorstellungen." (Children's drawings with the eyes open and shut: researches on kinesthetic images below the threshold of consciousness.) *Imago,* 17: 1931, 359–391.

(134) Spoerl, D. T. "Personality and drawing in retarded children." *Character and Pers.,* 8: 1940, 227–239.

(135) Sterzinger, O. "Zur Prufung und Untersuchung der kunstlerischen Veranlagung." (On the testing and examining of artistic ability.) *Psychotechn. Zsch.,* 6: 1931, 1–10.

(136) Stolz, A., and Manuel, H. T. "The art ability of Mexican children." *School and Soc.,* 34: 1931, 379–380.

(137) Takeda, T. "On the drawing of children." *Jap. Jour. Psychol.,* 9: 1934, 217–226.

*(138) Tiebout, C. "The Measurement of Quality in Children's Paintings by the Scale Method." *Psychol. Monogr.,* 1936, 85–94.

*(139) Tiebout, C., and Meier, N. C. "Artistic Ability and General Intelligence." *Psychol. Monogr.,* 48, 1936, 95–125.

(140) Varnum, W. H. *Selective Art Aptitude Test.* (International Textbook Co.: Scranton, 1939)

(141) Vernon, M. D. "The relation of cognition and phantasy in children." *Brit. Jour. Psychol.,* 30: 1940, 273–294.

*(142) Vernon, P. E. *The Measurement of Abilities.* (University of London Press: London, 1940)

(143) Vogt, W. "Zur Frage des Trainings." (The problem of training.) *Int. Zsch. f. Indiv.-psychol.,* 10: 1932, 146–151.

*(144) Voss, M. D. "An experimental study of the developmental processes in art appreciation." *Proc. Ia. Acad. Sci.,* 42: 1935, 173.

*(145) Voss, M. D. "A Study of Conditions Affecting the Functioning of the Art Appreciation Process at the Child Level." *Psychol. Monogr.,* 48: 1936, 1–39.

(146) Voss, M. D. "The Validity and Reliability of a Modified Form of the McAdory Art Test for Use at Lower Grade Levels." *Psychol. Monogr.,* 48: 1936, 68–84.

(147) Vydra, J. "Stammesunterschiede in der Begabung des Kindes fur bildende Kunst." (Racial differences in children's talent for pictorial art.) *4 Versamml. f. Kinderforsch.* (Bratislava: 1932) 311–314.

*(148) WALTON, W. E. "Empathic Responses in Children." *Psychol. Monogr.*, 48: 1936, 40–67.

*(149) WILEY, L. "The Validity of Certain Accepted Criteria of Design." (Thesis abstract. University of Illinois, Urbana, 1940)

(150) WILSON, D. J. "An experimental investigation of Birkhoff's aesthetic measure." *Jour. Abnorm. Soc. Psychol.*, 34: 1939, 390–394.

CHAPTER XXVII

STANDARDS OF VALUE IN ART [1]

RAY FAULKNER
Head, Department of Fine and Industrial Arts
Teachers College, Columbia University
New York, New York

I. INTRODUCTORY

Appraising art objects in an effort, often vain, to determine their value is one of the commonest art activities of the layman. Such an activity is not only of frequent occurrence, but is often exceedingly perplexing, if not downright confusing as well. Anyone who has listened for even a few minutes to visitors in an art gallery or to customers in a department store senses that the great majority of lookers and buyers feel compelled to pass judgment on anything that holds their attention for any appreciable period. In most cases, the time taken to make such judgments is remarkably short. Whatever the cause may be, 'snap judgments' about everything from paintings and sculpture to houses, tables, chairs, and dishes are made often, and apparently without deliberation. Perhaps the compulsion to judge many things makes it impossible to ponder over any single judgment.

However, some necessary judgments cause discomfiting moments. Such occasions arise when purchases are being made, for this is very different from hurrying through a department store or art gallery dealing out judgments without regard for consequences. As a rule, only when the object is to be purchased is the problem considered long and seriously — and painfully. Then the need for some sound basis on which evaluations can be made becomes acute. If this is a problem of major consequence in life, it is of pronounced importance to the art educator, for in his hands rest golden opportunities to guide and direct the artistic tastes of future citizens. The art educator does not act alone, fortunately or unfortunately as the case may be, because the motion pictures, magazines, newspapers, and other sources are potent

---

[1] Subsection III, "Philosophical Theories of the Nature of Esthetic Values," has been contributed by Ruth Raymond, Chairman, Art Department, University of Minnesota, Minneapolis, Minnesota.

factors in determining preferences, but it is his privilege and duty to be an active force.

That standards of value in art have had a long and turbulent history is a gross understatement. To be sure, critics, artists, and laymen, each talking and writing from points of view determined by special interests and backgrounds, have failed to agree on some issues, and, of course, arguments and disputes make far better news than do quiet, harmonious discussions. Much of the controversy that seems significant today quite naturally centers around what is loosely referred to as ' Modern Art.' Of the many striking examples of difference of opinion regarding the merit of given works of art, few afford sharper conflict than estimates of the paintings of Paul Cézanne. Thus, Willard Huntington Wright (38, p. 163) says: " Cézanne, judged either as a theorist or as an achiever, is the preëminent figure in modern art . . . Purely as a painter he is the greatest the world has produced "; while Royal Cortissoz, a critic of conservative taste, wrote (6, p. 130) that Cézanne was a painter who " never quite learned his trade, and accordingly in his dealings with landscape, still-lifes, and the figure was not unaccustomed to paint nonsense."

Similar examples of conflicting evaluations of the worth of art products could be multiplied almost endlessly, but we should not for a moment be led into believing that this is a new phenomenon. To be sure, the typical abbreviated history of art, written from one point of view, may make it seem that the works of all artists have always been accorded the importance now ascribed to them, but such an assumption is far from the truth. It is probably safe to say that the great majority of works of art that have any claim to significance aroused, in their day, some critics to vehement attack and others to staunch defense. Although this tendency may have become exaggerated in the period following the Renaissance, it is by no means new.

The reasons for such discrepancies are, of course, that critics hold different standards of value, look for different qualities in the work of art, and possess varying degrees of sensitivity. The standards they hold and the qualities they look for are determined not alone by their personal preferences but also in large part by the ' spirit of the times,' a point well illustrated by the difference in outlook between Victorian and contemporary critics. Consistent with the dominant tastes of their times (and to some extent responsible for them), the Victorians sought elegance, ornamentation, and the type of feeling that we now term ' sentimentality.' Contemporary critics, surfeited with Victorian excesses, are likely to praise strength, intensity, and simplicity. The following discussion aims to bring to a focus some of the major issues and controversies as a first step toward clarifying the nature and basis of art values as they affect not only the production but also the appreciation, criticism, and judgment of art.

II. Recent Issues in the Evaluation of Art

That there are many conflicts and controversies on issues of importance in the contemporary art field is often cited as evidence that the arts have lost their direction and are in a disorganized state. I believe that nothing could be further from the truth, for the presence of conflict in this case is interpreted as a healthy sign of interest and activity. When men are working on the frontiers of any field, meeting new situations, and solving new problems creatively, there are bound to be divergences of view and resultant conflict. Safety, security, and complete agreement are found only in issues that no longer are active in shaping men's lives. Thus, the issues discussed below show that contemporary art activities are not carried on according to formulas or absolute rules, but that they are of immediate and vital concern to many persons.

1. Imitation of Nature versus Distortion for Expression or Design

Whether or not art is, or should be, the ' imitation of nature ' is an ever-recurring issue, and recent art movements, particularly in painting and sculpture, have raised the blood pressures and adjectives of many critics. Some, including Ruckstuhl (29), Cortissoz (6), and Logan (21), have defended the idea that art should represent nature more or less literally. This is held to be an absolute rule, or law, from which deviations are not tolerated. The argument is usually based on the premise that nature is our great source of beauty, and that man can in no way improve on what he finds there. The beauty of the human figure, in particular, is held as an unsurpassable ideal that artists should seek to imitate to the best of their ability. Such writers praise highly Greek sculpture of the fifth and fourth centuries before Christ and the painting and sculpture of the High Renaissance in Italy, for during these periods artists exhibited great skill in portraying the human figure in stone and pigment. The art of these periods has become a standard, held more or less consciously, against which all other art is measured. The many art expressions in which the human figure (or other aspects of nature) was not given realistic representation —

the sculpture of Egypt, the early sculpture of Greece, the arts of the Middle Ages, and the arts of the Orient — are excused as representing periods during which the artists were striving toward the ideal but had not succeeded in perfecting their vision and techniques, or are briefly condemned, or merely ignored. Perhaps the greatest strength of the theory that imitation is the aim of art lies in its simplicity, for here is a rule that anyone can understand and apply in art evaluation. Much drawing and painting as well as ' picture study ' in the schools is firmly anchored in this criterion of verisimilitude.

Recently this standard of excellence has again been vigorously questioned by creative artists who do not wish to work within the prescribed limitations. Although there have always been some artists who did not conform, they were often dismissed as lacking sufficient talent to ' draw correctly.' But today relatively few artists hold simple imitation of nature as their aim, and their departure from imitative standards has been ably defended by such writers as Cheney (5), Pearson (27), and Wilenski (36), who stoutly maintain that nature may, and should be, modified, intensified, exaggerated, or distorted for the sake of greater intensity or more truly organic design. The controversy rose to sharp pitch concerning the work of such modern painters as Cézanne, Van Gogh, and Picasso, whose works show a tendency to distort or change nature for the sake of new compositions and meanings. In each case the work of these painters has been condemned, while new and unfamiliar, then begrudgingly, and finally enthusiastically, accepted.

In reality, the kernel of this issue is not *should* nature be distorted, but *what* and *how much* distortion will be accepted by critics and consumers. Even the most widely appreciated painters of the American Scene school — Grant Wood, John Steuart Curry, Thomas Benton — take considerable liberties with the appearance of their subject matter. To be specific, trees seldom if ever have the rounded, decorative quality with which Wood imbues the trees of Iowa; and men and women, even in Missouri, are not the elongated, knotty-muscled, dynamic persons that Benton places on canvas. Yet, in general, these deviations from normal appearances are accepted as not violating nature unduly or unpleasantly. Similarly, the most cursory glance at the history of art indicates that only a very small proportion of it is naturalistic. To mention but a few well-known examples, the sculpture of Egypt is imposing and memorable because of its solidity and simplicity, Gothic statues are exciting because of their aspiring, ascetic quality, and the sculpture of African Negroes has a dynamic organization of forces and movements that has seldom been surpassed in the history of art. To dismiss all such work as crude or immature is, indeed, a weak explanation.

Rather it must be recognized that art is a form of communication among men, and that the ideas, thoughts, and feelings communicated at different periods and by different artists have varied tremendously. Realistic statues on Egyptian temples would no more have accomplished their intended purpose than they would have around the portals of Gothic cathedrals. In the former, the ideals of permanence demanded that the human figure be treated in a solid, massive way. In the latter, the tenets of Medieval Christianity demanded that the human figure be shown, not realistically, as the pagan Greeks had done, but as creatures in which the physical attributes were of little consequence. It is logical in terms of the purposes for which these sculptures were produced that they should be as they are. To have forced them into an arbitrary imitation of natural appearances would have greatly diminished their significance.

What is true of the past is equally true of the present. Serving a wide variety of human needs, art expressions take many forms based on the idea to be communicated and the purpose to be served. For purposes of description and record, literal representations or copies may be the best solution, but for purposes of persuasion and stimulation the artist has every right to use all available means as he sees fit. The beauty of nature is acknowledged — but not imitated. In fact, the most glorious beauties of nature (sunsets, the Grand Canyon, or the Alps, for example) when transcribed literally to paper, canvas, stone, or metal invariably fail to convey much, if any, of their original power and appeal. Seeking to arouse in the observer a reaction similar to his own experiences, the artist, like the composer of music, selects and develops his material in a way that he believes will best convey his ideas. From the multitude of details before him he organizes those that are most expressive, shifting and changing where necessary so that the expressive qualities become effective. His work may thus range from a fairly close copy of nature to violent distortion or almost complete abstraction.

There are great differences in the ways in which distortion is carried out. At times it is merely carelessness or the result of incompetence in the technical handling of the medium, and as such is uncontrolled and meaningless. The distortions of El Greco give his paintings great power, while vehemence and elongation, when done by some one of lesser ability, merely look nervous; the difference is recognizable to those who care and know how to look for it. Sensitivity, integrity, talent, and many other factors operate to make distortion in some cases expressive, in others, of little significance.

As previously stated, the aim of the representative arts (to which this issue is related) is to transmit ideas from man to man. Their history shows clearly that the 'imitation of nature' is only one way of accomplishing this aim. The majority of artists have deliberately exaggerated, intensified, or distorted those qualities in their subject matter that are most essential to their communication. The idea to be expressed — not the appearance of the subject matter — should determine the degree to which art approximates nature. For some purposes literal representation is desirable or even necessary, but as a single criterion of excellence in painting and sculpture, the imitation of nature has no validity.

2. Subject Matter versus Style

The relative importance of subject matter and style is a venerable issue, having arisen early in the history of esthetics and showing every sign of having eternal life. In the representative arts, *subject matter* is generally used to describe that which the artist aims to represent (as a scene, incident, or person), and *style* refers to the distinctive or characteristic mode of presentation.

To some observers the subject matter is of paramount interest. At the extreme this point of view may manifest itself as a concern only for the literary or moral aspects of painting and sculpture. Great importance is placed on the 'story' told by the art object, and its value is judged primarily, sometimes entirely, on this basis. Almost any typical lesson in 'picture study' in the schools is an example of this approach to art. Similarly, those persons interested in art as a means of social reform, religious education, or political stimulation are usually deeply interested in the subject matter, often to the point of excluding style from their consideration. To them, art has a single, driving purpose that is to be accomplished through the subject matter, and that renders all else inconsequential.

To others, the style may seem vastly more important than the subject matter: *what* is painted is of less significance than *how* it is painted. Great attention is paid to mannerisms of drawing, special techniques of painting, or modes of composition, generally because the artists are not fired by any enthusiasm to influence human behavior in any substantial way. A certain manner of painting, certain combinations of colors and treatments of shapes, become popular, a *school* is established, and the subject matter is of consequence only because it provides a means of working in the established style. This is especially true of academicians, who devote much of their energy to following, and encouraging others to follow, stylistic precedents. Thus, at one extreme are those persons interested almost completely in subject matter — the scenes or incidents painted or carved — and at the other extreme are those interested almost entirely in the mode of expression.

The presence of such extreme points of view, in fact, the very existence of the issue between subject matter and style, betrays a superficial or distorted understanding of the way in which vital art is produced. As I have said, the representative arts are primarily concerned with communication and communion among men. The *idea* — the plan, nucleus, or preconcept from which all else develops — is the primary source of the communication and the basic force in motivating art production. An artist wants to relate his experiences and share them with his fellow men; and he begins with the idea. He may select persons, trees, apples, or abstract forms as subject matter by means of which his idea is communicated.

The *form* refers to the objective realization of the idea; in other words, to the totality of the finished art object. Only the creator has the idea, but all may experience the form. If the idea is strong and sincerely realized, the style of the art object develops as naturally and inevitably as a plant grows from a seed, for the idea carries within it the implicit form of the completed work. In any great painting — as, for example, Michelangelo's frescoes in the Sistine Chapel or Orozco's frescoes at Dartmouth College — the idea determines the manner of expression, even the colors chosen and the type of brush strokes employed. Less weighty art expressions, such as magazine covers or advertising posters, may also achieve this ideal balance between subject matter and style. As already pointed out, however, those artists who exaggerate the importance of either style or subject matter destroy this equilibrium, thereby impairing their art. Subject matter, interpreted broadly, is basic to style, but both are united in the art form to project the idea from the creator to the appreciator.

Thus, the *idea* is the beginning; the *subject matter* is that which is represented; the *style* is the characteristic manner of expressing the idea; and the *form* is the final product. In vital art production these four aspects are merged so closely that it is almost impossible to separate one from the other, to say nothing of attempting to establish arbitrary and fixed degrees of importance. All are essential and integral; one cannot exist without the others.

3. Art for Art's Sake versus Art for Society's Sake

Essentially this issue is whether art is a means or an end; or, more precisely, to what degree is art an end in itself. Such writers as Tolstoi (32) have seen art only as a moral force, while other writers, such as Dewey (10), Ducasse (11), and Read (28), find that art has meaning in its own right.[1]

4. Functionalism versus Eclecticism

Whereas the three issues thus far discussed refer primarily to the representative arts of drawing, painting, and sculpture, this fourth issue, although it also applies to painting and sculpture, most directly concerns those arts that serve utilitarian needs directly — architecture and the allied arts.

The nineteenth century was a period of revivalism in architecture, and in quick and uncertain succession the Roman, Greek, Gothic, Romanesque, and Renaissance styles of architecture were imitated in America. Even the Moorish and Turkish influences came into our ways of building, but they were so obviously unrelated to anything in our culture that they did little more than to produce a few ' Turkish corners ' in living rooms and a few temples of secret brotherhoods. Because the models from which eclectic architects drew their inspiration and details were admittedly great, this practice was defended by such eminent architects as Ralph Adams Cram, who designed, among other notable churches, New York City's Cathedral of St. John the Divine, and by the firm of McKim, Mead, and White, who were responsible for many buildings refined in the Renaissance manner. At times whole structures were copied as closely as funds and skill permitted, an example of which is the replica of the Parthenon in Nashville, Tennessee. At other times large portions of buildings were reproduced with only minor adaptations, such as the concourse of the Pennsylvania Station, New York City, which closely resembles a Roman bath. More often only details or ornaments were imitated.

---

[1] For further discussion of this issue, see Chapter XXVIII on " Art and Its Relation to Society," especially those pages dealing with " The Autonomy of Art " and " Art for Art's Sake."

By imitating, adapting, borrowing, and stealing freely from well over two thousand years of architectural history, architects placed along American streets buildings bewildering and often inharmonious in their variety, producing an effect described by Mumford as " solidified chaos." During the height of the ' Battle of the Styles,' as it was called, leaders rose to fame and fortune defending one style above the others as best suited to the times. The ' Victorian Compromise,' which decreed that banks and art museums should be Grecian, railroad stations and other public buildings should be Roman, and churches should be either Gothic, Romanesque, or Renaissance (but with emphasis on the Gothic), brought a certain agreement into the conflict and led to specialists not only in one style but also in one type of building.

Although such practices produced some buildings of undeniable beauty of proportion and detail, the weaknesses in this approach soon became self-evident. Borrowing styles that were developed by foreign cultures and that bore little or no relation to the American way of life could hardly be expected to produce vital, expressive architecture. Not only did eclecticism fail to give us a significant architecture of our own, but it also led men into faulty habits of thinking and false standards of taste. Beauty was seen only in buildings of the past or in those which resembled them, and culture became synonymous with that which was not only foreign but also dead. In favor of well-tempered adaptations, genuine originality was discouraged. That such thinking and practicing is quite at odds with the history of architecture seems not to have occurred to its proponents, who mistakenly thought of themselves as carrying forward the great traditions.

Because the buildings designed in this way were not related to American needs and ideals, architects like Louis Sullivan (31) and Frank Lloyd Wright (37) have waged a hard battle for an organic, developing architecture expressing America, a cause aided by such critics as Mumford (23) and Cheney (4). These writers base their arguments on two sets of facts. First, they point out that, in every great period of art, artists have dug deeply into contemporaneous resources to create appropriate forms in architecture, painting, ceramics, and the like. It is natural that each important social order should have art forms of its own, and although these will bear definite relations to those of preceding social groups, they will not be copies. In this way the phenomenon of a continuous, but ever-changing succession of styles occurs.

Second, no architecture derived from the past can be truly functional in contemporary society, for today we have problems to be solved and materials and methods of construction to be used that never existed before. Consequently, new solutions are demanded. The functionalist architect attacks any problem by studying in detail all aspects of it. If it be the design of a house, he becomes acquainted with the people who are to live in it so that he may provide for their ways of living. He considers the location of the property, and allows any outstanding natural features to influence his design in the same way that he takes into account the immediate neighborhood. He has at his command materials such as architects of no other generation had — large sheets of glass, glass building blocks, new composition boards, plywood, structural steel, and synthetic materials in addition to the customary wood, bricks, and stone. From these needs, conditions, and materials he designs the house. To be sure, he has profited tremendously from his study of other houses, present and historic, from which he has derived useful generalizations, principles, and theories. But he would no more think of designing a house in the tradition of Colonial Williamsburg than he would think of attiring himself in clothes characteristic of that civilization. He admits proudly that he is living in the twentieth century and designing for it, just as all great builders of the past built for their times. If his problem be that of designing a church, a railway station, or an office building, he follows the same general approach.

In summary, the eclectic chooses on the whole to cling tenaciously to the past, trying to preserve or bring to life something that has ceased to be functional and alive. He has a romantic nostalgia and veneration for the old order, often an ill-concealed hostility for the new. The functionalist, declaring that art ought to grow from and promote the spirit of the group creating it, adventurously solves his problems in terms of the living present, not the dead past. Fortunately, a number of factors — the need for stringent economy in building, a significant reorientation towards our own cultural resources, and the exhausting of Europe's well of inspiration — are combining to convince more and more persons that functionalism has many and decided advantages over eclecticism.

5. Summary

From this discussion of a few current issues it will be seen that the creation, enjoyment, and judgment of art are not simply the following of established rules, for the attitudes and philosophies on a variety of issues determine the manner in which creators and consumers view the field of art. Intelligent evaluation demands clear, incisive thinking.

Establishing a valid basis for judging art is one of the most important problems in art education, but one that has been conspicuously neglected in many art programs. Although, as will be seen, I believe firmly in the individuality of art judgments, merely ignoring the manner in which they are made is no assurance that intelligent individuality will result. The divergent points of view regarding the nature of art, reviewed in the next section, provide background material and suggestions for further reading.

III. Philosophical Theories of the Nature of Esthetic Values [1]

Thinkers since the days of Baumgarten have been making claims of value for art in accordance with the function they found it performing. Each of these claims is couched in the language of the age in which it was made. The early claims made by philosophers in ' ivory towers ' sound remote from everyday life and our vital concerns; today claims like the following are being advanced:

Art is a way of life, a way of doing anything.

Art is an intensification and interpretation of experience.

Art performs a healthy act of labor.

Art can give propitious form to matter, can make objects in our environment pleasant and significant.

Art, complementing and supplementing science, offers a valid form of knowledge of physical and human nature.

Art, though private and individual in one sense, is a communal activity.

Art provides a means of linking man with nature and with his fellow men.

Art, presenting these linkage opportunities, is of paramount importance for mental health in individuals and for mutuality in groups.

Art has thus been interpreted in a variety of ways, as serving numerous functions, and as having manifold values. Out of the variety of claims naturally grow differences of opinion concerning art values.

An analysis of one hundred definitions of art, chosen as typical of the claims made for art by writers from Baumgarten to Archibald MacLeish, shows that the individual claims carry varying degrees of social importance. Their emphases are significant of the temperaments and philosophical creeds of those who wrote them and of the opinions that prevailed and influenced their authors. Taken together, they fall

---

[1] This subsection is contributed by Professor Ruth Raymond, Chairman of the Art Department, University of Minnesota.

into a design that helps to clarify some of the confusion surrounding art values.

The significance of art lies not in the accomplishments of the past, but rather in the potential values that thinkers have discovered in those accomplishments. If there is justification in art for the claims made for it, art is more than a special field for those who have talents or skills. It becomes a pattern of direction for living.

It is possible to isolate more specifically a great variety of types of art values, of which the following are representative:

Art has value as:

(1) An expression of ideas and emotions.

(2) An expression of dreams and wishes.

(3) Expression as an end in itself.

(4) A means of modifying the environment in every ideal way.

(5) A way of reshaping the world closer to our desires.

(6) A means of giving significant form or design to formless matter.

(7) An intelligent and skillful way of dealing with natural things.

(8) A source of economic value.

(9) A communal activity in which experiences are shared.

(10) A universal language.

(11) A way of life.

(12) A form of knowledge.

(13) A way of discovering new aspects of life.

(14) A way of clarifying, interpreting, and objectifying experience.

(15) A method of teaching, or perpetuating and developing an idea.

(16) A moral influence.

IV. Standards in Art

Many kinds of values, sometimes diametrically opposed, have been sought for and found in art. This search for values is a major problem in art because, as Parker (26, p. 216) says:

> Our interest in art is seldom a matter of mere feeling or appreciation; usually it is a matter of judgment as well. Beginning in feeling, the esthetic experience passes over into comparison and estimation — into criticism, and there finds its normal completion.

If judgment of an art object is inevitable, or almost so, it becomes important to consider in some detail the basis on which such judgment rests. This raises several issues that are central to any discussion of art values. First, is it true that there is no disputing about tastes, or, are the judgments of some persons superior to those of others? Second, are there absolute standards or rules on which art may be judged? Third, are there any valid principles of art judgment? Fourth, can art judgments be improved, and if so, how? Fifth, what are some of the more common obstacles, or fallacies, that interfere with rational art judgment? Each of these issues will be discussed in turn.

1. Are the Art Judgments of Some Persons Superior to Those of Others?

The belief that every man's taste is as good — or bad — as that of every other man is so widely held that one does not need to read or listen for long to find examples of it. Believing that criticism and judgment are entirely personal, are subject to no standards, and rest on no foundation (other than that of the appreciator involved), the proponents of this theory assume that judgment is merely a matter of opinion and that there can be no science or study of values. Each art experience is regarded as unique and, consequently, incomparable and impossible to evaluate. This is in harmony with the Romantic emphasis on the individual and freedom from any sort of restraint or compulsion. Such a view is attractive in its emphasis on individuality, democracy, and freedom, but, if carried to its logical conclusion, would practically eliminate the intelligent study of art values. According to such a theory, sensitivity, knowledge, breadth of experience, and the like make no difference in the worth of the art judgment. Ducasse seems to favor at least the substance of this attitude when he says, " There is, then, no such thing as authoritative opinion concerning the beauty of a given object " (11, p. 284), and continues by saying that beauty cannot be proved by appeal to a consensus or to technical principles or canons.

Naturally, there is an opposing point of view to which most persons who have considered the matter carefully adhere. Drawing an illustration from another field, science, Dewey (10, p. 298) points out that there is great difference between what the tutored and untutored man sees when he judges natural events:

> Control of the subject matter of perception for ensuring proper data for judgment is the key to the enormous distinction between the judgments the savage passes on natural events and that of a Newton or an Einstein.

Santayana (30, p. 192) expresses a similar idea when he writes:

> There is consequently the greatest possible difference in authority between taste and taste, and while delight in drums and eagles' feathers is perfectly genuine and has no cause to blush for itself, it cannot be compared in scope or representative value with delight in a symphony or an epic.

In fact, most systems of esthetic theory are based on the assumption that reactions to art and judgments of it may themselves be evaluated, that all are not of equal merit. The sensitive observer sees more and different qualities in art than does the obtuse observer. Not only does he pay attention to different qualities of the art object, but his system of values more closely approaches a rational system of philosophy as well. According to almost any criterion, his judgment has greater merit, even though conclusive proof of this may be difficult. There are obviously several dangerous suggestions in this statement, of which the most serious are: (1) that there is an absolute basis of standards of value in art, and (2) that all persons should agree with those having superior judgment. The following discussions should demonstrate that the statement implies neither of these ideas, but rather calls attention to the manifold possibilities for individuality within a rational framework.

2. Are There Absolute Standards of Art Value?

a. Absolutism. ‘Absolutism’ in art is the theory that there are permanent, unquestionable laws or rules that govern the production and appreciation of art.

Mankind seems ever to be seeking security, not only as regards the practical necessities of life but as regards the higher truths as well. Perhaps it is a deep fear of the uncertain, a lack of the spirit of adventure, or perhaps it is simple laziness that causes most of us to look for rules that need only be learned and followed. Perhaps it is the simplicity of a dogmatic rule that exerts appeal. Whatever the motivating factors, there has been a long-continued search for absolutes in art, and not a few writers have claimed to have found the final answers.

Ruckstuhl (29), writing on *Great Works of Art and What Makes Them Great*, says that no one must criticize without proper standards, and refers somewhat enviously to the banker who knows the exact value of a piece of gold (seeming to forget that even the value of gold varies). His standards are the classic trilogy, the True, the Good, and the Beautiful, which, according to him, were unquestioned standards for art from the time of Plato and Aristotle down to 1860 — a date chosen presumably to represent the beginning of experimental, contemporary manifestations of the arts. It is clear from his vitriolic attacks on Impressionism and Expressionism that he feels the pattern for art was set by the Greeks, and that there should be no important deviations. The narrowness of his standards obscures for him any merit in art not conforming to the rigid pattern. This inflexibility, which makes adaptation to changing conditions and new art movements impossible, acts to limit seriously both art production and art appreciation. Growth and progress are hindered by insistence on conformity in a most undemocratic fashion. Under such conditions a rigid academy of taste is quickly established, and the creative impulse shrinks to midget stature.

But Ruckstuhl is far from being alone in believing that there are immutable laws — laws failing to give weight to such factors as the function of the object, the time and place in which it was produced, and the like — that can be applied to test beauty. Lessing, for example, believed that the laws laid down in Aristotle's *Poetics* were as certain in their application to the drama as were Euclid's *Elements* in their application to geometry. In spite of Lessing, the contemporary drama shows little concern for Aristotle's laws; it has, indeed, developed principles of its own quite at variance with Aristotle's.

A more recent effort to measure esthetic merit by absolute standards is that of Birkhoff (1) who provides a formula of intriguing, but misleading, basic simplicity: esthetic measure is equal to the *order* divided by the *complexity*. Analyzing the problem in scientific fashion, Birkhoff segregated his criteria, established a relationship between them, and then proceeded to develop prodigiously complex tables and tabulations. His approach is refreshing and may in time lead to progress. In its present state, however, the factors he considers are so small a fragment of meaningful art that any results from his ingenious equations must be viewed with proper scientific suspicion.

Taking their lead from such beliefs in absolute standards, many writers of art textbooks and manuals for instruction in the arts have either explicitly or implicitly laid down laws. In fact, most art texts give rules aimed presumably to develop proficiency — and conformity — in the production and judgment of art, and the absolutist regards these as laws. Many a great teacher has left behind a zealous group of acolytes who have proceeded, by way of showing their continued devotion, to freeze his inspiration into a rigid system, or method. By such means, direct and indirect, art in the schools not infrequently becomes reduced to a formula.

Concerning the absolutist point of view Santayana (30, p. 191) writes, " Dogmatism in taste has the same status as dogmatism in other spheres," and proceeds to point out that it becomes absurd when it assumes an absolute or metaphysical scope.

b. Relativism. ' Relativism ' is the hypothesis that there are no ab-

solute, immutable laws in art; that guides and principles are relative to
the particular situation under consideration. Thus, relativism is diametrically opposed to absolutism. In general, the belief today is less
in infallible standards than in an effort to formulate broad principles by
which judgments may be appraised and through which we may work
towards a greater understanding of tastes. Dewey (10) writes that it
is impossible to use standards in the physical sense in the field of art,
because each evaluation demands judgment, not merely comparison
with a given scale of values.

This does not imply that objective criticism and judgment are impossible. It means that art judgments and art principles are *relative*
to the immediate situation rather than *absolute*. It means that there
are no ready-made decisions that can be grabbed and applied unthink-
ingly. Munro (24) points out the danger of deciding any problem by
reference to fixed standards and urges that each problem be dealt with
frankly, in its own terms, by intelligent analysis. If this restriction is
carried to an extreme (which Munro does not), one is left with no system of values, but there is no reason to commit the folly of forcing the
limitation to that degree. Art experiences, although unique (as are all
other experiences in the final analysis), are not entirely divorced from
the past. Rather they are related to our funded stores of previous
experience. It is almost inevitable that through such past experience,
we shall come to have hypotheses about the effects of certain types of
form and color upon our appreciations, and that these may be predic-
tive guides to the future. They are guiding principles intended to
clarify and enrich future experiences, not laws aimed to narrow and
limit them.

Judgments may be relative to a number of factors, such as the aim
of the artist, the conditions under which he labored, the materials
with which he worked and the patron and social order for which he produced. Even this brief list illustrates an important characteristic of
relative judgments; namely, that they require a far deeper knowledge
and understanding of an object than do absolute appraisals. Seeing
the object in its context and determining how well or how poorly it
functions in its place are not easy tasks. They require rigorous and
lengthy study if done thoroughly, but it is in this way that superior
judgments are formed. Relative judgments result from an active study
of the situation as it exists. There are no rules-of-thumb, no codifica-
tions, that may be learned, stored safely away, and applied automatically when the need arises.

3. Are There Any Valid Principles of Art Judgment, or Criteria of Good Taste?

So far there has been no specific mention of what may constitute valid principles of judgment, or criteria of good taste in art, although the emphasis on individualism and relativity does not mean that we are without guides or principles. This is a point that engenders difficulties, beset as it is by the pitfalls of the dogmatic formula, the philosopher's vague generalization, and the Romantic's avoidance of organized principles. The academicians settle the matter quickly with rigid rules, while the philosophers generally exhaust their energies in discussions so general that the results have little, if any, value.

The attempts of a few writers to provide a basis for judgments are given next.

1. Birkhoff (1), searching for a rational basis for intuitive judgments, has evolved a scientific, quasi-objective formula based on the ratio of *complexity to order;* namely, esthetic measure is equal to the *order* divided by the *complexity*.
2. Torossian (33) gives two standards of criticism:
    (1) *Perfection,* which is based on
       a. Functional fitness for its work
       b. Pattern that is organic, relevant, and harmonious
       c. Clear and precise display of character
       d. Clear display and good use of material and technique
    (2) *Greatness,* which is based on
       a. Magnitude of subject matter
       b. Complexity of form
       c. Intensity of expression
3. Santayana (30) gives three basic considerations of taste:
    (1) Vivacity and volume of feeling
    (2) Purity and consistency of experience
    (3) Pertinence and width of appeal
4. Dewey (10) gives three criteria for judgment:
    (1) Form in relation to matter
    (2) Meaning of medium in art
    (3) Nature of the expressive object
5. Parker (26) states his general principles for judgment largely in terms of the object:
    (1) Complete use of medium (that is, using the fullest expressive possibilities of each medium)
    (2) Unique use of material (that is, exploiting the characteristics that make marble, wood, water color, and so forth unique)

    (3) Perfect use of medium in effort to give depth and breadth to the esthetic experience

He adds that no work of art can be judged without reference to its function.

It is impossible here to do more than thus to mention the salient points in each system of values and to refer the interested reader to the sources for more information. However, this listing of the salient points gives some indication of the types of statements made by those working from the philosophic or scientific standpoint.

4. Can Art Judgments Be Improved by Training?

In an attempt to provide students with a way of seeing, enjoying, and criticizing works of art, Faulkner and Ziegfeld have prepared (13) the following list of questions that can be addressed to any field of art. This is not intended as a formula, and, as will be readily seen, does not provide the answers. It is by no means the only way of attaining the desired goal. Its purpose is to suggest and arouse, to call attention specifically to issues and aspects that are pertinent and that might otherwise be overlooked or forgotten. The questions, and consequently the answers, are interrelated, and if followed consistently, the final evaluation depends on the pattern formed by the relationships among the items. The questions, followed by examples (each of which should be modified by the phrase, ' other things being equal ') to clarify their meaning, are organized under five major headings. The first refers to the *immediate reaction* to the whole object before and after the process of analysis. Second is the question of how well the object fulfills its utilitarian *functions*. The next classifications represent three fundamental aspects of the art object: *expression* refers to the idea, content, meaning, or purpose of the object; *organization* refers to the composition or design of the object; and *materials* refers to the actual things from which it is made.

Some Factors in the Evaluation of Art Objects

1. *The Whole Object:* What is your first reaction to the object as a whole?
    Example: Is it pleasing, displeasing, stimulating, etc.?
2. *Function:* Does the object fulfill its utilitarian functions efficiently?
    Example: A good chair is both comfortable and durable.
3. *Expression:* What is the purpose, idea, content, or meaning of the object?
    (1) Is its purpose clearly shown in its appearance?
        Example: An expressive factory looks like a factory, is not disguised as a pseudo-Greek temple.

(2) Does the object give you a new experience?

    Example: Since each painting or building is the solution of a unique problem, it should give the observer something new to experience.

(3) Is the meaning of the object expressed in terms of the medium?

    Example: A piece of sculpture is primarily a plastic expression in terms of stone, metal, or wood, and does not need to tell a literary story.

4. *Organization:* How is the object composed or designed?

  (1) Is the general composition well suited to the purpose?

    Example: Horizontal masses, suggesting repose, are well suited to domestic architecture.

  (2) Does it give the impression of one idea?

    Example: A unified building gives the impression of an organized mass expressing its purpose; it does not look like a miscellaneous collection of doors, windows, and other details.

  (3) Is there enough variety to hold attention?

    Example: A perfectly blank piece of paper is unified, but it is not stimulating enough to hold your attention for long.

  (4) Is the object easy and pleasant to look at?

    a. Are the weights and forces in a state of balance?

      Example: A living room in which all of the important furniture is against one wall or at one end seems uncomfortably out of balance.

    b. Are the parts emphasized in proportion to their importance?

      Example: In successful advertisements (or paintings) first attention is directed to the important parts.

    c. Does the whole design have continuity? (Are the parts rhythmically related?)

      Example: In Van Gogh's paintings foliage, buildings, and sky are all part of a continuous, rhythmic pattern.

5. *Materials:* How have the materials been chosen and worked?

  (1) Are they suited to the purpose of the object?

    Example: Chiffon is suitable for evening dresses, not golf suits.

  (2) Have the natural beauties of the materials been used to advantage?

    Example: If the grain of wood is beautiful, the wood may be finished so that the pattern is preserved.

  (3) Have the materials been skillfully handled from a technical viewpoint?

    Example: The brush marks in a painting may be skillfully directed to realize the form more solidly.

  (4) Are the materials beautiful in themselves?

    Example: Although good effects can be produced with unbleached

muslin for window curtains, linen fabrics are generally
more beautiful.
(5) Are the different materials used in one product harmoniously related?
Example: Because leather repeats to some degree the texture of
metal, it makes a harmonious upholstery for metal furniture.

Sensitivity to differences of the sort required to answer these questions and the ability to develop a pattern from the various responses
are dependent both on native art ability and training. Familiarity
with many examples of art, intelligent analyses of them, and creative
work are helpful means to these ends. Even so, there is still room for
healthy divergence of opinion, for each individual's judgment is of
necessity relative to his own background and experience. The best that
can be hoped for is sincere and intelligent consideration of all pertinent
factors before an appraisal is made.

5. What Characteristic Obstacles, or Fallacies, Interfere with Valid Art Judgments?

Even if it be granted that valid esthetic judgments should result
from serious study of the art object in its intended setting in life, yet
there are many false paths to confuse the unwary. Esthetic values and
satisfactions generally occur closely integrated with other life values
and satisfactions, and from such contacts derive their motivation and
nourishment. There is a possible danger inherent in this integration
that at times becomes a serious obstacle to esthetic interests — the
pressure of other interests may completely overshadow or obliterate
the esthetic. Arising out of this and other conditions are two fallacies
of esthetic judgment, reduction and confusion of categories, that Dewey
(10) considers major fallacies.

In *reduction* one part or constituent of the art object is isolated, and
the whole is reduced to the terms of this single component. The act
of isolating is in itself not harmful; in fact, it is probably essential to
anything more penetrating than a confused, goose-flesh state of over-
emotionalized appreciation. The danger is that the whole is obscured
by the part — a certain path to decadence in any field. This isolated
aspect may be the technique by which the work was produced, and
academicians are particularly wont to exalt technique above all else,
forgetting that art is basically a communication of an idea, not a display of dexterity. Historians and sociologists frequently err in considering nothing but the historical or political factors connected either

with the production of the work of art or with its subsequent history, and although such factors may be of importance, undue attention to them precludes a comprehensive understanding of the work in its entirety. Historians often fall into the pitfall of becoming so engrossed in documenting art objects that the merit of the object under consideration is forgotten in an intricate mass of trivial details, and the thoroughness of the documentation is not infrequently taken as an index of merit. In a somewhat similar way data about the life of an artist, his financial struggles, or his love life may provide the journalist with such newsworthy materials, as they did in the case of Van Gogh, that the art pales into insignificance. The technique, the political or historical incidents, the life of the artist, are factors of importance in arriving at relativistic judgments and ought not to be neglected, but concern with them to the exclusion of other characteristics fails to bring art into true focus.

Art teachers often fall into the habit of reducing art products to design principles, as though design were the beginning and end of art. This practice, when carried to an extreme (as it too often is), makes of art production little more than putting together forms and colors in a pleasing pattern, and of art appreciation little more than sensitivity to color and line combinations. Balance, proportion, rhythm, and the dozen or so other principles of design that have been formulated are isolated, and the whole work is reduced to these principles. The efficiency with which the object serves its purposes, the content or idea that it communicates, the way in which it harmonizes with and expresses its social and geographical environment, the manner in which the materials have been used — all these are overlooked.

From the layman's point of view, probably the most common example of this fallacy is reducing painting to its imitative aspects. In judging school art work the concern with technical dexterity also frequently prevents just appreciations. Technical excellence and imitation of nature are often considered inseparable — perhaps because academic teachers have failed to realize that a painting may be technically excellent without in any way being a copy of nature. Since many public-school art programs are founded on the concept that progress lies in gaining more accurate control of materials to facilitate representative drawing and painting, it is not surprising that many laymen, learning their school lessons too well, carry this mistaken notion.

In appreciating architecture and the allied arts there is a tendency to allow charm and decoration to become the primary considerations to such an extent that straightforward, vigorous, experimental forms are immediately rejected as not looking ' comfortable ' or ' livable.' As a result of the interest in imitating the historic, or period, styles there is also a tendency to reduce values in these arts to ' correctness,' to historical precedent. Thus, uncomfortable but correct chairs, inefficient but authentic cupboards, are admired, not for what they are or for what they will do, but for what they are supposed to represent. All is reduced to authenticity or conformity to the arts of the past.

In *confusion of categories*, which is similar to confusion of values, the esthetic experience and, consequently the esthetic values, are translated into other realms of experience. As Dewey points out, artistic substance is not identical with theme, and the theme may hinder our seeing the artistic aspect. Thus, in religious art the artistic content may be so completely overlooked in the interest of religious themes that painting, sculpture, and churches, trivial in treatment and poor in design, are insensitively accepted as worthy expressions of great faiths. Similarly, the intense patriotism that inspires the great majority of war memorials seems to act effectively in diverting attention from their artistic weakness. Ethical standards may also be substituted for esthetic ones, as in the ruling standards of Plato, Tolstoi, and the writers under the domination of several contemporary political theories. The Marxist interpretation of art is always in serious danger of finding no value whatever in art expressions that do not deliberately further the chosen economic theory, even though such art be a sincere portrayal of profound human experience. Nazi leaders, in a manner typical of their absolutist approach, have condemned the most significant recent art movements (many of which reached their highest development in Germany) on moral and political grounds. A confused notion of morality has at times led to a wholesale condemnation of the nude figure in painting and sculpture. There is still, however, a certain Puritan strain in most Americans, which causes them to be wary of sensuous pleasures resulting from art. Economic, when confused with esthetic, standards may lead to such curious beliefs as the one rather commonly held that the monetary value of an object influences, if it does not determine, its artistic merit.

A third classification of fallacies in esthetic judgment (which might be added to the two formulated by Dewey) is *excessive respect for authority* (24), the habit of ' following the herd,' which usually arises from a fear of being different or of not sharing the opinions of the group. The tendency to give to authority, in guiding and clarifying appreciations and appraisals, a position out of proportion to its actual value is a serious detriment to the formation of honest, personal evaluations. The desire for approbation through professing to have fashionable tastes not only in clothing, but in house-furnishings and even in painting and sculpture as well, places integrity and individuality in a precarious spot. During the past hundred years, and especially during the past few decades, the remarkable shifts in fashion from one period style of furnishing to another — shifts that have no relation to our ways of living, since one style is as remote as the next — have demonstrated how easy it is for manufacturers, decorators, magazine writers, and merchandisers, posing as authorities, to promote business by arousing in the consumer a real fear of being out-of-date. Tremendous enthusiasms can be created if leading interior decorators proclaim a revival of the Victorian, Biedermeier, or Colonial, or any other style they might happen to select. Similarly, painters become fashionable, are widely and loudly admired for a season or two, and then forgotten as the next luminary receives the spotlight of acclaim. Lacking any valid standards of their own, many persons flock to the banner raised most highly or waved most vigorously.

Not a few college curricula are planned to instill a blind and excessive respect for the authority of the past to such an extent that students are quite unprepared for contemporary art manifestations. The authority of the Greek, Roman, and Renaissance traditions, plumped out with the Romanesque and Gothic, sets the pattern for production and appreciation, as though all developments in art had taken place. Needless to say, the intelligent study of the history of art as a background for wise judgments is of great value, but the imposition of European traditions of scholarship and authority has taken a heavy toll of honest appreciation among college students.

A fourth cause of fallacy in esthetic judgments is *ignorance,* a sincere attitude toward the field of art, but an imperfect understanding of it. The ability to judge art effectively is undoubtedly rooted in innate factors, and may or may not require formal training, but it requires some kind of intelligent development. As a matter of fact, every person's ability to judge art is developed or changed by a great variety of factors — the opinions of relatives and friends, the art products in his environment, by magazines, newspapers, and motion pictures. While some of these experiences may be conducive to improvement, others may be equally detrimental in calling attention to insignificant factors by promoting false standards or by confusing fundamental issues. Each of the arts is a complex field, and while everyone cannot spend much time in study of it, intelligent orientation is desirable.

Owing to a mistaken notion that art is a ' universal language ' and therefore can be understood immediately by all, some observers defend their ignorance in a variety of ways. Disdaining learning and experience with the cliché that " It is all a matter of personal opinion," they defend their prejudices as judgments and their ignorance as highly personal, emotional sensitivity. When confronted with a work of art unintelligible to them, such observers may condemn it as not having sufficient breadth of appeal, clarity of statement, or human significance rather than admit that they simply do not understand it. Unlike science and medicine, fields which few profess to understand sufficiently to criticize and appraise, art is every man's domain. Ignorance, however, is as great a liability in art as in science, for art, like science, is a field of human activity that has a long history, a body of organized facts and principles, and the beginnings, at least, of a rational study of criticism. It is not to be expected that this can be understood without effort on the part of the individual. Man is born with certain capacities and sensitivities that may be developed through guidance.

V. In Conclusion

Those who incline toward the relativist point of view will at once give up the search for unchanging laws, but they will not give up the quest for a better, richer understanding of art, for principles that will aid them in interpreting, organizing, and evaluating art experiences. Merely taking the opinions of authorities, however, is far from satisfactory, for such practice leads to blind acceptance of formulas and makes the art experience a passive, secondhand affair.

The development of standards of value that have real vitality for the individual because they belong to him requires effort. Munro (24) stresses the need for descriptive study of two types as a basis for values: first, a careful analysis of form in art so that one will judge the whole work of art, not one part of it; and second, a thorough analysis of the individual self so that judgment is formed on the more permanent and basic elements in one's make-up, not on caprice or momentary excitement. If the art experience is an interaction between the *observer* and the art *object*, both require study.

The study of art requires consideration in general of the reasons underlying art creation, and in particular, of the effects of certain form and color organizations on human behavior, of the possibilities and limitations of materials, and the like. The study of self should naturally proceed hand in hand with the study of art, because taste is a matter of growth resulting from firsthand experiences with art. Good taste in art depends upon individual sensitivity and upon profiting from previous experiences. Each new experience provides one with new information concerning not only himself but also the external world. Each of these experiences can be refined by bringing it into sympathy with the whole pattern of thought; and if this is continued intelligently, each person is able to provide for himself a valid basis for understanding and evaluating art.

In the words of Santayana (30, p. 207):

> Good taste is that taste which is a good possession, a friend to the whole man. It must not alienate him from anything except to ally him to something greater and more fertile in satisfactions.
>
> Good taste comes . . . from experience in the best sense of the word; it comes from having united in one's memory and character the fruit of many diverse undertakings. . . . Chance feeling needs to fortify itself with reasons and to find its level in the great world. When it has added fitness to sincerity, beneficence to its passion, it will have acquired the right to live.

REFERENCES

(1) BIRKHOFF, G. D. *Aesthetic Measure.* (Harvard University Press: Cambridge, 1933)

(2) BRAGDON, CLAUDE. *The Frozen Fountain.* (Alfred A. Knopf: New York, 1932)

(3) BULLIET, C. J. *Apples and Madonnas.* (Covici: New York, 1930)

(4) CHENEY, SHELDON. *New World Architecture.* (Longmans, Green, and Co.: New York, 1930)

(5) CHENEY, SHELDON. *Expressionism in Art.* (Boni-Liveright: New York, 1935)

(6) CORTISSOZ, ROYAL. *Art and Common Sense.* (Charles Scribner's Sons: New York, 1913)

(7) CRAVEN, THOMAS. *Modern Art.* (Simon and Schuster: New York, 1934)

(8) CROCE, BENEDETTO. *A Breviary of Aesthetics.* Excerpt in *Philosophies of Beauty*, by E. F. Carritt. (Oxford: London, 1931)

(9) DEWEY, JOHN. *Experience and Nature.* (W. W. Norton and Co., Inc.: New York, 1925)

(10) DEWEY, JOHN. *Art as Experience.* (Milton Balch: New York, 1934)

(11) DUCASSE, CURT J. *The Philosophy of Art.* (Dial Press: New York, 1929)

(12) EDMAN, IRWIN. *The Philosophy of Santayana.* (Charles Scribner's Sons: New York, 1936)

(13) FAULKNER, R., and ZIEGFELD, E. *Art Today.* (University of Minnesota Mimeograph Department: Minneapolis, 1936)

(14) FIELD, JOANNA. *An Experiment in Leisure.* (The Macmillan Co.: Toronto, 1937)

(15) FIELD, JOANNA. *A Life of One's Own.* (Chatto: London, 1934)

(16) FRY, ROGER. *Vision and Design.* (Brentano's: New York, 1924)

(17) HAGGERTY, M. E. *Art a Way of Life.* (University of Minnesota Press: Minneapolis, 1935)

(18) HEARD, GERALD. *Pain, Sex and Time.* (Harper and Brothers: New York, 1939)

(19) HIRN, YRJO. *The Origins of Art.* (London, 1900)

(20) LEON, PHILIP. *Aesthetic Knowledge.*

(21) LOGAN, JOSEPHINE. *Sanity in Art.* (Kroch: Chicago, 1937)

(22) MACLEISH, ARCHIBALD. "Poetry and the public world." *Atlantic Monthly,* 163: June, 1939, 823–830.

(23) MUMFORD, LEWIS. *Architecture.* (American Library Association: Chicago, 1926)

(24) MUNRO, THOMAS. *Scientific Method in Aesthetics.* (W. W. Norton and Co., Inc.: New York, 1928)

(25) PARKER, D. W. R. *The Analysis of Art.* (Yale University Press: New Haven, 1926)

(26) PARKER, D. W. R. *The Principles of Aesthetics.* (Silver, Burdett and Co.: New York, 1920)

(27) PEARSON, RALPH. *Experiencing Pictures.* (Harcourt, Brace and Co.: New York, 1932)

(28) READ, HERBERT. *Art and Society.* (The Macmillan Co.: New York, 1937)

(29) RUCKSTUHL, F. W. *Great Works of Art and What Makes Them Great.* (G. P. Putnam's Sons: New York, 1925)

(30) SANTAYANA, GEORGE. *Reason in Art.* (Charles Scribner's Sons: New York, 1906)

(31) SULLIVAN, LOUIS. *The Autobiography of an Idea.* (Press of the American Institute of Architects: Washington, 1926)

(32) TOLSTOI, L. V. *What Is Art?* (Oxford Press: New York, 1930)

(33) TOROSSIAN, A. *A Guide to Aesthetics.* (Stanford University Press: Stanford, 1937)

(34) VEBLEN, THORSTEIN. *Theory of the Leisure Class.* (Viking Press: New York, 1935)

(35) WICKES, FRANCES. *The Inner World of Man.* (Farrar and Rinehart: New York, 1938)

(36) WILENSKI, R. H. *The Modern Movement in Art.* (Frederick A. Stokes Co.: New York, 1927)

(37) WRIGHT, FRANK LLOYD. *Autobiography.* (Longmans, Green, and Co.: New York, 1932)

(38) WRIGHT, WILLARD H. *Modern Painting.* (Dodd Mead and Co.: New York, 1927)

CHAPTER XXVIII

ART AND ITS RELATION TO SOCIETY

RAY FAULKNER

Head, Department of Fine and Industrial Arts
Teachers College, Columbia University
New York, New York

I. INTRODUCTORY

Walter Damrosch (5) has said that since Schubert, who was poor, and Mendelssohn, who was rich, both wrote good music, the ' conditions of existence ' must have little effect on genius. Some writers extend this idea to the point of saying that all art production, not that of genius alone, proceeds with little or no influence from society. In strong contrast is the belief that the arts are determined to a large extent by the social and economic systems in which they develop (6, 8, 11, 17, 20). To the educator, this has the familiar ring of the heredity-environment controversy.

The relation of art to society is not merely the concern of philosophers, but is also of vital import to critics, laymen, and, above all, to educators, because the manner in which this relation is understood and interpreted determines many of their attitudes, beliefs, and actions. Those who agree that society has little direct influence on art will not be concerned with controlling conditions in the interest of art production, but will rest content in the belief that art will develop quite adequately if left alone. In contrast, those who believe that social conditions significantly influence art production and appreciation will ever be seeking ways and means to bring about stimulating environments. The implications of these two divergent points of view reach into every phase of education in the arts.

Stephen Pepper, Head of the Department of Art, University of California, Berkeley, California, has contributed the following statement:

> There have been frequent attempts to correlate the values of art with social conditions. We find theories that art prospers most in a state of luxury or most under conditions of want, in times of peace or in periods of social turmoil, within an individualistic and free social atmosphere or under the protection of powerful patrons or in the service of a state or a

religion, in primitive society or in civilized society. An enumeration of the theories of such a correlation practically answers the question. Probably no such correlation exists.

Some sort of excellent art probably prospers under any social condition. It is obvious, however, that the form art takes will be greatly influenced by the social conditions, and it is probable that the quantity of good art produced is subject to these conditions. Bridges, skyscrapers, and cinemas could only appear in an industrial society, and fondly carved rattles and totem poles filled with magic, myth, and symbolism only in certain primitive societies.

Excellent art has a way of emerging in the most unexpected places, and is frequently missed by the critical eye of its generation. We are, perhaps, underrating the cinema today almost as much as the cultured gentlemen of Japan underrated the Ukeoye of their time. One might almost be tempted to state that the greatest art of a generation is the spontaneous and unrecognized movement that no one at the time takes to be art. Perhaps today our greatest art is our battleships and bombing planes, certain columns in our newspapers, certain messages and speeches of our presidents, prime ministers, and dictators. But to halt the march of this idea, which would rapidly turn into the economic theory of art, we need only think of the Horaces and the Blakes of almost every epoch. T. S. Eliot may also be one of our greatest artists, or some utterly unknown man so out of step with our time that he will only be discovered a century hence in a volume of poems that he had to pay to get printed.

The principal reason that statistical or pseudo-statistical correlations between art and social conditions are so difficult is the complexity of the problem of what constitutes excellence in art. If we are given any set of esthetic ideals, such as those of the Little Dutch School culminating in Vermeer, then its development in terms of the social conditions of Holland at that time can be easily worked out. We can perhaps also show why there was great interest in that school in New England in the late nineteenth century, and possibly why those New England painters did not attain the level of the Dutch. But such a study relates to only one set of ideals, and, as regards the relation of art as a whole to society, is not illuminating — may even readily become distortive. For what about Rembrandt or Winslow Homer?

Most theories of art in relation to society do just this sort of thing on a larger scale. They take the ideals of a school as a base — say the high Renaissance ideals of the Italians, or the new ideals of the modern French — and proceed quite truly to show how social conditions assisted or failed to assist in the development of these ideals. Such studies are interesting and often illuminating, but they must not be taken for more than they are. For instance, we are now ready to admit that there has been a great deal of sculpture quite equal to the fifth-century Greek. Hegel, for one, was simply taking the fifth-century ideals as a base and making some comparative literary comments of unquestionably stimulating interest. But these judgments were actually distortive in their intent. The Marxian theories in a subtler way appear to be doing the same thing, taking some sort of economic or social significance as a base.

In reaction, we have the purely historical and anthropological treatment of art in society, which purports to be free from all judgments of esthetic value except those which the artists or artisans themselves exhibit. Here art is treated as a cultural fact, like husbandry, the domestication of animals, or magic. So far as these studies imply no denials of esthetic judgments, or of the possibility and importance of other methods of studying art, they are all to the good. But just so far as this is true of such work, there is little of interest there for our topic.

The conclusion seems to be that there are no reliable correlations between art values and social structures, that the numerous theories offered to describe such relations appear to be inadequate and partisan, though often illuminating within their own field of vision; and that the historical and anthropological methods are irrelevant to the question, though serviceable in extending the range of materials for study.

Thus it becomes clear that the way in which the relations of art to society are interpreted is not a simple matter admitting an easy and quick solution. Rather there is a great variety of interdependent issues, conditions, and factors, all intricately interwoven.

Four major questions around which the remainder of this discussion will be focussed are: Is art an autonomous activity, or does it occur only as a by-product of other fields? Is art produced for its own sake? How and to what extent do social conditions influence the form of art? What are the major implications for education?

II. The Major Issues

1. The Autonomy of Art

Does the art impulse occur independently or is it always an outgrowth or by-product of play, sex, religion, and the like? Stated differently, is art one of the basic *components* integrating with other impulses to build society or is it a *reflection* of the social order and its activities? Because it is basic to many attitudes and practices, the issue of the autonomy of art is of strategic importance.

The concept of art as a mirrored image of social conditions and the artist as an especially sensitive person who follows and expresses social trends, without assuming active, influential leadership, is widely held by many persons, particularly those not directly concerned with the arts. A number of practices that lead to this attitude can be mentioned. The business man, interested primarily in increasing sales of his product, calls in a ' stylist ' to make his product more attractive in appearance, and thus to increase its sales appeal. At times the designer is given freedom to study and solve the problem in a comprehensive way, but often only minor changes, such as improving the spacing of stripes on a bath towel or designing a simple case to cover the mechanism of some complex product, are permitted. A dictatorial government may employ artists to popularize the face, name, or activities of its leader. Religious leaders engage artists to help persuade their congregations of the values of their religion. Because art is closely related to business and economics, education and religion, politics and government, play and recreation, it is frequently assumed that it is merely one of the tools to be used by these fields to achieve their ends. According to this belief, art has no independent existence or reason for being.

However, the continuity and persistence of art expressions in human history and the fundamental similarities of art products from widely varying cultural epochs point strongly to the theory that art is one of the basic types of human activity, closely related to other behavioral patterns, but having sufficient unique and positive characteristics to be regarded as one of the primary types of human behavior. This is the conclusion reached both by Hirn (10) who believes in the existence of an independent art impulse, although he is quite ready to admit that its appearance is concomitant with other activities, and also by Read who says (17, xiii) :

> But art, I shall maintain, is an autonomous activity, influenced, like all our activities, by the material conditions of existence, but as a mode of knowledge at once its own reality and its own end . . . as a mode of reaction, it is distinct and contributes in its own right to that process of integration which we call a civilization or culture.

Similarly, in developing his thesis Read points out that art is a mode of expression that makes use of many utilitarian things to convey its meaning, just as language makes use of paper and ink. He concludes his introduction with the following statements (17, xix) :

> In all its essential activities art is trying to tell us something: something about the universe, something about nature, about man, or about the artist himself. Art is a mode of knowledge as valuable to man — indeed, more valuable — than the world of philosophy or the world of science. It is only when we have clearly recognized the function of art as a

mode of knowledge parallel to the other modes by which man arrives at an understanding of his environment that we can begin to appreciate its significance in the history of mankind.

Although we may well question the statement that art is more important than science or philosophy, Read develops his argument convincingly by showing how art has served magic, mysticism, religion, and secular needs without losing its integrity.

In no sense should this be understood as implying that art dwells in an Ivory Tower (6) [1], that it remains aloof from other human concerns. The great variety of needs that the arts serve and have served gives ample proof of the manner in which art is woven into the social fabric. As in the field of chemistry we find unique chemical elements combining to form compounds, so in the social field we find special types of activities fused to produce the total pattern. In society as in chemistry the closeness of this combination should not dull us to the distinctiveness of the parts.

It is true that the special qualities of art are often obscured, not only by art's intimate association with other social processes, but also by the tremendous range of art functions and products; for the field includes sculpture, painting, and architecture as well as cooking utensils, dishes, and automobiles. Some of these provide more intense, or purer, esthetic satisfaction than do others. Thus, a painting by Michelangelo is hardly to be compared with the design on a magazine cover, any more than a typical gasoline filling station is to be compared with the Parthenon. The artistic values of a painting by Michelangelo and of the Parthenon are vastly greater than those of the magazine cover or the filling station because they appeal more forcibly to man's esthetic needs. Yet all four are art products, and the differences among them are quantitative rather than qualitative. It would be possible to arrange a continuous series of art products ranked according to the degree of their artistic content from, say, factories at one extreme to abstract paintings or flower arrangements at the other.

Through all these manifestations run the essential characteristics of art. Energy is directed and transformed into thoughtful action; nature is changed to produce new relationships that evoke a new emotional response. The result is identifiable as, (1) an expressive communication arising from qualities rather than facts of experience; (2) an orderly and significant organization of colors, forms, textures, and

---

[1] See Chapter by Laurence Buermeyer on " Art and the Ivory Tower."

spaces; and (3) a sensitive and sympathetic handling of materials. From these characteristics arises a direct appeal to man's esthetic sensibilities that results in a unique response — the esthetic experience.

Another aspect of this issue — the relation between the esthetic emotion and other emotional experiences, particularly in regard to creative or expressive activity — is discussed by Dewey (7, p. 78) as follows:

> Esthetic emotion is thus something distinctive and yet not cut off by a chasm from other and natural emotional experiences, as some theorists in contending for its existence have made it to be. One familiar with recent literature on esthetics will be aware of a tendency to go to one extreme or the other. On one hand, it is assumed that there is in existence, at least in some gifted persons, an emotion that is aboriginally esthetic, and that artistic production and appreciation are the manifestations of this emotion. Such a conception is the inevitable logical counterpart of all attitudes that make art something esoteric and that relegate fine art to a realm separated by a gulf from everyday experiences. On the other hand, a reaction, wholesome in intent against this view, goes to the extreme of holding that there is no such thing as distinctively esthetic emotion. The emotion of affection that operates not through an overt act of caress but by searching out the observation or image of a soaring bird, the emotion of irritating energy that does not destroy or injure but that puts objects in satisfying order, is not numerically identical with its original and natural estate. Yet it stands in genetic continuity with it. The emotion that was finally wrought by Tennyson in the composition of ' In Memoriam ' was not identical with the emotion of grief that manifests itself in weeping and a downcast frame: the first is an act of expression, the second of discharge. Yet the continuity of the two emotions, the fact that the esthetic emotion is native emotion transformed through the objective materials to which it has committed its development and consummation, is evident.

In summary, there is convincing evidence that art, in spite of its integration with other fields of activities and its widely varying functions and range of products, is a discernible and identifiable entity in the complex of social behavior. Art is not merely a reflection of society; it is one of the primary, determining components that make society what it is.

2. Art for Art's Sake versus Art for Society's Sake

The doctrine of art for art's sake, popular not many years ago, has recently been challenged on so many sides that today it is seldom mentioned with anything but scorn. While closely related to the preceding issue of the autonomy of art, this leads us more directly to a consideration of the purposes that art serves.

The theory has been attacked perhaps most effectively by the industrial designers, who, through their well-designed products, have called the attention of the public to the fact that most art products serve utilitarian purposes and that their value is to a large extent determined by the efficiency with which they function. Refrigerators, furnaces, kitchen pots and pans, and vacuum cleaners designed with full attention to intended function after careful study of present-day needs stand as evidence that art is not concerned with producing the useless. Even before the industrial designers came on the scene to proclaim art's usefulness, those architects who saw the weaknesses of eclecticism and meaningless ornamentation were laboring to show that architecture was not ' the decoration of construction ' but rather ' space enclosed for a reason.' Although the concept of architecture as a functional art is as old as the most ancient building, it had been obscured during the nineteenth century by unthinking veneration for the past and by a catering to the uninformed tastes of a new moneyed class, intent on displaying its wealth through useless decoration. Such excesses led Thorstein Veblen to conclude that " conspicuous waste," often in the form of decoration applied for ' art's sake,' was the criterion of art value held by many persons.

While architects and industrial designers have given tangible evidence through their works of the narrowness of art for art's sake, another group has attacked this belief, not with works but with words. Frequently, though not always, of Marxist leanings these writers see art vitally and usefully related to society and as a means of hastening the development of a new social order. Plekhanov (16, p. 33), one of the leading writers on esthetics from the Marxist point of view, quotes Chernishevsky as follows:

> ' Art for art's sake ' in our time is as fantastic an idea as ' riches for riches' sake,' ' science for science's sake,' and so on. All human affairs must have a useful purpose if they would not be vain and idle pastimes; riches exist for man's enjoyment, science for his guidance; art likewise must perform a certain utilitarian function and not engender mere empty pleasure. . . .
>
> Art, or poetry rather — because the other arts can accomplish little in this respect — diffuses among the mass of readers an enormous amount of knowledge and, what is even more important, an acquaintance with

concepts developed by science. Herein lies the great significance of poetry.

The contrasting attitude is illustrated by a quotation from Gautier's biographical sketch of Baudelaire in which he writes that Baudelaire " would not admit that poetry should have any end outside itself, or any mission to fulfill other than that of exciting in the soul of the reader the sensation of supreme beauty — beauty in the absolute sense of the term." To find sharper conflict of opinion would be difficult: Chernishevsky wrote that art must never be an end in itself but must always be subservient to other activities, whereas Baudelaire believed that art, always its own end, was harmed or weakened by serving other purposes.

Before proceeding to examine the validity of these two points of view, we may well consider Plekhanov's explanation of the origin of the cult of art for art's sake. It arises and grows strong, he writes, when artists feel a hopeless contradiction between their aims and those of the social group to which they belong. They must not only be hostile to the existing society but also see no hope of improving it through their own creative activity. By ignoring the social order and serving only art's demands they are then free to create work that seems to them important. While such withdrawal may act as a device protecting the genius in the pursuit of his work, it may also be merely an excuse for men of lesser talents to continue producing unintelligible or meretricious products.

Obviously there is much of value in Plekhanov's incisive analysis of the rôle of art in society. His many references to the importance of the ' idea ' behind the work of art, to art as a means of communication among men — in sum, his emphasis on art as an active factor in determining men's actions — is healthy and vigorous, inspiring to creators, and illuminating to consumers. The chief weakness of his philosophy, and of the others of which he has been chosen as representative, lies in his dogmatic decision that art expression must conform to a single preconceived sociopolitical pattern. If he believes that art may justifiably serve functions other than propaganda, he conceals this from the reader. He finds no place for those art expressions and experiences that exalt or stimulate men without ulterior motives. There is no place in such a system for simply enjoying the esthetic experiences afforded through contact with great paintings, sculptures, or symphonies as an important part of enriched, well-balanced living. To be stimulated and satisfied esthetically is not enough to him; in fact, he might even consider it harmful. By channelizing art expression he reduces a tremendous source of human satisfaction in that he prescribes, not for one or a few, but for all persons, what they shall enjoy. It is probably because such dogmatic narrowness strikes close to the heart of the democratic way of life that those who believe in the freedom of the individual resist such regimentation of art. Although art is one of the firmest bonds of communication among men, to limit its sphere of activity according to socioeconomic doctrine materially weakens its effectiveness.

Whether or not art is to serve utilitarian functions in life is not the kernel of the issue, because most persons agree wholeheartedly that art can and should be useful. The real issue is whether or not the functions that art serves are to be limited by anything narrower than the whole complex pattern of human interests and desires. When the purposes that art serves have been limited, it is a short step to prescribing the manner of expression as well. Regimentation of style follows closely on the heels of regimentation of content. Control is exerted not only over *what* ideas are to be communicated but also over *how* they are to be expressed. The tendency is generally in the direction of making the expression obvious rather than subtle and conventional rather than experimental, in the hope of thus achieving universal appeal. But to believe that one or a few types of art can carry significance to all persons shows a profound disregard for the remarkable variation in human nature.

In no case does the artist have complete freedom in his creative work, for his total environment brings unavoidable pressures that guide his activities and shape his products. But taking the interests and capacities of one group, or even the average of all groups, as a standard for art production to which all artists should conform is foreign to democratic respect for the individuality of the consumer and creator.

Although compromises often seem halfhearted measures, a comprehensive and sympathetic survey of the art field -- abstract and propaganda paintings, Expressionist sculpture and automobiles, modern houses and Greek temples, commercial posters and Chinese tapestries — precludes a wholehearted adherence to either extreme of this issue for the simple reason that the extremes have resulted from ignoring large and important sections of the art field and groups of people. To say that all art exists for its own sake, as an end in itself, is to ignore the magnificence of Greek temples, Gothic cathedrals, and Renaissance paintings as well as the more commonplace dishes, furniture, and clothes of everyday life. And to say that no art should exist or be enjoyed for its own sake is to turn our backs on the profound, deeply moving human satisfactions that come from our appreciations of the music of Brahms, Chinese painting, Negro or Egyptian sculpture, even though we may not understand the final significance of these expressions. Art production and appreciation suffer seriously when either extreme is in vogue. Those interested in enriching, enlarging, and expanding life do not make such needless decisions with their consequent limitations. Some art is, and should be, an end in itself; some art does, and should; serve many other fields.

3. The Influence of Society on Art

Even though we accept the idea that art is an autonomous field of human endeavor or has an ' original nature,' so to speak, there still remains the issue of the extent and the direction of the influence of the social order upon the art product. The relation between art and other fields of human activity seems at times to be inconstant. Thus, at certain periods, art of high esthetic merit flourished under the patronage of religion, and at other times art of the most maudlin type was equally well supported. Similarly, public buildings range in esthetic merit from the Athenian Parthenon to some Victorian courthouses and ' Renaissance ' movie palaces. If society does influence art production, it is important to determine which forces in society exert this power, and to what degree. It is possible that a complete range of art tastes and sensitivities exists at any given time in society, but the force exerted by different levels of taste varies tremendously from one period to another. Whereas during certain periods of Greek and Italian history those in control gave evidence of superior taste, at other times those who determined the dominant directions of art development have given evidence of markedly inferior taste. The determining effect of the social environment on art is closely paralleled by the psychological-biological problem of nature versus nurture.

First, we may consider the effect of society on the form or style of art. Taine (21), drawing a comparison from the plant world, points out that seeds of an orange planted in poor soil on a mountain will not produce trees such as will seeds planted in rich soil and a favorable climate. The trees will be small and misshapen in the one case, large and symmetrically formed in the other. Taine believes that artists, and consequently their products, are similarly affected (but not produced) by the social climate. The form of art products, like that of plants, is strongly influenced by the conditions under which they develop. An excellent definition of style is ' environment acting on form,' for styles in art do not spring into existence from nowhere, but result from long periods of adapting designs to meet human needs under differing social and geographical conditions.

The history of all art, but that of architecture in particular, gives ample evidence of this determining relationship (1, 8). The vast differences between the Egyptian and Greek temples, both built from stone by the post-and-lintel method of construction, are the natural result of differences in social and geographical forces. The Egyptian temple presents a strong barrier of almost unbroken wall to the observer, whereas the typical Greek temple, surrounded by its colonnade, is open on every side. Even if we had no other sources of information concerning the social systems of these two peoples, the stern, forbidding exterior of the Egyptian and the hospitable, open appearance of the Greek temples would tell us much about their builders. The grandeur of the Roman baths and basilicas, the heavy ornamentation often applied with little taste or reason, is clear evidence of the later Roman way of life. Similarly, the restless, surging verticality of the Gothic cathedrals, partially explained by climatic conditions, is a direct expression of the socioreligious beliefs of that age. In our country the differences in size and planning of New England and southern Colonial houses are due in large part to the different social patterns of the two sections. In each instance the basic impulse to build shelter for some purpose has been modified and shaped by trends dominant in that society. Painting, sculpture, and the allied arts would furnish many additional examples to substantiate this thesis.

Second, not only does the social climate affect the form of the product, but it often determines as well which artists will receive the encouragement and support necessary to creative work. No clearer example could be found than the present practices in the totalitarian states of dictating which artists are to create — and even which artists, living and dead, are to be enjoyed. The Nazi regime has cast disfavor on experimental, expressive art, with the result that most art produced in Germany today is academic and sterile. Similarly, while the Soviet powers have conducted broad experiments in government, economics, religion, and morals, they have not recently encouraged progressive efforts in the arts. The arts in these countries, painting in particular, are merely tools for popularizing social philosophy. Under such conditions art is nothing but a passive reflection of the dictated social ideology; in no sense is it a contributing factor.

In contrast, under democratic conditions art can be a lively force in shaping and developing the form of society. It can be an active, integrating ingredient in the social organization. Art in a democracy will not display the unity of dictated art, because it will always be seeking new, individual, more intense and more functional modes of expression. It is important to bear this in mind when considering the varied art expressions in the United States. Here society influences art, and art influences society.

4. The Major Implications for Education

The first implication for education is that the controversies, opinions, prejudices, and facts just briefly discussed deserve and demand far more attention, and more explicit attention, in education than they receive in the typical art class. Confined to the formula of imitative drawing, plus principles of design and color, plus stereotyped appreciation of a few ' Old Masters,' art in the schools has seldom plunged into these vital matters that ought to be at the basis of any sound approach to the field. Only when confronted with the necessity of correlating art with the social studies has the school art program been forced to consider the great social forces that nourish art production and consumption. The situation has commonly been dismissed cursorily with brief remarks about the lives of a few painters and a sketchy outline of the more superficial facets of art history.

The failure of the typical school art program to provide these experiences that demonstrate effectively the place of art in the total human economy has robbed art instruction of many potentialities and has tended to make it a thing of paper, pencils, chalks, and rules rather than a study and an expression of individual and group emotions and actions. Even at the college level — where the typical art curriculum bristles with specialized courses in fragments of art history — the so-called ' scholarly ' concern with the names, dates, and peculiarities of masterpieces diverts the students from the larger issues, and leaves them poorly equipped to comprehend major problems in contemporary art. It is time we realized that the imposition of diluted versions of professional art skills and the throwing out by the ' spray technique ' of vast amounts of patiently accumulated historical facts does little to promote a true understanding of art in its relation to social forces.

To be sure, the picture is not entirely black, for a number of schools, seeking to make education effective, have found the arts to be rich resources for gaining insights into present and past cultures. Spurred on by the recent government art projects in the United States, by contemporary artistic and political developments in Europe, and by the increasingly widespread enthusiasm for the arts on the part of the American public, educators in many fields are becoming increasingly sensitive to the rôle of art in the educative process.

No matter what one's personal beliefs and interpretations of the past and present of art may be, the complex interweaving of art and society, past and present, demands conscious attention, because, as already noted, the position taken by the educator on these issues will determine teaching procedures in many more ways than is generally recognized. For example, if, as the writer believes, art is an autonomous activity integral with science, religion, economics, and politics in producing a society, art in the schools should neither be isolated from other activities nor be dominated and submerged by them. Like an individual citizen in a democratic group, art is a component in the total cultural and educational pattern. Its fullest possibilities can only be realized when art is permitted to develop its unique contribution to the school program by relating it to other activities, at the same time allowing it freedom sufficient to develop its own qualities. This point of view has been admirably expressed by Munro (12), and has been carried out in one way by Stolper and Fenn (20). If, however, art is regarded as an activity so different from other human pursuits that it has little in common with them, art in the school program will remain aloof in the studio, seldom if ever condescending to associate with other subject fields. A third point of view, presumably the one that Marxist philosophers would defend, is that art, since it is subservient to the social studies, is nothing more than a tool. Having no independent validity or value, art would become only a handmaiden to them.

Nor is the effect of the teacher's philosophy of art limited to the more obvious relations with other departments. It penetrates into all teaching procedures. This is particularly true of the way in which art history is handled. If art production is interpreted as the outcroppings of sporadic geniuses drawing their inspiration and support from intangible sources, phenomena such as the Acropolis or the cathedral at Chartres will be inexplicable marvels before which we gape and wonder. In contrast, if art production is seen to be the result of certain conditions (all of which, it is true, may not be known), a careful study of these conditions will pave the road to an understanding of the products. Art products and processes will be perceived as deeply rooted in the social and geographical complex to which they belong.

Such illustrations could be multiplied many times to demonstrate more clearly how a philosophy, no matter how well or poorly formulated, affects teaching. As social conditions have affected, and will affect, the art produced and enjoyed by a society, so educational conditions will affect the art created and appreciated in schools. To a large extent, art at any given time is what society — and education — want it to be.

REFERENCES

(1) CHENEY, SHELDON. *A World History of Art.* (The Viking Press: New York, 1937)
(2) BOAS, F. *Primitive Art.* (Harvard University Press: Cambridge, 1927) The standard work today on the anthropology of art.
(3) BOSANQUET, B. *History of Aesthetic.* (Allen and Unwin: London, 1922) A book exemplifying the idealistic conception of the relation of art to cultural development.
(4) COULTON, G. G. *Art and the Reformation.* (Basil Blackwell: Oxford, 1928)
(5) DAMROSCH, WALTER. *NBC Music Appreciation Hour. 1932–33.* (National Broadcasting Co., Inc.: New York, 1932)
(6) DEWEY, JOHN, and Others. *Art and Education.* (Barnes Foundation Press: Philadelphia, 1929)
(7) DEWEY, J. *Art as Experience.* (Minton, Balch and Co.: New York, 1934) A book that stresses the intimate relation between art and society and the importance of each for the other. An antidote to all insulative theories of art.
(8) FLETCHER, BANNISTER. *History of Architecture.* (Charles Scribner's Sons: New York, 1921)
(9) HARRISON, JANE E. *Ancient Art and Ritual.* (Henry Holt and Co.: New York, 1913) A book exemplifying most of Tolstoy's fallacies, but hidden under a cloak of scholarship and erudition. Very valuable for making one aware of the pitfalls of esthetic-social thinking.
(10) HIRN, YRGO. *Origins of Art.* (The Macmillan Co.: New York, 1937)
(11) LIFSHITZ, MIKHAIL. *The Philosophy of Art of Karl Marx.* (Critics Group Press: New York, 1938)
(12) MUNRO, THOMAS. "Modern Art and Social Problems." *Art Education Today: 1938.* (Teachers College Bureau of Publications: New York, 1938)
(13) MUNRO, THOMAS. "Art and world citizenship." *American Magazine of Art,* October, 1938
(14) PARRINGTON, V. L. *Main Currents in American Thought.* (Harcourt, Brace and Co.: New York, 1927) A very fine book in which literary art is used as a means of showing the rationale of social movements. A model of its kind, for it describes the force and contents of works of art that have been influential as causes or effects of social movements and leaves open questions of esthetic evaluation.
(15) PHILLIPS, L. M. *Art and Environment.* (Henry Holt and Co.: New York, 1911)
(16) PLEKHANOV, GEORGE V. *Art and Society.* (Critics Group Press: New York, 1937)
(17) READ, HERBERT. *Art and Society.* (The Macmillan Co.: New York, 1937)

(18) SANTAYANA, G. *Reason in Art.* (Charles Scribner's Sons: New York, 1906) A good illustration of the spirit of a naturalistic approach towards the relation of art to society.

(19) SPENGLER, O. *Decline of the West.* (Alfred A. Knopf: New York, 1926) Good example of a widespread conception of social phenomena on the analogy of an organism that is born, matures, declines, and dies — with accompanying evaluations. Not to be too readily discarded as a complete absurdity.

(20) STOLPER, F. J. F., and FENN, HENRY. *Integration at Work: Six Greek Cities.* (Teachers College Bureau of Publications: New York, 1939)

(21) TAINE, H. *Lectures on Art.* (Henry Holt and Co.: New York, 1875)

(22) TAINE, H. *The Ideal in Art.* (Leypoldt & Holt: New York, 1869) *History of English Literature.* (Colonial Press: New York) The outstanding example of the identification of esthetic values with the cultural interests of social epochs. These books deserve careful study from the point of view of method however much one may disagree with expressed judgments on men and their works.

(23) TOLSTOY, LEO. *What Is Art* and *What Is Religion.* (Thomas Y. Crowel Co.: New York, 1898) Sincere, and mistaken, identification of art with religious movements, valuable as exemplifying all the fallacies of method in esthetics.

(24) VEBLEN, THORSTEIN. *Theory of the Leisure Class.* (Viking Press: New York, 1935)

SECTION III

ART EDUCATION:
ITS AIMS, PROCEDURES, AND AGENCIES

CHAPTER XXIX

PAST AND PRESENT TRENDS IN ART EDUCATION [1]

Royal Bailey Farnum, Robert Stose Hilpert, Grace Sobotka,
William G. Whitford, and Alma C. Field

I

THE EARLY HISTORY OF AMERICAN ART EDUCATION

Royal Bailey Farnum
Executive Vice-President, Rhode Island School of Design
Providence, Rhode Island

A study of the development of art education in this country must commence in the early decades of the nineteenth century, where we find drawing taught as a special and somewhat detached subject, advertised in local newspapers on the one hand by professional painters, who offered such instruction in limited classes with a definite vocational intent, and on the other hand by the boarding-school mistress, who "respectfully solicits a share of the publick patronage" for such "Ornamental branches" as "Drawing, Embroidery, Musick, and making a great variety of fancy articles" (12).

This segregation of drawing was the inevitable outcome of some four hundred years of separation between art and useful production. Up to the close of the Middle Ages and during the early period of the Renaissance, art was common to all processes of human manufacture and therefore was an integral part of the workman's training, learned through performance on the job or in the workshops of the various craft guilds. Design, color, and drawing were as fundamental to a man's experience as figuring, estimating, and tool manipulation. As organized society became more complex, as the guilds became less powerful, and as individual expression was fostered, the so-called 'Fine Arts' became separated from the crafts, and Schools of Art began to sprout.

It was then that architecture, sculpture, and painting became di-

---

[1] The titles and addresses of the writers of the five sub-sections of this chapter are given with the names of the writers at the head of their contributions. — *Editor.*

vorced from their traditional places in the general scheme of production and " were associated with the studio and the artist, and all other products were relegated to the workshop and the craftsman; and finally, with the advent of mechanized production, in the nineteenth century, the factory despoiled the craftsman of his traditional birthright as an independent creator of beautiful things for the needs of life " (42, p. 486).

So long as power machines were considered only as speedier methods for the reproduction of traditional handcrafts and classical ornament, art was conceived to be valuable to the wealthy patron alone or as a special accomplishment for the formal education of the few. It no longer was part of the common man's existence. For a few, the accepted approach to art in its newer and narrower sense was through drawing. In turn, drawing was confined chiefly to copy of the resurrected forms of Greek art by means of plaster casts of Classic sculpture and ornament. Even today one may find lingering aspects of this approach.

In the middle of the nineteenth century, however, a group of industrialists in Massachusetts came to the conclusion that skill in drawing and a knowledge of historic forms of ornament were essential to their manufacture, and later, in 1870, an act of the state legislature was passed permitting drawing ("industrial and mechanical ") to be " freely " taught in any city and town, and making " free " instruction compulsory in cities and towns of over 10,000 inhabitants (12).

At this stage of art education the esthetic welfare of children was not even remotely envisioned and such terms as ' correlation ' or ' integration ' did not exist in the teacher's professional vocabulary. Drawing, taught as an isolated subject, was dictated, geometric, and mechanical. But gradually the few leaders [1] who began to influence the situation realized the possibilities of a broader conception of what drawing symbolized. They traveled; they came in contact with thinkers in more general fields of education; they were affected by new teaching methods, by those early timid approaches in child psychology, and by the apparent need for a clearer understanding of art as it related to the rank and file of humanity. Drawing of geometric solids and historic ornament began to give way to nature drawing; then to study of form. Later color was introduced, and likewise some attempts at handwork were offered. Next came the possibilities of correlation with the more

---

[1] Henry Turner Bailey, Walter Sargent, Wilhelmina Siegmiller, Bonnie A. Snow, James Hall, Hugo Froehlich, Walter Scott Perry, Leslie Miller, Mrs. M. E. Riley, C. M. Carter, James P. Haney.

ambitious type of handwork called 'sloyd' (and later 'manual training'), with 'domestic art,' and in daring instances with history and geography. Recognition of two broad aims in drawing, cultural and industrial, soon pointed the way to a wider understanding of art values (28). Drawing and what it stood for might become a general, not a special, subject. Through this opportunity the child might be taught individual observation and independent expression. The values of appreciative understanding in the art expression of master artists and designers were slowly accepted. Opportunities for closely relating the services of art to other curricular activities became apparent. This was followed by a growing realization that the same values applied equally well and with similar practical relevancy in the child's home and in his general social environment (3).

II
CHANGING EMPHASES IN SCHOOL ART PROGRAMS

ROBERT STOSE HILPERT
Associate Professor of Art, University of California
Los Angeles, California

The examination of printed courses of study and actual classroom observation will reveal a confusion of philosophies, objectives, and procedures which weakens the points of agreement that could hold art educators together. This lack of agreement prevents art educators from establishing a unifying force akin to that found in school subjects on which educators have come to more definite agreement as to goals, purposes, and procedures. A clarification of purposes and programs of art in education must be carried out in terms of contemporary ideas of general education.

No doubt much of the current interest in general education has been stimulated by a reaction against the overemphasis upon specialization that has characterized some of the educational programs in the recent past. This same reaction against specialization is pertinently aimed at certain practices in art that recognized only the talented few and that largely ignored most of the pupils. The trend in outstanding schools is to relate education to the actual needs of all pupils as individuals and as members of contemporary society, and to meet existing problems in real life-situations. Art in education must follow this example more than it has to date and provide *all* pupils — not only the talented few — with opportunities to make art function as a vital part of everyday life. This is the challenge to art education raised by the current interest in general education.

As in other fields, there have been changes in objectives and procedures from time to time. As a result of each change there seems to be a definite carry-over of objectives and methods that we find persisting today. In some cases educationally undesirable procedures have continued through this sequence of periods to the present without a challenge comparable to that made by the recent emphasis on general education. No doubt much of the present confusion as to objectives and procedures is due to this carrying over of outmoded objectives unrelated to contemporary life and education.

I. Art for Art's Sake as an Educational Doctrine

The theory of Art for Art's Sake emphasizes art as a product for its own sake with no utilitarian, social, or moral purpose. Its advocates adhere rigidly, as did their teachers, to a narrow range of definite rules, technical skills, and historical facts held by their particular group. The different groups that continue to follow Art for Art's Sake disagree as to what procedures and what points of emphasis they advocate, but they do agree that art is a subject by itself and that the creation of beautiful forms is cultural activity for its own sake.[1] It is thought by some that this theory of art was an outcome of collecting and storing specimens of art in museums separated from the original environment in which they were created. Thus they have become detached from the life of their own time and environment and have become precious specimens of Art for Art's Sake, without indicating the political, religious, economic, and social factors that influenced or determined their form.

'Art for Art's Sake' was influential in establishing the 'training for skills and techniques' as an objective. This training was concerned with copying examples of art in museums from periods with characteristics that were not those of the present. Little or no recognition was given to experimental procedures or to the development of originality.

---

[1] For details, see Thomas Munro (55) and John Dewey (18). — *R. S. H.*

II. Appreciation as an Objective

As a reaction from the limitations of Art for Art's Sake the emphasis gradually shifted toward ' appreciation.' Appreciation is an objective emphasized today in most school systems having an organized course of study in art. The term ' appreciation ' is used very loosely, and the interpretation of it in art teaching is frequently limited in the elementary school to ' picture study,' with emphasis on ' stories pictures tell,' while in the secondary school emphasis is frequently placed on more detailed historical facts. The old limited concept of art as painting has continued in this popular procedure, but with the added erroneous emphasis upon literal, rather than upon esthetic, interpretation. In most cases picture-study lessons have been more or less arbitrarily developed and frozen into an accepted pattern. The pictures used are not only unrelated to the interests of children, but often unrelated also to any aspect of life today. The memorization of data concerning a picture and its artist can hardly be considered true appreciation.

In some high schools there has been an attempt to develop appreciation of art, not only in painting but also in sculpture, architecture, and industrial arts, in a sincere endeavor to recognize the esthetic values in these art expressions. Such an analysis of composition and art structure broadens the art experience from that limited to painting to include all the major fine arts. However, when taught by some teachers previously engrossed in Art for Art's Sake, the examples selected are largely from museum specimens unrelated to the interests and experiences of the pupils.

Some groups of art educators have followed a study of art examples of the past by a study of local good examples. While this still gives prestige to the past — usually to gallery specimens — it does attempt to lead pupils to observe, enjoy, and analyze the art objects in their own community. It is obvious that this whole procedure is more adapted to large cities than to average communities where there is a dearth of examples of the fine arts.

To offset the passive attitude on the part of the pupil-listener in art appreciation, art educators have introduced some manipulative exercises to aid the pupil in the analysis of composition of the art specimens discussed. Frequently this has resulted in a banal experience of attempting to copy, usually from mediocre small reproductions of paintings. The mediums used by the pupil are too often limited to inexpensive crayons or water colors that are not related to the medium used in the painting studied. Too much emphasis on a study of technique tends to oppose true appreciation, since art is primarily concerned with other factors than the methods of technique. The emphasis on imitation, rather than on creation, contributes very little to a sympathetic recognition of excellence in a work of art.

III. EMPHASIS UPON CREATIVE SELF-EXPRESSION

As a reaction against the overemphasis on technique and on imitation, other groups of art educators shifted the emphasis to 'creative expression.' Some held that appreciation could only be gained through participation on the part of the learner in creative work, while others sought only the immediate experiences of actual manipulation of some art medium in illustration, design, and the handcrafts. This emphasis on creation, although differently interpreted and developed, continues to be one of the major objectives of art in education today. 'Creative Self-Expression' is a title found in most courses of study, although there is little agreement among art teachers as to what is meant by the terms 'creative' and 'expression.' There is a dearth of concrete suggestions given in courses of study or in teachers' meetings to aid pupils or teachers in the development of this creative self-expression. Creative work for the pure joy of the experience is now held by many groups as the justification of art in education. To some, this is considered a reversion to the theory of Art for Art's Sake, but it must be admitted that the new objective does take into consideration certain current psychological and educational assumptions concerning the individual child as a whole — intellectual, emotional, social, physical.

IV. ATTEMPTS AT CORRELATION WITH ART

The 'correlation of art' with different subjects in the curriculum was a sincere endeavor to give some purpose to art in education other than for its own sake. The correlation of art with home economics and the manual arts in junior and senior high schools was probably more directly functional than that with other subjects. Some of the difficulties encountered early in this type of teaching were the limited experiences of art teachers in the other fields. Shop teachers, for instance, claimed the art teachers were not familiar with materials and tool processes of the manual arts. No progress can be expected in correlation with different subjects until art teachers realize the possibilities of art in every school activity.

V. Art in the Integrated Curriculum

In recent years the integrated school curriculum in the elementary school, as found in the activity programs of progressive schools, has sought to break down artificial boundaries between the different school 'subjects.' This has, in theory at least, changed the place of art as an isolated subject to one that enriches the project, unit of interest, or activity at hand. Ideally, the integrated curriculum should be well balanced with no undue domination of one aspect; but in practice art is frequently subordinated to the present emphasis upon the social studies. This has resulted in a very limited art experience. There has been little of outstanding educational or art value in such so-called 'integration of art' with other subjects as it has been taught in most places. This does not imply that integration does not have potential possibilities of high educational value. It must be admitted that much of the art in the integrated program has been a persistent interpretation of art as the illustration of factual material related to the unit and remote from and unrelated to actual experiences of the child. Thus the drawing of sphinx, pyramid, temple, or pueblo in relation to social studies leads directly to modified copies of illustrations from books or periodicals and does not call upon actual experiencing of art as an integral part of contemporary life in the immediate environment. Several cities leading in art education have recognized this limited use of art and have warned their teachers against forcing art where the subject matter of the unit does not inspire it. Art instruction that does not lead the learner to experience art beyond the four walls of the schoolroom is incomplete. It should lead each pupil to a desire to observe and experience firsthand the vital contributions of art to a normal everyday life.

VI. Stress on the Industrial Arts

In certain activity programs emphasis on the 'industrial arts' prevails. It was originally introduced into education programs some years ago as a reaction against art experiences limited to the fine arts. The activity of making things stimulated by the topic of interest affords the child opportunity to plan, execute, and evaluate his work with esthetic as well as functional values. Some of these early experiences of making choices in the color and arrangement of houses, for example, may develop an interest in the home that eventually leads to more specific art experiences in the upper grades and more specialized work in high-school art classes. A life interest in and enjoyment of architecture may be developed with the playhouse as a point of departure. Field trips to see how houses are built, how they form a part of a community as a whole, how they are landscaped and furnished makes, it may be hoped, for the development of observation and awareness of art factors in one of the largest areas of daily life.

Since art is not static, but dynamic, it changes with each generation. A new point of departure of art in education may develop out of the rapid changes characteristic of our present age. Thus it will be the concern of the art educator of each age to determine the interests and needs of the community and of the individuals within his groups, in order to develop an appropriate and vital art program worthy of its place in general education in a democracy.

VII. Summary

To summarize the more common emphases found in art education today, there is a continuance, to some extent, of the theory of Art for Art's Sake, with its emphasis on art as a product for its own sake. This theory carries with it emphasis on technical skills in drawing and painting, without recognition of the great mass of untalented pupils. As a reaction from art for the talented few an attempt to recognize all pupils has been made. Hence, *appreciation* has become firmly established as one of the major aims in the majority of published curricula, although its actual importance in school art practices is not always evident. To enrich experience, especially in the lower grades, the emphasis on *creative self-expression* has been justified on the basis of joy in the activity of exploring a wide variety of media. Other subjects in the curriculum have been enriched to some extent through the *correlation of art*, which has provided many pupils with an opportunity to experience art activities not otherwise provided in the school program. The activity program has been responsible for the increased recognition of *industrial arts* in the curriculum, thus providing opportunity for manual activities with esthetic and other values. In those schools that have attempted to break down artificial boundaries between the subjects by forming an *integrated curriculum*, art has been introduced as contributing to the enrichment of the curriculum, though at present it is usually subordinated to, and dominated by, the factual information of the social studies. Rich opportunities for this use of art will eventually be recognized as vital to every area of life. A few schools have taken the initial steps in this direction and hold as their objective the *integration of art with life*. Recent trends in general education indicate the possibility of providing an opportunity for all pupils at all ages to experience art through a program that develops *awareness* and *sensitivity* to the presence or absence of beauty, and *growth of fine taste* through critical evaluation and the making of choices. This theory, with the best of the preceding theories, gives promise of providing the basis for a comprehensive art program in general education.

III

OPINIONS ON THE AIMS AND METHODS OF ART EDUCATION

GRACE SOBOTKA
George Peabody College for Teachers
Nashville, Tennessee

This study is for the most part a report of several comprehensive research summaries made from 1937 on concerning what is now taught and what should be taught in art.

Whitford (77) wrote (a) that in most communities drawing, design, construction, modelling, and useful art knowledge and appreciation are regarded as a legitimate part of the required curriculum for the elementary school; (b) that the more purely technical phases of these subjects, including painting, elementary sculpture, the handicrafts, and more highly specialized work in the fine, industrial, commercial, and many other forms of art may be introduced into the elective art courses of the high school; and (c) that there is no general agreement in respect to actual subject-matter content or types of classroom activity that may be supplied under the various topics listed in the curriculum.

Moore (52) reported (a) that in the elementary school stress is usually placed on experiencing (becoming acquainted with) color, form, arrangement, and design through drawing, constructing, modelling, and blockprinting; (b) that in many schools each phase of the art work might be centered around such basic needs as food, shelter, clothing, utensils, tools, records, and community surveys; (c) that the curricula of the junior high schools usually include painting, sculpture, modelling, commercial art, simpler phases of interior decorating, and metal work, weaving, and pottery, with a little photography, in the industrial arts; (d) that the activities and phases of art work stressed at the elementary- and junior-high-school levels become more specialized at the senior-high-school level with emphasis on commercial art, architecture, architectural drawing, industrial art, design, painting, the relation of art to dress and home, and, occasionally, photography, modern industrial designing, and museum courses; (e) that high-school art topics follow too closely those of the art school, with too little correlation of art with other school work; and (f) that the logical, rather than the psychological, arrangement of art topics and courses too often predominates.

Regarding his study by visitation, D'Amico (17) wrote (a) that the elementary school has been most successful in establishing art on the basis of general educational needs and in relation to both individual development and integration; (b) that in the junior high school, art education has assumed the nature of an exploratory course in which the child experiments in many arts to acquire a broad experience and to discover his potentialities for any one kind of expression; (c) that art on the senior-high-school level is weak and ineffectual in both vocational and general education, while attempts to relate it to other subject matter are misdirected, and specialized training is superficial and formal, though creative work in art is developing in the direction of avocational and leisure-time interests, such as hobbies or clubs; (d) that in most colleges, with the exception of a few patterned after the progressive schools, the teaching of art is dogmatic and formal — an art school within a college with various segmented courses, as figure, landscape, composition, theory of design, and history of art; and (e) that with a very few exceptions, the teacher-training schools require the student to take courses in still life, representation, drawing, and painting as studio practice dominated by fixed, formal patterns in teaching.

Mitchell (50) wrote:

> 'Creative expression' takes the form of 'let the child do what he pleases, when he pleases, as he pleases,' or 'paint what the music makes you feel,' or 'make original designs using Chinese motifs.' The 'creative act' is scrutinized and attributed to all or a few. 'Creative expression' is assumed to be best achieved through large tools and plastic materials (thus barring those who easily and naturally create on a smaller scale and with more resistant materials). 'Integration' becomes merely the paralleling of subject-matter fields or the graphic representation of remote and vaguely conceived forms. 'Social problems' turn the second-grade child to drawing street-cleaners, horrors of war, or unemployment. Child-made murals and friezes that lack decorative and architectural value run

riot over classroom walls and corridors. 'Appreciation' is 'taught' by means of haphazardly organized notebooks filled with meager illustrative material and dictated notes, or it becomes a highly intellectualized consideration of abstract relationships in composition. It is even sought through such questions as "What do you suppose Whistler's mother is thinking about?" and "What kind of chair is Lincoln sitting in?" Those who cling tenaciously to the traditional art-school 'subject-matter-as-techniques' emphasis continue with amazing practices; trees must be mastered by third-grade groups, letters must be cut from squared paper in the second grade; center-of-interest, occult balance, and rhythm are singled out for drill exercises in high schools. Even 'the Modernists' have their pet stereotypes — "all painting must have form" — "be solid like Cézanne's" — "abstract design is preferable to pictorial design" — and "all art must be big and bold and free."

Several outstanding achievements have been made in developing new curriculum materials by the cities of Pasadena, California, and Wilmington, Delaware, and by the states of California and Virginia . . . . revealing tendencies toward integration and the development of creativeness. . . . These are exceptions, however. There still persists the traditional art school . . . content. . . . Tabulated lists of . . . subject matter . . . still rigidly prescribe what shall happen in all seventh-grade classes during the first week in October.

Whitford, Meier, and Moore (78) reported that (a) the emphasis is upon an educational approach to the teaching of art rather than the 'ultra-child-centered' concept, and also upon the significance of the creative effort; (b) the integration of art with social studies is making exceptional headway; (c) the 'unit' conception is used in organizing and administering the art curriculum, either as an independent subject or in interrelationship with other activities of the school; (d) art appreciation has been given a new significance as a broad phase of social understanding, not merely as picture study; and (e) visual education in the arts, with consideration of the motion picture and the radio, is of far-reaching significance.

Faulkner (34) wrote that in his experimental course contemporary life is the basis of the course content — that which is vital and important today is studied; historical art is considered when it has a bearing on the student's life; the students see and handle art objects repeatedly, experience them directly, analyze the problems and products of art, try to create, read about art, hear lectures, discuss. The emphasis is on individual enjoyment and understanding developed by direct experience and increased knowledge.

Munro (55) wrote that (*a*) specialized art teachers, who have learned art as a subject by itself, disagree widely as to whether students should draw from classical models and learn the methods of the old masters or be encouraged toward experimenting with materials and building up their own visual forms of representation; some insist upon ' art principles ' and rules of composition that others consider false and repressive; some insist upon memorizing facts of art history that others consider tedious and pedantic; all agree that the creating and enjoying of beautiful forms is an activity worth while; (*b*) teachers who emphasize the relation of art to social factors minimize esthetic form, are not interested in the directly perceptual aspects of art or in those elements dealing with exotic and unrealistic fantasies; they tend to depreciate the importance of art activities, including the traditional types of historical scholarship and technical skill as well as the products of free expression; all agree in finding significance and worth in art that deals clearly with social problems and favor emphasizing it in general education; all favor teaching social aspects in the history, appreciation, and production of art.

Concerning his own opinion, Munro wrote that the art teacher must put aside the trivial formulas learned from popular teachers' magazines, the dogmatic, false ' art principles,' the sentimentality and pedantic scholarship that have led to the present low estimate of art as a study for the higher grades. While recommending a fundamental integration of art with other subjects, he warned against the possible loss of distinctive art values in superficial types of integration. Art itself, he said, might well take a leading part in working out a desirable type of integration through showing the way in which many human activities and natural phenomena could be approached from an artistic point of view.

In an earlier article, Munro (54) outlined a set of basic principles for art instruction beginning with the thesis that ' education should aim at the harmonious development of native abilities.' He went on to specify the need of freedom for individual thought and feeling in esthetic growth, and for rational control and analysis as well. He proposed a thorough interrelating of the various arts in education, including ' fine ' and ' useful ' arts, and of art with other life activities. The sequence of steps in instruction should follow natural growth, but not in any rigid order. It should proceed from simple and easy to complex and difficult activities and art forms, from less to greater specialization, and from less to greater rational analysis and planning.

D'Amico (17) wrote that art education will require extensive as well as intensive training in the arts, and that the emphasis should be on a highly enriched curriculum of many arts to meet the personal needs of the student and to prepare him for emergencies that may arise in his experience.

Meier (48) reported that (*a*) in the period from the nursery school through Grade III the training procedure is mainly that of providing suitable material — finger painting, soft chalk, and clay — and favorable working conditions; (*b*) creative imagination is furthered by exposure to subject matter likely to enlarge the child's experience; (*c*) the teacher can also supply ideas for the solution of technical difficulties, when the child seeks help, although his rôle is primarily one of guidance; (*d*) the teacher can supervise activities, such as class trips to the bakery, to a farm, or to a fire station, in a way to enlarge the child's experiences with life and provide suggestions for subject matter for his artistic activities; (*e*) the central aim is always to make it possible for the child to initiate and project his own expressive activity and to permit him the satisfaction of being a cause of his own achievement; (*f*) in the period from Grade IV through Grade VIII the school should offer a varied program in art in order to offset the facts that during this period the child is likely to be aware of limitations in technique, that art interest suffers somewhat from the competition of other activities, and that the choice of subject matter will be complicated by the child's cognizance of a multitude of new objects and new interests; (*g*) in order to forestall the drop in interest in art that appears to come to the typical child at the beginning of the junior high school, the curriculum should be revised in such a way that the number and variety of art activities are sufficient to enable individual pupils to find some activities in which they may have particular interest and facility; (*h*) since every child will be a consumer of art, instruction should tend to promote a constantly deepening interest in the art aspects of life; (*i*) the art activities should more closely approximate the pupils' interests and the community's interests; (*j*) attention should be called to the art factor in many matters that usually escape the textbooks, such as design of automobiles, public buildings, manufactured articles of all kinds, as well as in caricature and other media of social control, movies, and advertising; (*k*) in the period from Grade IX through Grade XII, when large numbers of children avoid art, creative expression can be associated with innumerable activities, such as the rearranging of furniture, selection of an ensemble in dress, planning of a menu for a dinner, modelling of designs for cars and other equipment, construction of new advertising layouts, suggestions for a ' new ' architecture from Mayan or other forms; (*l*) the art curriculum in the senior high school should be revised, enlarged, and vitalized; and (*m*) the stereotype of the artist as a temperamental, erratic portrait-painter should be supplanted by a correct picture of the artist in modern life in such quarters as the motion-picture studio, the fashion designer's quarters, and the advertising office.

Faulkner (34) and Ziegfeld (83) wrote, and Moore (51) reported, that, though very few people have use for technical skills, all have need for art as it occurs in the vital fields of human activities — personal, home, community, social, business, and religious.

Tannahill (71) has contrasted the older and newer emphases in teaching art as follows:[1]

Old	*New*
Choice and Arrangement of Subject Matter	
Ideas of teacher imposed upon children.	Emphasis upon child interests, abilities, and ideas.
Set assignments with only the teacher's point of view considered.	Child expression, adaptation to individual variations.
Logical arrangement of subject matter by the teacher.	Subject matter psychologically arranged.
Limited subject matter.	Broad sources. Attention to contemporary aspects of life.
Art in Relation to Other Subjects	
Art an isolated subject, carried on independently of other school work or child's interests. (Some isolated work is needed, however.)	Art tied up with other subjects. Unit work, integrated subject matter. Activity program (too much of this prevents the more creative activity).
Technique	
Technique, the chief aim.	Technique, a resultant.
Formal, unrelated drill to obtain skill, whether needed or not.	Expression of creative ideas develops necessary techniques. Help is given where it is needed. (Sometimes it is necessary to take time for drill in needed skills.)

[1] Quoted from pp. 10–12 of Sallie B. Tannahill, *Fine Arts for Public-School Administrators* (Bureau of Publications, Teachers College, Columbia University: New York, 1932).

Old	New

The Teacher

The teacher, a taskmaster, one whose personality dominates the child, dictating to him from a superior (?) position. An academic artist who knows little or no child psychology.	The teacher, a guide, one who appreciates genuine child art, who inspires, helps when needed, plans work ahead intelligently so that aims are realized, but does not insist upon his plan if a better way unfolds — is ready to adventure.
A teacher of fine arts, not a teacher of children.	A creative artist, one who can perform as well as teach, has a philosophy of education and a knowledge of child psychology.

Use of Devices

Trick adult devices used in teaching drawing, a quick way of obtaining uniform results, even though little or no inner growth takes place. Teacher's drawings copied.	Devices made by adults are useless. Emphasis is placed upon real child expression, simple though it may be. The child's own ability to see should be developed.

Standard of Criticism

Adult perfection the standard.	Growth and development of the individual child. Childlikeness, not adultlikeness.
Emphasis upon external results alone.	
Realistic — lifelikeness.	Evidences of art quality — art-structure basis.

Results

Uniformity in results desired and definitely worked for.	Evidences of individuality in expression, consistent with personality.
Conformity to set patterns and formulas.	Dissimilarity, not similarity, the aim (should not be forced, however).
Static, lifeless quality of expression.	Vitality and strength of expression.

Time Allotment

A definite and short period given — no other time available.	Flexible program permitting art at times best suited to needs.

Effect on Children

Child becomes repressed, dull, loses interest in art, becomes a copyist and an imitator.	Child is freed from fear and inhibition, can express himself undisturbed by adult criticisms. His

Old	*New*
Dependent.	interest is live and keen. A desire to go ahead and do more.
Lacks real appreciation.	Independent, confident, shows initiative, self-respect, and increased art sensitivity.
Supercritical.	
Dissatisfied with own efforts.	
Self-conscious.	
Fearful.	Expansion of personality.

IV

SOME PRESENT AND RECOMMENDED PRACTICES IN SCHOOL ART

WILLIAM G. WHITFORD
Professor of Art Education, University of Chicago
Chicago, Illinois

The art curriculum in public and private schools today may be characterized as an experimental program adapting itself to new conditions and needs. The entire curriculum of American schools is undergoing more profound adjustment and reorganization than at any other time in history. For this reason the problem of the so-called ' special subjects ' must be approached from a new angle and with a new point of view. Little help can be secured by study and analysis of courses or classroom procedures of a past generation. The psychologist demands objectives and a curriculum based upon the characteristics of the developing mind of the child. The sociologist discusses the curriculum in terms of social adjustment without much regard for the nature of the individual child. The exponent of creativeness finds his objectives and a curriculum in the natural tendencies of the child to express himself through spontaneous activities of many kinds.

As an outgrowth of various theories and experimental practices, it is obvious that conflicting claims will be presented and wide diversity of educational ideals developed. But in general there is a growing desire to provide all pupils with a common, integrated body of habits, skills, attitudes, appreciations, and functional knowledge that will aid them in their adjustment to the world in which they live. A unified type of curriculum is being evolved in which integration functions by making use of subject matter in new ways. Subject matter, as such, is subordinated to educational concepts that are fundamental in promoting desired pupil achievement. In reality it is the basic concepts of the traditional subjects, and not the subjects themselves, that become the tools of the curriculum-builder.

Today educators are asking the representatives of all the special subjects to analyze their content material carefully and scientifically. In this way they will be able to suggest appropriate contributions to pupil adjustment through each subject field.

It has been the private schools, or specially organized public schools, in which the experimental work of curriculum reorganization has been carried far enough for appraisal at the present time. Data from available reports indicate that the integration of art with real life situations, and, consequently with other subjects, is developing rapidly throughout the country. This trend has resulted in an increased amount of time devoted to art, in increased budgets for the promotion of art activities, and in a greater variety and better quality of art supplies and equipment than was the case when art was administered as a separate subject of the school.

The academic, studio method of teaching art has been supplanted largely by a program of educational guidance. Reports of the National Survey of Secondary Education published by the United States Office of Education in 1932–33 revealed that the great majority of teaching procedures throughout the country were in some form of a controlled unit pattern. Art education in the lower grades is carried on largely through units of experience that aim to give pupils increased knowledge, appreciations, and skills. In the upper grades units of a more specialized type are being developed through which the pupil attains a well-rounded approach to the various arts. These units provide for general and technical information and for directed and creative activities. Educational balance is achieved by providing for (*a*) functional knowledge to be acquired as an aid in meeting the problems of the unit, (*b*) appreciation or enjoyable contacts with the art, and (*c*) a rich program of participation in productive and appreciative experiences. The unit conception of administering art instruction, either as a part of a unified organization in the lower grades or in the departmentalized courses of the higher grades, has occasionally resulted in a better educational approach to the subject.

Improvement in the present school program in art is dependent upon the following:

1. More intelligent interpretation of the educational objectives established by such organizations as the National Education Association, the Progressive Education Association, and the North Central Association of Colleges and Secondary Schools.
2. A realization that art education consists of two different but related types of instruction:
    a. Adequate education for all pupils of the school, the so-called ' consumer group,' based upon the social objectives of education.
    b. Adequate training for pupils with special talent who may become members of the professional, or producer, artist group, based upon the vocational objectives of education.
3. Development of better curricular patterns and classroom procedures to attain modern objectives. Research studies in all subject fields should be utilized for this purpose.
4. Better training of both the regular grade teacher for integrated programs involving art and for the art teacher in departmentalized work, particularly in respect to the fundamental concepts and their use in a balanced art education.
5. Better training of specialists in art who may be able to assist in both national and local problems of adjusting art education to modern conditions and needs. This is really a problem of proper supervision. Art today is being administered most effectively in those cities, counties, and states where regularly appointed supervisors are in charge of the work.
6. In order that art may not lose its identity, no matter what system of teaching is employed in the school, the ' minimum essentials ' or ' core fundamentals ' of art should be established and provision made for their incorporation into all types of school programs.

V

EFFECT OF RECENT INTEGRATIVE TRENDS ON A PUBLIC-SCHOOL ART PROGRAM

Alma C. Field
Supervisor of Art, Providence Public Schools
Providence, Rhode Island

In the year 1913 the Providence Public School System consisted of primary schools (Grades I through IV), grammar schools (Grades V through VIII), and senior high schools (Grades IX through XII).

Drawing was taught by grade teachers and supervised by four or five visiting art teachers, or supervisors. The course of study was planned by the supervisors, lesson by lesson, with no freedom of choice by grade teacher or child. All drawings were made by imitating the teacher or from observation of artificially set up still life or nature.

In 1917 the departmental system, or Gary plan, was started in a few grammar schools to accommodate the increased population in certain sections of the city. More ' drawing ' was taught under this plan, as it received more time and was taught by a grade teacher showing aptitude for the subject. Techniques improved as a result of more effective teaching. The plan was still fairly rigid as a course of study, but an increase in problems involving designs allowed the beginnings of creativeness. The making of craft articles to be taken home served in " trying to make drawing useful," but it continued as an isolated subject in the general curriculum.

From 1922 on, there came a conscious attempt on the part of supervising art teachers to allow in the lower primary grades freedom of expression in illustration, construction, and design and to allow in all grades the use of various media with large paper, big brushes, and plenty of paint. This was not due to any reorganization of the school setup but probably to the influence of Professor Cizek, of Vienna, and others like him. It was uphill, discouraging work, since the typical room teacher still preferred to rely upon the dictated or copy form of lesson and the use of patterns around which to mark.

In 1930 the ' activity program ' was introduced in the elementary schools and actively promoted by the administrative staff. This threw the door wide open for unlimited opportunities for ' Art.' The course of study became a skeleton framework of general objectives to be filled in with problems meeting the specific needs of particular projects, or activities, because construction fills a need as naturally as picture-making in the day's work. Art became ' alive ' — a term with real meaning here.

At present every elementary classroom finds art indispensable in the learning process. Art problems are being solved, art processes are going on, all sorts of media are being used, all as everyday affairs in the life of the elementary school. Integration is in full swing, but in looking ahead our problem is to rescue the child from too much integration in subject matter and to aim for integration of personality. The advantages in the platoon plan are a well-equipped art room with many media available to stimulate creativeness, and a trained art teacher on hand all day. There are disadvantages, however. Art is apt to be an isolated subject unless the art teacher sincerely feels that her subject should be at the service of the whole school. Integration of art and other studies becomes more difficult, since the art teacher must know the content of other school subjects; and while the definite time limits do not prohibit, they do hamper, many ambitious projects. On the other hand, these disadvantages become advantages when the right personality is in charge of the art room.

Junior-high-school work is now under the leadership of trained art teachers. It is conducted in adequately equipped art rooms, stocked to encourage experimentation with various media and to aid in whatever size or kind of problem is undertaken. Each year the rooms become less formal and more like workshops. The junior high school presents the widest diversification of interests of any school level. In theory we believe in the child-originated problem and, so far as human ability will allow and patience endure, we encourage original problems in the widest range of media. In practice the classes average some 45 pupils each, and the average junior-high-school teacher meets 450 different children weekly. While compromises have to be made by dividing the classes into groups, most of the pupils can be working out problems that interest them. The primary factor giving art an important, vital place in a junior high school lies in the personality, efficiency, and alertness of its art teachers. We have a course of study, but it is most flexible, made for beginning teachers and large classes where faulty organization can cause unfortunate results. In these years we try to acquaint the students with the various fields of art — such as sculpture, architecture, and the commercial, industrial, costume, and theater arts.

REFERENCES

(1) ANDERSON, L. F. *History of Manual and Industrial School Education.* (D. Appleton-Century Co., Inc.: New York, 1926) 251 pp.

(2) ASSOCIATION FOR CHILDHOOD EDUCATION. *Art for Today's Child.* (Association for Childhood Education: Washington, D. C., 1935) 32 pp.

(3) BAKER, JOY C. "Beautifying the farmstead." *National Education Journal.* 28: Sept., 1939.

(4) BENNETT, CHARLES A. *History of Manual and Industrial Education up to 1870.* (Manual Arts Press: Peoria, Ill., 1926) 461 pp.

(5) BIGELOW, KARL W. "The place of the arts in teacher training." *Western Arts Association Bulletin.* 24: 1940.

(6) BRADLEY, CHARLES B. "Art Education in the School of Today." *New York State Education.* February, 1935, p. 361.

(7) BROWNE, SIBYL. "Has school art a place in modern life?" *Teachers College Record*, 35: Feb., 1934, 396–406.

(8) BUTLER, N. M. " Drawing in the public schools." (U. S. Bureau of Education Circular of Information, No. 2, 1874) 85–96.

(9) CHILDS, JOHN. *Education and the Philosophy of Experimentalism.* (D. Appleton-Century Co., Inc.: New York, 1931)

(10) CIZEK, FRANZ. *Children's Coloured Paper Work.* (G. E. Stechert and Co.: New York, 1927) 24 plates.

(11) Clark, I. E., Editor. *Art and Industry.* (Bureau of Education: Washington, D. C., 1885–1898. 4 vols.)

(12) CLARKE, I. E. " Art and industry." *Education in the Industrial and Fine Arts.* (U. S. Senate Document No. 209, 46th Congress, 1879–80. Parts 1–4. Separate publication 1897–98.)

(13) COLE, NATALIE R. *The Arts in the Classroom.* (John Day Co.: New York, 1940)

(14) D'AMICO, V. E. " The modern art room." *Progressive Education,* 1931, 575–577.

(15) D'AMICO, V. E. " Toward a new art education." *Progressive Education,* 10: 1933, 461–465.

(16) D'AMICO, V. E., and Others. *The Visual Arts in Secondary Education.* (D. Appleton-Century Co., Inc.: New York, 1940)

(17) D'AMICO, V. E. " High Lights of a Study of Art in Our Schools." [In] *Art Education Today: 1936.* (Teachers College: New York, 1936) Pp. 1–16.

(18) DEWEY, JOHN. *Art As Experience.* (Minton, Balch: New York, 1934) 355 pp.

(19) DEWEY, JOHN, and Others. *Art and Education.* (Barnes Foundation Press: Merion, Pa., 1929) 349 pp.

(20) DEWEY, JOHN. " Education for a Changing Social Order." *National Education Proceedings,* 1934. Pp. 744–752.

(21) DIX, LESTER. " Aesthetic Experience and Growth in Life and Education." *Teachers College Record,* 40: 1938, 206–221.

(22) DIX, LESTER. " The Arts in a Progressive Education." *Teachers College Record,* 37: 1936, 698–705.

(23) DOW, A. W. *Theory and Practice of Teaching Art.* (Teachers College: New York, 1912)

(24) ECKFORD, EUGENIA. " Professor Cizek and his art class." *Progressive Education,* 10: 1933, 215–219.

(25) FARNUM, R. B. " Art Education." *Biennial Survey of Education in the United States (1928–1930).* (U. S. Bureau of Education Bulletin, No. 20, 1931)

(26) FARNUM, R. B. *Art Education: the Present Situation.* (U. S. Bureau of Education Bulletin, No. 13, 1923)

(27) FARNUM, R. B. *Art Education in the United States.* (U. S. Bureau of Education, No. 38, 1925)

(28) FARNUM, R. B. " Present Status of Drawing and Art in the Elementary and Secondary Schools of the United States." (U. S. Bureau of Education Bulletin, No. 13, 1914) pp. 29–35.

(29) FARNUM, R. B. " Art Education." *Biennial Survey, 1928–30.* (Bulletin No. 20, Department of Interior: Washington, D. C., 1931)

(30) FARNUM, R. B. "Art Education." *Biennial Survey, 1922–24.* (Bulletin No. 38, Department of Interior: Washington, D. C., 1925)

(31) FARNUM, R. B. "Art in Secondary Schools of the United States." *Biennial Survey, 1914.* (Department of Interior: Washington, D. C.)

(32) FAULKNER, R. "A research program in art appreciation." *Journal of Experimental Education,* 9: 1940.

(33) FAULKNER, R. "A research program in art appreciation." *Journal of Educational Research,* 33: 1939.

(34) FAULKNER, R. "Art in the General College." [In] *Art Education Today: 1938.* (Teachers College: New York, 1938) Pp. 91–101.

(35) FINCK, FURMAN J. "The Meaning of Art in Education." [In] *Art Education Today: 1938.* (Teachers College: New York, 1938) Pp. 31–37.

(36) FOX, M. "Art Appreciation for the High-School Student." [In] *Art Education Today: 1940.* (Teachers College: New York, 1940)

(37) GILES, MARY ALBRIGHT. "Working creatively in the visual arts with high-school students." *Progressive Education,* May, 1939, 320–330.

(38) GLEAVES, J. M. "Have ideals in art education changed?" *Design,* 37: 1936.

(39) GRUBERT, L. M. "A changing philosophy of art education." *Design,* 39: 1937, 3–4.

(40) Hartman, G., and Shumaker, A., eds. *Creative Expression.* (Reynal and Hitchcock, Inc.: New York, 1932) 350 pp.

(41) HANEY, J. P. "Art Education in the Public Schools of the United States." *American Art Annual,* 1908.

(42) HEATH, J. *Art Education in the Public Schools.* (Report of the United States Commissioner of Education, I, 1894–95) Ch. XVI, pp. 793–803.

(43) HOPKINS, L. THOMAS. *Integration — Its Meaning and Applications.* (D. Appleton-Century Co., Inc.: New York, 1937)

(44) KLAR, W. H., WINSLOW, L. L., and KIRBY, C. V. *Art Education in Principle and Practice.* (Milton Bradley: Springfield, Mass., 1933) 422 pp.

(45) MATHIAS, M. E. *Art in the Elementary School.* (Charles Scribner's Sons: New York, 1929) 180 pp.

(46) MATHIAS, M. E. *The Teaching of Art.* (Charles Scribner's Sons: New York, 1932) 356 pp.

(47) MEARNS, H. *Creative Power.* (Doubleday Co.: New York, 1929)

(48) MEIER, N. C. "The Graphic and Allied Arts." [In] *Thirty-Eighth Yearbook, Part I,* of this Society, 1939, 175–184.

(49) MCALISTER, JAMES. *Art Education in the Public Schools.* (Report of the United States Commissioner of Education, I, 1894–95) Ch. XVI, pp. 793–803.

(50) MITCHELL, EDITH. "Old and New Forces in the Art Curriculum." [In] *Art Education Today: 1937.* (Teachers College: New York, 1937)

(51) MOORE, J. E. "Art." *Review of Educ. Research,* 8: 1938, 7–10, 75.

(52) MOORE, J. E. "Art Education." (To appear in the *Encyclopedia of Educ. Research*)

(53) MOREY, ELIZABETH K., and YOUTZ, F. L. "Modern trends in the creative arts." *Progressive Education,* 9: 1934, 255–256.

(54) MUNRO, T. "A Constructive Program for Teaching Art." [In] *Art and Education,* by J. Dewey and Others. (Barnes Foundation Press: Merion, Pa., 1929)

(55) Munro, T. " Modern Art and Social Problems." [In] *Art Education Today: 1938.* (Teachers College: New York, 1938)

(56) Mursell, F. L. " Application of psychology to the arts." *Teachers College Record,* 37: 1936, 290–299.

(57) Payant, Felix. *Our Changing Art Education.* (Design Publishing Co.: Columbus, O., 1935) 93 pp.

(58) Pearson, Ralph. " The artist comments on teaching art in secondary schools." *Progressive Education,* 10: 1933.

(59) Pierce, A. E., and Hilpert, R. S. *Instruction in Music and Art.* (Bulletin No. 17, Government Printing Office: Washington, D. C., 1932)

(60) Pelikan, A. G. *The Art of the Child.* (Bruce Publishing Co.: New York, 1931) 123 pp.

(61) Pope, Arthur. *Art, Artist, and Layman.* (Harvard University Press: Cambridge, 1937) 152 pp.

(62) Powell, Mary. " Museum and School." *Western Arts Association Bulletin,* 24: 1940.

(63) Ragan, Mary E. " A Way of Teaching Art." [In] *Art Education Today: 1938.* (Teachers College: New York, 1938)

(64) Rusk, W. S., ed. *Methods of Teaching the Fine Arts.* (University of North Carolina: Chapel Hill, 1935) 220 pp.

(65) Ryder, Worth. " New Directions for Art." [In] *Art Education Today: 1938.* (Teachers College, New York, 1938) Pp. 11–19.

(66) Sargent, Walter. *Instruction in Art in the United States.* (U. S. Bureau of Education Bulletin, 43: 1918)

(67) Schoelkopf, Alice. " The arts in the new curriculum." *Teachers College Record,* 37: 1937, 383–387.

(68) Shaw, Ruth F. *Finger Painting.* (Little, Brown, and Co.: New York, 1934)

(69) Smith, B. K. *The Influence of the Modern Art Movement in the School.* (Address given before the Sixth International Art Congress, Prague, August 1, 1938)

(70) Stearns, Myron M. " Subjects or children? " *Survey Graphic,* October, 1939.

(71) Tannahill, S. B. *Fine Arts for Public-School Administrators.* (Teachers College: New York, 1932) 145 pp.

(72) Thayer, V. T., Zachry, C. B., and Kotinsky, Ruth. " A new education for youth." *Progressive Education,* October, 1939, 398–409.

(73) Tibbetts, V. H. *The Place of Art in the Modern School Program.* (pamphlet) (Binney and Smith and Co.: New York, 1934)

(74) Tomlinson, R. R. *Crafts for Children.* (Studio Publications: London, 1935) 120 pp.

(75) Tomlinson, R. R. *Picture-Making by Children.* (Studio Publications: London, 1934) 120 pp.

(76) Viola, Wilhelm. *Child Art and Franz Cizek.* (Reynal and Hitchcock, Inc.: New York, 1936) 111 pp.

(77) Whitford, W. G. *An Introduction to Art Education.* (D. Appleton-Century Co., Inc.: New York, 1937) 391 pp.

(78) Whitford, W. G., Meier, N. C., and Moore, F. E. " Art." *Rev. of Educ. Research,* 7: 1937, 464–466, 547–551.

(79) WINSLOW, L. L. *The Integrated School Art Program.* (McGraw-Hill Book Co.: New York, 1939)

(80) WINSLOW, L. L. *Organization and Teaching of Art.* (Warwick and York: Baltimore, 1928) 243 pp.

(81) WILE, IRA S. "Integration of the child — The goal of the educational program." *Mental Hygiene,* 20: April, 1936, pp. 249–261.

(82) WILLIAMS, WALTER R., JR. "Ohio's orientation program in the arts and industries." *Progressive Education,* Nov., 1939, 480–484.

(83) ZIEGFELD, E. "The Owatonna Art Project." [In] *Proceedings of the Western Arts Association: 1936 Convention.* Pp. 54–58.

CHAPTER XXX

ART IN GENERAL EDUCATION [1]

Leon L. Winslow, Ernest Horn, Edith L. Mitchell, Sallie B. Tanna-
hill, Jane Driver, Elmer A. Stephan, Walter H. Klar, Marion Quin,
Belle Boas, Victor E. D'Amico, Thomas M. Folds, Barclay S. Leathem,
Vincent A. Roy, Lester D. Longman, Ulrich Middeldorf, Helen McIver
Howell, Florence Tilton Ahlfeld, Gordon L. Reynolds, Alfred Howell
and Ann V. Horton, Edna Patzig, Dana P. Vaughan, and Royal Bailey
Farnum

I

CURRENT PRACTICES IN SCHOOL ART

Leon L. Winslow
Director of Art Education, Department of Education
Baltimore, Maryland, and
Lecturer on Art Education, The Maryland Institute

I. Some Objectives of Art in the School Curriculum

Art as a school subject should be regarded as an integrated part of
the school curriculum. In pursuing the subject the pupil grows in the
appreciation of art, and he acquires control over materials and processes, attaining thereby greater facility of self-expression. Gradually
he comes to assume desirable habits and attitudes that are largely the
result of sharing in the appreciative and creative experiences of others.
Although comparatively few pupils will become producers of art, all,
through effective teaching processes, can be brought to the recognition
and use of the principles of design in their daily lives.

The educational values most often ascribed to art in the school are
those concerned with individual growth in the control of the materials

---

[1] The titles and addresses of the writers of the twenty-three sub-sections of
this chapter are given with the names of the writers at the head of their contributions. For pagination of these sub-sections, the reader will find it useful to refer
to the Table of Contents. — *Editor.*

of an ever-changing environment. Sensitiveness to art and appreciation of it are important here. Advertisements, manufactured products, buildings and statues, paintings, and other man-made things in which beauty may be attained through the meeting of human needs all come in for proper emphasis. Such experiences as these make for improvement in the creative and in the recreative habits of the individuals, in their use of money, in the artistic choices they make, as well as in the care they take of themselves and of their possessions, and in the way they employ their leisure. Other curricular values generally ascribed to art are enrichment, unification, and evaluation, all of which are suggestive of the contribution that the subject makes continually to living. Through the services that it renders in the curriculum, art as a school study aims therefore to help boys and girls to live better the democratic life.

Art instruction concerns itself with the creative and appreciative experiences of human life as it is lived here and now, in the school, the home, the factory, and the market place. It is carried on in such a way as to meet both the general needs of the many for art appreciation and guidance and the special needs of the few for intensive training. Provision is made in the school for educative experiences that lead to social efficiency as well as to self-mastery — experiences that culminate in expressions of the fuller life, in increased happiness for all. Thus in the school, art functions as a way of living that is productive of emotional security.

Art experiences in the school promote balance in living. Since neither dominant change nor dominant stability is likely to bring about improvement of living conditions either inside or outside the school, the art education program will have to embrace something of both of these emphases. In it fancy will need to be included along with its opposite, reality, and there will have to be room in its design for both the radical and the conservative elements in education. Its planning will be regarded as an educational function, one involving democratic student participation and profiting by it. Tradition and reason both come in for their share of stress, and there is an equitable relationship between work and play, production and appreciation.

John Dewey (8) explains how an emotion can be transformed into expression by pointing out how an irritated person is bound to act to get rid of his irritation; how he may begin by arranging the furnishings in his room or the objects on his desk to secure this result. " As he puts objects in order," says Dewey, " his emotion is ordered." Whatever the irritated person decides to do constructively to bring order out of chaos will thus have an immediate and corresponding effect on his mental state, and it will also result in concrete art form. Thus, as the irritated person puts things in order does an art product result, even though it may not conform to the esthetic standards set by some who still believe that all art, to be genuine, should be put on exhibition somewhere in an art museum. What applies to the irritated person in the world at large applies with equal force to the irritated pupil in school. " As he puts things in order," in his manipulation of materials, of lines, of masses, of colors, " his emotion is ordered," and the result is an expression that is genuine, even though it may not rank highly as a work of art.

We are gradually coming to recognize in the prevailing unbalance in living a challenge to our efforts at educational planning for the general good. Were it not for the help that the schools may be relied on to give, the situation would seem to be hopeless. The principles of design, long familiar to teachers of the fine arts, will have to be used in the finest of all arts, the art of living. The urgent need is for a program of education that shall provide for the common art needs of all the people, both children and adults, both the artistically apt and the artistically inapt. Such a program must provide experiences of many kinds.

II. NUMBERS OF CHILDREN STUDYING ART

Figures are not available on the number of children studying art in preschools and elementary schools. It may be assumed, however, that most pupils do study art, since art activities of one sort or another usually form an important part of the educational program at the lower levels. The amount of this activity that may legitimately be classified as ' art ' varies greatly, of course, from school to school. In some school programs, art permeates all other subject-matter areas as naturally as it does in life situations, while in others art is segregated and limited to a few lessons in drawing or design. The quality of such activity varies greatly also. Under favorable conditions the art experiences grow naturally from the child in his environment and contribute to his total development. At the other extreme are formalized exercises imposed by teachers who have little training or sensitivity in art — exercises that may actually hinder the esthetic development of the pupils.

For high-school registrations in art, figures are available. According to Jessen and Herlihy (21):

In the high schools freehand drawing is the leader in registrations among drawing and art subjects both in seventh and eighth grades and in the last four years of high school; it is taken by nearly thirty percent of the pupils at the lower level and by 5.5 percent of those in the last four years. Most of the other art registrations are grouped under the heading ' art-craft-design.' Most frequently they were reported as art, but the classification includes some courses which were reported as crafts or design; in many cases, it was impossible to judge from the data given whether they ought to be classified under industrial work or under art. Commercial art and mechanical drawing were tabulated as industrial subjects, commercial art being included with the drawing and art group of studies and mechanical drawing being listed with the industrial subjects; a number of other studies classified under industrial subjects might with almost as much justification have been included with the drawing and art group.

Exclusive of mechanical drawing, the registration in drawing and art for seventh and eighth grades was two-fifths of the enrollment; with mechanical drawing it was over fifty percent of the enrollment. In the last four years of high school, one-twelfth of the pupils were taking art courses exclusive of mechanical drawing; with it included, over fifteen percent were registered in art courses.

In two states, namely, New York and Washington, the art-craft-design courses were more numerous than the courses in freehand drawing. Certain states, for instance, California, Indiana, New York, and Utah, have large numbers of schools offering various kinds of drawing and art courses; by contrast, some states report drawing and art taught in very few schools.

Thus, less than nine percent of high-school students studied in this survey enrolled in art courses, a figure much lower than that for enrollments in history, mathematics, foreign languages, or music. This relatively small enrollment at the high-school level is a real source of concern to art educators who believe art to be basic in the pattern of general education, and it brings to light a weakness in the high-school program. Of the many factors tending to prevent higher enrollments, the following are important: (*a*) college entrance requirements that do not give full credit to high-school art, (*b*) high-school art courses that are planned only for students showing special interests and abilities in art, rather than for the typical students, (*c*) programs of art in the elementary school that were not meaningful to children, (*d*) the pressure of family opinion " to enroll in solid subjects rather than in frills." Although few educators today regard art as a frill, this attitude persists on the part of the layman to a marked degree.

III. Problems of Method

The art-education program carried on in a school or school system should be planned with reference to the needs of boys and girls. It should provide for both art production and art appreciation. Production is for the most part concerned with creative expression, although some directed activity may be necessary in many of the units included in the course of study. Appreciation is often the result of activity that has been properly stimulated and motivated. The pupil comes to appreciate art through experiencing the processes of production as well as through examining critically the work of other children and of adult artists. If any distinction is to be made between art production and art appreciation, then a balance should be maintained between the creative work and the work in art appreciation, a balance requiring an equitable allocation of time and emphasis.

Wherever expression is involved, the pupil should be left entirely free to create, but the desire to create and the choice of theme for the creative problem should be the result of planful teaching in which a foundation of inspiration, technique, and skill has been acquired by the pupil through systematic teaching processes. If left to work out their own salvation uninspired and undirected, children cannot be expected to grow esthetically. Their art experiences must be constantly stimulated and enriched through methodical and enlightened teaching.

Instruction in design, representation, and construction should be sufficient to meet the child's needs at every level of his growth; the methods employed, those that secure the best educational results. To get such results, no single educational method should be prescribed. Whether, for example, the child should draw from memory, from imagination, or from objects is dependent on the nature of his problem, his interests, and his needs. Since the creative ability of children varies greatly at different grades and age levels, and within given grades, the methods employed at any level should be many and varied. To prescribe drawing from imagination, from memory, or from objects exclusively, at any particular grade level is to ignore entirely both the child and his art needs. All these methods of drawing are probably desirable at all the grade levels, at various times, and under various circumstances. A similar statement could be made about the methods employed in teaching construction and design. In short, instruction should be adapted to individual needs arising in connection with the problems of creation and of appreciation, as they arise.

Nor does any grade level have exclusive right to a particular art principle in the course of study. Repetition, emphasis, rhythm, proportion, balance, all are important, but none of them should be prescribed for exclusive treatment at any specified time. The emphasis of these principles is to be determined by the classroom situations arising that call for their use in connection with creative and appreciative experiences. Likewise line, mass, and color will each come in for its share of emphasis as the occasions demand.

It would be just as inappropriate to assign any medium to a particular grade level as it would be to assign an art principle or art element to a particular level. The time for teaching the use of a particular art medium is obviously when a problem arises that calls for its use. The art possibilities of pencil, crayon, charcoal, paint, clay, plaster of Paris, linoleum, wood, textiles, plastics, all are to be considered when occasion calls for their use in art expression and appreciation.

It should be kept in mind that art appreciation is closely related to art consumption, since one must be able to understand and evaluate art products if one is to select and use them efficiently. It is therefore essential that the needs of children as consumers of art products be given greater consideration in art teaching at all grade levels than obtains at the present time. Drawing and painting are not nearly so important in human life as most art course-of-study makers would have us believe. Architecture, both exterior and interior, furniture, costume, and numerous machine-made things and products of the handcrafts are of far more significance in the lives of most of us than are drawing and painting. Courses in design for both children and adults should, therefore, involve much more work in three dimensions than they do at present. Course-of-study makers should keep in mind these relative values and should aim to maintain a proper balance between them. Art appreciation should be broadly conceived, to include the selection, care, and use of products of all forms of visual art. Examples of these products or reproductions or pictures of them should be used extensively in art teaching to develop an understanding of art principles.

The art teacher should not be dependent on art interests that children already have, but should often stimulate children to acquire new interests that without art instruction they might never develop at all. Of course, interests should not be introduced that are too mature for the child to comprehend.

Individual differences in art are probably just as great as they are in any other field of education. The teacher of art should therefore recognize these differences and should adapt instruction to the individual child, making the methods, principles, and mediums fit his needs. In large classes children of similar interests may be grouped according to their interests but treated as individuals within a group. The growing tendency to increase the size of art classes is to be deplored; it gives rise to social problems of grave concern to the art teacher, who is still expected to instruct twice as many pupils as would be accepted in a class in home economics or industrial arts.

IV. The Organization and Administration of Art Education

Since art is a comparatively new subject in the school curriculum, its position there is not always thoroughly understood. The administrator of the art education program must see to it, therefore, that the importance of art in the educational system is made clear. In large communities the responsibility of promoting the art-education program is centered in a director or a supervisor working directly under the superintendent of schools or his assistants. In a small community the superintendent may have to rely on a single individual to teach art and in addition do such supervision as there may be time for. There is, of course, a wide variation between these two extremes.

From the standpoint of administration, art as a school subject may be regarded as coördinate with the other subjects of the curriculum. From the standpoints of content and of psychological method, art is somewhat, though not radically, different from the other subjects. It is concerned with the study of how human needs are satisfied through the transformation and use of materials and with the concrete expression of individual thoughts and feelings, to the end that life itself shall be richer and more satisfying. Obviously, its experiences with information and activities are not to be restricted to a narrow field of subject matter, but rather may be expected to grow out of the school curriculum taken as a whole.

It is necessary to keep in mind the needs of art, as these should be provided for not only in the curriculum, but also in buildings and equipment. It should be the policy of the person responsible for art in the school system to see that the architect is acquainted with the details of art needs both in the art rooms and also throughout the school buildings, including, where possible, provision for facilities for the display of works of art. All modern school buildings should be planned with these art education needs in mind. Art departments should generally be on the ground floor, preferably near the entrance of the building. They need not necessarily have a north light. Because of the quantities of materials used in art instruction the art rooms should generally be half again as large as other classrooms. If more than one room is required, they should be adjoining. Daylight should be admitted from one side only by large windows placed close together, as in studios. There should be adequate electric lighting for dark days and evenings, and an electrical outlet located near the back of the room for stereopticon and motion-picture machines. Daylight-proof curtains should, of course, be installed at all openings, including windows, transoms, and doors. There must be adequate display boards, preferably of cork, and display cabinets with glass doors, preferably built into the walls. There should also be running water and a large soapstone sink in each room. There should be a storeroom located near the art rooms for supplies for each school art department.

Because of the newer conception of the place of art in the educational system, it is slowly earning recognition as a major study, especially in the high schools. The art schools and the liberal arts colleges, too, are beginning to accept one or more credit units earned in the high school toward meeting their entrance requirements. Colleges for the preparation of teachers are also giving the courses in art and in art education a more prominent place in their curricula.

In the matter of time allotment, as pointed out elsewhere in this chapter, there still seems to be no uniform practice regarding the number of hours or periods to be given to art either in the elementary or the secondary schools. In most schools it is preferred to have all periods of equal length and the time given to an academic subject, such as history or English, is the same as the time set aside for art, although there is a tendency on the part of most school administrators to give double the time for art, or two single periods, often referred to as a ' double period.' This seems to be desirable since the materials used do not then have to be taken out and put away so often. There is, however, much to be said in favor of making art a major subject or a subject that meets every day even though the length of period may have to be less than ' double.'

In elementary schools art is generally a constant, or required, subject. This is also true in many junior high schools. In the senior high school, however, art is generally elective. It is maintained that, even where the subject is elective, it should be offered as a major subject if offered at all. In many of our senior high schools, however, art is still offered as a minor subject for one or more periods a week. It is here recommended that art be accorded the same credit as other subjects, with outside (homework) assignments if this is required for the other subjects.

The contribution of the elementary schools to art education as a means of individual and social adjustment is very significant, as it is at this level that creative expression and emotional reactions are least inhibited. It is here that the production and appreciation of art must have their beginnings in the child's experiences. In the junior high school, instruction in art is more specifically in the direction of exploration and guidance, both educational and vocational, although appreciation is still stressed as an objective. Here boys and girls become more fully acquainted with the significance of art and with its use in life. Although the senior high schools continue the exploration and guidance emphases, they also aim to offer special training for those pupils who should profit most by such specialization. It is suggested that they pursue a four-year sequence in which art is offered as a major subject.

When art is offered in the secondary school as a major subject in a special curriculum, it is probably advisable that a course representing the entire field of art be made available as a general exploratory subject in the ninth grade. The curriculum itself should present a balanced offering, and provision should be made, if possible, for the students enrolled in it to specialize in a single field, such as commercial art, in the eleventh and twelfth grades. Herewith is listed a suggested four-year curriculum for students majoring in art in the high school. It is recommended that even those students who plan to continue their studies in art school or college should enroll in the special art courses of the high school. The art subjects included may be regarded as constants; the academic and related subjects, as variables. The schools that pupils may plan to enter after graduation from the high school should influence the selection of subjects that they take other than art. It will be noted in the curriculum outlined that art appreciation as such is to be stressed in the courses in history. The constant art courses of the curriculum are: Grade IX, General Art; Grade X, Industrial Art and Painting; Grade XI, Commercial Art and Architecture; Grade XII, Sculpture and Theater Art.

The Four-Year Technical Art Curriculum
First Year
(Grade IX)

	Periods a Week	Number of Weeks
English	6	40
General Science	5	40
Algebra	6	40
General Art	5	40
(Painting, sculpture, architecture, industrial art and commercial art, with emphasis on general education and vocational try-out)		
World History	5	40
Music	1	40
Physical Education	2	40
Home Economics or Industrial Arts	4	
Activities	1	
Total	35	

Second Year
(Grade X)

English	5	40
Geometry	5	40
Industrial Art	5	40
(Handcraft and machine fabrication; textile, costume, millinery, and jewelry design; ceramics, furniture, and other branches of manufacturing; emphasis on creative work in design)		
Painting	5	40
(Pencil and charcoal sketches, pen-and-ink drawings, water color and oil paintings, etchings, book illustrations)		
Biology	5	40
Music	1	40
Physical Education	2	40
Total	28	

Third Year
(Grade XI)

English	5	40
Modern Language I or Physics	5	40

	Periods a Week	Number of Weeks
Commercial Art	5	40
(Advertising art, publications, display advertising, posters, commercial illustration, showcard writing, sign painting, pictorial photography)		
Architecture	5	40
(Community and home planning, interior decoration, landscape architecture, architectural drawing and design)		
English History	5	40
Music	1	40
Physical Education	2	40
Total	$\overline{28}$	

Fourth Year
(Grade XII)

	Periods a Week	Number of Weeks
English	5	40
Modern Language II or Chemistry	5	40
Sculpture	5	40
(Modelling in clay, casting in plaster and cement, wood carving, stone carving, casting in metal)		
Theater Art	5	40
(Contribution of all the arts to stage productions, including music and literature as well as architecture, sculpture, painting, industrial and commercial art; stagecrafts and scenic design)		
United States History	5	40
Music	1	40
Physical Education	2	40
Total	$\overline{28}$	

In the regular elementary schools today, as pointed out elsewhere in this chapter, art is generally taught by the regular classroom teacher, who has had little or no special training in art education. In the departmentalized and platoon type of organization a teacher is sometimes assigned to art classes only. These are generally regular grade teachers who have been especially successful in teaching art, although in some systems additional training in art and education is required. In the junior and senior high schools, in most localities, the art teacher is required to have special training equivalent to completion of a four-year teacher-training curriculum or the bachelor's degree with a major in art education. Some states require a master's degree of all high-school teachers.

Art education is a coöperative enterprise in which the supervisor, principal, and teacher have a share. It is important that all should have an adequate conception of art as a part of the curriculum and of school life in general. All should recognize the validity of the claim of art to sufficient time in the weekly and daily schedule of the school. All must be brought to realize that art involves experiences with ideas and feelings as well as with materials, that general experience is necessary to furnish a background for activities, that technical information and directed activities are necessary to the realization of superior creative work, and that consistent growth in art appreciation must be provided for. It must be recognized that art supervision, whether carried on by an art director or supervisor, by the general supervisor, or by the school principal, must concern itself with all these things, not alone with materials and processes, the media of art. It is largely for the general educator to see that vital school experiences are provided out of which the creative art expression will grow. In the elementary schools the general supervisor is often the only supervisor, and this makes it essential that he be trained to some extent in art so that he will have a basic understanding of the subject and its methodology.

Supervision of art education should stress the curricular purposes served by art as a school subject or area of experience. It should attain objectives of art teaching from the standpoint of the individual child, involving such items as orderly thinking, creative expression, recreation, self-realization, appreciation, guidance, taste, socialization. It should help the teacher to attain such curricular services as enrichment, motivation, integration, balance, unification, and evaluation. In accomplishing this, supervision should treat of such matters as: the improvement of instruction; types and means of supervision; function of the teacher; teacher growth; visiting the teacher; the organization and planning of a supervisory program; instructional materials; the major supervisory procedures; supervision and the child; demonstration lessons; in-service teacher education, including courses in art mediums; conferences; supplies and equipment; evaluating teaching; evaluating a school; supervisory errors; reactions to supervision; research studies in supervision; reports; evaluating supervision; the principal as a supervisor.

The principal may contribute a great deal to the success of the art work in his school. He may administer the art program efficiently and help to train his teachers to carry on instruction effectively. The principal should be familiar with the art course of study and should see that teachers use it as needed, should see that the art schedule is observed at all times, should confer with the art supervisor as often as necessary on general policies and on matters pertaining to teachers, pupils, instruction, supplies, standards, and exhibits, should get the advice of the supervisor in ordering equipment and supplies, and should see that his teachers participate in enterprises or projects sponsored by the Department of Education, such as the testing program, poster competitions, and exhibits. He may also improve the teaching of art by requiring that art education be carried on as an essential and integral part of the school program, by helping the teacher to become confident and independent, by encouraging good teaching and good art products turned out by the pupils, by observing art lessons, judging the teaching of them on the basis of desirable and undesirable classroom procedures and offering the teacher suggestions for improvement, and by giving art education a place in faculty meeting programs according to its needs. The principal may also help in the realization of art standards in the school building by seeing that such standards are maintained in the arrangement of written work, notebooks, and school work generally, that rooms and halls and their furnishings present a clean, inviting, and beautiful appearance always, that bulletin boards are kept up-to-date and present a balanced and harmonious appearance, that teachers and pupils share in improving and maintaining the efficiency and beauty of the premises, building, and equipment, and that pupils' art work is recognized as such and appropriately displayed in the building at all times.

In addition to the in-service training offered teachers through general supervision by the school principal and the art supervisor, provision is often made for improving their teaching by means of demonstration lessons, studio courses, exhibitions, and other agencies. These help to make up for the deficiencies in teacher education frequently occasioned by the meagerness of professional courses in art subjects prescribed by the normal school or the teachers' college. In some cities the programs of in-service teacher education vary from year to year. The program followed by the Art Division in Los Angeles in 1939–1940 consisted of three parts, as follows:

(1) A series of work meetings where teachers who attended worked under guidance on processes and subjects with which they needed to become more familiar. These meetings were conducted in various parts of the city and handled the following fields: clay modelling and pottery, stitchery, block printing, mask making, landscape and portraits, figure drawing.

(2) A large exhibit of painting, drawing, and crafts installed at the local museum, combined with a series of six meetings constituting a survey of procedure in arts and crafts in the elementary grades. The exhibit was carefully labeled to further understanding of educational viewpoint and actual procedure. Cases showing the steps in the processes, the finished work, and good exhibit arrangement covered the following fields: bookmaking, block printing (aprons, wall textiles, greeting cards, book linings, box covers, and so forth), costume decoration (for school programs, and the like), simple weaving, serpentine and twisted papercraft, stitchery, puppets, spray design, decorative papers, masks, clay, simple metal work. Institute credit was given to all who attended the meetings and the exhibit was open to all teachers for three weeks. The teachers' response to this procedure seemed of greater value than to the issuing of instruction sheets. The exhibit was very comprehensive and the superintendents coöperated with the Art Section in calling meetings of the school principals for discussion and explanation of the work.

(3) Short specific bulletins issued from time to time in response to definite needs.

V. The Art Program and Other Phases of the Curriculum

All subjects in the curriculum frequently present opportunities for reinforcing the art program. For instance, many topics in history are rich in scientific value as well as artistically significant. The suggestions generally given in the science course of study will aid the teacher in discovering and using the possibilities of coördination in accordance with the aims and content of the other subjects. Likewise, safety education and arithmetic may be interwoven with many of the art units, to the mutual strengthening of instruction.

1. Art and the Integrated Curriculum

Any *integrated* curriculum worthy of the name is also an *integrative* curriculum, since the effective integration of areas in the curriculum is aimed at integrative living, the integration of personality. Integration is the means that leads to this result. The attempt to organize experiences around a central core, such as social studies, history, or science is not enough; nor is the organizing of experiences around all the aspects of a many-sided life in the local community sufficient. Art should be integrated in the curriculum with whatever it is integrated with in life. Therefore the integrated curriculum cannot afford to be anything short of life itself, in which all the curricular areas contribute to effective living. The amount of integration of art and social studies should, for example, be about the same in school as it is in life. In no instance should such integration crowd out the integration of art and other areas. As pointed out by Leary (27, p. 49):

> Drawing as a formal, isolated subject is fast disappearing from the curriculum. In its stead in the elementary grades there is provided opportunity for creative expression in many mediums — clay, paper, wood, crayons, cloth, paints — the emphasis being upon the expression of ideas rather than upon perfection of the forms used.
>
> There is a marked tendency in recent courses, particularly at the junior-high-school level, to relate art to the home, the school, the community, industry, and all aspects of everyday living. They propose to make the child a better consumer rather than a better producer of art. The Delaware state course of study, for example, aims to develop the child's ability to enjoy and appreciate beauty as it occurs in nature and in man-made objects, and to develop his judgment and taste through an understanding of what constitutes beauty in daily living. Similar purposes are reflected by the courses of Minneapolis, St. Louis, El Paso, Joliet, Indianapolis, and other cities. Whatever experiences are provided — in portrait study, in design, in decoration and textiles, in creative art — are included for the contribution they can make to the development of an understanding and appreciation of the uses and values of beauty.
>
> The utilitarian aspect of art tends to be considered separately in industrial arts, although some schools introduce weaving, block printing, and similar experiences into the general art courses as a means of developing appreciation of color and design in everyday things.

There is no history, no geography, no science that is not intimately associated with the topics around which the art course of study is organized. The elementary teacher who instructs in all subjects should experience little difficulty in teaching art, which is so closely related to the other school subjects. The relationship of art to some of the other subject-matter areas will be discussed in the paragraphs that follow.

2. Art and History [1]

To make the past vivid and meaningful requires that it be recreated, brought back to life. Today one may walk through the streets of Williamsburg, Virginia, and be back again in Colonial America. A visit to the Maryland Wing in the Baltimore Museum of Art recreates the Federal period in American history. There are various places in the

---

[1] Contributed by Harry Bard, Supervisor of History in the Public Schools, Baltimore, Maryland.

United States where the curtain is drawn back and life is pictured as it once was.

But one need not go to Williamsburg or to the art museum in order to recreate the past. The classroom offers a splendid environment, and art is the obvious medium. For example, if the class is studying the Revolutionary War period or the post-Revolutionary period, it would be most important to recreate the man George Washington, who played so important a rôle at that time. What did Washington look like? Can we recreate him so that he seems to be in the classroom?

Fortunately, the portraits of Washington make this possible. Much history teaching can come from a study of the Washington portraits by Gilbert Stuart, Charles Willson Peale, John Trumbull, James Sharpless, and Edward Savage. The portraits by these painters are historical primary source materials; they help to recreate the man Washington. An interesting lesson with children is to have them refer to the diaries and letters of Washington and his contemporaries in order to see how true to life these portrait painters have revealed the man. At all times and in all countries painters have left visual records for posterity.

Cartoons, caricatures, and illustrations often add meaning to a historic point. A cartoon showing America as a melting pot adds meaning to the study of immigration in the United States. Illustrations of frontier life in early America make graphic the history of the West. Art, used in this way, adds meaning to the facts of history. Pupils like to illustrate what they are learning. This is particularly true of those children who enjoy projecting themselves into the study of history. Art is a part of the record of history. It is a means of recreating the past. It is an important phase of cultural history. It is a way of making history graphic. In short, art is essential to history, and history to art.

3. Art and English [1]

An art activity may be the natural outgrowth of an English experience, or an English activity may grow out of a stimulating experience in art. Because of the similar elements in both fields, a close correlation should not be difficult to accomplish. Both literature and composition abound in suggestive art outcomes. It is necessary, then, that the teacher of art be familiar with the English course of study, and that the teacher of English, not only be familiar with the art course of study, but also be aware of its possible outgrowths in English. A conference each

---

[1] Contributed by Edna N. Keefer, Art Teacher, Baltimore, Maryland.

term will reveal many possibilities of integration of these two subjects. Furthermore, the freshly motivated enthusiasm of the class should be of value when carried from either subject to the other.

Every opportunity should be utilized to impress the children with the fact that there are identical principles in each of the two fields. English, as well as art, has its dominance and subordination of character, its rhythm and balance in sentences, and its action and color in words. Literature and art both deal with the emotional side of life. The creative process whereby the writer expresses himself in literature is understood and reflected by the artist who illustrates his story. A good illustration, made by children, will result from a similar emotional understanding and interpretation of the author's purpose.

As to method, the teacher may show beautifully illustrated books to the class, emphasizing the unity existing between the author's creation of characters and plot and the artist's creation of suitable illustrations. That the artist has to know the story thoroughly before he can express in a picture what the writer expresses in words should be made clear. Good reading aloud at this point is one of the best ways of recreating the unity existing between the picture and the printed words. For example, an effective preparation for the creative interpretation of a poem by the children is a preliminary creative reading of the poem by the teacher. The poem selected should be appropriate, richly suggestive, and able to justify itself on the grounds of genuine merit. Emotional enjoyment of the poem is not complete if unknown words prevent the pupil from understanding the meaning of the whole. Any poem that requires the supplying of too much information should be discarded.

4. Visual Art and Music [1]

The correlative study of art and music is of great importance, since both have their roots firmly imbedded in measure, form, accent, and balance, and yet at the same time arouse feelings and emotions. Many types of lessons can make use of music to stimulate originality in visual art through illustration in which the child records an outward expression of his imaginings and feelings. An appreciation of the relationship between moods and colors may also be attained through such correlation.

Since one of the most difficult problems of an art course is the teaching of design, some pleasing and original arrangements of abstract

---

[1] Contributed by May R. Dixon, Art Teacher, Public Schools, Baltimore, Maryland.

forms may be brought about through music-stimulated design lessons. The integration of music and art should be promoted through many opportunities for free play of the feelings and the imagination.

5. Art and Physical Education [1]

Although the paths of art and physical education run side by side and often meet, teachers of these two phases of experience sometimes evidence little awareness of their kinship, common purpose, and possibilities. Fundamentally, the two are related, for both may be termed ' expressive activity,' the urge to give form, outwardly and creatively, to one's impulses and emotions. Some purposes common to each are enjoyment, appreciation for the beauty, form, and movement of the human body (the grace, the rhythm, the timing), design, and emotional release.

The fundamental rhythms, their combinations into dance patterns, and the folk song and dance place the child intimately in an art environment. The joyous spirit of the dance, its freedom of expression, its wholesome avenue of outlet for the creative impulse make it an esthetic experience. The games, athletics, sports, and the dances of man have permeated the art of centuries. We have only to turn to the sculpture, the paintings, the metal work, the engravings, and the tapestries of the masters to see examples of this.

Art is a creative process; so also is play; both are free and active pursuits that belong to the amateur as well as the expert. When the paths of art education and physical education run side by side or actually merge, there is an additional opportunity for appreciation of the beauty that enriches both.

6. Art and Health [2]

The human figure or themes of human interest constitute the most appealing subject matter to many students. This is why portraiture, figure study, and group composition rank high in their preference. This being the case, the study of the human body can be motivated by art, and the study of art motivated by health education. In appreciation lessons, the art teacher will often use the ancient Greek statues for examples. *The Discus Thrower* exemplifies the Greek ideal of manly

---

[1] Contributed by Dorothy V. Horine, Assistant Supervisor of Health and Psysical Education, Baltimore, Maryland.

[2] Contributed by Harriet C. Parks, Art Teacher, Gwynns Falls Park Junior High School, Baltimore, Maryland.

strength. The Greeks admired the graceful human body, and their
statues still show us the ideal figure. By training, developing, and
keeping clean the human body each Greek boy and girl tried to reach
this ideal.

Long ago, artists, in studying people for portraiture, realized that
costume was a part of personality, like gesture, posture, speech, gait,
habits, and other such attributes. Where costume is concerned, the
teacher of art becomes very important. With his knowledge of current
trends in clothing, design, color, line, and texture, he can contribute a
wealth of information to the solution of esthetic problems in this matter
of adornment. In this way the student can be guided to dress appropriately and neatly, artistically. When he is dressed well and his class-
mates approve of him, his self-confidence is augmented.

Students like to represent in their drawings the type of persons they
aspire to resemble. For example, girls will draw young men with pretty
faces and fine figures, while boys will draw muscular and powerful men.
Let us assume that " people " is chosen as a subject to awaken the student's sensitivity to the salient characteristics of different persons. The
student might then make sketches of various types of people in the
school, home, and community.

Campaigns are sometimes carried on to clean up the community.
Here, too, the teacher can take the lead in pointing out the beauty of a
clean house, a clean street, a clean dooryard. Children like to make
posters to interest the public in a clean-up campaign. In the inculcation
of civic pride the pupil is taught to take an interest in his school surroundings. Thus the arrangement and care of things in the school may
become a problem in art.

Art serves as a release to the child. He gradually gets a sense of
independence and a desire to be self-sustaining. While he wishes to
conform to a group pattern, at the same time he wishes to stand out
from it through some special ability or skill. Those with native ability
have this desire satisfied through the arts, but those who have special
interests in other fields can still derive satisfaction from art as an avocation, or hobby.

7. Art and Industry

" Culture that is genuine," writes Bonser (61, p. 36), " is founded
upon and vitally involved in utilitarian activities. It is but the expression of these most fundamental utilitarian and social relationships
in their idealistic aspects that gives us much of our most cherished art,

literature, and music." Gradually we are coming to appreciate the significance of art as an important factor in industries in which design is involved, as well as in households that are interested in the products of such industries as contribute articles of usefulness for homemaking. Industry is interested in art from the commercial side primarily, and it seeks to obtain designers, artificers, and artisans who can produce salable products. The household is interested in art from the utilitarian and decorative side, and it seeks to employ art in producing beautiful homes, beautiful furnishings, utensils, and clothing. To the modern household, the selection and arrangement of manufactured products in the home is of the utmost importance, and it is, therefore, with the setting up of esthetic ideals by which articles may be judged that the householder is concerned.

Art as a school subject relates to the transformation of materials into products; hence, it is concerned with this aspect of individual and of social life. The industries are sometimes grouped according to their products under the topics: food, clothing, shelter, records, utensils, tools and machines, light, heat, and power. Instruction in such topics as these is included in the art course because the course is concerned with the development of art intelligence and appreciation through understanding the things of the environment that have resulted from man's transformation of the raw materials about him into finished products. The purpose of this experience with materials is not the cultivation of technical skill, although some degree of efficiency will result from a proper gradation of the work and from careful teaching. The handwork included is for esthetic purposes, giving insight through participation. The subject matter embraces, in addition to the design and creative activity involved, the story of the historical development exhibited by the modern, as compared with the primitive, methods of transforming raw materials, the simpler principles involved in tool processes, and the influence of the art life of the people.

Some industrial arts that are perhaps typical of those that may best be undertaken in schools are as follows:

Bookmaking. Evolution of the book. Invention of printing. How books are made today. How to make a booklet, a Japanese book, a book of one signature, a book of several signatures, a portfolio, posters. Bookmaking as an art.

Papermaking. Early ways of perpetuating records. The invention of paper by the Chinese. Processes involved in papermaking. How to make paper.

Baskets and Boxes. Need for baskets and boxes in the commercial world.

Corrugated containers. Baskets of willow and rattan. How to make a woven basket, a woven basket over a form, a sewed basket, a padded box with cover.

Brick and Tile. The brick in history. Kinds of brick and tile made today. Process in brickmaking. How to make bricks for a toy house.

Pottery Craft. Use of clay in making pottery. Kinds of glazed pottery. Old and new methods of building ware. How pottery is made in the factories. Decorating of pottery. How to make a vase, a plaster-of-Paris form, a clay bowl, a square dish. Pottery as an art.

Cement and Concrete. Concrete as a building material. Manufacture of Portland cement. The aggregate. Water. Placing concrete in the forms. How to make a concrete box, a cement tile.

Textiles. Carding. Spinning. Weaving. Three types of weaves. How to make a loom frame, a harness frame, a shuttle, a rug. Art in textile fabrics.

Glass. Early uses of glass. Manufacture of glass in the United States. Variety of products. Processes of production and decoration.

Wood and Woodworking. Importance of wood and of things made of wood. Lumbering. Sawmilling. Drying. Furniture making.

Household art is emphasized in art courses of study because it helps boys and girls to be better home-makers. Houses take on a new meaning once their art significance is understood. If human needs are properly conceived and adequately met, beauty in the home will generally take care of itself. In order to meet the requirements of good architecture, for example, a house must be planned and constructed to fulfill the requirements of use. It must provide shelter and protection for all members of the household. This purpose will determine the size of the building and the number, size, and arrangement of its rooms, the kinds of materials used, and the processes to be employed in its construction. To meet our esthetic needs, a house that is also a home must not only be adequate, but it must also appear to be so, both inside and out, and this, as a matter of art, should be included in the art course.

8. School Exhibits and the School Museum

School exhibitions of pupils' work are educationally desirable because children are always interested in seeing what other children can do. Containing examples of the best work done, such exhibits provide criteria whereby the child may judge his own products, thereby furnishing an incentive to creative expression and to higher standards. School exhibits also help to keep visitors, especially the parents, informed of the progress in art that is being made by the children. Pupils may be encouraged to work out the plans for the exhibit as a project.

They will profit by learning to mount their own work and will enjoy doing it.

Exhibits should be continuous, if possible, changing every week or two, or on the completion of a given teaching unit. When the school maintains a continuous exhibit of pupils' work, the things shown are easily available at any time for a city-wide exhibit. Exhibits are sometimes inspired by holidays and are often scheduled to begin on days when there are to be special visitors or a P.T.A. meeting.

The place for exhibiting should be a prominent one in the building, and it should be a permanent one, easily reached, well lighted and ventilated. A room adjoining the principal's office is often appropriately used for exhibition purposes. When no other room is available, exhibits may be satisfactorily installed in the main entrance hall, which should be adequately lighted for the purpose. A special exhibition room in the school is desirable, though seldom available.

The school exhibit should be organized about one main topic or idea: for example, the work of one grade, a single lesson, a unit of teaching, a school subject, such as geography or science. At another time it might embrace original works or reproductions of works of artists, as for example, sculpture, commercial work, industrial art or crafts products of various kinds, and paintings. Such an exhibition of the work done by adult artists stimulates art appreciation.

The educational work being carried on outside the public-school system by museums has done much to focus the attention of school administrators and teachers on the educational importance of museum collections and on the desirability of displaying them in the schools. School exhibits should help to clarify the subject matter presented in the course of study, and to make curricular material more vital and interesting to the pupils. They provide much needed vicarious experience for the pupils, and through the careful selection and arrangement of the things shown, give esthetic pleasure, and encourage the development of taste. The need for school-owned collections is felt most keenly in the localities not reached by museum service. The collections lent by the public museum to the schools have, in most places, been few in number, while the facilities provided at the school for showing them have been inadequate. In addition to displaying the material lent by the local museums, schools should also build their own collections. Any school that is large enough and progressive enough to have a library should also have its own museum.

The inauguration of a school museum should not require the setting aside of a room specifically for this purpose, although in some schools this might be desirable. Floor space, suitable wall space, and display cases should be provided somewhere in the building where proper lighting obtains. All these matters should be included in the plans for every new building.

Art teachers, because of their preparation in design and the nature of their work, are experienced in arranging and labeling exhibits. It is therefore suggested that the art teacher or head of the art department in the school be designated by the principal to act as chairman of the school museum committee, which would be composed of teachers and pupils from other departments.

The work of the committee should include such tasks as the following: designating suitable places in the building for showing the exhibits, determining what adaptations or slight modifications would have to be made in the building to make effective displays possible, deciding what additional equipment and supplies would be required, determining the scope and nature of the exhibits, deciding where to borrow or otherwise obtain the collections of things to be shown, and working out a schedule of exhibits for the year. Once a school museum has been established, it is suggested further that sub-committees made up of pupils, each sub-committee working under a member of the faculty, be appointed to coöperate in building the collections and maintaining the museum generally.

II
INEQUALITIES IN OPPORTUNITIES FOR ART DEVELOPMENT

Ernest Horn
Professor of Education and Director of the University Elementary School
State University of Iowa, Iowa City, Iowa

I. Introductory

The selection and training of teachers for instruction in art must be considered from the point of view of the services that these teachers are expected to render and the situations in which they must work. Discussions of the problems of teaching art, including those pertaining to the curriculum, methods of teaching, and the preparation of teachers, commonly assume favorable conditions that are the exception rather than the rule. How limited the opportunities of most students are for development in art becomes apparent when one inspects the data on the communities in which they live, the various types of schools that they attend, and the amount and quality of art instruction that they receive.

Of the 25,976,306 pupils enrolled in public schools in 1937–1938, 19,773,611 (76.1 percent) were enrolled in elementary schools. The relative percentages of pupils in elementary and secondary schools are approximately the same if the enrollments in private elementary and secondary schools are included. Approximately half of this total enrollment in public elementary and secondary schools live on the farm or in communities of less than twenty-five hundred.[1]

The community environments of students in the total school population vary from those almost barren of artistic surroundings to those that are rich in such resources as public and private architecture, museums, exhibits, and the like; their homes vary from those that are illiterate to those that are highly cultivated; their opportunities for schooling, from the isolated one-room school, where no art is taught, to the large city high school with its elaborate curriculum, superb equipment, and highly qualified teachers.

It is obvious that there can be no one pattern for instruction in art. The only statement that is generally applicable is that every child has a right to good instruction. The means of providing this instruction will vary according to the type of school and the resources of the community.

II. SECONDARY SCHOOLS

Of the 24,590 public high schools in the United States reporting in 1938, 16.3 percent had an enrollment of fewer than 50 pupils, 23.2 percent an enrollment of from 50 to 99, 26.1 percent an enrollment of 100 to 199. About two-fifths of the high schools (39.5 percent) had an enrollment of fewer than 100, and about two-thirds, an enrollment of less than 200 pupils.[2] On the other hand, 6.9 percent had an enrollment

---

[1] *School Life,* 25: No. 7, April, 1940, p. 199. Also " Progress in Rural Education." *N.E.A. Research Bulletin,* Vol. 18; No. 4, p. 135. (Office of Education: Washington, D. C.)

[2] *Statistics of Public High Schools, 1937–38.* Biennial Survey of Education in the United States. Bulletin 1940, No. 2, Ch. V. (Office of Education: Washington, D. C.)

of over 1,000 pupils, and 50 public high schools had an enrollment of more than 5,000 pupils each.

In 1930, 42.7 percent of rural high schools for which information was available had an enrollment of less than 50; 33.1 percent, an enrollment of from 50 to 100; and 13.5 percent, an enrollment of from 101 to 150. More than three-fourths of these rural high schools enrolled not more than 100 pupils.[1] There has been a large increase in rural-high-school enrollment in the last ten years, and there is some evidence that the percentage of small high schools is decreasing.[2]

The small high school has many serious limitations: the small enrollment does not give flexibility in organizing classes, it has few teachers, and its instructional equipment is usually very meager. Yet it is to these small high schools or to junior high schools that most prospective teachers in secondary schools, regardless of their major subject, must expect to go for their first teaching experience. The art major will find little opportunity to teach in her chosen field, for in most small high schools no art is included in the program of studies. In a recent survey in one state, for example, only five of 375 consolidated high schools offered art at all, and these to very limited numbers. In the same state, only two of 449 cities of the third class included art in the program of studies.

It is obvious that students in small high schools are being deprived of opportunities for art development; even the occasional school that offers art at all usually does not provide a teacher whose training has been primarily in this field. Moreover, the students of these small schools are limited, not only because of meager educational facilities, but also by the absence of many important out-of-school influences, such as superior public and private architecture, libraries, art museums, and exhibits. Even students who wish to secure private instruction, and are able to pay for it, are unlikely to find a competent teacher in the small community in which these small schools are located.

Whatever appreciation of art or ability in it is developed in these small high schools is incidental to the study of other curricular areas, and these potential contributions will be limited, in most instances, by

---

[1] National Education Association. *The Outlook for Rural Education.* Research Bulletin, Vol. IX, No. 4, Sept., 1931, p. 281. National Education Association. (Washington, D. C.)

[2] United States Office of Education. *Economies through the Elimination of Very Small Schools.* Bulletin 1934, No. 3, p. 22. Superintendent of Documents. (Washington, D. C.)

the meager art training of the teachers. It is possible that, where the pressure of meeting entrance requirements for college permits, some art would be offered if there were more teachers who included art among the subjects they prepare to teach. In general, however, it is only in larger high schools that art instruction under reasonably well-qualified teachers is to be found.

III. ELEMENTARY SCHOOLS

Attention has been called to the fact that in 1936 more than three-fourths of the pupils enrolled in public schools were in the kindergarten and first six grades. More than two-thirds of the public-school teachers teach in these elementary grades. Nearly all these teachers are classroom teachers who teach art along with other subjects in the curriculum. Circular Number 178 (March, 1939), issued by the Office of Education, reports that this practice is followed even in cities of 450,000 and over and that " In none of these cities is there a special teacher of art clearly indicated below grade 7 except in platoon schools. . . . Nine cities report a supervisor, or director, or an assistant in charge of art education, with assistants ranging from none to 8 as the largest number." It is clear that the classroom teacher in elementary schools must teach the art and that supervisory assistance and direction is very inadequate.

There are no reliable data as to the percentage of schools that are organized on the platoon or departmental plan, and there is no reliable evidence regarding the relative efficiency with which art is taught under either plan as compared with its teaching by the regular classroom teacher. Few data are available on the amount of art training possessed by typical classroom teachers or by departmental teachers, but it is probably no more than is at present required for graduation from teachers' colleges, which is a very small amount. It seems very probable that the typical elementary-school child is taught by a teacher who is far from being qualified to guide his development in art.

There is a good deal of justification for the belief that art should be as competently taught in the elementary school as in the high school. In fact, there is some reason for believing that good instruction in the early years is even more important than in later years.

The principal reason for assigning the teaching of art to the regular classroom teacher may be administrative necessity or convenience. Nevertheless, other arguments are advanced in defense of the practice. Perhaps some of these arguments are rationalization of what is deemed to be inevitable. First, it is argued that, while the classroom teacher may not know art, she does know the pupils. This is valid only in the sense that she comes in contact with fewer pupils than does the special or departmental teacher of art, who goes from class to class. Second, the argument is advanced, especially in centers that stress integration, that the work in art is more readily integrated with the rest of the curriculum when taught by the classroom teacher. This is undoubtedly true; yet there seems nothing to prohibit the regular classroom teacher from integrating art with the curricular areas she herself teaches, even though a special art teacher may have charge of the art period. Certainly, within her limited competence, she could practice this integration as well as she could teach pupils in the art period. If she is incompetent in art, she can neither teach it nor integrate it with other curricular areas.

The typical classroom teacher has had little instruction in art, either in the elementary and the high school or in her college training. A fairly strong case can be made, therefore, for a modified form of departmental teaching in which art is taught by a teacher having special training in this field. In most departmental plans the teacher responsible for teaching art is also responsible for teaching one or more other fields. It is desirable, under such a plan, that the departmental teacher of art should have at least the equivalent of a minor in art in her college preparation. Even in schools that are not organized on a departmental or platoon plan, a teacher with art training sometimes teaches art in several grades in exchange for the teaching of other subjects in her own room. It seems wise to encourage this type of coöperation.

In most schools, however, the general classroom teacher is the teacher of art. This fact must be dealt with realistically, and efforts must be made to improve the teaching of art under the conditions that exist. There are two procedures, one or both of which may be followed: first, to encourage, or perhaps require, elementary teachers to take courses in art for certification or for graduation from teachers' colleges; second, to introduce a program for training teachers in service. Both of these procedures are discussed elsewhere in this volume.

IV. RURAL SCHOOLS

Attention has already been called to the fact that approximately half of all pupils in public schools live on the farm or in cities of less than twenty-five hundred. These pupils are almost completely deprived of any opportunity in art fields, either in the elementary-school or in the high-school grades. The conditions in most one-room rural schools are especially drab, and more than half of all public school buildings in the United States are of the one-room type. Surveys of instruction in these schools have repeatedly pointed out that, in most instances, the curricula are formal and narrow, and that instruction in art, as in music, is almost wholly neglected. Even when instruction is attempted, it is hampered by the absence of equipment, by the complicated daily program, and by the lack of training on the part of the teachers.

Approximately a third of all teachers of elementary grades in public schools are in rural one- or two-room schools. The teachers in these schools have, in general, the minimum of training that is legally acceptable.

Of the teachers in one- and two-teacher schools from whom reports were received in 1930–1931 in the *National Survey of the Education of Teachers,* 61.8 percent had not more than five years of training beyond the elementary school, and only 9.5 had more than two years of college work. In one state more than 10 percent of these teachers had no training beyond the elementary school.[1] The amount of college training received by rural teachers has apparently increased rapidly since 1930. In 1935, 24.2 percent of teachers in one-room rural schools had only a high-school education or less, and 42.1 percent an education embracing two or more years of college training. There has recently been a marked tendency to raise the certification requirements of all teachers, including those in rural schools.[2]

The typical teacher of a one-room school, in 1935, had not more than six years of training beyond the eighth grade. Even if she had attended a teachers' college for one or two years, she probably had not more than three hours of art. Her elementary-school and high-school education was obtained, moreover, in rural or small-town schools where no art was taught. She taught from twenty to twenty-five children distributed through eight grades, teaching from twenty to forty short periods a day. Her salary was a little more than $500. She had taught in rural schools about three years, and not more than one or two years in the same school. If she did not get married and was ambitious, she

---

[1] *National Survey of the Education of Teachers.* "Summary and Interpretation." Bulletin No. 10, Vol. VI, pp. 149–150. (Office of Education: Washington, D. C.)

[2] *Biennial Survey of Education, 1934–36,* Bulletin, 1937, No. 2 Vol. I, Ch. 5, p. 8. (Advance Sheets) (Office of Education: Washington, D. C.)

moved to a village school or continued her education, after which she taught in a village school.

The supervision that this typical teacher received was from the county superintendent, and this was poor both in quantity and quality. Less than half of the county superintendents had as much academic preparation as is represented by the bachelor's degree. The probability that this superintendent had college training in art is even less than in the case of the rural teacher.[1]

The picture of typical rural teaching and supervision drawn in the two preceding paragraphs is based largely on data provided for the years 1930 to 1935. While considerable improvement in rural education has recently been made in some states, conditions in most rural schools in the country at large are still extremely unsatisfactory. Gratifying results have been obtained in a few states where special art supervisors have been employed and where the general supervisors have developed a vision of the importance and possibilities of art instruction in rural areas.[2]

It is clear that most rural teachers are not qualified to give instruction in art, and that even if they wished to do so, they would receive little help from supervisory officers. There are scattered instances, however, where substantial beginnings have been made in providing art instruction, even under the difficult conditions that exist in one-room rural schools. Conditions are potentially better, of course, in states that require two years of training beyond the high school, with specified courses in art, and in a few states like California, where the minimal requirement is graduation from a four-year college course. Even in the few states requiring four years of college training, however, little

---

[1] National Education Association. *The Outlook for Rural Education.* Research Bulletin. Vol. IX, No. 4, Sept., 1931. (National Education Association: Washington, D. C.)

Biennial Survey of Education, 1934–36. Bulletin, 1937, No. 2, Vol. I, Ch. V, p. 9. (Advance Pages) (Office of Education: Washington, D. C.)

Salary and Education of Rural School Personnel, Status and Trends. Pamphlet No. 85. (Superintendent of Documents: Washington, D. C.)

[2] *Progress in Rural Education, op. cit.*

National Education Association. *The Status of the Teaching Profession.* Research Bulletin, Vol. XVIII, No. 2, March, 1940. (National Education Association: Washington, D. C.)

National Education Association. *A Policy for Rural Education in the United States.* Report of the Committee on Program and Policy, Department of Rural Education, Frank W. Cyr, Chairman. February, 1940. (National Education Association: Washington, D. C.)

is accomplished except under the encouragement and guidance of competent supervisors who recognize both the special limitations and the special resources of the rural school.

There is little hope for raising the general level of art instruction in rural schools without substantial changes in the whole structure of rural education, including the raising of standards for certification, the raising of salaries, the provision of more adequate instructional equipment, the consolidation of schools, and the improvement of the quantity and quality of general and special supervision.

There can be no question of the advisability of consolidation where it is feasible. The consolidated school attracts and holds better teachers, provides better equipment, and secures more competent supervision. Nevertheless, we now have, and for some years will continue to have, large numbers of one- and two-room rural schools. The limitations of these schools must be clearly recognized, but at the same time their potentialities must be fully developed. Among the most important steps to be taken to this end are: (*a*) the raising of certification requirements for teachers, (*b*) a professional preparation that definitely faces the special problems and conditions of rural schools, (*c*) the reorganization of the teaching program, (*d*) the provision of general supervisors whose training, like that of the teachers, has been focussed upon the needs and opportunities in rural schools, (*e*) the provision of instructional equipment fitted to the needs of rural schools, (*f*) the provision of special supervisors of art, and (*g*) the preparation of professional literature that deals explicitly with the problems of teaching art in rural schools.

It is perfectly clear from the evidence here reviewed that, for the majority of children in the United States, the opportunities for development in art approach the zero point. Communities that are most in need of the stimulation sound art instruction can give are wholly deprived of this stimulation. The leaders in art, in art education, and in education must develop a vastly increased concern with the problems of art instruction in rural and village schools.

III
ART IN THE ELEMENTARY SCHOOL

Edith L. Mitchell
State Director of Art
Department of Public Instruction
Dover, Delaware
and
Sallie B. Tannahill
Associate Professor of Fine Arts
Teachers College, Columbia University
New York, New York

I. Introductory

Having passed through many difficult phases of development, art has emerged, not without mark of conflict, into a fairly respected and dignified place in elementary education. It has been revived from the enervating effects of the pattern and busy-work periods of its intellectual and esthetic stagnation. It has weathered many isms of creative self-expression with resulting loss or gain of prestige according to their interpretations and demonstrated effectiveness to professional and lay groups. Recent forces outside the educational system have helped to keep it intact as an important factor in the shaping of the lives of American youth. Of these perhaps the most significant is federal support and furtherance of the arts, which has through its projects directed attention to native forms and resources and thereby created a more art-conscious public. Another force lies in the bond of understanding and appreciation being established between parents and children through adult-education activities in the arts. Still another is the evidence gradually being accumulated with reference to the therapeutic benefits of art experiencing.

There are still great differences of thought and practice that may easily be understood when one considers how few institutions responsible for the education of administrators, art, and classroom teachers have as yet made any real progress in coördinating and unifying their ideas about art with those of child study, general education, and producing art groups. Schools are still full of administrators who have had little experience in art, of classroom teachers whose inhibitions and limitations in art appreciation and experience become imposed upon their groups of children, of art teachers and supervisors who ride art hobbyhorses with reins of outmoded teaching techniques, and of local artists with holier-than-thou attitudes toward their own efforts.

In an effort to determine art objectives, one needs only to turn to the ideas and statements of outstanding individuals and groups to find educational objectives that may serve to direct the art educational program in the elementary school. Although specific emphases may change with different age levels, general objectives, including those of art, remain the same for all ages.

Art experiences provided for all children, irrespective of race, creed, social standing, or future vocation, should add to a desired completeness of living comparable to that set forth by the best educational thinkers. These experiences may be realized through expressive, appreciative, or technical avenues of approach and their relationships found through effective teaching. Many educators have found that early and well-guided participation in art activities requiring the use of a variety of art media and processes has laid a foundation for later taste and appreciation, as well as provided outlets for enjoyment and creative expression. The term ' creative ' as related to expression has often been given too limited an interpretation. Its implications here are broad and inclusive of many possibilities in child development. Creativeness has to do with thinking and feeling as well as with doing. It implies independence in the selection of medium, idea, and ways of combining them. It provides for desirable objectification of self — a means of self-knowledge and evaluation that makes for increased self-direction. It signifies an individual response and reaction to life and furnishes opportunities for growth in confidence and sincerity. A recognition of its characteristics lays a foundation of sympathy and tolerance essential to appreciation of the works of others. It develops alertness, freshness of outlook, imagination, and resourcefulness — qualities greatly needed in our rapidly moving modern civilization.

Appreciation of art grows out of situations requiring judgment relative to quality of material and form, and their relationship to their time and purpose. Wise teaching will provide many opportunities for the exercise and development of this discriminating power. It is toward this objective that illustrative materials, visits to art collections, shops, and nature may be used advantageously, but it should be remembered that the necessary feeling of kinship with all forms of beauty and fine art is strengthened by the actualities of related personal art experiencing. On this account, such instructional materials and experiences assume greater significance when preceded by creative planning and effort.

The technical problems of the elementary school may be solved as they present themselves. The realization of these must be the child's as well as the teacher's to insure concreteness of purpose. The need for assistance in solving technical problems is frequently an individual, rather than a group need. Techniques are valuable only as they lead to satisfactory developments in actual production commensurate with the experience and ability of the producer. A danger lies in their over-emphasis at the expense of fineness of plan and integrity of interpretation.

II. STANDARDS AND PURPOSES

Art experiences of children become richer and more vital when adequate standards are adopted for their selection and evaluation. Unfortunately, adults have for many years expected mature performance and techniques from children. Such imposition of adult standards has resulted in inhibited and distasteful responses to art. It is well to study investigations into the interests and abilities of children at different age levels. Findings in such studies will show that early enthusiasms for manipulating art materials, joy in color, and uniqueness of expression fade into drabness, timidity, and dependence as children grow with their school experiences.

A great philosopher of education has written:

> When I think of this fresh reaction of little children to the world, I am led to ask why it so soon gets dimmed, why it gets so soon covered up and a kind of mental rubber stamp or phonograph record takes its place. It may be thought absurd to demand originality of every one. But I think this idea of absurdity is due to having a wrong measure by which to judge originality. It is not measured by its outer products; it is rather an individual way of approaching a world common to us all.[1]

Little children in the primary grades are fearless in expressing themselves in line, form, and color, and they are not at all embarrassed if there is lack of proportion and reality in their work. No matter what adults may say, kindergarten and primary children are inclined to be satisfied with their efforts to express themselves.

Many teachers in the upper elementary school are greatly perturbed by the growing self-consciousness of the pupils and their dissatisfaction

---

[1] John Dewey (9), p. 4.

with their own art productions. The confident joy and spontaneous, natural work of early years seem to change to timidity and labored un-childlike expression. This change has been generally accepted as physiological and inevitable; the child's increasing awareness of natural phenomena and his growing analytical powers have been allowed to stand in the way of his growth rather than being directed into expressive art channels. But need this be? May not this condition be due to weakness in teaching? May it not be caused by unfortunate emphasis upon literal, realistic interpretations? It may be that we, as teachers, have not helped the child fairly and honestly to estimate the worth of his own endeavors; that we have made *our* dissatisfactions his and in this way have instilled in him a superficial, self-conscious attitude toward himself. Seeing more art work of other children would help pupils to find new interest and greater confidence in their own art activities.

Our scientific age has led us to see the fallacy of expecting to establish fixed formulas in education. Some teachers have resorted to the use of the recipe type of art teaching and have depended too greatly upon the short cuts or devices presented by persons and publications having limited concepts of art education. Their chief concern has been with the child's objective result in art form rather than with his development as an individual and growing personality. Belief in the latter emphasis requires the acceptance of standards such as these: *eagerness* to participate in art activity; *joy* that comes from individual satisfaction in art experiences; *confidence* that results from a self-revelation of powers of production; *sincerity* and *individuality* — expression consistent with personality and life; *courage* and *independence* in the selection and use of medium and subject matter; *discrimination* — informed and sensitized ability to determine art quality; *sympathy* and *tolerance* — an attitude toward art that aids, rather than checks, interest and appreciation; *realization* of the scope of art; and *respect* for its part in all of living.

If these standards for evaluating art education are accepted as adequate and if evidences of them are found in the productions, appreciations, and personalities of children, then surely art may be welcomed as an immeasurable force in education.

There is considerable difference of opinion among art educators with respect to determining *specific standards* of art learnings according to age levels. Written curricular materials have ranged from extremes of elaborate specifications of technical and subject-matter items to the most abbreviated generalities. Practice of the first type has resulted in stereotyped and mechanized teaching, while applications of the latter type have produced vagueness and uncoördinated planning, except in the case of the superior teacher.

It is of especial importance that some middle ground be found whereby sufficient interpretation and guidance may be provided in the form of written and graphic materials for the use of classroom teachers and administrators as well as for art teachers. Such materials must be sufficiently specific to reveal continuity and the ultimate purpose of an art program. In one section of a recent bulletin prepared for the teachers and administrators of the schools of Delaware (38, p. 19), Miss Edith Mitchell, State Director of Art, has dealt with this problem in the following manner:

> Art covers such a vast area of endeavor and experiencing, and its forms are so numerous, it becomes an almost impossible task to segregate specific types of activity and learning to the various age levels of school life.
>
> During the past year objective statements have been obtained from art teachers throughout the State in reference to their curriculum content and points of emphasis. Great diversity was revealed and there is every evidence that some coördinated efforts should be made to develop more comprehensive and functional art curriculum materials.
>
> To separate objectives from guiding philosophy, learning activities, and procedures contradicts the concept of integration. The following material may, however, be of assistance to classroom teachers and their administrators in clarifying major points of emphasis and basic concepts for their selection. Art teachers may wish also to use the material as a check against their own art teaching programs. It should be remembered that any statement of teaching objectives will need to be considered relatively since experiences, interests, and needs of children do not exactly coincide at any one age level. Mental, physical, emotional capacities and developments are interrelated and should serve as guides to the educator in determining content, method, and placement of teaching materials.
>
> Art in education aims to open up avenues of conscious enjoyment and inspiration. It strives to lay a foundation of taste and discrimination which will function throughout life. Its diversity of form, content, and technique should give it appeal to many for actual participation and use, while its respect for individual thinking and performance makes it an essential part of any democratic educational program. Specifically, art education in Delaware aims to attract all children to participate in one or many of its areas of experiencing. Through such guided experiences it hopes to deal with problems, technical and appreciative, which will de-

velop sensitiveness to quality in art and dissatisfaction for the lack of it. It places important emphasis on the use of significant, immediate experience and environmental stimuli as starting points. Contacts with related contemporary and historic art developments are sought to give fuller meaning to art contributions in human progress. Not the least of its intentions is to effect beneficial personality changes and adjustments through quickened interests and responses, and conscious individual achievements as a basis for group sharing and responsibility. Its therapeutic and diagnostic uses have only begun to be realized by educators. Art offers many ways by which other areas of learning may be clarified and enriched, and should establish itself as a functional agent in all school living, thereby laying a foundation for its expansion into the social, industrial, and civic life of the community.

The basic plan of organization under the headings Knowledges, Skills and Habits, Attitudes and Appreciations, is followed in this Delaware Curriculum Bulletin, with sub-headings that may further define these headings. No year levels are indicated, since the major part of the material is applicable to art teaching situations at all levels, but a simple progression will be noted, however, in each section. A few statements under each heading are given to illustrate the type of material that is included in the part of the Bulletin (38) dealing with art.

Knowledges

Materials and Tools. Knowledge of art tools and materials, processes, and techniques aids in planning for their use. Experimenting with these is a good way to start. One experience with an art medium does not exhaust its possibilities for future enjoyment and participation.

Nature of Art and Its Sources. There are many kinds of art (known as ' art forms '), such as a rug, a book, a poster, a textile, or a clay dish. All fine art has a plan. Plans vary because of material and function. The things you know best are the things best to use. Ideas can be used to show how you feel as well as what you see.

Processes and Work Habits. Talking and reading about art help to clarify its nature, technically and appreciatively. Measurement of achievement in art should be considered in terms of individual improvement over past performance. Performance does not necessarily mean actual making of something. It may be interpreted as meaning any type of art experiencing; such as research, selection and arrangement of forms and colors, or planning art activities and evaluating them upon their completion.

Composition and Design Elements. There are no fixed laws of design and composition. There are, however, common basic principles that can function in all art. Some of these are referred to as balance, rhythm, transition, opposition, emphasis, variety, and contrast. Order is related to art and is a part of it. Order can be achieved by putting things together that are somewhat alike and by the use of grouping. Using too many things alike will be orderly but tiresome. Interesting variations can be had by the use of a few elements that are different in size, color, form, or texture.

Mediums. Water color lends itself to a number of techniques. No one way is ' best.'

Motivating Sources. Religion, work, and play experiences of people have been powerful motivating factors in the production of art. Science has contributed much toward the achievements of art through the ages.

Relationships. Meanings should be attached to learnings in relation to the study of art of other peoples and times. Reasons for their art forms, materials, and techniques as well as their ideas and interpretations. An understanding of the uses made of such art. Familiarity with some of the industrial practices related to forms, materials, and processes experienced in school.

Skills and Habits

Materials and Tools. Increased power and diversity in their use.

Procedures. Noting techniques and information to be gained. Getting information and guidance when needed to maintain a high standard of work. Seeing with a purpose and an informed and inquiring mind. Seeing with conscious recognition esthetic elements in nature and art.

Applications. Continued use of art not only as a means of expression but also as it helps serve practical needs inside and outside of school.

Growth and Evaluation. Awareness of personal strengths and weaknesses in art through self-appraisal and attention to the constructive opinions of others.

Appreciations and Attitudes

Creation, Enjoyment, and Evaluation. Art may serve different people in different ways. To some, it becomes relaxation; to others, intense concentration and industry. Its enjoyment and participation help to establish a sort of balance in living. Realization that standards of taste are outgrowths of experience and education, and that borrowed ones are more of a handicap than a help. Art is like other areas of school learning in that reading, research, experimentation, review, and evaluation are essential to its fullest realization. It is unlike some in that there are no hard and fast rules. Expecting rather than resisting, changes in personal taste and preferences in art. Interest in new developments in art rather than opposition and distrust.

III. RELATION OF ART TO OTHER SUBJECTS [1]

No other field in the school curriculum so happily blends itself with the whole scheme of school life as does art. It vitalizes and enriches the

---

[1] This topic is discussed more fully by other contributors elsewhere in this Section of the Yearbook, especially in earlier pages of this present chapter.
— *Editor.*

work of social studies and literature; it colors the experiences of children in science and dramatic expression. Successful weaving together of the important strands of science, art, literature, and social studies into a fine and durable fabric of experiences for children undoubtedly results in economy and effectiveness of learning. This is possible only when there exists a spirit of happy and helpful interchange of ideas among classroom teachers, special teachers, and children. It is important to add, however, that unless work is presented in an inspiring and challenging way, little of joy or spontaneity will be found in the art. Children who are not thus inspired will ask, " Do we *have* to paint Mexico today? " There are many varied opportunities for art activities to provide amply for differences in interest and ability. These art experiences are excellent vehicles for strengthening powers of appreciation and attitudes toward the art of other peoples as well as the expressions of the children themselves.

In all elementary schools the *industrial arts and fine arts should be unified* insofar as is possible. This is being done in many school systems. It is impossible to divorce form from function, design from process, fine feeling from good workmanship, social values in the industrial arts from social values in the fine arts. There are many useful objects, however, that are not well designed; but everything that is fine in design is useful in the sense that fineness and refinement enrich life.

The difficulty in fusing fine and industrial arts is that a specialist in industrial arts may overlook or underestimate the value of fine arts. On the other hand, the fine-arts teacher who is fired with enthusiasm for design quality only may underrate the contribution made by industrial arts. A teacher who is responsible for both subjects should have a balanced conception of the importance of each. The one attitude emphasizes materials and processes; the other, looks or appearance — the design.

IV. The Distinctive Contribution of Art to the General Educational Program

Although it is evident that art can be used successfully to enrich and color other areas of learning, this is not its only purpose in the curriculum. Many a child is doubtless bored by the repeated insistence upon integration of art with other school activities.

Art should not slip into the rôle of a mere tool, for art makes a real contribution in the elementary school by giving boys and girls a chance to utilize their own ideas and experiences in art form — in clay, paint, crayon, wood, metal, cloth, and other media. Some of this type of work is possible, of course, when art is related to other school work, but there is a pressing need in our schools for more art work that reveals individual thinking and planning. The vital reason for this latter type of work lies in the sheer joy and satisfaction resulting from such types of experience.

Curricular material for use in the elementary schools of Wilmington, Delaware, under the title of *How Art Contributes to Our Daily Living,* makes use of this factor in its suggestions for activities and guiding philosophy. To quote: [1]

> This art program accepts art in its broader interpretation, its forms including articles familiar and useful in everyday living, the books we read and the clothes we wear, its materials ranging from wood to embroidery woolens, its tools from chisel to needles, its processes varying from stage lighting to linoleum cutting and printing, its styles symbolic, abstract, realistic, or fanciful, and its avenues of experiencing including enjoyment, research, creation, and evaluation.
>
> Variations in ability and interest are expected and provision made for them. There will be headdresses for a Hallowe'en party; costumes and programs for a class play; trips to parks, shops, and other class-rooms; gifts and toys for others to enjoy; arrangement of exhibits for visiting friends and relatives; a wall hanging to enhance a classroom, library, or corridor; a book of painted interpretations of trips and stories; table decorations for a party; colors to be mixed for scenery; dyes for costumes; mats and frames for paintings and drawings; explanatory notes for displayed collections and exhibits, controls for marionettes; lettering for a class book; and many other significant experiences. There is much for all.

V. PROBLEMS OF CURRICULUM-PLANNING

Scientific methods have greatly facilitated the work of curricular construction. Much thought and effort have been given to this aspect of education during recent years, often with splendid results. Written and printed curricular materials serve as excellent means for exchanging various points of view and practices and help to establish better understanding of developments in the field of art.

The form used should be determined by the type of school organiza-

---

[1] Edith L. Mitchell. " Basic Concepts. Art Education — How Art Contributes to Our Daily Living." (A Bulletin for the Guidance of Teachers, Grades 1–6. Preliminary Draft for Evaluation Only. June, 1940)

tion and the particular needs of the teaching groups. Where subject matter is integrated, all fields being brought together in broad units of activity, one course of study may be adequate for the entire school. This course of study should be planned by representatives from all departments of school instruction. Opportunities should also be provided for art work not fused with other studies.

But the discriminating school administrator will not neglect one vital consideration. Does the course of study function? Is it an aid and inspiration to fine teaching? It is disappointing when courses of study are found that seem easy roads to educational Utopia, yet fail miserably in their actual application. The weakness may lie in the course of study or it may easily be in the personnel of the teaching staff. Because of limited art experiences classroom teachers often feel the need of help in the many processes and techniques of art. Assistance may be effectively given by clearly expressed supplementary material formulated by the art teacher or art supervisor. Such material might include suggestions for working with clay, plaster of Paris, poster paints, transparent water colors, oils, colored chalks and crayons, wood, *papier-maché*. Ways of meeting problems in bookmaking, lettering, posters, block printing, costumes, stage sets, masks, marionettes, tie-dyeing, and color may also be made clear in mimeographed sheets to supplement the course of study.

VI. Guide to Curriculum-Planning

A successfully planned curriculum has the following characteristics:

1. It considers school, home, and play interests, abilities, and desires of children in selecting and arranging subject matter.

2. It states clearly the aims and hopes of achievement for the elementary school based on child interests, abilities, and talents and relates these aims to the general objectives of education.

3. It includes (a) opportunity for creative expression, (b) knowledge and appreciation of the art heritage of the race — contribution of art to civilization, to daily life, both modern and ancient, (c) opportunities for discriminating between the commonplace and the fine, and (d) aids for developing techniques needed for satisfactory achievement with tools and processes of art expression.

4. It provides (a) social experiences (group work), and (b) individual experiences (for self-expression).

5. It considers individual differences, especially (a) special opportunities for the talented child, and (b) work for the average child that he is able to do and that leads to further activity.

6. It is flexible and easily revised. It is impossible to predict what interests

will be aroused. Allowance should be made for choice of subject and materials, and for the unexpected, to suit various conditions and communities.

7. It is planned in advance. Even when the unit scheme is adopted and children's desires and interests are considered, it is well to plan work tentatively in advance, in order to avoid repetitions, omissions, and gaps and to be ready with enrichment material. The plan need not be adhered to if the unexpected necessitates a change, but there should be continuous growth and accomplishment of the aims and objectives.

8. It is made by the coöperation of the art supervisor with grade teachers, general supervisors, principals, and curriculum specialists.

9. It is suggestive rather than rigid. A great variety of possibilities for art expression is given, from which selections may be made.

10. It provides for the inexperienced teacher whenever possible. The art supervisor, however, through meetings, bulletins, and personal conferences, is able to give help to the new teacher.

11. It gives practical aid in regard to processes and techniques needed by all teachers.

12. It includes records of successful lessons or units as illustrations of good planning for child activity.

IV
ART IN A PUBLIC–SCHOOL CURRICULUM

JANE DRIVER
Director of Art Education
Wilmington, Delaware

Good curricular material is tentative material, and it can at least be said for the Wilmington art program that it is changing and growing to meet the needs of the teachers who use it. Although this account deals mainly with the elementary-school program, which has been more completely formulated than our other programs, it will also discuss secondary art units, in order that the curriculum may be considered as a whole.

We believe that developing curricular material on the spot is an ideal procedure, but feel that in situations similar to ours in Wilmington there is justification for written art units. A planned program, including preparation of art material, permits teacher participation, makes art an integral part of a school-wide curricular development, provides means of bringing stimulating material to the untrained, as well as to the trained, art teacher, keeps teachers and administrators in touch with the best thinking of the group, and coördinates modern philosophy of art education with common teaching practices.

Planning new art materials was part of a general program of curricular development inaugurated in September, 1931. Our part of this program began in September, 1934, under Professor Sallie B. Tannahill of Teachers College and continues under Miss Edith Mitchell, now State Director of Art Education in Delaware. In planning our art program, we discussed new methods of teaching, formulated a program of studies, and began our work on the units. Perhaps, like many other curriculum-makers, we overemphasized the importance of unit production and did not first prepare a thorough foundation on which to base our materials. We know now that good teachers are not necessarily unit writers, that the more important contributions from members of the group may well be investigations, reports of actual teaching experiences, testing of tentative materials, and careful evaluation of procedures. We are not ready to make a complete report on our program, but we can give a brief description of accomplishment to show how the art curriculum functions in our schools.

Our program is based on the interests of children that reveal their needs. Units are set up to provide for children's experiences through art activities; surveys, bibliographies, and enrichment materials help to familiarize the teacher with the fundamental concepts of the unit. The present plan is a tentative organization of elementary art material in three closely related divisions: (a) suggestive art activities growing out of children's experiences in social studies, language arts, and other areas, (b) a series of units on " How Art Contributes to Our Daily Living," and (c) materials for the teacher's use, such as a brief statement of philosophy, typical experiences of children, reports of teaching experiments, bibliography, and other materials.

Children have many and varied experiences that find expression in art forms. These expressions need not be limited to illustrating content material. This narrow interpretation of the function of integration may be responsible for the meticulous depiction of historic events through yards of frieze where no frieze is needed, for countless Indian heads that might have decorated a bygone tobacco store, for booklets and scrapbooks that violate all good book structure, and for many other kinds of busy work masquerading in the name of art. Children's experiences in these fields culminating in their natural desire for expression need not be neglected, but a plan should be sought that will satisfy these interests and that will direct the activities into work of a more creative character. Dramatic expression, with its allied art activities, offers a solution, and we have also found helpful the use of materials that involve ingenuity and resourcefulness, rather than too much concentration on painting and drawing, with undue emphasis upon representative types of art. For example, during a study of the city, a group of ten-year-old children block-printed a wall hanging, using the civic center and Wilmington's rider, Caesar Rodney, as design motifs. Printed in brown on natural-colored pongee it makes a rich and effective wall decoration. Boys, fourteen years old, carved from balsa wood small figures that have almost a folk-art quality. These interpret Bret Harte's " The Luck of Roaring Camp," the story of the miners' adopted baby, and their method of caring for it.

Although the series of units, " How Art Contributes to Our Daily Living," has a special emphasis for each grade, these points of emphasis are not limited to any age if pertinent experiences relating to them arise:

Grade I

Art relates itself to the child's home, school, and community experiences.

Grade II

Nature (or, in Grade IIA, the city) provides many forms and dramatic experiences that may be used in art expression.

Grade III

The arts make a significant contribution to forms of entertainment and recreation. Art provides for the development of unique interpretation and imaginative expression.

Grade IV

Environmental aspects of human living provide rich and stimulating material for art expression.

Grade V

Art contributions of other people and times influence our art expression today.

Grade VI

Art and the artist are significant in the life of the community.

Provision is also made for art activities growing out of interests in special occasions (for example, Delaware's Tercentenary Celebration), for art clubs and individual hobbies, for alternate units to suit the needs of certain central ideas, as " How Art May Contribute to the Entire Life of the School." This unit has challenged the ability of children in that it has created in them a desire to improve their environment and has provided ways for art to function in the school. Through art teaching of this kind children are becoming responsible for the appearance of school grounds, corridors, and classrooms; for bulletin-board displays and the arrangement of exhibitions; for signs, posters, invitations, and all forms of needed advertisement; for the production of stage scenery and decorations for special occasions.

The units for Grades I to VI are in one loose-leaf folder, with a general plan [1] and specific forewords for each grade. The units include suggested approaches with their activities and culminations. Child growth is evaluated in the following areas: information and understanding, appreciation, creative power, and techniques.

The interpretation of these units is an individual matter, but there are certain procedures that teachers agree are fundamental. Among these are the following:

(a) There should first be a period of orientation through approaches that lead into the unit and prepare the children for the term's work.

(b) Firsthand experiences through visits and excursions are desirable, but where local conditions make these impossible, other approaches are suggested, such as inviting artists to talk to the class and to show or demonstrate their work, bringing material into the schoolroom, arranging and talking about it, telling about experiences at home and on vacations, and planning work with children and teacher.

(c) The teacher next provides opportunity for a beginning activity in which all the children may participate. During this activity she learns the needs, interests, and abilities of the children and is ready to help with and advise about the individual and group problems that follow. Charles wants to paint what he saw on his visit to the zoo, Nancy wants to model her pet cat, some of the children are planning a wall hanging for the room. The possibilities are limitless.

(d) At the end of the term significant experiences are gathered together in some form of culmination that shows habits formed, interests aroused, powers released, appreciation developed, skills acquired that

---

[1] See Mitchell (39).

may carry over into the work of the next term, and, we hope, into the child's pattern of living.

The work of the seventh through the ninth grades is not described in detail here because it is being reorganized. This does not mean that children and teachers in this division are not doing any art work or that they are still working under a traditional system. Experiments are being carried on, new materials explored. The following units are under consideration:

Grade VII

How nature and science contribute to the art experiences of people.

Grade VIII

The relationship of arts. How we may understand people through their art.

Grade IX

The place of the arts in home, school, and community living.

Art work in the senior high school is elective, and students from different grades meet in the same art classes. To avoid repetition for any individual, we have set up a system under which two units, the one " Art," the other " Art Appreciation," are offered each term, and the program is repeated every three years. We do not defend this plan, nor do we apologize for it. We present our program for the reader's inspection, with the statement that at the end of our first cycle, February, 1939, we began to criticize, evaluate, and reorganize this material in a way that would eliminate titles such as ' Appreciation,' which throw monkey wrenches into every art discussion.

There has never been any intention of divorcing art and appreciation, even if that were possible, but in the latter approach we have sought to develop taste and discriminating judgment through varied art activities suited to all pupils, rather than to a limited group especially interested in art. These activities range from research to construction. They include art lectures, visits to art galleries, discussions, organization of school exhibitions, and experiments with various materials. We find, in actual practice, that our two types of units overlap, that procedures in the one may also enrich the other, and that material gathered and activities observed during three years' experience will prove invaluable in our future organization.

Among the activities that have grown out of pupils' interests in relation to high-school art units were the oil painting "From a School Window," a water-color painting, block-printed handkerchiefs, and etched metal buttons, which were made during the unit quoted above. A combination of balsa wood and papier-maché masks interpret " Macbeth and the Porter " from the unit " The Theater," and the dancing figure is from " Milestones in Art — Architecture and Sculpture."

Many other interesting things " just happen," as our teachers say. These I call ' by-products.' They add concrete evidence to our hopes that our children and teachers are not inhibited by a curriculum, but that through the broadening experiences that have accompanied its development they are enabled to understand the value of environmental forms as material for art expression. The mural was a ' by-product ' of the high-school art unit, " How Art May Provide for Social and Vocational Growth." It was painted in tempera on heavy gray paper by a high-school boy who came back to school after his graduation to finish it. He calls it " Events of the Year."

May I, very humbly, set down a few of the gains that have been made, advancement that we believe can be attributed to our use of new forces within the curriculum of the school? They are: more joy in art work, brought about by the acceptance of individual needs, interests, and expressions, aided by a wide range of art materials; an awareness by teachers and administrators of the function of art in the lives of children, including its enriching and expanding influence in all parts of the school; a more professional attitude toward teaching procedures, intelligent self-criticism, and efforts at improvement in preparation and methods; an improved appearance of school buildings through arrangement, new equipment, and decorations; the addition of art books to school libraries, the purchase of art curriculum collections for secondary art classes, and the establishment of teacher collections for all elementary schools; the beginnings of collections of art objects and materials in many schools augmented by loan collections from the supervisor's office and from the Delaware Art Center; an aroused interest in the community and the coöperation of city associations, especially by the provision of opportunities for interpreting our work through demonstrations, discussions, and exhibitions; better teaching programs, time allotments, and a revised report card; and finally a course on " The Arts in Contemporary Life," offered by the Department of Adult Education for teachers of the music and art departments and any others who may be interested.

V

ELEMENTARY ART ACTIVITIES IN A PLATOON SYSTEM

ELMER A. STEPHAN
Director of Art Education
Pittsburgh, Pennsylvania

A workable plan for the organization of the elementary schools around the child as the center of all activity has been evolved to the extent of combining both an activity program and a platoon organization.

In the first grade an activity program serves two purposes. First, there has always been a decided break between the freedom of the kindergarten program and the formality of the first-grade traditional school. The kindergarten emphasized freedom and self-expression with restraint only as the child was required to learn the meaning of living with other people. By putting the first grade on an activity program there has been effected a continuance of the delightful freedom exercised in the kindergarten, with only a gradual emphasis upon restraint as certain learning processes became necessary. Now that these processes are centered around a group activity in construction, the socialized influence of such activity is more and more emphasized and desire for learning becomes a child-made process through interest rather than adult-made through coercion.

Second, at the same time that the child is working through an activity program, we are developing reading readiness. In addition, many types of art activity are useful for early work with the learning child. This plan opens an entirely new avenue for art education in the first grade. Instead of having a definite time set aside for formalized art training, the child is thinking art all the time. His constructive activity in this program under the wise guidance of a successful teacher may be a thing of beauty. Art qualities can be indicated without overstressing skills and techniques, but art continues to be a basic factor.

In the Pittsburgh plan, from the second to the sixth grades all elementary schools are on a platoon basis in which, if the school is large enough, there is a special teacher for each subject. If the school is smaller, certain allied subjects are combined. From the standpoint of art education, this presents great advantages that may be briefly summed up as follows:

1. There is a trained art teacher in every school building. We shall have to assume that this teacher knows the modern point of view in art education. All art activities come under the guidance of this teacher, and if she is successful, since every child comes under her influence, the art work becomes an agency permeating the activity of the entire school.

2. Art education, because it means the life work of this one teacher, deserves and gets her full attention; she has no other subjects to prepare; her major interest is her life activity.

3. Because the child has a special teacher in each subject, he eagerly brings to the art room content material contributing to the art program. As long as the fundamental principles of art education are achieved, this content may be almost anything, providing it interests the child and is given at his maturation level. In the platoon organization we find that there are greater possibilities of integration and correlation because of this enthusiasm in the student body.

4. The tendency in many organizations to neglect the time allotted to art education does not appear in the platoon system because the child follows his schedule with regularity. He must go to the art room a given number of periods a week and a given number of minutes for each period. This is a decided advantage, especially in schools where the supervision might not be entirely sympathetic toward the art program.

5. Finally, there are certain physical considerations that make this organization ideal. All art supplies are kept by the art teacher in her own storage room connected with the special art room. These supplies are therefore not used indiscriminately for other purposes, and yet may be graciously shared by the art teacher if the need arises. The art room also becomes a shrine of beauty. It is carefully planned so that it has certain distinctive features of efficiency and beauty, and under the direction of a trained teacher the hanging of pictures, the display of exhibition material, the arrangement of flowers, and of even the furniture itself provide a constant lesson in design and an application of the principles of beauty to the development of the child's sense of appreciation.

At least for the present we are able to say that this plan of organization functions better for art education than any other plan we know, not only holding its place in the curriculum but being a vitalizing factor, even a dominating influence as well.

VI

ART IN SECONDARY EDUCATION

Sallie B. Tannahill
Associate Professor of Fine Arts
Teachers College, Columbia University
New York, New York

To the cause of better citizenship, art makes the following contributions: first, it adds greatly to the interests that may occupy leisure time in later life; second, it increases esthetic taste and discriminative ability, stimulating young people to more intelligent choices of the necessary things in life and to the betterment of civic art; third, but by no means the least important, it offers a field in which pent-up emotions may be released and the powers of invention encouraged, thus helping to round out the individual and develop personality.

I. Art As Recreation: Hobbies

In our present civilization, with work hours shortened and free time lengthened, the school's duty is to help lift recreation from mere idling and misuse of time to worthy employment during leisure hours. This function of the school, to provide the right kind of pleasure for free hours, is as important as any other function. The active mind must be busily engaged in some undertaking, and if it finds no attractive worthy outlets, it will find unfruitful, if not socially undesirable, ways of expressing its impulses. In numerous ways art can supply delightful pastimes and fields of expression, and it is in the junior high school, before the law allows the withdrawal of boys and girls from school, that such activities might well be put before them.

An adult who has a ' hobby to ride ' experiences release from worry, overwork, or strain. When other things go wrong, there is always the hobby to be depended upon for recreation. Joy and satisfaction may result from merely observing and coming in contact with works of art, from collecting, buying, and selling them, or from studying, lecturing, or writing about them, but the keenest pleasure is usually derived from actual participation in such creative work as lettering, bookmaking, embroidering, carving, painting, building, modelling.

II. Creative Opportunity and Critical Judgment

To undertake a rich and broad program in the field of art, it is necessary that equipment of the right sort be provided. A resourceful art teacher may in some cases discover ways of ' carrying on ' with comparatively little expenditure of money but it is difficult. Sometimes boys from the shop or those of a practical turn of mind can be of some help in making suitable equipment and in housing it. Money spent on equipment for this type of work is justifiable in the light of the rich returns to youth.

As children proceed from the elementary to the junior and the senior high schools, the emphasis in art education will be more and more upon developing appreciation, but the importance of creative expression should not be minimized. The adolescent youth is ready for adventure; he has an urge to ' leap in the dark '; he desires to construct and build. The field of art offers many and varied opportunities for boys and girls to invent and create in paint, plaster, clay, wood, cloth, metal, light.

In order, however, to make sure that creative activity will be of lasting and genuine value, something more than bursts of emotional expression is needed. To secure sustained interest, the expression should be accompanied and followed by serious thinking, weighing of values, critical judgment. Unless there is the combination of emotional and intellectual activity, growth in creative expression is likely to be stunted. This alternating process of " output and intake," of " construction and criticism," to use Dewey's words, should continue during the elementary school and the junior and senior high schools with even greater emphasis upon the " intake." Many ' progressive ' schools that have overemphasized the creative and emotional side need the balance given by discrimination and judgment. Because of the neglect of the intellectual for the purely emotional, many older children in progressive schools lose interest and give up art entirely. For instance, Munro (44) tells of a remark that was made by an American boy of considerable talent in modelling who had given up the work to spend his spare hours at mechanical engineering:

> The art classes had been fun, he remarked with a superior air, but were just ' fooling around '; he wanted to ' learn something ' and ' get some where.' A few years of toying with art materials had been enough to exhaust its attractiveness as a game, and he had come to demand something more substantial to bite down on mentality, some intellectual food for his growing curiosity about the world. For this next step in development,

the free expression method had no help to offer him, nothing but the vague advice to keep on being himself, and doing whatever he wanted.

III. The Average and the Talented Youth

The average high-school youth may produce nothing of outstanding merit in art, but if he derives happiness in his attempts, then this inner satisfaction is all-important. His work should be judged from the standpoint of his present ability, needs, and interests, and not from the point of view of expert workmanship. The average, or untalented, youth should be given work in general appreciation, in experiences that will help him understand how art permeates his daily life today. Historical art study, as it affects the present, is important, but chronological facts that focus the attention only on ancient times are not necessarily important. Youth is concerned with today; he wants to know about modern industrial design, how art affects machine production, streamlining, skyscrapers, new and contemporary types of advertising. The average youth should be helped to see that art is a fundamental in general education, that no one is fully educated who is not aware of this vital part that art plays in daily living. And not only is it necessary to be aware of the place of art in life; the youth should also practice art so that his own life will be richer and fuller.[1] The relation among the various arts — painting, sculpture, architecture, crafts, the dance, music, and the theater — should be discussed and felt.[2]

For the talented youth, the more opportunity he has to work in art media, the better; he considers technique of great importance and finds that as he creates, skills are developed. He must have skills in order to produce satisfying results.

> When our secondary schools give adequate attention to the expression of the creative impulse, we shall be amazed at the contributions which you will make, not only to the material well-being of the world, but also to those intangible values which constitute durable satisfaction.[3]

IV. Art Processes and Activities of Special Interest

Boys and girls in the junior as well as in the senior high school are interested in drawing or painting one another, and in making portraits of themselves as viewed in the mirror, so that drawing or painting them-

---

[1] See Faulkner (12).

[2] See Mursell (47).

[3] Department of Superintendence, Sixth Yearbook, *Development of the High-School Curriculum.*

selves, their parents, sisters, or brothers may be a new source of delight to them. Human interest is keen at this age and should be stimulated. In connection with this work a study of portraiture, including drawings and paintings in which the human figure is dominant might be undertaken; thus their own interest would lead to related fields of modern and historic art, and latent ability in portraiture or cartooning might be discovered.

Modelling and carving are an adventure for youth and appeal strongly to those who have a feeling for form and wish to express their ideas in three dimensions. Life-sized busts of friends or of famous characters, as well as sculpture for architectural settings, are of great attraction to young people. The use of stone, wood, and plaster is recommended.[1]

All phases of the arts of the theater appeal to youth. Stage-sets, costumes, masks, lighting, posters, and programs present problems of great value for the release of creative power and for development in appreciation of design and color. Perhaps there is no subject related to art that, because it provides a chance for everyone to serve, is of more social and individual value and has greater possibility for correlation with other departments than has stage work. This type of work develops group consciousness to a marked degree.

Printing, etching, lettering, and posters are also sources of great satisfaction to the adolescent. High-school boys and girls will want to carry these forms of expression much farther than in the lower school; they will want to unite the work in the print shop with that of the studio and thus bring together two types of work that should never be divorced. Attractive printing is as important as correct printing; the latter without the former may be easily and clearly read, but the printed page, the announcement, the menu, the program, must have art quality besides.[2]

Both boys and girls, especially the latter, are vitally interested in themselves and therefore in costume design, in their clothes, the becoming style, the right line, the color that suits them best, the ensemble. Girls who have appeared nonsocial have been given a complete change in outlook by wearing new and becoming clothes. Boys need this work,

---

[1] See "An Interview with Oronzio Maldarelli, Sculptor," in *Art Education Today*. (Bureau of Publications, Teachers College, Columbia University: New York, 1940).

[2] See "Printing as an Art Industry," by Mary L. Davis, in *Art Education Today, 1938*. pp. 21–30.

too, for they are concerned these days with color combinations of hat, shirt, tie, suit, overcoat, and gloves.

Boys are especially interested in architecture because of their interest in construction. Potential architects are often discovered through these studies and, furthermore, interest is aroused in civic betterment and public housing.

Today photography is a most interesting occupation for young people. As an art project it includes much more than the clicking of the camera, the development of the negative, and the making of the print. The most fascinating part of photography is in its challenge to work with unusual materials, to select outstanding compositions, and to find specimens of effective dark and light arrangements. The subject matter may be very ordinary, but design, lights, and shadows may combine with it to make an unusual and attractive result. Photography plays an important rôle in advertising, and it is possible for some young people to develop real ability in this work while in school.

Color photography and motion pictures, both of great interest, may well be utilized as vital parts of the art program. In some schools boys and girls have written their own scenarios, have taken their own moving pictures, and have derived a great deal of pleasure, enlightenment, and growth, both individually and socially, in working together to make a production.[1]

V. The Art Program Should Be Linked With Large Areas of Living

Art in the junior and senior high schools should not only relate to present school life but should also reach out beyond the school to wider life experiences. Subject matter should be subordinated to the needs, interests, and purposes of students. Content of the curriculum must be altered as social changes occur, and the tendency should be toward organization for broad areas. The areas of living proposed by Harap's committee in *The Changing Curriculum* (18, p. 96) are living in the home, leisure, citizenship, organized group life, consumption, production, communication, and transportation.

It may readily be seen where art experience is involved in these eight categories. As is pointed out in the book just cited (18, p. 94), "Esthetic life permeates the whole of human experience." And again (18, p. 11), "The trend toward integration in the schools has made it desirable or necessary for teacher-representatives of two or more broad

---

[1] See Tierney (70); also Newhall (48).

fields to pool their respective resources and to engage in correlated or coöperative teaching." Indeed, the desired end may not be achieved without personal and whole-souled coöperation among teachers and pupils.

VI. Field Trips, Visits to Shops and Museums

In connection with the exploratory work, it is necessary to provide time in which to visit stores, museums, and other collections where young people may see the actual things they have been discussing and studying in the class. Schools equipped with small museums and plenty of illustrative material may not need to plan trips to museums, but most schools will need to set aside time for visits to shops, public buildings, parks, and so forth. Most department-store managers are willing to coöperate by permitting classes to visit their stores. These visits are particularly helpful in developing discriminating taste. In these stores may be displayed the poor, the mediocre, and the fine in clothing, furniture, lamps, rugs. Since children of high-school age are interested in selecting their own clothing and in helping to choose the home furnishings, much good should come from these visits. A natural situation is created when a class is taken to a department store to judge the art value of objects.

Trips to the museum are needed, too. Boys and girls should become acquainted with the finest things in the museum in order to improve their standards of taste. The museum helps to link the art of the past with contemporary art; it shows the development of present-day art and the relation of one form of art to another. The museum trips help to furnish a background for class discussion and further research.

To find time for these trips is often a problem, but when their importance is realized, it will usually be possible to arrange schedules for them. Some schools have ' activity periods ' at the end of the afternoon, and all field trips and shop museum visits are planned for that time.

VII. Art Club and Assembly Programs

Well-organized clubs are another means of bringing high-school pupils together in groups to carry on types of interesting work that may not come under the regular art program. Since these activities, if carried on successfully, demand serious work, they should be integral parts of the regular program. They may be scheduled during class periods. Following is a list of activities prepared and used by a high-school art teacher in the Columbia High School, School district of South Orange and Maplewood, New Jersey.

September

Sketching trip — picnic supper — demonstration of lettering, artistic effects for quick advertising

Art in and around Columbia High School

Search for special art features of building; discussion

Puppets

October

Sketching trip — animal sketching at deer paddock

Color — demonstration of dyeing

Experiment with certain colored dyes on various colors and materials (Mothers invited)

Costume party

Cartoons

November

Museum trip

Story hour — water-color sketching, illustrating some bit of prose or poetry

" Modern Art — What Is It? " (Lecture)

Silhouettes

December

Decorative papers — demonstration

Making of crackled, cornstarch, marble, cork-printed, and batik papers

Exhibition of Christmas package wrapping

Studies of Christmas pictures — those of Raphael, Botticelli, Da Vinci, etc.

Block-printing — Christmas cards

January and February

Art play — for assembly

Making of stage sets; study of lighting effects; costume designing; camouflage in costuming (study of inexpensive materials that give the effect of more costly velvets, silks, etc.)

Trip to the theater

March

Blackboard drawing

Soap-carving

Processes of reproduction — study and demonstration

Engraving, etching, lithography, aquatint, etc. (Guests invited)

Fashion parade — Art through the Ages

April

Color schemes for table decoration
Competition in table decoration (Tea served in faculty dining room)
Art number of the *Columbian* (school newspaper)
Story hour — quick sketching at large easel

May

Development of architecture in America
Sketching trip
" How I Furnished My Summer Camp "
Art in and around South Orange and Maplewood
Snapshots and sketches, nicely mounted for exhibit

June

Sketching trip
Masks and mask-making
Flower arrangement
Study of Japanese flower arrangement
Contests of original arrangements

It can readily be seen by glancing over the ten-months' program of this particular school that it comprises a wide range of club activities. A considerable part of high-school art might be achieved in this way through active and popular club organizations. The teacher would then be able to give her time wholeheartedly to these organizations instead of having to add such work at the end of a full day's program.

In recent years spacious auditoriums have been provided in many schools in which various types of art work may be demonstrated before the whole school body. Art has many contributions to make to assembly programs. It is through these that the school can keep informed on what is going on in art as well as in other subject-matter fields. The following are suggestive of the various types of art assemblies possible for high schools: fashion shows; home furnishing demonstrated through the use of borrowed furniture and accessories, arranged in different ways to show how a home may be furnished economically and in good taste; plays and pageants; lantern-slide talks on various phases of art appreciation; famous pictures shown in tableaux; motion pictures that have to do with art; demonstrations of various techniques, such as making an etching, a block print, a cartoon, a poster, a Christmas card, a mask, a textile design, and the like.

VIII. Art Service

The art department in a high school has opportunities to render service in many ways where art is needed. This kind of activity is, however, usually unorganized, and for that reason it is not effective; it interferes with regular class work and frequently requests for posters and similar material are expected to be met overnight. While the boys and girls are willing to give their time to meet these requests, the result is often a decided loss to their artistic growth, as it means mere repetition of former experiences.

The following are forms of art service found in certain high schools:

(a) All kinds of advice about the school building and equipment: the color of the walls; the buying and hanging of pictures; the selection and placement of sculpture and mural paintings; the selection and arrangement of furniture; the color, design, and suitability of curtains; the layout of booklets, menus, and so forth.

(b) Care and arrangement of bulletin boards, show cases.

(c) Advertisements, posters, signs, tickets, programs for lunches, dinners, games, plays. Coöperation is needed here between the print shop and the art department.

(d) School magazines, annuals. Making cover designs, and sheets, page decorations, illustrations, coöperating with the English department and the print shop.

(e) Decorations for parties, receptions, dinners, lunches, commencement.

(f) School plays: the art department takes an important part in making the stage sets; arranging color schemes; studying the effect of lighting, designing costumes; coöperating with the property man.

Art service is an essential part of the school life, and may be made an important part of the art teaching. Such work may be handled through clubs or through art-service committees organized as special art classes or units under the guidance of an art teacher. If possible, such a group should meet within the school day, and the teacher in charge should be given full teaching credit for time spent on the work.

IX. Vocational Guidance

The high-school youth is vitally concerned with what will happen to him after graduation. The school needs to guide and advise him. In the junior high school a foundation should be laid for making a more definite choice later. The exploratory courses given in the eighth and the ninth years should serve as a general survey of the art field that will demonstrate to pupils the possibilities in vocations where art is essential, as in art professions and also in vocations and trades where discriminating judgment and good taste are at least assets. It is obviously desirable, then, to acquaint our talented high-school youths with the various fields of work open to those who have specialized in art. Data on salaries, hours of work, and advantages and disadvantages will help young people to decide more readily in what field they would like to specialize in preparation for a vocation.

VII

ART AND THE JUNIOR HIGH SCHOOL

WALTER H. KLAR
Supervisor of Fine and Industrial Arts, Public Schools
Springfield, Massachusetts

The junior high school was planned to serve the needs of pupils during their transitional years between the elementary grades and the senior high school. The original five objectives are still very much in evidence, although changes are being made in many of the junior high schools because of changed objectives.

The effect on the art program of the original junior high school has been as follows:

1. Courses in art appeared on the regularly printed programs of the junior high school. This was an advantage to the subject, as the mere printing of it alone tended to give it a certain status among the other school subjects.

2. The time allotment was definitely stated at, for example, one or two periods a week. This was an advantage over the former organization, because with a less definitely presented program, there were classes in art in some seventh, eighth, and ninth grades and no provision at all for art work in others.

3. The staff of teachers within the junior high school became familiar with the fact that art was now a regularly listed subject on a similar basis in some respects to that of other subjects.

4. With the development of the junior high school there came the question of qualifications of teachers. Many school systems, at such times as the junior high school was being developed, were confronted with a situation in regard to the employment of teachers of art that was difficult to meet. A practice that

then became current in many of the eastern states, and possibly throughout the country, was to require that such teachers as desired to teach art in a junior high school should have taken at least 12 credits in their special field. To require a teacher of art in a junior high school to have 12 credits was a step in advance, but the result of this requirement was far from satisfactory. Many teachers became special art teachers with an insufficient art background. Such teachers succeeded well with the average and less-than-average groups of pupils, but in many cases they were no match for the unusually gifted children of the junior-high-school age.

5. The placing of art education on a plane comparable to that of the other subjects brought about the recognition of the need of specially designed and equipped art rooms — surely a step in advance.

6. In many junior high schools there have been developed art clubs, and in some schools a certain day and hour is set aside for club activities. Pupils are permitted to organize their own clubs, and ideally to have them presided over by members of the group rather than by the teacher. While it is true that the club period has been one during which children may work in the subject they like best, it is also true that one period per week out of a possible 25 or 30 periods is a very small amount of time to be given to the field they enjoy most.

7. Art education as an elective subject, by serving the needs of those pupils who are not in the college preparatory group and who are not required to take other subjects for senior-high-school entrance, has benefited greatly by the junior-high-school organization. One now finds work at the junior-high-school level being done with this type of pupil that only a few years ago could not possibly have been approached at the senior-high-school level.

The foregoing outcomes are on the whole more favorable than unfavorable to supplying opportunities in art education in the junior high school. This is not the whole picture, however. In actual practice, many schools had made provision for art on their program of study, had employed special teachers, and had supplied them with well-appointed rooms in which to work, yet many of the pupils in the junior high schools had only slightly more opportunity to study art than they had had under the previous, more traditional school organization of the grades in question. This situation grows out of the distinction between ' constants ' and ' variables,' as some schools designate the subjects, or between ' required ' and ' elective ' subjects. The fact that we now had a junior high school in place of Grades VII–IX did not change college entrance requirements for senior high schools, and by the same token, did not change at all the senior-high-school freshman entrance requirements. Consequently, in the field of art education we have over and over again met this situation: foreign languages for students who are later to go to college, mathematics for students who are later to attend the technical high school, and certain courses in arithmetic or mathematics for students who intend to pursue a commercial course in the senior high school have appeared as required subjects at at least the eighth-grade level, with the result that probably over half of the junior-high-school pupils do not have any opportunity to elect art. Under the earlier organization the conditions were not universally better, because some school systems followed a plan of eight grades for the education prior to the high school, succeeded by a four-year high-school course, with art a more or less required subject during the eight grades but entirely elective in the senior high school.

Thus far, art educators have found no way of holding, in the eighth and ninth years of the junior high school, a large number of boys and girls who cannot take the subject because of requirements to be met later on or because of immediate pupil and teacher program situations.

The educational philosophy responsible for the origin of the junior high school and for its continuance has been of distinct value to art education for the following reasons: first, it has assisted in formulating objectives in art education and has so stated these objectives as to make evident the value of art education at the junior-high-school level; second, the advocates of this philosophy have seen within their individual school buildings the functioning of art education in connection with the daily work of the school; third, the principals of the junior high schools have on the whole been men and women somewhat in advance of the former type of grammar-school principal and have recognized the possibility of suggesting to many pupils that they explore the art courses; and fourth, many teachers of art in the junior high schools have been assisted in improving their methods of teaching through conferences with their school principal.

These favorable comments cannot be negatived by any parallel series of unfavorable ones. The junior high school as an organization has undeniably succeeded in rounding out personal development. Boys and girls attending the junior high school are within an institution manned by specialists. Grant that art, industrial arts, home economics, music, physical education, and science teachers are specialists; so, too, are the teachers of English, mathematics, social studies, and languages. Each of these specialists sees the educational merits of his own bailiwick. Therefore although, as has been said, there are many pupils in the junior high school who do not have an opportunity to take art, it is also true that some pupils are permitted and persuaded to elect so many periods of art that there is danger of their losing their educational perspective. I have seen boys and girls in the junior high school so thoroughly interested in art that they neglect other desirable or needed subjects. This is a weakness of the junior-high-school organization. Attempts are being made through courses in guidance to overcome it, but guidance alone cannot be the answer. Counselors within the field of guidance attempt to assist a larger number of pupils than is possible within the time devoted to the work. Personality development is an ever-continuing process. Pupils need something more than opportunities to proceed at their own rates of ability; they many times need the intimate guiding hand of the old-fashioned nonspecialist school teacher.

VIII

A SENIOR–HIGH–SCHOOL ART PROGRAM

Marion Quin
Lincoln School of Teachers College
New York, New York

The art program in the senior-high-school division of the Lincoln School of Teachers College at present has the following six-fold purpose:

1. To operate a fine arts studio as an opportunity for living completely in the democratic spirit.

2. To capture the interest of every child for experience and expression in as many media as possible.

3. To offer adolescents a daily opportunity for emotional release and integration through art activity.

4. To develop and enrich appreciation of beauty in the simple things of everyday living and to discover beauty in all activities as of equal or more importance than its recognition in highly developed forms.

5. To provide a continuous experience of appreciation until esthetic sensitivity becomes a habitual attitude in everyone. The opportunity for a continuing life interest in any art expression will grow out of this.

6. To encourage and guide the potential professional producer of art.

The present art program in Lincoln School is an experimental attempt:

1. To accomplish these purposes by offering the entire program on a basis of free choice, thus preserving the free and sincere spirit of the artist.

2. To discover all points at which art activities are effectually and naturally integrated with other subject matter and educational activities.

3. To discover teaching techniques by which beginners at all ages may find immediate satisfaction in art activities and thus be motivated to continue their esthetic growth and seek technical help as necessary.

4. To learn how to create an atmosphere under school conditions that releases tensions and induces in children that relaxed but vital state in which the esthetic experience comes into being and thrives.

5. To help children to recover a healthy mental and emotional status whenever this has been disturbed or prevented by unfavorable cultural conditions — the more specifically therapeutic aim.

It may be of general interest to set down a few classroom episodes to show how these aims are attained. Such illustrations as can here be included will be drawn from recent activities in the secondary school in which I have directly participated. The aims of the elementary school are not fundamentally different, and its work leads sympathetically to the later experience.

The illustrations that follow have been interesting to observers for various reasons. One common reaction is astonishment at finding every student in an eleventh grade enthusiastically producing an idea in a medium of fine arts. For many young people adolescence is the barren age in art activity. This is strange and challenging to the teacher, for there is no time of life when there is a greater need for creative and expressive activities. But it is all too common to find high-school art activity limited to a handful of persistent youngsters devoting a few periods a week to continuing a special interest acquired in childhood. The others crawl into their shells and grow up wondering what such phrases as 'Art is a way of life' can possibly mean to anyone. They spend their lives and their money gathering around themselves all the wrong (for them) kinds of possessions. They die never knowing that any relation exists between themselves and the cultural expressions of the age in which they have lived. This is a sorry state — one of the unhappy aspects of a complex civilization, and perhaps a problem peculiar to a technical and industrial society; at any rate, the isolation of vast numbers of the people from art expression does not exist in primitive cultures. We have the same basic needs for participation, and it is a special problem of American art teachers to learn how to meet such needs in our society and time.

In order to meet such needs in growing students by giving them experience and practice in integrating activities, Lincoln School uses, among other means, ' general ' courses. The general course (sometimes called the ' integrated,' or ' core,' course) is taken by all students and is planned and taught coöperatively by teachers from several fields. In our school it usually includes teachers of English, social studies, and art, with others on call whenever their help will improve the teaching.

Art activities carried on as part of the general course may be of many varieties. Sometimes they are the outgrowth of expressed student needs.

Last year the tenth grade was studying Primitive Man. Interest in the study had risen to the point where some kind of expression was inevitable, and the students were composing primitive chants under the leadership of the English teacher. At this time they had the opportunity to spend a Saturday re-visiting a farm where, during a two-weeks' excursion the previous year, they had planted about a thousand seedling trees. They were interested in checking the success of their forestry. To the art teacher it seemed also a fine opportunity to seek for materials of primitive decoration — berries, seed pods, shells, stones for implements, and the like. This proved to be an excellent suggestion. When the students returned on Monday their eyes sparkled. In addition to the things suggested, they had found bones! And one group had found a skunk, not too long dead! One of the girls had drawn some animals with blood from the skunk on bits of slag. One of the boys brought home the skull and the tail. These he cleaned, boiled, and mounted on a well-weathered stick to make a chief's scepter. The entire collection formed fine decorative material. Before the class met that day one boy decided to make a primitive mask. His decoration would not be complete without it. When he told the class of his intention, the whole group of forty-seven wished to make masks, too. The masks were quickly modeled in clay, the papier maché pressed into the moist forms, the masks completed and painted in three days. The culminating expression of the entire activity took the form of a tribal meeting and feast. Each group, appropriately costumed, took its turn in expressing the primitive spirit.

At another time four weeks had been devoted to a study of the rise and fall of the Roman Empire. The coöperating faculty group decided that a good way to explore the understanding of the period by the students would be to let them depict symbolically their conception of the Roman culture. In order to allow their work to be quick and free, the medium used was chalk. Curiously, in the eyes of the staff, the students almost unanimously expressed the idea that the entire Roman Empire was driven by the desire to spread Christianity. The expression showed the faculty members clearly that a wrong emphasis had been made, and they at once set about correcting the situation. It is to be noted that to the faculty group this expression was an evaluation of their own work. They, and not the students, had failed.

On another occasion, during a study of the Middle Ages, a teacher read from Chaucer. As the reading went on, I slipped from the room and returned with art materials for the entire group. As the reading ended I whispered my plan to the teachers. Twenty minutes remained of the period. I suggested to the student group that since the Wife of Bath, the Friar, the Knight, and all the rest had stalked this very room, it might be fun quickly to record our conception of them. No pictures of any of these characters were in evidence.

At lunch hour we put all the drawings above the blackboard in the home room. Teachers who had taught these boys and girls in the elementary and junior high schools found themselves being escorted to Room 413 " to see what I did this morning." Many of the group had returned from lunch and were sitting in the center of the room admiring the other fellows' work with generous and vocal enthusiasm — but with eyes constantly straying silently and rapturously to their own.

In this experience we have an exceptionally good example of the reconstructive and therapeutic effect of art activity. Diffidences shown by their worried remarks at the beginning were left behind. For a number of the students a needed social prestige was gained or restored. Emotional impasses were surmounted. In one case there was the beginning of a relief from stuttering. In the opinion of several teachers who had been working with them for two years, this was the first instance for several of these students when a learning situation was met easily and comfortably. And for many of the group the enthusiasm shown on this occasion was a new phenomenon. It is significant that other teachers drawn in by these students to see their work were in more than one case teachers with whom they had had some difficult relationship or with whom they felt a need to bolster up their status.

The thing that is most important in such activities is the common denominator of sustained ' interest,' ' motivation ' (or whatever term you wish) that has been generated within the students by their experience, that they have built up themselves without any intent of expressing. Nevertheless, the pressure is there and the essence of method is to catch this readiness and to use media that are simple and quick, thus allowing expression to be as unimpeded and natural as impression has been. So used, the medium and the technique truly become an extension of the artist's neural structure. He shows what he has seen as easily as he has seen it and while his feeling for what he has seen is still strong within him. Natalie Cole, in her recent *The Arts in the Classroom*, says " children cannot create out of a vacuum." Nothing more true was ever said. In these illustrations the motivation was a group experience but each student expressed what was in him in his own way. In the elective art classes the entire process — motive, idea, medium, and method — is completely individual. But even in the work of the general course, where expression grows out of a common experience, there is no necessity for duplicated or imitative results. A further very important consideration is that successful experience in these easy media leads many a child on to far more difficult, tedious, and complex projects and techniques; as for example, wood carving, design and weaving of tapestry, design and making of stained-glass windows.

Let no one think that because this process has been an easy and happy one for the student there is any loss of quality. Such work, because done ' at white heat,' preserves its vitality and has the expressive quality of all work in which nothing gets in the way of the flow from impression to expression. The medium has been employed as efficiently as the child uses his own muscles. This is truly integrated activity, in which the artist, his idea, and his tools become one working unity, and every critic knows that this is the pattern of all good art. Many of these sketches are as excellent in technical performance as anything these students will ever do, and many of the masks, referred to at an earlier point, could have been, in the opinion of competent observers, a respected part of the exhibition of masks that was then showing at the Brooklyn Museum.

The teacher who utilizes these free methods is not less interested in good art than those whose students constantly and laboriously plod through technical drill and dictated exercises. She knows that it does not promote growth in a student to overrate his work because it is his. But she also knows that the artist's work comes alive when technique is forgotten under the drive of free-flowing expressive performance. For this reason I am convinced that techniques must at all times remain servants of the expressive process, not only in the highly competent and mature artist but equally in all the growing processes of the student. There is a place for real labor with techniques, but growth will be stopped or hampered whenever a concern with techniques is allowed to become master.

It is not only that a free method tends to capture all students; such a method is the best assurance that students will improve in the quality of their work as rapidly as they are individually capable of doing. The mediocre have their chance; the previously undiscovered talent blooms with great rapidity, and we have the testimony of many exceptional artists that the extraordinary talent is, more than any other, helped by a method of instruction that allows it great freedom. It is important also to note that such free methods used in the group work of the general course seem to awaken art interest in many students and lead them to enroll individually in elective art classes, as is indicated in the growing enrollment of elective art students shown in the accompanying table. Art has always been a part of the general course but the stress on a free method has been greatest in the last three years. And these have been years of rapid expansion of elective art classes in Lincoln School.

NUMBER OF ELECTIVE ART STUDENTS — SENIOR HIGH SCHOOL

Year	Total Enrollment	Number Electing Art	Percentage of Total
1936–37	143	24	16.8
1937–38	145	14	9.6
1938–39	152	39	25.7
1939–40	139	54	38.8
1940–41	135	60	44.4

The all-important thing in art is the learner's gaining familiarity with nature, both within himself and outside himself, and with the materials and media that attract him. The hardest part of the guiding process is for the teacher to keep sufficiently out of the way of the learner to give him a chance to deal with experiences in his own way. Art is an emotional experience reconstructed by the learner's own unique way of working.

Adolescence is a time of jerky development, irregular ups and downs, unpredictable spurts of activity and inactivity. The individual awakens gradually. Routine methods are completely out of order. Individual treatment elastically adjustable from day to day — from child to child — is needed. The teacher is a guide or counsellor in the painful struggle against inferiority and persecution complexes, phobias, loneliness, and guilt feelings. Wrong treatment can be devastating, leading to permanent maladjustments and atrophy of the creative talents. The reason art activity is so important in personality development is that it carries to the child his own measure of worth. He is not required to compete or to meet a given standard or to please the teacher. The essential requirement is that he be himself and thus come to respect and defend his own integrity.

The function of the teacher is to guide the development of the child's abilities — to help him organize his own emotional experiences, not in graphic and plastic forms alone but in any medium. To teach in this way, the teacher must have far greater understanding of the developmental process, far greater skill in working in and out of that process, far greater patience and faith in the capacity of everyone for art development, and far more capacity for building in the learner a confidence in his own power than is necessary for the traditional teacher of art skills.

IX

SOME PROCEDURES IN ART TEACHING

BELLE BOAS
Chairman, Art Department, Horace Mann School for Girls, and
Assistant Professor of Fine Arts, Teachers College
Columbia University
New York, New York

The procedure in every schoolroom is a mirror of the teacher's point of view as well as of his personality. His point of view affects everything concerned with his school life, the atmosphere of his classes, his guidance, and his planning. Without definite convictions, he will fall under the spell of every passing theory that promises quick and facile results, to the detriment of the slow, gradual ripening of the pupils entrusted to him. If neatness, for instance, is his only god, he will make obeisance only to it, forgetful of the many richer meanings in life. If the teacher considers himself a superior officer ruling a regiment of obedient robots, he can hardly expect a quickening of the fire of their creative impulse.

If, on the other hand, he believes profoundly that art in its truest sense can be fostered only in a free atmosphere of friendliness, experimentation, and discussion, he will find means of creating that atmosphere. Not only will work be planned to develop creative ability and self-knowledge, but there will be nurtured as well an intelligent understanding of the place of art in life.

Informality in no sense means license or waywardness on the part of pupils. It is rather a freedom of expression to state an opinion honestly, knowing that the opinion will be respected. It means that encouragement will come easily to the teacher's lips and that respect for all honest work will be maintained.

There is a need for honest convictions on the part of both the teacher and the pupil. Because of his convictions the teacher will have standards of design and workmanship, but he will also realize that his own standards have taken years to develop and cannot be expected of untrained pupils. Therefore, there will be tolerance of every sincere effort, but through discussion, praise, and questioning, by the use of fine illustrative material, he will gradually raise the standards of his group. His direction will be constant though unobtrusive. A class of junior-high-school students, surrounded by the commonplace realism of the cheap magazine cover, will need long and patient guidance to carry them a few steps further towards finer design and color, but if fine design and interesting color have meaning for the teacher, he will find ways of introducing opportunities of dwelling upon them. He cannot force sudden understanding; his means will be questioning, discussing through comparison, and exhibitions that will focus attention upon certain important aspects of which his pupils would otherwise have been unaware. The teacher given to dictation will see in this only a slow, halting method, but actually, by allowing free, sincere comments, he permits the learner to grow gradually into self-confidence and appreciation.

Discussion is one of the best means of encouraging confidence. This does not mean that discussion supersedes handwork or that argument is the goal of art instruction. Often the most sensitive and ablest students are the most reticent. But the value of a good open discussion clarifies meanings and opens up new approaches, enlightening the teacher as well as the pupils.

Discussions arise naturally in all planning as a means of solving problems. For example, the choice of a color for a particular room; the presentation of historical subjects, such as the causes of the shift from Gothic to Renaissance painting; the development of new ideas, such as the study of the place of plastics in industry — all these will inevitably create discussion.

Let us take a single illustration in more detail.

In a high-school class studying display, a unit on posters was taught. After several lessons, two posters were pinned on the wall, one advertising the Milan Fair of 1933, the other the Paris Exposition of 1937. The class knew that a poster should be easily understood, that simplicity of statement is therefore desirable, that contrasts of value aid in effectiveness. Various students admired the Italian poster for its message, almost brutally conveyed by the huge blue head of Mercury in startling contrast to the orange background. They admitted its telling symbolism and dominance over its neighbor. Then, as they looked further, the quiet French poster ingratiated itself into their consciousness. They noted that the symbols, while less bold, were more subtle; the color grayer but more unusual; that the further one looked, the greater enjoyment one gained from the delicacy of color and subtlety of idea. The conclusion was that, when seen often, the Italian poster would become tiresome in its very insistence. Discussion in this case produced deeper understanding and sensitiveness.

Again, discussions arise as a means of solving problems.

A tenth-grade group looked about its new quarters with distaste, having left a freshly painted room. " Can't anything be done with this dreadful place? " they demanded of the art instructor. Through consultation, committees were formed, one to make plans for a more efficient and pleasing arrangement of furniture, one to plan color schemes for the twenty feet of burlap bulletin board, the third to submit sketches for a frieze. Each committee, after presenting its plans to the entire group, received criticisms and made modifications. Furniture was moved around, large color samples were discussed and voted on, trial sketches were pinned up and criticized. The final results were pleasing in that they were fresh, cheerful, and approved by the group.

What actual values were there in the product of this discussion? First, the situation was genuine, containing difficulties similar to those that would face the children in their own homes. There was an obvious gain in the pooling of ideas, in the adjustments and compromises common to all group decisions. Finally, an attitude of self-assurance pervaded the class from the pleasing result of their work.

Here one may well ask, Does the art teacher always follow the desires of his class? Is there no underlying plan from which lessons achieve a continuity, a progression? Is it all a hit-or-miss hodgepodge? Certainly a paper plan is not the main concern. The chief goal is growth in esthetic experience. Therefore, whatever will help in bringing that about is utilized. Plans are made and changed in accordance with needs. For instance, much of the art in Grade X in the Horace Mann School is based upon American life. Consequently the esthetic elements that enter into that life are studied insofar as students of that age are capable of understanding them. It may mean a motion-picture production or the contribution of WPA artists; it may be based on early American architecture and furniture or on contemporary advertising and display; it may even be concerned with American dress design or the construction of model airplanes. Whatever in this study is adapted to the abilities and interests of this group is used, always provided there is inherent in it an esthetic experience.

Does this imply that art must always be tied to social studies or utilitarian needs? The imaginative life is as real at certain times as the physical life, but imagination is not exclusively concerned with fairy flowers, or lollypop trees, or particularly of fantastic creations. Imagination also plays with the materials of real life, transforming them into new and unusual arrangements of beauty. An artist like Burchfield makes a mean street in a mining town into a painting made rare by his imagination and deep emotion. Fantasy has its rightful place, as all of us who love Mickey Mouse know, but it must not supersede the life of reality. Hence, when coördination with social science or music offers significant material, significant in that pupils can grasp its meaning, the art teacher utilizes whatever in it will enrich the art program.

To achieve coöperation means teamwork in planning. For example, in the ninth grade, when a study of the Renaissance is to be pursued for some months, each teacher concerned receives a tentative outline of the main themes, not only the historical causes and developments, but also certain concepts, such as the increased importance of the individual, or the widening of geographical and mental horizons. After studying the themes, each teacher makes his contribution to the unit. Because of the great interest in personality at this period, there is suggested a study of the portrait, both as a creative activity and as a means of widening appreciation. Here is an opportunity to present the change from the flat literal likeness of the fourteenth-century portrait to that of the idealization of the sixteenth century. Perspective and the study of space take on new meanings in this historical study. Of course, unless the contribution has intrinsic value to the class, it is omitted, lest a forced correlation do more harm than good.

Everyone lives both a group life and an individual life. Therefore the art teacher will give the pupils opportunities to participate in group performance. But there are also the individual's personal interests to be guarded and fostered. There are many occasions in painting, designing, or modelling when a pupil, in order to express his personal feelings and opinions, works alone. That is his undeniable right. The teacher's obligation is to allow for both types of lesson.

Not only is there both coöperative and individual work, but there is also a third plan in which all the class is engaged in designing posters or making floor plans or painting portraits, lessons designed by the teacher but growing out of genuine needs. In large classes the organization for this sort of group work is undoubtedly simpler, and today no undue regimentation is expected. Even when teaching so standardized a subject as perspective, variations are encouraged. It is no more illustrative of a general principle to draw a receding row of telegraph poles or trees than to draw a file of men on horseback or the return of laborers from the mill. Group organization need not negate individual differences. Naturally in the matter of technical demonstrations, such as printing an etching or glazing a pot, individual teaching is a waste of precious time. Often, too, in large classes there is a lively criticism and interest in each other's work that makes for progress.

When individual interests are to the fore, several methods are used. In the high school, pupils often write out a plan of work. Elementary children tell what they want to do and do it. This necessitates careful arrangement of the studios for various activities (painting, pottery, and modelling, or printing of many kinds) that will encourage choosing among these activities. This arrangement, while difficult in many schools, does give scope for individual desires, in that pupils pursue their own interests unhampered and become independent and self-reliant. Careful supervision has to be maintained to insure improvement and experimentation. Careful checking will discover weaknesses that need to be strengthened; weakness in design or technique or drawing, for instance.

In the primary grades there are times when the eagerness to paint is so intense that no restraint should be put on pupils. Let them start at once. At other times, one gathers them to the front of the room, all sitting informally on the floor, and chats with them. One may talk about their pets at home, their vagaries and tricks, or about their walk to school and what they saw on it. It is simply a question of concentrating their memories in a specific channel so that instead of wandering or repainting the same row of flowers, they may paint their personal experiences after thinking about them. At this point criticism consists only of praise. " How fine and large John's dog is; it fills the whole paper! " " See how Mary has echoed her colors in all parts of her picture! " These children have revived a real memory that they are able to express because it is personally real. When all art lessons proceed out of intimate experiences, copying will no longer be a problem.

One of the best ways to stimulate art interests is the use of carefully prepared excursions that will enrich the pupil's experiences. With younger children the trip may be taken to increase their knowledge of their environment. With older children, after preliminary discussion of the purpose of the visit, mimeographed sheets are sometimes given to each one with directions for procedure or questions to be answered. For instance, a tenth grade is to go alone to the American Wing of the Metropolitan Museum to study early American interiors. A sheet that reads as follows is given them:

Go to the top floor of the American Wing and visit the various rooms. (1) What kind of wood is used in the furniture? (2) What kinds of furniture do you find? (3) Is most of it curved or straight? Why? (4) What decoration is used? (5) What evidences of comfort do you notice? (6) Describe the room you like best.

Go to the floor below. (7) What differences do you notice in the wood and the style of the furniture? (8) Compare this floor with the floor above in comfort. (9) Can you give any reason for this change? (10) What evidences of Classic motifs do you find?

One may object that a lecture would have produced the same knowledge in far less time. But a lecture would have been a teacher's performance with the pupils as passive listeners, whereas in the excursion there is a greater amount of genuine self-instruction, the result of thinking as well as of looking. And even in this case, the learning goes deeper if discussion of the visit takes place later on. The children have learned to see and to think about what they have seen. Since doing is an active procedure, teachers must seize upon significant material that will stimulate it. The teacher's part is to draw out the meaning of the trip, to dwell upon its many aspects, and often to emphasize its visual importance. This development of the idea is all important, if there is to be any worth-while projection of it later, no matter whether the result be in stage design or landscape painting. Assimilation of the idea must precede the outward expression.

This brief statement is merely an indication of some procedures common to many schools — procedures that rise out of the psychological theory that all learning is self-learning, that the teacher plans and guides towards the pupils' self-development.

X

ART AND INDIVIDUAL DEVELOPMENT ON THE SECONDARY-SCHOOL LEVEL

Victor E. D'Amico
Head of the Fine Arts Department, Fieldston School
New York, New York

Art instruction at the Fieldston School attempts to meet two major requirements: the specific art needs of each individual and the integration of art with the student's general education. The specific needs of the individual vary from spontaneous interests, such as making a poster for a particular event or painting a picture for emotional satisfaction, to the prolonged three-year specialized study under the Fieldston Plan for the student of professional interests. Integration of art with the student's general education involves fusion of the art experience with the general needs and interests of students and certain correlation of subject matter. It is essential to emphasize that the latter is only a means to the former. So many schools make the error of believing that they are providing integrating experiences because they are relating subject matter in courses or units.

The method of instruction is plastic, individual, and coördinating in order to achieve the objectives just mentioned. It is ' plastic ' in the sense that it allows for a variety of materials and ways of doing things, taking into account also the difference in concept, in pace, and in the time of each student. It is ' individual ' in the sense that it recognizes individual choices, habits, and abilities. It is ' coördinating ' to the extent that it realizes motivations and meanings beyond the initial art expression and seeks, therefore, to tie up the specific art experience with other interests of the student and with broader fields of cultural backgrounds.

In operation, the method works somewhat as follows: The curriculum is different for each student. The student selects his own subject matter and materials. When he is not resourceful in finding these for himself, they may be recommended to him by the teacher. The student proceeds to work in the way best suited to him, discovering this way through exploration rather than by dictation from the teacher.

When the student fumbles or becomes mired, the teacher helps him to find the correct way or to work out a solution. In a totally new situation, the teacher acquaints the student with the general qualities, procedures, and tools before the student attempts to explore in his own way. For example, in the making of an etching, the teacher will first go through the process and indicate the values that comprise an etching. From this general information the student proceeds ' on his own.' There is, therefore, no set curriculum for the entire group, no prescription as to what shall be done from day to day, no set problems or projects to correlate with historical periods or the changes of the seasons. The program evolves with the growing concepts and capacities of each individual. It may be said that there are as many curricula as there are students in the school. In the junior high school the method is based on spontaneous interests and choices. That means that the student selects what he wishes to do most and when he completes this, follows with another choice. It is the teacher's responsibility to see that the choice is one that provides an adequate learning experience and that each experience leads toward greater meaning and growth. In the seventh grade, for example, a student may desire first to make a painting, then a sculpture or a piece of pottery, or he may make three paintings in succession, each requiring more competence than the preceding one.

On the senior-high-school level, the advanced student of art is expected to select a problem of greater challenge and to plan his work with some perspective. He selects a problem that may demand from a week to as much as a year or more, depending on his ability and concentration. He records his problem on a special form called a ' contract,' in which he states his choice of subject matter, material, sources of study for research, areas of correlation, progress made, difficulties encountered and their solution. For example, one student in the senior year chose to study mural painting, involving the study of composition and oil painting as the primary objectives. He completed a 35-foot mural in a space reaching to the ceiling in the school lunchroom. The mural depicted the story of how the big city gets its food from the farmer to the consumer. The project covered a period of more than six months of intensive work. Other projects included a study of graphic processes, smaller murals, water-color painting, compositions of various subject matter, character studies, pottery throwing, various phases of stage design from the mask to the making of stage models. Students who undertake short projects may do several of them and explore a wide area. The longer projects are chosen by those who have discovered a desirable field they wish to study intensively. Group projects are worked out in the same manner.

This method of procedure provides a way of teaching, in which the student becomes the motivating force of his own education, and the teacher at the same time finds opportunity for deeper and more extensive teaching. Teacher and student act as partners in the enterprise, like master and apprentice. The individual student can proceed as far as his abilities will permit.

In addition to his awareness of the variety of individual capacities and interests, the art instructor takes into account the general pattern of growth from younger to older adolescence. This pattern includes three stages, the first two roughly classified as the exploratory period, the second as the specialized period.

In the first stage (roughly Grades VII and VIII) the emphasis is on a general and wide exploration. Art is required for all, and each student explores a variety of art — fine arts, shop, printing, household arts — and his creative potentialities in the use of visual and plastic media. The second stage (approximately Grade IX) entails extensive exploration in one art field — fine arts, shop, household arts — for the entire year, and in the fine arts there is a deeper orientation to the general field. The third stage covers the training of the older adolescent, both the special student of art and the general student (approximately Grades X–XII). The training of the special student is developed under the Fieldston Plan, which is probably unique. The student with particular aptitude for art is trained by a special teacher, and his interest becomes the basis for his entire education. The other studies, such as social studies and science, correlate with the art interest. Thus history in the high school clarifies for the student the reasons for the feeling and thinking processes of the creative man and the effect of his ideas on society; chemistry and physics explain and analyze for him the materials and tools of the artist; literature offers him a wide field for reading and discussion about the lives and work of other artists in relation to their time and place. Thus, the special field becomes a means of enlarging the interests and experience of the student, rather than narrowing them, as in ordinary vocational education. The emphasis of these later years is largely cultured and technical, but at no time is the mastery of techniques made more important than the cultural experience.

The emphasis in training the general student is mainly cultural. He does not come under the Fieldston Plan but is given opportunity according to his interests and propensities for art. In this respect the arts act as a correlating factor of the special and general interests. By ' cultural ' is meant a broad understanding of the arts of the past and present as they relate to the social, political, and economic experiences in the hope that they will help the individual in his own development and adjustment to society. In the upper grades the intellectual and philosophical phases of the arts as they relate to other fields of experience are stressed, since the student at this stage is disposed to such learning. Thus the student is constantly encouraged to see art as a part of a total social pattern and his particular ability as a contribution to society.

The general aims of the Art Department are rather like those of other schools based on the tenets of Progressive Education.

(*a*) To develop the individual capacities of each student to their full extent.

(*b*) To keep individuality and creativeness of expression as the most important values of the art experience.

(*c*) To acquire an awareness and mastery of the esthetic laws that govern all arts as they apply to all life.

(*d*) To develop a growing awareness and appreciation through the modern and traditional arts.

(*e*) To develop skill and discipline through the use of visual arts.

(*f*) To enrich the personality of the student and contribute to his emotional, mental, and physical health.

(*g*) To help the student to derive more from his daily experience and contribute more to it.

(*h*) To discover or augment the professional possibilities of the individual.

(*i*) To broaden the cultural background of each individual.

The Art Department at Fieldston is attempting to evolve a practicable plan of instruction that shall be in keeping with modern educational philosophy and the requirements of the times. The aims and processes described are the result of more than a quarter of a century of exploration in art education on the secondary level in the Ethical Culture Schools. Some phases of the work have had the test of time; others are of recent vintage. The most important characteristic of the process is its experimental nature. While much remains to be desired in our work, we feel that our efforts are working toward a solution of the many problems that confront all teachers of the arts at this level.

XI
ART IN BOYS' PREPARATORY SCHOOLS

Thomas M. Folds
Art Director, The Phillips Exeter Academy
Exeter, New Hampshire

Not many years ago the eastern college preparatory schools for boys represented the last line of defense against the advance of art education. Now, however, nearly all of these schools, including the most conservative, have yielded at least their curricular outposts to some form of visual-manual instruction.

What is significant about this change is the fact that essentially conservative schools of this type, with an educational policy dedicated primarily to the purpose of getting boys into a small group of eastern colleges, are nevertheless willing to include art instruction in their curriculums, even though it has little to do with book learning and still less with college-entrance requirements.

Art doesn't fit comfortably into the college-entrance system, principally because it is not included among the "examinables." There is no such thing, for instance, as a college-entrance examination in art; and, if art instructors in the preparatory schools have any say in the matter, there never will be. Inasmuch as we are devoted primarily to stimulating art appreciation through each student's own creative expression, a college-entrance examination in art would measure, at best, merely certain learned facts that we consider of secondary importance. Moreover, it would eventually imprison the art course itself within an *a priori* theory of education that would not make those necessary allowances for adventure in learning lying at the root of all true art appreciation.

If we deny the student this adventure, most of the art we feed him is so much ' spinach,' which he will eventually disgorge. He must be given freedom to explore problems and media within the range of his own abilities and interests. Boys interested in contemporary commercial art, for example, should be encouraged to develop this interest — to become acquainted with the achievements of modern designers, like Cassandre, Herbert Bayer, Kepes, or E. McKnight Kauffer — before they are introduced to Japanese prints, Greek vase drawings, or other well-pedigreed art of the past. In other words, we see no reason for subjecting our students to a course in art history, since much of this ground belongs within the scope of general history teaching, where it can be properly integrated with other aspects of various cultures or in the college level where it can serve as a *culmination* of prolonged creative activity in the school.

And this creative activity can follow many different paths. Most of us teaching art in the preparatory schools believe in the old saying that what is " one man's meat is another man's poison." We assume that, although it is good for some boys to paint in oils, it is better for others to paint in water colors, or not to paint at all, but to build, to carve, to use the camera, or explore other media. Since there are many approaches to general art appreciation, we believe it is our responsibility, no matter how exasperating this may prove at times, to help each student follow that approach which develops his own natural ability.

One way of doing this is to combine activities in different media within the walls of a single studio. If you were to poke your head into the average preparatory school workshop, you would probably see many different projects in sculpture, drawing, painting, display technique, and architecture carried on side by side — some of them individual projects, others collaborative efforts. There is room here for the boy with leanings towards science as well as for the boy interested principally in history, economics, or even athletics. The main value in such a program lies in the informal learning it encourages for each boy is curious about the other fellow's problems. And one of the art instructor's tasks is to stimulate this curiosity without resorting to the formalized lecture pattern with which most colleges must put up. In this way the young architect gradually learns something about sculpture or industrial design or even the comparatively restricted field of map-making and exhibition technique.

Now, up to a certain point, this method of teaching is similar to that developed by the Progressive schools; and we freely acknowledge our debt to their pioneering work. At the same time, however, we are aware of certain weaknesses in this type of teaching — of its tendency for example, to rob creative activity of discipline by offering the student too much freedom. Well, we have no intention of extracting discipline from studio activity. We have no intention of using art as an aspirin tablet for curricular headaches, as a cure for regimented teaching in other subjects. But, if the framework of our teaching is flexible, if it makes those necessary allowances for individual aptitudes and interests, there is no reason why it cannot offer *both* freedom and discipline.

Perhaps the kind of discipline needed most today is the discipline of *coöperative, constructive thinking*, which we sometimes lose sight of in our enthusiasm for encouraging individual talent. ' Rugged ' individualism has been corroding democracies for a good many years. Certainly it has not husbanded natural resources or created beautiful communities: above all, it has not promoted that group enthusiasm for community ideals that is the backbone of any healthy culture.

One way to develop such group enthusiasm, such coöperative constructive thinking, is through education in community planning. But where in the secondary-school field can you find evidences of such activity? Very few courses in art, civics, social studies, or history include it in their programs. Yet there are certain rudimentary studies in community planning that are quite as necessary for the development of sound citizenship today as are the elementary principles of law and economics that we customarily include in the high-school education of every American boy and girl.

How can this type of work be done? Obviously not by tacking a one-year art course onto the fringe of the curriculum and offering it to a small number of gifted or maladjusted students. Art is a complex language that can be learned only over a period of many years. Logically, it should be a continuous training, ranging from kindergarten up through the secondary school into the college, changing in content as the child or adolescent changes, growing with him until it becomes an integral part of his mental habits, of his whole conception of life. And if art is a language — a universal language — then why should it be restricted to only a few privileged people? Why should it not become a basic topic in the framework of every adolescent's education — indeed, of every child's education?

In a democracy, communities are not built by the privileged few, but by the people as a whole; and when better communities are built, the people will build them. Without their group enthusiasm for better planning and building, without their tolerance of new forms and their general art appreciation, city-planners and architects must file away their drawings and blueprints in despair, for we no longer live in the comparatively simple communities of the seventeenth and eighteenth centuries, which reflected the harmonious thinking and will-to-style of the people themselves, rich and poor alike. The early American community was the product of a single living tradition in design, from the mills by its river to the town common, the church, and the homes. It had not yet been flooded by great backwashes of stylistic clichés handed down from cultures long dead. And, for this reason, the teaching of art or the study of community planning was not needed in the early American school; the town itself was a work of art and a daily lesson in color, texture, and form to every one of its inhabitants.

The art course today is a modern invention designed to answer modern needs. And one of the greatest modern needs is the generation of real art appreciation among the masses. Stimulating interest in community planning must be our next move. Teaching boys and girls how to dabble in paint or plasticene is only a small part of the program. If the school is going to develop good American citizenship, then it must reorganize its art and history courses to include the study of people — how they live and how they build. What meaning has a course in American history if it overlooks the character of the early Yankee community or of its formal contemporary in the old South? Here are the visible symbols of those much misunderstood words ' freedom ' and ' liberty.' What meaning had they then, and what meaning have they now? The textbooks young people read ignore this aspect of history. They tell of beautiful Washington, but not of its obsolete Baroque military plan that stubbornly resists a century's industrial expansion. They tell of Boston, breeder of revolution and early American patriotism, but not of Boston clinging pitifully today to its past, chopped into narrow, tortuous streets and infected with malignant slums. Here is the history of degeneration in esthetic conviction and civic pride — the result of a hundred years of rugged individualism run to an extreme. Why have the history books overlooked all this?

The same question might be asked of our art teaching. Too often it is limited to only three or four fields, particularly those of the pictorial and plastic arts. Yet there is always a certain number of students whose talents lie in planning and building; and it is important that the curriculum develop these talents. Fortunately this is being done to a certain extent in many of the eastern preparatory schools. A year ago, for example, a small group of boys in one school made a two-year study of architecture and city planning, pooled the information they gathered in a series of three-dimensional wall displays, then finally designed and built a scale model of a hypothetical modern American community that included stores, school, parks, community center, and housing units for varying income groups. Boys specializing in exhibition technique designed the wall displays; those primarily interested in painting worked on murals for the community center; and fledgling sculptors designed reliefs for the entrance to the school. In this way the study of community planning became the focal point of a considerable variety of different creative activities as well as an extension of the school's history courses. It was a new approach to secondary-school education.

If we are going to prepare young people to recognize the importance of the arts in modern life and to participate intelligently in the planning and building of their own homes and communities, then projects of this kind must be extended throughout each level of the secondary schools and woven into the fabric of both art and history teaching. And though there is no one way to do this, because individuals, schools, and local traditions differ from one another, yet I believe that the stimulation of coöperative constructive thinking in the field of the arts, which form the stuff of our visual and physical environment, should be an important part of every school's program, for the reason that this kind of teaching lays the groundwork of democratic culture.

XII
THEATER ARTS IN SECONDARY SCHOOLS

BARCLAY S. LEATHEM
Professor of Drama and Theater, Western Reserve University
Cleveland, Ohio

Far from being a frill, the theater is one of the most vital forces in American life. As a synthesis of the arts it provides a means of bringing to a focus the diversified activities of the secondary schools. Costuming, lighting, scenery construction, publicity, business management, acting, stage decor, creative writing, music, and the dance appeal to students of every variety of aptitude and interest. Leaders in Progressive Education have used stage arts as a way of stimulating studies in history, English, civics, and related subjects. Important to the educator is the fact, now well established, that the learning process need not be painful or dull. Students soon learn that it is more fun to act the part of Mussolini or Chamberlain in an original classroom dramatization of the Munich Conference than it is to write a report on the same theme.

The techniques of drama enliven any subject to which they are applied by properly trained teachers.

I. Stress on Educational Values

It is noteworthy that the best work in stage arts is being done in those schools that stress the educational value of participation in plays. The activity is justified not by its relation to possible future employment in commercial theater, radio, or cinema, but by development of personality and by enrichment of the student's awareness of artistic values. Being in a play teaches coöperation, resourcefulness, self-discipline. It improves speech and posture. It stimulates imagination. It directs attention to color, form, and other elements of design. These new interests are carried over to life outside the school. The student who has helped to arrange the furniture in a stage setting or to select the colors for stage properties will not thereafter be apathetic to his own environment.

II. The American Educational Theatre Association

The theater is one of the latest of the arts to achieve academic respectability. Beginning as a student activity, it has won recognition as a curricular subject, and it is gaining steadily. One indication of this was the formation in 1937 of the American Educational Theatre Association to represent the common interests of teachers of dramatics throughout the educational system. Another evidence of drama's rising popularity in the schools is the support given to it by the Rockefeller Foundation, which has contributed to universities approximately $500,-000 to improve teacher training in stage arts. Included in the grants of the Rockefeller Foundation is a subvention to the National Theatre Conference. This organization, with offices at Western Reserve University, Cleveland, Ohio, maintains a placement service, publishes a *Quarterly Bulletin,* awards fellowships, coördinates regional conferences, strengthens library facilities, obtains reductions in royalty fees on recommended plays, and conducts surveys on current theater problems. Records of the National Theatre Conference show that stage arts are being fostered in at least 5,000 high schools, and the number is increasing yearly.

III. Extremes of Merit

At the lowest level, the work is limited to an occasional class night play, operetta, or pageant. Supervision is entrusted to teachers whose training has not equipped them for the task. The performance is given to raise money for other school projects. Principals and superintendents control selection of plays and refuse to authorize payment of royalty fees. Usually only farces without literary value are given. Under these conditions stage arts cannot thrive. Students leave such schools with perverted concepts of the drama.

At the highest level, play production is a recognized course of study in the school curriculum. Teachers are appointed who have earned a master's degree in the theater arts at any one of the twenty-eight universities specializing in this field. The plays are selected from the best in period and contemporary dramatic literature. Students are educated to a critical evaluation of all aspects of stage production.

IV. FAULTY STAGE DESIGN

One of the handicaps to progress in secondary-school dramatics is faulty design of stages by architects. This in turn affects adversely the standard of stage décor. Writing for the *High-School Thespian* in January, 1938, Leslie Allen Jones says:

> Scenery today is shrouded in mystery to most high-school groups. Following the fashion of sixty years ago, high-school auditoriums have been equipped, if at all, with stock scenery and a few borders and drops which are forever after held to be inviolate. When you add to this fact stages with polished floors and impossible proscenium widths the average group is pretty badly handicapped in an attempt to mount plays with a feeling of real theater.

Unfortunately even schools in wealthy communities have inadequate stages. Architects have adapted for school auditoriums the most expensive, but not the most practical, elements of commercial theater design. Their answer to criticism is to point to all the other secondary-school stages that have been poorly designed. The stage newly completed is usually a synthesis of existing mistakes. One exception is the stage now being built for the Glenville High School of Cleveland, Ohio. In this instance the architect consulted Eugene Davis, the high-school teacher of dramatics and carried out Mr. Davis's ideas. Another example of a well-constructed school auditorium is at Shorewood, Wisconsin.

There is no longer excuse for such bad practice among school architects. Advisory services are available through the United States Office of Education and through the National Theatre Conference. Moreover, there are examples of sound design in many community and university theaters. Among the best are the University of Indiana, the University of Wisconsin, Stanford University, the University of Iowa, the Cleveland Play House, and the Pasadena Community Playhouse.

V. Evaluation of Current Practice

For an evaluation of current practice in the visual arts of the theater in schools, adequate source materials are lacking. The two magazines that emphasize high-school dramatics are *Players Magazine* and the *High-School Thespian*. Many teachers doing excellent work are too busy to submit to these journals pictures of their designs. From the limited evidence certain generalizations may be offered.

Type of *stage settings* has been influenced by the decided preference of the high schools for realistic plays. To reproduce as closely as possible the original setting used in the New York production has been the norm. Even when schools attempted period plays, little attention has been given to the architecture of the period in the design of sets. A notable exception is Webster Groves High School, Missouri, where a scene designer has been employed to work with Eugene Wood, the director.

Innovations in the past few years have been the unit set and space staging technique. There is a definite movement toward more simplified staging, cyclorama, and units replacing the traditional realistic box set. The popularity of *Our Town* in high schools this last year encouraged this tendency. Its influence may be far-reaching in its emphasis upon imagination as a substitute for complete details. The choice of play still remains largely the one- or two-set interior or exterior, realistic, modern mystery, comedy, or farce. However, there are indications to point the way toward production of multiple-set classics through nonrealistic, simplified staging. The work of the technical director and the importance of stagecraft have been growing steadily in prestige and importance.

New features in the *High-School Thespian* indicate trends in staging. Professor Earl Blank, of Berea College, Kentucky, conducts a column entitled " Staging the High-School Play." In it, Professor Blank describes a different play in each issue and submits floor plans for its staging. For instance, *The Importance of Being Earnest* is described in a unit-set staging. Drapes with a single double-center entrance are used in all three acts with variations of furniture. In the same magazine Leslie Allen Jones, Lecturer in the Extension Division, Brown Uni-

versity, edits a department called " The Technical Director's Page."
It is supplemented with a section on " Questions and Answers."

" We have rather a small stage and have overhead lights and foot-
lights. We desire some specific lighting for about thirty or forty dollars. Would you please give us some advice on this matter? " This
question defines at once the problem and the opportunity of the high-
school drama teacher in the field of *stage lighting*. In only a few
schools is there modern equipment or a teacher skilled in its use. The
contribution in lighting, then, must depend upon the ingenuity with
which adequate effects can be achieved with simple, often homemade
materials. Results are good in schools that provide supervision. As
in other aspects of play production, good leadership stimulates achievement. Only during the past decade has adequate training in stage
lighting been available in universities. It will be some time before the
effect of this training will be widespread in the secondary schools.

In *stage costuming*, high schools have made notable progress. The
work of Alberta Johnson, of Wauwatosa High School, Wisconsin, is a
conspicuous example of what can be done to link student and community enthusiasm with sound artistic accomplishment. She has experimented successfully with designing by groups. Acting as coördinator,
Miss Johnson selects the materials, keeping the requirements for basic
interpretive and pictorial design clearly in mind. Students, working in
committee, then consider the characters, the research, and the ensemble
requirements in relation to fabrics before them. All major costume features are allocated to each character as ideas are shared by the student
designers. The sketches are made by many different students who undertake to add detail to a chosen costume. Creative ability is thus expressed within limits set by the needs of the play as a whole. In this
way individual responsibility and satisfaction are retained, though the
play benefits by a basically fluid design and a free pooling of the best
ideas. After an apprenticeship in one major production, the most talented designers are ready to try alone a problem in design. They realize
that sixteen-cylinder-thinking is in order in the theater. Execution of
the costumes is entrusted to a more or less permanent committee of
mothers in the community, thus utilizing talent both within and without the school in creating the permanent wardrobe of the Drama Department.

The popularity of operettas and of such commencement pageants as
those written by Walter Bissell of the Central High School, Cleveland,
has led to the building up of costume collections in many schools.

Teachers and students of home economics collaborate with dramatic directors and art teachers in increasing the number and quality of costumes.

An encouraging recent tendency is the effort of art teachers to learn the special problems of theater esthetics. Limitations of the naturalism of Zola and Antoine were first assailed by Nietzsche. In pointing the way to fresh concepts of design, Adolphe Appia and Gordon Craig gave the theater of Europe a provocative visual impetus. From this foreign influence American designers quickly evolved their own methods.

In *The Stage Is Set*, Lee Simonson stresses the essential differences between graphic arts that exist in space, either two or three dimensionally, and stage arts that exist in both time and space. Movements of actors and of light influence scene design. One fundamental test of a stage setting is its effect upon the movement of the actor in relation to the play itself. Teachers of art whose training emphasized other applications of design need to learn the process by which a performance is evolved from the first analysis of the playwright's script. That they are doing this, either through taking courses in the arts of the theater in universities or through consultation with experienced play directors, is revealed by the improvement in the scenic investiture of school plays.

To raise standards of stage arts, *the critical faculties of the students* must be developed. Gary High School, Indiana, is pointing the way. There, the school auditorium is used every period for some kind of dramatic activity. After the performance there is an analytical discussion, guided by teachers, but presided over by students. The curtain is raised; the cast is assembled on stage. It is not unusual to hear a fourteen-year-old member of the audience object to the tempo of a scene or criticize constructively the visual details of setting, movement, color, line, and mass. This is far in advance of doing *Mr. Pips from Pipsville* with untrained students directed by untrained teachers in an effort to raise money to buy sweaters for the basketball team. The students at Gary are being educated to discriminate between good art and bad; they are being trained for purposeful enjoyment of leisure.

Historically, the theater has flourished at peak moments of cultural achievement. Drama vivifies man's noblest efforts. From Aeschylus to O'Neill it epitomizes the communal art of its day. It does not exist apart from life, but stems from it and reflects it. A man is educated when he is truly aware of his past and his present, when he has a way of living as well as a way of earning a living. To these ends, appreciation and practice of stage arts are essentials of modern education in America.

XIII

COLLEGE ENTRANCE REQUIREMENTS IN RELATION TO SECONDARY–SCHOOL ART

Vincent A. Roy

Supervisor of Art Education, Pratt Institute

Brooklyn, New York

College entrance requirements present a serious problem in the advancement or even the maintenance of art education on the part of all concerned, for unless something is done, the entrance requirements, as they now exist, may bring about a continuously increasing curtailment in our present art-education program.

To indicate the background of the situation briefly, it may be pointed out that college entrance examinations and requirements date back to 1642 when they were first introduced at Harvard University. In 1895 a committee on College Entrance Examinations was appointed by the National Education Association and their report subsequently did much to bring the colleges and secondary schools closer together in their practices. At present, the College Entrance Examination Board, which has been very influential in securing and maintaining uniformity in the courses and nature of instruction offered in secondary schools, is made up of representatives of forty-one colleges and universities throughout the country and the representatives of three accrediting associations. Thus does this Board continue to have contact with practically all the secondary schools and colleges of the country. The Board prepares, administers, and rates examinations in all the academic subjects.

Until 1871, the only means of passing from the secondary school to college was by examination given at the college in prescribed subjects. Now, less than twenty-five percent of the colleges require examinations as the only standard of admission. A much larger percentage — 63 percent of 517 schools (National Survey of Secondary Education, Monograph No. 10) — will accept a transcript of the record of the graduates from accredited secondary schools, without examinations.

Despite the change in emphasis from examination to certification and other means of admission, the influence of the College Entrance Examination Board is still felt in that the same subjects that have been the basis for examinations all these years are still the subjects considered in certification. About 80 percent of the 118 institutions studied designate specific units required in high-school work. It seems that the college entrance examinations and college entrance requirements are commonly thought of as synonymous, even though the latter are much broader, including in addition to the College Entrance Board examinations, other examinations, as well as high-school subject certificates, high-school diplomas, certain rank in high school, intelligence tests, principal's recommendations, other recommendations, personal interviews, and character and personality rating.

The purposes of college entrance requirements are very simple; namely, first, to prevent from entering college classes, students unfit to pursue the work to their advantage; second, to protect the scholarly standards of both secondary school and college; third, to stimulate and keep the secondary school vital and purposeful; and fourth, to improve selection so that it may become better in guiding students correctly toward their life's work.

The advantages of strict entrance requirements are: first, they build up standards of instruction in the secondary school, and tend to keep the colleges themselves up to certain standards; second, they make possible a certain desirable uniformity of standards in secondary schools and colleges; third, they insure the admission of better-prepared students — the stricter the examinations, the better prepared are the students; and fourth, they stimulate, because the knowledge that he must meet and pass the requirements motivates the student, and passing gives him added self-confidence.

It must be admitted that the purposes and advantages of the college admission requirements are fine and desirable in themselves. There is, however, a serious menace that needs to be removed as soon as possible if art education is to become the constructive force it is capable of becoming in our society. The essence of the difficulty lies in the subject-matter requirement. Of the fifteen or sixteen units required from the secondary school, at least ten are definitely specified academic subjects, and for the other five or six units that the student may offer as electives, the subject of art or drawing is not recognized in the majority of colleges as of any value whatsoever. Also, superintendents of schools and secondary-school principals are too often intent on requiring all students to take the college-preparatory course, regardless of their needs, interests, or abilities.

Thus we see that in college entrance requirements as they exist at present there are certain definite disadvantages for art in the secondary school. These disadvantages, put briefly, are six in number.

First, a great many secondary-school students are deprived of their rightful opportunities for art education by the present arbitrary college entrance requirements.

Second, secondary-school students are forced to drop art or be exposed to a mere smattering of it in favor of a subject that is recognized as meeting the college entrance requirements, but that may maladjust the student to any future education.

Third, the study of art has thus been depreciated in the minds of the students to the status of a minor subject.

Fourth, many students are committed to a life of mediocrity who could otherwise become outstanding contributors to our society if they were permitted and encouraged to develop their talents.

Fifth, the present requirements apparently deny the major importance of the permanent value of art — to the future lives of the students, to the satisfaction of their esthetic nature, and to the increased happiness gained from well-rounded educational activities.

Sixth, it is commonly recognized that the present requirements refuse to recognize the changing curriculum and philosophy of contemporary education. They hold to the idea of the secondary schools and colleges as they were originally founded " to provide a classical education for the privileged few." As a youth remarked during the coöperative conference of youth and administrators at Harrisburg, Pennsylvania, February, 1938, " We want education to prepare us for life, not for a college we're not going to."

To eradicate these difficulties and improve the situation, the following five suggestions are proffered.

1. The colleges and universities should be approached to secure their acceptance of art as a required major subject on the basis of its cultural values or to permit the use of art units to satisfy at least three, if not more, units towards electives. There will be at least these five definite values to be gained from their so doing:

   a. The college will benefit by admitting students who have had training in esthetic judgment and mental and motor coördination. These students will possess a broader background than those with a purely academic training.

   b. The college art departments will benefit because of the advanced training of the entering students. Much college art work is not above, if equal to, the level of work done in high schools where the study of art is encouraged.

   c. Students who plan to enter art fields after graduation from the high school should be allowed to start their art education at an early date, for basic skills developed in the elementary grades need to be improved by those showing potentialities if newly gained abilities for growth are to be realized. Also, unless definite training is given, they will be unable to qualify for entrance into a professional art school. Satisfactory progress in technical work can be made at college level under these circumstances only if the student has acquired a good foundation at the secondary level.

   d. Increased recognition of art education in the secondary schools by the college entrance boards and officers of admission would result in those institutions securing a greater number of students qualified through ability and natural aptitude to undertake careers in one of the fine or applied arts, as well as giving the students a richer cultural background.

e. Students who have been permitted to prepare for art fields in secondary schools, but who decide upon graduation to go to college, may find that they do not have the established requirements for admission. This frequently prevents future artists from broadening their cultural backgrounds. This suggests provision being made for accepting such students as specials or for liberalizing admission requirements.[1]

2. The College Entrance Examination Board should be approached to enlist its influence in taking or suggesting steps that will lead to having art recognized as an elective, if not one of the major subjects. That the Board is cognizant of change in our educational setup is evidenced by the secretary's annual report of 1938, in which he points out that the lack of uniformity in admission policies of the forty-one universities making up membership in the Board demands more or less flexibility in its program.

3. The superintendents of schools and the principals of the secondary schools should be approached to secure a liberalization of the course requirements for their students. . . . As was pointed out in the recent Regents Inquiry in New York State (reported in *Education for American Life,* " The high schools have been ' college preparatory ' institutions. Now that only one-fifth of those in high schools do, as a matter of fact, go on to college, the time has come to make over the high schools so that they will also be useful to the four-fifths who finish their formal schooling when they leave the secondary school." This means that high schools as well as colleges can help the situation. Included in the one-fifth who go to college are those who study at professional art schools (which do require art as a subject for admission), as well as those who will study art at a liberal arts institution as a deflated minor because they were deprived of sufficient high-school training to enable them to enter an art school. These two groups are maladjusted when placed in the usual college-preparatory course. . . . The superintendent likewise needs to understand, and be able to show to the parents of children with artistic ability, the desirability of having such children prepare for art schools, instead of for the traditional type of academic institution.

The New York State Board of Regents in 1934 took a big step in the right direction by revising and broadening the provisions for the granting of a state high-school diploma. They now provide that nearly any subject field may be studied so long as definite sequences are followed that permit a student to elect art as a major subject to the extent of as many as five college entrance units.

---

[1] It remains to be seen whether the eight-year study of the Commission on the Relation of School and College of the Progressive Education Association will bear fruit in the general broadening of specific entrance requirements and whether art will receive just recognition.

4. Another, and perhaps a most fundamental, approach is the matter of curricular and methodology revision in the field of art education. To be accorded the same recognition as other courses, it will undoubtedly be necessary, eventually, to give subject matter and its presentation more meaning and practical and cultural value. It will need to possess real consumer values with definite thought-provoking materials as well as artistic exercise that promotes growth on a par with abilities developed in chemistry, physics, or other subjects. The subject will definitely need to be ' sold,' not only to the school children, school officers, and teachers, but to the parents as well.

5. A concerted effort in each of the foregoing directions by all individuals and educational agencies possible — The National Education Association, The Eastern Arts Association, The Western Arts Association, The Pacific Arts Association, The Southern Arts Association, The Progressive Education Association, and others — is the only way in which progress can be made in this problem of securing just recognition for secondary-school art.

XIV
ART IN COLLEGES AND UNIVERSITIES

LESTER D. LONGMAN
Head of the Department of Art and
Professor of the History of Art
State University of Iowa
Iowa City, Iowa

I. STATISTICS ON GROWTH

The study of art, which once grasped with uncertain hold the fringe of higher learning, in recent years has defied the depression, multiplied the number of its followers, and moved steadily nearer the heart of the curriculum. Today art is taught in two-thirds of our colleges as compared to one-half in 1925, and enrollments have increased in similar proportion. It is most favored by colleges for women, in nearly all of which it is found, while it is provided in but half the men's and in two-thirds of the coeducational. The demand for able teachers and the erection of new buildings prove that the upward trend continues.

II. CAUSES OF GROWTH

There are many causes of growth, but among them the most direct is the priming of the pump, for which we are indebted to the Carnegie

Foundation. Its scholarships have supplied a generation of well-trained, enthusiastic teachers, and its temporary grants for salaries and equipment have inaugurated art in scores of smaller colleges where otherwise it could not flourish. Another cause not less direct has been the spread of the philosophy of Progressive Education, which fosters learning by doing and finds art most useful to its methodology. Among less specific causes may be cited the popularity of visual imagery in general, as evidenced by public appreciation of the motion pictures, of profusely illustrated magazines, and the candid-camera hobby; and the genuine public interest in well-designed industrial arts, which in common parlance are known as 'streamlined.' The average man, more sensitive now to visual values, makes art in advertising pay, buys bath-tubs if they are well designed, subscribes to magazines to see Van Gogh, reads books that tell him what art is, takes courses that reveal its story, and sometimes seeks to find in art a means of self-expression.

III. Objectives and Methods Still Undefined

In spite of progress made, however, the proper place of art in higher education is still not well defined. In every institution history, literature, and science are taught, and serve a common function. Courses everywhere are fairly uniform and standard texts are used. Art's case is different. In the lowest third of our colleges no art is taught at all, while in the middle third it still receives the scantiest support. Some one hundred and fifty institutions, usually those with highest academic standards, provide a major course of study; a few require a course in art of all their A.B. graduates; and in rare instances the enrollment in the Art Department is first or second highest of all departments. Objectives are equally varied and often nebulous; standard textbooks are few; courses with common titles are not comparable; and the diversity of course offerings is bewildering. What would a student be like if subjected to the following curriculum: Merchandise Display, Blackboard Drawing, Wall Hangings, Silhouettes, Flower Arrangement, Penmanship, Demonstration Drawing, Art of the Mask, China Painting, Color in Wood Finish, and Art of the College Annual! These courses, culled from college catalogs, confirm the suspicion that in college nothing is studied that is not taught, and that the best school is too often assumed to be the one with the thickest catalog. The department of art holds no monopoly on this mischief, but it ranks among the leading offenders; and the trend toward an indiscriminate multiplication of courses in specific techniques, baptized with the most diversified titles, seems far from halted; it makes credit-transfers vexatious, ranks as a major evil in art teaching, and proves art a fledgling in university circles still needing to consolidate its gains.

IV. Ideal Conditions for Art Instruction

1. Administration

Doubtless some advantage may accrue in itemizing those conditions that predispose toward healthy growth in art instruction; thus current ills may be revealed and suggestions given for their betterment. One critical problem, which, if left unsolved, will surely compromise the evolution of a common purpose and a reasonably standardized curriculum throughout the nation is the Herculean task of securing everywhere the most favorable administration. An improper one can hardly ruin a good teacher, but it can greatly lessen his effectiveness. It is simple to pronounce that ideally art should be taught in art departments, but to consummate the ideal will require protracted effort. Art is still a new arrival in university environments, the offspring of such patronage as circumstance allowed. One finds it sheltered under the wing of classics, archaeology, philosophy, education, home economics, architecture, and engineering. Thus art is not regularly taught for the sake of art, but is often a suffix to the dominion of some other department — a profitable royalty, certainly, but a dangling appendage with a suitable bias, a tenant that must pay rent. In truth art is not " art for teachers," nor is it at home with engineers, though both teachers and engineers will do well to become exposed to it. It should appeal to all students, but men are not home economists and girls are shy of architectural draughting rooms. While home-makers and architects should certainly come to terms with art, neither has an exclusive right to its management. Both its popularity and its quality suffer when art is under a foreign bondage. Four separate patrons offer no adequate solution, for each one fights the others with eager propaganda, the university pays for duplication of effort, and art is still not taught for its sake alone. Surely another decade will see a vote of thanks extended to all these hospitable patrons, and art, now come of age, will set forth upon its own adult career. In no other way can it achieve distinction.

This is not to say that, once an independent art department is established, a course in art for engineers should not be given by the engineering college and like policies be continued elsewhere. This, indeed, may be desirable if it can be afforded, but art's true and independent home must be established in the college of liberal arts, where the general student body will be attracted, and where the menage is no longer supervised by a prejudiced mother-in-law.

On occasion art has been welcomed in the university for its own sake, but with reservations. It is accepted for a special purpose that restricts its potential function. Then one finds it in the catalog in departments labelled Applied Arts, Industrial Arts, History of Art, Art Appreciation, Graphic Art, Design, Commercial Art, and the like. These limitations of the scope of art will sometimes be removed, for art is all of these and more. The proper title for the department of art is "The Department of Art."

Students in colleges of liberal arts should have easy access to the study of art, and our future artists should not be denied access to a liberal education; yet both results are compromised when art is taught in a separate college, where technical specialization is extreme (the condition often comparable to the average art school), and ' artisans,' not artists, leave the halls of ' learning.' If a separate college of art is to be maintained, every effort must be expended to give the art students a liberal education, and every facility must be extended to associate the art courses with the courses in the college of liberal arts, so that art may play its proper rôle in general education.

Art instruction is often narrow when practicing artists are in charge of art departments, for they frequently stress technique at the cost of education, misunderstand academic objectives, and prove themselves incompetent administrators. Ideally, art should be taught in a Department of Art, in the College of Liberal Arts, under the direction of a liberal educator, one who understands the university scene and who will not, through prejudiced convictions, confine the range of art to nothing but art history, or nothing but painting, or commercial art, or crafts, or art appreciation.

2. Good Teachers and Sympathetic Administrators

Besides the problem of administration, there are other serious issues that affect the quantity of student interest and the quality of production. There are still many university instructors who are poorly trained as artists, largely uninformed in the history of art, or ineffective in the art of teaching. Specialists in pedagogy often need content; young art historians forget to learn to lecture; good artists teach mannerisms. When the teaching is good, progress may be starved by presidents and deans who understand science and fail to value art, or who, valuing it, plead poverty, or who, impoverished, lack the imagination to enlist the aid of large foundations or wealthy patrons in supportable projects of art development.

3. Extra-Curricular Support of Art

The staff of a prospering department of art will promote extra-curricular activities. Some sponsor art clubs and annual exhibits or bazaars of student art; others provide lending libraries of prints, reproductions, or original paintings, and present series of travelling exhibitions. Some offer night classes, hobby classes, free instruction in crafts, and sessions for criticism of paintings by amateur enthusiasts; others specialize in public lectures and demonstrations, forums, and conferences. All this is valuable and more common today than it was ten years ago.

4. Nature of the Student Body

The character of the students often prescribes limits to growth. If they are largely from a single state, the university must help to make art available in all that state's high schools or forego progress. Wealthy students can afford a general education and will generously elect courses in art history; needy students require a utilitarian curriculum and force the university to more practical courses. An intelligent educational policy must respect these divergent purposes and interests.

5. An Adaptable Curriculum

In most institutions the students are neither uniformly rich or poor, nor in other ways standardized when they arrive. Therefore a standard curriculum will regiment unduly and will circumscribe quality. A liberal choice of curricula is usually a condition of healthy growth, especially in art education where individuality must be respected. The usual A.B. course is too theoretical and too centrifugal for some minds, and often it prohibits the election of practical art in the freshman year or permits so little as a maximum that it dampens the ardor and enthusiasm of the most talented students. For these promising artists a Bachelor of Fine Arts degree, allowing reasonable specialization from the very beginning, will prevent an interruption in their professional development, make their progress more purposive, prevent them from renouncing the university to seek the too narrow training of technical schools, and secure to the most gifted as broad an education as they are able to absorb. In the same way, when strictures upon the M.A. course prevent stress upon technical competence as an artist, or when this degree is used for art history alone, a Master of Fine Arts degree may draw good artists to the university and aid them to broaden their education and discipline their thinking.

6. Value of a Course in Art Appreciation

Limitations in objectives put shackles on enrollments. In most situations a well-taught survey course in the history and appreciation of art will serve the useful purposes of enriching the lives of multitudes of students and of supplying a large audience of enlightened amateurs to patronize our future artists. Some colleges disclaim this reasonable responsibility or allow a poor job to suffice. So profitable a course, and one so vast in scope, should be conducted by a well-trained art historian, equipped with thousands of good slides and prints, lacking which the content will be so meager as to fail of college caliber. Its stress should be on values, not on facts.

7. Balance between Art History and Studio Work

The prosperity of an art department and the quality of results achieved depend to a very large extent upon the integration of historical, critical, and practical studies. The ideal solution requires a balanced curriculum. To neglect the history and criticism of art and place excessive stress on studio production — a common fault — is a disparagement of the dignity of the university and a repudiation of a proper function peculiar to the university, the only institution society has invested with the power, and commissioned with the duty, to cultivate in unbiased manner the highest intellectual pursuits. Moreover, worthy teaching of art history enriches and invigorates the practice in the studio. To satisfy these purposes, a survey course is merely a beginning; a major sequence in art history is but a normal expectation.

On the other hand, some studio experience will enrich the study of art history. Yet in some colleges and universities only the history and criticism of art is taught, either because of insufficient funds to realize an ampler purpose or unwillingness to countenance the practice of art in college halls. American art is the loser. Scarcely any graduate of these colleges, however talented and intelligent, will ever become an artist, and the art history is likely to be mechanical. To offer laboratory experiments in varied studio techniques, to copy several masterpieces or imitate the line of Botticelli, and thus to supplement the lectures on appreciation is a frequent, but inadequate solution. The approach must be creative; the objective, commendable results; the courses, numerous. The studio cannot prosper as the slave of lecture courses, its power dissipated by servility. A like penalty, of course, is paid when the history of art is but a store of tips for artists, which I fear is still more prevalent a delinquency.

V. Art History, Its Present and Future

In perhaps a score of institutions a student may obtain a good general education in connoisseurship and methods of research. Such intellectual pursuits have recently received additional momentum through the fortunate arrival of many German scholars who have joined our college faculties. Princeton, Harvard, and New York University are the foremost representatives of this thorough European training in art history and offer the most complete post-graduate curricula. Good departments are also to be found at Chicago, Columbia, Oberlin, Dartmouth, Smith, Vassar, Wellesley, and Bryn Mawr, and perhaps a dozen others, mostly in the East. Some also offer studio work, but in a strictly minor rôle. In recent years the middle-western universities and some far-western ones have supported the history of art with greater generosity (for example, the state universities of Wisconsin, Illinois, Iowa, Ohio, and Minnesota, Northwestern University, and Washington University in St. Louis), but in the Middle and Far West in general and in the South as well, the early bias for the practical still dominates curricula. More liberal assistance to art history may clearly be anticipated in days to come, since what is done is visibly inadequate, but few will try to emulate the present leaders. For the anti-intellectualism that in recent years is sweeping over Europe finds a natural echo in historically pragmatic America and promises to represent the drift and tenor of the next decade. The cause of history cannot prosper where knowledge for its own sake and a liberal education are a jargon without sense. We have not reached this pretty pass as yet, but we manifestly give our clamorous applause to that knowledge which leads the most directly to informed and useful practice. Let us hope this movement will not go too far and a new dark age of mechanized power drive out unbiased search for truth.

VI. Current Faults in Teaching

There are two extremes of recent pedagogy that, by now, perhaps have passed their crest of popularity. Some teachers still contrive to make the history of art as dryly archaeological as statistic reports on Shakespeare's use of commas. Their students have no more genuine and substantial understanding of esthetic value than do the victims of a nicely packaged and beribboned art appreciation. If their preparation for connoisseurship is well fortified with facts, their singular bewilderment before the totally unfamiliar in art reveals a meretricious education in the principles of criticism, and lacking genuine understanding, even their connoisseurship is subject to correction and reproach. Being thus deplorably unschooled in the study of esthetics and equally unpracticed in the processes of art creation, such students know little of contemporary artists and current art activities in America and sympathize still less with them. They would make befuddled exhibition judges and are unable to apply their art in daily life.

An opposite pedagogical extreme is represented by the recent custom deliberately to integrate art with other studies and with daily life. This is good only in proportion as the integration is by way of elucidation of basic principles. But one cannot expect to illustrate esthetic value in all its multitude of ramifications. It is a Herculean task merely to convey to students wherein esthetic value consists. Moreover, the more intelligent and sophisticated students, by virtue of this wit, are able to apply essential principles to new and varied practices, and thereby integrate successfully for themselves. Recently the methodical stress upon art in relation to life and upon codified appreciation has too often replaced education in the fundamentals. Such a policy of superficial appreciationism is useful only in schools not highly selective in admitting students or in the lower forms when the youth of the students or the terminal character of the teaching may make it suitable. It goes without saying, however, that the employment of esthetic principles in homely practices should somehow be assured, whether through intelligent student awareness, or by abundant illustrations, or by instruction in predigested art appreciation — the method depending upon the intelligence and maturity of the students. Some art departments overestimate the mentality of their pupils and hence omit to mention obvious helpful hints on art and daily life or art's relation to geology; but currently the more usual offense has been to underestimate the sagacity of their scholars and thus to deprive them of a sounder education.

VII. Trends and Forecasts

1. The College Art Association Comes to Life

The trends of today are forecasts of the future, and it is both feasible and salutary to investigate their nature — feasible because so much is evident upon analysis, and wise and salutary so that our aspirations may not be preposterous or extravagant, our ideals merely private prejudices, and our achievements quixotic. First, of all, we may reasonably feel encouraged that progress will continue. This we know not just because enrollments in art are constantly increasing, but also because in recent years the College Art Association has been experiencing a new birth, evolving a national consciousness, expanding its activities into new fields of service, enlarging its membership, and realizing a new variety and a heartening vitality in the annual conference program. Ten years ago the conference speakers came from but a handful of our universities; today they may be from nearly every state and speak on far more varied subjects.

2. New Enthusiasm for American Art

The university reflects the recent popular enthusiasm for contemporary American art. Exhibitions and lectures on the subject are abundant, and at some institutions — for examples, Wisconsin, Illinois, Iowa, Dartmouth, Mills, Stephens, and the Claremont Colleges — professional artists who once would not have been at home in university environments have been engaged as teachers, or as " artists-in-residence " with obligation to do no more than paint, welcome studio visitors, and give occasional lectures. The long-standing rift between artists and halls of higher learning is gradually being closed and mutual compliments replace the customary interchange of jeers and ridicule.

3. Professional Art Accepted in the University

To state the case more clearly, it appears that art in the university is becoming professional and artists are becoming respectable. This circumstance reminds one of the day when science sought admission to the university, when laboratory work was frowned upon, and adroit administrators devised B.S. and Sc.D. degrees to supplement A.B.'s and Ph.D.'s, and thus effect a most productive compromise. One wonders whether there existed then a person called a " scientist-in-residence," to do no teaching, but to welcome laboratory visitors. More recently law and medicine were similarly assimilated, appropriate degrees were given, and private schools were abandoned or merged with universities. As this meant progress then, so now this process should improve the quality of American art, even though art be less intellectual a study than law, or medicine or science.

In any case no one can stop this trend. The faith America has al-

ways placed in formal education as the source of all authentic progress
and reform will impel art into its orbit, whether for good or evil, as
though by powerful magnetism. Conservative educators will object;
many artists will rebel at seeing brother artists educated; and private
art schools will declare a deadly war against this new and formidable
competitor, armed as it is with vast financial resources, unusual cultural opportunities, an atmosphere of intellectual discussion, the power
to grant degrees, control of teaching positions, and a new will to produce America's leading artists of the future. As the larger universities
lead the way, art schools will strive to liberalize curricula, seek power
to grant degrees, and consolidate with universities; normal schools will
strengthen content and professionalize their faculties; smaller colleges
will see art enthroned by the side of science as its equal and will prepare to meet the cost; and conservative institutions, postponing the
evil, will continue their good work of educating those intelligent audiences and discriminating patrons, those scholars and curators that
democracy always postulates and that our future artists must require
if the coming ' American Renaissance ' in art is to be realized.

4. The Ideal Art Department of the Future

Those universities that in the future will be called superior in the
teaching of art will soon adjust curricula to our changing social needs
and will support a comprehensive course of studies. This means that
every effort will be made to educate an audience of genuine amateurs.
But it also means an intensified professionalism, and not in one, but
three areas — adapted to the purposes of scholars, of teachers, and of
artists — and carrying the ablest students through the doctorate degree.

5. Training Creative Artists

A semi-professional curriculum for artists, closely associated with
the college of liberal arts, will attract talented students to the university, which will be to their advantage and to the advantage of society. B.F.A. and M.F.A. degrees will mark their progress.

6. Training Creative Art Historians

The parallel between art and science is not exact, for the study of
art history is more validly autonomous, of larger scope, and more rewarding than the history of science; and therefore a professional course
that leads to the doctor of philosophy degree in scholarship, yet pro-

vides some knowledge of techniques and a limited experience in art production, must be regarded as valid in superior institutions, into whose
hands society has placed the obligation to preserve unbiased historical
research. Emphasis should be placed on creative scholarship, not reproductive, just as in the studio the work should be as creative as possible and not reproductive or manneristic. At present, less than half-
a-dozen universities are offering a commendable Ph.D. degree in
scholarship.

7. Training Creative Teachers

Not less respectable, because it is first of all a social duty rather
than an intellectual responsibility, is the function of preparing teachers
adapted to our present circumstances. Most colleges cannot afford to
engage specialists, and generally request men or women reasonably
well prepared to lecture on the history and criticism of art and instruct
in the studio. Even where specialists are possible, colleges are happy
to find teachers sympathetic to both the history and practice of art.
Not many universities as yet have faced this reasonable expectation
and organized curricula appropriately to gratify it, slighting neither
aspect, emphasizing catholicity, and yet not sacrificing superior quality. Yet it can be done. For men are never fully educated when degrees are granted, and by the inspiration of broad and far horizons they
can be inspired as youths to seek a specialized maturity for themselves.
An imagination thoroughly excited to explore the beguiling, fruitful
vistas and the puzzling labyrinths of the history of art can be depended
on to continue the search when formal training stops. Were this accomplished by our teaching, as it seldom is, some dates and places and
chronology could well be sacrificed, in order that students might acquire an equal preparation to explore the world with painter's brush
and pencil.

The art teacher, like any other, is today compelled to have advanced degrees, and will certainly be no less obligated in this matter in
years to come, while art repeats the course that other subjects followed
in establishing themselves securely in the university. High-school
boards as well as universities demand it, and increasingly expect art
teachers, however poorly paid, to obtain the Master of Arts degree or
its equivalent. This policy sometimes promotes good teaching, but
with equal potency it so depreciates the quality of the degree that soon
no greater honor will pertain to it than the A.B. degree now enjoys.
This trend cannot be stopped, but an M.F.A. degree of more substantial

character is now given in a group of leading universities, and this can more easily be controlled and seems a logical solution. The degree is now meant primarily for college teachers; it is awarded either in the history or the practice of art, but could well be given in recognition of high quality in both, and thus become a professional degree for artists who aspire to be associated with colleges and universities.

8. The Ph.D. Degree

The question whether the Ph.D. degree may be similarly employed is destined to become the subject of most lively debate. It may logically be held that the demand for the Ph.D. on the part of colleges is artificial and should be frowned upon in the field of art except in the study of art history. It is certain that genuine or creative scholarship and genuine or creative art seldom are found together in the same individual. For most potential artists, creative scholarship is too analytical and critical, though short of the Ph.D. degree the sharpening of one's critical powers should be good for the majority of artists, or else Dewey is badly mistaken and art is incurably romantic or perhaps a mere technique.

To my knowledge Ohio State University is the only one that has yet awarded a Ph.D. in which the major emphasis was on creative art; two such degrees have been given. The University of Iowa has laid out the curriculum for such a degree, but so far has awarded none and is skeptical of using it except in the rare case when an isolated mind fails to follow the norm and shows strange powers of creativity in both scholarship and art production. Such white blackbirds are rarely met.

Fortunately no university has yet proposed to give a Ph.D. degree for high achievement in studio work alone or for work two-thirds of which, for example, is in the studio. If one is to give a doctor's degree for such a course it might as well be an M.D. as a Ph.D. This is not because artists by and large are not as worthy as scholars, but it is a matter of calling a spade a spade.

The requirements for the degree at Ohio State and Iowa are similar. At the University of Iowa the candidate must show a comprehensive knowledge of the history of art (equivalent at least to an undergraduate major and an M.A. degree in this subject), a reasonable understanding of such correlative intellectual pursuits as philosophy and history, languages and literature, experience in the scientific method in the history of art as evidenced in independent research, a knowledge of French and German, a professional competence in painting or in sculpture, and superior ability in the use of a variety of media. There are written and oral examinations, but the thesis may be a creative art project. At Iowa, before presenting himself for final examination, as evidence that he has reached a professional level of technical and expressive power, the candidate must certify that he has had his work accepted by the juries of at least four approved exhibitions of national scope. This is a stiff set of qualifications, and cannot be met by second-rate students who need a degree to get a promotion. The intellectual character of the Ph.D. is retained, but encyclopedic erudition is sacrificed to technical instruction. The art thus produced may be charged with being too intellectual, but it would not have to be if the student were well balanced intellectually and emotionally. At present, it remains to be seen whether such a degree is worth while, even for a chosen few, and whether it will be imitated or neglected.

VIII. Summary

The past decade has seen an increase in enrollments, in courses taught, in number of schools engaged in art instruction, in quality of teachers, and in quality of art produced. But art has not yet found its place in higher education or recognized many of the conditions that predispose toward healthy growth. The terminology of courses is hopelessly confused, and art is kept in bondage to serve most varied departments. Or when art is taught in art departments, sometimes but one aspect of the subject is promoted, and the curriculum is limited to a standardized progression to a single degree. Many colleges do not yet offer a major curriculum, some spend more time in integrating than in teaching fundamental principles, and others forget that art is alive. The next ten years must witness the consolidation of objectives and procedure, which, to judge by current trends and social needs, involves a recognition of the parity of art and science in the university, and an acceptance of the obligation both to enlighten the public in esthetic values and intellectually to discipline and liberally to educate the artists of the future.

XV

ART EDUCATION IN THE UNIVERSITY [1]

ULRICH MIDDELDORF
Associate Professor of Art, and
Acting Chairman of the Department of Art, University of Chicago
Chicago, Illinois

What does an average university today do in regard to art education? First, it is charged with the education of scholars for various purposes, for pure research, for the administration of museums, for teaching in the same kind of institution from which they have emerged.

Second, there is the task of training creative artists in many fields, which may include all the different kinds of applied and commercial arts. This is a special and important problem to which I shall return again.

Third, as important as the preceding activities and closely connected with them, is the education of teachers of art for elementary and high schools. Before we can approach this problem with profit, we must turn to the main task that confronts us in every university and college, and in every other school where we can expect any interest in art at all.

The three tasks of the university in art education are very specialized ones. And they will appear limited, indeed, the moment we ask ourselves: Must we not do something for the student body in general, for the many boys and girls who are interested in art without having any ambition ever to specialize in it? We can help such a student to understand and appreciate the large artistic inheritance that has accumulated through the centuries and that is at everybody's disposal, provided he can make use of it. But he will be able to make use of it only after he has learned how to do it. Understanding and intelligent appreciation of art is a thing that must be learned. Furthermore, we

---

[1] Presented as a lecture at the Annual University of Iowa Art Conference, April 21 and 22, 1939. I am grateful to the organizers of this conference, and especially to Dr. Lester Longman, for their kind permission to publish this lecture. — *U. M.*

The editor regrets that limitations of space have compelled abridgement of Professor Middeldorf's excellent article. — *G. M. W.*

can make our pupils aware of what is happening around them; we can help them to the understanding of the art of today. That also needs a good deal of intelligent preparation, a thorough development of the critical judgment, if the individual wants to find his way through the complicated and endless controversies that inevitably accompany even the most modest and moderate exhibition of contemporary art. But we can give to the student even something much more practical; we can develop his taste by making him acquainted with the basic principles of art as expressed in the works of the masters, ancient and modern. And thus we can help him to make an intelligent choice of the things offered him in our vast market of arts, crafts, and entertainment. We can thus enable him to shape his surroundings and his life into a certain dignity and beauty.

Turning now from generalities to more concrete considerations, let us first look at our undergraduate students with reference especially to the reasons that lead them into the art classes. Among these students I think we can definitely distinguish two different types. There is first, of course, the boy or girl who has some talent and who dreams about becoming an artist. Then there is also the student whose interest in art is stimulated by a casual acquaintance with it at home or elsewhere or who has discovered through his study of music, literature, and philosophy that art is an integral part of culture. Some of this second group of students go into scholarly work; the majority of them, however, will form the main bulk of the group of students to which I have alluded.

How many of the high-school students and the undergraduates who attend our art classes do eventually become serious professional artists or craftsmen? Very few, perhaps not many more than go into pure scholarly work. Now this rather limited group, in view of its gifts and ambitions, needs a very good training; as a matter of fact, the best training in the practice of art we can afford. These students belong in a specialized school, in a real art school that can develop its own high standards, unhampered by considerations of the general education of large masses. Such a school need not necessarily be part of a university, but may be one of the famous old independent professional schools.

I think it is clear that the future scholars and artists form a very small minority compared to the students who seek education in art without having the ambition to become either scholars or artists. I am convinced even that general interest in arts would be still more impressive if students were not so easily scared away from our art departments by the notion that we want to make them into either art historians or artists. How many students hesitate to take work in an art department because they know they lack creative talent? But these are just the ones to whom we really could and should give — perhaps even as a compensation for this lack — a knowledge and an understanding of art.

The problems we discuss here are by no means confined to the universities. What we think right to be taught in a university should also be right for a high school, in a more elementary form. In other words, whatever we decide to do in the universities will be of the greatest importance for the high schools; or, what we do in the universities ought to be to a certain extent determined by what is needed in these other institutions — an obvious thing, if we consider that among our own students there is a not inconsiderable number who eventually want to become high-school or college teachers. Now these future teachers form a group of students of which we want to take especially good care. After all, the high-school student is the prospective university student. Art education in a high school and in a university may, accordingly, vary in thoroughness, but in no basic difference, since in both kinds of institutions the student body has a similar constitution. Consequently, what is valid for the university teacher is valid perhaps in an even higher degree for the high-school or college teacher.

What can we now do in this situation? Doubtlessly we shall always find a number of students, who, though not seriously interested in the practice of art, would like to make it their hobby. These students ought to be encouraged and every guidance should be given to them to make them into pleasant dilettanti. In my opinion almost any university will therefore offer some instruction, with studios and other technical facilities, in the practice of art. But one ought to draw a sharp line between such students and the professionals. The studio activity of the former can be considered scarcely more than any other extra-curricular activity that helps the student to enjoy life. We should not give too much credit for such courses. How can we give to the students that education in taste, in the knowledge of art, in the understanding of the principles of art, that I described before? At the University of Chicago we try to do that by means of courses in the history of art. We do not understand history of art as a simple accumulation of facts, of boring dates, statements of influences, or of developments, and the like; rather we stress the real understanding of all this factual material. By a special method of analysis and comparison, we try to grasp in a work of art the general principles underlying the different manifestations of the arts. We welcome everybody in our classes, since we are convinced that almost everybody can find an approach to art by our method. We are convinced that we can increase the enjoyment of art and improve taste, and we are convinced that here lies one of the great values in the history of art.

We do not, however, neglect another approach to the appreciation of art. Fully convinced that technique plays an important part in all the arts, we expect our students to get acquainted in our studios with the principles of the various techniques; that is, with those of the ancient masters. So we have another field for our teachers in practice, and I must say that our practical teachers at the University of Chicago conceive their task in just this sense and carry it out very successfully. But we certainly do not want to overestimate the importance of these technical exercises. Technical ability is essential for the creation of a work of art, but is it not subservient to something much more important, the spirit that inspires the artist?

There is another thing that should be mentioned. I said before that too much stress on practical work may scare away a student. But it would also be disastrous if, in our practical work, we allowed the level of our teaching in the practice of art to be lowered by bothering too much about hopeless cases. There are definite limits to an education in creative production, much narrower limits than there are for an education in the understanding of art. There is more harm done in flooding the country with persons who have a wrong estimate of their own creative abilities than with persons to whom the occupation of art means a more or less successful intellectual pursuit. In short, I dread nothing more than the all too visible achievements of a want-to-be artist of bad taste and inferior gifts. And I am afraid of nothing more than that such 'half-baked' aspirants should be let loose on the children in our schools. And to say it again, I am convinced that we can help almost everybody in the intellectual, reasoning appreciation of art, that we can instill into everybody at least some of the principles of good taste.

In the high school the problem of practical instruction in art has to be reconsidered, in my opinion. From studies in educational psychology we know that the happy age in which every child can express his personality like a real artist comes to a very early end, almost at the point when the child leaves the kindergarten. After that, we encounter the division into the two unequal groups that has featured the preceding discussion. We ought to consider that fact more than we do in planning the program of art education in the high schools.

The problem of introducing the freshman and sophomore to the study of art has, I think, been successfully tackled in our university in the large humanities survey courses. There the fine arts are dealt with on the same basis as are literature, music, or philosophy; they are included in a brief outline of the history of human thought. In this way the student is also made acquainted with the philosophical foundations of the critical judgment.

As for collegiate degrees for the art student, I have certain opinions.

Today, when the A.B. is losing more and more of its importance in daily life, we ought to insist on its being as little as possible a degree for a specialized vocational education.

With the second step, the master's degree, we come to the difficult problem of how to express in it these different forms that art education has to take in a university. Our solution is to use the master of arts as the other departments use it; that is, grant it to those of our students who approach the field from the intellectual and scholarly angle. For the students who want to fulfill their requirements for the State Teacher's Certificate and who want to take a corresponding program of practical and historical courses, we could award a " Master of Art Education " or, as we in Chicago have just formulated it a bit lamely, a " Master of Arts in Art Education." For achievements in practice, the University of Iowa awards the " Master of Fine Arts," which I think underlines very well the differentiation I have in mind as the ideal.

There remains the doctor's degree. In the Humanities it has the same general character as the M.A., only on a higher and more exacting level. I do not see that we need to modify the original meaning of this degree. We had better continue to apply this degree to those who find their vocation in critical studies and research. The creative artist has no need to be decorated with a degree, which fits his build so little. I think we acknowledge the unique individual character of the artist's personality much more if we do not try to measure him with such a yardstick, which somehow puts the mark of the academician on him. The artist will grow to fame by his achievements. If for some reason not inherent in his art he needs one of the purely academic degrees, let him take some academic work to deserve it. As I see the future of art education in this country, such a procedure in regard to the degrees would be highly justified.

XVI
ARTISTS IN RESIDENCE IN COLLEGES

Leon L. Winslow

It is now five years since the Mexican painter Orozco delivered at Dartmouth College his series of ' lectures ' in the form of the paintings that may be seen on the walls of the reading room in the Library. Orozco, while at work there, aroused great interest among the undergraduates and that interest is still strong. In 1934, the University of Iowa engaged as its resident artist the American painter, Grant Wood, with the title of Associate Professor in the Department of Graphic and Plastic Arts. Another distinguished American painter, John Steuart Curry, is Artist in Residence at the College of Agriculture of the University of Wisconsin, and Thomas Laman is working at Wesleyan University, Middletown, Connecticut.

In the smaller colleges the plan is new.[1] Few, indeed, among them have yet taken up with the idea, presumably either because the function of the resident artist has not been clear or for fear that the limitations of the budget might forbid.

The Concert Project has been instrumental in arranging an experiment of this kind at Olivet College, Michigan. Here George Rickey is installed for the season. A similar project has more recently been begun at Hendrix College, Conway, Arkansas. The artist there is Louis Freund.

The experiment consists in this: The college engages the artist to live in residence and, while there, to undertake any piece of work that will be appropriate to its history, its traditions, and surroundings. The artist, asked only to keep his doors open to all who may be interested, lays out a mural decoration or some other painting that admits of collaboration. He sets before the students the problems involved, he opens their eyes to the research that will be needed, asks them to contribute sketches and ideas and, when the plans are ready, invites them to join in the execution.

---

[1] "Visits by Faculty Artists and Peripatetic Professors." (American Association of Colleges, 19 West 44th St., New York, 1939–40.)

Theoretically, the artist does no teaching; that is, he is supposed to carry forward his creation without being involved in the conduct of formal courses. Actually, by making colleagues of those whose keenness he has whetted, the artist is doing teaching of the finest kind — he is applying in a modern form and for a limited time the ancient principle of apprenticeship. He communicates his subject to others through his sincerity in working.

Apparently there is no lack of able artists, congenial and temperamentally suited to campus life, who would welcome free residence on a Board Fellowship if assured a certain amount of cash (from $750 to $2000, according to their circumstances and family needs) at the end of the academic year. To the conscientious artist, a college roof overhead and a place to work are more than a haven; his activity there gives him the spirit of the craftsman executing a commission, doing something wanted.

The college that engages an artist in residence stands to gain far more than the visible result of his efforts. In general, the college is making of itself in this twentieth century what the patron was in the eighteenth, what the Monastery was in the Middle Ages — the center of artistic activity for miles around. Much has been said and written of the opportunities that every college has for leadership in its community. The artist in residence is a natural focus for artistic thought and activity on the campus and in the surrounding country, and so the college finds this leadership thrust upon it.

In particular, the resident artist is a valuable addition to the faculty because he exemplifies creation — one important aspect of the arts that is generally neglected in colleges. His very presence helps to clarify a long sequence of questions that the conventional instruction in art provokes and leaves unanswered.

Where college art consists only in courses about it, its history, and how it should be estimated and esteemed, can much remain long in the mind? Does not most of it soon wash away leaving only a sediment of the lingo? Indeed, could any attempt at a short cut to artistic understanding through a vicarious experience result in anything more than admitting people to a cult? Is not the actual experience at firsthand necessary in order that the student may grasp the problems the artist faced and overcame? Should not this experience come first? Science, which deals in determinable facts, needs the laboratory where those facts may be verified. But in art, where facts about it are secondary and feeling is all-important, is it not more likely that the activity itself is the subject, and the talk the laboratory? In short, is any student really ready to be told about art until he has not merely received some practical instruction, but has also actually tried something himself?

The creative artist meets with many students besides those who are enrolled in art courses and gives them the opportunity for firsthand contact with his undertaking by inviting them to join in it. As this work proceeds simultaneously with the established classes, it cannot fail to show that real art is something even greater than appreciation, history, and practical instruction — it is a contagion. It is a contagion that may affect mentally and physically, not alone the students of art, but also those many more who, nowadays, are too often left in outer darkness, blind even to the pictures that the college hangs upon its walls.

At Olivet College it has been clear almost from the beginning that, if the experiment of letting students learn art by collaborating with the artist is to succeed, it must bring about a profound change in the regular courses in fine arts. President Brewer, when introducing George Rickey, pointed out that " the teaching of art appreciation is, in most instances, an agglomeration of parts of courses in other subjects, such as archaeology, esthetics, sociology, and even optics. This deadly situation undoubtedly came about through the pious effort to make of art a respectable academic subject. Possibly the time has come to render back to those disciplines the life-giving elements of which they have been bereft. Then perhaps we shall be free to look at art and to see it."

XVII

CONTINUITY OF PROGRESSION IN ART EDUCATION

HELEN McIVER HOWELL
Instructor in Art, Hollywood High School
Los Angeles, California

In attacking the problem of bridging gaps, eliminating inconsistencies, and developing a desirable continuity of art education between the various school units — elementary, junior high, senior high, college, and university — two important premises must be taken into consideration. First, in today's art education the unfolding of the individual pupil's esthetic nature — his love of beauty and his understanding of the meaning of beauty as it functions in all of living — is the basic objective, rather than his achievement in paint or clay. Second, all decisions as to standards, requirements, sequences of studies, or even specific objectives for any pupil group must be kept in a state of continuous development and change, responding sensitively to the changing needs of pupils and the communities of which they are a part. Consequently, the problem cannot be met by compiling lists of fixed standards in terms of skills and techniques for certain age-grade levels. The following instance will serve to illustrate what we have in mind.

In a junior-high-school social studies class, near the end of the semester, the pupils developed an active interest in civic art in their own community and an eagerness to find out more about the design of the modern buildings, bridges, and lampposts about them, the layout for the new civic center, the need for regulation of billboards, and the improvement of ugly shopping districts. When these pupils entered the art appreciation course required in the senior high school the following semester, their teacher struggled in vain to arouse them to an active interest in masterpieces of painting. To be sure, modern architecture was a unit in this teacher's course of study, but it came later on in the semester after many of the pupils had definitely concluded that all art study was a bore.

Too numerous to mention are such easily avoidable misunderstandings and mistakes, wherein is evident failure of some lower unit to prepare adequately for art work to follow or a feeling of pupils that they are wasting time in needless repetitions.

The best means of avoiding these mistakes is obviously the frequent conferring in each school neighborhood of the teachers of units in adjacent school levels. Junior-high-school art teachers need to be familiar with the entire elementary-school program, not alone with its art offerings. Junior-high-school teachers of social science and of many other fields need to see what the elementary school is doing in making art function throughout its activities; senior-high-school teachers need similarly to know the ideals and activities of the junior high schools.

Providing for such coördination of the various school units, of course, is an essential part of the supervisor's function. With his view of the entire picture, from the nursery school through the college, the supervisor is in a position to help teachers to a wider perspective of understanding as well as to arrange the practical matter of local teacher conferences. Without such help, however, initiative in calling groups together may be taken by principals, district superintendents, or probably best of all by the teachers, themselves. Such conferences should not be held with the idea that the higher school unit wishes to dictate standards to the lower one. On the other hand, the teachers of the upper unit might well go to those of the lower one, sincerely asking for their assistance in explaining the needs, capacities, and backgrounds of their pupils, the good things started, and the interests awaiting further guidance.

Through such conferences, many valuable teacher and pupil helps may be worked out. Committees of teachers may work upon specific objectives and compile lists of community art needs, interests, and resources. They may make plans for the best form of cumulative pupil record cards. They may prepare joint exhibits or exchange exhibits of pupils' work, arrange for intervisitation of pupils and teachers, and plan for teacher and pupil speakers from the higher unit to enlarge upon the usual work of the school counselors. Some of the meetings might be devoted to exchanging ideas on making art a functioning part of experiences in many areas of study. In that event teachers from all departments should be urged to attend.

There are several large responsibilities resting upon every teacher in doing his part to prevent gaps and deficiencies, inconsistencies, and wasteful overlappings. These responsibilities should be discussed in group conferences, but each teacher should assume them individually as well. He should examine his concept of the principles of general education and of art as a part of all education and all of life. In this way, upon each level of development each pupil will be receiving preparation for various kinds of subsequent art experiences, individual needs will not be neglected, and art will be an active part of the pupil's whole life.

The teacher must also assume the responsibility of making clear to his pupils the meaning of the laws of composition as they function in his experiences in appreciation and his uses of appreciation in practical activities of life, as well as in his creative expression in clay or paint.

Probably most important of all is the teacher's responsibility for guiding his pupils to an intelligent concept of the purpose and meaning of his own esthetic growth. The pupil who has been led to look upon his education in art as a gradual unfolding of his creative powers and of his capacities to understand and use beauty will not toss his head with a superior air, saying, " Oh, I've had that," when an activity appears similar to one in which he has engaged before. Instead, he will feel that he never is standing still but always going forward.

He will see with increasing clarity that art is an indispensable means to rich personal development and valuable social adjustment.

Art record cards may be of great value in meeting the needs of individuals. A brief statement of a pupil's principal art interests, special abilities, and kinds of work done in an earlier school unit can be exceedingly helpful to the teacher of the following unit. Such comments might be added on general record cards when it is not possible to have cards for art alone. This sort of aid is very useful when pupils transfer from one school district to another.

In the junior high school, the problem of sequence generally is solved satisfactorily by placing in the first year a course required for all students. This course serves also as a prerequisite to elective courses.

In the senior high school, a year of basic work often is required before art students may enter most of the specialized elective fields. Here, rules must be sufficiently flexible and subject matter sufficiently adaptable to meet the needs of the individuals, particularly those of the student who is not majoring in art. In one senior high school, a number of students who are eager to do craftwork and who need the educational benefits it brings them are unwilling or unable to take the time for a prerequisite course. This school solves the problem by waiving the prerequisite but devoting the first part of the semester to an intensive study of design. The good design quality of the craftwork done in these classes is proof of the success of this method of teaching.

In one large university, all art major students are required to take a number of foundation art courses, after which each may select from one of several groups of art specialization. Within each group there are further requirements and a number of electives. Free electives for all groups also are available. Much individual guidance and frequent group conferences on the part of members of the art faculty help to make this plan serve the students' needs. Graduates from such a department are outstanding for their sound understanding of basic art matters, their ready adaptability to changing art needs in the world about them, and their well-developed creative power as individuals.

An art major curriculum in the secondary school, university, or professional school depends for its strength very largely upon its carefully organized sequence of courses leading to advanced work. The presence of outstanding teachers in advanced specialized fields in university or professional school, for example, cannot make up for the deficiency in an art department in which strong basic courses in art structure and in needed techniques are lacking.

XVIII
TEACHING ART IN RURAL SCHOOLS

FLORENCE TILTON AHLFELD
Art Supervisor of Rural Schools
Sussex County, Delaware

The nation has been aroused in recent years to the ever-increasing difficulties of the farm and village family in securing sufficient income to purchase the products of our industries. There is one phase of this problem to which all too little thought has been given; that is, the ability of our rural population with its limited purchasing power to choose wisely manufactured articles. This problem of consumer choices must be governed by quality in manufactured articles and the consumer's ability to recognize quality in design, material, and construction. This has been an almost totally neglected field in rural education.

I. OBJECTIVES THAT APPLY TO THE RURAL SITUATION

'Art appreciation' sounds to many a rural taxpayer like something quite apart from the necessities of life that he works so hard to obtain. If our public schools will approach this problem of raising appreciative ability from the consumer's point of view, our thoughtful farmers will realize its importance in our school system. School patrons must first of all be shown that art instruction will yield for their children an enriched living. It is of the utmost importance that all art teaching should keep in mind the following objective: " to develop in the individual the ability to meet intelligently art problems which confront him in daily living." [1] This general objective has three major phases of importance: (*a*) to assist children to develop ability to create artis-

---

[1] *South Dakota State Curriculum for Elementary Schools*, p. 1350. (Lena Wetner, Art Chairman, directed by Grace Baker, Colorado State College of Education, Greeley, Colorado.)

tic environments for themselves, (b) to make art vital to them through contacts with beauty in nature, industrial products, and in the fine arts, and (c) to assist children in the development of imagination through free expression with art media.

If art education fulfills these objectives, the problems arising from the unfamiliarity of the population with works of art, the persistence of puritanical beliefs that still hamper artistic development in isolated districts, and remoteness from art centers can gradually be solved. The farmer is close to nature; he is often a deep thinker on problems of elementary importance. The art teaching must not be a rehash of curricula and methods found in cities, or formal, dictated lessons and silly 'busy work'; it must rather appeal to the country dweller's love of nature, his ability to use his hands, and his craving for beauty.

This instruction can be related to the home interests, and, in the schoolroom, to other curricular fields that may be greatly enriched by art. In addition, opportunities for individual expression and the development of individual tastes must be found in the school and in the rural community. The tying of art instruction closely to the community life, as by making home and school grounds attractive, by making suggestions for redecorating churches, community centers, homes, and schoolrooms, helps to solve some of the most vital psychological problems in art teaching. The small school can capitalize on these opportunities much better than can larger schools where administrative problems complicate art instruction.

Among the psychological problems that art instruction faces is this one: Can all persons draw? Art instruction that meets the objectives cited is not greatly dependent upon the ability to draw. Development of skills is not of major importance except to that rare individual who will one day earn his living through some phase of artistic endeavor.

II. The Selection and Training of Rural Teachers

One of the greatest problems faced by rural art education is that of inadequate art ability on the part of teachers. Even the so-called 'art specialist' teaching in rural America is in all too few instances a creative artist. It is the conviction of many persons who have had experience in training art teachers that no person should hold a specialized art position who cannot do really creative work in some phase of art.

The elementary teacher needs to have good art instruction in at least one course in her training period. Teachers' colleges must see to it that no teachers are certificated to teach in the elementary school who cannot teach art as well as they teach such subjects as arithmetic and reading.

How can rural schools secure better teachers for their art work? The answers are numerous. Many interesting experiments are being made in widely separated parts of America. In many consolidated and township schools administrators do not feel that art work is sufficiently important to employ a full-time specialist. They try to solve the problem by a combination of two specialties, as art and music. Art is often taught by a high-school teacher who also teaches mathematics, English, or home economics. In rare instances we find an elementary teacher who is employed to spend a portion of her time teaching art in other elementary grades. Most of these combinations are quite unsatisfactory. The music-art combination often results in stilted, uncreative teaching in one or the other of the specialties, because the two talents are not often found to a marked degree in one person.

The combination of high-school subjects and art is likely to be poor because teachers' colleges train teachers for either secondary or elementary work. This type of individual may be a good high-school teacher but be quite at sea with the problems of elementary-school art supervision.

For teaching art in elementary schools, the combination of art with elementary subjects is usually a far happier solution, because the person who elects such a position is frequently an adequately prepared elementary teacher who enjoys creating with art media.

In Delaware, and in other parts of the United States as widely separated as Minnesota and California, successful work is being done by special art teachers teaching in two or more schools. Each consolidated school gets the benefit of the services of an individual who is an artist, adequately trained in educational theory to meet the problems of art education and the problems of assisting elementary teachers who do the major portion of the actual teaching. In Pennsylvania and Delaware, the work of these special teachers, teaching in a group of schools, is carefully supervised by a state supervisor who plans curricula, materials, and equipment for all the consolidated schools of the state. In other sections, such as California, a county supervisor directs the work of special teachers who teach in two or more township schools. In still other instances there is no state or county supervision, but special teachers with adequate preparation plan and direct instruction in a group of schools.

Whatever the individual administrative plan may be, these special teachers in remote districts are badly in need of supplementary help in their work. All too often the contributions of leaders in art and art education are locked in remote libraries. The present county library program may assist by providing essential references. Teachers need illustrative materials and definite help on curricula and methods of instruction. Art teachers in rural schools cannot take their children to an art museum, as can the art teachers of Chicago, Cleveland, or St. Louis. Some plan must be worked out to bring pictures to them.

III. Special Problems of the One-Room Rural School

The hardest situation facing leaders in art education is the one-room rural school, which still exists, and will of necessity continue to exist, in many sections of the United States. There one teacher is expected to teach all the elementary subjects including the special subjects.

This problem was studied by the author in Hennepin County, Minnesota, which presents a typical situation.[1] Forty schools in the county were visited. The number of children taught varied from seven to thirty-eight. Ninety percent of the teachers had attended rural or small village schools in their childhood. In none of these had there been a special art teacher or supervisor. Not a single one of the teachers had had any art instruction at the high-school level. Only 57.5 percent had had even one course in a normal school or teachers' college. Four percent had had more than one course. Fifty-seven percent of the teachers confessed that they used patterns for their work. Only one teacher had any definite art helps available. The sources of inspiration for their work were almost entirely lacking in a creative viewpoint. None of the teachers had any large newsprint or Manila paper. In only one or two instances were the teachers using any materials except colored wax crayons and 9 x 12 Manila paper. There was a total lack of interesting, large, colored reproductions of really fine paintings. There was little evidence of any appreciation of the basic art principles or of their application to daily living in the classroom.

This sort of situation can be remedied and is being remedied in many places. County art supervision in Pennsylvania, Ohio, Delaware, Missouri, California, and in some sections of other states gives the teacher assistance.

---

[1] Florence Tilton. *A Field Study of Art Teaching in One-Room Rural Schools of Hennepin County, Minnesota*, 1936. (An unpublished study carried on under the direction of Dr. Leo Brueckner and Dr. Wesley Peik, of the University of Minnesota.)

I never think of one-room rural schools without hearing in my imagination the rhythmic singing of colored children as they played on the school grounds of the colored schools of Sussex County, Delaware. I hear that singing because it is so closely allied in my memory to the lovely, free, colorful, rhythmic patterns they produced in chalk, paint, and crayon during the delightful art periods that I had the privilege of guiding. In my memory linger the eager questions of white and colored teachers of one-room schools. They were hungering and thirsting after help in art work. They wanted illustrative material, help in their social studies activities, knowledge of how to guide children in their illustration work. They wanted to know how to letter; they were grateful for the alphabets I drew on blackboards for the technical art lessons I gave those children. Art teachers! if you want a thrill, go to work as a county art supervisor.

There are under way other movements to assist these one-room teachers. Notable among these is the Rural Traveling Art Exhibit, started by Mrs. Nellie Schlee Vance, of Nebraska, and made possible through the generosity of the Carnegie Corporation. Every state and every county in every state should have the benefit of such a traveling exhibit.

Again, there are in many communities persons well fitted to assist in the teaching of some craft. Thus, in North Dakota are Norwegian grandmothers who learned to weave in faraway Norway. In Indiana are home pottery workers. In any rural area there are likely to be persons who have had technical training. If school administrators would seek out such persons, many of them would be glad to assist the rural teacher.

Occasionally one finds a teacher who, with little or no background of art training, has caught the vision of expressional opportunity.

I am thinking now of a lovely little white schoolhouse set on a hill surrounded by a wood in Hennepin County, Minnesota. The instant I entered that doorway I knew I had entered a school where art was a part of daily living. The formal set arrangement of desks so common in one-room schools was banished. Instead, desks were grouped. All along one wall was a large frieze with figures painted in what was very evidently child work. The color scheme was restful; the teacher was dressed in good taste; well-arranged books added color to the room; there was an air of happy comradeship as the children made covers for a history booklet. The teacher began plying me with art questions. She was concerned about how appreciation was to be developed without pictures. She expressed the opinion I had long held that arranging a display of child work was something children should do themselves because they could learn thus how to balance sizes and shapes of paper in a given space.

She was aware of the opportunities for teaching color in their daily life. When questioned about how she organized her work, she said she taught one subject such as lettering to the entire group, but varied the work, giving simple applications to the small children, more difficult ones to the fourth, fifth, and sixth grades, and the most difficult applications to the seventh- and eighth-grade children.

In this school art is an integral part of living. Children are taught to be conscious of beauty in all things. They endeavor to make their environments beautiful. They accept appraisals of school work for its artistic merit as naturally as they accept appraisals of speech. They believe that all things, to be effective, must be beautiful. They learn how to create beauty through daily choices in dress, the arrangement of their books and playthings. They enjoy color, simplicity of line, dark and light pattern and forms of many kinds through association with beauty. These they find in nature, in pictures, in sculpture, in architecture, and in manufactured articles. They experiment with modelling in clay, in wood, and in plaster. They weave simple patterns on looms they themselves have made. They express their imaginative ideas both as individuals and as groups. Through working together to accomplish common objectives of beauty for their school, they learn how to subordinate selfish desires to group objectives. They are developing hobbies and interests. When a study is made of a foreign country, they learn what types of costumes are worn, what are the typical color arrangements, how the forms of artistic expression of a people are influenced by their geographical background, the facts of their history, their emotional characteristics, and their economic status. In all social studies the contributions of art are studied. The teacher thinks of art as one of the areas of learning, developed through four approaches; namely, the appreciative, the creative, the informational, and the technical. There is a well-adjusted balance between work designed to foster self-expression and opportunities to make art choices. All work is child-originated. There is no dictation, no tracing, very little copy work; but much imagination, much work for the development of mental images. The power to do things skillfully is kept growing throughout the school period. The children are taught those knowledges and abilities judged by experts to be most socially useful. This teaching is by the rural teacher, not by a special art teacher.

The successful teacher of art in rural schools exemplifies good taste in her personality and in her clothing. She considers the school environment in her personal choices. She plans her art work as carefully as she plans the reading instruction. She knows what work is generally accepted for inclusion in the art program and how it should be placed according to abilities. She organizes her school into different groups, not necessarily following the eight-grade plan. The primary grades form one group, the intermediate grades, a second; the seventh and eighth, a third. In order to assist her school with technical difficulties, she presents art lessons occasionally when the subject for the three groups is similar, but the accomplishment planned is suited to the ability of each group. She gives specific help in drawing people, nature forms, trees, lettering, and animals. She provides for a definite increase in ability to design, to use color harmoniously, and to construct. Children initiate ideas in individual expression and in group projects. The methods employed for accomplishing results in art are similar to those employed in teaching other school subjects.

The care of the school grounds and the arrangement of the schoolroom is made a pupil project for the entire school. Each age level has some part in this plan. Through discussions of how to arrange the furniture with the lines of the room, how to create a balance with the objects, principles of design are learned. The planting of a flower bed is a color problem. The problem of how best to make the windows attractive eliminates cluttered, fussy decorations. Grouping of clippings, prints, and the like, on well-placed bulletin boards is one of the ways of developing a knowledge of simplified arrangement of lines, areas, and colors. Children mount their own school work; by so doing they struggle with the principles of design: dominance, proportion, rhythm, and balance. They discover that colors show best against neutral backgrounds, that titles printed below may detract from the object displayed if not kept simple and orderly.

One or two pictures are displayed. These are chosen for beauty in color, interest to the group, and artistic merit, regardless of period in painting or patriotic motivation. The frame does not detract from the interest of the picture. It is carefully hung with wires corresponding to the lines of the room and at a height suited to children. This picture may be one of a group owned and exchanged by a group of districts. Children thus have an opportunity to enjoy for a month one really fine reproduction of a picture of artistic quality, even though the funds available to a given district are limited. The hanging of the picture is a group interest participated in by all of the school. The children will not be expected to know many facts of the artist's life.

Exhibits consist of several types: (*a*) the exhibition of school work for the benefit of parents and friends, (*b*) exhibits of objects of beauty, such as Swedish weaving, Mexican pottery, from the homes of the pupils, and (*c*) when the interest in a particular phase, such as pottery, has been prevalent, the display either of pieces of pottery loaned to the school by manufacturers or of pictures borrowed from libraries and museums. Exhibits should be supplemented by excursions to see things of beauty in the community, such as an especially beautiful doorway, and by discussions of objects of beauty seen by individual children in their travels.

The constructive work has two objectives: first, to assist the child toward a normal physical and muscular development; second, to assist the child toward an understanding of the problems of construction in an age when most production is outside the home. This involves (a) simplified constructive processes which have been expanded and multiplied by the invention of machinery, and (b) thinking in terms of design and color relationships. In accomplishing these objectives, the children will make such things as booklets, Japanese-bound books, simple case-bound books, rugs, pocketbooks, and the like. The equipment for bookbinding and weaving is made by the children. They model out of clay jolly imaginative figures; they make bowls, learning the process used even today by southwestern Indians. Their interest in a party provides the motivation for making a series of objects constructed from paper. They also make toy movies, puppet shows, games, and costumes for dramatizations. All these constructive activities originate with the specific situation in mind and are not the result of following descriptions of how to make things. Personal experimentation and originality of ideas are the educational objectives most stressed. Designing is thought of as planning from the beginning to the end, not as decoration applied to an object.

Illustrations, at all age levels, are characterized by self-expression. When successful, illustration presents an idea in a forceful way. It may be executed in any one of a number of graphic materials.

At this level, color is one of the most important phases of art teaching. The following phases of color are considered fundamental in the enrichment of the rural-school curriculum:

1. Enjoyment of color in nature, in clothing, in man-made surroundings, in manufactured articles of all kinds, and in works of art.

2. Understanding of (a) the three qualities — hue, value, intensity, and (b) color mixing and blending in light and in pigments.

3. Experimentation with color in dress suited to personal coloring and personal traits, in outdoor surroundings, in interior environments, as well as in drawing with such media as colored chalks, paints, and crayons.

4. The techniques and skills necessary for successful harmony of color in these experiments must have been mastered. These would include how to use fabrics, how to plant seeds for a flower garden, how to select objects of varying

materials and textures for given color effects in an interior, as well as how to use crayons, paints, and chalks.

Group projects will have originated through child experiences guided by the teacher. Each child taking part will share in the responsibility for well-arranged parts, for correctness of realistic representation, and for beauty of color. Every child will do original work throughout.

Lettering will be simple, direct, and freehand, made with the two objectives: (a) functional effectiveness, which includes ability to be read and to take its place as an element in the total plan of the project, and (b) the conscious striving for beauty of proportion and spacing. To accomplish these objectives, the teacher limits to one or two the number of kinds or forms of alphabets taught. She plans for each child to have had a variety of experiences with each of them. All charts, unless of a very technical nature, are pupil-made charts. Through making these, as through printing signs and invitations and making posters, the children secure practical experience in lettering.

Variety in kinds of materials used is the important characteristic of art work in the school at this level. Colored chalks, charcoal, opaque and transparent paints are better than wax crayons for little children. Pencils are used only by the most advanced of the upper-grade children and are not combined with other media. All expression is directly in the final medium. The children do large work on paper pasted over blackboards, on large drawing boards, on the floor, or on tables, whichever fits in best with the working conditions of the room. In this school there are one or two easels for the use of beginners for free expression.

Work is judged for merit as follows:

1. Originality of idea expressed.
2. Forcefulness of the expression.
3. Use made by the child of the opportunities he has had for acquiring knowledge, appreciations, and skill.
4. Functional effectiveness of the results. Has the child satisfied his own conception? Has he realized his objectives? Does it fulfill the purpose for which it was created?
5. Does the work indicate that there had been enjoyment in its development? Can we enjoy it?
6. Does it show organized thinking?

The following are *not* major considerations: (*a*) neatness, (*b*) pleasing results judged by adult standards, (*c*) skillful use of the tools and materials, and (*d*) does it look real?

The work found in any given school will include (*a*) some constructive processes and materials, such as wood, cloth, clay, and weaving materials, (*b*) some modelling materials to develop the feeling for three-dimensional form, and (*c*) some graphic materials, such as charcoal, opaque and transparent water paints, ink, pencil, and colored chalk.

The room has a wide space in some one place that can be used for group activity. There may be many pupils, but if there are, they are successfully grouped on at least three levels of ability for art work. The desks are movable, or at least adjustable. The aisles permit the use of drawing boards big enough to increase the size of the desk for effective art work. There is either a separate workroom or a storage cupboard that will permit the use of adequate materials.

XIX

AN EXPERIMENT IN THE DEVELOPMENT OF ART JUDGMENT

GORDON L. REYNOLDS
President, Massachusetts School of Art
Boston, Massachusetts

We must, in our educational processes, work for critical judgment, not as an enemy of creative production but as its friend and ally. We all have accepted that an originality of mental attitude is possessed by many human individuals; also, that education may either preserve and encourage this attitude or relegate it into obscurity. Those of us into whose hands educational responsibilities have been placed may well ask ourselves: Are we really aiding the development of minds that are genuinely productive? Are we successfully sponsoring minds that can efficiently engage in discrimination among values? Are the graduates of our educational institutions capable of disentangling the fine from the poor, the good from the bad in any field at any time? Ability of this type has been the basis for the growth of civilization. It has made possible advancement in all phases of life.

Recently at an experimental school there was introduced into the art curriculum of the fifth and sixth grades a series of discussion periods on the process of construction and criticism as related to functional art today and tomorrow. The staff was not satisfied with the elements of the existing curriculum. The creative work was not sufficiently analyzed by the children after completion, nor were the problems varied to the extent that any consideration was being given for art as it serves man today. Yet there were problems familiar to many, such as imaginative compositions, compositions growing out of the child's experiences, designs applied to three-dimensional creations, practical applications of lettering, and numerous color experimentations with their practical applications.

On the whole, the philosophy and thought behind the work was sound enough, in that expressions were growing out of life in the school, home, and community. But a very simple observation made one day in the sixth-grade classroom drove home the fact that the child, as a part of this vast social order, is continually encountering products of industry and industrial design. The observation took place during an art lesson, when the children were creating jungle scenes. Two adjacent boys lacked interest in this problem. The supervisor discovered that a popular scientific magazine revealing streamline forms by Norman Bel Geddes had attracted these boys from the realm of the imaginative back to science as it is serving in our present day and as it will serve tomorrow.

The first thought of the supervisor was that periods for evaluating many of the modern forms with which the pupils were familiar might be arranged; that is, that they might try to discover the element of creation on the part of the artist-engineer-designer. Some of his colleagues in other departments intimated that this would be impossibly difficult for sixth-grade boys and girls, that scientific analysis involving materials and functional qualities would not appeal to them. But this supervisor had noted that these children could think creatively in many forms of artistic expression. Why should one exclude the opportunity for sound judgment in the realm of modern functional art, an art that was serving these children materially every day?

The supervisor's only fear was that knowledge of terminology and of some of the advanced phases of science entering into the pattern of attack by our designers might present insurmountable difficulties. Before a month had passed, however, the children could converse intelligently on industrial design, functionalism, machine-shop practices, tools of execution, the ultimate consumer, alliance of artist and machine, and the sound use of streamline forms. Some of the children could explain the theory of aerodynamics with a vocabulary that would make most adults stand in wonderment. It was only possible in many of the cases to analyze the principles involved and call attention to the industrial requirements for their use. The first objects considered were simple in use and form, but gradually attention was turned to the field of transportation, lighting, radio, heating, electrical appliances, and even the classroom itself.

In all cases it was made certain that the creation under discussion was one that would be familiar to the child. In some cases research was necessary on the part both of the child and of the teacher. The instructor did not attempt to evaluate each piece personally but avoided superimposing his interpretation on the child. He did adjust his vocabulary to the children's age level and through skillful questioning led them to an understanding. New words and forms aroused interest and soon became a part of the everyday conversations of the children. Ability to analyze increased as the children moved from one problem to another. They introduced new problems for class discussion and decided in what order they would be attacked.

An impartial jury made the following observations after following this experimental addition to the curriculum. The child discovered:

1. That the artist of today can be something more than a painter or a sculptor.
2. That art qualities exist in many of the common, everyday products of the machine.
3. That a new type of beauty is the result of the wedding of mind and matter and is growing out of a new order of things — a new age.
4. That these many objects about us may be a type of living art.
5. That this new art is a useful one.
6. That adventure is possible in exploring the creative values of his day and age.
7. That the pupil had gained new understanding and ability in three-dimensional design.
8. That he looked with new eyes at the world about him.

We should realize that this experiment was not designed to produce or lay the foundation for producing expert designers. The objective was to aid the majority of these children to become, eventually, intelligent consumers — consumers who understand because they exercise critical judgment. Let us all aid in the manifestation of this creative mind.

It is not my intention to leave the reader with the impression that a cold, scientific approach to modern creations should be the one and only procedure used with the child. We must not forget that certain learnings are desirable and that emotional release serves the child as well as the man.

We profess consideration for individual differences, but are we really providing opportunity for individuality and sincerity in our art? In following courses of study the teacher many times establishes the media and subject matter instead of allowing the child to develop courage and independence by making his own choice. Satisfaction, pleasure, and a realization of growth should be included in our aims. All these elements can be strengthened by wholesome classroom discussion. This statement seems obvious, but many teachers have not discovered that learnings such as self-reliance, faith, and an inner harmony, learnings that the art product will never reveal, grow so readily under the interpretation of art experiences.

In the field of art education, as with most departures from old forms, the pendulum swung to the other extreme. Complete neglect for all technique and the encouragement of total freedom have been responsible for legitimate criticism on the part of educators. These extreme procedures have prevented in many cases the supporting of a progressive art program on the part of the conservative element in our profession. Complete neglect of intelligent analysis in art is a misconception of the aims of the new school.

As Munro has pointed out in *Art and Education* (44), " Reliance upon freedom and self-expression may be carried to excess. Artistic power is increased by intelligent analysis and reflection properly directed. Art and standards of testing should not be treated as matters of pure impulse and emotion, but discussed and analyzed to a considerable degree."

XX
ART APPRECIATION BY RADIO IN THE SCHOOLS

ALFRED HOWELL
Director of Art in the Cleveland Public Schools
and
ANN V. HORTON
In Charge of Museum Instruction, Cleveland Public Schools
Cleveland, Ohio

The general radio program of the Cleveland Public School System, including all major subjects, reaches age levels from the kindergarten through the high school, to faculty groups. In this comprehensive program art has been allotted a fair proportion of time, which is devoted entirely to appreciation, rather than to phases of creative work.

This art appreciation program, beginning in Grade VIb, has been built upon interests of age levels as nearly as such may be determined, through Grade XIIa. Grades VIb and VIa have fourteen radio lessons each semester; grades above this have four each semester. The general plan is indicated as follows:

Exposure to Many Types of Design

6B *Picture Study*. Masterpieces of painting and drawing.

6A *Beauty in Daily Surroundings*. Nature forms, toys, ceramics, textiles, and metal work.

Design in the Minor Arts

7B *Representation*. " Artist does trick with ruler "; " Artist goes to Zoo."

7A *European Influences*. " Let's go to the Land of the Middle Sun," and similar art journeys.

8B *Crafts*. Textiles, ceramics, cut paper.

8A *Application of Design*. Linoleum, stitchery, ceramics, metal.

9B *Elements of Composition*. Line, dark and light, color.

9A *An Artist at Work*.

Design in the Major Arts

10B *Everyday Art*. Modern homes, average interiors, industrial design.

10A *Cleveland's Debt to the Past*. Relation of historic architectural styles to present-day architecture.

11B *The Lens versus the Paint Brush*. (A comparison.)

11A *Ways of Representing.* Realistic, decorative, abstract, styles of painting.

12B *Graphic Arts.* Fine drawings, Japanese brush work, etching, wood blocks.

12A *Plastic Arts.* Everyday uses of sculpture, plastics, casting, monumental works.

For each semester's theme a manual of instruction suited to each age level has been prepared and sent in advance to teachers. This states the objectives of each lesson, the dates and hours of each broadcast, preparation preceding lesson, suggestions for follow-up and further use of the lantern slides that accompany each broadcast and remain for the entire semester at the school. Teachers are thus prepared to participate actively and to direct pupils' alert reception of lessons.

The fear that radio teaching may supplant the classroom teacher is no longer expressed. Such apprehension is particularly groundless in art radio lessons for several reasons. First, appreciation is only one phase of art teaching, and the periods allotted to its enrichment by radio are too brief and too infrequent to usurp the major duties of the art teacher. Second, good radio lessons are not monologs of the 'take-it-or-leave-it' type. Rather, by providing for the timely participation of the classroom teacher and pupils, the broadcaster makes classroom activity as essential as the voice on the air.

There is further evidence that radio lessons do not take the direction of art appreciation from the hands of the classroom teacher in the fact that every lesson is based on visual material, sets of lantern slides, which the teacher may use *ad infinitum,* while the radio uses them fifteen minutes only. The number of lantern slides chosen for a lesson varies from two to eight. Each school is supplied with an identical box of slides. Obviously, the brief statement made by the broadcaster cannot exhaust the inspiration to be derived from this carefully selected visual material that is placed at the service of the classroom teacher. These three points are emphasized by facts of procedure, which are in general as follows:

The broadcaster is usually the teacher who has written, tested, and revised the script of the lesson. At a scheduled time, this person presents the lesson at the microphone from the central radio station at the school headquarters. Through sound-proof walls of glass he can signal the operator for music or sound effects and can be directed for voice control by the technician. While the script is necessarily before him, the broadcaster, if an experienced radio teacher, 'just talks the lesson,' and perhaps extemporizes a bit to relieve all tension and make the teaching as natural as possible.

As the lesson proceeds and pictures appear on the screen, questions that raise discussion are interjected, as: " What particular mood did the artist try to express in this portrait? " (20 seconds allowed.)　" Your answer to the next question must be pointed out at the screen. ' Where did the artist show foreshortening? ' " The value of such class activity depends upon the alert direction by classroom teacher, even more than upon the voice on the air.

When junior-senior high schools tune in for their appointed schedule, the number of groups receiving varies from eighteen to thirty. In these groups, several classes may be combined. When an elementary radio lesson is scheduled, about one hundred schools receive the lesson. A natural classroom atmosphere is more easily maintained if the group is limited to one teacher's class.

Frequently the concluding words of the lesson suggest subsequent activities for pupils. Classroom bulletin boards and many subsequent drawings bear evidence that the radio exposures have been effective.

That a technique for radio teaching must be developed is obvious. Its demands are inherent in the nature of the plan. Its success requires that the classroom teacher make use of the manual provided and be alert to catch the objectives of the lesson. Of pupils it requires direct thinking and challenges them to clean-cut answers. It can be a definite aid to preventing inept and inaccurate habits of response. Of the radio teacher it requires hours of painstaking writing, trial, and re-writing, and such experience with the entire situation that he may, with conversational ease, keep word and tone vibrant with interest.

From the point of view of the learner, we have found the following definite outcomes:

1. Increased enthusiasm for works of art and nature, determined by close observation during broadcasts and subsequent material gathered by students.

2. Pride in being able to recognize works of art; ability to distinguish between works of different masters as to subjects and technique.

3. Increased interest in visiting the Art Museum, where many of the originals for slides shown in the broadcasts are to be seen.

4. Enrichment of vocabulary — a decided advantage in the pupil's confidence in self-expression.

From the point of view of the classroom teacher, there is evidence that the advantage of radio teaching outweighs its obligations. We have noted the following:

1. More teachers of secondary schools are availing themselves of material for follow-up activity, such material being supplied by the Public Schools Education Museum and from the lending collections of the Cleveland Museum of Art.

2. Coöperation with parents often releases exhibits characteristic of home-land tradition, so that social as well as artistic outcomes are secured.

3. Appreciation is expressed for the economy of effort whereby the results of research and the compiling of material by one teacher or group of teachers are made available to many teachers.

4. Certain intangible values in the general cultural enrichment and teaching techniques are traceable to the radio teaching.

5. Finally, with television just around the corner, the anticipation and readiness of teachers' responses should be taken for granted.

Generally speaking, then, the radio program has proved to be a real stimulus and is eagerly looked forward to by pupils and teachers alike. It is also responsible for the accumulation of a rich body of visual material that must inevitably serve as an inspiration for creative effort, thus developing an ideal of art appreciation based upon seeing and doing.

XXI
WAYS OF EVALUATING STUDENTS' ART WORK [1]

Edna Patzig
Associate Professor of Art, State University of Iowa
Iowa City, Iowa

I. Grades and Examinations

The complex nature of art ability makes the problem of evaluation by means of grades and examinations in art courses much more difficult than in most subjects. Competent art teachers who are aware of the relative abilities of their pupils frequently find that results in examinations do not show attainment equal to that shown in freer work done with a purpose.

Development in art does not depend solely on acquiring information and developing skills. There is involved an emotional factor that

---

[1] See also the following section (XXII) of this chapter, by Dean Vaughan. — *Editor.*

is responsible for expressiveness, including originality of thought, spontaneity, and interesting handling of media. The emotional drive stimulates thought, personal effort, integrity of expression, and self-criticism. As yet no tests have been devised that can measure this all-important factor, and there are grave doubts that there ever can be.

The acquisition of art knowledge and the development of skills are very necessary in art training, and growth in parts of these areas may be measured with a fair degree of accuracy. The understanding of art principles undoubtedly aids progress toward esthetic values in art expression. There are several standardized tests [1] that aid materially in showing students' ability to judge the application of these principles.[2] The fact remains that a product may embody all the accepted principles of good proportion, balance, rhythm, and emphasis and may be well executed technically, yet fall short of real art quality. In efforts to obtain measurement of progress, one must not lose sight of this immeasurable, but important, factor.

II. Practical Need of Some Evaluation

In spite of the difficulty, perhaps impossibility, of measuring art ability accurately, the practical need of some evaluation is apparent. The study of students' progress or lack of progress leads to a critical analysis of teaching methods and helps to determine whether or not courses are meeting their objectives. A check on work done shows the pupil his individual needs. A realization of accomplishment deepens interest and stimulates greater effort.

The very fact that schools are recognizing the importance of the emotional factor and are encouraging more pupil initiative and greater freedom of expression makes even more important a careful evaluation of students' work. There is danger of ' art for fun,' playing with materials, with insufficient study of goals and estimate of progress toward them. Types of evaluation that students can readily comprehend, combined with a clear notion of desirable outcomes, will promote self-discipline in a subject that might encourage indulgence in personal whims. Every endeavor needs to be made to encourage rigorous effort toward higher standards of attainment.

---

[1] Cf. discussion of art principles, tests, and evaluation in Chapters XXI and XXIII. — *T. M.*

[2] See N. C. Meier and C. E. Seashore (37), also Margaret McAdory (32).

III. Present Standards

Research has been done in an attempt to analyze the nature of art ability and to discover conditions that will encourage its development. The drawing scales,[1] tests in art judgment, and tests in fundamental abilities [2] are typical results of this research. A very good beginning has been made, but these tests are not yet sufficiently inclusive or dependable to be of material help to the teacher in making a fair rating of art ability, or as a basis for reorganization of courses of study.

Certain art educators [3] have adapted materials from these tests and enlarged or combined them in an effort to widen their scope, to relate them more nearly to their objectives, and to include more of pupil initiative. The ' work-sample ' type of test used at the Cleveland Museum of Art [4] recognizes the importance of the emotional factor in any evaluation and gives the child " a chance to construct a complete independent form of his own," in various tasks involving the abilities considered essential.

There are certain courses in which the measurable factors of knowledge and skills dominate. Color charts, definitions of art principles, standards of proportion, definite steps of drawing, and memory of facts in the history of art comprise the greater part of these courses. Judged by the results of objective tests and drawing scales, certain pupils ought to rate high, but actually fall far short in their grasp of the broad aims of art education.

Efforts to avoid the shortcomings of stereotyped courses and to place value on personality development rather than on objective results are shown in suggestions for a very different basis of evaluation. For example, a university bulletin [5] recommends a check list including (a) initiative, (b) concentration, interest, and motivation, (c) judgment, and (d) coöperation. An art course for elementary schools [6] suggests the importance of originality, sincerity, vigor of production, richness of content, and similar points in judging children's drawings.

A clear analysis of objectives to determine specifically what skills and esthetic values instruction should attempt to develop and what in-

---

[1] L. W. Kline and G. L. Carey (24). S. A. McCarty (33).

[2] A. S. Lewerenz (31) and A. J. Knauber (25).

[3] W. Nicholas, N. C. Mawhood, and M. B. Trilling (49) ; W. G. Whitford (77) ; and Leon L. Winslow (78).

[4] T. Munro (42, pp. 77–78).

[5] J. W. Grimes and E. Bordin (16).

[6] Los Angeles City School District, *Art, Elementary Schools,* 1929.

formation is needed will do much to determine the types of evaluation that may be profitably employed. Standards may be set up in those areas where students will unquestionably benefit by definite procedure and definite information. Having in mind the very important, less easily measured esthetic values, the informal subjective type of evaluation should also be employed.

The habit of appraising the results of each unit of work on the basis of the specific objectives may be of greater value than any elaborate system of tests with scoring. If students are allowed to compare their work with that of others in the group and to discuss their successes and failures, they will reveal their understanding, their growth in discriminating judgment, and their immediate accomplishment.

IV. ATTAINMENT AT VARIOUS LEVELS

With the present differences of opinion in art education and lack of convincing evidence to substantiate the superiority of one approach over another, it is impossible to say just what can, and should, be taught at different levels of age and instruction. To set up too rigid standards of attainment, in the light of our present knowledge, would very likely lead to stereotyped teaching.

Certain commonly held theories as to what should be done at various levels may be questioned. There is need for investigation and experimentation, followed by careful evaluation of results concerning the time when certain phases of art instruction may be introduced most advantageously. This evaluation should be based not only on immediate objective results, but also on pupil growth over a period of years.

The theory that art training through the first three grades of school should consist chiefly of providing materials and encouragement, and the frequently expressed opinion that children lose their interest and vitality of expression above the third grade are points that need thorough study. The reason generally given for loss of interest in the upper elementary grades is the growing self-consciousness of the child and his inability to perform to his own satisfaction. There is some evidence and strong reason to believe that if the child could, during the earlier years, acquire more skill, understanding, and knowledge along with his freedom of expression, he would gradually build up an ability in expression that would give him greater satisfaction a few years later when he is more logical and critical.

V. Cumulative Records

One of the best methods of evaluating students' art work, as has already been suggested in this Yearbook, is that of keeping cumulative records. Examples of pupils' work may be kept from week to week and from year to year. If, with this, can be kept careful case-histories, including interests, attitudes, and achievements, there will be a rich source for studying not only the relative ranking within a group, and the progress of the individual over a period of years, but also the degree of success in the teaching of the subject. Where progress ceases, it will be well to search for the cause.

Time and space may not permit this plan of cumulative records in public schools where the teachers have hundreds of pupils each day and very few free periods. If it could be done in smaller schools and in research centers, much light might be thrown on the problem of evaluation.

XXII

SYSTEMS OF GRADING

Dana P. Vaughan
Dean, Rhode Island School of Design
Providence, Rhode Island

Thousands of records are stored away, collecting dust, throughout the educational institutions of the country. Tons of paper are used annually, and hours upon hours of time that involve many people and much financial burden for the institutions that otherwise might have been used for direct teacher-student improvement, office space, and storage space. All are part of the effort to evaluate students' work. The technique required for carrying out this activity can all too easily overshadow the reason for which it is required. The questions can be rightly asked, Is it worth the price? And if it is worth the price, what is the real problem in evaluating students' work, and does it accomplish its purpose?

The educational field is primarily theoretical; reality does not truly function, and natural measures of accomplishment are not easily determined. In the majority of the situations in institutionalized education where standards are to be upheld and where students are to be conscious of logical development, some theoretical estimate or measuring stick is necessary.

The problem specifically stated seems to me twofold: first, such an estimate is a measure of accomplishment, the primary value of which is that the student may know relatively what has been accomplished by his efforts and at what rate he is progressing; second, any institution that offers a certificate, a diploma, or a degree indicates automatically that standards are considered, and standards cannot be considered or held to unless definite evaluations are made of students' capacities. These may be made in minute proportions or may only be made in very large blocks of accumulated accomplishment; but whichever the method, they are basically founded upon relative evaluations.

The evaluating of students' work in the art field is no less a problem than in the academic field, and has many elements that make it more difficult. The art field not only must cover a factual knowledge, but in addition an emphasis on skill and emotional content — these factors are not constant qualities or quantities, and in most cases they are far from positive. Art schools of any appreciable size, in order to be sure of meeting the industrial situations that must be considered in relation to the study of art as a functioning part of life, find that some evaluations of the student's accomplishment must be made in one way or another, so that a clear understanding of capacity may be gained, standards upheld, and information for future use made available. A few hundred transcripts from high schools and colleges and art schools at first glance show very little uniformity in the evaluation of students' work, whether in the academic field or in the art field. Some use the symbols *A*, *B*, *C*, and *D;* some use numerical ratings; others use ' high,' ' low,' and ' average '; others use relative standing in the class. Even where a simplified form has been attempted, and only ' passed ' or ' failed ' has been resorted to, other additions and notations indicate that even these two designations are not sufficiently adequate.

One uniformity, though, is apparent in the great majority of records; namely, that there are in most cases at least three or four levels and that, regardless of the symbol used to indicate them, they seem to pivot on ' average,' with ' high,' ' low,' and ' failed,' and varying degrees of intervening steps above and below the average. Upon studying records from different institutions and noting the relation of their evaluations to the relative accomplishment of the students, it is evident that the standards for ' average ' vary, but once this is established, the other gradations fall into line.

In explanation, assuming that the symbols *A, B, C, D,* and *F* (failure) are used, it appears that *C* represents 70 to 80, on a numerical scale, and that is generally considered the average accomplishment. Then, in some institutions the actual accomplishment of the student with a *C* grade may be actually very mediocre; in others, very high. In some of the most successful colleges, to gain a *C* or a *B* requires a high quality of work, whereas in other institutions a *B* or even an *A* does not require any higher standard. This situation is equally true when brought down to the evaluations of a given subject. One teacher's average acceptable standard may be much higher or much lower than another's. The art grades in transcripts are generally high in proportion to academic subjects.

The problem of evaluations is increasingly complicated by the point of view of the individual in evaluating the student's work. The aim of one instructor may be to use the evaluation as a direct means of encouragement or discouragement for the individual student — in other words, using it as a whip or as a reward, according to the individual's needs. This is a perfectly legitimate point of view; but on the other hand it will quite seriously upset the use of these records in an institution where meeting of standards is the emphasis required. Where the standards must be met, the student has his work evaluated in relation to what should be accomplished as a standard, rather than what he might or might not have accomplished in relation to his capacity.

Another point of view from which teachers often evaluate is the progress of the individual in relation to his or her estimated capacities. Here again this approach to the problem can be very constructive to the individual, but destructive in relation to the development of the standards of the institution.

An attempt to work out a system that might give a clearer and more rounded evaluation so that both the individual and institutional standards may be considered has been tried with some success. The following diagram shows the attempt, in working out this system, to form a basis for evaluations that will bring in some uniformity and yet be constructive, and will also be easily interpreted in whatever symbols may be required.

	F	*D*	*C*	*B*	*A*
Native Ability	0 1 2	3 4	5 6	7 8	9 10
Quality of Accomplishment	0 1 2	3 4	5 6	7 8	9 10
Quantity of Accomplishment	0 1 2	3 4	5 6	7 8	9 10
Concentration	0 1 2	3 4	5 6	7 8	9 10

The first of these items (estimated native ability) and the last one (concentration) act as apparent causes for the quantity of accomplishment and the quality of accomplishment. This sort of uniform analysis of the one record mark used for a specific subject, has in most cases clarified and standardized the instructor's estimates of the problem rather than complicated it. A series of such records, particularly when accompanied by notes and comments, can give a fairly comprehensive evaluation of a student's real accomplishment as well as of his relative ability and effort — all important factors that are usable and yet easily converted into conventional symbol records and transferable into symbols to serve as a specific record in relation to the standard of an institution.

In illustration, suppose a student has native ability estimated at 8, quality of accomplishment estimated at 8, quantity estimated at 4, and concentration estimated at 2. Only the quality and quantity are considered as the group standard. When reduced to the conventional symbols of A, B, C, and D, the addition of the 8 for quality of accomplishment with 4 for the quantity of accomplishment makes 12; dividing by 2 for an average, leaves 6 or an actual C accomplishment.

It is obvious on looking at the complete record that the student has capacity, but through lack of concentration is not making the best of the opportunity and accomplishing only a C according to the group standard.

Like all systems involving estimates based entirely on human judgment and involving such intangibles, the degree of accuracy is variable, yet it can give a relatively accurate picture over a period of time and a series of records.

It is doubtful whether the progress in the mechanical fields of our present generation could be at its high level of accomplishment were it not for numerous and minute measurements, tests, and standards. Is it not reasonable to feel that evaluations should also be made necessary in the educational field? It would seem that a scientific approach is the only one to meet the needs of a scientific age.

The problems of evaluating and comparing everyday work in the matter of development are of course as varied and effective as are the individuals teaching, whatever the subject. The aims are often confused and complicated, the system and technique confusing and irritating. In spite of the cumbersomeness of the problem of evaluating students' work, in spite of the endless piles of records that probably will never be touched for any purpose and the usefulness of which is out of proportion to the effort involved in compiling them, in spite of some educators and students who decry any evaluation as a waste of time or a system of false goals, it nevertheless seems a necessary evil in educational procedure if progress is to be constructive and standards are to be progressive. The problem is more one of emphasis upon the use of the material compiled from evaluations than upon the technique of the compiling. As long as education remains theoretical and educational outcome is remote from reality, some method of evaluation is inevitable, and our problem will always be to seek continually a wider and broader use through a simpler and more comprehensive method.

XXIII

SCHOOL PROGRAMS IN OTHER COUNTRIES

Royal Bailey Farnum
Executive Vice-President
Rhode Island School of Design
Providence, Rhode Island

Europe, during the first half of the nineteenth century, was making a beginning in the introduction of art as a part of elementary national education. Sporadic attempts had been made somewhat earlier both here and abroad to make drawing a part of the academic study of young people. In our own country Benjamin Franklin, in 1749, associated drawing with writing and arithmetic in his " Proposed Hints for an Academy." [1] Perhaps he was influenced by his knowledge of customs in Europe, for by the end of the first quarter of the century the Prussian schools [2] were experimenting with " the arts of drawing and designing" and by 1838 the work was well under way. In 1842, Ireland had recognized the value of linear drawing in its relation to other school subjects such as " geography, geometry, mensuration," and so forth, and similarly drawing had been introduced in certain schools of Belgium, Holland, and Germany.[3]

It must be remembered, however, that these earlier attempts to

---

[1] See *Barnard's Journal of Education*, Vol. 27, 1877.

[2] Report of Professor Stow to Ohio Legislature, 1838, on Prussian Schools.

[3] Isaac Edwards Clarke. *Art and Industry*, Part I, p. 11. (Washington, D. C.)

make drawing a part of the regular school curriculum were based in the main upon a conscious desire to apply the knowledge thus gained to problems of industry. R. R. Tomlinson [1] points out that when, in 1835, the Government of Great Britain appointed a " Select Committee" to study the best procedure for extending art and design among the people, it was especially for the " manufacturing population." It was not until educators began to see other services that drawing and art might render that the industrial point of view became only one of several objectives. Then, general observation, historical knowledge, appreciation of nature, and later the development of skills, memory training, the exercise of imagination and the creative faculties, and other psychological and sociological aims came to be recognized as important contributions in general education.

Today, owing in part to the international exchange of ideas by means of art and educational publications and art congresses, the nations abroad have many common objectives. Programs are of interest because of similarities rather than of differences, and in viewing exhibits of school work at international congresses one is struck by the evidence of current educational influences centering on new experimentation and discoveries in child psychology.

Among his conclusions following his study of the international situation, Mr. Tomlinson [2] notes the following:

(*a*) the recognition of the importance of design in drawing, painting, and handwork,

(*b*) the introduction of new media and materials for art purposes throughout the world,

(*c*) the replacement of small sheets of paper by large ones of various proportions, and the consequent increase in the size of drawings and in the freedom of expression,

(*d*) a growing use of the linoleum block for children,

(*e*) a recognition of the importance of creative thinking and art expression among children,

(*f*) the importance of having in each country a national gallery of children's art.

Generally speaking, the trend of thinking in most countries has swung completely from a critical analysis of details in classroom procedure to the more fundamental study of the philosophy underlying

---

[1] R. R. Tomlinson. *Picture Making by Children.* (The Studio Publications 1934.)

[2] *Op. cit.*

human tendencies in self-expression. Professor Zaher, Chief Inspector of Drawing, Cairo, Egypt, in a paper on " The Manual and Visual Tendencies of Children," said: [1]

> The various modern educational methods, aiming at the development of the child and respecting his personality, tending to develop his natural aptitudes, and advocating freedom and natural life for him, need to be studied carefully to see how far they tend to ameliorate his conditions and to what extent they could be utilized to forward our aim.
>
> The degrees of aptitude of children in drawing vary according to their intelligence and environment. The teacher's special concern should be the child whose subjective expression is poor and whose psychological functions are not fully developed. Such a child is found in every school, and I here again repeat that he needs special treatment and attention. His drawings made spontaneously, but guided by the teacher in the most unobtrusive manner possible, would show a steady development, a widening experience, and a fuller conception of things and ideas. With children, in general, one is inclined to adopt this attitude in the first stage; the teacher's rôle should be to create an atmosphere of freedom and to try to understand the child's point of view.

Speaking before the same International Congress,[2] Hiraku Kawanami, Instructor in the Japanese Middle School at Mukden, said:

> Historically speaking, manners and customs of the Japanese, Chinese, and Korean races are said to have been much the same as 1,500 years ago. . . . At present, fifteen centuries later, remarkable differences have come to exist, because, during the long period, each race has had to adapt itself to its topographical circumstances. Hence the development of characteristics of his own, entirely different from one another. This theory is feasible and leaves little room for any challenge.
>
> This development of characteristics of each race is strikingly reflected on pictorial works by young children and the experienced eye of an artist is able to correctly guess, at a glance, which race the juvenile artist belongs to. Works by Japanese children are generally varied in colors, with discreet curves and delicate suggestions, whereas Manchu boys draw bold lines in such primary colors as red, and secondary colors as vermilion and yellow. Again, Korean children prefer light colors in limited kinds that remind me of a calm moonlight night.
>
> As seen from the above mentioned observations, it is nothing unnatural that children, who are being brought up in an atmosphere assimilated

---

[1] Paper presented at the VIII International Congress on Art Education, Drawing, and Art Applied to Industry, Paris, 1937.

[2] See Footnote 1.

to natural surroundings, and who have come to possess a sensibility directly influenced by nature, should demonstrate their own characteristics in their works. Moreover, these characteristics are themselves interesting objects of art and no one is allowed to come to a hasty conclusion that this sense of art is desirable and that is undesirable.

This fact should always be kept in view on the part of parties concerned in art education. In any case, works should not be looked at from a biased angle. No matter whether an art educationist is a mere appreciative spectator or a responsible leader, he ought to be thoroughly acquainted with characteristics of the race with which he deals and then he should endeavor to foster and cultivate them as far as possible.

At the same time, as long as it is admitted that the home life is an invincible factor breeding a second nature of children, the art educationist is urged to extend his sphere of operations from the scholastic compound to the home life, so as to attain the ultimate aims of art education and thus to promote the zeal of each race on a joint basis of beauty and love. The art educationist is responsible for endeavors on this line.

Perhaps this point of view is summed up in an earlier statement of the German, Dr. Gunther von Pechmann,[1] who wrote:

Art education is not only the training of creative powers, but is an education of judgment and right estimation. The *new school* battles against dead ideals, against empty models, the overestimation of technical skill and the underestimation of the living powers of heart and soul. It is guided by the belief that all works will be good if their form be a true expression of a noble-minded humanity.

Charles H. Sawyer, who made a study of twelve English public schools in 1936, reports as follows:

Today the purpose of practical instruction in the visual arts in the English schools, as suggested by comments of both the art masters and their superiors, may be summarized under the following heads, which to a large extent supplement each other: (1) increased powers of observation, (2) the development of skill in the use of the hands, (3) a balance and relaxation from purely intellectual subjects, and (4) the development of the " creative " powers of the individual . . .

Differences of opinion concerning the essential purposes of education in the arts, which explain some contrasts in procedure, appear frequently to be a question of relative emphasis rather than of basic differences in educational philosophy.

---

[1] Director, Department for Modern Arts and Crafts, Bavarian National Museum. " New Ways of Art Education in Germany " — a catalog of children's exhibitions issued by the American Federation of Arts, 1929.

On the other hand, there has been a growing interest in again relating certain aspects of art education to the industrial progress of our modern era. Art principles for the sake of better taste in the selection of common consumer goods and, in turn, the influence of improved taste upon the design of mass production enter into this next picture.

Poland, Czecho-Slovakia, Italy, Germany, Denmark, and Sweden are outstanding examples of nations that have advanced to an international recognition of unusual art merit in their industrial products. Sweden probably leads all other countries in her intelligent handling of education in art for this purpose. She has not only revived her native handcrafts with great financial and social success, but, through educational programs, she has also related the native characteristics and fundamental principles of these crafts to modern industrial needs. Thus, the earliest reasons advanced for the introduction of drawing in general education are again finding firm ground for support today.

In the totalitarian countries similar objectives prevail, but, in addition, art expression is permitted, if not directed, to develop along propaganda lines. This is particularly true in Russia [1] where, at the same time, steps have been taken, theoretically at least, in a most enlightened way to offer opportunities for general art education in all its branches.

Every effort is made to have the child respond to the new life developing around him, to reflect his emotional reactions to aviation, to industry, to coöperative farming, to the ideals of the Communist Socialist State. It is asserted:

> Today, every one of the millions of young inhabitants of the Soviet Union has the right to real childhood. The point is not the number and magnificence of the toys they have to play with, but the fact that child labor in the Soviet Union is absolutely forbidden. All children attend school. A country which was so recently universally illiterate is now universally literate. Every child enjoys the legitimate and inalienable right to play, sing, dance, draw, model, and find an outlet for his aptitudes and tastes. Family, school, and kindergarten eagerly foster and encourage any aptitude shown by children for drawing, music, or dancing. In every part of the country there are Palaces of Young Pioneers, clubs, and child art centers with studios, classes, and circles of all kinds. No conditions are set for admission to the art, music, dramatic, or dancing classes; any child can join who wishes. Take any youngster who joins one of these

---

[1] See S. Marshak. *Children and Art in the U.S.S.R.* (Foreign Languages Publishing House: Moscow, 1939.)

art classes. He has everything at his disposal, all the paper, crayons, paints, and modelling clay his heart may desire. Side by side with him there are other boys and girls who draw, model, and make toy airplanes and gay masks and carnival costumes. He has instructors to advise him how to use his material, to suggest an interesting theme and unobtrusively to direct the lively imaginative play of the young pupil into artistic channels.

As the children grow older, their aptitudes begin to differentiate. . . . Gradually his taste turns into a definite channel. He undertakes tasks of increasing complexity. And if he is not armed in good time with a certain knowledge and skill, and if his imagination is not supplied with richer nourishment, his young talent may be extinguished.

At this stage the studio comes to the child's aid. This is not a professional art school; its chief purpose is to foster the child's creative activity; but it definitely sets out to arm the child with a certain knowledge, proficiency, and skill.

For children who display definite talent, there are the junior departments of the schools of art. These classes, studios, numerous contests, and expositions are designed not only to discover and develop gifted children but also to raise the general artistic level of the rising generation.

Of course, by no means all the children who exhibit talented work at contests or expositions will become professional artists. But one thing, at least, is certain; they will grow up with a genuine appreciation of art and a keen faculty of observation of the life around them.

In Germany, the changes in education, apparently, are still going on. In a recent report of our own Office of Education [1] the statement is made: " Nationalism is manifest in the 101 hours, or 37 percent of the total, that are taken up with German studies. German youth are to know and take pride in Germany through much study of the mother tongue, and the history, geography, art, and music of their country." Apparently, great emphasis is being placed upon the utilization of all subject matter for the glorification of the National Socialist regime.

One would be inclined to think that, under the circumstances, art work must naturally follow the trend and that, while the fundamentals of drawing and basic principles of design are taught, the objectives must be thoroughly imbued with nationalist propaganda.

A democratic nation is more concerned with that type of education which develops all the capacities of a boy or girl as an individual than with a mass attack for the sake of race consciousness or state aggrandizement. American philosophy in art education, therefore, seeks per-

---

[1] Alina M. Lindegren. "Education in Germany." (Bulletin, 1938, No. 15)

sonal revelation through creative effort and emotional response to beauty as a means toward cultural progress for each human being, on the theory that an enlightened and intelligent citizen, free to think, free to speak, and free to express, is the strongest possible unit in a commonwealth governed by democratic principles.

Observation has clearly shown, in the various International Art Congresses dealing with art education, that American exhibits indicate wider ranges of creative opportunity, greater latitude in subject matter, untrammelled art leadership, and a total lack of political propaganda as compared to many other national displays.

At the same time, most foreign countries appear to take their art programs, in so far as they relate to that technical proficiency essential for the craftsman in industry, far more seriously than we do, especially at the secondary-school level and beyond. Teachers, free from the American bug-a-boo of collegiate credits in unrelated academic fields of higher learning, are rigorously trained in art knowledge and technical craftsmanship over an extended period of time, and are subjected to searching technical examinations. The boys and girls, also, instinctively recognize the value and importance of real study and prolonged hard work, perhaps because in the more congested countries life itself is a harder battle for existence.

References

(1) American Federation of Arts. *Art School Directory.* (Vol. 1. The Federation: Washington, D. C., 1939) 159 pp.

(2) Association for Childhood Education. *Art for Today's Child.* (The Association: Washington, D. C., 1935) 32 pp.

(3) BARNES, E. A., and YOUNG, B. M. *Children and Architecture.* (Bureau of Publications, Columbia University: New York, 1932)

(4) BOAS, B. *Art in the School.* (Doubleday, Page: New York, 1924) 124 pp.

(5) CLAPP, E. R. *Community Schools in Action.* (Viking Press: New York, 1940) 430 pp.

(6) Committee on the Function of Art in General Education for the Commission on Secondary School Curriculum. *The Visual Arts in General Education.* (D. Appleton-Century Co., Inc.: New York, 1940) 166 pp.

(7) COX, G. J. *Art for Amateurs and Students.* (Doubleday, Doran and Co., Inc.: New York, 1931)

(8) DEWEY, JOHN. *Art as Experience.* (Minton, Balch: New York, 1934) 355 pp.

(9) DEWEY, JOHN. *Construction and Criticism.* (Columbia University Press: New York, 1930)

(10) DIX, L. H. "Aesthetic experience and growth in life and education." *Teach. Coll. Rec.,* 40: 1938, 206–221.

(11) "Education through Art." [In] *Modern Trends in Education.* New Education Fellowship, Proceedings, 1937, pp. 216–237.

(12) FAULKNER, R. "Art in the General College." *Art Education Today: 1938.* (Teachers College: New York, 1938)

(13) GIBBS, EVELYN. *The Teaching of Art in Schools.* (Greenberg: New York, 1936)

(14) GLACE, MARGARET F. S. *Arts in the Integrated Program; an Analysis of the Art Content of Some Units of Activity in Grades Four, Five, and Six.* (Cullom & Ghertner Co.: Nashville, Tenn., 1934) 93 pp.

(15) GRAY, WILLIAM HENRY. "The Psychology of the Fine Arts." [In] *The Psychology of Elementary School Subjects.* (Prentice-Hall, Inc.: New York, 1938)

(16) GRIMES, J. W., and BORDEN, E. "A Proposed Technique for Certain Evaluations in Art." *Educational Research Bulletin,* xviii, Jan. 4, 1939 (Ohio State University: Columbus)

(17) GUPTILL, ARTHUR L. *Sketching as a Hobby.* (Harper and Brothers: New York, 1937) 150 pp.

(18) HARAP, H. *The Changing Curriculum.* (D. Appleton-Century Co., Inc.: New York, 1937)

(19) Hartman, B., and Shumaker, A., Editors. *Creative Expression: the Development of Children in Art, Music, Literature, and Dramatics.* 2d. Ed. (E. M. Hale, 1939) 350 pp.

(20) HOBAN, C. F., and ZISMAN, S. B. *Visualizing the Curriculum.* (Cordon: New York, 1937) 300 pp.

(21) JESSEN, C. A., and HERLIHY, L. B. *Offerings and Regulations in High School Subjects,* 1933–34. Bulletin 1938, No. 6, p. 19. (Office of Education: Washington, D. C.)

(22) KEPPEL, F. P., and DUFFUS, R. L. *The Arts in American Life.* (McGraw-Hill Book Co.: New York, 1933)

(23) KLAR, WALTER H., WINSLOW, LEON L., and KIRBY, C. VALENTINE. "Art Education in the Rural Community." [In] *Art Education in Principle and Practice.* (Milton Bradley Company: Springfield, Mass., 1933)

(24) KLINE, L. W., and CAREY, G. L. *A Measuring Scale for Freehand Drawing.* (Johns Hopkins University Press: Baltimore, 1923)

(25) KNAUBER, A. *The Knauber Art Ability and Vocabulary Tests.* (University of Cincinnati Press: Cincinnati, O., 1935)

(26) LASCARIS, P. A. *L'éducation esthétique de l'enfant.* (Alcan: Paris, 1928) 508 pp.

(27) LEARY, B. E. A. *Survey of Courses of Study and Other Curriculum Materials Published since 1934.* Bulletin No. 31, 1937. (Office of Education: Washington, D. C.)

(28) LEMOS, PEDRO J. *The Art Teacher.* (The Davis Press: Worcester, Mass., 1931) 491 pp.

(29) LESTER, R. M. "Arts Teaching Equipment for Colleges and Secondary Schools." [In] *Review Ser.* No. 24, pp. 227–308. (Carnegie Corporation: New York, 1937)

(30) LEVY, F. M. *Art Education in the City of New York: a Guidance Study.* (School-Art League of New York: New York, 1938) 148 pp.

(31) LEWERENZ, A. S. *Tests of Fundamental Abilities of Visual Art.* (California School Book Depository: Hollywood, Cal., 1927)

(32) McADORY, M. *The McAdory Art Test.* (Teachers College: New York, 1929)

(33) McCARTY, S. A. *Children's Drawings.* (Williams and Wilkins: Baltimore, 1924)

(34) MATHIAS, MARGARET E. *Art in the Elementary School.* (Charles Scribner's Sons: New York, 1929) 180 pp.

(35) MATHIAS, MARGARET E. *The Beginnings of Art in the Public Schools.* (Charles Scribner's Sons: New York, 1924) 119 pp.

(36) MATHIAS, MARGARET E. *The Teaching of Art.* (Charles Scribner's Sons: New York, 1932) 356 pp.

(37) MEIER, N. C., and SEASHORE, C. E. *The Meier-Seashore Art Judgment Test.* (Bureau of Educational Research and Service: Iowa City, Iowa)

(38) MITCHELL, E. L. "Curriculum Experiences for Elementary Schools." *Delaware Curriculum No. 1,* September, 1940.

(39) MITCHELL, E. L. "Old and New Forces in the Art Curriculum." *Art Education Today.* (Teachers College: New York, 1937)

(40) MUNRO, T. "Adolescence and Art Education." [In] *Bulletin of the Worcester Art Museum,* July, 1932; [also in] *Methods of Teaching the Fine Arts,* ed. by Rusk. (University of North Carolina Press: Chapel Hill, 1935)

(41) MUNRO, T. "The art museum and the secondary school." *Progress Educ.,* 14: 1937, 521–534.

(42) MUNRO, T. "Art Tests and Research in Art Education." *Proceedings of the Western Arts Association.* Dec. 1, 1933.

(43) MUNRO, T. "The Fine Arts in the Elementary and High School." [In] "International Understanding through the Public-School Curriculum." *The Thirty-Sixth Yearbook, Part II,* of this Society, 1937.

(44) MUNRO, T. "Frank Cizek and the Free Expression Method" and "A Constructive Program for Teaching Art." [In] *Art and Education.* (Barnes Foundation Press: Merion, Pa., 1929) Pp. 217, 311.

(45) MUNRO, T. "A Graded Program in Comparative Arts." [In] *Art Education Today: 1936.* (Teachers College: New York, 1936)

(46) MUNRO, T. "A Psychological Approach to College Art Instruction." *Parnassus,* November, 1933.

(47) MURSELL, J. L. "Some Generalizations concerning Art Education." [In] *Art Education Today: 1937.* (Teachers College: New York)

(48) NEWHALL, B. *Photography, a Short Critical History.* (Museum of Modern Art: New York)

(49) NICHOLAS, F. W., MAWHOOD, D., and TRILLING, B. *Art Activities in the Modern School.* (The Macmillan Co.: New York, 1937) 379 pp.

(50) NYQUIST, FREDERICK V. *Art Education in Elementary Schools.* University Research Monograph, No. 8. (Warwick and York., Inc.: Baltimore, 1929) 160 pp.

(51) O'HARA, E. *Art Teachers' Primer: Forty-four Assignments to Art Classes with Eighteen Blackboard Diagrams.* (Minton, Balch: New York, 1939) 180 pp.

(52) PATTEN, MARJORIE. *The Arts Workshop of Rural America.* (Columbia University Press: New York, 1937) 202 pp.

(53) PATZIG, EDNA. "Art education in rural schools." *Midland Schools, 50:* March, 1936, 213–214.

(54) PAYANT, FELIX. *Our Changing Art Education.* (Keramic Studio Publishing Co.: Columbus, Ohio, 1935) 93 pp.

(55) PERRINE, VAN DEARING. *Let the Child Draw.* (Frederick A. Stokes Co.: New York, 1936) 88 pp.

(56) PERRY, EVADNA KRAUS. *Art Adventures with Discarded Materials.* 4th ed. (Noble and Noble: New York, 1933) 169 pp.

(57) POORE, H. R. *Art's Place in Education.* (G. P. Putnam's Sons: New York, 1937)

(58) POPE, ARTHUR. *Art, Artist, and Layman.* (Harvard University Press: Cambridge, 1937) 152 pp.

(59) Progressive Education Association. *Creative Expression; the Development of Children in Art, Music, Literature, and Dramatics.* Gertrude Hartman and Ann Shumaker, Editors. (John Day: New York, 1932) 350 pp.

(60) RUGG, H., and SHUMAKER, ANN. *The Child-Centered School.* (World Book Co.: Yonkers, N. Y., 1928) 359 pp.

(61) RUSSELL, J. G., and BONSER, F. G. *Industrial Education.* (Teachers College: New York, 1912)

(62) SAUER, D. *Everyday Art at School and Home.* (Bridgman Publishers: Pelham, N. Y., 1930) 244 pp.

(63) SAWYER, C. H. *Art Instruction in English Public Schools.* (Phillips Academy: Andover, Mass., 1937)

(64) SCHULTZ, H. "Changing the Attitudes of Secondary-School Students toward Artists and Their Art." Bulletin of the Department of Art of the National Education Association, Vol. V, 1939, pp. 20–24.

(65) "Selected References on Secondary School Instruction: Art." [In] *Selected References in Education.* (University of Chicago Press: Chicago, 1934–39)

(66) SHAW, R. F. *Finger Painting.* (Little, Brown, and Co.: Boston, 1934)

(67) SOBOTKA, GRACE. *Art Instruction in the First Six Grades.* (Edwards Brothers, Inc.: Ann Arbor, Mich., 1935) 35 pp.

(68) SWEENEY, F. G., BARRY, E. F., SCHOELKOFF, A. E. *Western Youth Meets Eastern Culture.* (Columbia University: New York, 1932)

(69) TANNAHILL, S. B. *Fine Arts for Public School Administration.* (Columbia University: New York, 1932)

(70) TIERNEY, L. "Teaching Photography in the Art Department." [In] *Art Education Today: 1939.* (Teachers College: New York)

(71) TODD, J., and GALE, A. V. N. *Enjoyment and Use of Art in Elementary Schools.* (University of Chicago Press: Chicago, 1933)

(72) TOMLINSON, R. R. *Crafts for Children.* (The Studio: London, 1935)

(73) TOMLINSON, R. R. *Picture-Making by Children.* (The Studio: London, 1934)

(74) ULP, C. M. "Models in motion: A study of materials and procedure best adapted to teach dynamic drawing." *Jour. Higher Educ.* 4: 1933, 19–22.

(75) U. S. Office of Education. *Good References on Art Instruction, Especially Helpful to Teachers in Smaller Schools.* Bibliog. No. 59, Comp. by M. R. McCabe and W. H. Gaumnitz. (Washington, D. C.: 1939) 12 pp.

(76) WADSWORTH, B. M. *Selling Art to the Community.* (Davis Press: Worcester, 1929)

(77) WHITFORD, W. G. *An Introduction to Art Education.* (D. Appleton-Century Co., Inc.: New York, 1939)

(78) WINSLOW, L. L. *The Integrated School Art Program.* (McGraw-Hill Book Co.: New York, 1939) 238 pp.

(79) WINSLOW, L. L. *Organization and Teaching of Art.* (Warwick and York, Inc.: Baltimore, 1928)

(80) WOMMELSDORFF, O. *Wandschmuck für Schulen.* (Pädagogischer Verlag: Düsseldorf, 1930) 136 pp.

SUPPLEMENTARY LIST OF BOOKS ON ART SUITABLE FOR CHILDREN OF ELEMENTARY-SCHOOL AGE [1]

Author	*Title*	*Publisher*
Bailey, C. S.	Children of the Handicrafts	Viking
Berry, Ana	Art for Children	Studio
Brown, Paul	Black and White	Scribner's
Bruce, Marjory	Book of Craftsmen	Dodd
Bryant, L. M.	Children's Book of Celebrated Sculpture	Appleton-Century
Chandler, A. C.	Treasure Trails in Art	Hale
Conway, A. E.	Book of Art for Children	Macmillan
Deucher, Sybil	Giotto Tended the Sheep	Dutton
Deucher, Sybil	Millet Tilled the Soil	Dutton
E-Yeh-Shure	I Am a Pueblo Indian Girl	Morrow
Furniss, Dorothy	Drawing for Beginners	Bridgman
Gaba, Lester	On Soap Sculpture	Holt
Gibson, Katharine	Goldsmith of Florence	Macmillan
Hamilton, E. T.	Handicraft for Girls	Harcourt, Brace
Hamilton, E. T.	Popular Crafts for Boys	Dodd
Hillyer and Huey	A Child's History of Art	Appleton-Century
Holme, Geoffrey	The Children's Art Book, Second Edition	Studio
Lamprey, Louise	The Story of Weaving	Stokes
Langdon, W. C.	Everyday Things in American Life	Scribner's
Leeming, Joseph	Fun with Paper	Stokes
Lutz, E. G.	What to Draw and How to Draw	Dodd
Naramore, Elizabeth	William and His Friends	Viking
Oliver, I. B.	First Steps in the Enjoyment of Pictures	Holt
Perry, E. K.	Art Adventures with Discarded Materials	Noble

---

[1] This list of books suitable for elementary-school libraries was prepared by the Director of Work with Children, The Enoch Pratt Free Library of Baltimore.

Author	Title	Publisher
Robinson, E. F.	Houses in America	Viking
Rogers, Frances	Big Miss Liberty	Stokes
Smith, S. C.	Made in Mexico	Knopf
Smith, Susan	Made in America	Knopf
Smith, Susan	Made in France	Knopf
Steedmen, Amy	Stories of the Painters	Nelson
Van Loon, H. W.	The Arts	Garden City
Wheeler, I. W.	Playing with Clay	Macmillan
White, W. C.	Made in Russia	Knopf
Whitford, W. G.	Art Stories, 3v.	Scott
Wilhelm, L. M.	With Scissors and Paste	Macmillan
Winslow, L. L.	Elementary Industrial Arts	Macmillan

CHAPTER XXXI

THE EDUCATION OF ARTISTS

Royal B. Farnum, Milton S. Fox, Florence N. Levy, C. Valentine Kirby, Arthur Pope, E. Raymond Bossange, Clifford M. Ulp, Gilbert Rohde, L. Moholy-Nagy, James C. Boudreau, William Longyear, Alfred G. Pelikan, and Vincent A. Roy [1]

I

THE GENERAL AND TECHNICAL EDUCATION OF THE ARTIST

Royal Bailey Farnum
Executive Vice-President
Rhode Island School of Design
Providence, Rhode Island

Man is the only living being endowed with the powers of invention and intelligent creation. It is the successful attainment of these powers, resulting in complete efficiency for human service, that we term 'art.' The artist is a person who achieves this result; and, as his expressions cover all fields of visual form, he should not be confined in one's mind to the painter of pictures alone. The artist is a designer whose scope of activity is quite unlimited. In this chapter the term includes, among others, the architect, painter, sculptor, industrial designer, commercial artist, photographer, and illustrator.

Opportunities for artists and designers today are legion compared to yesterday. Moreover, they are multiplying yearly like the proverbial rabbit. But, alas, the right artists and designers who are needed are not available for the opportunities that exist. And therein lies the crux of the whole situation. With all the art schools and colleges in the land turning out students as art graduates by the hundreds each year, why is it that so many enter the ranks of the unemployed if opportunities do exist?

---

[1] For the titles and addresses of these contributors, see the section contributed by each one. For the general plan of the chapter, see the Table of Contents.
— *Editor.*

Let us consider for a moment this new social order of ours. First, it is an age of change, of speed, of rapid communication, of technology, of science, of power machinery, of esthetic upheaval, of practical economy, of research, of synthetic manufacture, of markets, of labor, and of men.

It is a world unconsciously seeking beauty, and demanding it in the useful and common forms of living; a world wherein the opportunity and the desire for the quiet contemplation of a single great work on canvas, for example, finds little or no room. This is to be regretted, but, for the time being, life's struggle forbids time and proper interest for such luxury.

The new social order is one, then, in which art finds its best expression in practical daily living. It is there that we find the art graduate's opportunity. While I believe that we truly are art conscious as a people, we are not painted-picture conscious. There is, therefore, great hope for the nation; some day great paintings as well as great sculpture will return to grace our culture. But, heaven be praised, that will come through a great public educated to fine expression in common things and ready, therefore, for the higher spiritual values.

What, then, is wrong at present? Just this: education in art, as in everything else, must take due cognizance of the structure of the society for which it educates and must prepare to meet its needs. American community life today requires artists so educated that they may be of real and vital service now. Therefore, any youth narrowly trained and equipped solely to paint a picture or to model a head is as ill prepared as would be the twelve-year-old if he received instruction only in the three R's. Likewise, the student given a background limited just to drawing, art history, and paper design has no pertinent place in our present society. He just is not wanted unless by a tragic series of failures he finally gains the knowledge of his world that his school failed to give him.

The opportunity exists, therefore, for those who can qualify, who can meet the specifications written clearly and frankly by society itself. And, to qualify, a new point of view must be taken in our professional art institutions. They must achieve wider scope and offer a broadly scheduled curriculum that educates the artist to be fully aware of the present social demands.

The art graduate of today, if he is to be equipped to take advantage of opportunities that actually exist, must, of course, have a high degree of facility in creative expression, in the use of his media, and in the handling of his tools. But more than that. he must be made aware of the dignity and the importance of commerce and manufacture. He must be conscious of market demands. He must be informed and intelligent about such problems in industry as labor relations, sources of raw products, mass production, costs of material, consumer demand and acceptance, trends in design, and types of transportation. Unless he is conscious of the many limitations of his art problem set by manufacture and distribution, how is he to plan intelligently for it?

Also, he must know what applied research means as distinguished from fundamental research. He must be taught the value of time, the importance of work. Over one thousand sketches were made before the final theme center, the Perisphere and Trylon, at the New York World's Fair, was evolved. Finally, he must have some of that culture which English and the social studies give.

It is generally expected that an art school should teach the use of tools and modes of expression in art. The world today demands other factors, also, but fails to be articulate about them before the graduate lands in its lap. And the world is too busy to come to the school and tell it its business. The school, therefore, must be ever watchful, alert to changing trends, ready to learn; it must be flexible enough to change or to broaden its base, stable enough to maintain the true ideals of art, and ready to make their application in lowly places more often than in high. The new graduate must be as well educated for his profession as the lawyer, the doctor, the executive, or the engineer is for his.

Roughly, the outlet for the artist's work is of two different types; one of these calls for imaginative planning and original designing; the other requires the pictorial and mechanical preparation of any design or form that may be desired. In either case, technical proficiency is essential, but there has arisen a special demand for a better and more broadly educated artist, a man of greater intellectual power with a better appreciation of the economic, cultural, and industrial problems of society. Consequently, an inventory of courses and educational requirements for the education of artists is called for throughout the country. Already some schools [1] have taken the initiative in this mat-

---

[1] For example, the Berkeley College of Arts and Crafts, Berkeley, California; the California Graduate School of Design, Pasadena; the Chicago Art Institute; the Massachusetts School of Art, Boston; the Moore Institute, Philadelphia; the Museum School of Industrial Design, Philadelphia; Pratt Institute, Brooklyn, New York; the Rhode Island School of Design, Providence; and the School of Design, Chicago.

ter and some of them already have introduced so-called 'liberal' or 'cultural' courses to supplement the usual professional instruction.

A great deal more, however, must be done to prepare the designer for the tremendous advances that are being made in the field of new, especially synthetic, materials, in new human services, and in new public demands. The general education of the artist, therefore, must include English and specialized work in the field of social studies, related science and mathematics, the elements underlying economic structure, a working knowledge of psychology and sociology, and some work in philosophy.

One might well ask, "If all this is necessary, should not a regular liberal-arts education precede the technical professional training in art?" The answer is "No" if the two types of education are pursued separately, for, on the one hand, the "liberal-arts" course of instruction is often a relic of the past, both in content and method, and, on the other hand, any technical instruction in art conducted exclusively on a hand-performance basis is equally narrow and impractical. There must be a wedding of the two. Approaches must be creatively planned with less weight given to memorized knowledge. Painting and the historical development of the art should proceed simultaneously; for example, drawing and the science of visual perspective and orthographic projection must go hand in hand; design, color, and the use of tools and materials in current industry must synchronize with modern economics, a study of consumer markets, of the sources of raw products, of methods of manufacture, of advertising and selling.

This demand for broader training with related and integrated courses, of necessity, calls for students of at least average intelligence. A high-school art department that is a logical preliminary step leading to professional training is no longer a place to dump the low intelligence group on the excuse that its courses require little or no mental effort. Moreover, such a department should no longer seek to cloak itself with the questionable glamor of a foreign atelier where art, with a big A, may isolate itself from the life stream of general education and student activity. It behooves all guidance teachers to familiarize themselves with these trends toward a more serious view of the purposes and requirements of art education, and to appreciate the importance of guiding the right student into this exacting profession.

The technical education of the artist, likewise, involves a broader and more extensive training than that which prevailed in former years — especially in fields of applied and industrial design. Even in fine-arts courses the concentration of effort upon a single form of technical instruction is wholly inadequate if the artist is to meet, with competence, the requirements of current demand. Historic style and a critical analysis of nature are important as a background of knowledge (but not, as formerly, as a point of departure in creating new forms).

Technical courses for the prospective artist, therefore, should include the use of various materials, a mastery of different tools and tool processes, and an understanding of the esthetic and functional services of art.

Two distinct approaches or methods of education for artists prevail in the professional schools.

The first method is more or less based upon traditional procedures that approach the ultimate goal through the copying of classical examples of art by means of meticulous and dictated rendering with charcoal, pencil, crayon and paint, advancing as proficiency is indicated, or a given period of time is completed, to still-life groups and finally to the human figure. This method of imitative rendering is supposed to prepare the student for imaginative and creative effort after he has mastered an imposed technique. It is similarly administered to the sculptor, painter, and architect as initial steps in their professional preparation; it is then supplemented by separate lectures on perspective, composition, anatomy, and possibly color, and is followed by extreme concentration in the separate fields of specialization. The majority of schools are breaking away from this narrow approach in favor of a broader and more integrated method.

The second method is based upon the idea that experimental freedom in the beginning, by means of which principles of design and technique are evolved through self-discovery, accompanied by expressions in various materials with the use of related tools and processes, is a sounder approach to the desired objective. Therefore early steps involve the handling of both two- and three-dimensional materials at the start. Discussion, guidance (rather than imposed ideas), and self-discipline lead the student to a clearer understanding of the demands of art expression than the more traditional and outmoded approach.

In this second method theoretical considerations of color, composition, perspective, anatomy, and the accepted canons of esthetic understanding are woven into the general pattern and are taken up as they naturally arise during the development of the student's powers in artistic expression. At the same time the relationships of art and design to esthetic and useful demands in modern society are gradually clarified. This approach requires real teaching ability, a physical equipment far more extensive in scope than the average school provides, and any or all materials now available in modern manufacture. Simple hand tools are not enough; power machines are essential. Paper designs must be followed by three-dimensional models. Traditional techniques must be supplemented by new applications to new uses. Related study in such fields as economics, sociology, manufacture, marketing, distribution, science, business ethics, divisions of labor, and other phases of modern life are essential to the education of the professional designer, but such study should not be presented in the typical academic manner. Only those elements having some bearing upon the problems of the commercial artist and the industrial designer should be presented. And the same holds true for the less restricted artist if he is to serve, with understanding, the client of today.

Finally, projects of a practical nature, preferably solicited from outside the institution and directly related to human needs, should become the program of advanced students. These should involve the procedures and restrictions of current usage; they should demand solutions that satisfy modern consumer demand; and they should recognize the importance of careful research in a thoroughly businesslike and scientific manner.

Modern life, with its highly complex structure, is rapidly finding a definite and vital place for art, especially in industrial or mechanized activity. This trend is rapidly increasing, partly because of the speed of science and invention. The application of new discoveries to useful purposes has forced a demand for the services of both artist and engineer, and schools of art must prepare themselves to meet the situation.

It is obvious to the art educator, at least, that traditional and limited courses of an academic nature can never meet the situation. The following general outline is suggested, therefore, as a trend in the building of more extensive curricula and as fundamental to these new demands. The typical art school usually recognizes the importance of a general, or foundation, course during the first year. Some schools require two years for all students before they begin to specialize. The tendency is to continue this common base, but at the same time to introduce experience of an exploratory nature that will help to discover special abilities and interests in a number of directions. Therefore the newer foundation course would include the following:

1. Drawing by means of different media from imagination. Manufactured forms and nature, including the human figure — both freehand and mechanical.
2. Design for two- and three-dimensional purposes, using a variety of mate-

rials, such as paper, textiles, metals, wood, and plastic media involving carving, modelling, and building.

3. Lettering and the development of letter forms in two and in three dimensions with the use of pens, carving tools, and structural material.

4. Principles of drawing, design, and color educed through discussion and analysis.

5. English and history.

6. Elementary principles and laws of science as related to mechanical, physical, and chemical needs.

Specialization in the field of visual art is necessary today because of marked divisions of professional activity in modern life. But there is much overlapping. For example, the artist-designer might be given a problem, the solution of which requires a knowledge of modelling, painting, display, structural design, mechanics, and mass production. Such a demand is not unusual; on the contrary, it is becoming increasingly common. Consequently the school of art must give recognition to the trend.

Advanced courses therefore should include the following:

1. A major amount of concentrated work for two or three years in each specialized field, such as painting, sculpture, architecture, graphic arts, textiles and clothing, jewelry and silversmithing, interior design, industrial design, glass and ceramics, illustration, photography, theater arts, or any other important division of visual art.

2. Related work from such of the foregoing fields as may be desirable, sufficient in amount and in technical process to meet satisfactorily the broad requirements of the major.

3. Advanced design study including composition and color, current and historic style, and ornament.

4. Freehand drawing from the human figure.

5. Mechanical drafting; *i.e.*, working drawings.

6. Related science, economics, and problems of manufacture and research.

7. Cultural and academic courses, including English, history, mathematics, and esthetics.

8. Special courses that may bear directly upon the work of the major subject, such as illumination, electricity, mechanical processes, consumer trends, art in merchandising, related phases of engineering, properties of natural and synthetic materials, professional ethics, markets at home and abroad, and other phases of human progress that determine new and old directions for art service.

A minimum of four years is probably the desirable period of time for foundation and advanced work in training the artist of today on what might be termed an undergraduate basis. In addition to this there appears to be a trend in the direction of graduate work for one or two years, during which time actual production of a professional character would be carried on, financed by an outside client and promoted on a supporting fellowship basis similar to graduate work in fields of science, engineering, and business administration.

II

AIMS AND METHODS IN PROFESSIONAL ART–SCHOOL TRAINING

MILTON S. FOX
Instructor, The Cleveland Museum of Art
Instructor, The Cleveland School of Art
Cleveland, Ohio

I. INTRODUCTORY

A great deal has been said in recent years about methods and theories of art education in the grade and secondary schools; recently the subject of college art education has become popular. But the literature on the training of the professional artist is scanty and tentative. One almost comes to assume that all the problems have been solved, that except for one or two minor changes — the addition of some academic subject, for example — the end of the evolution has been reached, and that all that remains is to turn out a steady stream of competent creative talent. Yet this obviously is not true. Economically the situation of the artist is wretched; socially he remains a difficult problem. In actual fact, the whole field is badly in need of systematic study; methods, aims, curricula, and theories must be overhauled. If something of the sort does not happen, the college art courses may soon attract a large part of the clientele heretofore trained in our art schools.

The trouble lies in the fact that the art school has refused to take stock of itself in the light of general educational principles that in recent years have transformed teaching methods elsewhere. It is still an institution given only to the training of skills directly concerned with the execution of some limited and specific task. With rare exceptions, it ignores the need of continuing the general education of its students just out of high school. The training it gives is based on cerain *a priori* assumptions that are now to an important degree no longer valid; its aims and standards were set up by artists and theorists who flourished under another dispensation, and by a patronage of conservative and not always discriminating taste. It has not even been genuinely conservative of the traditional best, but merely of a pallid and reactionary yesterday. Its 'sound' views rest on a specious notion of tradition. What are impressively called 'enduring fundamentals' turn out to be nothing but the methods and techniques approved by some particular group.

For the last hundred years and more the training of the artist has progressively narrowed the interests of the student. He was to be a creature of 'inspiration'; the less he knew, apparently, the less adulterated would be these urges. He was taught technical proficiency of a kind, and, driven by 'moods,' his inspiration led him to search for subjects of an illustrational or literary kind — especially things old, picturesque, novel, distant, or odd. This extreme nineteenth-century view has yielded pretty much to time, yet the methods (and the implied conceptions of art and the functioning of the artist) largely persist. They are based on the pathetically amateur esthetics of practicing artists, given *ex cathedra*. This would not be a great evil if it did not reveal to what an alarming extent the art curricula of the last few generations have been determined by artistic nonentities.

The course of study was — and still is — based on the drawing of the nude — a relentless drill in the rendering of the visible, the dehumanized, the still. The student is loaded with all the paraphernalia of 'realistic' perspective (which becomes a shibboleth) and the restrictions of 'correct' drawing and proportion. He worries about 'centers of interest' — a device by which one may allow the eye, a lens, to supplant the mind. Design and composition are largely matters of 'pleasing' arrangement of real objects (outdoors one changes the position of one's easel). The selection made, artistic creation then becomes a matter of rendering the objects in the student's usual technique. The student has almost no idea of broad esthetic principle, of the psychology of art, of the functions and uses of art, of the relation of the artist to his community and to society. He is usually unaware of the different types of artistic effect and composition, of the uses of materials, of the variety of subject material and interests. The net result is the creation of an individual who has mastered certain skills, but whose imagination has been allowed — almost encouraged — to atrophy, and whose general cultural development proceeds fitfully, if at all, in his odd spare moments.

We need in our artists more of the ideal of the Renaissance: the man of parts. The artist of that time spent years in learning the niceties of manipulation and materials before he embarked on self-expressive ventures. While still quite young, he came into contact, either directly or indirectly through his masters, with the poets and philosophers of his community; and the very nature of painting at the time made it necessary for him to know something of architecture and other adjacent fields. He tried his hand at poetry, perhaps at music, and dabbled with the leading ideas of his day. His training was really a continuous broadening process; when he was ready to paint, his mind was well stocked with ideas, his imagination was alive, and technique was integrated as the smooth and effective vehicle of his conceptions. Renaissance artists went to nature for their themes, so to speak, but their art was the art of variations — the expressions of cultivated minds. The same, in general, may be said of the practices of the Orient.

Art-school curricula must become more realistic and practical, and, at the same time, more visionary; but soundly based on the psychology of real people, and directed to the satisfaction of real needs. This, however, cannot be accomplished by rote training of artists, by training students to turn out ' good ' or ' acceptable ' art works rather than intuited (or otherwise apprehended) experience formed in the depths of cultured minds and given body in visual terms. A system of routine tasks that all students are forced to undergo constitutes a restrictive or subtractive process. This method assumes that all students are capable of the same training, and that any person so trained is a qualified artist. In the field of the so-called ' applied ' arts, as well as in the ' fine ' arts, assignments are to a large extent unreal and grandiose in nature. Because of the disillusionment sure to come, they are harmful rather than helpful in the long run. To be sure, teaching should have some glamor about it; yet it is wrong to train commercial artists, for example, mainly to make ' smart ' posters, designs for World's Fairs and so on, when for years after the student leaves school, he will be called upon to make pen drawings of perfume bottles, scrubbing brushes, and blankets. Similarly, young students should not be encouraged to think in terms of murals and great decorative pieces before they have any idea of the real difficulties and complexities in painting, both in conception and execution, as well as some idea of the social significance of large-scale public painting.

The art school should exist to fulfill four main functions: (*a*) to bring about the cultural enrichment of the student; (*b*) to impart to him full experience with art forms, techniques, materials, and methods; (c) to develop the faculties related to the production of works of art — perception, imagination, a large repertory of visual shapes and experiences, esthetic effects; and (*d*) to give him an understanding of his society and his place in it.

I propose to discuss briefly the training of future artists and craftsmen under the following heads: (*a*) The Creation and Production of Art Works; (*b*) The Cultural History of Art; (*c*) The Social Setting of the Artist; (*d*) His Professional Advancement; (*e*) His Cultural Background; and (*f*) The School Itself.

II. THE CREATION AND PRODUCTION OF ART WORKS

1. The Psychology of the Artist [1]

One of the major objectives of all art training should be development of a great sensitivity to visual phenomena and a rich repertory of visual experience.

a. Perception. To this end there must be a thorough exercise of perceptive abilities. Perception (or observation, as it was called in certain seventeenth-century academies), so far as the art student is concerned, is taken to mean the noting and awareness of visible characteristics of things or events. The student should be trained to discern both the obvious characteristics (and their relative importance in the visual whole) and the less obvious characteristics, those slight, but important, peculiarities that make particular things and events unique. For example, he should be able to describe or to picture such things as the various types of clouds, formations and textures of trees, postures of different kinds of bodies, different stages of running, the effect on the color of a given face of different kinds of light, of different directions of light, and so on. In this practice, which should be very intensive during the early years of schooling (but continuing throughout), there should be little emphasis on artistic creation; all emphasis should be placed on increasing the sensitivity of eye and mind to visual stimuli. This sense training should include some of the other senses, as in the feel of wind and rain on the face, odors, tastes, and tactile, haptic, kinesthetic qualities.

---

[1] This section is supplementary to the general discussion, in Chapter XXII, of the psychology of artistic creation.

This perceptual training may well replace what seems an altogether disproportionate and ill-considered use of the nude in life-classes. I am not suggesting that drawing from life should be discontinued at any stage of the game. It is suggested that there are more important things than life-drawing during the early stages, that, while the human body remains perhaps the greatest interest of human beings,[1] there are many other beautiful or notable things in nature. Too many artists and art students are visually callous to nature. Their training with the nude has not been used as a means of sharpening observation and sensibility, but as a means of acquiring techniques and factual data.

b. Visual Memory. Since one of the major objectives of the methods of training here proposed is the development of a repertory of visual experiences from which to draw, it follows that the training of visual memory will be important. Sooner or later all emotional transformations of nature are traceable back to a stock of memory images. In order to develop this ability the student would be asked to describe or draw from memory such experiences, for instance, as the appearance of his breakfast table or some adventure of the previous summer. This practice parallels that reported from Japanese schools, where the student observes the model for a few moments, then turns the other way and draws from memory, thus developing a feeling for the essentials of posture, motion, bearing, and other striking characteristics.

c. Imagination. Immediately connected with both perception and visual memory is imagination, which, as used here, will include the assignment of feeling-tone, emotional response, and empathy to the stimulus. There is obviously a wide range of types, or divisions, of imagination. Perhaps these processes might be designated as the ' will to recreate.' Imagination may be restricted in the extent to which it creates new configurations from the stuff of experience, or it may be free and independent. Rembrandt's type of imagination would seem to be of the first sort; he leaves certain things out, emphasizes others, and yet does not do violence to the ' real ' appearance. We recognize the effect as typical, in the first instance, of Rembrandt, and not of natural objects. At the other extreme we have the fantasies of young children, who will consciously disregard natural appearance. Paul Klee and many of the Surrealists will allow their imaginations to take complete hold.

---

[1] Is this perhaps not academic itself? Does modern art in general confirm that artists have found it so — for representational purposes, at any rate?

Without imagination there can be no art. We do not wish to know merely that there is an outside world; we wish to know how persons and periods regard that world. But the artist who has, to use a critical cliché, " something to say," allows this imaginative, re-creative activity greater scope — even encourages it to have its own way. Art students must be trained to develop this ability, to be aware of the constant presence of this tendency to ' read into ' nature or experience; and to know how to direct it, to increase their ability to respond to it, and to transform it into esthetic objects.

The mind of the student should accordingly be well stocked with material of all sorts, from the humanities, from current affairs, from imagination. The normal mental process is largely one of the discovery of *correspondences and associations* (discovery does not necessarily mean willed or conscious) ; everything strikes us as like something else, or reminds us of something else, or as carrying overtones or undertones. And it is through this characteristic that one object or presentation may be made by the artist to carry the feeling, or the overtones or undertones of something else, gaining thereby weight, richness, or significance. It is not suggested that the student deliberately prepare a stock of visual similes, metaphors, or puns, that he learn to liken everything to something else. Much of this he will do in any case, as any human being will. It is asked, however, that he realize the eternal presence of interplay in most of his perceptions, and to give it its due and controlled place when he is at work. Our art training should foster this tendency. The artist should learn from poetry that " jocund " day can stand " tip-toe " on a mountain top, that gardens can grow in faces. He will thus come to feel free to rearrange parts, to invent, to distort; he will learn that one draws or sculptures, in the best practice, for some reason other than, or in addition to, the fabrication of a merely agreeable object.

d. The Selection of Qualities. Since, as the student will discover, he very seldom gives a complete account of phenomena because of the intrusion of feeling, attitude, imagination, and the like, he should have training to help him learn which qualities will have to be sacrificed, which emphasized, in order to bring out the qualities that seem important. The artist is discovering, or revealing, something that had heretofore lain unrevealed. In the light, then, of various prior considerations, the art student should be trained to account for phenomena in terms especially suited to those considerations. He must learn to select, emphasize, and even to distort. He should be shown the kinds of selection made typically by different kinds of artists. But in the last resort, this form of activity should be developed from the standpoint of his own experiences.

e. *Interests.* Finally, in this brief discussion of some of the psychological needs of the artist, there must be a word about interests. These are to a large extent established by the time the student decides to come to an art school, but now is the time to deepen and broaden them, in order that his perceptions may become more meaningful and revelatory, that his memory may become stocked with images and visual experiences, that correspondences and associations of an imaginative sort may come to mind.

2. Esthetic Effect; Techniques

Thus far I have discussed in a general way the training of the artist as related to the psychology of art. But perception alone is of little use to the artist. The development of the artist's faculties must be directed also to greater expressiveness in terms of the materials he will use, and to the effects that he will be able to get with these materials. The artist is also a craftsman, no matter what his medium or métier; he deals with some sort of physical stuff, and he must be able to control this to produce in actuality the equivalent of what he has in mind. The esthetic or plastic effects and the techniques by which the artist manifests his insights are interlocked closely with his perceptions.

The only way the artist can present the felt qualities of an experience or intuition is to devise symbols and stimuli that are esthetically suited to those qualities. The artist's main business, therefore, is to know a great range of esthetic effects obtainable through line and color, and so on. The student should practice making all kinds of lines, different kinds of modelling effects, color effects. Before he is asked to measure off a nude into accurate proportions, he should be asked to draw lines that move gracefully, that are jerky, that are varied in many respects, and that are relatively serene. The Chinese had elaborate textbooks and guides for artists showing lines carrying with them implications of various sorts. It is true that after generations of insistence upon these implications the various lines would carry with them the qualities assigned, but it is to be doubted that the implications were in the first place assigned arbitrarily. At some time the quality of a certain line must have seemed so delicate and sinuous that it was called the "floating thread" line, another the "chasing clouds and running water" line. Even to us cultural outsiders, the poetical rightness of these designations is clear. No advertising artist or illustrator would use the Chinese " floating thread " line for rendering an explosion. The student should be referred to good advertising art, to fine art, to nature, to develop a feeling for these matters. He should be asked to draw various kinds of rugged shapes, to be able to secure effects of blockiness and high polish, blockiness and shimmer of light (so far as is possible). He should practice various ways of suggesting distance; color for emotional effect, color to suggest superficial surface application, color to suggest integration with substance. Let him take an apple, a book — anything — and make it present a variety of stimuli. With lines and light and dark, he might make configurations that will be static and restful, others disturbing or violent. The works of many modern artists will serve as text; so will the works of Oriental artists. The importance of this practice cannot be overemphasized; the art student must know the ' music ' of esthetic effects, for only so will his work have artistic life.

The study of esthetic effects necessarily means also training in manipulative and technical effects. The student should know thoroughly all possible treatments of water colors, for instance; what happens with more, what with less, water; in each case, what happens if the paper is more or less moist. How do gouache, or poster colors, behave under similar treatments? How many different ways can water colors be manipulated — wash, stipple, crosshatch, scrub, blot, stroke, underpaint, dry-brush — and what are the ' feelings ' associated with these treatments? In addition, the student should be required to devise at least one original variation on the more familiar handlings.

The same systematic and thoroughgoing procedure should be undertaken with all the artist's and craftsman's materials, and all art students, regardless of ultimate intention, should have this manipulative drill. It does not do to say that the artist will sooner or later pick up a good deal of this experience. I know from personal experience and from conversations with many artists that much time and energy are wasted trying incidentally to learn something that should be a cornerstone of one's training. Some schools now include training in manipulation, but as a rule it is tentative and unsystematic, whereas it should be basic. Again, the students should be informed of new artistic materials — for example, fluorescent pigments, various trick crayons, et cetera — and he should try them out at once. Of course, manipulation must not be allowed to become an end in itself; it is a means for esthetically expressive effects.

3. Devices and Methods

Art schools of the past have erred in not providing enough information of the how-do-you-do-it sort; the result again is lost time for the student, and usually the adoption of any methods conveniently to hand. The student should be taught the tricks of the trade. How should a painting be begun? Should all types of painting be begun in the same way? Is a sketch merely a stage on the way to a finished work, or may the sketch itself be the finished work? How did sculptors of the past start their work? What steps are best in making pottery or carving wood? Students should know how artists of all esthetic persuasions and of various periods have worked; how leading artists of the day work. They could learn much from a careful examination of original notes, sketches, and jottings, the subsequent elaborative stages, and finally the finished work. What changes occurred along the way? What were the possible reasons for the changes? Were these for the better? What do the early stages have that the final lack, and vice versa?

There are other devices that should be studied and used by the student. It seems silly at this time, when a geometrical and mechanical environment is so much a part of our consciousness, to denounce mechanical aids to art. They were used in the past by great artists, but the nineteenth century disapproved of them. There is no sound reason why artists should not use in their art, the rule and compass, or the pantograph, the spotlight, airbrush, camera, or any other device that will aid in getting the effects desired.

Less time should be spent on such routine matters as perspective, anatomy, and the like, which are really devices rather than ends. Perspective, it should be made clear, is merely a convention of tentative value. Other forms of perspective have always been used; more and more, isometric and other forms of perspective effects have been challenging the supremacy of the old-fashioned optical method. Similarly, anatomy might well receive less emphasis, and the morphology of movement more. For portrait painters it might be well to study lighting, borrowing tricks from photography in order to rescue this once noble art from its present dismal, backward (even though anatomically correct) state. Indeed, all art students should be required to become thoroughly familiar with the esthetic effects and devices of good photographers. It has been done before; it is even more necessary now.

III. The Cultural History of Art

We deal next with a phase of the art student's training, now relatively casual and unimportant, that should be placed on an equal footing with other phases. The student should know intimately how to look at art works, to analyze them, criticize them. His treatments, oral and written, should be accompanied by numerous sketches to bring out details, technical bits, plastic qualities, and other subtleties. Far from being casual, these activities should be carefully devised and closely integrated with the other activities in the course of training. The student should at the same time become acquainted with the whole evolution of the making of images through a type of art history that might be described as a blend of art history and cultural history. We should not be concerned with imparting dates and all the other minutiae that beguile the scholar. Art history can be handled in such a way as to impart the greatest amount of pertinent information for the art student. This ' appreciative cultural history of art ' will bring to the student the techniques and esthetic niceties of the great artists of history. It should open up many new vistas suggesting new ways of attacking artistic problems.

Appreciation should be closely related to the creative activities. The student should try his hand at various manners; this is probably the best way really to get at the gist of the style. He should, as a matter of fact, be required to copy the works of other artists, among them some whom he does not happen to like at the time; and these copies should follow as closely as possible the procedure, methods, media, brushing, and so on. Exercises should be devised in which the student will create new things in the manner of some certain artist in order to demonstrate that he has perceived and grasped the essential esthetic and technical peculiarities. Not only will careful study of art works yield valuable information on techniques and esthetic effects; it will also increase the student's imaginative range and perceptual abilities. In short, the whole history of art should be made his textbook, and the great masters his mentors. All students should be required to assemble notebooks or scrapbooks of reproductions, cartoons, photographs, casual drawings — anything that has some sort of esthetic interest, either positive or negative; to jot down critical comments, and to sketch possible alterations.

IV. THE SOCIAL SETTING OF THE ARTIST

The students should know, as all educated people should, where they fit into the social scheme of things. What are the social functions of an artist in this time? What is he to do for society and what may he expect from society? For whom is he painting and sculpturing? These questions are troublesome to the average student who must think of his work as a means of livelihood, and yet who enters the field because he " wants to express himself." There should be a thorough and systematic treatment of the whole problem; otherwise we shall continue to turn out a high percentage of social and artistic misfits. The student should know something of the outstanding problems and beliefs of his time, and something of the ideal of social service, particularly since it is evident that many artists will continue to be engaged on collaborative or joint projects for the public. How will this affect his individuality? Are all individualities best expressed in works of ' fine ' art, no matter how poor?

The school should help orient the student with regard to his abilities and society's needs. Where are creative talents likely to be needed in the next few years? Shall we need more portrait painters or more architectural sculptors? More painters of ramshackle old barns, or more city planners, or mural decorators, or landscape designers? To effectuate such guidance and advisory assistance, art and craft schools throughout the country ought to come together in some sort of organization in order to set up some kind of machinery through which curricula, aims, needs, materials, methods, student aids, and other subjects will be thrashed out, and to establish a central board to study trends.

V. HIS PROFESSIONAL ADVANCEMENT

The school should not leave the student in ignorance about exhibitions, sales, contracts, business methods. Most artists learn these things only fragmentarily, and then at a loss of time and energy. Students should be advised of exhibitions to which they are eligible and in which they have a chance of acceptance, and perhaps should be helped to ship entries jointly. They should be advised about dealers and commissions. Should they draw up a contract for a portrait? What happens if the sitter declares the finished work unsatisfactory? Is the artist entitled to compensation? The whole matter of the economics of art and artists should be studied so that the student will know what he is undertaking.

VI. His Cultural Background

From what has already been said, it is clear that the cultural background of the student must be as broad as possible. He should know something of architecture, of music, of literature, particularly English poetry; he should have some knowledge of social theories, current affairs, science. His experience of music and literature should not be limited to mere listening or reading, but extended to analysis and critical appreciation. The analogies in the devices, structure, and esthetic effects in these arts and the visual arts should be pointed out. The student should be led to see the relation between the arts as forms of personal expression and as forms of social expression.

VII. The School Itself

While this is not the place to go into the question of plant, it may be said that libraries should be expanded in their scope to contain a large collection of photographs, reproductions, and heterogeneous material like that which goes into the making of a newspaper morgue. There should be adequate space for laying out materials for study and work in the library. The collection should also contain motion pictures demonstrating techniques and motion, as well as a collection of musical records. The auditoriums should be equipped for the projection of motion pictures and designed to facilitate audition and note-taking, especially if there is to be, as has been suggested, greater activity in the form of lectures by teachers, manufacturers, teachers of the humanities, and so on.

The faculty should be more varied in artistic aim and esthetic principles than is common now, yet should be more coöperative. Conflicting personal biases need not interfere with general objectives; when the student has achieved his preliminary training, he will be allowed to choose his mentors. The whole program should be smoothly integrated, so that there is a minimum of waste motion or confusion to the student.

III

OPPORTUNITIES FOR TRAINING AND FOR EMPLOYMENT IN APPLIED ART

Florence N. Levy
Director, Art Education Council
New York, New York

Art is not confined to pictures in gold frames or to monumental sculpture, and a knowledge of one or more artistic techniques — drawing, modelling, color, design — is necessary for many occupations. Applied art is not on a lower level than painting or sculpture; it is merely different. And it is not reached by a shorter road.

Some young people ask: " Where can I learn in the shortest time, at the lowest cost, so as to earn the most? " This is not the right attitude. Success comes slowly through systematic study and by working up through related tasks.

If art is being considered as a life work, it is necessary, after securing a good fundamental training in drawing, design, and color, to consider carefully what phase of art seems to hold the greatest interest and the greatest likelihood of success; what, for example, are the opportunities in local occupations for a career.

The first step up the ladder from high school to the professions is sometimes attained through scholarships, many of which are available in professional art schools. [1]

The School Art League of New York City, since 1911, has awarded 613 scholarships to graduates of the high schools there for the study of applied art at professional art schools. Many of these young men and women have achieved success, particularly in such fields as advertising (only a few women), illustration (about two-fifths specializing in fashion illustration), teaching, interior decoration, display, industrial design, textile design, and costume design. In the last named field, only a few are really successful, but at least two enjoy annual salaries in five figures.

---

[1] See *Art School Directory*. (The American Federation of Arts: Washington, D. C., 1939)

The first job is the most difficult to locate. Typing and stenography or selling sometimes serve as an entering wedge. Some of the first jobs for fashion illustrators are with the dress-pattern publishers; for textile designers, in textile studios; for advertising designers, in advertising agencies. With this type of experience as a basis, it should be possible to secure a staff position with a well-established firm or to undertake free-lance work. Earning power depends upon the ability and the reliability of the individual.

The larger art schools maintain a placement department but cannot guarantee positions. Most jobs are secured through personal contacts or through recommendations. Positions under Civil Service require passing an examination. In New York City, the National Alliance of Art and Industry, at 119 East 19th Street, maintains a well-organized placement section; the Artists' Guild, composed chiefly of illustrators, handles sales of work by its members. A limited number of positions are secured through newspaper advertisements. A study of advertisements that appeared during October, 1934, in the Sunday edition of 85 newspapers in 68 cities showed 414 " Help Wanted " and " Situations Wanted " in which a knowledge of some form of art was required for 19 different occupations.[1] A similar study made during March and April, 1936, of 47 newspapers from 36 cities revealed 1861 advertisements involving 24 different occupations.

I have been conducting guidance in art education for many years. During 1938, I answered inquiries from 511 individuals (169 men and 342 women) regarding 67 occupations. Information was given in 341 conferences and through correspondence with 170 who made inquiries by mail.

The Occupational Information and Guidance Service of the United States Office of Education, in Washington, is working on a list describing 55,000 jobs. *The Book of Opportunities,* by Rutherford Hayes Platt, in the 1933 edition, gives information about some 3,500 occupations, and the index of this book has been checked for the field of art.

The following list covers occupations that require a knowledge of line, space, form, design, and color — either of one or of several in combination — but does not include techniques and courses of study. The aim has been to confine the information to occupations and not to include the training required. It may be noted here that in most of these occupations, the position of assistant is a requisite step toward the

---

[1] This study was made by the Federated Council on Art Education with the coöperation of the Institute of Women's Professional Relations.

higher grade; thus, Assistant to the Art Director in an advertising agency may lead to the position of Assistant Art Director and, finally, to Art Director.

Occupations that Require Training in Art

1. The Assembling Arts: Display, Interior Design, Landscape Architecture, Theater Arts (including Theater Costume and Sets, Motion-Picture Costume and Sets).

2. The Constructive Arts: Architecture, Costume.

3. The Graphic Arts: Advertising, Illustration, Mechanical Drawing, Photography, Print-Making (hand), Print-Making (mechanical).

4. The Handcrafts: Ceramics, Leather, Metal, Paper, Textiles, Wood.

5. Industrial Design: Ceramics, Leather, Metal, Paper, Plastic, Textile, Wood.

6. Painting.

7. Sculpture.

8. Miscellaneous Fields: Lecturing, Library Work, Museum Work, Selling, Scientific Work, Teaching, Writing.

IV

A LIST OF VOCATIONAL OPPORTUNITIES IN THE VISUAL ARTS

C. VALENTINE KIRBY
State Director of Art Education
Harrisburg, Pennsylvania

Air-Brush Operators.

Architects: Landscape, Marine.

Art: Teachers, Supervisors.

Bronze: Founders, Chasers.

Cartoonists: Political, Comic, Motion-Picture.

Carvers: Furniture, Architectural Stone, Monumental Stone, Picture Frame, Wood.

Colorists: Lantern slides.

Decorators: Glass (etched and cut), Interior, Furniture, Mural, Porcelain, Pottery, Tile.

Designers: Architectural, Automobile, Basket, Bookplate, Book Covers, Book Jackets, Ceramic, Commercial, Container, Cotton Prints (textile), Furniture, Garden Furniture (iron, cement, and terra cotta), Glassware, Fashions (men's and women's), Hardware, Jewelry, Lace, Lighting Fixtures, Lettering, Machine, Millinery, Motion Picture (sets and properties), Pageant, Poster, Radio Cabinets, Rugs and Carpets, Sheet Music Covers, Shoe, Show-Card Writers, Silk Prints (textile), Stained-Glass Windows, Tapestry, Theatrical (stage sets and costumes), Tile, Toilet Articles, Wallpaper, Window Display, Woollen Prints (textiles), Wrought-Iron Work.

Draughtsmen: Anatomical, Archeological, Architectural, Biological, Botanical, Conchological, Entomological, Ethnological, Pathological, Paleontological.

Engravers: Commercial, Jewelry, Map, Mezzotint, Steel, Wood.

Etchers: Decorative (metal and glass).

Glass Blowers: Art, Botanical Model, Zoölogical Model.

Illustrators: Agricultural, Books, Juvenile, Commercial, Magazine, Newspaper.

Letterers: Motion-Picture Titlers, Illuminated Letterers.

Lithographers.

Model-Makers: Anatomical, Biological, Ethnological, Historical.

Modellers: Architectural (terra cotta), Leather, Decorative (papier mâché), Decorative (plaster).

Mosaic Workers.

Motion-Picture Art Directors.

Museum: Background Painters, Building Superintendents, Curators, Guards, Guides, Instructors, Librarians, Model-Makers, Preparators, Registrars, Supervisors of Circulating Exhibits, Taxidermists.

Ornamental Iron Workers.

Painted Glass: Cartoon Designers, Painters, Cutters, Fitters.

Painters: Landscape, Mural, Portrait, Sign, Science.

Photographers: Portrait, Motion-Picture, Photo-Engravers, Photo Retouchers.

Picture Dealers.

Picture Restorers.

Plaster Workers: Decorative.

Sculptors.

Silversmiths.

Stage-Lighting Effects.

Toy-Makers: Decorators.

Weavers: Hand, Basket.

V

THE GENERAL EDUCATION OF THE ARTIST, ART TEACHER, AND CURATOR

ARTHUR POPE

Professor of Fine Arts, Harvard University

Cambridge, Massachusetts

In matters of education, one cannot lay down any hard and fast rules that can be applied to all cases, for there are many ways of acquiring an education, and even the professional knowledge and skill required in an art like painting may be arrived at from various starting points and by various routes. Nevertheless, if I were asked to advise a boy who was planning to become a painter, I should tell him, first of all, to get as good a general education as possible, especially in literature, history, and philosophy, as well as in the general history and principles of art, so that he might have some idea of the significance of his technical skill in relation to a philosophical and cultural background. In going to exhibitions of contemporary paintings, one is constantly struck by the evident lack of interest shown by the artist in what he is saying — in what he is painting. Subjects seem to be chosen merely for the sake of a display of technical skill or cleverness in arrangement — there is no enthusiasm for the subject as such. I believe that without this primary enthusiasm for what one is saying or what one is representing, art becomes an empty thing — a medium for technical display, or an attempt at self-expression, an aim that has been so much overemphasized of recent years. To quote Gilbert Murray: " I think that there is almost no more dangerous doctrine to be preached to young poets and artists than this doctrine that art is self-expression. It makes them think of the one thing of all others which they ought to forget. The artist ought to be thinking of his subject and his work, and not of himself at all." [1]

Speaking especially of portrait painting, Booth Tarkington (20) writes:

---

[1] Gilbert Murray. *The Classical Tradition in Poetry.* (Harvard University Press, 1927) p. 243.

A painter, moreover, cannot paint anything the salient significance of which he is incapable of perceiving. He may record it, more or less as a camera would; but he cannot paint it for the eyes of those who ask painting for more than surfaces. A master craftsman is, of course, not necessarily an artist, and, though the portrait painter who is an artist needs to be a craftsman, the portraits he paints must come out of the inside of his head, not merely from his deft hand and measuring eye; he must know his man.

In a sense, this means that it needs a great man to paint a great man truly: the painter must at least be great in his comprehensions.

The necessity for comprehension holds for all painting. Therefore, I should advise a boy to get just as much of a broad foundation of knowledge and understanding as possible, for the broader one's interest and knowledge, the deeper the meaning that one is likely to find in one's subject or put into one's handling of it. Art is the product of thought about relationships of all kinds, and the measure of artistic value might almost be said to depend directly on the amount of thought, or meaning, that an artist can crowd into a given number of strokes or a given amount of manual effort.

All this means that, under ordinary circumstances, and especially in this country, a prospective painter (and the same thing would apply to a prospective sculptor) should continue in school and go to college before devoting himself more exclusively to professional training. In some colleges, at least, he can, along with his general studies, obtain a foundation in theory and practice, as well as in the history of art, so that he will have lost little time, if any, even from the point of view of technical practice.[1]

It may be objected that in the Renaissance a prospective painter entered the master's workshop when he was twelve or fourteen and certainly received nothing approaching a modern school or college education. But, as I have observed elsewhere, it must be remembered that cities, like Florence, Bruges, and Venice, were comparatively small, and that at least the leading artists were friends of the scholars and poets, if, indeed, they were not poets and scholars themselves. They were often leading citizens, too. Leonardo was an engineer as well as a scientist, and in the seventeenth century Rubens played an active rôle in international affairs. Painters and sculptors were often learned and thoughtful exponents of the fundamental ideas of their time. Of course, conditions of life were entirely different then; today, we must

---

[1] See Philip G. Clapp, quoted in Pope (16, p. 85).

adapt our education to present conditions. It is difficult for any of us to acquire an education in the informal manner of the Renaissance.

After college, I believe that a painter ought to be able to pursue his advanced training in a graduate professional school, as in the case of law or medicine. No such school exists now [1]; so the student must either enter the best art school he can find or pursue his studies independently. Much may be said for the latter course.

There is another reason why I should advise any boy interested in painting to continue with school and college rather than to go into an art school at an early age. In an art school — at least as most of them are conducted at present — one spends practically one's whole time in practice, on the supposition that in an art like drawing or painting the technique is so difficult that one must begin very early to acquire technical skill and must devote one's whole time to it if one is going to get anywhere. Even granted that this were true — and it probably is not — and even granted that the technical training in the art school be satisfactory — which likewise it probably is not — there is one great difficulty with this exclusive training. Its entire aim is to turn out a painter well equipped technically to become a professional artist. Suppose, however, that the student, after acquiring all this great technical ability, decides that he is not really interested in becoming an original artist — that he has little really that he wants to say, or that there is no prospect of a satisfactory demand for what he wants to say; and yet he wishes to make a living, marry, and live a normal life. He is definitely interested in art, but would like to pursue that interest in some other way than as a professional painter. There are all sorts of other careers in the general field of art besides that of the professional artist.[2] Suppose, for example, he decides that he would prefer to go into museum work or into teaching. He suddenly finds himself at a terrible disadvantage, as compared with others of his own age, in that he has devoted a number of precious years to exclusive technical training and has acquired almost none of the general background necessary for work of a more scholarly nature. He finds that he has to start all over again almost at the beginning.

This is no mere hypothetical case. Students are constantly emerging from art schools to find themselves in exactly this situation. Some of these are in a position, financially and otherwise, actually to start

---

[1] The reader will find a more extended discussion of a possible graduate school in *Art, Artist and Layman* (16).

[2] See, for example, Mr. Kirby's list in the preceding pages. — *Editor*.

over, and they come to the university. I have known a number of such
persons in recent years. There are probably countless others who are
unable to do this.[1] They find themselves forced to continue somehow in
the practice of art as a profession. As second-rate painters, many of
them help to swell the mass of artists who have to be supported by the
government; others, disappointed and disillusioned, turn without enthusiasm to the practice of ' commercial ' art.

Few students at the ages of fifteen to eighteen or nineteen years can
be certain of their qualifications for a specific profession like painting.
I think they should be encouraged to obtain first of all a genuine cultural background; they will need it in any case. In many instances,
this procedure will not only save years of work, but often prevent real
tragedies as well.

For students who are planning to become teachers in universities
or curators in museums, it goes without saying that study in college
should be followed by work in a first-rate graduate department of art
in a university. I believe that in connection with their study of the
theory of art, all such students should do a certain amount of drawing
and painting, for actual practice in the terms of an art gives an understanding of quality of performance that it is difficult to achieve in any
other way. This does not mean necessarily original ' creative activity '
on which, of late, so much emphasis has been placed. What we want to
find out is how painters have worked to express their ideas, the kind of
' vocabulary ' they have used; and for this purpose studies made after
the drawings and paintings of different masters are of much greater
value than attempts at original composition. In fact, one begins to
wonder whether much of the preliminary training, even of the professional artist, should not be of this sort. Chinese painters, for example,
(and Renaissance painters were trained in much the same way) began
the practice of painting by learning a vocabulary of strokes.[2] This
vocabulary of strokes represented an accumulation of visual knowledge
acquired by many previous generations of painters, and, what was most
important, provided a means and a method of acquiring new knowledge
on the part of the new generation. This is the essence of tradition.
Some way will have to be found to give painters something of this accu-

---

[1] One of these walked into my office just as I was reading this over: a young
man with great technical ability, but, frankly, with nothing that interests him to
paint. To make a living, he has turned to commercial photography.

[2] Mention of this aspect of Chinese art training will be found earlier in this
chapter. — *Editor.*

mulated knowledge of the past, and something of a vocabulary of expression, before we can expect much in the way of a new renaissance. With every painter attempting to ' start from scratch ' to express something entirely original and personal, the content of art becomes thinner and thinner. At any rate, a knowledge of how it has been done in the past is the important thing for the teacher or curator.

Knowledge of art itself, rather than of reproductions, is also important for the teacher or curator. Therefore, the student should pick out a university, especially for graduate work, where original works of art are available. This should, as far as possible, be supplemented by travel and study in Europe. While war is on, this is naturally out of the question. In the meantime, more and more works of art of fine quality are becoming available for study in this country. For students of moderate means, fellowships provide the opportunity for necessary travel. But in this, as in other fields of learning, there is not much place for mediocrity. I am convinced that a student should be pretty sure that he can be first-rate in some phase of the subject before undertaking the study of art as a career.

VI

COURSES IN SKETCHING FOR COLLEGE STUDENTS

E. RAYMOND BOSSANGE
Dean, School of Architecture and Allied Arts, New York University
New York, New York

Technical work in the arts in an academic college is of value if the purpose of the course is to train observation, develop appreciation, and stimulate an emotional reaction to works of art, nature, and, in fact, to life itself. When, instead of that, the purpose, as is often the case, is to produce work that can be shown or exhibited, the results are often rather poor. In the latter case, such attempts are based on the false premise that because the student has a cultural background, he may be able by clever short cuts to avoid the drudgery of mastering technique and still produce something to exhibit. If the production of such work gives the student pleasure, that is something, but time can be spent to better advantage by adopting a different method.

There is an important difference between a fundamental course in chemistry, for instance, for a man who proposes to make that field his profession, and a general course adapted to give the layman an insight into that phase of knowledge and some valuable information. The same is true in art. Freehand drawing, for instance, for the student with professional intentions, involves a long apprenticeship in drawing, usually from cast, until the fundamentals are mastered. The layman, however, would get much more benefit in the same time from a course in making simple sketches.

I emphasize *simple* sketches, for to do a simple sketch the student must observe and carefully study the spirit of the object, must determine the relative importance of the elements, and must eliminate the unimportant. Thumbnail sketches (a scale which makes details impossible) done at any time and anywhere when a good subject is found are a splendid exercise. A few lines to express an attitude or the movement of a figure, regardless of the lack of pencil facility, are more important than labored drawings.

A simple color sketch of a painting, giving the principal masses of color in their right relations, the main values, and the composition of the picture, is of much greater educational importance than a painstaking imitation of any example. Such a sketch requires study, the careful weighing of the elements, and the determination of what counts most in conveying the message. To study a building and then make a simple sketch that tries to show the character (monumental, religious, domestic, civic, or utilitarian), the composition, the relation of voids to solids, the proportions and distribution of ornament, the expression of materials and how the building functions, necessitates concentrated efforts that lead to understanding and appreciation.

Sketches are even more valuable if done from memory. Students who try to draw a building, a picture, or a statue from memory will immediately discover how very little they have observed and how relatively unimportant is what they do remember. The importance attached to drawing from memory by the Japanese is well known. The object is shown for a few minutes, then taken away, and the child draws what he remembers with as few lines as possible. And what wonderful results this system produces! Not only are their sketches reduced to the essential lines, but the students have felt the spirit of the object so thoroughly that they are able to substitute for a group of lines one line that gives the action or character even more truthfully, although very often that line does not exist in the object itself.

Whistler is said to have arrived at simplicity of expression by a very different method. His preliminary studies for an etching were completely drawn, hardly a single detail omitted. Then he would erase all insignificant lines, and thus he achieved the effect of simplicity. Sargent required as many as eighteen sittings for a portrait. During seventeen of them, he studied the drawing, values, color, brush strokes, and so forth. Then, having scraped off nearly all the paint, with intense concentration and dexterity, he painted it all over in the last sitting, thus giving the portrait the boldness, dash, and vitality of a rapid sketch but with all the knowledge and study he had put into the preparatory work.

I do not hesitate to advise memory sketching as the best way to train observation. To feel the spirit of the subject through discriminating observation that simple sketches require — that is the main purpose.

VII

TECHNICAL AND LIBERAL COURSES IN THE ART SCHOOL

Clifford M. Ulp
Director, School of Applied Art
Rochester Athenaeum and Mechanics Institute
Rochester, New York

The objectives of the specialized art school are generally accepted as dealing primarily with the mastery of skills and techniques of drawing and painting and the application of these to individual creative art work. The training is usually designed to give the student the necessary equipment to fill the specifications of individually selected goals, yet broad enough to qualify the student for a constellation of jobs.

While there is a divergence of opinion on the best methods of teaching the skills and techniques, there is common agreement that they can be taught and that certain items — the study of action, line, form, perspective, color, and design — are basic.

The crafts are not usually given major importance in the technical art school. It is evident, of course, that for such work there must be specialized technical courses. Pratt Institute, Rhode Island School of Design, Philadelphia Museum School of Industrial Art, Alfred University, the School of Applied Art of the Rochester Athenaeum and Mechanics Institute are some of the technical art schools offering both art and craft courses. In the area of original creative art work, we find the use of the tool (drawing and craftsmanship) employed in a variety of ways, such as illustration, poster design, lettering and layout, commercial design, industrial design, typographic design, architectural decoration, modelling, landscape, portrait and mural painting, to mention only a few.

While these two areas, mastery and use of the artist's means of expression, are of paramount concern to the technical art school, there is a growing awareness of the importance of the liberal component in technical art training. This means that the technical art school has recognized the need of a wider educational program emphasizing the place of liberal subjects in the curriculum. This continues to present a very real problem to the technical art school. Recognizing this difficulty, some art schools have frankly offered no formal liberal courses, and this has led to the charge of narrowness in art schools where the technical art training is excellent.

Some art schools have contended that an art course is a liberal course in its very nature and that it is best not to introduce formal classes in liberal subjects. It is only within the last ten or fifteen years that any effort to introduce the liberal component has been made. Some educators have proposed that the curriculum in the art school should be one-third liberal and two-thirds technical. In other schools a proportion of one-sixth liberal to five-sixths technical has met with a measure of success. The recognized technical art schools are making a vital contribution to the field of general education. Students who have taken these courses have gained competence in art pursuits and are filling positions of importance in the art world. It is perhaps true that the responsibility of the art school to the student would be better discharged if liberal courses were included in all art-school curricula.

VIII
APTITUDES AND TRAINING FOR INDUSTRIAL DESIGN

GILBERT ROHDE
Industrial Designer
New York, New York

Before we even consider training for designing, we should think of natural aptitudes. Native endowments manifest themselves long before the time when specialized training for industrial design is to be entered upon. I might rate the native abilities that are necessary as follows:

First, thirty percent ability to see where things could be better and an instinctive ingenuity in thinking of ways in which they might be made better. All of us meet with various annoyances in the use of certain products or in conditions to which we are exposed; the faucet or the vacuum cleaner may not work right, or the room may be too hot or too cold or too dry, but most of us go no further than expressing our annoyance. If you are one of those few who say, " Now why can't this be changed or improved? " and then can think of a way of doing it, you have the most important natural aptitude. This may be manifested at a very early age in respect to simple objects.

Second, thirty percent of what can be called either ' sales ability ' or a sense of mass psychology — a sensitivity to demand, the ability to sense what most people will like.

Third, twenty percent scientific-mindedness, especially in the shape of a feeling for materials and construction. This trait also should be manifested at an early age. If as a child you never took a clock apart or made some construction with levers for lifting things, you will be handicapped as a designer.

Fourth, for the last twenty percent, a native sensitiveness to esthetic form. It may surprise you that I place that last; but I do so because, with this aptitude but without the other aptitudes, you may be either an artist or a craftsman but you cannot be a successful industrial designer.

It still remains for someone to devise a group of aptitude tests to measure these traits satisfactorily.

As for training for industrial design, this has not yet been crystallized, and it is fortunate that it has not been at this early stage. One must know more about the requirements before training for industrial designing becomes as rigid as that for some of the older professions. A few schools have made a fair start, but the opportunity is still there to do a better job.

The training must include some fine arts, pure drawing from figure, pure composition, and, above all, sculpture, because the industrial designer must think in three dimensions.

There must be some study of the history of art, but it is here that we strike what is probably the greatest difficulty, because despite all that has been written on what is the matter with art education, very little change has taken place. It still tends to be taught in the *Beaux Arts* manner, as if art were an isolated phenomenon, unrelated to other experience, as if the 'styles' sprang full-blown from the head of Jove. If we can forget all about styles and get a sense of art as merely one human activity conditioned by wars, climate, geography, distribution of wealth, trade, religion, raw materials, invention, and temperament of local potentates, we will have a much better feeling for the appropriateness of form in our culture. I recommend reading Dewey and Van Loon on this point.

There must be a fair degree of training in the commercial form of graphic arts needed in the profession, for example, in rendering. The designer who succeeds in establishing himself in business is not likely to do his own rendering, but rendering is the most valuable asset for getting a first job. And then the designer must have a sense of what is bad, in order that he may judge the work of others. There must be sufficient instruction in the making and reading of working drawings for the designer's purpose. This need never be carried to the point of making the complicated drawings necessary for the working parts of machines, for the designer is never called upon to do that.

There must be considerable training in the technology of materials and fabrication, but there is as much danger there of giving too much as too little. If a young man were subjected to a full course in engineering, physics, and chemistry, his imagination would be completely blocked. On the other hand, he needs a little of all of these, particularly the study of material and fabrication. As far as I know, there is no fully developed course of this kind at present.

The student must actually work with materials or power machines.

This would be done in connection with the making of models of his own design. Model work is much more important than paper work.

There should be some study of advertising, publicity, and sales methods. Photography is useful, but not necessary.

Some architectural study should be included in every industrial-design course. And then the sooner we include some product-design work in every architectural course, the sooner we shall break down the artificial distinctions that now exist between the designer of buildings and the designer of those things that go into a building. Of course there must be specialization, merely because of the time factor in every man's life, and there will be a difference in emphasis, but there need not be the mutual exclusion that exists today with its concomitant jealousies.

The question of how to study design, how much to work with abstractions and theory, and how much to work on application of design to actual commercial problems is a controversial one. The answer, of course, lies somewhere in the middle ground. Here the ingenuity and personality of the teacher is probably as important as the curriculum itself, for no routine can effect the transfer of theory to application.

Theoretically, every teacher in the design department of a school of industrial design should be a practicing designer. Obviously, this is not possible. But there must be at least one man in the school who has had much experience in various fields and who constantly keeps his hand in commercial design.

IX

EDUCATION IN VARIOUS ARTS AND MEDIA FOR THE DESIGNER

L. MOHOLY-NAGY
Director, School of Design
Chicago, Illinois

In 1903, Frank Lloyd Wright launched in Hull House, Chicago, an offensive against Ruskin and Morris. He proclaimed the machine the legitimate tool in the hands of the creative artist. This was a brave challenge to the governing ideas of that time, as the potentiality of the machine for a genuine production was not yet discovered, and very few people were yet able to see the real issue that lay behind Morris and Ruskin's fight against the machine. It is true, the machine was then employed for imitating craftsmanship. Objects used for generations by the well-to-do class were poorly reproduced for the low-income groups. Morris and Ruskin, who kept a clear sense for formal and organic values, saw in the old craftsmen the personification of all creative work and were horrified at the low quality of industrial mass production.

They declared that the machine had to be eliminated. Wright quickly grasped the mistake of such a conclusion. He understood the machine as being pliable to man's needs; not as an imitator of hand tools but as an instrument for genuine creation. Of course, the machine must be studied and understood in order to be used rightly.

From that time on, creative artists of America and Europe, the German *Werkbund* and the *Bauhaus* followed this principle that already had set Europe in motion through the work of Van de Velde and others.

The *Bauhaus* especially took up a systematic investigation of how the potentialities of the machine age could be incorporated in an educational and production program. Gropius stated " art and technique is a new unity." This stood for his era, and the statement became the slogan for his generation; however, not without a struggle. The factory owner as well as the consumer resisted the ideas, sometimes against their own interest. But the opponents were eventually won over by better design, more efficient architecture, intellectually and emotionally fruitful art movements, motion picture, airplane, radio, television, and the new forms of communication, transportation, and distribution. The esthetic mastery of the machine, the principles of functional mass production, became commonplace knowledge.

At that stage, the *Bauhaus* already grew beyond this program. Trying to found a new mentality needed to handle the machine, the *Bauhaus* worked out a new educational approach. This education laid a great emphasis not only on the technological elements, but also on the sensory experiences that are important sources of human expression. In this way, the emotional and intellectual balance of the individual and his inventive capacity were developed. The surprising finding was that this work has brought forward a new goal; namely, the mastery of the machine, not only from the point of view of design but from the human point of view as well. In other words, the forty years that have elapsed since the Wright manifesto have shown that the discovery of the machine as a means of genuine creation changed essentially the quality of products but did not change the economic and social conditions of the masses. On the contrary, the rising production brought more people under the control of industry than ever before, and it seems that our present civilization and culture are largely the projection of *a partly misunderstood* mass production. Our metropolitan dwellings are stone jungles and are nearer to slums than to nature; our eight-hour work day is crippling in one way or other; the time-consuming transportations daily are inescapable sources of fatigue.

The conveyor belt, efficiency engineering with its snapshot conclusions drawn from hurried tests, the neglect of our integrating forces make life more cruel in its psychological effects than the hardships of unregulated labor of twelve to fourteen hours a day in the early period of the Industrial Revolution.

We do not yet have any suggestion that enables us to master this situation. But the solution must be congenial to our biological requirements embedded in a technical civilization, as the machine cannot and should not be eliminated. It is a neutral tool that can be used for the benefit of mankind. The problem is, how can we use it without complete exhaustion of creative energies.

The ' why ' of our actions and the ' how ' of our departures will emerge slowly when everything will be centered around the welfare of the human being and around his sensibility and active participation in the affairs of our world. Man as a biological unit and not as a money-making mechanism is the integrator of every activity and must become the long disregarded yardstick again. So the healthy functions of man's organs and their development and his need for recreation and leisure will be the keys in the future to the mastery of the machine and with it of his surroundings. The great edifice of science, art, and technology will receive its justification through his happy and balanced status.

An integrated education, the integration of art, science, and technology, may produce the genius needed to solve this problem. This is not any more a question of the education of the designer, but rather of the general education to which all specialized forms of education have to be subordinated.

The School of Design in Chicago is founded upon the principles and educational aims of the *Bauhaus*. The idea of this education was born out of the conviction that designs for mass production and modern architecture, with extensive use of steel, concrete, glass, plastics, and so forth, need new men with fresh mentality to handle them. Exact knowledge of material and machine is equally necessary to give the product organic function. The School of Design trains men and woman practically and theoretically as designers of handmade and machine-made products in wood, metal, plastic, glass, textiles, and for stage, display, exposition architecture, typography, photography, modelling, and painting. The School of Design aims, also, to educate architects, art teachers, and photographers, and to carry into the ranks of professionals and interested laymen the principles of a new type of education that develops a new type of designer, able to face every requirement, scientific and technical, social and economical, not because he is a prodigy but because he has the right method of approach.

Of course, a great hindrance to self-expression is fear. One is limited by the fear that someone will laugh at him, will think him ineffective. This fear is increased by an anachronistic system that teaches the student that he must walk in the shadow of the genius of the past. In the School of Design, the student's self-expression is never compared with the work of some great master in the past. On the contrary, he is encouraged and urged to study what the great man himself studied in his day — those fundamental principles and facts on which all design of all times is based. The student must build upward for himself, gaining that happy status of self-experience and experimentation that is the true source of creative achievements. Then he is ready to study tradition and the contributions of bygone geniuses, enriching his own knowledge by the fruits of their discoveries.

The education of the student at the School of Design is carried on in theoretical and practical courses in the classes and workshops of the school. The school year is divided into two semesters. Each student must spend two semesters in the preliminary courses and six semesters in a special workshop. After the successful completion of this training, he will obtain a diploma and he may receive the architect's degree by continuing four semesters (two years) in the architectural department.

First Year. The preliminary curriculum offers a thorough test of the student's abilities in the different types of art work. It helps him to make genuine decisions, when confronted with tools and materials, with the fundamentals of expression. The course is divided into three main parts:

1. Basic elements of workshop training, leading to the mastery of the means of expression: (*a*) hand tools, (*b*) machines, (*c*) materials, (*d*) surface treatment, (*e*) volume, and (*f*) space.

2. Basic elements of plastic representation, leading to the visualization of plans and ideas so that other persons can read their meaning: (*a*) life drawing, (*b*) color work, (*c*) photography, (*d*) geometrical drawing, (*e*) lettering, and (*f*) modelling.

3. Sciences, leading to an understanding of those things that control all life: (*a*) life sciences, (*b*) social sciences, (*c*) physical sciences, and (*d*) intellectual integration.

Parallel with these subjects will be given: (*a*) survey of contemporary art, (*b*) music appreciation, (*c*) gymnastics, and (*d*) contact with outside activities; exhibitions, museums, factories, building sites, and so forth.

Briefly, the preliminary curriculum embodies the essential components of the training that will be given afterwards more elaborately in the special workshops. Also, it gives the student ample opportunity to find his likings and to make a careful choice of subsequent specialized work in one of the workshops.

Second, Third, and Fourth Years. After passing the examination in the preliminary course, the student enters one of the six specialized workshops: namely, (*a*) wood, metal (object design), (*b*) textile (weaving, dyeing, and fashion), (*c*) color (murals, decorating, wallpaper), (*d*) light (photography, film, typography, commercial arts), (*e*) modelling (glass, clay, metal, stone, plastics), and (*f*) display (theater and exposition architecture, window display).

In the *Fifth and Sixth Years* architecture is added.

As for examinations in the School of Design, the following plan is followed.

First Year. After the first half-year of the preliminary course, the first examination will be held in the form of a students' trial exhibition. After the second half-year, a similar exhibition will be held as the final examination in the preliminary course.

Second, Third, and Fourth Years. Workshop, tools, and machines, bookkeeping and estimating, drawing, scientific subjects (including social sciences), elementary lectures in architecture (constructions and statics), with final examination for a diploma, make up the schedule.

Fifth and Sixth Years. The examinations deal with architecture, landscape architecture, town-planning, and scientific subjects. Problems are set that pertain to kindergarten, grade, high schools, and colleges, and to such social services as hospitals, recreation, leisure and hobby organization, with an additional thesis for the degree in architecture.

In the School of Design the teachers are not only chosen for what they know but also for what they are doing. They are creative personalities, engaged in projects of their own as well as in teaching. The inventive student will discover that these instructors sympathize with his problems because of their own experiences and will guide him skillfully into correct methods of study and into the fruitful attitude of experimentation.

These are general facts about the School of Design, the program of which may stand for similar institutions. But there is still another important factor. This School is not simply a school for designers. It tries to be, too, the nucleus of a cultural community, with the hope that equilibrium is fostered in everyone's life. The school tries to remodel the whole meaning of art itself, as a form of expression in which everybody can participate, though to different degrees.

The struggling young people who want to be artists will receive all the assistance possible from the school; but if they are someday artists, it will be their own personal responsibility and private achievement. As long as they belong to the school, they must think in terms of needs, functions, tools, and materials. They are educated as designers and craftsmen to earn their living. Any other course would be a gamble. And earning one's living by means of a job that one has thoroughly mastered for the benefit of the community is a clean and productive kind of existence. Should a student's expression develop into the sphere of the great arts, which means the most genuine expression on the highest level of the time, the pleasure will not only be his but the school's and the community's as well.

X

TECHNICAL EDUCATION OF ARTISTS FOR COMMERCE

JAMES C. BOUDREAU
Director, School of Fine and Applied Arts
Pratt Institute
Brooklyn, New York

Every period in the history of man is marked by definite major interests that associate themselves inseparably with each civilization. The Greeks were a great art-producing and art-loving people. The Romans were soldiers and lawgivers. In the Middle Ages, impelled by strong religious feelings of the people, there flowered the marvelous houses of worship known today as the Gothic Cathedrals of France and England.

Our own American civilization is expressed in commerce and industry. It is the function of commerce to distribute to you and me and all other Americans the many things the industrial plants produce. An important phase of commerce is advertising, or acquainting possible buyers with information about products that have been manufactured. Within the field of advertising are vital positions for alert, qualified artists who are capable of illustrating industrial products, such as foods, clothing, machines, and books, so that the public will want to buy them. One who makes these pictures is called a ' commercial artist.' Within recent years his title has changed to ' advertising artist,' although his duties remain the same; namely, making pictures that help sell manufactured goods.

Advertising art offers two kinds of employment; one, the steady salaried position where one works by the week and in return receives a specified weekly pay check. Here the artist has but one employer, who keeps him busy making pictures for his firm. Most of these regular positions are with advertising agencies, although there are many opportunities for this type of steady art work with large department stores, mail-order houses, and even some manufacturers who market their own products direct.

The other employment outlet is called ' free lancing.' The free-lance artist has his own private studio and is on call at all times to work for anybody or any firm that desires his type of picture-making. He is paid on the per-drawing basis. While most commercial artists aspire to be free-lancers, it is highly advisable for the beginner to accumulate two or three years' experience in steady employment before setting up in business for himself.

Candidates who will succeed with adequate training must have five essential qualifications before they enter upon their professional preparation. First, they must have the creative impulse. This should be evident in their past drawing experiences. The ability to represent things is not enough. More important is the ability to present ideas. Second, a high mental capacity evidenced by an outstanding scholastic record on the high-school level, including academic subjects as well as art, is a vital asset. Third, social adaptability is an essential. Working with others presents itself throughout school and in the profession. Commercial art itself is a highly social medium. Fourth, a super-abundance of enthusiasm is needed, an exuberance that is not easily dampened. Fifth, the candidate must have the spirit of the perfectionist, an unquenchable thirst for improvement and development in many directions.

An art-school entrance examination is essential if these qualifications are to be ascertained. Such an examination will include graphic performance in drawing and design; a high-school scholastic record; 'citizenship' in the high-school period, evidenced in extra-curricular activities like clubs, school magazine, athletics, music, and dramatics; and letters of recommendation from persons qualified to evaluate the candidate in terms of these five essentials. Following the assembly and study of the above data, a personal interview is highly advisable before final selection.

Granted that qualified candidates have been invited to prepare themselves for professional commercial-art opportunities, we are now ready to outline an adequate program of training. Since the prevailing practice in America calls for three years of intensive post-high-school study, that length of time is accepted in presenting the following sequence of studies.

The first year may well be devoted to a solid foundation in drawing and design. Color theory and perspective are vital foundational subjects. At least once a week students should receive instruction in the history of art. In the second year, a transition from general basic art toward commercial art should be effected. While continuing drawing, design, and art history, such professional subjects as layout, lettering, typography, and reproductive processes will find their places due to this transition. The third year will again continue general drawing and design, permitting, however, more time for commercial-art major content. Advanced study in lettering is strongly urged. Advertising problems should become more complex and more inclusive. At least one campaign with a comprehensive spread incorporating letterheads, small and twenty-four sheet posters, booklets, newspaper and magazine space should be developed.

It is most important that the commercial-art content be subject to continuous change, so that it synchronizes with the best contemporary professional practices. A stereotyped program repeated year after year is fatal. Where the size of advanced enrollment permits, it is highly advisable to offer students an option within the advertising field. Such options could well include layout, display, packaging, fashion, photography, or lettering. The option elected should not, however, interfere with the typical third-year program outlined.

Round-table discussions led by outstanding advertising and business personalities comprising a wide spread of activities will prove most helpful toward a professional orientation. These guest speakers should meet the seniors in the latter part of their last term.

Of course, it is expected that adequate and comfortable classroom and studio space, with proper equipment for the various activities listed, will be provided in the physical plant of the art school. Makeshift adaptations of rooms poorly fitted for a particular subject prove a serious handicap for successful results.

Such a selected student body, housed in rooms appropriate for the curriculum outlined, presents a real challenge to a strong faculty. Selection of the teaching staff should entail even more care than that of the student body. All staff members should be professionally active in the subject they present, in the highly specialized advanced subjects presented in the second and third years. Part-time instructors will, accordingly, constitute much of the faculty. While this part-time staff will complicate administration of the program, the rewards are greater than the difficulties. In addition, it is possible to attract leaders for two to four half-days per week. Such a plan offers an opportunity for service without the economic or professional loss that naturally accompanies full-time instruction. Furthermore, it facilitates faculty adjustments as changing programs require.

Experience has proved that a successful combination of the factors mentioned — students, program, plant, and faculty — does provide an

adequate training for careers in commercial art. The graduate will
have acquired a good understanding of commercial art as a business
and will have reached at least a minimal professional level in his work.
There will be no gap to bridge between his school experience and his
job. This desirable status is the accumulative result of three years of
apprenticeship under professionally active leaders, augmented by practical conferences with outstanding business and advertising specialists.

XI

UNRECOGNIZED ART SCHOOLS IN AMERICA [1]

WILLIAM LONGYEAR
Department of Advertising Design, Pratt Institute
Brooklyn, New York

The *American Art Annual* lists and describes briefly several hundred
American schools of art and architecture. These are often classed as
recognized art schools, although many are on the border line. There
exist hundreds of art schools not listed in the *Art Annual*. These may
be found, one or more, in American cities and towns from coast to coast.
' Unrecognized ' herein applies to the school with meager faculty and
facilities, the school with shifting curricular policy and student acceptance standards, and the school run for private profit, without state
support or adequate endowment.

The policies of unrecognized art schools are generally geared to the
business of income for existence and private profit. Policy, if any, is
frequently changed to meet the occasion. Policy is shaped to the interests of the school rather than to those of the student. Tuition may
be as much as ' traffic will bear.' Extras, model fees, laboratory fees,
and unexpected assessments are levied on the student who is able to pay.

The faculty may consist of one or more qualified or unqualified
teachers. One instructor may teach several widely different subjects.

---

[1] This article is not the result of a survey. It emanates from observation,
personal experience, and from repeated testimony received over a period of years.
It is intended to give a picture of the field in general, although attention is called
to the exception. Facts conveyed herein are known within the art education profession but have seldom appeared in print.

Student teachers are often used. Widely recognized, 'big' artists are often printed in the catalog as inducement, though they usually make little or no contribution by teaching.

The buildings, more often the rooms, of the unrecognized art schools are not designed for their purpose; they are inadequate in space, lighting, ventilation, and heating. In the larger cities, schools are located in loft or business buildings, whereas in the towns, private residences are used. Equipment is meager. Because of expense, modern furniture, instruments, tools, and properties are lacking.

Courses are generally published in booklets. They are chosen as a result of popular demand from potential students who do not have a knowledge of industrial or social needs. Students seeking courses not listed are seldom turned away. Such students are either absorbed into regular classes or are given a pretense for the course demanded. Because these courses do not have to meet state or other requirements, they are often nothing more than impractical 'busy work.' Courses run for a length of time in proportion to the student's financial resources. Actual instances are known of schools that have withheld graduation from students who refused to take repeated extension courses as suggested by instructors. Such students were classed as 'unqualified for professional work' and the threat of 'no recommendation' was held over their heads.

Students patronizing unrecognized art schools are generally poorly advised, ignorant of conditions, or financially helpless. The layman or parent finds it difficult to obtain ratings in this elusive and specialized branch of learning. Students are attracted by glamorous catalogs and high-pressure advertising. Talent sometimes survives the unfortunate training given by the poor school, but much damage has been done to the student in loss of time and in the inculcation of bad habits of thinking and technique. Many comprehend their error too late, after time and money have been dissipated.

The tuitions of unrecognized art schools vary greatly. They may be zero for fashionable students accepted for their drawing power and contacts. They may be excessive. The low cost of tuition required by many schools precludes good instruction or other facilities. Instructors are poorly paid and give accordingly. In larger cities schools offer elaborate 'fronts' in the form of catalogs, reception rooms, and exhibits. Names of prominent patrons and advisory committees are published. Placement and professional opportunities are often the bait held out to prospective students. The school lists its successful graduates, who upon investigation may turn out to have received little or no help from their alma mater.

What I have said amounts to an indictment against the unrecognized art school, but long experience and extensive knowledge of conditions justify the statements I have made. To be sure, there are some ' unrecognized ' or unheralded art schools, imbued with sincere purpose, that are really fulfilling a need in their localities. These schools should not be condemned. They are frequently operated at a loss or at least without profit by a management that serves a worthy purpose.

XII

COMMERCIAL CORRESPONDENCE COURSES IN ART

ALFRED G. PELIKAN
Director of Art, Milwaukee Public Schools and
Director, Milwaukee Art Institute
Milwaukee, Wisconsin

In discussing briefly the training of the artist in contemporary society, it is advisable at the start to state that the word *artist* is used to denote a person properly trained and qualified to take his place in the community on a par with men in other professions, such as the doctor, the lawyer, the architect, the teacher, and others whose right to practice in their chosen field depends on meeting definite requirements established by the state or by some other governing body. All the professions have steadily increased their requirements in order to keep out incompetents, to raise the standards of attainment, and to protect the profession.

In the old days of the guilds, with their system of progressive steps from apprentice to journeyman and then to master, the standards established in the arts and crafts were high and the reputation of the guild jealously guarded.

Today few artist craftsmen have the opportunity to receive their training in the *botega,* or workshop, but must depend on qualified art schools.

So far, no short cut to the mastery of a. y subject has been found, but there are always those who, unwilling to make the sacrifice necessary for attainment in any field, fool themselves with the belief that they are able to master art or music in " twelve easy lessons." It is in this connection that certain types of correspondence courses and unrecognized art schools do much to lower the standards of the profession of art by their frequent misrepresentation and disregard of the student's ability and preparation to meet the demands of the professional artist. These practices have lowered professional standards, so that much building, designing, and painting are done by improperly trained incompetents.

Clearly the recognized art schools and the colleges with qualified art departments ought to conduct an educational campaign that will help protect young people from falling prey to false promises, as well as to establish and maintain standards that will equip their students to qualify as professional men and meet the demands expected of them.

Note by the Sponsor of the Chapter. I have been asked many times concerning the value of correspondence schools. Unquestionably their value is limited. No one can contend that indirect, impersonal, written criticism is comparable with personal, direct instruction in classes wherein concrete results are studied daily. Moreover, art instruction by mail must always be limited primarily to two-dimensional material. Nevertheless, some valuable education may be obtained from the few reliable and idealistically maintained correspondence courses. Even more may be gained where small groups in the same community have been able to work together on the same courses. It requires patience, unusual persistence, and a willingness to sacrifice social intercourse and normal activity if the work is to be accomplished with the maximum of good. But, even so, the student must be made to recognize the fact that the best correspondence course can never educate him adequately to become a qualified artist or designer. At best, it becomes a spur to urge him on and shows him some of the simpler techniques, purely on an imitative basis; however, for a truly creative approach or a proper study of three-dimensional form by means of hand and power tools and all the various materials involved, it is, of course, impossible. — *R. B. F.*

XIII
THE FREE-LANCE ARTIST AS A TEACHER OF ART

Vincent A. Roy
Supervisor of Art Education, Pratt Institute
Brooklyn, New York

The free-lance artist is unattached to any organization or studio; he is entirely independent as far as effort and achievement are concerned. He has usually had art-school training, although some are ' self-made.' Some free-lance artists establish a reputation and secure commissions through their own initiative in making contacts. Others employ a business agent, while a third group works through several agencies.

Although most graduates of the practical or commercial art schools start out on a free-lance basis, their first jobs are likely to be in a regular studio.

In any event, very few such artists consider at the outset the possibility of teaching. As a result, when they need more income and turn to teaching as a possible source of it, their ability or inability to teach becomes important. From the point of view of technical art education in an art school or a vocational high school, the free-lance artist finds that knowledge of subject matter is not sufficient. Furthermore, accustomed as he is to considerable freedom in the way he works, he finds difficulty in meeting the routine of the average school. He has little understanding of the students' complete program or of the students' ability or capacity. In fact, most of his difficulties concern the student and the school rather than art technique.

But the free-lance artist does bring or could bring to the classroom new and vital ideas and inspiration. He knows his specialty thoroughly. He knows the entire field in which he works — its possibilities and limitations, its characters, current trends, practices, processes, and what people do and do not want. He has a wealth of information that the classroom student needs and could use to advantage if he could be helped to acquire it.

All of which sums up to the fact that, as an agency in art education, the free-lance artist-teacher's basic need is for an understanding of students at the level at which he is teaching. However, as a beginning, granted that he knows his subject thoroughly, and that he has his educational job well in mind, he may be acceptable as a teacher, provided he can at least converse readily and clearly about the work of the artist. Then, if he wishes to continue and devote more time to teaching, he definitely needs to make a conscientious effort to understand some of the fundamental concepts of education and psychology — whether they be formally acquired or not is unimportant. He should know something about the simpler methods of presenting lessons to a group and of helping students to develop and assimilate the skill or knowledge involved. He needs to master the simple mechanics of classroom management.

In other words, if the free-lance artist can and will master the teaching technique, he will prove to be a valuable addition to any art staff.

XIV
PROFESSIONAL ART PROGRAMS IN OTHER COUNTRIES

ROYAL BAILEY FARNUM

Centralization of control and regional coöperation are paramount in the organization and conduct of art schools throughout Europe. In a recent English report on " Industry and Art Education on the Continent," [1] which discusses various schools in Austria, Czechoslovakia, Milan, Germany, Zurich, and Paris, the following conclusions are drawn:

> Abroad, the central and not the local authority generally seems to be responsible for the appointment of the principals and staff and for the administration of the schools, and the system of finance is planned with this condition of affairs in view; for example, in Czechoslovakia, we saw that the State, which is responsible for making appointments, pays the salaries of the teachers, the municipality generally paying for the provisions and upkeep of the school buildings.
>
> The existence of an elaborate system of day continuation schools in several of the countries visited is, of course, due to the necessity of making

---

[1] Written by E. M. O'R. Dickey and W. M. Keesey for the Board of Education, London, England.

provision for apprentices who are required by law to attend classes generally for one full day a week for three years. Provision for this purpose has had to be made on a very big scale, and, as has been stated, the standard of much of the work seen was impressively high, particularly in view of the fact that all the apprentices in a given locality were under instruction, and not only a small band of enthusiasts, as is generally the case at evening classes in this country.

The industrialists generally seemed to have a big say, except that the controlling power of the State is always there to prevent the employer from having it all his own way. The School of Art and Crafts at Munich, however, appeared to be independent of the industrialists' direct supervision and control, though it is understood that ex-students were well received by business men. There was no place where the experimental type of design for modern conditions in the schools of the highest category was said to be looked upon with unanimous approval by the majority of business men. The State saw to it, however, that proper attention was given to this vitally important aspect of the work.

While in a few places a hostile attitude, as is too often found in many parts of this country, exists towards the production by the schools of work which might be held to compete with trade production, there were many notable exceptions. It has already been explained that the decoration and furnishing of rooms by the School of Furniture and Interior Decoration at Prague was not regarded by the industry as objectionable, because they believed in the usefulness of the school and felt that it was a good thing that the instruction should be given this realistic bias, and, in some of the important art and crafts schools visited, commissions are undertaken by the students and carried out in the school.

In marked contrast to the type of provision made in this country [England] are the schools which serve the interests of a single artistic industry or group of industries, and no other purpose, such as the Pottery School at Karlsbad, the Textile School at Berlin, the Munich Dress School, or the Glass School at Zelezny Brod. We saw in the Berlin Textile School and the Munich Dress School examples of monotechnics which deal with the training of designers for specific industries who may obtain posts anywhere throughout the whole country, whereas the Karlsbad Pottery School and the Zelezny Brod Glass School deal with particular districts only. The monotechnics which were seen in some cases provided the most advanced type of work in that particular line, and, in other cases, provision was made at a central institution for the highest type of work.

There is no comparison between the spacious and lavishly equipped schools on the continent, notably in Czechoslovakia, Germany, Zurich, and Milan, and our schools at home. Even taking into account the necessity for making provision for very large numbers of apprentices in attendance at day continuation schools and the natural desire of an important capital of a prewar state or kingdom to build an impressive academy, such as that at Munich, there is still no comparison. The " Higher Institute for Artistic Industries," at Monza, housed in the Royal Palace which was presented for the purpose by the King of Italy and surrounded by magnificent grounds, can only be described as superb, and our own Royal College of Art [London], with infinitely less room for its 400 students than is provided for the present total of 66 at Monza, offers a striking contrast.

Reference has frequently been made to the staffing of the art and crafts school which serves industrial requirements where the members of the staff who have the title of professor play the chief part, generally with workshop instructors working under them. For example, at the Higher Institute for Artistic Industries, at Monza, the pottery section is in charge of a professor who is the art director of a big pottery firm and only attends the school for one day a week, whereas a workshop instructor is employed full-time and is always on the spot. Owing to the fact that the professor of design is generally very conversant with industrial conditions, the presence of the workshop instructor as such is, however, not always necessary. Many of the professors in Czechoslovakian schools, in Germany, and in Zurich, had originally been trained in the Art and Crafts School at Vienna, and there seems to be no doubt that this famous school has served as an important nursery for the best German-speaking teachers of industrial design for many years past.

The history of art, taught in a way which makes it a useful part of the education of practical artists and craftsmen, formed an important part of the courses in many of the schools visited. It has been noted that the teachers of this subject appeared often to have been trained in art schools in the ordinary way and then to have taken a course in the history of art at a University. We may look to the newly founded Courtauld Institute [London] to play a useful part by providing courses of this kind for art-school teachers who wish to supplement their practical knowledge by a special study of the historical and theoretical aspects of their subjects.

The difficulty of securing the services of practising artists or craftsmen of high ability as teachers in the provincial schools is, as we have seen, tackled in Czechoslovakia and other countries by the provision of amenities in the shape of studios and sometimes living accommodations for these teachers. The full-time professor in the majority of the schools visited is given every opportunity to continue practising his art or craft by the provision of a workshop or studio on the spot and, especially in the central institutions, is also given a considerable measure of liberty in arranging with his students when they will receive instruction.

There were many examples of the employment of prominent practising artists or craftsmen in such places as Paris, Berlin, or Munich as part-time teachers in the same way as they are employed in London at the Royal College of Art, at the Slade, and in the London County Council Art Schools. The principals of schools in large centers were generally emphatically in favor of the part-time employment of practising artists.

History may show that the Austrian, German, and other Continental art and crafts schools have owed their origin largely to the pioneer work done by Morris in this country, but it is true that the type of art and crafts school to be found at Vienna, Prague, Munich, and Milan today is different from our own Royal College of Art both because facilities are provided for practical work in the study of design for industry on a more ambitious scale, and also because special arrangements are made for training designers for specific industries who may often become teachers of design for industry, as in Professor Drahonovsky's class for intaglio engraving on glass in the Prague Central School of Arts and Crafts. It did not appear that the education of the whole man as an artist in the widest sense was by any means neglected, although the degree of specialization in the later stages of advanced courses was often marked.

While we number among our teachers in the English art schools some admirable artists and craftsmen who have an excellent knowledge of industrial or commercial conditions, there is unquestionably room in this country for better arrangements for producing more artists of the first quality, with a real understanding of industry both as to the technique of manufacture and the conditions under which goods are produced and distributed, who shall be of service both as designers and also as teachers of industrial students.

The best teachers in the art and crafts schools visited were all keenly alive to the importance of keeping in touch with the latest ideas and passing them on to their students, and the future craftsmen and designers are thus encouraged to show initiative in this respect after they leave the school. It was interesting to find a definite organization for the purpose of keeping industry in touch with the probable demands of the luxury trade in connection with glass articles and accessories for dress, and the like, through the bureau established for this purpose at Zelezny Brod. This bureau, as has already been explained, is actually independent of the school organization, but is housed on the school premises, and the professors keep in touch with old pupils who have set up for themselves, in order to supply them with fresh ideas about design.

It seems that the Continental academies of ' fine art ' must always have depended for their success largely on a clientele of foreign students, and that, under present conditions, the numbers of foreigners could scarcely be expected to keep up. Hence the fact that in some of the institutions of this type the numbers had dropped and the staff had been cut down. . . .

It was impossible not to form a general impression that where an art and crafts school and an academy existed side by side, the work done in the former was often much livelier than that in the latter. This disappointing character of the achievements of some of the professors and students of painting in certain academies may be attributed, in part, at any rate, to the fact that on the Continent there has apparently been no equivalent to our Slade School. In this country, during the last thirty or forty years, an excellent standard of drawing has been firmly established in many quarters as a result of the teaching of the Slade. The progressively minded student who intends to become a painter has thus a fine standard of draughtsmanship to look up to as a goal worthy of his attainment, whereas his contemporaries on the Continent, lacking such an incentive, have no alternative to following in the footsteps of abstract artists without troubling to learn to draw first, or, on the other hand, being content to be trained in an academic atmosphere perhaps tinged with pseudo-Modernism.

An exceptional academy was the "Academy of Graphic Art" at Leipzig, which, as we have seen, provides courses for those who intend to work for reproduction and as designers of type, bookbinders, and so forth. The Academy is very adequately equipped with various kinds of machinery for this purpose and workshop practice forms part of the course for all students, and it has already been noted that the provision of equipment for practical work was considered so essential that duplication of some of that already provided for the trade students in the adjoining school of printing was permitted.

The most important points for comparison with our own system [England] may be briefly summarized as follows: —

(1) The significance of the part played by the State in emphasizing the importance of good design in all branches of education for industry, more especially in the encouragement of the study of contemporary design in relation to modern methods of manufacture.

(2) The ease with which regional organization and coöperation between schools can be effectively planned under a system of centralized control.

(3) The compulsory release of apprentices for day instruction, which is made possible by the complete organization of industry on an apprenticeship basis.

(4) The existence of a system of training teachers who shall at the same time be good artists and have a thorough understanding of industrial conditions, which is not paralleled at home, and the fact that future art-school teachers are not required to take a course of pedagogy.

(5) The planning of courses bearing a clear and definite relation to one another and to varying types of industrial requirement, including full-time foremen's or masters' courses of a type scarcely, if at all, known in this country.

(6) The provision of spacious buildings and very complete and up-to-date equipment, as well as studios and workshops for the principal teachers.

(7) The existence of many schools of a monotechnic type organized solely in connection with particular artistic industries or industrial groups, covering both the scientific and artistic aspects and staffed by artists of ability who have an intimate knowledge of industrial conditions.

The report of Alina M. Lindegren on " Education in Germany " [1] gives the following information on the training of artists in other countries:

The history of art may be studied in many different phases, such as Christian art and archeology, geography of art, Asiatic art, Islamic art, and so forth, at all the German universities and in the divisions of architecture in some of the technical high schools. In the universities it may be either a principal or a secondary subject in attaining the degree of doctor of philosophy. At the technical high schools of Dresden and Karlsruhe, it may be presented as a major or minor toward the degree of doctor of technical sciences.

The ten special schools of art are a second group of institutions whose requirements for admission, except for applicants for training in preparation for the examination for teachers of drawing at secondary schools, do not include a certificate of maturity. Like the high schools of music, the high schools of art demand for admission talent, previous training in art, and sufficient general information. Admission as a regular student is dependent on success in an entrance examination, followed by one or two semesters of study on probation. The age for admission varies at the different schools from 16, 17, or 18 years, to not over 30, 35, or 40 years. Generally, also, the applicant for training, particularly in architecture or sculpture, must present evidence of practical work and training in manual art from a master craftsman (*Handwerkmeister*), manual arts (*Handwerkschule*) or industrial architectural school (*Baugewerkschule*).

State High School of Art Education at Berlin (*Staatliche Hochschule für Kunsterziehung zu Berlin*). This was formerly the State School of Art (*Staatliche Kunstschule*) at Berlin, founded in 1828 by Frederick William III. It is an institution for the training and examination of

---

[1] Bulletin, 1938, No. 15 (Office of Education, Washington, D. C.)

teachers of drawing for secondary schools in Prussia, and, also, for teachers of industrial art (*Werklehrer*).

United State Schools of Free and Applied Art at Berlin-Charlottenburg (*Vereinigte Staatsschulen für Freie und Angewandte Kunst, Berlin-Charlottenburg*). This institution was established in 1924, by combining the former Academic High School of Plastic Art (*Akademischen Hochschule für die Bildenden Künste*) founded in 1696, with the Institute of Instruction of the State Industrial Arts Museum (*Unterrichtsanstalt des Staatlichen Kunstgewerbemuseums*) founded in 1867.

In its three divisions — architecture, free art, and applied art — the school aims to offer ' all-round ' training in plastic arts and auxiliary sciences, in architecture and interior construction with decorative plastic and painting, and in the industrial arts.

Academy of Fine Arts at Dresden (*Akademie der Bildenden Künste zu Dresden*). This was founded in 1705, as an Academy of Painting (*Malerakademie*). It is a State high school having as its aim the theoretical and practical training in painting, graphic arts, sculpture, and architecture, of young people of talent who select art as a career. It is organized into study rooms (*Studiensäle*) and individual schools (*Einzelschulen*).

State Academy of Art at Düsseldorf (*Staatliche Kunstakademie Düsseldorf*). The Academy was established in 1796, as a private school of painting. In 1777, the Elector of the Palatinate made it an Electoral Academy of Art. During the Napoleonic period, it gradually ceased to exist, but was reëstablished in 1819 by Frederick William III. In the lower division future architects, sculptors, painters, graphologists, workers in industrial arts, and teachers of art at secondary schools receive common instruction in drawing, painting, etching, wood-cut engraving, modelling, lettering, and linear drawing, anatomy, perspective, technique of painting, general lectures on architectural and artistic form, and the history of art. The upper division is devoted to specialization in particular fields: architecture, sculpture, painting, decorative painting, graphic art, stage art, typography, and printing.

The Baden State School of Art at Karlsruhe (*Badische Landeskunstschule Karlsruhe*). The Baden State School was established in 1920 by uniting the Academy of Fine Arts (*Akademie der Bildenden Künste*), founded in 1854, with the Industrial Arts School (*Kunstgewerbeschule*). It offers training in free and applied art, including training for teachers of art at secondary schools. The school has five divisions: painting, graphic art, applied art, architecture, and sculpture (and drawing), each with three classes: preparatory, special subject (*Fachklasse*), and master class (*Meisterklasse*). Candidates for the examination for teachers of drawing in secondary schools receive theoretical training in a special division and practical training in the special subject and master classes.

State Master Studios of Art at Königsberg, Prussia (*Staatliche Meisterateliers für die Bildenden Künste in Königsberg*). The State Master Studios opened in 1845 as a high school of architecture, painting, sculpture, and graphic arts. Its main instruction includes courses in drawing, painting, modelling, etching, copper engraving, lithography, architecture, and glass painting. Supplementary instruction is offered in courses like history of art, linear drawing, descriptive geometry and perspective, anatomy, applied graphic art, lettering, and technique of painting. Practical shop instruction includes pasteboard, wood, metal, and art needle work.

State Academy for Graphic Arts and Bookmaking at Leipzig (*Staatliche Akademie für graphische Kunste und Buchgewerbe*). The State Academy was founded in 1764. Since organization in its present form in 1901, instruction has been devoted exclusively to graphic arts and bookmaking. It offers training for the furtherance of art and skill in all phases of the bookmaking industry, particularly for the training of graphologists, illustrators, and book industrial artists.

Academy of Fine Arts at Munich (*Akademie der Bildenden Künste in München*). The Academy was founded in 1770 as a school of painting, completed the following year as an Academy of Painting and Sculpture, and reorganized in 1808 as an Academy of Arts. Since 1911, it has had the status of a high school for painting, sculpture, and graphic art (*Hochschule für Malerei, Bildhauerei, und Graphik*). In addition to courses in painting and graphic art, technique of painting and knowledge of materials, and sculpture, it offers supplementary courses in general history, history of art, human anatomy, anatomy of animals, applied perspective, and drawing from living models. It offers, also, special or professional instruction in wood engraving and lithography.

Württemberg Academy of Fine Arts (*Württembergische Akademie der Bildenden Künste*). After its founding in 1761, the Württemberg Academy became a faculty of the Carl High School (*Karlshochschule*), which was dissolved in 1794. It was refounded in 1829, by King William I. It offers training in sculpture, painting, and graphic arts. Attendance in each of the schools of drawing and painting is limited to two years; in the school of composition, to three years; and at the Academy, to seven years.

State High School of Architecture, Manual and Fine Arts at Weimar (*Staatliche Hochschule für Baukunst, Handwerk, und Bildende Kunst Weimar*). The State High School has three divisions: (1) State High

THE EDUCATION OF ARTISTS

School of Architecture (*Staatliche Hochschule für Baukunst*), (2) State
High School of Fine Arts (*Staatliche Hochschule für Bildende Kunst*),
and (3) State School for Handwork and Applied Art (*Staatliche Schule
für Handwerk und Angewandte Kunst*). Its purpose is to offer training
in all fields of art to talented young men and women that will prepare
them for independent practical and professional work.

REFERENCES [1]

(1) BLAKE, VERNON. *The Art and Craft of Drawing.* (Oxford University Press:
London, 1927) 163 pp.

(2) BLAKE, VERNON. *Drawing for Children and Others.* (Oxford University
Press: London, 1927) 163 pp.

(3) BOWIE, HENRY P. *On the Laws of Japanese Painting.* (Paul Eeder and Co.:
San Francisco, 1911) 117 pp.

(4) The Conference on Art Occupations in Industry. *Proceedings: New York,
1936.* (Institute of Women's Professional Relations: New London, Conn.,
1936)

(5) DE DOISBANDRAU, H. L. *Training of Memory in Art and Education of Artist.*
(The Macmillan Co.: London, 1914)

(6) GOULINAT, J. G. *La technique des peintres.* (Payot: Paris, 1922) 259 pp.

(7) GROPIUS, WALTER. *The New Architecture and the Bauhaus.* (Faber and
Faber, Ltd.: London, 1935) 80 pp.

(8) Institute for Research. *Art as a Career.* Research No. 97. (The Institute:
537 Dearborn St., Chicago, 1940)

(9) KAHN, E. J. *Design in Art and Industry.* (Charles Scribner's Sons: New
York, 1935)

(10) LÖWENFELD, VIKTOR. *Nature of Creative Activity.* (Harcourt, Brace and
Co.: New York, 1939) 272 pp.

(11) MAYER, R. *The Artist's Handbook.* (Viking: New York, 1940) 592 pp.

(12) MOHOLY-NAGY, LADISLAUS. *The New Vision.* (W. W. Norton and Co., Inc.:
New York, 1938) 207 pp.

(13) O'HARA, E. *Art Teacher's Primer.* (Minton, Balch and Co.: New York,
1939)

(14) PEARSON, RALPH M. *Experiencing Pictures.* (Brewer, Warren & Putnam:
New York, 1932) 225 pp.

(15) PEVSNER, NIKOLAUS. *Academies of Art, Past and Present.* (Cambridge University Press: London, 1940) 323 pp.

(16) POPE, ARTHUR. *Art, Artist and Layman.* (Harvard University Press: Cambridge, Mass., 1937)

(17) PRICE, MATLACK. *So — You're Going to Be an Artist!* (Watson-Guptill:
New York, 1939) 168 pp.

(18) SAKANISHI, SHIO. *The Spirit of the Brush.* (E. P. Dutton & Co.: New
York, 1939) 108 pp.

(19) SIRÉN, OSWALD. *The Chinese on the Art of Painting.* (H. Vetch: Peiping,
China, 1936) 261 pp.

[1] Additional references are given in the footnotes of this chapter. — *Editor.*

(20) TARKINGTON, BOOTH. *Some Old Portraits*. (Doubleday, Doran: New York, 1939)

(21) THOMPSON, E. S. *Training Girls for Art Vocations*. (Irwin Clark: Toronto, 1935)

GUIDANCE PAMPHLETS

Vocational guidance pamphlets that bear upon art as a career are obtainable from the following:

(1) Federated Council on Art Education, Now dissolved; address 14 College St., Providence, R. I.

(2) Institute for Research, 537 So. Dearborn St., Chicago. (Careers)

(3) Morgan, Dillon & Co., 5154 N. Clark St., Chicago. (Success, Vocational Information Series)

(4) National Occupational Conference, 551 Fifth Avenue, New York.

(5) Quarrie Reference Library. W. F. Quarrie & Co., Chicago. (Vocational Monographs)

CHAPTER XXXII

OTHER AGENCIES IN ART EDUCATION, FORMAL AND INFORMAL

Royal B. Farnum, Thomas Munro, Morse A. Cartwright, Huger Elliott, Dorothy F. Cruikshank, Ella Bond Johnston, Iris Barry, Elias Katz, and Dawn S. Kennedy [1]

I

MUSEUMS, GALLERIES, AND EXHIBITIONS

Royal Bailey Farnum
Executive Vice-President, Rhode Island School of Design
Providence, Rhode Island

Exhibitions of art in galleries and museums in our country have been steadily gaining in attendance by young and old alike over the past quarter century, and have recently become important as agencies for the development and promotion of art education. A recognition of the importance of esthetic values to be found in more common forms of utilitarian service and in the display of three-dimensional objects, such as furniture, silver, ceramics, glass, wood, metals, and synthetic materials, has given healthy impetus to museum attendance. Furthermore, new ways of lighting and a better understanding of methods of display have greatly improved the public presentation of art. The museum is no longer a place of dead storage. Taking a lesson from the modern department store, it has become a delightful center for the display of beauty.

What effect upon public taste this increase in attendance may have is difficult to tell. Unquestionably a keener appreciation of line, form, and color must result from even brief visits. Add to this the direct educational service of our museums in the form of bulletins, docent talks, study groups, music programs, and lectures, and without doubt contemporary public taste is being greatly enriched.

[1] For the titles and addresses of these contributors, see the part of the chapter contributed by each one. For the general plan of the chapter, see the Table of Contents. — *Editor.*

In a recent number of the *Museum News* [1] it was reported that the Art Institute of Chicago was offering a Monday afternoon series of lectures under the title of " A Clinic of Good Taste," concerned with ways and means of making the home beautiful; in the Boston Museum of Fine Arts a series of lectures on design in the home was announced; and the Toledo Museum offered on Monday and Wednesday afternoons a course in art appreciation, with music appreciation programs Tuesday evenings and Wednesday mornings.

These are but a slight indication of the types of museum activity that are going on from coast to coast, south as well as north. They would seem to constitute potent agencies for the education of public taste. Whether they have any marked effect upon the producers of art, either as its quantity or its quality, is something still open to question in the comparatively short period that they have been operative.

II

THE EDUCATIONAL FUNCTIONS OF AN ART MUSEUM

Thomas Munro
Curator of Education, The Cleveland Museum of Art
Cleveland, Ohio

How much educational work, and of what kinds, should an art museum undertake? What relative emphasis should be placed upon such work, and how should it be related to the museum's other functions? In the last few years the museum has come to take its place as an active teaching agency along with schools, colleges, and art academies, yet the general question of its proper relation to them has never been adequately thought out.

There is no tradition to provide an answer, for the work in its present form is a new and unprecedented development. It has come about, not as a result of much conscious, long-distance planning, or from any theory that the museum ought to do certain things, but step by step, in response to particular demands of the public. This itself is some indi-

---

[1] October 15, 1939. (Published by the American Association of Museums, Washington, D. C.)

cation that the services rendered meet genuine needs, and the lack of plan has helped to avoid fixed preconceptions.

Museums have come to differ widely in the extent to which they have undertaken educational work; all the way, indeed, from large proportions to none at all. Such work tends to begin with certain typical services and then to ramify along divergent paths. The first step may be gallery guidance; this leads to the advance announcement of gallery talks on particular exhibits. Clubs and groups of friends request talks, then series of talks, then systematic courses on some particular art or historical period. New exhibitions bring throngs to the museum and call for repeated explanatory talks. More formal lectures on art, by visiting authorities, are presented in the museum auditorium; these lead to an annual series that someone must plan and manage.

Meanwhile, teachers are bringing children to observe examples of some art or past civilization about which they have been studying. As more come, their visits must be scheduled in advance; and this itself can become a task of considerable magnitude. Many teachers feel the need of assistance in explaining museum exhibits and ask that museum instructors be assigned to meet their classes. Some alert teachers call for courses on the use of museum materials, on art history, and on appreciation in general. Children come to sketch in the museum; a special class is started for members' children; an empty room is used as a studio for painting and modelling; talented children from the schools are admitted, then other young and eager applicants, until some hundreds may be coming each Saturday. Qualified special teachers are engaged as part-time assistants. Marionette shows, motion pictures, and illustrated talks are given by and for the children. Classes in music and folk dancing may be added as special privileges of membership. Parents and other adults may wish to use their hands in amateur drawing or in craftwork; advanced students may call for professional technical instruction.

Outside demands may call forth an extension of services to still wider circles in the community. Speakers on art are called for by clubs, schools, parent-teachers' associations; a local newspaper may print each week the picture that is to be discussed over the radio. The schools clamor for visual materials to be brought to the classroom; lantern slides, photographs, color prints, small plaster casts are acquired and lent; then small works of foreign handicraft, and ancient artifacts not quite important enough for the main galleries, yet significant for historical study. Works of local artists are presented to the museum, to be circulated among schools and libraries. Distributing, arranging, and caring for these exhibits, and scheduling them in advance, come to demand the whole time of one or more persons.

Thus, under favorable conditions, museum educational work can develop in a few years into a surprisingly elaborate mechanism. On the whole, the cultural value of these functions is so obvious that there has been little disposition to question them. Yet occasional misgivings have been expressed, especially by foreign visitors with very different conceptions of what a museum should be.

For example, it has been said: " Why do any teaching in a museum at all? Let the works of art speak for themselves. Don't interfere with people's enjoyment of art by asking them to listen to any lectures." But no one urges the mature visitor to be educated against his will. Furthermore, as a matter of fact, many persons find that art does not always speak for itself, fully and distinctly. Especially with the recent tendency of museums to acquire examples of exotic, primitive, and modernistic art, there has developed a persistent demand for some clue to their understanding and appraisal. Advanced students, moreover, wish to penetrate as deeply as possible into the technique, the esthetic form, the cultural background of what they see, not merely to enjoy it in a casual and superficial way. It is in answer to such legitimate demands that museum teaching develops. School children's visits are in a sense involuntary, like all the rest of their studies. But anyone who watches their behavior and expression during museum visits will realize that most of them are having a very good time and want to know more about the strange and fascinating things they see there. Of course, much depends on what is said and how it is said; dull facts and sentimental praise can kill their interest and are worse than no talk at all, but the capable instructor can heighten their enjoyment by pointing out interesting details and qualities, and by giving only the right amount and kind of information as a background.

Does museum work make the artist a mere imitator of the past? Will children, in particular, be more creative if kept away from the museum? There again, the answer depends on the kind of instruction. Museum objects can be used, not in excess and for imitation, but for occasional suggestion and stimulus to free imaginative construction. The artist can gain an understanding of how past ages and artists expressed themselves in appropriate forms, and thus of the fundamental meanings of art, but he does not need to copy these symbols literally in expressing modern life or his own personality.

Are American museums developing educational work at the expense of scholarship? This charge, which has been made abroad, is meant to imply that advanced research and writing on the part of curators, in art history and archaeology, has been neglected in favor of popular mass education in simple art appreciation. It may well be that in all subjects we in America have tended to overemphasize mass education at the expense of advanced scholarship. Certainly, popular lectures and children's classes have been much to the fore and doubtless undue satisfaction is often felt in securing large audiences. Advanced research is usually regarded as a function, not of the museum educational department, but of the curators in charge of the collections; small advanced courses are regarded as the task of university graduate schools. There seem to be no inherent reasons, however, why such lines should be drawn, or why any of these functions should interfere or compete with the rest. It may be necessary in some places to protect museum curators against too persistent demands for popular lectures, and to insure them time for study. It may be necessary to urge museum trustees and supporters not to judge the success of educational work too much in terms of number of persons taught, and to approve as well the spending of time and money on advanced work that reaches a very small public.

If these cautions are observed, the development of museum educational work should go hand in hand with scholarship. In Cleveland, no sharp lines are drawn between museum departments, or between museum and university. Curators from various departments give occasional public talks, but not enough to interfere with their other work. Certain courses given by the educational staff and attended by museum members are open for credit to university students; these and other advanced courses are maintained by the museum in spite of their small attendance. Researches and scholarly writing are encouraged in the case of staff members who wish to undertake them.

Again, it has also been suggested that an undue emphasis on education may tend to lower the quality of works of art acquired, because funds will be diverted from purchases to education, and mediocre objects will be purchased to fill in historical series and thus provide materials for teaching. As to the first point, it may seem that every dollar spent for education is one less available for purchases, but the appearance is misleading. Money comes to museums for educational purposes, through gifts and grants, fees, and paid memberships, that would otherwise not come at all; indeed, gifts of art works and money for purchases are not infrequently stimulated by the knowledge that a large public will learn to appreciate them. On the other point, it is the duty of the museum administration to resist any pressure toward lowering of standards. For study, inexpensive casts and color prints can now be secured in great variety and much-improved quality.

Lastly, it may be asked whether the museum is not stepping out of its proper field into that of the school or college when it becomes in part an educational institution. Should it not emulate the public library and be content to provide material for outside teachers to use; that is, should it not merely collect, exhibit, and preserve works of art? Certainly, there can be no doubt as to what should be its primary function; but conditions may justify its carrying on education as a secondary function, just as the school or college often buys and exhibits illustrative materials or even starts a small museum of its own. Rigid specialization is not always the best way for an institution to be socially useful.

For each museum, the extent and character of the educational work it should carry on will be determined by the whole educational structure of its community. If other institutions are at hand that are willing and able to carry on a particular branch of art education as well as the museum could, there may be no reason for the museum itself to attempt it. For example, in Cleveland the Art Museum makes no attempt to conduct a school for the training of professional artists, although several museums elsewhere do so. This is due to no objection in principle, but simply to the fact that such an academy already exists nearby. In certain other cities, the proximity of a well-developed institute for popular lectures and courses on art releases the museum from this duty, so important in the Cleveland Museum. The nature of art instruction in the local schools and college must also be considered, with the aim of avoiding unnecessary duplication. At the same time, there may be worse things than apparent duplication of services within a fairly large community. Competition, instead of monopoly, is sometimes wholesome, and two ways of teaching the same subject may lead to very different results.

As a center of art instruction, the museum has certain definite advantages over all outside institutions. First and foremost is the fact that art can there be taught in fairly close contact with the indispensable materials for teaching it properly. Teaching it without original works of art, by means of textbooks, or even with lantern slides and photographs, is a poor substitute. Another advantage is the power to coördinate work for all age levels.

But should the museum employ its own teachers, and conduct its own classes, or merely open its doors to teachers and classes from outside? Either or both may be the wise course, according to local conditions. At Cleveland, the situation is flexible and diversified. Outside teachers and classes come freely and in large numbers. Some teachers, paid by the public school system, are permanently assigned to museum service, where they meet and teach classes, and whence they take art materials for demonstration in the schools. Some teachers, employed by the museum, have their salaries for special instruction paid in part through appropriations by outside schools, colleges, and clubs. Some are paid entirely out of the museum's operating fund, for instruction to members, their children, and the general public. Such flexibility of arrangement permits great freedom of adjustment to varied and changing local needs. A nucleus of educational personnel permanently employed and supervised by the museum administration is, however, essential for the sake of directing and coördinating all the manifold activities, including teaching, scheduling, arranging study materials, and advising the outside teacher how to use the museum to best advantage.

The future may bring still further development of the museum as an active teaching agency, or a tendency for other institutions to take over more actively the work of teaching in museums, or such close coöperating between the museum and other agencies that all present lines of demarcation will be obscured. Meanwhile, the museum is actually doing valuable pioneer work along lines that would formerly have been considered out of its field. In many communities, this would have remained undone if the museum had not been at hand, ready and adaptable to the taking on of new functions.

III

THE PLACE OF THE MUSEUM IN ADULT EDUCATION

Morse A. Cartwright
Director, American Association for Adult Education
New York, New York

The first museums in Europe, and in this country as well, were collections designed primarily for the use of the initiated. They catered to a highly esoteric audience — one that in numbers approximated only a minute fraction of one percent of the population. The early museum curator, whether in the field of science or of art, occupied the position of high priest of a cult. His job was to arrange and to classify and to increase his collection. The early museum in this and in all countries was for the very few, those who either by reason of wealth or position, on the one hand, or of extraordinary knowledge on the other, possessed membership in the cult itself. The fact that in Europe many of these museums came into existence by royal decree helped to create the royal fiction that only the élite were fit to view such treasures.

I regret very much to state that both in Europe and in America there are yet museums whose curatorial staffs and whose boards of trustees evidently still adhere to this archaic concept of the function of the museum in community and national life. Such museums have no place in adult education and — I would go one step further — no place, in my estimation, in modern life.

There are many points of similarity between world's fairs and museums. They both rely largely upon visual methods. They both attempt to tell a story in graphic form or to exhibit materials of interest or of artistic value to the thousands who flock to their doors. It is true that many museums owe their origin to fairs and expositions. Certainly, the museum movement in the United States has been stimulated successively by each of the expositions that has taken place since the Philadelphia Centennial in 1876.

The main difference, as I see it, between the educational effect of a museum exhibit and that of a world's fair exhibit lies in the opportunity that exists for a continuing process of educational enrichment that is inherent in the museum exhibit, but totally lacking in the fair exhibit by reason of its ephemeral nature.

The museum is primarily an educational institution and only secondarily (even if importantly) a scholarly or research institution; it is a medium for recreation and amusement and an agency for the housing and improvement of collections. It is only through the acceptance by museum authorities of such a concept that the museum can be on the way toward taking its rightful place in the forefront of the great and growing adult education movement in this country. After all, there are only three great institutional agencies for adult education that possess physical plants available to the people of this country. They are the public school, the library, and the museum. The museum must be, as the library and the school must be, adult centers as well as centers for children. They must be open, not as most museums are during the daylight hours only, but a full sixteen hours a day, thus making their educational opportunity available to the bulk of the adult public that is either employed or otherwise occupied during most of the hours the museum is now open.

I see the museum of the future as an active educational force, not interested primarily in formal education, but making use of every opportunity for informal teaching (which is by far the best teaching) that offers itself and that can be brought to the attention of an eager public.

The museum of the future will have contact with churches, with clubs, with hobby groups, with the labor movement, with business and industrial organizations, with parent-teacher organizations, with foreign-language groups, with racial minorities, with all the hundreds and even thousands of classifications of allegiances that go to make up the American community of today. I see a promotional task done in a dignified and at the same time attractive manner, designed to interest these groups in what the museum has to offer. I see a similar promotional appeal addressed to the individual who prefers not to cast in his lot with the group. This is a reaching-out process and one to which the museum staff will have to address itself increasingly as the years go on.

I think the museum, too, must realize its responsibility as an agency for molding, as well as for reflecting, public taste and opinion. I think it must move out on its own initiative, and that, in addition, it must be ready to serve as auxiliary to other agencies working for adult education in its multifarious forms within the community.

IV

EDUCATIONAL ACTIVITIES IN MUSEUMS OF ART

HUGER ELLIOTT
Director of Educational Work, The Metropolitan Museum of Art
New York, New York

There are few works of art of so universal an appeal that some knowledge of the social backgrounds that conditioned them is not helpful to the layman. And when we turn to the matter of esthetic appraisal, we find that in this self-conscious age the man in the street, overwhelmed with photographs of every known object, is confused by the multiplicity and diversity of the material confronting him; he does not know what to think.

Fortunately, it is in no wise the task of the museum to tell the layman what he should think. But since the turn of the century the conviction has been growing that it is the duty of the museum to offer the visitor some information concerning the religious, political, artistic, or other trends that gave a work its particular character. Gallery talks are offered for those who wish to attend them. From the reports of the museums of art in this country, it appears that museum visitors are attending such talks in ever-increasing numbers. The museums are evidently meeting a very definite need.

In this age of the newspaper and the radio we are so busy keeping up with current affairs that there is little time in which to become familiar with the life and thought of people of past ages. Yet it is obvious that the appeal of many of the objects displayed in our museums depends to a large extent upon how much is known about the conditions under which they were produced. Everyone who has talked in a museum gallery recalls the surprise and pleasure expressed by visitors who find this or that topic or display becoming deeply interesting when studied as a part of a given civilization. It is as though new worlds had been opened to their view.

The problem confronting one who speaks to a group in a museum gallery differs greatly from that of the college professor. The latter addresses, week by week, a class more or less equally prepared in the subject; whereas, save in rare instances, the museum speaker ' starts from scratch.' One auditor may be an expert in the given field and another quite ignorant of the first rudiments of the matter in hand. The subject must be so handled that the interest of the average listener is aroused and he yearns for further knowledge. It is an exacting and a stimulating task.

A talk about a work of art in the presence of the object itself has a special significance. In the educational programs of the museums there is occasional mention of the fact that a certain lecture is to be given in a lecture hall or classroom. This is done that material in other localities may be discussed with the aid of lantern-slide illustrations. In the majority of cases such a talk is followed by a visit to the gallery in which are to be seen the related works of art in the museum's collections — it is a logical procedure.

Those who are interested may obtain from the various museums copies of current lecture programs and annual reports. In the latter will be found the statistics concerning the attendance at the gallery talks and lectures given for the public. It will be evident that year by year the educational work of our museums of art is being broadened in scope.

V

THE MUSEUM AS A COMMUNITY CULTURAL CENTER

DOROTHY F. CRUIKSHANK
Worcester Art Museum
Worcester, Massachusetts

If the town hall is the center for the political administration of a community, then the art museum ought to be the cultural center for the same citizenry. Each in its own way should touch the lives of all the people without regard to race, creed, or occupation. The town hall, of course, already does this. It has been the axis around which the civic affairs of the community have revolved since towns began, but as yet the museum has done little more than scratch the surface in the task of making itself a part of the inner lives of the people. It is time that it began to take its place as the inspirational center for creative thought and the social center for cultural activities.

Is a museum justified in maintaining elaborate galleries and sponsoring exhibitions for a select few? Members of the professions come readily enough to see a good film or even to a free public lecture or special exhibition if the advertising for the event has been tactfully planned and widespread. Yet, to almost every citizen, to the factory workers, office and store clerks, bus drivers, and workers in trades, our gallery highlights, including Bellini, Gainsborough, Winslow Homer, or even the recently publicized Dali, are much stranger than fiction, and our usual museum programs of lectures, cinemas, and musicals do not attract them. Such museum activities cannot compete with the motion-picture theater, the clubs, lodges, and church organizations that these people attend, for these people are essentially joiners, and much of their spare time is absorbed by the different groups with which they have become affiliated.

Our museums, however, have something very real to offer to the mass of our citizens. Since we cannot hope to gain their patronage, at once, as individuals, their group interests may suggest our first point of contact. An enterprising chairman of any program committee will heartily welcome a museum's printed list of proposals for suitable club entertainment, and it is not unlikely that he will respond if the educational significance of the programs is not overemphasized. Whether this first contact is made by a visit to the museum or through a talk by a staff member at the club, the desire, on the part of the group, to repeat the experience, depends upon the ability of the speaker to be ' human,' to talk with members of the group on their own ground and from their own point of view. There is a time and a good place for everything, and a good place for informality and warm hospitality is in a museum of art.

VI

MUSEUM CIRCULATING EXHIBITS FOR SECONDARY SCHOOLS

Dorothy F. Cruikshank
Worcester Art Museum
Worcester, Massachusetts

The exhibitions offered for use in secondary schools in the vicinity of the Worcester Art Museum are based upon the required reading lists for college entrance credit. They complement the work of the classroom and attempt to give a cultural background for the humanitarian subjects studied in the average secondary curriculum. As to topics, there are exhibitions devoted to various phases of American history, to Homer, to the age of Pericles, to Rome in the time of Vergil and Caesar (with authentic material rarely included in textbooks), and to the secular and ecclesiastical traditions of Europe in the Middle Ages and the Renaissance. Literary associations have been particularly stressed in the exhibitions of English life in the time of Shakespeare and of the eighteenth-century elegants. The Grand Siècle exhibitions illustrate the France of Racine and Molière; the dramatic occurrences of the French Revolution are shown by unusual and distinctive plates. The civilization of the Orient is likewise illustrated.

Each exhibition is accompanied by a selected bibliography for the teacher, and lantern slides supplementing the material are furnished on request. The exhibits are circulated free of charge, save for express charges.

The material comprising twenty exhibits may not be without interest to museums and to schools.

1. *Art and Life in Ancient Egypt.* Wall paintings from the tombs at Thebes illustrating the religious and cultural background of the time. Scenes from everyday life, such as banquets, vintage time, funerary customs, hunting, fishing, and so forth. Also photographs of Egyptian architecture, sculpture, and faïence. Especially colorful.

2. *The Homeric Poems.* Illustrations of scenes and events in the *Iliad* and the *Odyssey* as found in the Roman wall paintings of the first century before Christ. Scenes from the Palace of Minos at Knossos, Hagia Triada, and the Palace at Tiryns. Mycenaean objects — gold masks, cups, bronze daggers inlaid with gold — unearthed by the famous archaeologist Schliemann.

3. *Greece in the Time of Pericles.* Views of the Acropolis built under the leadership of Pericles after the Persian Wars. Photographs of the Propylaea and the Temple of Nike, the Doric Parthenon and the Ionic Erechtheum, with various sculptural details from the Erechtheum and the Parthenon Frieze.

4. *Vergil and the Aeneid.* Wall paintings found in the House of the Tragic Poet and in the triclinium of the House of the Vetii depicting scenes from classical mythology. Photographs of Pompeii and Herculaneum and the Hellenistic mosaics found in Corinth. Illuminated manuscripts of the *Aeneid* from the fourth to the fifteenth centuries, including the famous illustrations in the Vatican Codices and Petrarch's copy of Vergil illuminated by Simone Martini.

5. *Bible Illustrations from the Earliest Times to the Renaissance.* The development of religious and artistic expression as seen in the illuminations of the fifth and thirteenth centuries. Byzantine, French, Flemish, English, and German illumination taken from such manuscripts as the Joshua Roll, the Vienna Genesis, the Godescalc Book of Gospels, the Psalter of St. Louis, the Gospel Book of Otto III. Especially colorful.

6. *The Minnesingers.* Illustrations in the great Heidelberg manuscript showing imaginary portraits of the Minnesingers with their coats of arms; twelfth and thirteenth centuries. A small exhibition, but colorful.

7. *Chivalry and Courtly Life in the Middle Ages.* Illuminated manuscripts from the British Museum portraying aspects of medieval life and scenes from *Romance of the Rose.* Drawings of English armor of the sixteenth century. Illuminated pages from Froissart's *Chronicles* (fifteenth century). French drawings by Francois Clouet (sixteenth century) and French, Flemish, and Florentine tapestries. Especially colorful.

8. *Mediaeval Life of the People.* Illuminated manuscripts showing the

Occupations of the Month and the Signs of the Zodiac. Flemish Calendar. Illustrations of the sixteenth century and a series of miniatures by Simon Bening of the same century. French tapestries of the fifteenth and sixteenth centuries. French drawings by Jean and Francois Clouet. Colorful.

9. *Mediaeval Minor Arts.* An exhibition showing the various materials and objects used to recount Biblical history, not only in the colorful stained glass of Chartres Cathedral but also in the enamels, the metal work, the tapestries, textiles, the ivories, and the illuminated manuscripts of the time. Especially colorful.

10. *The Bayeux Tapestry.* Large mounts containing excellently colored reproductions of the famous tapestry or embroidery portraying vividly the history of Duke William's Conquest of England in 1066 and giving a continuous view of the entire tapestry.

11. *Shakespeare and Tudor England.* Photographs giving a panoramic view of Tudor England, showing the famous castles of the fifteenth and sixteenth centuries. Views of the Globe, Fortune, and Swan Theaters (the latter the only uncontested evidence regarding the form of the English playhouse). Title page of Shakespeare's first edition of plays, 1623. Also portraits of important men of the time by Hans Holbein and others.

12. *Le Grand Siècle.* Fifteenth-century architectural engravings of the Louvre, the Palace and Gardens of Versailles, and numerous chateaux. Scenes in artists' workshops engraved by A. Bosse. Engravings from the plays of Voltaire, Cardinal de Richelieu, Molière, and Corneille. Drawings and paintings by Boucher, Robert, and Chardin.

13. *The French Revolution.* Contemporary paintings and engravings portraying the important historical characters and events, including scenes of the Bastille, executions, the Revolutionary Tribunal, and the costumes of the clergy, nobility, and the third estate.

14. *American Art of the Colonies and the Early Republic.* Photographs showing the development of early American architecture and furniture. A drawing, *Natives at a Meal,* by John White, sixteenth century. The Freake portraits by an anonymous artist, and paintings by Badger, Gullager, Stuart, and Copley. Historical engravings and paintings of men and events.

15. *Mohammedan Art.* Persian miniature painting of the fifteenth and sixteenth centuries and Indian miniatures, Mughal School, of the sixteenth and seventeenth centuries. Illustrations from chronicles, romances, moral tales, and fables showing the customs, architecture, and costumes of the age and including scenes from the lives of the kings.

16. *Far Eastern Art.* Portrait, landscape, animal, and flower paintings from the fourth to the nineteenth century showing the artistic expression of the various dynasties in China. Also fresco paintings of Buddhist legends.

17. *Development of Modern Painting.* A selection of twenty-six fine color reproductions beautifully framed. A comprehensive survey, tracing the de-

velopment of modern painting from the seventeenth century to the present time.

18. *Processes of Art.* An exhibition showing how the following prints are made: aquatint, dry point, engraving, etching, lithograph, woodcut, and wood engraving. This exhibit comes in seven cases, each case being provided with plates, proofs, and explanatory notes on one process.

19. *The Story of Bookmaking.* Twenty-five photographs showing the most significant events in the development of bookmaking, beginning with ancient techniques and concluding with modern typography. Prepared with full explanatory notes by Dr. Otto Bettmann.

20. *Worcester Architecture.* A group of seventy-six photographs of examples of Worcester architecture from 1720 to the twentieth century. Includes simple farmhouses of the first settlers, dwelling houses, churches, commercial buildings, and public buildings. Made by Henry Russell Hitchcock, Jr., Professor of Architecture, Wesleyan University.

Miss Minnie Goldstein, Secretary for School Service at the Worcester Art Museum, writes as follows:

I am glad to report some specific results growing out of the work in connection with our Circulating Exhibitions for Secondary Schools. . . . We have no means of determining directly what these exhibits have meant to the students themselves, but we can assume, since more schools are requesting this material, that teachers feel it is worth while.

At first the loan of our sets was limited to the boys' private schools of New England. Later, on request, the service was extended to the public schools of New England. During the past year we have allowed the exhibits to go anywhere in the United States. The South and Mid-West have responded especially well.

As one direct result, a group of boarding schools organized the " New England Arts Association of Preparatory Schools for Boys," the sole purpose of which is to promote art interest among their students by preparing each year sets of circulating exhibits. . . . Private schools in other sections have followed the lead of New England schools.

VII
ART EXHIBITS IN PUBLIC SCHOOLS

ELLA BOND JOHNSTON
Director, Art Association
Richmond, Indiana

In Richmond, Indiana, forty-two years ago an Art Association was organized by local citizens to coöperate with public-school officials in securing exhibits of works of art for the education of the community. This Art Association is organized democratically, with various types of citizens as officers. It is incorporated as a nonprofit organization and has no paid officials.

The School Board furnishes the gallery, with heat, light, and janitor service; the Art Association secures and installs the art exhibits and does educational work for both the schools and the community. The expenses of the exhibits are met by the dues of the Association, supplemented by contributions from the School Board and the Common Council.

After several years of holding exhibits by Indiana artists in June (at the end of the school year when it was possible to transform a schoolhouse into an art gallery) three things became clear: first, there was a substantial interest in art in the school and the community; second, the coöperation with the public schools was of decided value and seemed likely to be available in the future; but, third, we could not meet the large expense that would be incurred if we had annual June exhibits of the work not only of local artists, but also of artists of the East (which we felt essential to our growth in art appreciation).

Here arose the idea of inducing other cities in the state to make up a circuit that would divide the expense of exhibitions of American paintings. Finally, in 1910, six cities joined Richmond in taking an exhibit by New York painters, a plan that continued for about twenty years and included cities not only in Indiana but also in adjoining states. It fulfilled a need of the time, was early in the field, if, indeed, not the first of its kind. The exhibits were installed in schoolhouses where that was possible, otherwise in empty storerooms, church parlors, courthouses, public libraries, club rooms, and the like.

In 1911 the Richmond Art Director, acting as the Chairman of the State Federation of Women's Clubs, organized a similar circuit of the smaller Indiana towns to take an exhibit of paintings by Indiana painters. These two pioneer circuit exhibits have been followed by a continuous growth of art interest and organization in the state, notably in the higher institutions of learning.

The development and results of the art movement in connection with the Public Schools in Richmond, Indiana, a city of 35,000 inhabitants, stands as a model and inspiration to the smaller cities of the country that cannot establish art museums such as are found in our great cities. After holding exhibits for 14 years in a public-school building, we decided that the effectiveness of the work with the children was reduced because it was not possible at the end of the school year to secure the benefit of follow-up work on the exhibits.

At this time the Art Association and the school officials asked the School Board to include an art gallery in a new high school — something unheard-of before. This building, dedicated in 1910, contained on the third floor three large galleries with skylight, electric trough light, and suitable background for displaying works of art. Now a dozen different collections could be exhibited during the school year — not only circuits and local painters' exhibits, but also collections of graphics and reproductions, of pictorial photography and drawings, of art work by school children, and exhibits of many crafts both domestic and foreign.

From the beginning we have arranged an annual exhibit by Richmond painters with prizes and sales. The last catalog lists a jury-selected group of one hundred paintings by forty-five painters, many of whom produce work accepted in the most important exhibits in this country.

For the past seven years the Art Association has sponsored an exhibit of pictorial photography under the chairmanship of a local photographer who is both a national and an international prize-winner. Prizes are given for local work, and in connection is shown an exhibit of prints from some distinguished photographer, who often can be secured for a lecture on the subject.

Among our high-school graduates who took the art course and who were devoted to the gallery are many who are known in the art world today. We like to think that these young people are where they are today in part because of their contact with the art gallery in the Richmond High School.

We think we have demonstrated that an art gallery in a public high school is as needful, as useful, as reasonable, and as sensible to supplement the work of an art department as a library is to the English department, or as an auditorium is to the music and drama, or a gymnasium to the physical training department.

Both our high school and our art association have outgrown their building and now new and larger quarters are being erected on a beautifully situated twenty-acre plot of land. Two units of this new plant are already in use — the large Civic Hall and the Academic Hall. The third unit being built this year (1940) is the Art Building; it will contain a small auditorium, four art galleries, and the school art and music rooms. A local citizen who has been a patron member of our Art Association for many years donated $50,000 to supplement the city's funds. Later, when other funds are available, it is planned to add rooms for the crafts of printing, wood work, metal work, and the like.

When this building is finished, occupied, and in use; when the Dramatic Society stages plays; when the chorus, orchestra, and band give their concerts; when the art collections are displayed in the galleries and current exhibits are being shown, then may we not say that here, at last, the arts have found their rightful place in public education?

VIII

ART EXHIBITS BY COMMERCIAL ESTABLISHMENTS

ROYAL BAILEY FARNUM

Commercial art exhibits also have assumed their share of responsibility in aiding art education. For many years publishing houses have made a business of sending carefully mounted sepia, black and white, and color prints of famous paintings to public schools where they have been displayed. Admission charges often are made for two purposes, to defray the expense of installation, and to raise funds for a school purchase for decorating one or more rooms. Not a few public school buildings have been decorated by this means.

More recently some of the houses have been instrumental in collecting and distributing exhibits of children's work, a helpful and fine example of coöperation between business and education.

One of the most important of the travelling exhibits under the auspices of a commercial organization is the annual " Scholastic Competition," first held in Carnegie Institute, Pittsburgh, during the early spring. The exhibit consists of art work selected from some thousands of examples submitted by high schools throughout the country and covers a wide range of media, including ceramics, sculpture, and modelling, jewelry, metal work, weaving, drawing, etching, and painting. Following the Pittsburgh showing, the work is separated into smaller exhibits that are then circulated among the different states. Much of the material is of exceptionally high quality, even professional in character. A number of the professional art schools offer annual scholarships to graduating students who show unusual proficiency in this national competition, which is conducted by the *Scholastic Magazine*.[1]

Commercial and industrial activities have always had a strong and, at times, a dominating influence on art education in the public schools. At one time commercial houses dealing in art supplies even shaped the courses of study and to a large extent controlled the demand and supply of art teachers. The conditions today are completely changed, and leading art supply houses are doing valuable service in their coöperative efforts to assist by every legitimate and ethical means in promoting art education. Scores of commercial houses furnish art lecturers, many of whom carry concrete examples of art to show both teachers and children. Members of these houses speak before town and city service clubs, such as Rotary, Kiwanis, and Lions, and do valiant work in presenting the practical as well as the esthetic values of art in general education to the taxpayers of the country.

A number of firms issue regular house organs designed primarily to give help and information on art to teachers in the schools. Two notable examples are *Everyday Art*,[2] a twenty-four page magazine with cover and many illustrations in full color, and *The Drawing Teacher*,[3] a sixteen-page folder in black and white. The magazine consists of timely discussions by leaders in art education on general topics, more specific articles on the uses of various materials, and news and comments in the art-education world. The folder mentions a wide variety of news items from different sources and carries carefully developed and freely illustrated lesson plans for different grade levels.

---

[1] *Scholastic*, 430 Kinnard Avenue, Dayton, Ohio.

[2] Published by the American Crayon Company, Sandusky, Ohio (C. W. Knouff, Editor).

[3] Published by Binney and Smith Company, New York City.

There are many other industries and commercial activities that offer less intensive service to art education, but that nevertheless are important agencies in influencing public taste. Among these are the publishing houses that issue the popular national magazines. They carry many articles pertaining to art. The illustrations are in the main accurately reproduced in color and often present material having unusual art merit. Many of the advertisements in such publications offer constant sources for esthetic interest, satisfaction, and judgment. Unquestionably they are a very vital factor in supplementing the more formal approach to art education offered in schools and colleges.

Add to these illustrated magazines of a general nature the special group covering home and garden interests, clothing, travel, and current events, and we get some notion of the constant bombardment of illustrations and ideas that serve to focus public attention on art qualities, if not on pure works of art.

In this same field of publications are the added influences found in the daily newspapers, many of which have art columns, sections, and illustrated Sunday supplements of unusual interest; in books, whose illustrations and jackets have a strong influence; and in other examples of design to be found in display cards, posters, and billboards. Current trends in design are reflected in practically all mail-order catalogs, which in turn add their bit to the art propaganda of the day.

Another strong influence upon public taste is found in store windows and counter displays within the building. In any progressive small shop and in the large department store much time, energy, and money are often expended in order to display merchandise attractively; so that today window-shopping commands as much attention from a far wider clientele than most of the so-called ' art exhibits.' In fact, many windows exemplify the most expert use of fundamental principles of design and in their merchandise present objects of high art quality. But an added factor, wholly unknown and unnecessary in a museum gallery display of art, is essential in the store window. This is the factor of speed. As Kiesler remarks (32) :

> We want to be informed about things quickly. . . . Our age is forgetting how to hear and how to listen. We live mainly by the eye. The eye observes, calculates, advises. It is quicker than the ear, more precise and impartial. The evolution of the show window is due to one fact: speed. For this reason the show window is a modern method of communication. The special manner in which the display manager communicates: therein lies his art. The communication itself — the show window

— is the most direct method of all methods by which the store-owner can bring into contact passer-by and merchandise. Selling through the glass is becoming more and more important.

Still another source of influence for art education is through the direct sale of art material with guides or lessons for their use by means of both store-retailing and mail-order departments. An incorporated organization in Boston, known as " Fellowcrafters," is typical of this movement. In reply to a request for information the following was re-received from W. B. Pollock, Jr.[1]

We are members of the Related Arts Service, which is an association of manufacturers that exists for the purpose of developing and disseminating a philosophy of arts and crafts education in an effort to assist educational administrators in seeing the value of arts and crafts education in communities where art is not taught, or else is inadequately taught because school administrators need help in convincing the taxpayer that art education is worth while.

Coupled with this work, we, as members of the Related Arts Service, coöperate in efforts to assist teachers in developing courses of study in craft work and in training teachers to carry out these courses of study in a fashion consistent with the philosophy of art education that we are attempting to develop and spread.

It has been our consistent policy in the sale of materials for craft work to sell materials in such a form that the student has ample play for developing and executing original forms of decoration. Since each medium in craft work has peculiarities that condition the type of design suitable for execution in that medium, we have endeavored to furnish suitable designs for various media to serve as models for the student in developing his own design.

So long as movements of this kind are honest in their desire to aid amateur talent, so long as they base their ideas on sound principles, employ art experts, and try to foster the best in public taste, they should find a legitimate field for their activity. Like correspondence schools of art, they may be the means of stimulating hidden talent, but in any event they are one positive means of affecting public taste.

---

[1] Sales Manager, Fellowcrafters, 385 Boylston Street, Boston, Massachusetts.

IX
MOTION PICTURES AND RADIO IN ART EDUCATION [1]

Royal Bailey Farnum

I. The Motion Picture

To what extent the motion picture has influenced the taste of people in America it is difficult to measure at the present time. While the utilization of educational principles in the making of public entertainment films has been lacking, these pictures unquestionably have had a very important and real bearing upon public taste, particularly during the past decade when sound, lighting, and the composition of sets have all been so beautifully perfected. The time must soon come when the trained educator will be given full recognition as a necessary principal in the arrangement and presentation of films for motion pictures, for they are a potent educational force in American life.

The value of pictures to education already has been recognized by the industry. Within the past year a valuable catalog of noncurrent 'shorts' has been issued by an organization called "Teaching Film Custodians, Inc.," [2] for the purpose of making carefully studied and selected films available for school use.

Meantime smaller organizations, industries, and individuals have been making films for educational purposes. A few have been made to cover certain phases of the art field. The Metropolitan Museum [3] has issued twelve or more films for teaching art appreciation, covering certain special exhibits. The University Film Foundation has made eight technical pictures [4] to show artists at work. The Harmon Foundation

---

[1] For additional discussion of the motion picture as a form of art, see Chapter XIV. Mention should be made here also of the extensive Motion Picture Project of the American Council on Education and the reports of its Committee, Series II, "Motion Pictures in Education." (1937) — *Editor.*

[2] *Catalog of Films for Classroom Use.* (Teaching Film Custodians, Inc., 25 West 43rd Street, New York City. 50¢.)

[3] Metropolitan Museum of Art, Museum Extension Division, Fifth Avenue, New York, New York.

[4] The University Film Foundation, Harvard Square, Cambridge, Massachusetts.

issued a film,[1] directed by Alon Bement, to show how art entered every phase of human life.

Columbia University has also displayed an interest in art-education films. One particularly valuable one in the technical field demonstrates an individual technique of water-color painting.

Taking advantage of the pictured motion of animated form, the late Charles H. Woodbury conceived the idea of having students draw from the screen, thus bringing life into the classroom in a very simple, but most efficient, way. Under the direction of Mr. Woodbury and Mrs. Elizabeth Ward Perkins, and as a result of their experience with drawing classes,[2] the Eastman Kodak Company prepared fourteen short reels for this purpose, making a scene for each one ten feet long, but repeated ten times on a hundred-foot roll. Thus, when the student fails to grasp the significant facts by means of his pencil the first time, he is able to view the same action ten times in succession without interruption. As a teaching tool, it has valuable possibilities and is used in a number of professional schools with marked success.

II. The Radio

The forms of art considered in this Yearbook are wholly visual. It has been difficult for the radio to adapt its services to a program of art education until recently when its limitations and possibilities have been more thoroughly investigated. In the fall of 1939, the National Broadcasting Company offered a series of dramatized broadcasts entitled " Art for Your Sake." [3] Ten foreign and two American artists, one living, were presented to the listening audience by means of sound effects as well as clever spoken lines. At the same time each broadcast tied in with a series of five color reproductions of paintings that were made available by the National Art Society [4] at a nominal cost. A second series of thirteen programs was given in the spring of 1940. These broadcasts met with phenomenal success; many thousands of the color prints were sold, and volumes of letters of appreciation were

---

[1] *We Are All Artists.* The Harmon Foundation, 140 Nassau Street, New York, New York.

[2] The Woodbury Training School in Applied Observation, Boston, Massachusetts.

[3] National Broadcasting Society, R. C. A. Bldg., Radio City, New York; Dr. Bernard Myers, New York University, commentator, and author of the critical brochures accompanying the reproductions. " Programs in the Public Interest." Vol. II, No. 3, and others.

[4] National Art Society, 30 Broad Street, New York.

received at the N.B.C. studio. It would seem to indicate that public interest in pictorial art, perhaps already aroused by the numerous other agencies at work, was ready for this radio experiment.

In November, 1940, the National Broadcasting Company announced a forthcoming series of Sunday afternoon broadcasts to be entitled *Pageant of Art,* and to be prepared in coöperation with the American Association of Museums and the Metropolitan Museum of Art in New York. Predominantly dramatic, the series showed the interrelation of art and changing civilization and presented the artist and his works as the expression of the life of his time. Many of the broadcasts featured brief comments by directors of American art museums and by other experts in related cultural fields. A group of radio writers, headed by Richard Morenus, was engaged to furnish the scripts in collaboration with Francis Henry Taylor, Director of the Metropolitan Museum. Program subjects dealt with a long list of important periods in art and cultural history. The program was under the direction of Dr. James Rowland Angell, President Emeritus of Yale University, Director of Educational Activities at the National Broadcasting Company.

X

THE WORK OF THE MUSEUM OF MODERN ART FILM LIBRARY

IRIS BARRY
Curator, Museum of Modern Art Film Library
New York, New York

At the time the Museum of Modern Art was founded in New York in 1929, the Director, in his preliminary report to the Trustees, already envisaged for the future a department of motion pictures. The only new art form of modern times, the motion picture — though too commonly regarded as an ephemeral entertainment only — in fact provides a significant reflection of contemporary manners and moral values, while its influence is far-reaching.

The Museum of Modern Art Film Library was founded in 1935 with the aid of a grant from the Rockefeller Foundation. It is an educational institution created primarily with the purpose of instituting a considered study of the motion picture, of the history and of the functions of this new art.

Originally, the motion picture was regarded purely as a recording instrument, as an extension of experience, as a means of portraying the external world. Its dramatic possibilities were dimly perceived in those early years only when the photographers turned from the everyday world of reality to improvise bits of low comedy or melodramatic incidents as naïve as they were brief. Fantasy was introduced next, through trick films that utilized stop-motion photography to contrive magical disappearances and transformations — qualities that were afterwards adapted to the uses of the animated cartoon. The availability of the medium for a wholly original type of narrative communication was not discovered until the joining together of apparently disassociated photographic images — as in the celebrated " Great Train Robbery " — first suggested a technique that for the future the motion picture was largely to adopt.

The capacity of this new medium to juggle with time and with space, and the opportunity it affords the spectator to furnish out of his own experience and imagination a considerable portion of the film's total content are, even today, only imperfectly understood, whether it be in the realm of fact (newsreel and educational documentary) or in the film of make-believe. It is still not entirely understood that a film, both in essence and in its effects, is radically unlike still photography, literary narrative, or theatrical representation, no matter what elements it may have in common with these. A truly creative use of sound, introduced over a decade ago, likewise remains largely undeveloped. Yet in this profane art, whose history is so strikingly unlike the history of the other visual arts, a remarkable and fertile creativeness has been apparent, and this new method of communication has developed apace. The stages through which it has developed and the potentialities that lie before it afford a field of large interest.

One of the major obligations undertaken by the Museum of Modern Art Film Library was, accordingly, to " create a consciousness of history and tradition within the new art of the motion picture — so that it might be studied and enjoyed in the same manner as the older arts are commonly studied and enjoyed." With this purpose, it became clear that its first task would be to trace and acquire as many as possible of the outstanding films of the past, so that they might be preserved permanently. This was all the more important since, normally, films are singularly evanescent. Generally speaking, a film three years old is, under ordinary circumstances, a film that will rarely be seen again. Imagine trying to study literature if only new books were available or painting if only recently executed canvases were visible.

The Film Library, therefore, undertook to collect, preserve, and to make available to colleges and museums for examination the greatest possible number of meritorious or original films from the four and a-half decades of motion-picture history. Such an examination was bound at least to strip the motion picture of forty years of prejudice, legend, and ballyhoo that had hitherto delayed its full recognition as an art significantly characteristic of our era.

Speaking more specifically, since its foundation in May, 1935, the Museum of Modern Art Film Library has formed a collection of nearly 2500 films produced between 1895 and 1937. These include a considerable proportion of the memorable films both of the United States and of Europe. From its constantly growing collection of motion pictures the Film Library has already assembled seven complete series of film programs for circulation to museums, colleges, and educational groups to serve as study material on the history and influence of the motion picture. Any educational or cultural organization may obtain the programs (which average two hours in length) for educational purposes for a rental fee of $30.00 for 35-mm. and $15.00 for 16-mm. films, by writing to the Film Library and arranging a suitable exhibition date. Each program includes the films themselves, program notes of a critical or descriptive nature for each member of the audience, and printed music for pianoforte accompaniment of all silent films. A complete set of the thirty-eight program notes, bound, may also be purchased separately for one dollar plus postage.

The first of the series of films, " A Short Survey of the Film in America, 1895 — 1932," provides the groundwork for a general study of the history of the motion picture — how the films progressed from fact to fiction, from sensation to emotion, how they gained in length, in meaning, and in technical resources as more and more of the potentialities of the medium were discovered. The third series deals with " The Film in Germany and in France." The fourth and seventh series continue the survey with representations of outstanding Swedish and Russian productions. Intervening series continue to provide further examples of important American work in this field, which will again be extended by an examination of the very rich realm of American film-comedy in a forthcoming series. Additional programs depict the nature and progress of the nonfiction or documentary film, trace the development of the animated cartoon, afford a detailed study of the work of pioneer directors, and preserve the efforts of such great theatrical figures of the past as Bernhardt and Duse as they lent themselves to explore the medium of the screen.

Plans for the extension of the Film Library's past activities have developed especially towards the provision of more advanced and detailed study material that should be the more welcome since the motion picture has lately assumed new importance in the academic world.

The Museum of Modern Art Film Library last season had circulated its programs to 287 institutions throughout the country. It is remarkable that these have been used in a surprising diversity of ways and by diverse groups, for example, by departments of economics and sociology, by departments of drama, by departments of fine arts, by foreign-language departments, and by local film societies, founded in certain centers — usually as a result of the combined efforts of an art museum and a university — to hold joint showings.

In addition to its work in the compilation of film archives and the preparation of programs of films for circulation, the Film Library has also, necessarily, assembled an immense amount of collateral material that is constantly being supplemented, as, for example, a collection of 1500 books on the cinema; also still photographs, posters, and original designs for costumes or for film settings (ranging from Leopold Survage's designs in gouache for an unexecuted abstract film, planned as long ago as 1913, to samples of the paintings on celluloid from which recent Disney cartoons have been photographed). An important group of original scenarios is also being collected, together with many original documents and analogous items of interest, such as biographical data on outstanding producers, directors, and artists, much of which has been recorded from word-of-mouth and never before set down. All this unique material is freely available to students, to journalists, and to authors.

During the past three years the Film Library has also conducted a course on the History, Esthetic, and Technique of the Motion Picture for the Department of Fine Arts, Columbia University. With the assistance of lecturer-experts, a small class of students each semester has undertaken an examination of the physical, intellectual, and psychological bases of the motion picture. An introduction to the practical elements involved in production (studio methods, camera work and lighting, cutting and editing, sound-recording, laboratory work, scenario preparation, music) has been paralled by a study of the diverse theories of composition and of the functions of the various executants. The financial structure of the industry and the esthetic peculiarities of the medium have come under survey as well as the history of its development and of the international exchange of technical and of ideological influences that it has undergone. This course is still necessarily experimental in nature but it is to be observed that among the students enrolled were a number of graduate students and young professors who seek to continue the work among the numerous colleges and universities now having permanent cinema divisions. Others among the students came from or are already active in the film industry proper or in the fields of documentary or of amateur film production.

While much has been accomplished by the Film Library since its foundation in the summer of 1935 — to a very considerable extent because it had the good fortune to earn the interest and support of the film industry as a whole and of generously coöperative members of the industry, — much remains to be done. The institution is a pioneer in an unexplored field, and the recovery and preservation of motion pictures is not merely a lengthy and a costly undertaking, but also one that has encountered unforeseen obstacles.

XI

THE PLACE OF MOTION PICTURES IN ART EDUCATION

ELIAS KATZ
Director, *Art Films*
New York, New York

In recent years, motion pictures have come to take a place of increasing importance in art education. Evidences of this trend are many. Teachers are requesting information as to the location and quality of art teaching films. New methods of using art films are being studied. Courses in appreciation of the art of motion pictures are being offered. Art classes and art clubs are producing films as creative art projects. The present article summarizes progress in this field and indicates possible further developments.

I. Motion Pictures for Purposes of Art Instruction

It may be a surprise to some art teachers to learn that there are at least several hundred motion-picture films at present available for art teaching, and that these films may be purchased or rented at reasonable cost. Films are available on such subjects as the community, design, graphic arts, architecture, painting, sculpture, arts and crafts, as well as an indefinite number of miscellaneous subjects dealing with peoples and places over the world. This vast store of visual aids is gradually becoming known to art teachers everywhere. In some schools, art teachers make much use of films, particularly in a number of high schools in New York City and Los Angeles, and in a few progressive schools elsewhere in the country.

The content of art films is gradually improving in instructional value and in technical quality. Certain aspects of art study have many films; for others, for example, in aspects like home, school, office, theater, costume, color, and the printing and advertising arts, little has been available. This discrepancy is being met by the producers of films. On the question of how to use art films most effectively few reports are available.

In summarizing the use of motion pictures for art teaching purposes, it is evident that, although progress has been made, much remains to be done. Perhaps the most crucial lack is in the matter of supplying art educators with information as to what art films are available, where to get them, and how to use them. One solution to the problem may be the setting up of a national committee or organization for the purposes of (a) keeping art teachers informed as to the location, quality, and cost of art films, (b) reviewing and evaluating existing art films, (c) making recommendations as to further production of films for the art field, and (d) publicizing methods of effective teaching of art with films.

II. Making Motion Pictures as a Creative Art Activity

The production of motion pictures as a creative art project for art class or art club is an activity that is neither difficult nor expensive, and is intimately related to the objectives of art teaching. Films have been produced for as little as $25.00, and after being shown in school assemblies, at a small admission charge of five or ten cents, the original cost has been covered, with enough to spare to go to the production of other films.

A fine motion picture can be produced by students if, during the course of the production, they are made aware of fine design in the rectangular surface of the screen, the art principles of dominance, balance, rhythm and harmony, and the interrelation of art elements of line, dark-and-light pattern, and color in conveying a mood or in communicating an idea. In fact, the production of films calls forth the utmost in knowledge and appreciation of art and provides an unexcelled opportunity for making the art experience a vital one.

We may mention only a few points in connection with motion-picture production.

The necessary materials for such a project are the camera, a tripod, a photometer (light meter), lights (if necessary), and the film. Most school projects are made on 16-mm. film, which can be exhibited in classroom or auditorium. Once the theme is selected and worked out, the scenes are photographed. Then they are edited into their appropriate sequence. These stages require the exercise of creative ability and artistic judgment on the part of the participants. Each scene must be designed in accordance with art principles. The story must be developed in rhythmic periods leading to a climax. The editing of visual sequences demands the ability to integrate the whole story in visual terms. Finally, the designing and building of settings and costumes demand creative expression of the theme in art terms.

Films have been produced as creative art projects by schools all over the country; to mention a few, at Lincoln School, Horace Mann School, Ethical Culture Fieldston School, Greenwich (Connecticut) High School, University of Minnesota, and many others.[1]

III. Appreciation of the Art of Motion Pictures

Most teachers are aware of the profound influence that motion pictures exert on their students. However, it has not been until recently that organized efforts have been made in schools to train children really to understand and appreciate films.[2] An important force in this direction has been the establishment of the Film Library of the Museum of Modern Arts, New York City.[3]

---

[1] A worth-while bibliography of material published on this subject up to 1936 appears in the section on " School-Made Films " in *Motion Pictures in Education*, by Dale, Dunn, Hoban, and Schneider.

[2] For several years the Committee on Motion Pictures of the National Council of Teachers of English, and the Committee on Motion Pictures of the Department of Secondary Education of the National Education Association have been actively engaged in developing units of study on motion-picture appreciation.

[3] See the preceding section (X) of this Chapter. — *Editor*.

Among the art qualities to be studied in motion pictures, there must first be considered the principles of design (rhythm, dominance, balance) and the elements of design (line, dark and light, and color). Then comes a study of the applications of principles and elements of design in lighting effects, camera angles, settings, costumes, and atmospheric treatments. There should also be some study of the rhythmic organization of scenes, and the interrelationships of sound and visual image. Throughout the study, the stress should be on the art qualities inherent in the film studied, and the extent to which these qualities have been realized by the director and actors.

IV. Summary

In this section I have briefly considered the place of motion pictures in art education. Films have been shown to be of value as instructional materials, as creative art projects, and as an art form to be studied and appreciated like painting or sculpture. Alert art teachers and supervisors are coming to realize that their art work can be enriched and vitalized through the introduction of films and the study of films as a part of the art curriculum.

To facilitate the work of art teachers who want to use films to illustrate or to study principles of art, there is appended information as to sources of supply.

Some Distributors of Art Instructional Films

Art Films, 96 Charles Street, New York, New York.
DeVoe and Reynolds Co., 34 Olive Street, Newark, New Jersey.
Eastman Classroom Films, Rochester, New York.
Erpi Classroom Films, Inc., 3511 35th Avenue, Long Island City, New York.
Walter O. Gutlohn, Inc., 35 West 45th Street, New York, New York.
Harmon Foundation, 140 Nassau Street, New York, New York.
Metropolitan Museum of Art, Fifth Avenue and 82nd Street, New York, New York.
Museum of Modern Art Film Library, 11 West 53rd Street, New York, New York.
Teaching Film Custodians, 25 West 43rd Street, New York, New York.
Young Men's Christian Association, Motion Picture Bureau, 347 Madison Avenue, New York, New York.

See also *Eastern Arts Association Bulletin,* Feb. 1940, pp. 32–34, and the following magazines:
Design. (Motion-Picture Section published monthly.) 32 Warren Street, Columbus, Ohio.
Educational Screen. 64 East Lake Street, Chicago, Illinois.

XII

COMMUNITY ENTERPRISES AND NATIONAL ORGANIZATIONS INFLUENCING ART EDUCATION

ROYAL BAILEY FARNUM

I. COMMUNITY ENTERPRISES

There are many activities throughout the country that in one way or another make valuable contributions to education in art. Among these are enterprises, under different auspices, that materially affect the community as a whole. " Swarthmore College includes in its program for the school year a number of art exhibits, lectures, musical programs, and selected motion pictures, all of which are open to the community," writes Miss Ethel Stilz, acting chairman of the Department of Fine Arts. This is typical of a great many college and university centers where art services of a similar nature are freely offered to the general public.

Elsewhere local clubs and associations set up opportunity classes in art and handcrafts, bring art and music lectures to the community, and in many ways foster the arts. On the West coast, San Bernardino, Riverside, Pasadena, Santa Barbara, San Diego, San Francisco, Seattle, Portland, and Los Angeles are among the most active cities.

The Community Art Project of Providence presents a slightly different point of view as a local activity. Most organizations expect the public to come to them. This Project reversed the common practice and proposed going out into the community. Established eight years ago with Carnegie Corporation funds administered under the joint direction of a committee from the Rhode Island School of Design and Brown University, it at once proceeded to place exhibits of art in strategic locations, such as libraries, schools, store windows, and other places where groups of people would gather.

As the state is so small, the ' community ' comprises all of it and adjacent towns and cities. Exhibits, transported by the Project's station wagon, are changed every two or three weeks and include a great variety of art expressions.

In addition to the ' shows,' the Project issues monthly during the winter a three-fold ' calendar.' The material on one side of this sheet consists of the art, music, and dramatic events for the coming month within a radius of forty-five miles, and also the exhibits in the museums and galleries. On the other side is an illustrated article written locally upon some art subject, which makes the calendar worth while preserving. There also are illustrated lectures loaned free to responsible individuals and organizations in the state; the borrower defrays the cost of transportation only.

The Rhode Island *League of Arts and Crafts* [1] supplements and adds to the work of the Community Art Project by holding classes in handcrafts daily and in the evenings at its headquarters. At times its products become exhibition material for the other project.

Among other New England enterprises should be mentioned the new *State of Maine Industries,* an incorporated body organized primarily to market Maine handcrafts. In 1939 they erected a handsome colonial building [2] where are exhibited " hundreds of articles, the handicraft of Maine folks made in their own homes or small shops."

New Hampshire presents one of the most interesting and effective of state community activities in the field of handcrafts. It is worth quoting what Miss Jessie Doe, Secretary and a member of its commission, writes about the *League of New Hampshire Arts and Crafts.* [3]

Three sections of the country are outstanding for handcraft: first, the Southwest, where Indian weaving, pottery, and beadwork are found; second, the so-called ' Southern Highlands ' of the Middle South, where in the remote mountain fastnesses the linsey-woolseys were still being woven when the mountain schools were established, and weaving, whittling, and other crafts were taught and reëstablished as a means of paying tuition in return for learning to read and to write; and third, but not least, New England, where industrialism and modern machinery had crowded out handcraft until there was little left other than a few basketmakers, some ' fancy work ' embroidery, and the famous hooked and braided rugs. It remained for New Hampshire to develop the first state-sponsored handcraft organization in the country — The League of New Hampshire Arts and Crafts.

It sprang from the little town of Sandwich in the foothills of the White Mountains, where, under the guidance of Mrs. J. Randolph Cool-

[1] Address, 30 Benefit Street, Providence, Rhode Island.

[2] On U. S. Highway 1, east of Saco; address, R. F. D. No. 2, Saco, Maine.

[3] Jessie Doe. "The League of New Hampshire Arts and Crafts." *Yankee Magazine,* July, 1939. (Minor omissions and alterations have been made in our quotation. — *Editor.*)

idge of the town, the Sandwich Home Industries had flourished for five years. Here was a shop to sell what the townspeople made with their own hands and a tearoom kept going by volunteers to pay the small rent.

News of this good work reached the Governor's ear, not once but many times. . . . He appointed a commission of representative men and women of the State to look into the educational and economic possibilities of arts and crafts. As a result, in 1931 the League of New Hampshire Arts and Crafts, the first state-wide organization to be sponsored by the Legislature for all the people's benefit, was organized with an unpaid, governing council of eleven, and a paid, full-time director, who, when not on the road, occupied the main office in Concord. Groups similar to the original one in Sandwich were developed in different parts of the State.

What was the main purpose? The records of the League state that "the State appropriation shall be applied to instruction, standards, and production in arts and crafts, including administration, for the economic and educational advantage of all citizens in the State." It was recognized that, to carry out this policy, close, friendly contact was needed between all officers, from the director to the last member of a local board, with the producing members. Each "Home Industries" group has its chairman and committee who know the neighbors and what they can do. They start classes in the making of articles most needed to round out production for the League as a whole. Many of the groups maintain small shops run by local members for the sale of League-made goods. Expenses are kept down by volunteer help and civic interest so that these shops are self-supporting. There is an interchange of goods made by all groups to these League shops and a small commission is charged for necessary upkeep.

The League is fortunate in receiving from the Federal Smith-Hughes fund, through the State Board of Education, half the expenses of its teachers. Since a high standard of instruction is one of the greatest values of the League, the director spends much time in selecting teachers of superior training and ability. Each teacher is itinerant; that is, he or she may spend a few days with one group, then go to another, then another, and then repeat the circuit throughout the winter months when the shops are closed and the State is supposed to be more or less 'hibernating,' though as New Hampshire becomes more and more a winter playground, more shops stay open throughout the winter.

From the beginning the jury has been a most important feature. Besides the local jury that passes on all articles made by the local members before they may be accepted for the local shop, there is a State jury that endeavors to give constructive criticism as to design, workmanship, suitable material, and salability. This jury decides whether articles may be accepted by the main office for distribution among the League shops, and it seeks to educate and encourage by suggestion, remembering that the League is expected to help all and also realizing the latent possibilities in many. The League has a committee to encourage young craftsmen in the groups.

A Craftsmen's Fair has now become an annual event. This year will be the sixth of these midsummer festivals, which have been held in successive years in different places.

Visitors come from everywhere to these fairs, and come again. But best of all to the New Hampshire people is the knowledge that what the Legislature established eight short years ago as a pioneer adventure has proved its worth and is helping the people economically as well as enriching their lives through the joy of creation.

Mention should also be made of county, state, national, and international *Fairs and Expositions*. These numerous annual fairs usually have departments of art where prizes are awarded for exhibits of homemade articles. Often beautiful products, especially of needlework, are displayed, and many children are undoubtedly stimulated to attempt artistic production. Little, however, is done to guide or properly direct these efforts. Moreover, since the exhibits usually come from rural districts, mutual influence upon the teaching of art in the schools is seldom felt, for art education in our country schools is deficient in both teaching and supervision.

International expositions, however, can and do accomplish a great deal in educating the public in art, not only through the collections of great masterpieces, as exemplified in the recent Chicago, San Francisco, and New York shows, where world treasures were gathered together under a single roof, but also through the architecture of buildings, the murals and sculpture, the landscaping, and the innumerable examples of refined and beautiful machines and machine products. An international exposition is essentially an experience in the broad field of visual art.

II. National, Professional, and Regional Organizations Interested in Art

Within a number of professional organizations and many specific club activities, art education is a dominant factor either wholly or in part. Art teachers and professors naturally confine their programs to the furtherance of art among their own membership. One body, however, the *Eastern Arts Association*, organized in 1936 a Junior Division, comprising art students in art schools, colleges, and universities, grouped by chapters, and designed to carry on active work during the year.

There are four regional bodies that serve the school art teachers of this country.

The *Eastern Arts Association* covers the territory east of Ohio and north of Virginia. Its purpose, typical of the other three sections, are " to promote the interests of art education and art educators by — (1) gathering and disseminating pertinent information; (2) undertaking research and other projects; (3) bringing its members into contact with leaders in educational work; and (4) arranging at least one gathering annually in the spring of the year where questions pertaining to Art and Education may be discussed and where members may meet for the interchange of ideas and engage in coöperative activities." In addition, through committee work, exhibits, annual gold and silver awards for outstanding service of its membership, and the lively thirty-six page bulletin issued six times a year, this Association offers effective professional support in art education.

The *Western Arts Association* functions most effectively in a similar way and serves the Middle North and West, thereby covering a somewhat larger, though more sparsely settled, area.

The *Southeastern Arts Association* and the *Pacific Arts Association* likewise have similar objectives. Though smaller in membership, they compensate for this by their enthusiasm and their vigorous programs.

There is, in addition to the regional groups, an *Art Department* of the *National Education Association*, which promotes two annual meetings, one at the time and place of meeting of the American Association of School Administrators, and one at the annual summer convention of the N. E. A. Its bulletin publishes some of the convention papers but it is comparatively inactive during the interim between meetings.

The *Progressive Education Association* also has its special art-education activities that are emphasized at the annual meetings and in one issue of its magazine.[1] Unquestionably, the experimental efforts of the membership of this Association, whose teaching is largely in private elementary and secondary schools, has done much to energize and stimulate the work of the public schools. Their service to art education cannot be overestimated, for they have been able to test and stabilize new methods and new policies when the machinery of the public system

---

[1] *Progressive Education*, 221 West 57th Street, New York, New York.

of education finds it impossible to do so, through no lack of desire or willingness to experiment.

The *College Art Association of America* functions from a more theoretical and historical standpoint. Its annual meeting is usually held during the Christmas holidays and papers deal largely with art and archeological research, the philosophy and the history of art. It publishes the magazine *Parnassus* and the scholarly quarterly called the *Art Bulletin*.

There is need for an adequately supported clearinghouse consisting of a small, carefully selected group or cabinet of persons chosen to represent different levels of art education whose function would be to give information on current trends, to coördinate detached and widely separated enterprises working toward similar ends, and to assist in clarifying and promoting on a nationwide basis the values to be recognized in the field of the arts.

There is no organization in the country, unless it be the American Federation of Arts, that is broad enough in its aims and scope of activity to maintain such a coördinating cabinet or council. At one time it was hoped that the Federated Council on Art Education, organized in 1925 with representation from the major art associations, might accomplish this larger service, but, after publishing a number of reports and doing an all-too-meager service in vocational guidance, it was found that it could never do the valuable work so urgently demanded without being far better financed.

The *American Federation of Arts* was organized in 1909 and incorporated in 1916. Its membership is made up of individuals and organizations, the latter called ‘ chapters.’ It publishes the foremost art magazine in the country, *The American Magazine of Art*. The Federation, for many years, has handled travelling art exhibits, and annually publishes the invaluable *American Art Annual*, a volume comprising the descriptive listing of art organizations, museums, galleries, and schools of art. There is included also a list of important art sales and an obituary. In past years it contained a directory of men and women in a variety of art professions. More recently the Federation has issued a separate volume on *Who's Who in American Art*.[1]

Like the other associations, the *American Federation of Arts* holds an annual convention at which individual and chapter members are brought together for formal papers, round-table luncheon discussions, and special visits to art shrines, exhibits, and private homes.

In addition to these regional and national groups there are groups

---

[1] Published by American Federation of Arts: Barr Building, Washington, D. C.

of art teachers who form local divisions of state and municipal teachers' associations. Their discussions most naturally concern concrete studies of immediate problems, less general than those of the larger bodies.

But there are many other influences that bear on art education; for instance, those represented in avocational activities, like garden clubs, home study groups, and the like. Education in the principles of good design and color may be presented through flower arrangement, garden design, interior decoration, and dress, and by means of club papers or outside lectures.

Then there are other enterprises wherein the members participate in some form of art activity either in the pictorial arts or in handcraft. The *Artklan* of Toledo, Ohio, is in this group. Founded in 1912, it is now an incorporated organization governed by officers and a board of control elected annually in June. Limited to twenty active members, its object is to provide an opportunity to draw and paint from life as well as to provide a meeting place for social contact with fellow-artists.

The *Business Men's Art Club* of Chicago is another group activity open to business and professional men. It began its class in 1920 with eighteen members. No proficiency is required for membership. Evening classes and outdoor sketching trips are in its program. In one of the club's yearbooks the following statement is made: " If you do not make your living by the practice of art and are thirty years of age or over, you fulfill the qualifications for membership." This club has been the inspiration and often the godfather of other clubs of similar nature, a thriving one at Milwaukee, for instance.

Other nation-wide movements are in the field of handcrafts. Because of the depression many ' leisure-time ' activities sprang up all over the country. The arts suggested a logical outlet, and among the classes organized were many in handwork. This in turn called attention to hobbies, which appealed not only to collectors but to dabblers in the manual arts as well. Hobby Shows were instituted with craftsmen at work; dealers in supplies issued literature telling how to make things; and thus emphasis was given to the design and making of three-dimensional form.

More recently leaders on the Eastern seaboard have visualized the possibilities of doing even more to promote art understanding by means of national handcraft organization. The latest effort is known as the *National Guildcrafters*, a nonprofit educational society incorporated under the laws of the District of Columbia.[1] It is designed to offer

---

[1] Located at 20 South Third Street, Columbus, Ohio.

home-study courses in a wide range of crafts. The organization supplies the lesson plans, the materials, and the criticism.

Another national crafts group whose purpose is somewhat different is the *American Handcrafts Association,* which is still in a preliminary stage, but is developing plans for a long-term program for the coordination of craft activities, the planning of a national exhibition based on the study of native crafts and their place in the history of our country, with a forecast of the part they may be expected to play in the future. Among its objectives are the development of a high level of achievement in design and craftsmanship, cooperation with other groups working locally to this end, and the cultivation and promotion of a public demand for the highest type of craftsmanship. Such a coordinating organization is greatly to be desired, especially as many, little-known, but high-grade groups of craftsmen are working throughout the country with improper recognition and inadequate support.

In still another field is to be found the *Amateur Cinema League,*[1] which tends to fill a fast-growing need for aid because of the extensive use of films by the amateur. The managing director, Mr. Roy W. Winton, in answer to a request for information, writes the following:

> The Amateur Cinema League, Incorporated, founded in 1926 by Hiram Percy Maxim, the late inventor and author, is devoted to the service of persons who make their own motion pictures for nontheatrical purposes. By the publication of a basic text on personal movie-making, the maintenance of a monthly magazine, *Movie-makers,* the provision of booklets and other specific data, the preparation of filming plans, and the criticism of completed motion pictures, it aids individual filmers in making better movies.
>
> The League is committed to the proposition that the motion picture is a new art form and not a composite of older arts. It believes that the technique and procedure of movie-making constitute a corpus of knowledge about this new art form and that the development of an esthetic of the movies is a definite possibility, which has, to some degree, already been attained.
>
> Therefore, the Amateur Cinema League, in its publications and in its relations with its members, continually seeks to build up esthetic canons in addition to technical information. It has analyzed, from time to time, the factors that constitute the artistic bases of motion pictures and it seeks to give them wider public understanding.

Many national groups organized for other purposes also serve their members indirectly in some art education capacity. Notable among

---

[1] Located at 420 Lexington Avenue, New York, New York.

these are the *American Association of University Women*, the *General Federation of Women's Clubs*, the *Association of the Junior Leagues of America*, the *National Recreation Association*, the *Boy Scouts*, the *Camp Fire Girls*, the *Girl Scouts*, the *Girls' Friendly Society*, and the *Boys' Clubs of America*.

REFERENCES

(1) ADAM, T. R. *The Civic Value of Museums*. (American Association for Adult Education: New York, 1937)

(2) ADAM, T. R. *The Museum and Popular Culture*. (American Association for Adult Education: New York, 1939) 177 pp.

(3) BACH, R. F. "Museum on the march." *Jour. Adult Ed.*, 11: 1939, 65–67.

(4) BACH, R. F. "Neighborhood circulating exhibitions." *Museum News*, 12: No. 15, 1939, 7–8.

(5) BARTON, J. E. "Education of public taste." *Museums Jour.*, 34: 1935, 297–309.

(6) BEATON, WELFORD. *Know Your Movies: the Theory and Practice of Motion-Picture Production*. (Howard Hill: Hollywood, California, 1932) 192 pp.

(7) BENSON, E. M. "Educational Program." *Phil. Mus. Bul.*, 34: Nov. 1938, 1–12.

(8) BLOOMBERG, M. *Experience in Museum Instruction*. (American Association of Museums: Washington, D. C., 1929)

(9) Carnegie Institute. "Sketching is fun; Adult education classes at Carnegie Institute look forward to another successful year." *Carnegie Magazine*, Nov. 1937, 177–179.

(10) CLARK, G. G. "Young art students turning to commercial work." *Design*, 40: Sup. 2. Feb., 1939.

(11) COLEMAN, L. C. *The Museum in America*. (American Association of Museums: Washington, D. C., 1939) 3 v. 730 pp.

(12) Committee on the Function of Art in General Education, for the Commission on Secondary-School Curriculum. *The Visual Arts in General Education*. (D. Appleton-Century Co.: New York, 1940) 166 pp.

(13) COOPER, R. M. "Measuring industrial design." *Design*, 39: June, 1937, 15–18.

(14) CURRELLY, C. T. "The museum and the radio." *Museum News*, October 1, 1937, 9–11.

(15) DALE, EDGAR. *How to Appreciate Motion Pictures: A Manual of Motion Picture Criticism Prepared for High-School Students*. (The Macmillan Co.: New York, 1933) 243 pp.

(16) DALE, EDGAR, DUNN, FANNIE W., HOBAN, CHARLES F., JR., and SCHNEIDER, ETTA. *Motion Pictures in Education: A Summary of the Literature; Source Book for Teachers and Administrators*. (H. W. Wilson Co.: New York, 1937) 472 pp.

(17) DAVIDSON, M. "Government as a patron of art." *Art News*, 35: October 10, 1936, 10–12.

(18) Eastman Kodak Company. *How to Make Good Movies*. (Eastman Kodak Co.: Rochester, 1938) 230 pp.

(19) "Education for Democracy: Cross Section of the Community Reached by Educational Program." *Worcester Museum News Bull.*, 5: (4), Nov., 1939.

(20) EVANS, E. I. "Not Bread Alone." *Cincinnati Mus. Bul.*, 10: 1939, 80–83.

(21) FRARY, I. T. "Retaining the public's interest." *Museum News*, Sept. 15, 1936, 7–8.

(22) HAGGERTY, M. E. *Enrichment of the Common Life.* (University of Minnesota: Minneapolis, 1938) 36 pp.

(23) HITCHCOCK, H. R. "Museums in the modern world." *Arch. R.*, 86: 1939, 147–148.

(24) HOLME, GEOFFREY. *Industrial Design and the Future.* (The Studio: New York, 1934) 160 pp.

(25) HYDE, DORSEY W. "Educational aims of the community museum." *Museum News*, May 1, 1938, 7–8.

(26) KATZ, ELIAS. "Educational possibilities of motion-picture films in art courses." *Educ. Screen*, 13: 1934, 97.

(27) KATZ, ELIAS. "A listing of motion pictures for art teaching." *Design*, 41: Dec., 1939.

(28) KELEKIAN, D. "Four memoirs of the growth of art and taste in America: the dealer." *Art News*, 37: Sup. 67–68, Feb. 25, 1939.

(29) KENNEDY, D. S. "Art and consumer education." *Design*, 41: Feb., 1940, 8–10.

(30) KENNY, J. B. "Films in the art class." *Design*, 41: Oct. 26, 1939.

(31) KETTELL, R. H. "Art Exhibitions at Private Schools." [In] *Worcester Art Museum Annual*, Vol. II, 1936–37, 99–101.

(32) KIESLER, F. *Contemporary Art Applied to the Store and Its Display.* (Brentano's: New York, 1930)

(33) LEWISOHN, SAM A. "Four memoirs of the growth of art and taste in America: the collector." *Art News*, 37: Sup. 69–70, Feb. 25, 1939.

(34) McBRIDE, H. "Four memoirs of the growth of art and taste in America: the critic; collecting from a critical viewpoint." *Art News*, 37: Sup. 65–6, Feb. 25, 1939.

(35) McMAHON, A. "Trend of the government in art." *Parnassus*, 8: Jan., 1936, 3–6.

(36) MENDELOWITZ, D. M. "Motion pictures and art education." *Design*, 41: Dec., 1939, 8–11.

(37) MUNRO, T. "The Art Museum and the Secondary School." [In] *Progressive Education*, xiv, xv, Nov., 1937, 7.

(38) MUNRO, T. "Art Museum Work and Training." [In] *Women's Work and Education.* (University of North Carolina: Greensboro, N. C., Feb., 1934)

(39) MUNRO, T. *Educational Work at the Cleveland Museum of Art.* (Cleveland, Ohio, 1940) 32 pp.

(40) MUNRO, T. "The Function of the Museum in the New Art Education." [In] *Bulletin of the Department of Art Education of the National Education Association.* Vol. V, 33–43.

(41) MUNRO, T. "Museum Educational Work for the General Public." *Cleveland Mus. Bul.*, 26: 1939, 132–136.

(42) MYERS, E. E. "Community art activities." *Design*, 41: Jan., 1940, 8–10.

(43) PARKER, T. C. "The artist teaches." *Progressive Educ.*, May, 1938, 387.

(44) PARKER, T. C. "Community art centers." *Museum News*, 15: Oct., 15, 1937, 7–8.

(45) PATTEN, MARJORIE. *The Arts Workshop of Rural America: a Study of the Rural Arts Program of the Agricultural Extension Service.* (Columbia University: New York, 1937) 202 pp.

(46) PELIKAN, A. G. "Amateur paints." *Design*, 38: 1937, 20–21.

(47) PERKINS, E. W. "Drawing from motion pictures." *Educ. Screen*, 10: 1931, 105–107.

(48) PUDOWKIN, V. I. *On Film Technique.* (Camelot Press: London, 1929) 204 pp.

(49) RAMSEY, G. F. *Educational Work in Museums of the United States.* (H. W. Wilson: New York, 1938) 289 pp.

(50) REA, P. M. *The Museum and the Community.* (The Science Press: Lancaster, Pa., 1932)

(51) READ, H. E. *Art and Industry.* (Harcourt, Brace and Co.: New York, 1935) 143 pp.

(52) ROBINSON, E. S. "University training and the museum worker." *Museum News*, Nov. 1, 1936, 7–8.

(53) ROHDE, G. "What is industrial design?" *Design*, 38: Dec., 1936, 3–5.

(54) ROTHA, PAUL. *Celluloid: The Film Today.* (Longmans, Green, and Co.: New York, 1931) 259 pp.

(55) ROWDEN, D., Ed. *Handbook of Adult Education in the United States.* (American Association for Adult Education: New York, 1936)

(56) SANBORN, P. "Museum radio talks." *Museum News*, Oct. 1, 1937, 11.

(57) SCHOEN, E. "Industrial design, a new profession." *Mag. Art*, 31: 1938, 472–479.

(58) SYMONS, L. R. "Children in the museum." *Cincinnati Mus. Bul.*, 9: July, 1938, 86–92.

(59) TAYLOR, F. H. "Museums in the changing world." *Atlantic Monthly*, Dec., 1939, 785–792.

(60) TEAGUE, W. D. *Design This Day.* (Harcourt, Brace and Co.: New York, 1940) 291 pp.

(61) ULP, C. M. "Models in motion." *Journal of Higher Education.* 1931.

(62) Zentralinstitut für Erziehung und Unterricht. *Museum und Schule.* (Hobbing: Berlin, 1930) 152 pp.

SECTION IV

THE PREPARATION OF TEACHERS OF ART

CHAPTER XXXIII

SOME PROBLEMS OF AIM AND METHOD IN TRAINING ART TEACHERS

Otto F. Ege
Head of Teacher Training Department, Cleveland School of Art
Assistant Professor of Art, School of Education
Western Reserve University
Cleveland, Ohio

The preparation of teachers of art cannot be properly oriented until there is a more general agreement among administrators and educators as to the value and function of art in their educational philosophy and in their programs. At present, one group of educational leaders places great emphasis on technical achievement and vocational objectives; another group, on personality adjustment and social consciousness; and still others, on leisure-time avocations, intelligent consumers, alert appreciators, and similar worth-while and significant objectives.

There is, however, a general consensus that the prime function of the art teacher today is to mold, refine, and enrich the emotional life of every child, not merely to train the hand or inform the mind. To meet this challenge, our training program for art teachers must be radically changed. At present, unfortunately, nearly half the art teachers in secondary schools of the United States teach another subject — English, music, history, or even physical education — in addition to art.

The art teacher should possess certain qualities and abilities to a degree not necessary for some other teachers. He should have a keen awareness of the world and life about him, should possess the ability not to teach, but to experience, the art lessons with his pupils, should be endowed with a sensitive and creative imagination, and should have a sympathetic understanding of emotional conflicts and be able to release tensions and inhibitions through opportunities for self-expression.

In training teachers of art it is necessary not only to develop competence in art, but also in techniques of teaching. A philosophy must be developed to make teachers conscious that they are not merely to teach art, but are also to bring about desirable adjustments in their pupils through art experiences. The art course makes unique contributions to this adjustment.

Opinion is again divided as to the type of school that can best prepare teachers of art, and also as to the number of teachers needed for it. Twenty-five years ago, most art teachers were trained in art schools; now most of them are being trained in universities and teachers' colleges. Each type of training has advantages and disadvantages. The art-school atmosphere is apt to create teachers who are more interested in skill and in the production of art than in the broader aspects of the art program. The teachers' colleges, on the other hand, have rarely been equipped with proper studio facilities or personnel to give the students power and facility in drawing, painting, modelling, design, and the crafts. Furthermore, the art faculty in an academic school is frequently chosen on the basis of academic degree rather than on one of art ability. Since so many teachers of art will inevitably be trained in teachers' colleges and universities, it is essential that the faculties of the institutions include teachers of outstanding ability in art. Another alternative is to have an art school coöperate with a teacher-training institution and thus to have art subjects taught by practicing artists with the proper facilities, and academic and professional subjects taught in academic halls. This seems logical and rational, and finer results from the art instruction of teachers so trained are already clearly evident. We feel, however, that in several important centers the error is being made of grouping the training thus: three or four years given to art work, then one, two, or three years devoted entirely to academic work. It seems more reasonable for the two types of preparation to run concurrently, with the emphasis in the first few years on art, and in the latter, on education.

Again, the proportional division of these two types of training is a matter of continual controversy, since the art teacher with the integrated program must know " more and more about more and more." Art schools grudgingly arrange for the minimal required professional hours and feel that they are liberal when one-fourth of the art program is " sacrificed." The schools of education frequently resist any attempt to raise the art hours, required and elective, from the proportion of one-third to one-half the total number of hours. The solution seems to lie in a continuous plan, combining undergraduate and graduate work. The undergraduate program is to give rich experience in, and mastery of, several fields of art expression, while the graduate program is to be devoted largely to art history, theory, and practice.

In some of the coöperative courses, five, or even six, years are required for the undergraduate degree. Although this length of time seems justifiable, it has frequently deterred the more capable art student from entering the field of teaching. He checks his potential earning capacity as a teacher with that of the industrial designer or advertising artist. The latter, with only four years of training, may in three or four years reach the salary maximum for which a teacher must work from seven to ten years, after the completion of a longer course of training. Furthermore, the salary increments of a teacher often cease at this point, whereas there is no limit in the other fields. With this competition it is difficult to secure the right type of man, dynamic and skilled, to assume duties in the schoolroom. The proportion of men to women in the art teaching field is lower than in most of the other subjects in the secondary-school curriculum.

The professional preparation of the art teacher falls roughly into three divisions: first, the acquisition of technical skill and the ability to express significant concepts; second, the understanding of art education, its problems and its objectives, as well as its relation to the educational program as a whole; the development of professional self — the " cultured use of the capacity to relate oneself and one's service to people in need " — the art of teaching art; and third, the acquisition of a cultural background, including the mastery of English.

Techniques and skills, overemphasized in the past, are frequently apt to be minimized in the present. Technique does not mean hand skill only; in the fuller meaning, it implies the ability to see, to analyze, to evaluate, to remember, to design, and to interpret our reactions to the world about us through design and graphic expression. The art teacher needs to be taught a number of techniques and processes — not how to " handle and teach " charcoal drawing, water-color or tempera painting, enamelling, or pottery building, but rather how to equip himself with the means to express concepts more fully and help others to do likewise. Good drawing and good design are necessary fundamentals for any art medium and problem, and the lack of these cannot be redeemed by the glamor of etching ink, or the setting of a semiprecious stone in silver. The art of drawing is more important than the craft of drawing. Certainly, to transmute our impression of nature, to catch the rhythm of life about us, is far more important than to achieve a realistic illusion of nature. For this art of drawing numerous techniques are necessary. In the field of teaching design, the mind as well as the eye should be satisfied; functional form should be combined with decorative form. The object conceived should work well and look well.

Again, still other techniques are necessary for the art teacher to succeed in the fields that include such subjects as textiles, wallpapers, advertisements, stoves, and automobiles. Technique in itself, no matter how well manipulated, is not a means of development unless sublimated with ideas and ideals. It is evident that the range of subject matter presented is continually expanding. With new objectives and better-trained art teachers, graphic expression — the greatest joy of the child in the elementary level — is no longer displaced by design problems in the secondary schools. Theories of color, of perspective, of design, are no longer semester courses, but means to an end, introduced when and where needed. Graphic and design problems have real significance for the child; in these problems, the thinking experience and the feeling experience have the same value as the doing experience.

The theory and practice of art teaching — the what and why, and the when and how — form an ever-changing pattern. Growth is most clearly evidenced by a broader viewpoint. Tabulations of objectives frequently advanced in the recent past would include many minutiae, with emphasis on minor phases. Such lists look absurdly inclusive and presumptuous or seem platitudinous and indecisive.

A broad generalization of the objectives in the field of art might well be limited to a few areas and aims, as follows:

First, to contribute to the growth of the student's personality in a way suitable for social living. To accomplish this, the student teacher should study the psychology of the emotions for therapeutic as well as pedagogical ends. He needs to know about the will, inhibitions, tensions engendered by age, sex, race, health, religion, environment, and numerous other factors.

Second, to give to every student art experiences that contribute to the joy and richness of living. To stimulate those creative acts that give inward satisfaction, relieve tensions, instill confidence, arouse new interest. To develop awareness and a keener appreciation of nature and of the social state, as well as of the fine heritage of the arts.

Third, to discover, conserve, and develop the specially gifted child, not, however, at the expense of the average pupils in the group or of those with very little aptitude for this subject. All are capable of creating on various levels; all are capable of enjoying certain types of emotional experience in art programs.

These objectives may be realized by a variety of means. One teacher may be able to arouse keen interest, hold sustained effort, and reach high attainment and produce excellent results through figure-drawing and illustration; another may be equally successful through advertising art and industrial design with the senior-high-school group. The next year, the same classroom might require a different motivating force. No ideal curriculum can be printed or demanded. The teacher must be well equipped to organize and direct, as well as to reorganize, his program continually for the fullest realization of our ideology.

The teacher also needs to know the normal growth of the normal child with relation to his graphic expression; how to anticipate and pre- pare for the next phase; how to accelerate that growth when feasible and desirable; and how to aid those whose growth is retarded. He needs to know corrective procedure for the one-subject child, the light- ning-sketch ' artist,' the small-drawing type, the afraid-to-start group, the copyist, the neurotic type, and others that are found in every class.

The art teacher in training may have this fundamental theoretical and practical training, but he must also be a good showman, one who in- spires confidence by his numerous demonstrations. In addition, he must also be a good salesman of each lesson and of his program as a whole. Otherwise, he is apt to fail in the bigger issues. Lacking good showmanship and good salesmanship, he might, with pressure, obtain acceptable tangible results, a fair school exhibit, but he would not be able to inspire and help the child to truly creative work and thereby to attain that valuable and somewhat intangible result, a better-adjusted personality.

This brings us to the final point, the development of a professional self — to engender in the embryo teacher a process of development that must go beyond that required of the average person or of the average teacher. A professional self should emerge that possesses new and greater potentialities for relating oneself to other people, for assuming responsibilities with patience, and for making knowledge support ac- tion. Knowledge and skills must be coördinated with attitudes. At- titude and teaching skill cannot be checked in the lecture hall, but only in real situations when the trainee is allowed full responsibility, under supervision, in a variety of classes. The practice teaching period, to be the touchstone for success, must be long and varied.

The ideal art teacher cannot be selected with assurance by any ex- isting art test, by checking scholastic records, or even by personal in- terview. The applicant's intelligence ratings should place him in the upper third of any group of students, and his poise and personality should create a favorable impression on the interviewer — yet with all such things in his favor he may be a failure in the crucial test of the classroom.

Many of the most promising trainees have disappointed us. We did not, or could not, discover their emotional inadequacy for the profession of art teaching, their inability to be flexible, to grow, to meet new challenges, to be leaders, or to think and plan for themselves instead of repeating their training program. Let us who are responsible for the training of students be sure that we, too, are continually expanding our horizons and deepening our insight through the actual doing of art and actual contact with children, so that we may understand the tasks that will face the younger generation.

REFERENCES

(1) Committee on the Function of Art in General Education for the Commission on Secondary School Curriculum. *The Visual Arts in General Education.* (D. Appleton-Century Co.: New York, 1940) Ch. 5: " The Art Teacher: His Qualifications and Preparation."

(2) DeLuce, O. S. " The Background of Art History and Esthetics of the Art Teacher." [In] *Bulletin of the Department of Art Education, National Education Association,* Vol. V, 1939, 159–162.

(3) Lamb, N. W. " A Critical Evaluation of the Academic Requirements in the Training of the Art Teacher." [In] *Bulletin of the Department of Art Education, National Education Association,* Vol. V, 1939, 154–156.

(4) Poore, S. " Training Tomorrow's Art Teacher." [In] *Bulletin of the Department of Art Education, National Education Association,* Vol. V, 1939, 147–154.

CHAPTER XXXIV

CURRICULAR PATTERNS OF SOME INSTITUTIONS PREPARING ART TEACHERS

GEORGE S. DUTCH
Professor of Art, George Peabody College for Teachers
Nashville, Tennessee

School administrators seeking teachers of art have the choice of the product of the art school, the teachers' college, or the university. It is well to recognize the differing emphases of instruction in these institutions. The teacher of art coming from the art school is often long on technical art training and short on general education and educational theory and practice, whereas the reverse emphasis is frequently true of the teachers' college product. Universities, on the other hand, often furnish a type of art teacher who is overloaded with art history and theory, to the detriment of a sound grounding in technical training and art education. Ideally, the art teacher is the happy combination of a roundness of education and experience that comes through work in all these fields. An examination of several selected curricular patterns for the preparation of teachers of art that will serve to indicate different types of practice can be made by consulting the catalogs issued by art schools, universities, and teachers' colleges. In this chapter I have indicated the sources whence such information may be secured for five important schools for the training of teachers of art, and have quoted comments made upon their respective curricula by officials of each of them.

I. THE SCHOOL OF THE ART INSTITUTE OF CHICAGO

One of the world's largest art schools, the School of the Art Institute of Chicago, includes a Department of Art Education of approximately one hundred active students. The following information is taken from the 1940–41 catalog of the School, which should ' e consulted for details about the required courses.

The immediate objective of this Department is to prepare students technically and philosophically to meet the art teaching requirements of public and private schools. Every student is given an opportunity to develop his technical understanding before adding intensive courses in pedagogical method. This double responsibility toward the artistic ideal and toward the manner of its presentation to young students is met in the curriculum here outlined.[1] The obvious advantages of working with students in other departments of the School and using the collections of the Institute are an additional strength in the organization of this Department.

Observation in the Saturday children's classes and practice teaching in Chicago and suburban schools are a necessary part of the Department's activity, serving to give student teachers direct contact with children at various age levels.

Students entering the Art Education Department are expected to work toward the Degree of Bachelor of Art Education, which meets certification requirements in most states.

Serving as a broad introduction to the problems confronting all artists, the Introductory Degree Course constitutes the first year's work with the following offerings:

	Term Points
Drawing and Composition	9
Figure and Cast Drawing	9
Design, Pattern and Three Dimensional	9
History of Art	4
English Composition	6

Gertrude M. Hadley, Chairman, Art Education Department, discusses the degree requirements in a letter that is here quoted in part:

Of course, we believe a strong art background is essential for a teacher of art, and so the four-year course is divided into approximately three years of technical art and one year of academic study. This enables our students to meet the majority of State Certification Requirements upon graduation . . . we assist [students] with their programs and advise sequences that will meet specific requirements to the best of our ability. We believe this assistance to be of major importance. . . .

Our Technical Art program is flexible and will vary according to individual interests. One may wish to major in Painting; another in Advertising, Ceramics, etc. Any specialization generally follows the first two years. We do not advise too specialized a course, but a more general one for a beginning teacher, and stress the need of continued schooling. Our students seem to feel the need also, and our records show that a good percentage of them continue in summer schools over the country.

---

[1] Here omitted.

All academic courses may be taken at any accredited college or university, but the New Plan enables a student to carry an academic course each term with his technical art courses. He attends late afternoon classes — 4:15 to 6:15 — two days a week, earning a major, a course, or 3 semester hours per term, according to the school he attends (University Downtown College, Y.M.C.A. College, DePaul University Downtown College, or Northwestern McKinlock Campus).

A Master of Art Education Degree is also offered by the Department of Art Education. The academic and professional qualifications beyond the Bachelor of Art Education Degree are stated in a special folder.

II. THE CLEVELAND SCHOOL OF ART AND WESTERN RESERVE UNIVERSITY

While the School of the Art Institute of Chicago has been able to develop a program of teacher education on a degree-granting basis by the acceptance of academic credits from neighboring colleges, the Cleveland School of Art has organized with Western Reserve University an art-education curriculum leading to a Bachelor of Science degree.

The degrees of Master of Arts and Doctor of Philosophy may be taken in the Graduate School of the University. Part of the work for these degrees may be done in advanced courses at the Cleveland School of Art. Courses in art history and theory at the University are required for a graduate degree.

For a description of the Art Education Curriculum, the reader may consult the *Bulletin of Western Reserve University* (1940), from which the following excerpts are quoted:

> The Cleveland School of Art offers jointly with the School of Education a four-year course in the training of teachers and supervisors of art. The first two years are devoted to a general art course in the Cleveland School of Art. The advanced art, academic, and professional courses are given during the Junior and Senior years in the Cleveland School of Art and the School of Education. The purpose is to train teachers who will be able to participate in the general life and activities of the modern school, and to coördinate their work with that of other departments, as well as to develop appreciation, critical judgment, and the power of expression in art. Upon completion of the curriculum, the University grants, through the School of Education, the degree of Bachelor of Science, which entitles the student to a Four-Year Provisional Special Certificate in Art.

A total of 126 semester hours is required for the degree. . . . Not less than 30 semester hours must be taken in residence at the School of Education.

The courses in Education are supplemented with directed Observation and Participation in the Saturday Morning Classes at the Cleveland School of Art, composed of elementary- and high-school students. Practice teaching is provided in the Cleveland Public School system. There is also opportunity for electives to permit the student to specialize in a particular field.

Comments on this coöperative arrangement between an art school and a university are furnished by Otto F. Ege, Head of the Department of Teacher Training in the Cleveland School of Art, and Assistant Professor of Art at Western Reserve University:

You will note that the first two years are devoted to a regular general program at the Art School. In the third year the students devote half of their time to academic work and the other half to an art program with one elective. The handicraft can be either metalry, enamelling, jewelry, or ceramics. In the senior year it is the hope that students have decided on a special field for high-school teaching. These choices include advertising art, illustration, industrial design, crafts, portrait painting, or interior decoration.

Only one day devoted to organization and management and curriculum construction is included in this program. In the second semester the students spend half of their time in practice teaching mostly in the junior high schools of Cleveland, and four afternoons are spent in their elective field. In addition to this second semester program they are required to do a serious piece of research in art education as a final project. During their third and fourth years the students are also expected and required to observe and participate at least eight Saturday mornings during each year in our Saturday Morning Classes for children.

There are also a few students who are financially able and interested in supplementing this required training with summer study and evening extension work, so that they acquire a Minor in English, History, or some other subject, or else take courses in supervising the intermediate-level art program.

This program of some ninety hours in art, thirty hours in professional and academic work, is, of course, criticised by some State Departments of Education as not giving the student cultural viewpoints, but we feel that we have trained better art teachers than those institutions that are limited to forty or sixty hours in art training.

Class enrollment in the Teacher Department is limited to approximately twenty students. A few more are admitted on trial, but frequently eliminated at the end of the first semester of their third year.

The students holding our B.S. degree can continue their studies for their M.A. In this program the amount of practical art experience and training is somewhat limited on the theory that the cultural aspects should be stressed. This graduate program includes a number of elective courses in History of Art, Esthetics, and Educational Research Problems. Next year some emphasis will be placed on teaching art appreciation with the radio — its problems, its scope, and a check on its results.

III. The State University of Iowa

One of the several objectives of the School of Fine Arts of the State University of Iowa is to offer training adapted to the needs of those who expect to teach the fine arts.

Students preparing to become art teachers are advised to enroll for the B.F.A. degree. In order to secure a special art certificate in the state, they are required to have a minimum of 30 semester hours credit in art. We advise a minimum of 40 semester hours in practical art courses with 18 semester hours of history of art.

In addition to credits in art, they must have credit in general psychology, principles of American government, and the following courses in education: Introduction to Education, Educational Psychology including Measurements, Methods in Art, Observation and Laboratory Practice, electives in education.

Our students preparing to teach frequently register for Observation and Laboratory Practice in the High School, or Practice in the Elementary School, or a course with practice at both levels.[1]

The Bachelor of Fine Arts Degree [2]

This semiprofessional course is intended primarily for talented artists with a professional interest in fine arts, or design and commercial art. It may also lead to elementary and high-school teaching, or, after further well-chosen graduate studies, to college teaching. Students proceeding to this degree must specialize in practical art. A minimum of 18 hours of history of art is required.

In addition to the Bachelor of Fine Arts degree, the University of Iowa offers work leading to the degrees of Bachelor of Arts, Master of Arts, Master of Fine Arts, and Doctor of Philosophy.

---

[1] From a letter from Edna Patzig, Associate Professor, Department of Art, University of Iowa.

[2] From a mimeographed statement on the *Department of Art, University of Iowa.*

IV. George Peabody College for Teachers

Courses in George Peabody College for Teachers are designed for the effective preparation of educational leaders and teachers for every large type of teaching position, including in the arts, instructors in colleges and teachers colleges; teachers, directors, and supervisors of the arts; and classroom teachers. The basic organization in the college, " The Professional Unit, composed of the junior, senior, and first graduate years, is devised to encourage greater continuity, thoroughness, and scholarship in the education of teachers through the integration of courses. Students completing the Professional Unit will receive the M.A. degree. Those completing only the first two years (the junior and senior years) will receive the B.S. degree." For several years the offerings at Peabody in fine arts and industrial arts have been organized under one heading, The Arts.

The student majoring in the Arts on either the undergraduate or graduate level is helped to adjust his program to his individual needs in relation to his previous training and experience. A wide range of courses is offered under the general headings of Appreciation, Techniques, and Arts Education. A statement of the philosophy of the Arts as presented in a recent Peabody Bulletin indicates the general character of the Departmental offerings. The following are excerpts from this *Bulletin:*

> " The Arts " at Peabody College is a phrase that deliberately stresses the oneness of all the arts to the extent that students are encouraged to secure as wide a range of contact with all the related arts as is possible without sacrifice of quality of performance. Particular emphasis is placed upon seeing art as vital to a rich and satisfying life. . . . .
>
> Art conceived in these terms makes necessary an understanding of how to enhance appreciations, increase opportunities for satisfying experiences in art, and integrate curricula so that they achieve unity of purpose.
>
> Qualitatively there is a vast difference between the inception of the ability to discriminate and the achievement of the creative artist. Both secure enjoyment, not necessarily according to the quality or the degree of their participation. Recognizing this range of capacity and interest of individuals, Peabody aims to provide curricula for the individual interested in art experiences as general education, avocation, or recreation, as well as for the student planning a professional career as art teacher or director.
>
> Satisfaction in the arts requires mastery first of hands, then of tools,

then of machines. Paint, clay, soap, plastics, metals, textiles, leather, and wood are representative of the media for fascinating opportunities in this process of mastery.

Drawing is the language of industry. Every person specializing in the arts must know the rudiments of this language and possess the ability to " talk with a pencil." This applies alike to the mechanic, the artisan, the craftsman, and the artist.

V. TEACHERS COLLEGE, COLUMBIA UNIVERSITY

" General Arts " is used as a title to include the Department of Fine and Industrial Arts and the Department of Music and Music Education at Teachers College, Columbia University. Major programs leading to degrees and professional diplomas [1] are arranged in each of these departments. The fields of specialization in Fine Arts and Fine Arts Education are: Teaching and Supervision of Fine Arts; Drawing, Painting, and Design; House Design and Decoration; and Costume and Theater Arts.

The requirements for the degree of Doctor of Philosophy or Doctor of Education are determined largely on the basis of individual needs. Courses include practical and theoretical work in the arts, psychology, education, and related subjects.

Ray Faulkner, Head of the Department of Fine and Industrial Arts, points to certain features in the Teachers College program:

> Both art and music courses are listed under the heading of General Arts and have been organized in a similar fashion to facilitate the planning of courses in art and music.
>
> The Departments of Fine and Industrial Arts have been combined, and although majors in each field are offered, a combined major is available. We hope that, as times goes on, the arbitrary and foolish distinction between the Fine and Industrial Arts will lessen. Our second move toward breaking down subject-matter boundaries is evident in regard to the Department of Music. Our third step forward is the special preservice group, which I believe marks a significant development in teacher training.

The program of the special pre-service group mentioned by Faulkner offers such profitable suggestions on the professional development of the prospective teacher of art as to warrant quotations:

---

[1] For the course offerings in Fine and Industrial Arts, in Fine Arts for the B.S. degree, Fine Arts Education for the M.A. degree (including the requirements for certification in New York State), and for the Ph.D. and the Ed.D degrees, the reader is referred to the appropriate publications of the University. — *Editor*.

The Pre-service Group was set up as part of the study being conducted by the General Education Board on the improvement of the training of teachers. It enrolls for the most part those students coming from liberal arts colleges who have had intensive subject-matter training and wish to become teachers. There are also students who have had education work as undergraduates but who wished another year of training. All students are working for the master's degree.

The courses taken by the students include both work in education and in their subject-matter fields. The courses in the latter depend on the previous training of the students and the state and departmental requirements they had to meet. The education work taken is the same for all. All meet in a central seminar, Foundations of Education, concerned with the sociological foundations of education, philosophy of education, educational psychology, and history of education. The group divides into smaller sections, or Divisional Seminars, according to fields of specialization. Of these, there are six, Art and Music, the Social Studies, the Humanities (English, French, Spanish, and Latin), Science and Mathematics, Home and Community Life, and Elementary Education. These groups meet with representatives of each of their departments for discussion of work in these fields. While the division of groups is on the basis of broad fields, it is not the plan of this study to indicate that as being the only, or even the best, type of organization for secondary education. From time to time these divisional seminars subdivide further when matters concerned only with their particular field need consideration.

Concurrently with the above, all students are enrolled in practice teaching, which for most of them continues throughout the year. Thus the study of general methods, special methods, psychology, and philosophy of education goes hand in hand with observation and actual work in real situations. The integration that results is apparent as the students bring their own experiences to bear in their work in the seminars, and their particular problems become a basis for much class work and discussion.

An intensive personnel program is also carried on with all of these students. They are given several diagnostic tests, and all have a series of interviews with personnel workers. Those students with particular problems are given special help.

The whole study represents an attempt to organize the pre-service training of teachers into a large, well-knit pattern.

CHAPTER XXXV

COURSE REQUIREMENTS FOR TEACHERS OF ART IN FIFTY INSTITUTIONS

Walter E. Hager
Secretary, Teachers College, Columbia University
and
Edwin Ziegfeld
Assistant Professor of Fine Arts
Teachers College, Columbia University
New York, New York

I. Tabulation of Data

In order to determine the general pattern of college requirements for the preparation of prospective teachers of art, a tabulation was made of required courses in fifty colleges and universities. The group selected for study included eighteen state universities, nineteen state teachers' colleges, and thirteen colleges and private schools. The results appear in the following four tables, showing the requirements of art, art education, other prescribed education courses, and general or academic work, respectively.

In the tabulation it was found that similar courses appeared under various names in different institutions. Such courses have been placed in one classification. In other instances courses have been grouped under one heading because it was impossible to tabulate them separately, as with Drawing and Painting, or Design and Color. All tabulations are in semester hours.

II. What the Tables Show

It is well to bear in mind in studying the tables that the pattern of requirements of any college is obscured by grouping the courses that it requires along with those of forty-nine others. Many apparent irregularities can be explained when the pattern of requirements of the 'irregular' institution is studied. For example, the one institution that does not require any courses in drawing or painting provides for twenty-four semester hours in art courses to be planned by each student's major adviser. These would almost certainly include one or more courses in

735

TABLE I. — COURSES IN ART PRESCRIBED IN FIFTY COLLEGES AND UNIVERSITIES
FOR PERSONS PREPARING TO TEACH ART

| | | Of the Institutions Requiring the Subject | |
Subject	No. of Inst. in Which Required	Median Requirement in Semester Hours	Range in Semester Hours
Anatomy	6	2½	1–6
Architectural Design	5	3	3–6
(incl. House Design and House Planning)			
Art Appreciation	24	3	1–12
(incl. Appreciation of Art, Introd. to Art Environment, etc.)			
Commercial Art	17	3½	3–6
(incl. Commercial Design, Advertising, Poster Design, etc.)			
Clothing Design	11	2	1–6
(incl. Dress Design, Costume Design, etc.)			
Crafts — Handcrafts	27	5	2–11
*Bookbinding	3	2	1–6
*Metal Work — Jewelry	3	3	2–6
*Pottery — Ceramics	11	2	2–4
*Weaving	4	2	2–3
Design and Color	50	8	3–32
(incl. Design, Art Forms, Art Structure, Color Theory, etc.)			
Drawing and Painting	49	12	3–36
(incl. Sketch, Representation, Life Drawing, Water-Color Painting, Oil Painting, Painting, Cast Drawing, Landscape, etc.)			
Esthetics	6	6	1–6
History of Art	41	4	1–8
(incl. History of Painting, Architecture, Sculpture, Furniture, Ornament, etc.)			
Industrial Art	9	3	2–6
Interior Decoration	15	2	1–10
(incl. Interior Design)			
Mechanical Drawing and Lettering	27	3	1–9
Modeling and Sculpture	17	3	2–7
Theater Art	7	3	1–5
(incl. Stagecraft, Theater Design, Stage Design, etc.)			
Required Art Electives	6	3	1–24
Summary for Art Courses	50 †	45.5 ‡	24–93 §

* Figures for this subject included in figures for preceding group heading.
† Number of institutions investigated.
‡ Median of total semester hours required in the 50 institutions.
§ Minimal and maximal semester hours required in a single institution.

TABLE II. — COURSES IN ART EDUCATION PRESCRIBED IN FIFTY COLLEGES
AND UNIVERSITIES FOR PERSONS PREPARING TO TEACH ART

Subject	No. of Inst. in Which Required	Of the Institutions Requiring the Subject	
		Median Requirement in Semester Hours	Range in Semester Hours
Methods in Art Teaching (incl. Art Methods, Art in Education, Art Curriculum, Art Teaching in Elementary, Junior High, and Senior High Schools, Teaching of Mechanical Drawing)	47	3	1–12
Practice Teaching (incl. Practice Teaching and Observation, Student Teaching, Cadet Teaching, etc.)	50	5	3–16
Summary for Courses in Art Education *	50	9	5–22

* To be read like similar summary in Table I.

drawing or painting. One of the institutions that requires no education courses of a general nature provides for an unusual number of courses in methods of art teaching. These latter would doubtless include a consideration of the problems covered in the more general education courses in most schools. But, even though there may be a few inaccurate impressions of that sort, the tabulation of requirements does permit a useful study of the general status of college requirements for prospective teachers of art.

1. Agreement on Required Courses

There are few instances of unanimous agreement on the courses to be required. English, Design, and Practice Teaching are the only ones required by all schools. Forty-nine schools require courses in Drawing and Painting; 47, Methods in Art Teaching; 49, Educational Psychology; 48, courses in Philosophy of Education and General Teaching Methods; 41, courses in the Sciences; and 40, courses in the Social Sciences.

Every school requires one or more courses either in Art History or Art Appreciation. Courses in these two fields overlap in many instances. The titles, however, may represent different approaches. Judged both by frequency and median requirements, Art History receives the greater emphasis.

TABLE III. — COURSES IN EDUCATION OTHER THAN ART EDUCATION PRE-
SCRIBED IN FIFTY COLLEGES AND UNIVERSITIES FOR PERSONS PREPARING
TO TEACH ART

Subject	No. of Inst. in Which Required	Of the Institutions Requiring the Subject	
		Median Requirement in Semester Hours	Range in Semester Hours
Educational Psychology	49	4	2–10
Philosophy of Education and General Teaching Methods (incl. Introduction to Education, Philosophy of Education, Teaching Methods in Secondary Schools, etc.)	48	5	2–12
History of Education (incl. Study of Local and State Systems)	22	3	1–5
Electives in Education	13	4	1–11
Other Courses in Education (Introduction to School Administration, Educational Guidance, Educational Sociology, Extra-curricular Activities, Guidance, etc.)	12	3	1–3
Summary for Courses in Education *	50	13	6–22
Summary for Courses in Art Education and Education *	50	24	13–35
Summary for Courses in Art, Art Education, and Education *	50	68.5	39–113

* To be read like similar summary in Table I.

The only other courses that are required by more than half the schools are Psychology, the Crafts, and Mechanical Drawing.

2. Range of Requirements

Striking in the four tables is the wide range of requirements in practically all subjects. The largest requirement may demand from two to twelve times as many hours as the smallest requirement in a particular subject or group of subjects. Thus, the requirements in Design range from 3 to 32 semester hours; in Drawing and Painting, from 3 to 36 semester hours; in Methods in Art Teaching, from 1 to 12 semester hours; and in Practice Teaching, from 3 to 16 semester hours.

That this variation is not compensated for in programs in individual

TABLE IV. — GENERAL AND ACADEMIC WORK PRESCRIBED IN FIFTY COLLEGES
AND UNIVERSITIES FOR PERSONS PREPARING TO TEACH ART

Subject	No. of Inst. in Which Required	Of the Institutions Requiring the Subject	
		Median Requirement in Semester Hours	Range in Semester Hours
English	50	9.5	5–20
Social Science	40	10	5–21
*Geography	5	3	2–6
*History	16	6	4–13
*Economics	2	3.5	3–4
*Sociology	7	3	2–6
*Political Science	7	3	2–6
Science (Physiol. and Biol.)	41	8	3–16
*Biology	5	4	2–7
*Zoölogy	2	7	6–8
Psychology, General	27	3	1–8
Phys. Ed.; Health Ed.; Hyg.	32	4	1–8
Foreign Languages	14	10	6–16
*French	2	10	10–10
Humanities	5	8	5–10
Mathematics	9	3	3–7
Music Appreciation	5	4	2–6
Speech	14	3	1–4
Academic Electives	31	18	3–36
Other Miscellaneous Requirements:			
Dramatic Art	1		6
Orientation Courses	5		1–2
Philosophy	1		3
Thesis	1		2
One Minor	4		12–20
Two Minors	1		33
Minimum Out of Division	1		16
General Electives	9		13–38
Summary for Academic Work †	50	45.5	17–77

* Figures for this subject included in the figures for the group heading.
† To be read like similar summary in Table I.

schools is shown by the range of total requirements in each of the classifications on which the tables are based. The totals of required courses in Art range from 24 to 93 semester hours; in Art Education, from 5 to 22; in Education, from 6 to 22; and in the three categories combined, from 39 to 113. It is startling that such great variation exists among schools that are preparing students for the same teaching positions.

The median requirement in art courses (45.5 semester hours) seems quite understandable and defensible. It is hard to understand how an art faculty can with confidence send out teachers of art with no more preparation in all phases of art than is represented by 24 semester hours! And it is quite as difficult to understand why so many as 93 semester hours should ever be considered the minimal acceptable preparation in the area.

3. Requirements in Art Courses

Courses in Art History and Art Appreciation, one or both, are required by all schools. Forty-one require courses in Art History (median, 4 semester hours; range, 1 to 8). In some instances these courses are on the history of specific phases of art, such as furniture, ornament, or sculpture. Art Appreciation is required by fewer institutions (twenty-four), and the median requirement (3 semester hours) is less. The emphasis in many of these courses is on the chronology of art, which links them closely with art history.

Drawing and Painting is required by 49 colleges and universities (median, 12 semester hours; range, 3 to 36). This is both a reflection and a determinant of typical public-school practices with their heavy emphasis on representational drawing and painting.

General Design and Color, required by all schools (median, 8 semester hours; range, 3 to 32), ranks just below Drawing and Painting. These two categories comprise about half the total requirements.

Conspicuous is the small number of schools requiring courses in specific fields of design, as for example, Clothing Design (11 schools), Interior Design (15 schools), Architectural Design (5 schools), and Commercial Art (17 schools). These fields may be treated in many institutions under General Design, although the impression received from studying the course announcements in bulletins is that most courses in General Design and Color are concerned with design principles, such as balance, emphasis, and rhythm; design elements, such as line, form, dark and light, texture and color; principles of color combination; and the creative and expressional aspects of design and color. This emphasis on the abstract concern over design and color is reflected in the art work in most public schools; that is, design appears as a study in itself, instead of occurring in the making of something.

Another fact shown clearly in Table I is the small amount of emphasis placed on art experiences with three-dimensional materials. Crafts, Modelling and Sculpture, and Industrial Art are the only three categories in which a student is assured work with three-dimensional material. It may occur in other courses, such as General Design or Theater Art, but it is certain that art training in schools at all levels has had a tendency to become largely a paper-and-pencil, two-dimensional matter, and this is clearly shown in the kind of requirements set up for prospective art teachers.

4. Requirements in Art-Education Courses

Three schools do not require special methods courses in the teaching of art. This subject is presumably covered in other education courses or in educationally professionalized art courses. It may well be questioned whether such treatment is effective in preparing a student to meet the problems he will face in a teaching situation.

There is also a tendency to confine the methods courses of major students in art education to a consideration of problems at the secondary-school level, despite the fact that many persons prepared to teach art find their first positions in small communities where they conduct one or two art classes at the high-school level and also supervise or teach art in the elementary grades.

All schools require practice teaching. Both in methods of art teaching and practice teaching, the range of requirements is striking.

5. Requirements in Education Courses

Courses in Educational Psychology, Philosophy of Education, and General Teaching Methods are required in nearly all schools in the study. In the schools that form the exceptions, the requirements in art-education courses are particularly heavy, so that these courses probably include discussion of the more general problems of Education and Educational Psychology. History of Education is required in less than half the schools. Twelve included in their requirements courses in such fields as School Administration, Guidance, Educational Sociology, and Extra-curricular Activities, and thirteen made provision for electives.

In Art Education and all other Education courses combined, the median requirement is 22 semester hours (range, 15 to 42). The minimum and the median are no doubt defensible. It is a little difficult to understand why so many as 42 semester hours of work in all areas of Education need ever be required in a program totaling no more than four years.

6. Requirements in General and Academic Subjects

It is gratifying to note that in all the fifty institutions the desirability of insisting on some breadth of preparation is now recognized. The minimal requirement in general or academic subject matter (17 semester hours) is undoubtedly low. Only five colleges, however, require less than 30 semester hours, or one-fourth of the total program, in these general fields. The maximum reported requirement in general and academic work (77 semester hours) is disturbing. Noting a requirement so large as this and recalling that the minimal requirement in education, including art education, is fifteen semester hours, one wonders whether the student can possibly develop competence in the field of art.

The only general or academic subject required in all of the fifty art-teacher education programs is English. The median requirement in this field (10 semester hours) is commendable. Even the minimum (5 semester hours) probably can be defended.

Most of the institutions included in the study prescribe some work in social science and in natural science. However, nine institutions do not require the former, and eight omit the latter. Since art expressions so frequently and so appropriately reflect the problems, the thinking, and the aspirations of groups or individuals in society, it is difficult to defend the omission of the social sciences from the work required in preparing art teachers. Although the case for requiring some work in the natural sciences is not quite so clear, the contributions of science have certainly affected art forms as well as modes of living. Some knowledge of these contributions is desirable.

It is admittedly unwise to work for complete uniformity of requirements. It seems clear, however, that in every program for the preparation of art teachers there should be included some work in English, social science, and natural science.

Apparently intrenched interests or pressures of some kind influence the requirements in certain institutions. Otherwise it is difficult to explain the prescription of such subjects as mathematics, philosophy, and probably foreign language, even though the latter is required in nearly one-third of the institutions studied. It is difficult to understand why knowledge of a foreign language is so vital in the preparation of art teachers that it must be required of all of them.

III. Summary

In the four large areas studied, the median requirements for the preparation of art teachers do not seem large or excessive. Open to question are the lack of agreement as to what shall be included in the education of an art teacher, and the wide range that exists in all the required courses. While complete or even close agreement is not desirable, the great variation in the amount of work required and in the types of courses themselves indicates that very differently equipped teachers are being produced to fill the same kinds of positions.

A large proportion of the art courses are devoted to drawing, painting, general design, and color, while only a few deal with specific aspects of art production, like architecture, interiors, and clothing. The courses in general design are perhaps based on the belief that knowledge of the principles of general design will transfer to specific fields. Apparently there is little opportunity for students to work with three-dimensional materials.

The need for breadth of preparation is recognized in all the institutions. The programs of certain of them would be strengthened by increasing the amount of work required in the less definitely professional areas. Since the work that prospective teachers of art take in college affects directly what and how they teach in their positions in the public schools, the pattern of courses recommended or required in colleges and universities merits serious study in terms of directions and practices in all art education.

CHAPTER XXXVI

THE TECHNICAL PREPARATION OF THE ART TEACHER

ROYAL BAILEY FARNUM

It is logical to expect that a teacher or supervisor of art should be able to demonstrate his professional understanding and ability by concrete performance as well as by administrative planning and classroom teaching, just as one would naturally expect a teacher of music to give audible demonstration by his own singing or the playing of some instrument.

While professional ability on the part of the art teacher is expected, alas, the exigencies of the present situation relative to his preparation are such that the opportunity for any adequate acquisition of real skill is seriously curtailed.

The technical equipment necessary for the success of the teacher of art is not ordinarily obtained in his earlier schooling, either in quantity of art expression or in the exercise of skill. Therefore, he must obtain this in conjunction with his professional courses in art. It is even more true if he is to instruct in special classes of high-school children. Moreover, professional skill in this field is dependent upon a special and natural coördination of hand and mind, a combination that the rank and file do not possess and that the teacher of art must have cultivated in his training courses.

During the past decade or more, all educational requirements for teachers in public schools have been drastically increased. This has caused considerable hardship to the art teacher and supervisor who, perhaps with marked success, have been in harness for some time. College credits and degrees based upon scholastic standing not only began to determine the professional status of these teachers, but the salary scale, in many cases, was also made dependent upon them. Consequently, instead of journeying to places rich in art treasures, attending art classes, or perfecting their own abilities, wherein they could increase their art knowledge and skill, art teachers were forced to fit into the groove gouged for the general teacher. This meant a professional lag in art from which we still continue to suffer, for seldom does one find a professor of education, a superintendent, or a principal who recognizes or seems to appreciate the equivalent values of serious and mentally exacting concentration in creative expression in the arts as compared to lecture courses and book study on subjects that have little or no direct bearing upon the real job of the supervisor or art teacher. But ' credits ' must be earned.

Unquestionably, a broad and comprehensive knowledge in educational and ' cultural ' subjects is essential in teaching, but hardly at the terrific sacrifice of professional art training so essential for the art teacher, inasmuch as the practical demands made upon these teachers who are on the firing line are primarily in their professional art fields. The following percentages [1] indicate the distribution of time and credit to different groups of subjects in six eastern schools where art teachers are prepared:

1. Carnegie Institute of Technology: Educational Subjects, 17; Cultural Subjects, 28; Technical Art Subjects, 44; Electives, 8; and Physical Education, 3.
2. Massachusetts School of Art: Educational Subjects, 27.2; Cultural Subjects, 11.2; and Technical Art Subjects, 61.6.
3. Pratt Institute: Educational Subjects, 16.5; Cultural Subjects, 40.5; and Technical Art Subjects, 43.
4. Rhode Island School of Design: [2] Educational Subjects, 36.1; Cultural Subjects, 17.9; and Technical Art Subjects, 46.
5. Syracuse University: Educational Subjects, 23.9; Cultural Subjects, 21.7; and Technical Art Subjects, 54.4.
6. University of Wisconsin: Educational Subjects, 29.7; Cultural Subjects, 36.7; and Technical Art Subjects, 33.6.

The time allotted to " technical art subjects " should be spent in a study of art in history, in learning the use of a variety of art media, and in the acquisition of a high degree of technical skill in a few media. In the graphic area, the teacher should be equipped to handle with ease and expertness crayon, pencil, and brush, and in other lines he should have an elementary knowledge of the manipulation of such materials as paper, cardboard, wood, soft metal, clay, plaster, and textiles. In the three-dimensional area, he should know two or three materials with a considerable degree of skill. In some one line of art expression, he

---

[1] A comparative analysis of six institutions prepared in the Teacher Training Department of the Rhode Island School of Design, December, 1939.

[2] The course is five years with the degree of Bachelor of Art Education.

should hope to excel; this might be drawing, painting, handcraft work, design for reproductive processes, sculpture, interior furnishing, costume, or some other creative field wherein he could demonstrate a high degree of proficiency.

Requirements in time and credits for courses in art history and in education are just now decidedly out of balance in many teachers' colleges. It is the same old story of overemphasis on book material and factual acquisition. Art teachers must be equipped to meet current problems, which depend less upon what *has* happened and more upon what *can* and *is* to happen.

The trend to penalize the special gifts and the enthusiastic interest of the art teacher for the sake of college credits based upon a procedure evolved by schools of liberal arts for subjects of a different character is not only unfortunate; it also works seriously against the progress of the arts in education. Steps should be taken to study and to analyze the content of high-grade courses in professional art training with a view toward assigning to them similar or equivalent credits, thus eliminating the necessity for the progressive art teacher to study irrelevant courses, either in college or later, merely for the sake of ' credits ' as we know them today.

Any standard in the realm of the arts, however, should be maintained upon as high a plane as the highest standards in book-studied programs. Such standards can be attained, but the regrettable aspect of the situation lies in the lack of comprehension and understanding on the part of some of the leaders who now control the program of education and attendant credits through accrediting and examining boards. Many persons enjoy the lecture method of education and delight in reading and library study. Perhaps on this account learning through doing, knowledge obtained through following native talents in the creative field of the arts, and vigorous research in three-dimensional activity are considered inferior in value to courses requiring the study of books. Art expression erroneously appears to be simple of attainment, and consequently, it is felt, cannot have equivalent cultural, disciplinary, or intellectual value. There is, furthermore, the distinct feeling in some centers of education that traditional lecture courses in narrow fields of the fine arts, such as Early Renaissance painting, should receive college credit, whereas equally strong courses along such lines as the evolution of textiles, the history of graphic arts, costume and its contribution to modern civilization, and industrial design as an economic

factor in history are not acceptable for such credit.[1] But actually the
concentration and intellectual requirements demanded in serious hand
expression, whether in representation of form or in creating design, are
fully as exacting as any courses in so-called ' liberal ' arts.

The amount of technical work essential for the preparation of a public-school art teacher, however, may properly be considerably less than
that demanded by the future requirements of the professional artist.
The preparation of the art teacher, therefore, cannot focus narrowly but
must make some sacrifice of technical proficiency for the professional
teaching equipment required. It would seem that, at present, the sacrifice is far too great if the current demands upon the art teacher and
supervisor of art are to be maintained, and even more so where, as in
many localities, these technical requirements are being expanded and
increased.

---

[1] I once experienced such a distinction in subject recognition. A lecture
course on "Colonial Architecture" was approved, but a course on the history,
significance, and social value of type and the printing press was unacceptable!
Colonial architecture affected a small area of this country over a short period of
time; the printing press affected the whole world, and continues to do so; but this
fact was not deemed pertinent.

CHAPTER XXXVII

THE ART TEACHER'S PREPARATION IN ART HISTORY AND ART EDUCATION

MARGARET F. S. GLACE
Head, Teacher Education Department
The Maryland Institute
Baltimore, Maryland

I. SOME TYPICAL CURRICULA

An analysis of catalogs from institutions engaged in the preparation of art teachers throughout the United States revealed many and varied curricula. In order to facilitate comparative analysis, the institutions were grouped into three general classes; namely, professional art schools, liberal arts colleges or universities, and state teachers' colleges. Examination was made of the curricula of 10 art schools, 28 liberal arts colleges or universities, and 34 state teachers' colleges. These 72 schools are located in 33 states, thereby representing the different geographical sections of the country.

It is very evident that many factors influence the content, length, and arrangement of the curricula, in particular, state requirements for teachers' certificates, prevailing educational philosophies, sectional demand for teachers of art, attitudes toward teaching and the administrative personnel within the institution, and the background of the students.

Recent literature as well as unpublished research studies were investigated for the purpose of including any material that would clarify or supplement the analytical data. The limitations and difficulties of a catalog interpretation are obvious, so that at best only general conclusions can be drawn.

II. WHAT PROSPECTIVE ART TEACHERS NOW STUDY ABOUT ART HISTORY AND ESTHETICS

In every institution, large or small, the same general curricular pattern provides for the professional preparation of the art teacher. This organization includes: (a) the technical art subjects; (b) professional courses in education, psychology, special methods, practice teaching, and observation; and (c) cultural courses.

749

Art history is usually considered a component of the technical art subjects. It appears under various titles, like Esthetics, Art Appreciation, History of Art, History of Fine Arts through the Ages, American Art, Introduction to Art, History of Fine Arts, Current Arts, Development of Modern Painting, Contemporary Trends in Art, Appreciation of Fine Arts, Essentials of Art, Art in Everyday Life, Appreciation of Decorative Arts, Art of the Book, History of (various periods) — a well-nigh endless list.

TABLE I. — COURSES IN ART HISTORY AND ART EDUCATION IN SEVENTY-TWO TEACHER-PREPARING INSTITUTIONS

	Teachers' Colleges	Liberal Arts Colleges or Universities	Art Schools	Total
Number of Institutions Investigated	34	28	10	72
Percentage Investigated of Total Number	.47	.39	.14	
Range of Semester Hours Required for Graduation	120–128	120–136	124–150	120–150
Average of Semester Hours Required for Graduation	123.60	127.20	129.20	126.70
Art History				
Range of semester hours required	3–12	6–24	2–12	2–24
Average of semester hours required	7.20	11.30	7.70	8.70
Percentage of total hours required for graduation	.06	.09	.06	.07
Art Education				
Range of semester hours required	6.7–22	5–17	12–32	5–32
Average of semester hours required	15.40	11.10	18.80	15.10
Percentage of total hours required for graduation	.12	.09	.15	.12

By analysis we find (Table I) the range, the average, and the percentage in the teachers' colleges, the liberal arts colleges, and the art schools. The requirement in art history in all institutions varies from 2 to 24 semester hours, averages 8.7 semester hours, or .07 of the total number of hours required for a degree. In many instances the hours required in art history or allied subjects appear out of balance with the total number of hours required in the major field. The tendency to overemphasize art history seems particularly prevalent in the liberal arts colleges.

It is to be deplored that in the preparation of art teachers there exists the necessity for seeming overspecialization in technical subjects. This occurs, of course, at the price of a broad, general education. Because of the failure of the secondary school to provide adequate basic courses in art, it devolves upon the schools of higher education to compensate for the deficiency. This results in increased requirements in the subject-matter fields. That the teacher-preparing institutions are responding to these demands is shown by some data (2) published in 1933, according to which 94 percent of art majors took history and appreciation to the extent of a median of 4.1 semester hours. The median of 8.3 semester hours (catalog analysis) for 1939–1940 would indicate the upward trend, although it is certainly not conclusive.

III. What Prospective Art Teachers Now Study about Art Education

The data (2) published in 1933 inform us that 94 percent of the art majors devoted a median of 5.6 semester hours to gaining a knowledge of *special methods* in art. In attempting to determine the status of special methods in art (reported as one part of the general division termed " Professional Courses ") one is again confronted with diverse and often obscure terminology. The usual titles include Principles of Art Education, Theory and Philosophy of Art Education, Fine and Industrial Art Education, Art Methods, Introduction to Art Education, Organization of Public-School Art, Elementary- and Junior-High-School Art, Teaching of Art in the Elementary Schools and the Secondary Schools, Art Curriculum and Supervision, Theory and Practice of Teaching Art, and the like. There was even greater difficulty here in endeavoring to isolate the specific courses in art education.

The art schools (Table I) stipulate the highest percentage of required hours in art education, and the teachers' colleges next highest. The teacher-preparing institutions, taken as a whole, demand 5 to 32 semester hours in art education, with an average requirement of 15.1 semester hours, or .12 of the average number of hours necessary for graduation. The extreme instances of 32 semester hours in art schools and 22 semester hours in teachers' colleges must represent much work of a character to be found classified under professional courses in education and psychology in other institutions.

IV. Recommendations

The program of any institution educating teachers of art should not only include provision for the professional equipment of the student but also give opportunity to those with special talent to continue their individual development. " According to the almost unanimous reports of artists themselves, there is no substitute for participation and self-expression through some of the recognized art media. Important as courses in art appreciation may be, real appreciation comes from the experience of creation " (3, p. 52). Art history and appreciation courses should be taught as the interpretation of our social and cultural heritage in the light of the place of art in modern life. Catalog descriptions of present courses indicate emphasis of factual period data devoid of contemporary implications.

The content of art education courses should be arranged so as to meet adequately the public-school teaching needs. " Education today is an integrated process, with activity programs in the elementary schools and interrelated activities in secondary schools. It calls for a well-rounded, broadly trained teacher who may understand and enter the study and discussion of a wide range of subjects " (1, pp. 160–161). This plea for synthesis in our teacher-preparation curricula is not limited to the art field. The success of isolated instances leads us to hope for more general adoption of the plan on the college level.

A regional survey [1] of teachers in service reveals that in reply to the question, " What aspects or experiences of your art training have you found most helpful in your teaching? " an overwhelming majority of 418 teachers mentioned different phases of art education, like methods, integration, lesson-planning, and curriculum-planning.

All these needs (life, individual, public-school teaching) must be effectually provided for while maintaining a balanced program of professional and cultural training. The solution appears to be that of greater professionalization of articulated content courses.

References

(1) Kirby, C. V. "Vitalizing the Art Curriculum for More Effective Service." [In] *Problems in Teacher Training.* (Prentice-Hall: New York, 1936)

(2) U. S. Office of Education. *National Survey of the Education of Teachers.* (Bulletin 1933, No. 10, Vol. III)

(3) Watson, G., Cottrell, D. P., and Lloyd-Jones, E. M. *Redirecting Teacher Education.* (Bureau of Publications, Teachers College: New York, 1938) 105 pp.

---

[1] *A Survey of Needs of Practicing Art Teachers in Nine Northeastern States.* (Manuscript Report of Research Committee, Eastern Arts Association, 1939)

CHAPTER XXXVIII

COURSES OTHER THAN ART AND EDUCATION FOR THE PROSPECTIVE ART TEACHER

ERNEST HORN

Professor of Education and Director of the University Elementary School
State University of Iowa, Iowa City, Iowa

The published data concerning the courses now taken by prospective art teachers are far from complete. Even such data as are available are difficult to interpret because of the impossibility of determining the content and quality of what is taught under a given course title. The impression obtained from an examination of catalogs of institutions that prepare art teachers is one of great diversity in the amount and nature of the requirements in art, in art education, in education, and in courses outside these three fields. This diversity is far greater than is warranted by differences in local needs or facilities; it reflects the divergent opinions, otherwise manifested in articles on teacher education, as to what the education of art teachers should be.

What courses the art teacher should take, as an undergraduate, outside the fields of education and art education depend in part upon the nature and amount of instruction required or permitted to be taken in these two fields. In one school, for example, courses in esthetics, in anatomy, in industrial arts, or in theater arts may be offered outside the art department. In another institution these courses may be offered by the department of art. In fact, it is sometimes necessary that the art department provide such courses, either because suitable courses are not offered in other departments or because they are not available to art majors because of prerequisites. When taught in the art department itself, these courses are probably more closely related to the needs of the art teacher than are the more specialized introductory courses offered in these same areas in other departments. In many instances they may also be more broadly cultural because they are likely to be more nearly adapted to the needs of the average person. To the extent that this is true, these courses provide, therefore, excellent preparation for teaching in elementary and secondary schools.

Just what the pattern of courses should be in any given institution,

753

outside of art and art education, is dependent in part upon the type of position in which the student expects to teach, as well as upon the facilities of the institution and the relationships that exist between the departments of art, departments of education, and other departments. Nevertheless, there are fundamental requirements that must be given careful consideration by any institution that attempts to prepare art teachers.

The courses that meet these requirements fall into four main groups: first, courses that contribute to the personal development of the student, irrespective of the specialized requirements of art teaching; second, courses in related areas that are essential for giving the teacher proper perspective for his own field of work; third, courses that will enable him to relate his instruction to that of other teachers; and fourth, courses that provide the beginning teacher with minor fields that he may be called upon to teach in small schools, to which inexperienced teachers frequently must go for their first experience in teaching.

Precisely what courses any individual student will need in these four groups will depend also upon his previous experience in secondary schools. For example, the most gifted graduates of secondary schools with strong art departments frequently demonstrate abilities in one or more fields of art that are far above the average attainment of art students in college. Such students need fewer college courses in art and may well elect, therefore, more courses outside of art. Other students electing a major in art have developed so little ability in creative work that an extensive election of art courses is required to meet even the minimal qualifications for art teaching.

It seems reasonable to assume that any course offered in a college of liberal arts and of interest to the student will be valuable for his personal development. Since the total number of hours a student may take is limited, however, it seems desirable to give preference to fields intimately related to the teaching of art rather than to fields that have little such relationship. Among the courses that are especially profitable for the art student to pursue as a means of reinforcing and orienting his work in art are the following: history, especially history courses in which cultural and social aspects are emphasized; English, American, and comparative literature; dramatic arts; industrial arts; psychology; philosophy; esthetics; science; and home economics. Such courses not only strengthen the teacher in the work for which he is specifically responsible but they also enable him to coördinate his work with that of teachers in other fields. The present trend toward integration in the curriculum as a whole requires the art teacher to understand the relation of art to the various curricular areas.

Attention has been called to the fact that many students who major in art find it impossible to secure their first position in a large high school in which they may devote all their time to teaching art. It is common practice for large city systems to require teaching experience as a prerequisite to appointment. This experience must be obtained in smaller schools, sometimes in departmental teaching in the inter-mediate- or junior-high-school grades, and sometimes in small high schools. Since small high schools, even when they offer art at all, cannot afford a teacher who teaches art alone, it is advisable for prospective art teachers to prepare themselves to teach in one or more additional fields.

Church [1] reports that, of 155 California junior and senior high schools with an enrollment of four hundred or less, 19 had a full-time art teacher; 23 required the teaching of one additional subject; 27, two additional subjects; 22, three additional subjects; 20, four additional subjects; 14, five additional subjects. Thirty of these schools offered no art instruction. The full-time art teachers were undoubtedly found in the largest of these high schools.

In the high schools reporting in connection with the National Survey of the Education of Teachers, the other subjects most often taught in high schools by the art teacher were trades and industries, English, mathematics, and home economics. [2]

The needs and limitations of smaller schools should be given far more consideration than is the case at present by those responsible for the education of teachers. As pointed out elsewhere in the report, about two-fifths of the high schools in the United States reporting in 1938 had an enrollment of less than a hundred, and about two-thirds of the schools, of less than two hundred pupils. Of the rural high schools reporting in 1930, more than three-fourths enrolled not more than a hundred pupils. These small schools obviously cannot employ a teacher to teach art exclusively. It is conceivable that the best plan for encouraging the teaching of art in small schools where art instruction is not now given is to provide teachers who have either a major

---

[1] Idella R. Church. *Art in the Village.* Department of Art Education Bulletin (National Education Association), Vol. V, 1939.

[2] *National Survey of the Education of Teachers,* Vol. III, Bulletin 1933, No. 10, p. 231. (U. S. Office of Education: Washington, D. C.)

or a minor in art combined with preparation for teaching in one or more other fields.

Wide differences are found among institutions in the amount, as well as in the nature, of the work required outside of art. It is admittedly difficult to determine the proper balance between courses promoting efficiency in art itself and courses in art education, in education, and other curricular areas. Certainly, the amount of work required in art education, in education, or in other departments should not be so large as to prohibit the prospective teacher from becoming reasonably proficient in art itself. Neither within the art department should the history of art, art appreciation, and other theoretical courses crowd out the badly needed courses in drawing, painting, sculpture, design, and other courses in the creative use of visual media. The fact that most students come to college with very little proficiency in creative art makes it especially important that such training be not curtailed in college. The teacher of art should himself be a productive artist in order to have an understanding of the creative process he seeks to stimulate and guide in his students.

For this reason and because of the large amount of time required to attain reasonable proficiency in drawing, painting, sculpture, design, and other phases of creative art, it seems advisable to require a substantial number of hours in such courses. It is probable that at least a third of the students' total time should be devoted to studio courses. Part of the hours needed for this increase in the major might well be obtained by sharply reducing the exorbitant number of credits that are frequently taken in education, art education, and in the history and theory of art. Teachers' colleges tend to give too few hours to art courses, in proportion to the requirements in other academic fields in art education and in education; art schools tend to give too many such hours.

CHAPTER XXXIX

THE ART TEACHER'S PREPARATION IN THE THEORY AND PRACTICE OF EDUCATION

ERNEST HORN

An examination of the information presented in earlier chapters will show that the courses in the theory and practice of teaching are commonly listed in two divisions — art education and education. The courses most frequently required in art education are Methods of Teaching Art and Student Teaching. Among the courses most frequently taken in the department of education are Educational Psychology, History of Education, and Principles of Education. It seems both advisable and feasible to achieve much more complete coördination and coöperation between the art department and the department of education than commonly exists. Such a plan would undoubtedly eliminate a great deal of useless overlapping and would probably result in a desirable reduction of the total number of hours taken at the undergraduate level in these two closely related fields.

It is difficult to appraise the value of courses given under the present titles because of the great variation in both content and quality of courses under a given title. It is possible, however, to present in brief outline the chief types of problems a prospective art teacher must be prepared to meet.

The most important groups of problems are:

First, problems that the art teacher faces in common with all teachers, such as, the cost and support of education, the administrative and supervisory organization of the school, relation of the teacher to the community, and problems of state and national education.

Second, problems in the psychology of learning and student development, with special emphasis upon learning and development in art.

Third, problems of the curriculum and methods of teaching in art.

Fourth, problems pertaining to the general organization of the secondary curriculum.

Fifth, problems in the methods and curricula in elementary schools — for students who, in addition to teaching in high school, may supervise the teaching of art in elementary schools.

757

I. Problems That Art Teachers Face in Common with
All Teachers

These problems may make up the content of the course under such titles as Principles of Education or Introduction to Education. The problems fall roughly into four divisions.

a. First, every beginning teacher should have some knowledge of requirements for certification for teaching, of the procedures that must be followed in securing a job, of all the responsibilities that will be given to teachers, and of such items as teaching combinations, extra-curricular activities and their general relationship to community activities, working conditions, opportunities for careers, and rewards in the teaching profession.

b. The second major area might be designated " Concepts of Education," including such matters as the general objectives of education, the contrasting objectives in totalitarian and democratic states, the issues regarding the relation of the individual to society, the school's part in social change, the relative importance of present and future needs, and finally, in the light of all these considerations, an explicit statement of objectives for the schools of the United States.

There are certain aspects and implications that should be emphasized in the consideration of objectives: equality of educational opportunity, compulsory education, the determination of the amount and character of education for elementary and secondary schools, requirements pertaining to teacher qualifications, state and local sovereignty in school control, including taxation, changes in school enrollment, private interests in education.

c. The third general area to which all teachers should be introduced might be entitled " The School System of the United States," including both the development, organization, and character of the elementary- and secondary-school programs and a knowledge of the development and present status of the junior-college movement.

d. The fourth area that should be considered in the introduction to education is the organization, cost, and support of education. This may include the rôle that the federal government plays, or should play, in the support, organization, and control of education, including the factors tending to produce an American system of education; the rôle of state governments in the administration and control of education; the rôle of the local school unit, including the local district organization, and its relation to the state; and the nature and function of the local board of education, the superintendent of schools, the principal, supervisory officers, and the teacher.

The study of the problems of financing education should include the increasing educational services demanded by the public; the competition with other public services, such as highways, charities, police protection, eleemosynary institutions, social security, and old-age pensions; distribution of school cost among salaries, capital outlay, debt service, operation of plant, and other areas; contribution of the total cost of education made by the federal government, the state governments, and local school districts, including equalization of the cost of education, enlargement of units of taxation, and more equitable taxation methods. All problems in this, and in other areas, should be viewed historically.

An intelligent grasp of the problems in these four areas will not only contribute to effective coöperation with the professional staff of the school but will also enable the teacher to interpret the policies of the school to patrons. The art teacher, no less than other teachers or supervisors, is responsible for developing intelligent public opinion concerning educational problems and policies.

II. Problems in Learning and Student Development

Educational Psychology or some equivalent course is almost universally required for prospective art teachers. This requirement reflects a wholesome appreciation of the importance of knowledge of how students learn and develop. It must be admitted, however, that in many institutions these courses are somewhat disappointing to prospective art teachers, sometimes because they are vague and general in character, but more often because they contain so little that seems to the student to deal with learning and development in art. There is no reason, however, why courses in Educational Psychology cannot be made both vital and helpful to prospective art teachers. There can be no doubt of the importance of giving these prospective teachers a firm grasp of the data and principles pertaining to learning and development.

The trend of evidence at the present time seems to indicate that learning and development in art follow the broad patterns of learning and development in other curricular fields. It is to be expected, therefore, that art teachers will profit from the explicit treatment of learning in these other fields. Nevertheless, learning and development in the production and appreciation of art involve many problems that are different in important respects and much more complicated than in the case of such subjects as typewriting, spelling, or arithmetic. Among the problems that need much more explicit and practical treatment than is usually given are the nature and extent of individual differences in art abilities and their significance for instruction, the nature and development of creative imagination, motivation, emotion, meaning, and thinking.

In addition to the problems commonly treated in Educational Psychology, there are certain topics more often treated in general psychology that can be set forth to advantage for the teacher of art; for example, color vision, adaptation, and contrast; the nature of perspective, tri-dimensional vision, spatial illusions, and the like; and the simpler aspects of esthetics.

The best guarantee that the course in Educational Psychology will meet the needs of the classroom teacher is to provide it with an instructor who has a thorough knowledge of the theory and evidence pertaining to learning in various curricular fields, including art, as well as an intimate acquaintance with the problems of classroom teaching. If in any institution the course in Educational Psychology does not give the art student guidance in directing learning and development in the field of art, either it should be modified to do so or it should not be required.

In institutions where the number of prospective art teachers warrants a special section, it should be possible to deal much more explicitly with the problems of learning and development in art, reviewing the theory and evidence relating to learning in other curricular areas.

III. Problems of Methods in the Teaching of Art

The attack on these problems should be made in two ways: (1) through a systematic course in methods of teaching, and (2) through directed observation and student teaching. Obviously, these two approaches to teaching should be closely coördinated.

1. Special Methods in Art

The purpose of the course in special methods in art is to assist the student in organizing what he has learned in art and education and to focus this organized knowledge upon the practical problems of classroom teaching. The less the previous work of the student has been coördinated, the more difficult and crucial it is so to organize it that the work in its entirety shall form a basis for methods of teaching.

The teacher of special methods cannot even assume that his students, although majors in art, have a thorough understanding of basic principles in all phases of art or have related the separate courses they have had in art. They may, for example, be very hazy in their information about basic letter forms or the control of qualities of color. They may fail to relate their course work in design to their study of drawing, painting, and lettering or their course in perspective to simple problems of drawing. A good course in special methods of art is likely, therefore, to be a good course in the fundamentals of art itself, stressing the interrelatedness of all art expression and appreciation and the wide application of art principles to everyday living. In order to assist students in coördinating and utilizing all of their art courses toward the best teaching of art in the schools, the teacher of special methods must of necessity be competent in art as well as in education.

The course in special methods will need to harmonize the work in art with the work in education. The teacher of art education should be familiar with the problems treated in courses in education as well as with those emphasized in art courses. This organized background needs to be utilized in giving specific help on such problems as the following:

1. Determining objectives.
2. Choosing essential content to be taught in the limited time available.
3. Determining the method of approach and phases of work to be emphasized at different age levels.
4. Planning and developing units of work.
5. Providing for individual differences.
6. Evaluating pupil progress.
7. Selecting material and equipment with consideration of costs.
8. Knowing the sources of reference and illustrative materials.
9. Planning attractive classrooms and exhibitions.
10. Participating in the art activities of the community.

While the course must deal adequately with the practical problems of class teaching, it will not consist in mere detailed devices for teaching but will stress rather the fundamental principles in art and in learning. There need to be a careful consideration of objectives and an emphasis on the understanding of basic art principles that will permit wide application and future growth. It is a thorough grasp of these fundamental matters that will enable the prospective teacher to adapt his training to various types of teaching positions and to solve the innumerable problems that arise in different classroom situations.

Many persons who majored in art education find their first teaching positions in small cities where they teach one or more courses in the high school and supervise art in the elementary school. In such instances, the course in methods should deal adequately with problems of teaching in the elementary schools as well as with those in secondary schools.

In order to avoid theory that is not fully comprehended, the course in special methods should include carefully directed observation of excellent teaching that will illustrate how the principal problems treated in the course are dealt with in the classroom.

2. Student Observation and Teaching

The observation of skillful teaching and actual practice in teaching are now common requirements for certification and for graduation from teachers' colleges and other institutions that prepare teachers of art. These requirements reflect the recognition of the difficulty, if not the impossibility, of making courses in education and in art education vital and understandable apart from the opportunity to observe teaching activities and to participate in them. Systematic observation and practice teaching are sometimes combined into the same course requirement. The observation of classroom teaching should not be limited to that done in such a course. Every required course in education should include systematic provision for extensive observation of classroom practices pertaining to the problems treated in the course. Such provision is more commonly made in connection with the courses in special methods and the value of observation in such courses is obvious. The necessity for well-planned observations in connection with courses such as Principles of Education and Educational Psychology is not so commonly recognized. Attention has already been called to the fact that these courses frequently impress students as too general and too far removed from their problems to be either interesting or understandable. Well-planned observation of teaching contributes materially to making these courses more vital and practical. Not the least of the contributions made by classroom observation is that it stimulates both students and instructors to view the problems of the course in their relation to typical classroom situations. It is doubtful whether any course should be required, either in education or in art education, that does not include some plan for the observation of classroom activities related to the most important problems of the course.

The directed observation of skillful classroom teaching gives a clearer grasp of teaching procedures, creates an enthusiasm for teaching, and gives the prospective teacher greater confidence and assurance of success in his first efforts in teaching. It is entirely possible to give a prospective art teacher an opportunity to observe the ways in which each of the principal problems in the teaching of art is met by skillful teachers.

Skillfully directed observation should precede practice in teaching, but additional observation should be encouraged as problems arise in practice teaching. The beginning teacher can scarcely hope to engage efficiently in teaching activities which she has not seen demonstrated and for which she has not been specifically prepared in other systematic course work. Without such preparation, the beginning teacher flounders and is deprived at the outset of a sense of achievement.

There is some difference of opinion as to the relative amount of time that should be given to directed observation and to directed teaching. Where practice in teaching has been preceded by systematically planned observation, less time will be required by the prospective teacher to attain reasonable proficiency. How much time should be spent upon observation in a course specifically organized for that purpose depends in part on the amount of observation provided in such courses as Special Methods, Principles of Education, and Educational Psychology. Certainly six semester hours, or one twentieth of the student's total credits, are the very minimum that should be required in observation and practice teaching.

IV. Problems Pertaining to the General Organization of the Secondary Curriculum

Every teacher of art should view her work in its relation to the rest of the curriculum. This need is particularly crucial when one considers the amount of emphasis given at the present time to interrelationships between subject-matter areas — the integration, or coördination, for example, of the social studies and art.

Teachers of art need information concerning the general problems faced by teachers of other subjects, such as mathematics, history, science, and English. If the boys and girls are to be considered in the educational plan, it seems necessary that all teachers have some knowledge of the problems and difficulties faced by their students in other fields in which they are participating.

A course in the secondary-school curriculum should deal with such problems as the present curricula, their evolution and status; the aims and functions of secondary education in relation to other school units; contemporary points of view and issues; methods of determining the specific objectives; problems of method; and efforts at reconstructing the content and organization of the various secondary fields, such as English, social studies, science, mathematics, foreign language, fine and practical arts, vocational subjects, health and physical education, and extra-curricular activities.

The emphasis given throughout the course in the secondary curriculum should focus on the common problems facing all teachers in all curricular fields, with special consideration of the outstanding problems peculiar to the teaching of special subjects. It should deal with these problems in the light of the needs of the beginning teacher. In this course, as in all others, liberal use should be made of observation of desirable school practices.

V. PROBLEMS OF CURRICULA AND METHODS IN THE ELEMENTARY SCHOOL

Problems that concern the elementary school are particularly crucial to the prospective teachers who may, during the first year or two of their teaching experience, in addition to teaching in high schools, either supervise art in the elementary school or teach art in a departmental organization. Such students should be made familiar with the methods and curricula in the elementary school as well as with the peculiar and difficult problems of teaching art in the elementary grades. Special attention should be given to the integration of art with other fields, since integration is usually more thoroughgoing in the elementary grades than at higher levels.[1]

There are two problems to which those responsible for training teachers and supervisors in art should give special attention. The first is the reduction of the number of hours frequently taken in education and in art education at the undergraduate level in order to provide for a better-rounded, more thorough preparation in art itself and in other related departments. The second is the closer coördination of the work of all instructors responsible for the courses in art, art education, and education. The impression given from a study of the institutions that train teachers is that it is common practice for instructors in education, in art, and in art education to work independently and in some instances at cross purposes. One of the most glaring instances of lack of coöperation, with consequent confusion of the student, is found

---

[1] For a discussion of the problems of art in the elementary school, see various parts of Chapter XXX.

in situations where practice teaching in the demonstration school is supervised by persons who have had little or no training in art and whose directions to students are at variance with those given by the instructor in special methods. It seems essential that the person responsible for teaching special methods in art should also be chiefly responsible for the supervision of observation and student teaching. These responsibilities include, however, the effective harmonizing and coördination of instruction in art with the practices and policies of the school as a whole.

CHAPTER XL

GRADUATE WORK FOR THE ART TEACHER

ERNEST HORN

Graduate work for prospective or experienced art teachers contributes to the student's development in several ways. First, it enables him to continue his work along the lines begun in his undergraduate work in art. Second, it gives him an opportunity to explore other areas of art not yet experienced, since, in the limited time available, it is impossible for students to get even an introduction to all the fields of art during their four years of undergraduate work. Third, it makes possible the more thorough study of advanced thought and practice in art education. Fourth, it affords the student an opportunity to continue his development in fields other than art, either by continuing an undergraduate minor or by selecting other courses that will broaden his general culture and reinforce his special field of work.

The opportunities to secure desirable work in other departments are seriously curtailed by a lack of flexibility in institutional requirements, chief among which are the refusal to give graduate credit for introductory courses, the rigidity of minor requirements in other fields, the setting up of prerequisites, and the traditional requirements for advanced degrees. The needs of the student should be the primary consideration. If the quality of the student's work and the maturity of his methods of attack in an introductory course are satisfactory, he should receive graduate credit for it. In many instances both the interest of the student and his educational history clearly indicate the value of certain introductory courses in other departments.

Very frequently the requirements set up for minors in other fields are so arbitrary and so frozen to a peculiar pattern that they do not serve the needs of the graduate student in art. There is no reason why a more flexible adjustment to the needs of the student cannot be made in the minor department without sacrificing vigor or quality of work. Again, there is much to be said, especially in planning a minor for the master's degree, for a distributed minor, that is, one in which the total credits are equal to those of the regular undistributed minor, although

767

the courses are taken in several fields to meet some legitimate purpose of the student. Where institutional requirements for graduate work make this impossible, the student's needs should be met by accrediting to the major certain clearly needed courses in other fields.

Often a graduate student in art is denied admission to courses in other departments because he has not taken certain 'prerequisite' courses. It is the feeling of this Committee that a very large proportion of these prerequisite requirements, in both graduate and undergraduate courses, cannot be justified. In most instances superior students are perfectly capable of taking the courses they need without having taken the specified prerequisites.

One of the most important problems confronting those who direct graduate work in art arises from the fact that the qualifications traditionally demanded for securing the master's or doctor's degree are different in important respects from the qualifications that the creative artist seeks to attain. The traditional pattern of graduate requirements may be met without much difficulty by the student whose primary interest is in the history of art, the theory of art, or art education, but the student whose chief interest is in enlarging his abilities in creative art cannot meet the traditional pattern without seriously sacrificing his major interest. The same problem, in principle, arises, of course, in related fields, such as dramatic art, music, and creative writing. The traditional requirements for a thesis for the master's or doctor's degree are particularly ill-adapted to the student who wishes to devote most of his energies to the development of creative ability.

In some institutions the requirement of a thesis for the master's degree is abrogated, although this practice is not generally favored.[1] There have been many promising developments, in the case of both degrees, in the direction of allowing students to offer an exhibit of creative work in lieu of the traditional thesis. Similar departures from the customary concept of the thesis are also found in music, dramatic arts, and literature.

There are troublesome problems — the evaluation of the creative project, for example — involved in such plans, and it will probably take some time to evolve one that would work as smoothly as the plan that has been developed over so long a period in the case of the traditional

---

[1] "Problems of the Master's Degree." *The Report of the Committee on the Master's Degree Presented to the Association of American Universities on November 9, 1935, Ithaca, N. Y.* William J. Robbins, Chairman. (University of Minnesota Press, Minneapolis, Minn.)

thesis. Such a plan as is advocated would seem to offer great promise, however, in encouraging students to continue development in creative fields with the prospect of academic recognition comparable to that received by candidates who attain degrees in the customary fashion. Because of the emphasis upon the possession of advanced degrees by teachers in colleges and universities, some such adjustments must be made if adequate preparation for the teaching of creative art is to be encouraged.

The writing of a scholarly thesis in art history, in art theory, or in art education is time-consuming, and if the creative artist must meet this requirement, he must of necessity leave off his creative work for one or more years while his research and writing are under way. The neglect of creative work for so long a period may prove to be a very serious matter. One cannot view with unconcern the prospect of the graduate student, in the most advanced stages of his work, devoting his energies almost exclusively to work outside the creative fields.

More good is accomplished by recognizing the interdependence of art theory and art history on the one hand, and of creative art, on the other hand, than by setting these fields in opposition to each other. Nevertheless, as matters now stand, a greater contribution to the quality of art teaching in public schools would doubtless be made by requiring all candidates in the history of art to offer evidence of creative ability than by forcing the creative artist to do a thesis in the history or theory of art. Those responsible for graduate work in art should follow closely the developments in meeting similar problems in other creative fields, such as music, dramatic arts, and creative writing. At the present time art departments seem to lag behind these fields in recognizing the importance of creative ability.

Some graduate students, on the other hand, may look forward to a career in teaching the history of art. Such students will be primarily historians, dealing with art as a branch of history and using the recognized methods of historical research. For these students the conventional type of written thesis is entirely appropriate, but even they will profit from at least an elementary training in studio courses. Other students may look forward to appointment to a one-man art department in a small college. For such students either the creative or historical thesis may be appropriate, but the emphasis in course work should be upon studio courses.

Other students may prefer a career in art education, either as a college instructor in this field or as a teacher or supervisor in the public schools. For such students either the creative or the written thesis is appropriate. There is an urgent need for a more critical investigation of many problems in art education, and these investigations may properly constitute a thesis. It must be admitted, however, that not many of the current theses in art education contribute significantly to the solution of the basic problems of learning in this field. A good many of them could be written by students having little personal experience with the fundamental processes in creative work. The thesis in art education should not be a refuge for students who cannot meet the requirements for either a creative thesis or a thesis in the history of art. It should be undertaken by those who are primarily interested in problems of art education and competent to investigate them. It would be a fine thing if more students seeking a career in art education should be able to demonstrate the type of proficiency required for the creative thesis. Certainly such students should develop a strong and varied proficiency in studio courses.

What has been said applies primarily to the needs of the graduate student who is majoring in art. Departments of art, however, should give careful consideration to the organization of courses to suit the needs of graduate students in other fields. All that has been said about the need of flexibility as to prerequisites and minors in other fields applies in principle, and with equal force, to minors and other course work taken in art by majors in other fields. It is the opinion of this Committee that the place of art in general education would be enlarged and improved by encouraging graduate students majoring in other fields, especially students majoring in school supervision and administration, to elect courses in art.

There has been too much fear of the loss of institutional prestige in making necessary adjustments to the varied needs of graduate students. It is quite possible to maintain the highest standards in making these adjustments. Indeed, adaptations to the needs of students elevate, rather than lower, academic standards in the mind of the serious student, to whom many of the present arbitrary requirements seem petty and unreasonable. The impression should not be given, however, that inflexible requirements are found only outside departments of art; often the most arbitrary and unreasonable requirements are found within the art department itself.

CHAPTER XLI

RECOMMENDED EXPERIENCES IN ADDITION TO SCHOOL AND TECHNICAL TRAINING

C. VALENTINE KIRBY
Chief, Art Education
Pennsylvania Department of Public Instruction
Harrisburg, Pennsylvania

The desirability of broad culture and experience in the art teacher or art supervisor can hardly be questioned. His field is so broad, his subject so deeply enveloped in past civilization and so interwoven with present-day life that he should be able to draw from a rich store of culture and experience almost continually. He must work and associate with broadly educated people and enter intelligently into their fields for coöperative enterprises. Working together on integrated programs requires much more than a narrowly specific art training on the part of the art teacher.

The art teacher is expected to be well informed in regard to contemporary art. He must not only be able to develop an appreciation of the great architecture, sculpture, and painting of the past, but he must be alert also to all that artists are doing today — new art forms to meet new world demands. Reading is not enough; the art teacher should travel to the galleries, museums, and churches here and abroad, and catch the thrill of facing the original in its appropriate setting and its historic atmosphere. How much more impressive is the teacher who can say to his pupil, " I saw this with my own eyes."

One must not overlook the fact that for many with limited means tours to foreign galleries and cathedrals are out of the question, but one's immediate environment may have treasures that have been overlooked. Local buildings may re-echo some style of great architecture. Fine color-printing makes it possible to possess faithful reproductions of great art. The radio and motion picture bring suggestions for new enterprises in school drama, and the nearest museum is presumably " free to the people."

It is particularly important that the art teacher and art supervisor be acquainted with all that goes on outside of school in the way of vocational art activities. This should not be restricted to any one art. The teacher should seek direct acquaintance with the whole range of arts discussed in Section I of this Yearbook, including architecture, city planning, industrial design, and commercial art, as well as painting and sculpture. He should observe the buying and selling of art as well as its production.

Knowledge of the social and business life of the community — what shops offer, what people buy — all are guides to a timely and interesting art program. The art teacher is particularly in need of the stimulation and inspiration that travel, museum visits, and a generally broad cultural experience give. Altogether the art teacher or art supervisor strengthens his position by personal acquaintance with the world of art outside of the classroom and this acquaintance with existing conditions will lead to an art program in the schools related to, and consistent with, the whole range of contemporary art.

Visions must be broadened through personal contacts with inspiring workers in wood, marble, metal, and precious stones. Those who would make life more colorful must appreciate the meaning of the struggle for success and the stimulations that come from failure. They must see these currents moving, not only in the field of art, but also in the field of music, in industry, in social groupings, in the professions — law, medicine, theology. The teacher must see with a discerning eye these currents as they manifest themselves in all people and in all institutions. The experience of the art teacher outside of the school must be catholic, or sufficiently broad to encompass all men's activities.

The technical education that every art teacher will receive in well-defined experiences within accredited institutions must necessarily be supplemented by practices, methods, and procedures gained from intimate contacts with the world of production. A foundry is a storehouse of inexhaustible knowledge, and the silk mill hides the artistry that must be brought to light. In the factory and in the store are the visible manifestations of the techniques taught in the institution. The art teacher will not be satisfied with the mere mastery of techniques. Real satisfaction must come from the experiences as they are found in all of life — in the home, in the church, in the family, in industry, and in the school.[1]

Every teacher or supervisor of art should be a producer of art in some form — painting, sculpture, or handcrafts. It is not unreasonable that people should lose faith in a teacher of art who can do no more

---

[1] Contributed by Henry Klonower, Director, Teacher Education and Certification, Department of Public Instruction, Harrisburg, Pennsylvania.

than talk about art. On the other hand, the art teacher who carries on some form of creative art work — and there are many who do — wins the admiration and respect of children, school directors, and school patrons alike. This personal expression of art in one or more of its numerous forms and materials is not done with the thought of competing with professional artists, but rather as a means of stimulating one's imagination and developing one's own powers through doing. The art teacher who has returned from a summer school of painting may in turn lead his pupils on a sketching expedition and all of them work together.

In music, the drama, the dance, and the visual arts may be found not alone common principles and elements of beauty, but also an intimate relationship. An understanding of one supplements that of the others. The art teacher may properly be expected to exhibit the culture that familiarity with these arts connotes. Furthermore, the school, in its musical programs and its dramatic presentations, will require the services of the art teacher, and he must be competent to meet such demands.

CHAPTER XLII

THE TEACHER OF ART IN COLLEGES AND UNIVERSITIES

GEORGE S. DUTCH
Professor of Art, George Peabody College for Teachers
Nashville, Tennessee

Any discussion of the requirements of teachers of art in colleges and universities must be considered in relation to the basic purposes of the various types of collegiate institutions. As far as art is concerned, junior colleges, general colleges, and liberal arts colleges are often regarded as nonprofessional or nontechnical in nature, whereas the teachers' college and the university are generally to be classed as professional, even on the undergraduate level. There are, however, a great number of liberal arts colleges in which the art offerings follow the professional specialization of an individual professor of art, resulting in courses that are narrowly professional and that fail to meet any 'liberal arts' purpose.

The current term ' general education,' used to designate the newer programs in many liberal arts colleges, embraces all that is implied in the older terms ' cultural education ' and ' liberal education.'[1] Art usually finds its place in this ' general education ' curriculum, of either the two-year or four-year college, in a humanities ' survey ' course that cuts across the fields of the arts: architecture, sculpture, painting, literature, drama, the dance, and music. Such a course aims to lead the student to understand and enjoy these fields better, to familiarize him with the heritage of the past in relation to the appreciation of the present.

It is evident that the teacher qualified to fill the position comprehended by the general-education program is a person broadly prepared in the humanities as a whole rather than in any one or two restricted aspects of the fine-arts area. This statement is not taken as meaning that art finds its only place in the college as a part of the ' humanities '; many junior colleges and general colleges, as well as a considerable

---

[1] For a comprehensive treatment of " General Education in the American College," the reader is referred to the *Thirty-Eighth Yearbook, Part II,* of this Society.

number of liberal arts colleges, offer a distinctly ' studio ' type of art program. It might be better if such offerings were broadened into an arts-laboratory form that could be articulated with the humanities course. A college of sufficient size to make possible a laboratory set-up will require a person technically well-prepared in the range of the graphic and plastic arts, a person who is the graduate of the professional art school. Only in the larger college should a staff of trained specialists in the several arts and crafts be considered; the ' one-man ' art faculty member must be many-sided in his technical education, in addition to being eminent in some one special field of art expression.

The art department in a university should represent the right balance of the historic, esthetic, and technical elements in the rounded development of the art student. An example of this type of program, its organization and personnel, is presented in a statement by Pepper (3) for the University of California at Berkeley:

> The art department in a university must face several long-established conditions. There is a tradition within universities so strongly intellectual as to be suspicious and even hostile to the full development of esthetic values. In the appreciation of beauty in nature or art, three sets of values are roughly involved: (a) the sensuous and emotional, (b) the discriminatory and recognitional, and (c) the informational.
>
> The most effective methods of developing sensuous and emotional appreciation seem to be exposure to quantities of beautiful materials, discriminating comments, contagious enthusiasm, emulation, and admiration for the richness of perception of a cultivated person and for the creative powers of a talented one, stimulation of a desire to make things, presence in the company of others engaged in making things, and practice in making things. Another condition is the attempt to turn an art department into a vocational school or professional art school. This condition arises with the advent of professional artists to represent the sensuous, emotional, and discriminatory values and to teach the practice courses. A third condition is the artistic temperament, a fact as proverbial as the absent-minded professor. At the University of California at Berkeley we are working to eliminate these conditions.
>
> The first thing was to see to it that neither the historical idea nor the professional-school idea got possession of the art department. We offer a number of courses in history and archaeology, given by professors of these subjects, and a number of other courses in practice and appreciation, given by professional artists who have attained recognition in their field, for whom learned degrees are not required or, in general, considered desirable.
>
> The solution of the problem of artistic temperament is along the same

lines. The greatest value of the artist is his individual personality. We want to encourage in each artist the full expansion of creative power and secure a variety of contemporary vital expression.

The third group of art courses lies between history and practice courses. They are those in theory and criticism. At California these courses are taught by artists who have special esthetic interests. Besides the strictly theoretical interest in the detailed esthetics of the visual arts, this field could train people for a profession of criticism that would raise the standards of present journalistic criticism.

Such is our aim, in Berkeley, to obtain all values of history, theory, criticism, and practice from the most expert men in each field and so to organize the department that the differences among these men and their aims will enrich both students and faculty.

It should be noted in the foregoing statement that Pepper says, " The greatest value of the artist is his individual personality." This may be putting it a little strong, but certainly, if all other things are equal, the teacher with a stimulating personality should be the first choice of an administrator.

Lamar Dodd, Head of the Department of Art of the University of Georgia, emphasizes this position in a reply to a letter asking for his point of view on the requirements of the teacher of art in the university:

I made the statement repeatedly that I considered personality one of the prime requisites for the applicant. I am sure you know many who, according to their academic training, are well qualified to teach art — persons whose training can be evaluated on paper. We do not overlook the importance of such preparation, but I feel that we need a person of intelligence and one who will prove an inspiration to the students with whom he works. I have found so many who, according to the academic statement, are well prepared, but who as teachers have proved a miserable failure.

The focus of the department of art in the teachers' college should be upon a practical program of art education that will meet the needs of the prospective elementary- and high-school teachers. This is no small order in the limited time usually allotted for such a purpose; therefore the art teacher should scrupulously avoid the temptation of diverting his instructional time into various attractive, but irrelevant, art offerings — at least until he is certain that his obligations to the field of art education are fully met. Of course, the college of such size as to warrant several members of the art faculty is justified in offering a range of courses meeting the ' general education ' objective as well as providing for the professional development of the high-school art teacher.

The requirements of the teacher of art in the teachers' college are not different from those of his co-workers. Requirements cited by Evenden (1, pp. 287–290) are (a) knowledge of the individuals to be taught, (b) a broad cultural background in the principal fields of organized knowledge, (c) a broad scholarly mastery of the field or fields to be taught, and a supporting knowledge of the most closely related fields, (d) an understanding of the relationships between education and society, (e) an understanding and mastery of the professional knowledge and skills needed for successful initial teaching experience, (f) a well-rounded and well-integrated personality, such as will assure a position of leadership in the school and community in which he works, and (g) a guiding philosophy of education and of life.

Russell (4, p. 307) contributes an additional standard by saying, " In all other respects, with the possible exception of ability to do research, the teachers-college staff should be fully the equivalent of the faculty of the better colleges of liberal arts and the universities of its region."

Little of a concrete nature is to be found on the preparation of college teachers of art and art education. The following contribution to the problem comes from the effort of a committee of college art teachers (5) in Baltimore:

> Undergraduate major in fine arts (preferably the history of art and esthetics), consisting usually of a general survey of the entire field, strengthened by intensive study in one aspect of each chronological subdivision (e.g., ancient art, medieval art, renaissance art, post-renaissance, and modern art), or one form (e.g., architecture, sculpture, painting), or undergraduate major in art education including courses in the following: (a) advanced technical courses; (b) additional courses in art history, philosophy of art; (c) independent research in art education, museum work, archaeology; (d) minor subject matter field; (e) written summary of research, necessary for degree (seminar).
>
> The special college teacher of art or of art education should also possess one or more years of graduate study in the history of art, in the theory and technique of one form (painting, sculpture, architecture), or in art education, leading to the master's degree. (No college teacher can expect a rank much beyond that of an instructor without a master's degree or special evidence of extraordinary ability.) The value of graduate study lies in the intensive training in method of acquiring and organizing information, in increased maturity of judgment. Skill in techniques

needed for the teaching of creative art at the college level must be backed by an understanding of the value of creative art for the undergraduate as an outlet for the expression of his ideas comparable to written reports and exercises commonly required in literature courses. These techniques can probably be acquired faster and more efficiently by the prospective teacher at the graduate level than at the undergraduate level. The undergraduate college undertakes to train a critical public, as art patrons, rather than the creative artist.

Graduate work provided at the art school should embrace intensive study in art history and design, advanced work in psychology and other educational courses, and individual research with written summary report.

This curricular pattern for the prospective college teacher of art and art education is open to serious criticism. It is a question whether the implied emphasis upon the history of art and esthetics will be productive of the kind of teacher demanded by colleges and universities attempting vital programs of superior general education. How can such a narrow pattern meet the challenge of the broad concept of the art area presented in Section I of this Yearbook? Surely here is a problem requiring the studied consideration of college administrators and teachers of art. The tendency toward the vogue of adding the ' artist in residence ' to college staffs must be suggestive of the desire to bring much-needed new blood into the academic atmosphere of many college departments of art.

REFERENCES

(1) EVENDEN, E. S. " What is the essential nature of an evolving curriculum of a teachers' college? " *Proceedings of the National Education Association,* 76:1938, 285–295.

(2) KIRBY, C. V. " Vitalizing the art curriculum for more effective service." [In] *Problems in Teacher Training.* (Prentice-Hall, Inc.: New York, 1936)

(3) PEPPER, STEPHEN C. " Art among the liberal arts." *Proceedings of the National Education Association,* 77: 1939, 403–404.

(4) RUSSELL, JOHN DALE. " What is the essential nature of a teachers' college instructional staff? " *Proceedings of the National Educational Association,* 76: 1938, 295–307.

(5) " The training of teachers of art in Baltimore and vicinity." *Report of the Mayor's Art Survey Committee.* (Baltimore, 1938, mimeographed)

CHAPTER XLIII

THE TRAINING OF COLLEGE TEACHERS OF ART HISTORY AND APPRECIATION

FRANK JEWETT MATHER, JR.
Director of the Museum and Curator of Renaissance and Modern Art
Princeton University, Princeton, New Jersey

I. THE PRODUCT DESIRED AND THE QUALIFICATIONS OF THE PRODUCER

Before planning ways and means of production, it is well to have a clear vision of the product at which we aim. What kind of young man or woman do we want to teach our college students anything? We evidently want, first of all, a person who loves his subject well enough to master it by hard and enthusiastic work. In the case before us, we want a scholar who loves the work of art enough to learn its history thoroughly, a process involving much toil and some inevitable tedium. We want a teacher who, apart from abundant accurate knowledge about the work of art, has wide and eager experience of the work of art itself. Finally, we want a generous and self-respecting teacher, generously communicative enough always to give his students of his best, self-respecting enough to avoid mere platform tricks or autointoxications induced in the much abused name of appreciation. The greatest asset of such a teacher is the warmth of his knowledge. He must be a scholar when he begins and must remain a scholar to the end — not necessarily a productive scholar, yet at the least he must ever keep alive a scholarly curiosity, industry, and probity. Any collegiate teaching of the history of art that is other than this, or that falls short of this, is simply the crackling of rhetorical thorns under the academic pot.

Let me add that there is plenty of legitimate place for that vague and too often windy gospelling that is called 'appreciation,' but its place is in university extension and in popular lecturing in colleges or elsewhere. It is easy to be contagiously enthusiastic about what you know very badly, but it is impossible, in any proper sense, to appreciate what you do not know well.

What has been written above about the collegiate teacher of art is equally applicable to the collegiate teacher in any of the historical disciplines, and I suspect it may even have some relevance to the parallel field of the sciences. The aspirant for teaching in art on the college level will do well to take a reasonable number of undergraduate courses in the history of art, and will naturally continue his training in the best graduate school that will accept him. I have written advisedly a " reasonable " number of art courses, since as things go in most of our American colleges he would actually do better to follow the best courses he can find in languages, literature, and history. In our Princeton Graduate School, as a result of long and bitter experience and in the interest of our students, with the exception of those from colleges that can probably be overcounted on the fingers of two hands, we have to treat our new students who have followed a formidable schedule of undergraduate courses on history and appreciation of art as if they had learned nothing of either. We find they know nothing accurately and concretely, and we have them follow our undergraduate curriculum in order to qualify themselves as full-fledged graduate students. That they have after all profited somewhat by their inadequate work in their own colleges is suggested by the fact that they generally cover satisfactorily our three-year departmental curriculum in a single year. But from our point of view the promising applicant is the Bachelor of Arts who can actually read French, German, and Latin, and knows something of the respective literature and history. If for these accomplishments he has foregone much history and appreciation of art as they are generally taught, we feel he has done well by himself and by us.

One should not deny to this run-of-the-mill teaching the merit of interesting many students in art. But since we are considering professional training, it would be simply blinking the facts to admit that, with the exception of a handful of American colleges, anything that seriously furthers scholarly training in the history of art can be achieved in our undergraduate courses on art.

II. The Method of Training

Coming to graduate training in the history of art, it in the main must follow the well-beaten highroad of the historical disciplines generally. It has the advantage over ordinary history in that it studies the actual data of past effort, the work of art itself, instead of studying such data by old description or hearsay; it has, at least in our country, the disadvantage in comparison with the history of literature that the work of art must ordinarily be studied in reproductions of one sort or another, whereas the poem and the prose masterpiece may be read in the original. This evident disadvantage of graduate study in the history of art may be offset by travel, by accessibility of great museums and private collections, by availability of college or university art museums.

1. The Availability of Works of Art

I feel that it is foolish for an American student to follow graduate studies in the history of art at any institution where fine original works of art are not reasonably accessible, and that it is a sheer waste of money and effort to set up a graduate department in the history of art in universities remote from fine art collections — unless, indeed, the foundation comprises an adequate local museum. All the needed graduate instruction in the history of art for many years to come could be provided in not more than nine or ten graduate departments of suitable geographical location. The congestion of good graduate departments in and around New York is, while natural, considering the richness of our great Atlantic cities in works of art, perhaps detrimental to our studies throughout the nation, because it encourages the foundation of weak and ill-equipped departments to meet an apparent geographical need. In short, in a better-managed academic world, Columbia, Harvard, Princeton, New York University, and Yale would draw cuts to see which two departments should go West and grow up with the country. As it is, they will do their bit in manning such Southern, Middle Western, and Western departments as may need strengthening or may be founded.

2. The Scholarship and Pedagogical Competence of the Staff

Naturally, the student who is choosing a graduate school will consider primarily the scholarship and teaching capacity of its staff. Here the advice of recent graduate students will be better than any of mine. Indeed, a directory of outstanding scholarship and exceptional teaching talent, as of 1940, would be both invidious and futile, for a dozen deaths or retirements would radically change the whole situation. In general, the budding graduate student will properly consider richness of museum resources. This would indicate in first line New York and Boston, and only less Chicago, Baltimore, Philadelphia, Washington, and perhaps Kansas City in some near future. Cost and confusion of living must be weighed against such choices. A student might reasonably accept more remote museum facilities for living in the dignified and civilized way possible at the Princeton Graduate College. Yet even in a cafeteria art may be successfully pursued.

3. Content and Style of Instruction

I may be expected to say what the graduate school should teach the future college professor of art. I shall not do anything of the kind, for I don't think subjects of courses really much matter provided the teaching is thorough and generous. What is essential is that the graduate student should leave with a reasonably complete knowledge and experience of the whole history of art. No university can teach the whole history of art explicitly on any research basis, but it can make sure of the student's teaching himself the essentials by imposing examinations sufficiently rigorous and comprehensive.

For the rest, there are many ways, and the last thing we want in graduate studies is regimentation. For example, the very staple of our graduate studies at Princeton is the seminar. Yet we have to admit that, with a very limited use of this method, Harvard gets excellent results in scholarship by superadding a very odd series of *tête-à-têtes* between professor and student, officially " 20 " courses, to the very rich undergraduate curriculum; while New York University gets results from courses that to an outsider, or even to one who, like myself, has given them, look like a kind of super-university-extension effort.

To speak of study abroad in these days is to indulge a bitter irony. The general principle seems to hold that a year in a good American graduate school will save an enormous, sometimes disastrous, amount of lost motions in the *Wanderjahr*.

I have purposely avoided the ever-burning issue of the historical versus the practical approach. What it really comes down to is, probably, the type of the student's mind. The field is so vast that the student who has the theoretical — that is, the scholar's — mind, will have little enough time for practical work; at most can do the equivalent of a modicum of Sunday painting. A few graduate students are lucky (or unlucky) enough to have the empirical mind, which means that they are incapable of drawing from any experience except their own. Such students frequently develop into excellent connoisseurs and museum officials, but they are simply misfits in any place devoted solely to historical scholarship. They should seek such generous and patient fellow empiricists as conduct museum and practical courses. On the whole, this problem affects rather the museum than the college, for the staple of any really effective college teaching in the history of art will necessarily be a sound historical scholarship.

The record, whether in productive scholarship or in teaching, of the rising generation of college professors of art, a group perhaps some two hundred strong, that has emerged from various sorts of university training, suggests that such training, however various, has been effective.

I have said nothing about the specific training of the graduate student in teaching, because I believe direct methods are time-wasting and inefficient, while the ordinary routine of written report to the seminar, journal club, and learned society already give the student excellent training in the essential matter of clear presentation. Beyond this, the graduate student who is really conscious of his future vocation will naturally sample the undergraduate classes of any professors, in any subject, who are known to be superior teachers. If the student lacks this amount of initiative, I believe he is beyond the aid of any direct pedagogical training.

CHAPTER XLIV

THE PREPARATION OF THE ART SUPERVISOR

C. Valentine Kirby
Chief, Art Education
Department of Public Instruction
Harrisburg, Pennsylvania
and
Leon L. Winslow
Director of Art
Department of Education
Baltimore, Maryland

I. The Need for the Supervision of Art

Progress in art education has been measured for the most part by the high points of achievement in those towns and cities where may be found adequate art supervision and competent instruction. In the country as a whole, however, the classroom teacher, usually with little or no preparation and no supervision, is required to teach whatever art is taught, and, worse yet, millions of children are deprived of any art instruction whatsoever.

Provision for competent supervisors of art, endowed with personal qualities of sympathetic understanding and professional leadership, would appear to be nothing short of a crucial necessity. The supervisor of art is not only indispensable in giving guidance to classroom teachers who are well disposed but incompetent in art, but he also stimulates and makes possible the growth of teachers who are more able. The school administrator, perhaps less familiar with art than with other areas of education, may look to the supervisor of art to assume full responsibility for the art program and the selection and use of art materials.

A good supervisor of art is an investment in every sense of the word. The current tendency to dispense with supervisory services in this field must be regarded therefore as a seriously mistaken administrative policy. Particularly crucial is the provision of adequate supervision of art in rural schools.

II. Desirable Training and Qualifications of the Art Supervisor

The field of art education is making increasing demands, and new responsibilities must be assumed by the supervisor of art. Supervision is a profession and requires a professional preparation.

The successful art supervisor today must be professionally minded, alert to the underlying philosophies and practices in the field of general education, as well as in art. He must be coöperative, businesslike, creative, imaginative, and enthusiastically desirous of enriching the school, home, and community life. He should be technically competent in some field of creative art or craft expression, should be able to assist in the costuming and staging of school plays, and in displaying art exhibits, and should be an active influence for art in the community generally.

The art supervisor should possess certain desirable personal traits and qualifications that are essential. He should first of all be filled with an enthusiastic desire to enter the teaching profession. He should have good mental and physical health, balance and poise, and not an overdose of the 'artistic temperament.'

There are two types of professional institutions that are preparing teachers or supervisors of art — one, the art school with a curriculum in art education; the other, an art curriculum established in a teachers' college. One provides teacher preparation in an art environment, the other an art curriculum in an educational environment.

Curricula for the preparation of art supervisors include such subjects as English, social studies, biological science, education and educational psychology, student teaching and conferences, as well as a wide experience in art techniques and art appreciation.

It is desirable that the supervisor of art should receive some preparation in general supervision and administration, and it is equally desirable that a general supervisor of elementary education should have sufficient art instruction to be of assistance to the classroom teacher.

III. Problems and Responsibilities of the Art Supervisor

The supervisor of art is not only a teacher but also an executive who plans and guides the art program both in individual classrooms and in a group of schools.

In this executive position, problems arise in regard to the economic and efficient distribution of one's time and effort. Consideration must be given to the size of the district, and the number of schools, teachers, and classrooms to be served and visited.

The responsibility of the selection and economic distribution of materials and supplies belongs to the supervisor of art who, likewise, assumes some responsibility in the selection of equipment, including appropriate objects of decoration, for the art room.

The supervisor of art has among his responsibilities, if we may include some that have been touched upon already, (a) guiding the preparation of courses of study in art, (b) conducting meetings for teachers in service, (c) assisting in the preparation and display of art exhibits, (d) applying art to the service of the school and the life of the community, and (e) assuming responsibility for assisting in all matters affecting the attractive appearance of schoolrooms, buildings, and grounds.

Since those who are preparing to teach art will in most cases be called upon to supervise the teaching of art or to consult with elementary teachers who teach art along with other branches, it is desirable that some training in the supervision of art should be offered in our teachers' colleges and art schools, especially at the graduate level.

A survey of the field at the present time discloses that, although a course in supervision as such is seldom offered, some institutions do offer courses that more or less parallel such a course. Nearly all the other institutions offer courses in the teaching of art at the elementary- and secondary-school levels. Since these are ' methods ' courses that stress procedures, they do contribute something to the supervisor's equipment, but they are not sufficient to meet the peculiarly difficult problems of the supervisor of art. A special course in art supervision is needed.

Some instances of courses that are in point may be mentioned.

The Colorado State College of Education, at Greeley, provides a course, called " Curriculum Content and Administration in Art Education," that gives considerable help to the prospective art supervisor, as do also the courses called " The Art Curriculum," given at the Milwaukee State Teachers College, called " Administration of Art Education," at George Peabody College for Teachers, " Curriculum-Making," at the Rhode Island School of Design, and " Problems in Art Education," at the University of Minnesota. In Ohio, where a new state regulation requires that supervisors of art must have a master's degree, the College of Education of the Ohio State University offers a course, called " Problems in Art Education," that is intended to make art supervision more effective. Ohio University at Athens offers " Art Supervision and Curricula," described as follows: " Art objectives. Projects in teaching and supervision in various types of schools and suggestions for growth toward the ideal situation." The State Teachers College, at Buffalo, gives a course entitled " Secondary Art Curriculum and Supervision," in which is included " the work of the supervisor or special teacher." The Northern Illinois State Teachers College, at DeKalb, offers a course in " Art Organization," in which are included such topics as art-testing procedures, experiments, research, and curriculum integration.

Courses in Art Supervision appear to be offered by very few institutions; only five of the ninety-six institutions responding reported such a course. In all instances where such courses are offered, two or more prerequisites are required; that is, the student is expected to receive a foundation in methods of teaching and in the observation and practice of teaching before being allowed to pursue the study that relates to the supervision of teaching.

" Art Supervision " (3 semester hours) at Western State Teachers College, Kalamazoo, Michigan, is, according to the catalog: " A study of the school curriculum and its needs in art activities. A course of study will be outlined and administrative problems discussed. Collections of illustrative material will be cataloged, and supplies and equipment planned."

" Supervision of Art Education " is a four-hour course at the Delta State Teachers College of Cleveland, Mississippi. The course includes: the history of art education, principles of teaching and supervising art, courses of study, materials for art teaching, and guidance for more advanced study and professional growth.

" Teacher Preparation and Supervision in Fine Arts," a ' three-point ' course offered at Teachers College, Columbia University, is for students with experience in art teaching approved by the instructor. It includes: " The function and qualifications of supervisors and heads of departments. Conferences with teachers, teachers' meetings, rating teachers. The place of art in the curriculum. Organization of subject matter for elementary, junior, and senior high schools, normal schools, and teachers' colleges. Tests and measurements in fine arts. Art and social reconstruction."

The School of Education of Indiana University offers " Methods and Practice Work in Supervision of Art " as a three-credit course.

The Pennsylvania State College's School of Education offers also " Art Supervision " as a three-credit course that includes: " Problems of supervision, such as ideals and objectives of supervision; the improvement of instruction; classroom supervision; teachers' meetings; evaluation of classroom results; and choice and budgeting of materials, together with a bibliography."

IV. RECOMMENDATIONS

In school systems employing one or more art supervisors, the supervision is of course taken care of in a special division of the school system thus set up for the purpose. In small school systems without such a special division, the elementary supervisor, or the school principal, or both, must give whatever supervision of art is possible under such circumstances. This supervisory service should aim to accomplish the functions of supervision as they apply to the improvement of administration and instruction in the art field.

The supervision of art education, whether carried on by a special supervisor or by a general supervisor or school principal, should also be concerned with numerous matters that bear more or less directly upon the general task of making pupils sensitive to beauty; as, for example, the decoration of the classroom, the appearance of bulletin boards, of the playground and premises, the arrangement of exhibits, the visiting of museums, the purchase of art supplies, and the like.

Courses in the supervision of art should be offered in those teacher-training schools that are preparing students who are likely to be called upon to supervise the work of teachers, even though most of their own work will be teaching. Graduate schools should offer such a course, and it is desirable that it be offered for either undergraduate or graduate credit.

Dr. Henry Klonower, Director of Teacher Education and Certification, State Department of Public Instruction, at Harrisburg, contends that when art teachers have demonstrated competence, especially to assume leadership, they should be selected for special education that will enable them to supervise the teaching of other art teachers. Only those with superior abilities, sympathetic understanding, and far-sighted vision should be selected for supervisors.

CHAPTER XLV

RURAL ART SUPERVISION AND TEACHERS' EXTENSION CLASSES

HAROLD GREGG
Supervisor of Art
Sonoma County, California

Most of the pupils of our rural schools are the children of workers, and will become workers. It is altogether out of place for us to try to develop in them proficiency in the techniques of any of the arts. There are those who will have concern about the children's preparation should these pupils wish to continue art training in the high school. This fear is unnecessary, for if the child has a background of creative training, he can quickly develop proficiency in the finger skills and techniques. Teachers should be more concerned with the children's attitude toward art and their understanding of the interrelation and background of all its forms. The responsibility of the art supervisor is to help teachers set up a program of art that will accomplish this.

A program of supervision must be built upon existing conditions, particularly such conditions as the number and kind of schools and their geographical location, the quality of the teaching staff and its attitude toward supervision, the various attitudes of the communities. Of these conditions, most important is the quality of the teaching staff.

Sonoma County, California, has 112 rural schools. Seventy of these are one-room schools; the remainder are two- and three-room, with a few four- and five-room schools.

Teachers in our county schools are as varied as teachers could possibly be. Their indicated training varies from the county examination certificate to the M.A. degree. Their ages vary from fresh young things 'just out' to those many years past the retiring age. There is no apparent correlation between youth and good training on the one side and good art teaching on the other. We find that the best general teachers in the county are also the best art teachers. This " best teacher " group is made up of teachers from every level in the age and training scale. Neither is there a direct relation between the natural physical environment and good art teaching. It might be said of our county that good art teaching is not dependent on the age of the teacher

793

or on the kind of training, on the size or age of the school, on the natural physical environment, or on the size of the school budget. Good art teaching is dependent on the teacher's and the parents' attitudes toward art and their understanding of art. The supervisor must treat each school as a separate problem to be helped and directed in a manner peculiar to its own needs.

During the past three years we have been building an art program in the schools of Sonoma County. At first, there were many discouragements; now the program is taking direction and moving forward on a sure footing. The following paragraphs will deal with the activities of the art supervisor and the program of art education in these California rural schools.

In 1938, our first job was to set up some general philosophical guide for the thinking of the entire group of teachers. This took the form of a mimeographed bulletin on art. It dealt with the general techniques of teaching art in the rural schools. It was simply written, profusely illustrated with line drawings, and designed to put teachers at ease concerning the teaching of art in their schools. Along with general statements on the principles of art education, the bulletin contained simple problems, examples, ideas, and suggestions for carrying these theories into practice. This bulletin was bound in such a manner that new materials could be added from time to time. Each additional mimeographed folder presenting some new craft, medium, or technique has its own introduction, background, and suggestions for integration with the whole course of study. During the next two years many of these additional helps were printed. This supplementary material was given only to those teachers who expressed a desire for it. Consequently, those who did receive the material read it, and soon we were receiving many requests for new ideas.

Our next step was to make many brief calls on the schools of the county. Just a stop — " Hello " — " Can we help in any way? " A short conversation with the pupils, and a promise to help them get started with any new project. These many calls gave us an understanding of the particular needs of many teachers and pupils. Their greatest needs seemed to be how to develop a broad understanding of the possibilities of art, how to obtain a knowledge of materials, and an acquaintance with many simple art techniques, and — most important of all — how to converse freely about self-expression in general until fear of art could be eliminated. This, we decided, could best be accomplished by holding *extension classes for teachers.*

The outline shown in Table I was followed for the four extension classes held that year in the north, south, east, and west of the county. It gave to all those who attended a basis of understanding and a foundation for future art planning.

TABLE I. — COURSES IN ELEMENTARY-SCHOOL ART GIVEN IN SONOMA COUNTY EXTENSION CLASSES IN THE SPRING OF 1939

Contents of Course (Tentative)	Techniques
Introductory Sessions *	
Background of art	
Art in living	
Art's place in elementary education	
Creativity in children	
Integration with school program	
Plan for a year's work in art	
Preschool and Primary	
Beginnings of appreciation	Modelling and Clay
Acquaintance with art media	Cut-Paper and Cloth Work
Releasing creative impulse	Powder Paint
Building an art-form vocabulary	Crayon Work
Intermediate	
Development of appreciation	Water Color
Fostering growth of imagination	Soap Carving
Fostering growth of creativity	Potato and Inner-Tube
Review of art forms, color, and lettering	Printing
Simple crafts and techniques	Spray, Spatter, and Toothbrush Painting
Upper Grades	
An art background	Block printing
Growth of appreciation	Puppets
Integration of art and subject matter	Outdoor sketching
Crafts and techniques	Review and open discussion

* All those interested in taking this course should attend these introductory discussions.

The county was divided into four sections. ' Extensions ' were arranged in two of these sections in the fall and in the other two sections in the spring. The classes ran for fourteen weeks; twelve weeks would have been better. Each teacher paid one dollar for the entire course. This made it possible to supply the class with plenty of art materials. It also gave the teachers a feeling of belonging to the class. We made out our course of study for the extension program in keeping with the commonest needs of the group. Its contents were as follows:

a. A background of art
b. The interrelationship of all art forms
c. The integration of art in education and life
d. The important relation of art to our own county, people, environment
e. Art media and techniques in the primary grades
f. Art media and techniques in the intermediate grades
g. Art media and techniques in the upper grades

Paralleling these extension classes were many visits, talks to clubs, and, wherever possible, small school art exhibits. On all sides we heard such remarks, usually whispered, " Why, my class does that sort of work with no guidance at all." One of the reasons for exhibits is to bring about the realization that much art is natural and simple; thus examples displayed in our County Office were not necessarily the best we could find, but were examples of good, original, honest, childlike art. The value of these simple little exhibits should not be underestimated. We believe they are a most powerful factor in stimulating interest for an art program in county schools.

At the last meeting of each extension course we discussed further needs of the group. The teachers felt they now had a foundation for thinking in the field of art education, and they all seemed to want definite instruction in some one form of expression.

The second year's extension courses were built on the pattern shown in Table II.

TABLE II. — EXTENSION COURSES GIVEN SONOMA COUNTY RURAL TEACHERS IN THE FALL AND SPRING OF 1939–40

Course	Duration
Outdoor Sketching Course (embodying a wide range of general art principles)	4 Weeks
Craft Groups (working on their particular interests)	4 Weeks
The Arts of Christmas	2 Weeks
Room Environment (beauty corner and arrangement of room)	2 Weeks
Craft Groups (working on their own interests, weaving, clay, puppets, printing)	4 Weeks
Outdoor Sketching (embodying all the principles of art in general)	4 Weeks

Teachers carried the work of the extension courses into the classrooms. As we introduced the many possibilities of art expression through the lowly crayon, the teachers permitted their pupils to experiment in the full range of crayon technique. The same week that our teachers' classes took to the fields with a stiff cardboard, a few pieces of drawing paper, two clothespins to hold the paper from flapping, and a pocket full of crayons, approximately seventy little groups of children took to the fields with their own pockets bulging with broken crayons. This regimentation was encouraged only during the first experimental period of outdoor sketching with crayon. We feel it would be deadly to an art program if used as a steady supervisory diet.

Each week the teachers brought in the work of their classes for general criticism and for mutual benefit. This, more than ever, brought out the many different styles and effects to be obtained through use of a common medium.

The four weeks of crayon work were planned in steps. The first day we tried all possible ways of using the crayon — light-dark, soft-heavy, smooth-rough, thin-broad, pure areas of color, combinations of several colors. We also attempted blocking-in sketches on a clean sheet of paper. For our second meeting we walked over fields and talked. We discussed the possibilities in nature for inspiration. We started many sketches that day. There was so much to see. The third time our class went out we selected subject material and went to work. At the end of that period we discussed our drawings, and suggested ways of improving them. The fourth field trip was one of complete freedom for the teacher. It was her business to choose her subject, start, and finish her drawing. In the fall we started the second part of our extension work, the crafts. Each teacher selected a craft with which to work. The class divided into four sections: puppetry, weaving, clay work, and printing. Each teacher worked with one group for four successive weeks. In this way each one gained a self-assured knowledge of one craft and an understanding of the other three. This part of the extension took on a very pleasant social atmosphere. Each time a new idea was introduced and found to be practical, it was mimeographed and transmitted to all the group. Again the children of each little school followed the teacher's work in their own school work.

During all this craft period constant reference was made to the original discussions of art appreciation and of the relation of the work we were doing to the whole background of crafts and art through the history of man.

The remaining two weeks of this course were devoted to the arts of Christmas. All the teachers brought ideas, and we used the class as a clearing house of suggestions for the holiday season. Stained-glass windows, Kleenex Santa Clauses, decorations, gifts, packages came to class. The teachers seemed to enjoy this part of the course very much.

After Christmas vacation the course was started in the other two centers of the county. The seasons now would be reversed; so we reversed the outline of the course and started with seasonal art and room arrangement for the first two meetings. The second part of this program was given over to crafts, and for the last four weeks we enjoyed outdoor sketching during the full beauty of an early spring.

These extension classes were well attended. About 140 teachers were enrolled in the four sections of the county. However, many teachers were not reached by these classes. There were some who were just " not interested." Their schools were visited, and the pupils helped directly by the supervisor.

During the two years of the extension classes many teachers came to the office to talk over their art problems and many worked out individual art courses of study.

At the end of the two-year period, it was evident that the art program in the county schools needed some integrating project. Many of the teachers were asking for more courses, but for the most part they were the ones most interested in art and best able to carry on an art program without such help. We decided on an art exhibit for the whole county — an exhibit compiled from all the rural schools in the county.

We started the program in May of 1940. In our County Superintendent's monthly bulletin all teachers were told of the plan. We requested them to gather all the art work done in the previous two years and have it ready soon after school opened in the fall. The local newspaper ran a fine story of the coming exhibit. Notices appeared in the County Superintendent's bulletin in June and September. Each notice described the kind of art examples wanted, how to label them, and where the materials should be delivered. Personal calls were made — the most effective way, of course, to insure coöperation.

For several weeks before the ' dead line,' the supervisor drove the roads, ' tagging ' schools. " Hello, I just stopped to remind you of the art exhibit. Oh, of course you have! Look at that sketch on the wall. And you probably have many more just as good. Yes, crafts, too. Anything that is original. Well, be sure to send in those pieces, anyway! Goodbye."

The work came in. Hundreds of pieces. All sizes and shapes and kinds. The principal of the school where the exhibit was to open offered space and pupil-help for the long, tedious job of sorting, mounting, and arranging the art work into an interesting, as well as informative, show.

The major purpose of the exhibit was to give a graphic representation of the course of study in art for Sonoma County rural schools. The exhibit was arranged according to grade level. The first-grade examples demonstrated the child's earliest concepts of the most important things in his young life. His development from early concepts to the sharpening of his observations and the development of better muscular coördination was made evident. Each grade level illustrated examples of steady growth of art concepts and of skill in performance. The exhibit was truly a clearing house of suggestions and ideas, as almost all known school art media were represented. Teachers visited and took notes. Many teachers brought in their classes to study various phases of the exhibit.

In the supervision of rural schools there must be some way to bring about an exchange of ideas; some way to indicate the strength and the weakness in the art program. The *travelling exhibit* is doing just that. Some teachers are astonished to find how well their children are able to express ideas; how original, how free and confident they are in the use of certain art media; how they, as teachers, have neglected entirely the introduction of many art media. Thus, it is helping the teachers discover their own strength and weakness. From the moment the exhibit was hung, it became apparent that there is great strength in crayon technique, but that water-color instruction is greatly needed throughout this whole county.

This travelling art exhibit will be shown for one week in each of eight different centers of population in this county. During its stay in a center the supervisor will work in the schools of that area. He will invite all teachers to come on one afternoon and, as a group, discuss the exhibit with the next year's art program in mind.

When the exhibit has been shown in eight centers of the county, it will be returned to the County Office, and there be broken down into about eight small but complete exhibits for distribution to any of the schools wishing an art show of its own. The best of this county art work will be sent to the State Capitol for exhibit there. This will be an added incentive to our art program.

The art section of our recent County Institute proved an excellent means for giving teachers a broad view of the whole art program. A dramatized art course of study was also presented. Panels measuring 4' × 7' were hung on the center of each wall of a large classroom. Each panel contained an explanation and examples of our art work, illustrating the aims, characteristics, and the procedures of teaching art in the primary, intermediate, upper, and secondary levels. Below each panel were tables and chairs and easels. Children were working in media ranging from clay, easel painting, and chalk in the primary level to vocational and avocational art media in the high-school and junior-college level. True, it sounds much like Barnum's Best Three-Ringer, but it did spread before the people, in its entire scope, the growth of the art idea through the grades and into adult life. The art section brought out the importance of long-time art planning in the schools.

The function of the art supervisor is rather to challenge interest than to teach the purely artistic. It embraces public relations, parental understanding of the child's work, and the teacher's attitudes toward art. Actual demonstrations and art teaching are incidental. Each school, each group of pupils, each teacher, is an individual problem and must be handled accordingly. If we were to list the important activities of a rural art supervisor, these items would certainly be included:

Establishing an art philosophy for each particular area
Exhibits — many small; a few large, inclusive, explained exhibits
Extensions — that give the teachers self-assurance
Bulletins — for suggestions, aids, " How-to-do "
Talks — to parents and teachers
Demonstrations — meetings for teachers and parents
Demonstrations — in the classroom
Newspaper articles
Radio broadcasts
Many office conferences

These listed supervisory activities may seem hard, cold, and without a spark of inspiration. This is far from true. These one-two-three steps are always carried out with reference to, and in keeping with, our original philosophy. All our talks, demonstrations, and exhibits are related and help to interpret our thesis for art in rural areas.

Rural life can be, and often is, a life of monotonous drudgery — a life of drudgery against the most inspirational, most beautiful background the world affords! It is a life that many times seems aimless and bereft of hope, and yet in no other kind of living are there to be found such deeply rooted traditions. People have but to glance up from their work, they have but to stop and look around them, to feel the great natural store of inspirational materials. Herein lies the responsibility of rural art supervisors — to aid rural people in looking up, seeing, and acquiring the self-assurance and ability to interpret their environment to their own satisfaction and contentment.

CHAPTER XLVI

PREPARATION OF THE GENERAL CLASSROOM TEACHER FOR TEACHING ART

Edwin Ziegfeld
Assistant Professor of Fine Arts
Teachers College, Columbia University
New York, New York

Any consideration of the preparation of the general classroom teacher for teaching art must depend largely on the answer to two questions: first, what are the present responsibilities of the general classroom teacher concerning the teaching of art and the prospects of the future, and second, what is the training in art that he now receives? This section will begin with a consideration of these two questions, and will be followed by recommendations for a program of art training for the general classroom teacher.

I. The General Classroom Teacher and the Teaching of Art

In Chapter XXX, Horn, in his treatment of " Inequalities in Opportunities for Art Development," has described the situation that prevails in elementary and rural schools relative to the teaching of art. The discussion clearly indicates first, that the classroom teacher who is not responsible for the art instruction of his class is the exception rather than the rule; second, that in most instances he, and he alone, is responsible for the art program, and that its quality, good or poor, is dependent on him; and third, that there are no immediate prospects that there will be any significant change in the present situation. Present trends appear to be leading away from the platoon system and departmentalized instruction, which means that more classroom teachers than previously will have to assume the responsibilities of art teaching. There is also a tendency toward increasing class size that will require even more competent teachers to achieve satisfactory results.

II. The Art Training of the General Classroom Teacher

The second problem for investigation is the art training that the general classroom teacher receives. Fortunately, a thorough study of the education of teachers (29) done recently by the United States Department of Education includes a great deal of information that bears on the immediate problem. Following are data taken largely from that survey dealing with art training, both in the high school and in the college, of prospective classroom teachers. In most cases figures on other subjects besides art are included for purposes of comparison, but in none of the data from the *National Survey of the Education of Teachers* are the tables reproduced in their entirety. Tables I and II are concerned with the art training that prospective elementary teachers receive in high school. Tables III to VI show the training prescribed by teachers' colleges and universities according to an analysis of catalogs. Tables V and VI show the work actually taken by students graduating from teachers' colleges and universities, according to an analysis of their records. When the tables deal with college credits, the figures are in semester credits.

TABLE I. — COURSES TAKEN IN THE HIGH SCHOOL BY PROSPECTIVE
ELEMENTARY TEACHERS

(Work taken in the high school by 71 prospective teachers of the intermediate grades graduating from teachers' colleges in 1931. [29, Vol. III, p. 76])

Subject	Percentage Taking the Subject in the High School	Percentage of All the Work Taken
Art	16.9	1.2
English	100.0	21.5
Mathematics	98.6	16.0
Music	38.0	2.7
Science-Biology	60.0	3.5
Science-General	28.2	1.8
Science-Physical	64.8	5.2
Social Science-History	100.0	16.4

TABLE II. — TRAINING IN ART RECEIVED IN THE HIGH SCHOOL BY PROSPECTIVE
ELEMENTARY TEACHERS

(Art training in the high school of 82 students at the University of Minnesota preparing to become kindergarten or elementary teachers. Data collected in 1938 by the writer.)

Years of Art Taken in High School	Number of Cases	Percentage
0	74	90
1	7	9
2	0	0
3	1	1

TABLE III. — TRAINING IN TEACHERS' COLLEGES PRESCRIBED FOR PROSPECTIVE ELEMENTARY TEACHERS

(Size of prescription in art, industrial art, music, and English, according to an analysis of catalogs of 66 teachers' colleges and normal schools [29, Vol. III, pp. 517–524].)

Subject	Four Years				Three Years				Two Years				One Year			
	No.	P.C.	R.	Md.	No.	P.C.	R.	Md.	No.	P.C.	R.	Md.	No.	P.C.	R.	Md.
Art																
Elementary *	21	95	2–9	5	8	100	3–9	5	11	91	1–6	3				
Intermediate	18	89	3–7	5	8	100	3–6	4	15	93	1–5	3				
Kinder.-Primary	30	80	3–12	6	13	100	3–11	5	21	90	1–6	3				
Rural	11	82	1–6	5	5	80	3–5	4	19	95	1–4	3	5	80	1–2	2
Industrial Art																
Elementary	21	5	2	–	8	13	5	–	11	0	–	–				
Intermediate	18	11	1–3	–	8	13	3	–	15	13	1–3	–				
Kinder.-Primary	30	27	1–5	3	13	46	2–5	3	21	19	1–3	2				
Rural	11	27	1–3	2	5	0	–	–	19	21	1–3	2	5	0	–	–
Music																
Elementary	21	100	2–12	4	8	88	3–10	6	11	100	1–8	4				
Intermediate	18	89	1–8	4	8	100	3–7	5	15	87	1–5	3				
Kinder.-Primary	30	83	2–12	5	13	100	3–10	5	21	100	1–6	3				
Rural	11	82	1–8	4	5	80	3–6	4	19	84	1–5	2	5	100	1–2	2

* The first line is read thus: Of the 66 teachers' colleges and normal schools studied, 21 offered four-year majors in elementary education. Of this number, 95 percent prescribed art courses, the size of these prescriptions ranging from 2 to 9 semester credits with a median of 5. Eight of the institutions studied offered three-year majors in elementary education, 100 percent of them prescribing art courses, etc.

Three important facts emerge from these six tables. First is the small amount of art taken by students planning to become general classroom teachers. It is apparent that most of them enter college with no art training beyond the elementary grades, and many may not have had it there. In perhaps no other subject that they will be called on to teach do these students enter college with a less adequate background, judged in terms of training. Furthermore, as is shown in Tables I and II, the number who elect art in the high school is exceedingly small. Of the two groups studied, only seventeen percent in the one and ten percent in the other had taken any art work during their high-school careers. A comparison with other subjects in Table I demonstrates how little time comparatively is devoted to art in the high school. All members in this group took English and history; apparently all took one or more courses in science; and all but one enrolled in mathematics.

TABLE IV. — ART COURSES IN TEACHERS' COLLEGES TAKEN BY
ELEMENTARY TEACHERS

(Work taken in art, industrial art, music, and English by graduates of 20 teachers' colleges who have majored in intermediate, kindergarten-primary, and rural education [29, Vol. III, pp. 525–529].)

Subject	Four Years				Two Years			
	No.	P.C.	Range	Md.	No.	P.C.	Range	Md.
Art								
Intermediate *	75	68	1–57	6	100	77	1– 8	3
Kinder.-Primary	75	92	1–25	6	100	90	1–18	4
Rural	—	—	—	—	100	70	1–33	3
Industrial Art								
Intermediate	75	25	0–10	2	100	5	1– 3	2
Kinder.-Primary	75	17	1– 8	3	100	5	1– 5	2
Rural	—	—	—	—	100	9	1–15	2
Music								
Intermediate	75	73	1–74	6	100	78	1–39	3
Kinder.-Primary	75	79	1–34	5	100	86	0–27	3
Rural	—	—	—	—	100	69	1– 7	3
English								
Intermediate	75	100	5–37	21	100	96	3–27	10
Kinder.-Primary	75	99	5–42	18	100	97	2–25	9
Rural	—	—	—	—	100	98	2–32	8

* The first line is read thus: Of the 75 students majoring in a four-year course in intermediate education, 68 percent took courses in art, the amounts varying from 1 to 57 semester credits, the median being 6 semester credits, etc.

TABLE V. — TRAINING IN COLLEGES AND UNIVERSITIES PRESCRIBED FOR
PROSPECTIVE ELEMENTARY TEACHERS

(Size of prescriptions in fine arts [including music], English, and foreign language according to a catalog analysis of 16 colleges and universities [29, Vol. III, pp. 530–533].)

Subject	Percent Prescribing	Range of Credits	Median of Credits
Fine Arts (including Music)	50	4–10	6
English	94	6–48	12
Foreign Language	81	6–18	12

In contrast, only one-sixth of the group were enrolled in art courses. While only 1.2 percent of the total time in the high school of these students was spent in art, over one-fifth was spent in English, one-

TABLE VI. — COURSES IN COLLEGES AND UNIVERSITIES TAKEN BY
ELEMENTARY TEACHERS

(Work taken in fine arts [including music], English, and foreign languages by 100
prospective elementary teachers graduating from colleges and universities [29,
Vol. III, pp. 534–536].)

Subject	Percent Taking Subject	Range of Credits	Median of Credits
Fine Arts (including Music)	85	1–24	5
English	99	7–36	17
Foreign Language	73	2–31	12

sixth in mathematics, one-sixth in history, and about one-tenth in the
sciences. Over twice as many members of this group had courses in
high-school music as in art. Because of the paucity of art training in
the high school of these prospective teachers, teacher-training institutions are faced with the problem of providing these students with the
necessary art knowledge, skills, and appreciations to enable them to
teach art effectively.

But even in college, not all of these prospective classroom and rural
teachers enroll in art courses. In the teachers' college group (Table
IV) only 68 percent of those in the four-year elementary group had art
training in college. The high figure is 90 percent — that being the
percentage of two-year kindergarten-primary teachers who took art
in college. About four-fifths of them appear to take art courses, and
about the same number take music. The amount of art taken represents about five percent of the total college credits. In addition, some
work in industrial arts is taken by a very small percentage of this group.
In comparison with English, the same situation exists that was reported
for the high-school programs. The student is, indeed, the exception
who does not include English courses in college, and that, it must be
remembered, after four required years in the high school. Not only a
far larger percentage of students take English than art in college, but
on the average they also take three times as much.

Table VI, on the work taken in colleges and universities, shows that
85 percent of the group are indicated as having taken fine arts with
a median of five credits. This classification, however, includes music
as well as art, and there is no way of determining the relative amounts
of each. Assuming that the time was equally divided between the two
subjects, it would mean that only about two percent of the college time

of those students who took art was spent on that subject. The comparison with English is similar to the situation in teachers' colleges.

The second fact that is apparent in the data is the discrepancy between the prescriptions of the teacher-training institutions and the courses the students actually take. While these differences might be due to the errors of random sampling, they might be due to other factors. As is shown in Table IV, the number of graduates of teachers' colleges and normal schools who took art is slightly smaller than one would expect from the number of institutions prescribing it. On the other hand, the number of students graduating from colleges and universities who actually took art courses is much greater than one would expect from the frequency of the prescriptions. This might well mean that these young people, knowing the job that was ahead of them, attempted realistically to take courses that would aid them in this job, even though it meant going out of the prescribed schedule. If that is true, it is a healthy sign, but it is only a sign of direction and not in any sense a goal.

The third major fact indicated by the tables is the meagerness of the requirements in art for prospective classroom teachers. This is particularly evident in the data on colleges and universities in Table V. Only one-half, exactly fifty percent, of the institutions require that their graduates, who it is known are planning to teach in the elementary grades, take courses in fine arts. The figures that are available include both music and art, so that the amount of art that is required is perhaps only about three semester credits. The situation is critical. Of the students entering the university to become elementary or kindergarten teachers, only one out of six (at the most) has had art instruction in the high school. In the positions where they will be placed, from eight to ten percent of the class time will probably be spent in art activities. Yet only half of the colleges and universities preparing young people to teach in the elementary grades require that they receive instruction in a field that they will all, with few exceptions, have to teach. Even in the cases where art is required, the amount is generally small and inadequate.

In discussing prescriptions and electives, relative to the exhaustive study of teacher education, the authors of the *National Survey of the Education of Teachers* state (29, Vol. III, p. 291):

> It seems important that teachers should take at least appreciation courses in music and art: art should be more emphasized for its cultural and recreational values, for its importance in practical life as well as for

the enrichment of an increasing amount of leisure that it gives. The life situations of today call for more fine-arts prescriptions, even at the expense of some of the more traditional requirements.

Very few instructors opposed the statement that a general education should include fine arts and music. The opinion was frequently encountered that college people, whether they engage in teaching or not, are lacking in knowledge of past and present art, in artistic taste, and in appreciation of visual beauty, and that college requirements and courses do not sufficiently stress fine-arts experiences.

The need is recognized, then, but many of the institutions of higher learning apparently do nothing about it.

A comparison of the prescriptions in art with those of foreign languages is most interesting. Table V shows that eighty-one percent of the colleges and universities studied prescribe foreign language for elementary-education majors, compared to fifty percent for art, and furthermore that the prescription is twice as much as for fine arts, perhaps four times as much as for art alone. The inclusion and size of this requirement is undoubtedly part of the plan to give all teachers a good cultural training. The value of foreign languages as aiding the achievement of this goal is doubtlessly valid, but their contribution in producing better elementary teachers is highly questionable. If the criterion of cultural value is used to determine many of the college requirements, one is certainly safe in insisting that art can qualify as an indispensable subject.

Prescriptions in teachers' colleges and normal schools as shown in Table III are more liable to include art than those in colleges and universities, and the amount of the prescription is also greater. In this respect these institutions show a more realistic approach to the problems of a teacher than do the colleges and universities. One curious phenomenon is noticeable, that as the length of the training period increases from two to four years, either the relative amount of time given to art or the percentage of institutions prescribing it decreases. Apparently, the ' higher ' the education the prospective teacher receives, the less need he has for training in art. It is a striking example of what art educators know all too well: that art is not academically respectable to the scholars and administrators, themselves trained entirely on subjects that deal only with words, who control largely the offerings and requirements of institutions of higher learning. Art is available to students who have one or two or even three years in which to prepare themselves for teaching, and who must be practical about the matter.

But as soon as a student becomes a candidate for a Bachelor's degree, he becomes also a candidate for verbal culture and art becomes a less attractive subject. The student is given in increasing amounts science and mathematics and foreign languages and English and all the other subjects that are summaries of our cultural heritage. Art, which can boast of an equally attractive ancestry and can help the classroom teacher to lead a fuller and richer life, is neglected.

In summary, it appears from these studies that far too many prospective teachers graduate from their professional training with no contact with art. This is especially serious since art is a subject taken by only a few in high school. Prescription of art courses for prospective elementary-grade teachers is by no means general, and it is particularly low in colleges and universities. The amount of art, either prescribed or taken, is small when compared with other subjects taken in college. It appears, in colleges and universities at least, that students take more art courses than are prescribed. If this is true, it might be interpreted as a demand on the part of students for training for which they feel a need, a tendency that administrators might well heed.

One other point should be borne in mind in appraising the foregoing data. The figures give no indication of the kind or quality of the art training received by those who take it. In many instances the prescribed art course may be one in the history of art, which, though contributing to the general culture of a student, is of limited value in helping him teach art to young children. The ' appreciation ' course often required of teachers in training is also likely to be factual art history with little or no relation to present-day life, either expressed or implied.

This entire situation of the art training of the general classroom teacher is crucial and the lack of teacher preparation in art in the elementary grades would be countenanced in few, if any, other subjects in the curriculum. It explains much of the poor art teaching that takes place in schools all over the country. Teachers for the most part are willing and eager for experiences that will make them better teachers. In few subjects does the typical teacher feel less secure than in art, and it is the duty of teacher-training institutions to increase and improve instruction in this field.

III. Recommendations for the Training in Art of the General Classroom Teacher

Having discussed briefly the status of the general classroom teacher in art and the training in that subject which he now receives, the following section will be concerned more specifically with the nature of that training. These recommendations are in no sense revolutionary or impossible of achievement. It is realized that many institutions now provide adequate training. At the same time, there are many more in which the training in art available to this group is far from adequate. These recommendations are offered in the hope that they can act as a guide in enlarging and making more effective these latter programs.

1. General Recommendations

a. Make Art a Part of the Training of All General Classroom and Rural Teachers. The members of the Committee preparing this Yearbook urge *strongly* that training in art be a required part of the education of all general classroom teachers. They feel that no one should teach art who has not had training in it. The present situation of requiring the teaching of art by teachers without art training is unfair, not only to the teachers, but even more so to the children.

The more training possible for these prospective teachers, the better — provided it is good. Some individuals in the high school receive training in art that is equal or superior to some art training in college. When such is the case, it should be accepted and the student released from comparable courses in college. However, since so few elect art in the high school, it becomes the duty of the college to supply it. If art training at the high-school level becomes more common, it will affect the amount and type of art training necessary for these students. However, with the situation as it is at present, with only a small percent electing art in the high school, we had best proceed on the assumption that the college is responsible for the art training of prospective classroom teachers.

The amount of training desirable is not easy to determine. That the quality of the training is more important than the quantity, and that some persons respond more quickly to training than do others are both valid statements, but they both beg the immediate question. The matter is further complicated by the fact that the general classroom teacher must prepare himself in many subjects other than art, and in all of them a competent performance is expected. Probably not as much time could be given to art as a group of art educators might desire, but it is obvious that there could be an improvement of present requirements.

Six semester credits, while not large, might be considered a minimal requirement in a four-year curriculum, with proportional amounts for shorter curricula. This would provide for the four-year student a full year of training if a three-hour course were taken each semester (or quarter), and a shorter period could hardly be adequate for the complexity of the task. A six-credit requirement is slightly more than appears to be required now in teachers' colleges and normal schools, and considerably more than is required in colleges and universities. It might be necessary in some instances to lighten requirements in some of the more traditional subjects, as is suggested in the *National Survey of the Education of Teachers* (29, Vol. III, p. 291). Certainly, as mentioned above, it seems pertinent to question requirements for elementary teachers in such subjects as foreign languages or mathematics, particularly when they have a tendency to reduce the amount of art in teacher-training programs. General art courses are as cultural as many they might replace, and also have the advantage of giving the prospective teacher a background for the activities he will pursue.

The most immediate problem is getting all institutions that prepare classroom teachers to include art in their requirements. Superintendents and principals should insist that teachers who work in their schools have art training and that it be comparable in quality and amount to the other subjects they teach. Art education can be no better than the teachers who control it, and their training must be improved if art is to assume and maintain the position of importance in the schools that the general educators have indicated for it.

b. Develop Special Courses in Art for Elementary and Rural Teachers. The art needs of elementary and rural teachers constitute a special problem in higher education. They differ, on the one hand, from those of the nonprofessional student, and on the other hand, from the needs of the art-education major. Only in a general introductory art course would the needs of students in the three groups be similar and any professionalized emphasis demands that the elementary teachers be placed in a group of their own. In many institutions the practice prevails of placing these students, together with students majoring in art education, in classes emphasizing participation and methods. This is highly unfortunate. In participation courses it tends to discourage the person in elementary education by placing him in competition with students much more skilled than he, and nothing is more detrimental to art expression than a feeling of inferiority. The difficulty of combining the two groups in methods courses is that most art-education majors are planning to teach in the secondary grades, and their problems are very different from those of elementary teachers. The knowledge and abilities that prospective elementary teachers must acquire are so varied and broad in scope and the amount of time generally is so short that everything possible must be done to facilitate learning. This can best be accomplished by arranging classes in which the time can be spent entirely on the problems of the students enrolled.

c. Clarify the Relationship between Fine and Industrial Arts. A rigid distinction between fine and industrial arts exists in many schools. It is based largely on a nineteenth-century conception of the nature of art that differentiated sharply between art concerned with human expression and emotions and that which dealt with the needs of everyday life. This dichotomy is also expressed as ' fine ' and ' applied ' arts, ' fine ' and ' practical ' arts, and ' fine ' and ' useful ' arts. Translated into the school program the fine arts become concerned only with ' expression' in drawing and painting, and the work has a tendency to become superficial and divorced from reality. Industrial-arts programs take as their sphere such fields as food, shelter, and clothing. The emphasis on their practical and industrial nature often leads to a preoccupation with processes and the work produced often lacks art value.

A sharp division between the two fields implies a specialization that is neither feasible nor desirable at the elementary level. Actually, the line of distinction between the two fields is almost impossible to draw. It seems more reasonable to consider art as one large field, at times more concerned with practical problems than at others, but with many constant characteristics always present. This point of view is gaining rapidly in acceptance in school practice. The tendency at present to organize instruction in the elementary grades around a center, a topic, a problem, or a theme has also tended to break down this distinction. In the training of teachers, it seems better to teach art as one large unified area, entering in various ways into many activities, for that is the manner in which art appears to function best in elementary programs.

d. Acquaint Prospective Teachers with the General Classroom Situation in Art. Far too many classroom teachers graduate from teacher-training institutions without having had contact with art as taught in the public schools. Their student teaching and observation of classes are often concerned entirely with the so-called ' major ' subjects of the elementary grades, with little or no attention paid to ' special ' subjects. This lack of experience works a hardship on them when, after obtaining positions, they are faced with the necessity of conducting a program in art in their classes. It is recommended that teacher-training institutions acquaint prospective classroom teachers with the classroom situation in art in such ways as observing special demonstration lessons in art taught by competent teachers, observing classes in art in a variety of situations and involving a variety of activities, and practice teaching in art, with provision for observation, criticism, discussion, and evaluation by competent critic teachers or supervisors.

2. Specific Recommendations

In making any specific recommendations for the training of the general classroom teacher in art, it seems reasonable to discuss them in terms of what the teacher will have to do in the classroom situation. What will he want to know? What will he have to do? What particular abilities should he develop? The answer to such questions, based on his present and possible future status and the art training that he receives before college, will go a long way toward determining a realistic course.

The knowledge needed by the general classroom teacher may be discussed under three heads: first, what he should know about art; second, what he should know about the child and his development in relation to art; and third, what he should know about the teaching of art. The logic and convenience of the categories justifies their individual consideration, despite their close interrelations.

a. Knowledge of Art. The well-prepared classroom teacher will have a sound and workable philosophy of art. There is a growing tendency to consider art as an all-pervasive activity integrally related to the whole fabric of life. This concept has been admirably developed by Dewey (9) and Haggerty (13, 14). The teacher will have favorable attitudes toward new tendencies and developments in the arts (8) as well as toward historic periods and products. Unfortunately, it is often true that pupils in elementary classes have a greater appreciation of new art manifestation than do the teachers, who may thus retard and inhibit appreciation. The teacher's appreciation and understanding of art must naturally go well beyond names and dates (3); it must be built on meaningful experiences, must be based on a sound philosophy, and must be general enough that he both makes art an integral part of his own life and appreciates the art expressions of children as well as those of the great masters. The concept of art as a creative enterprise, related to all the aspects of life, demands that it become an integral part of the lives of these prospective teachers. They should live art as they will teach it.

The concept of art as something that permeates all activities of living implies that art extends far beyond the narrow fields of painting and sculpture, which for many years have exerted a virtual monopoly on art in the schools, and includes such fields as architecture (19), community planning (2, 20), and industrial design (23, 26).

Thinking of art in terms of the living present rather than the dead past means that the teacher will be familiar with contemporary developments — what is happening today in community planning, in housing, in painting, in sculpture — for it is those developments that operate significantly in the lives of people today. Knowledge of the art of the past is desirable, with particular emphasis on how it affects art today (4, 6).

Some skills in art are necessary for the prospective classroom teacher, but these need not be highly developed. Indeed, in the short time available for the training of these teachers, an overemphasis on the development of skills will result in an underemphasis on other important phases of their training. Most necessary is having experience in the production of art products, realizing how these problems are solved, feeling how art materials are manipulated, and above all, experiencing creative activity. Tannahill writes that teachers of the elementary grades need " actual experience in the joy of creating or expressing themselves " (25, p. 70). If we hope to develop creative ability in children in the elementary grades, then it is necessary that the teacher have a definite understanding of what it is they are to develop. Far too many teachers have little or no concept of what creative activity in art is and often reject those products of children that represent new ways of projecting their experience.

Skills in art materials should not be limited to those in two dimensions, such as drawing, painting, and lettering, but should include experiences in the three-dimensional arts — architecture, interior design, community planning, garden design, industrial design, and modelling. These contacts should not be dull, academic exercises, but should be outgrowths of life and effective in it.

Contacts should be provided for the prospective teacher with a wide variety of products. These can be firsthand contacts with buildings, parks, stores, factories, and museums in order to increase awareness of the many different aspects of art. Utilization of community resources is as important in art as in social studies and the teachers should discover the many possibilities that exist.

b. *Knowledge about the Child.* Every teacher-training program includes instruction on the developmental aspects of childhood, characteristic modes of behavior, children's interests, how children learn, and the like. In general, all this knowledge is related to the child and his art experiences. There is however much he should know that relates specifically to the child and art. Art, for the child, is a direct means of expression and can play an important part in his emotional development (22). Zachry, in her recent investigations, was impressed by the significant rôle that art plays in personality development (31) and its relation to mental hygiene (32). Art can be used as an approach to the emotional problems of children (24) and some aspects of it are a reliable guide to the measurement of intelligence (12).

Art is an intensely personal means of expression for a child (7, 15). The prospective teacher will become familiar with his characteristic forms of expression (21, 27, 28) [1]; he will know the various stages of development through which children pass as they develop in drawing ability. For example, Eng (10) has prepared an interesting account based on the drawings made by her niece over a period of years. Other investigators have formulated so-called ' stages of development ' (1). The prospective teacher will realize that he must respect the sincere and direct art expressions of the child and neither impose nor expect adult standards. The experimental literature on child development in graphic and allied arts has been summarized by Meier (18).

c. *Knowledge of the Teaching of Art.* The prospective teacher of art in the elementary grades will have, along with his understandings and skills in art, the ability to make these function in a classroom. He will know how to set up learning situations in art, how to stimulate and guide art activity (5, 16), and how to relate art instruction to the life of the child, to the school, to the community (15, 30, 33). He will know the difference between using drawing in relation to other school subjects as a record and drawing as a means of expression. In many systems where art is closely related to the social studies, it becomes merely a series of exercises in representation where verisimilitude is stressed above everything else. Representative drawing is one of the functions of art in a school program, but only one of many. Others are equally valid, if not more so.

The teacher will also realize the relative importance of such devices

---

[1] This is certainly best done by direct observation or by working with children rather than by looking at books. The references quoted are collections of children's work, and while the ones chosen for reproduction are highly selected and therefore not typical of the work that a teacher might expect from an average class, they nevertheless show the characteristics of art work by children.

as technique or the principles of design and color. There is often a tendency to emphasize technique, to impose ' tricks,' to work for flashy results. Technique is a by-product of art expression, not an end, and it should be treated as such. Art also is frequently presented, even to small children, as a series of principles of design. These principles are formalizations and abstractions, generalizations of art theorists, and, as such, have little place in the teaching of young children. When used, they should be considered as means to expression, never as ends, or as reasons for expression. A problem of repetition, or balance, or use of line can have little meaning or validity for a young child, meaningful as it might be to the mature and experienced mind of the art teacher.

The use of patterns is a matter that should be clarified. Many teachers make use of them in art work, often on the rationalization that it permits the less-talented pupil to secure results that sustain his interest. Fortunately, this pernicious practice is being abandoned, although it is still far too common. The use of patterns contributes little to the growth or development of a child because he is called upon only to follow directions, and all his thinking is done for him. It ignores consideration of individual differences, and has a tendency to make him dissatisfied with his own original products. The same criticisms can be leveled against other sorts of dictated lessons wherein the child is called upon only to follow directions.

The use of different media is another matter that may puzzle the classroom teacher. It is often felt that media can be graded in the same way as books in reading are graded as to difficulty. A sounder point of view is that the problem is not so much which media are suitable as what results can be expected from them when used by children of different ages. It is true that there are media obviously not suited for use by young children; they can hardly be expected to do sculpture in marble or intricate metal work. But most available media can be handled satisfactorily by children and adults at all levels of maturity. For example, clay can be modelled by kindergarten children and by famous sculptors. Furniture construction is a highly developed craft for cabinetmakers, but the making of chairs and tables of orange crates by first-grade pupils is a thoroughly satisfactory activity. Crayon and certain types of paints are usable over a wide range of school years, and the same is true of many other materials. Children themselves often bring from home many materials that they are familiar with and can use to advantage. The problem is not so much a matter of certain materials being uniquely suited to certain age or maturity levels as an understanding of the results that children can achieve with them. It is important, therefore, in teacher-training programs that the prospective teachers not only become acquainted with a variety of media, but also become familiar with the performances of children with such media.

The teacher also will know how to provide for the individual differences that exist in the typical class. This is not satisfactorily done, generally, by having all the students in each class do the same sort of problem. Many of the new techniques of instruction developed for general classroom use are uniquely suited to art. Any large topic of instruction, whether it be restricted to art or related to nature study or the social studies, can generate a multitude of art activities that can suit many and varied interests and abilities. The teacher must realize that, above all, he is developing individuals, and that art, like all other subjects, is merely a means to this great aim. He must, therefore, know how to develop each individual to the fullest extent of his capacities by recognizing him as an individual. However, no individual exists alone; he is always a member of a group, and art lends itself well to coöperative group projects. The teacher must be familiar with ways of organizing groups that can work efficiently and harmoniously on group enterprises.

The foregoing discussion of the qualifications desirable in a general classroom teacher in order that he may teach art effectively does not by any means exhaust the possibilities. Those were selected for discussion that seemed most important, but many points are conspicuous by their absence.[1]

3. Suggestions for Simplifying the Difficulties of the Recommended Program

One may well ask how all of this can be accomplished in the short space of time generally allotted to art in most institutions. Certainly the need for a thoroughly disciplined course is clear. The three following points are included as suggestions for simplifying a most difficult task.

a. *Art Is a Normal Human Activity.* There is nothing any more mysterious or obscure about art than about other human activities. Each of us has capacity in art, as each of us has capacity to read and write, and all of these capacities can be developed through training.

---

[1] Some of the issues raised receive fuller treatment in Chapter XXX, " Art in General Education."

The amounts of the capacities and of the ultimate abilities vary from person to person, but that is a framework within which to operate, not a deterrent to action.

Dewey (9, p. 80), in commenting on the relation of art to life, writes:

> The problem of conferring esthetic quality upon all modes of production is a serious problem. But it is a human problem for human solution; not a problem incapable of solution because it is set by some unpassable gulf in human nature or in the nature of things. In an imperfect society — and no society will ever be perfect — fine art will be to some extent an escape from, or an adventitious decoration of, the main activities of living. But in a better ordered society than that in which we live, an infinitely greater happiness than is now the case would attend all modes of production. We live in a world in which there is an immense amount of organization, but it is an external organization, not one of the ordering of a growing experience, one that involves, moreover, the whole of the live creature, toward a fulfilling conclusion. Works of art that are not remote from common life, that are widely enjoyed in a community, are signs of a unified collective life. But they are also marvelous aids in the creation of such a life. The remaking of the material of experience in the act of expression is not an isolated event confined to the artist and to a person here and there who happens to enjoy the work. In the degree in which art exercises its office, it is also a remaking of the experience of the community in the direction of greater order and unity.

b. *All Art Expressions Have Basic Similarities.* The different fields of art, such as painting, architecture, and ceramics, are expressions of closely similar creative impulses. They differ from one another because they are created from different materials and because they serve different functions in life. Products within any single field also vary because they are produced at different times under different conditions. Through them all run the same underlying principles, the same desire to bring order to our existence, the same will to express our needs and our desires. If art is taught and understood as one large field of human expression instead of many, the attitude of the student to the field will be clarified and made easier.

c. *Sound Training Will Be an Incentive to Continued Growth in Art.* Even if we could foresee all the situations that a prospective teacher would have to meet in the classroom, there would not be time to teach him specifically how to meet them. All we can hope to give him is a solid framework of attitude, ability, and knowledge that will enable him to meet new situations effectively. This framework must not be composed of vague concepts and generalizations, but rather constructed from rich and meaningful experiences. This framework, furthermore, will not be as an enclosure, but instead it will be an opening up into unexplored fields that will encourage the teacher to continue his education in the arts in his daily life, in his job, in his recreation, in school. Art, perhaps even more than other subjects, demands that a person grow and develop constantly.

REFERENCES

(1) AYER, F. C. "Present Status of Instruction in Drawing with Respect to Scientific Investigation." *Eighteenth Yearbook, Part II,* of this Society, 1917, pp. 96–110.

(2) BAUER, CATHERINE. *Modern Housing.* (Houghton, Mifflin Co.: Boston, 1934)

(3) BOAS, GEORGE. "What Is Art Appreciation?" [In] *Art Education Today: 1940.* (Bureau of Publications, Teachers College, Columbia University: New York, 1940) pp. 3–7.

(4) CAHILL, H., and BARR, A. H., JR. *Art in America.* (Reynal and Hitchcock: New York, 1935)

(5) CASWELL, H. L., and CAMPBELL, D. S. *Curriculum Development.* (American Book Co.: New York, 1935)

(6) CHENEY, SHELDON. *A World History of Art.* (Viking Press: New York, 1937)

(7) Commission on Secondary School Curriculum, Progressive Education Association. *The Visual Arts in General Edcation.* (D. Appleton-Century Co., Inc.: New York, 1940) Chap. IV.

(8) COX, GEORGE J. "Give Us Art in Our Time." [In] *Art Education Today: 1935.* (Bureau of Publications, Teachers College, Columbia University: New York, 1935) pp. 34–39.

(9) DEWEY, JOHN. *Art As Experience.* (Minton, Balch and Co.: New York, 1934)

(10) ENG, H. *The Psychology of Drawing.* (Harcourt, Brace and Co.: New York, 1931)

(11) FOX, L. M., and HOPKINS, T. L. *Creative School Music.* (Silver Burdett Co.: New York, 1936) Chaps. II and III.

(12) GOODENOUGH, FLORENCE L. *Measurement of Intelligence through Drawings.* (The World Book Co.: Yonkers-on-Hudson, N. Y., 1926)

(13) HAGGERTY, M. E. *Art a Way of Life.* (University of Minnesota Press: Minneapolis, 1935)

(14) HAGGERTY, M. E. *The Enrichment of the Common Life.* (University of Minnesota Press: Minneapolis, 1938)

(15) HARTMAN, G., and SCHUMAKER, A. *Creative Expression.* (The John Day Co.: New York, 1932)

(16) HOPKINS, L. THOMAS. "A Point of View in Art Education." [In] *Art Education Today: 1935.* (Bureau of Publications, Teachers College, Columbia University: New York, 1935)

(17) LÖWENFELD, VICTOR. *The Nature of Creative Activity.* (Harcourt, Brace and Co.: New York, 1939)

(18) MEIER, N. C. "The Graphic and Allied Arts." [In]·*Child Development and the Curriculum.* Thirty-Eighth Yearbook, Part I, of this Society, 1939, pp. 175–184.

(19) MUMFORD, LEWIS. *Architecture.* (American Library Association: Chicago, 1926)

(20) MUMFORD, LEWIS. *The Culture of Cities.* (Harcourt, Brace and Co.: New York, 1938)

(21) PELIKAN, ALFRED. *The Art of the Child.* (The Bruce Publishing Co.: New York, 1931)

(22) PRESCOTT, D. A. *Emotions and the Educative Process.* (American Council on Education: Washington, D. C., 1938)

(23) READ, HERBERT. *Art and Industry.* (Harcourt, Brace and Co.: New York, 1935)

(24) SANDERS, B. "Art as an Approach to Children's Emotional Problems." [In] *Art Education Today: 1938.* (Bureau of Publications, Teachers College, Columbia University: New York, 1938)

(25) TANNAHILL, SALLIE B. *Art for Public-School Administrators.* (Bureau of Publications, Teachers College, Columbia University: New York, 1932)

(26) TEAGUE, WALTER D. *Design This Day.* (Harcourt, Brace and Co.: New York, 1940)

(27) TOMLINSON, R. R. *Crafts for Children.* (Studio Publications: New York, 1935)

(28) TOMLINSON, R. R. *Picture-Making by Children.* (Studio Publications, Inc.: New York, 1934)

(29) United States Department of Education. *National Survey of the Education of Teachers.* Bulletin, 1933, No. 10.

(30) WOFFORD, KATE V. "Art in an integrated program." *Design,* 41: June, 1940, pp. 7–8.

(31) ZACHRY, CAROLINE B. "The rôle of art in personality development." *Mental Hygiene,* 17: January, 1933.

(32) ZACHRY, CAROLINE B. "The Rôle of Mental Hygiene in the Arts." [In] *Art Education Today: 1940.* (Bureau of Publications, Teachers College, Columbia University: New York, 1940) pp. 31–36.

(33) ZIEGFELD, E. "Developing a functional program of art education." *National Elementary Principal,* 18: July, 1939, 289–295.

INFORMATION CONCERNING THE NATIONAL SOCIETY FOR THE STUDY OF EDUCATION

1. PURPOSE. The purpose of the National Society is to promote the investigation and discussion of educational questions. To this end it holds an annual meeting and publishes a series of yearbooks.

2. ELIGIBILITY TO MEMBERSHIP. Any person who is interested in receiving its publications may become a member by sending to the Secretary-Treasurer information concerning name, title, and address, and a check for $4.00 (see Item 5).

Membership is not transferable; it is limited to individuals, and may not be held by libraries, schools, or other institutions, either directly or indirectly.

3. PERIOD OF MEMBERSHIP. Applicants for membership may not date their entrance back of the current calendar year, and all memberships terminate automatically on December 31, unless the dues for the ensuing year are paid as indicated in Item 6.

4. DUTIES AND PRIVILEGES OF MEMBERS. Members pay dues of $3.00 annually, receive a cloth-bound copy of each publication, are entitled to vote, to participate in discussion, and (under certain conditions) to hold office. The names of members are printed in the yearbooks.

Persons who are sixty years of age or above may become life members on payment of fee based on average life-expectancy of their age group. For information, apply to Secretary-Treasurer.

5. ENTRANCE FEE. New members are required the first year to pay, in addition to the dues, an entrance fee of one dollar.

6. PAYMENT OF DUES. Statements of dues are rendered in October or November for the following calendar year. Any member so notified whose dues remain unpaid on January 1, thereby loses his membership and can be reinstated only by paying a reinstatement fee of fifty cents, levied to cover the actual clerical cost involved.

School warrants and vouchers from institutions must be accompanied by definite information concerning the name and address of the person for whom membership fee is being paid. Statements of dues are rendered on our own form only. The Secretary's office cannot undertake to fill out special invoice forms of any sort or to affix notary's affidavit to statements or receipts.

Cancelled checks serve as receipts. Members desiring an additional receipt must enclose a stamped and addressed envelope therefor.

7. DISTRIBUTION OF YEARBOOKS TO MEMBER. The yearbooks, ready prior to each February meeting, will be mailed from the office of the distributors, only to members whose dues for that year have been paid. Members who desire yearbooks prior to the current year must purchase them directly from the distributors (see Item 8).

8. COMMERCIAL SALES. The distribution of all yearbooks prior to the current year, and also of those of the current year not regularly mailed to members in exchange for their dues, is in the hands of the distributor, not of the Secretary. For such commercial sales, communicate directly with the University of Chicago Press, Chicago 37, Illinois, which will gladly send a price list covering all the publications of this Society and of its predecessor, the National Herbart Society. This list is also printed in the yearbook.

9. YEARBOOKS. The yearbooks are issued about one month before the February meeting. They comprise from 600 to 800 pages annually. Unusual effort has been made to make them, on the one hand, of immediate practical value, and, on the other hand, representative of sound scholarship and scientific investigation. Many of them are the fruit of co-operative work by committees of the Society.

10. MEETINGS. The annual meeting, at which the yearbooks are discussed, is held in February at the same time and place as the meeting of the American Association of School Administrators.

Applications for membership will be handled promptly at any time on receipt of name and address, together with check for $4.00 (or $3.50 for reinstatement). Generally speaking, applications entitle the new members to the yearbook slated for discussion during the calendar year the application is made, but those received in December are regarded as pertaining to the next calendar year.

5835 Kimbark Ave.   NELSON B. HENRY, Secretary-Treasurer
Chicago 37, Illinois

PUBLICATIONS OF THE NATIONAL HERBART SOCIETY

(Now the National Society for the Study of Education)

PUBLICATIONS OF THE NATIONAL SOCIETY FOR THE STUDY OF EDUCATION

PUBLICATIONS

PUBLICATIONS

PUBLICATIONS

Distributed by

THE UNIVERSITY OF CHICAGO PRESS

CHICAGO 37, ILLINOIS

1952